CALENDAR OF
INQUISITIONS POST MORTEM

and other Analogous Documents preserved in the
Public Record Office

Vol. XVIII
1-6 HENRY IV (1399-1405)

Edited by

J. L. KIRBY

LONDON
HER MAJESTY'S STATIONERY OFFICE
1987

ISBN 0 11 440202 7

CONTENTS

PREFACE

This volume of the *Calendar of Inquisitions Post Mortem* covers the first six years of the reign of Henry IV (1399–1405).

The text is based wherever possible on the Chancery class of Inquisitions post mortem, Henry IV (C 137/1–51). Gaps and deficiencies have been made good from Exchequer Inquisitions post mortem, Series I (E 149/71–88), Exchequer Enrolments of Inquisitions (E 152/344–407) and in one or two cases from Exchequer Escheators' Accounts Enrolled (E 357/14). Reference is made where appropriate, to Common Pleas, Feet of Fines, Series I (CP 25(1)), and to printed Calendars.

With the beginning of a new century small modifications have been made to the method of calendaring. Only the modern form of place-names is used in the text of this volume (as in the *Calendar of Inquisitions Miscellaneous*, volume VII, *1399–1422*) although all the spellings which occur in the manuscripts, apart from straight Latin translations, have been included in the Index of Persons and Places in brackets after the modern form. Dates have also been modernised. Regnal years and references to saints' days have been retained only where doubts might arise in the translation to the modern form. References to the four quarter days, Lady Day, Midsummer, Michaelmas and Christmas, and also to Candlemas, Hockday, Lammas, Martinmas, and similar dates are, however, given in these anglicized forms.

Names of jurors and, with certain exceptions, of escheators are still omitted as in the past, but annual values and extents of manors, omitted from previous volumes, are now included. In most cases knight's fees were said to extend at the conventional figure of 100s. a fee, multiples and fractions of fees being assessed in proportion. These figures have been omitted, and in the absence of a value in the calendar it may be assumed that they were so assessed. All other values attached to fees, together with the values of advowsons at the occurrence of a vacancy, have been included.

Writs of *diem clausit extremum*, and *precipimus. . . die quo obiit* (which differ only in the fact that the tenant is not newly dead) are described simply as 'Writ'. Writs asking for further details appear as 'Writ, *plenius certiorari*' or '*melius sciri*', and where it is suspected that the tenant held more than was found in the original inquisition as 'Writ, *plura*'. Writs for the return of knight's fees and advowsons (*Volentes certis de causis certiorari super vero valore feodorum. . .*) are described simply as 'for fees', and writs for proof of age and assignment of dower are so described.

The whole volume, both text and indexes, is the work of Mr. J.L. Kirby, who also saw it through the press.

Public Record Office

LIST OF ABBREVIATIONS

TABLE SHOWING THE PRESENT REFERENCES TO ALL DOCUMENTS FORMERLY INCLUDED AMONGST THE INQUISITIONS POST MORTEM OF THE PERIOD COVERED BY THIS VOLUME

The old reference is given in the first column, the new references in the second, third or fourth as the case may be.

The numbers in this volume appear in the fifth column.

Documents which cannot now be traced are marked 'Missing'.

		Inquisitions Post Mortem Henry IV (C 137)	Inquisitions Miscellaneous (C 145)		Numbers in this volume
1 Henry IV	1			Missing 1821	1
	2	1			2
	3A	1			3
	3B			Chanc. Extents for Debts (C 131) 49, no. 1	
	4	1			4–6
	5	1			7–9
	6	1			10
	7	1			11
	8	1			12
	9	1			13–15
	10	2			16–19
	11	2			20–7
	12	2			29
	13	2			30
	14	3			34–6
	15	3			39
	16	3			40–1
	17	3			42–8
	18	4			49
	19	4			50–2
	20	4			53–5
	21	4			56–7
	22	4			58
	23	4			31–3
	24	4			37–8
	25	5			59–63
	26	5			64–7
	27	5			68
	28	5			69

	Inquisitions Post Mortem Henry IV (C 137)	Inquisitions Miscellaneous (C 145)		Numbers in this volume
29	5			70–1
30	5			72–6
31	6			77–80
32	6			81–3
33	6			84
34	6			85
35	6			86
36	6			87
37	6			88
38	6			89–90
39	7			91–6
40	7			97
41	7			98–9
42	7			100–2
43	7			103
44	7			104–6
45	8			108–15
46	8			116–7
47	8			118
48	8			119
49	9			153–66
50	10, 11			123–52
51	12			167–89
52	13			190–204
53	14			205–6
54	14			207–11
55	14			212
56	14			213–4
57	14			215
58	14			216
59	14			217–8
60	14			219
61	14			220
62	14			221–2
63	15			223
64	15			224
65	15			225–9
66	15			230
67	15			231
68	15			232–3
69	15			22
70	15			234
71A	16			264–89
71B	17			290–307

	Inquisitions Post Mortem Henry IV (C 137)	Inquisitions Miscellaneous (C 145)		Numbers in this volume
72	18			235–59
73	19			8
74	19			309
75	19			310
76	19			311
77	19			312
78	19			313
79	19			308
80		272		
81			Chanc. Extents for Debts (C 131) 49, no.2	
82		272		
83			Chanc. Extents for Debts (C 131) 49, no.3	
84		272		
85	19			314
86	19			315
87	19			316
1 Henry IV part 2 1	20			326–34
2A		273		
2B		274		
2C		274		
2D		275		
2E		276		
2F		277		
2G		278		
2H		278		
3	17			307
4	11			152
5	9			166
2 Henry IV 1	21			335
2	21			336
3	21			337
4	21			338–40
5	21			341
6	21			344
7	21			345–6
8	21			347
9	21			348
10	21			349–50
11			Missing 1821	351–2

	Inquisitions Post Mortem Henry IV (C 137)	Inquisitions Miscellaneous (C 145)		Numbers in this volume
12	21			353
13	21			354–5
14			Missing 1821	
15	21			356–9
16	21			360
17	21			361–4
18	21			365–6
19	22			367
20	22			368–9
21	22			370–1
22	22			372
23	22			373
24	22			374
25	22			375–8
26	22			379
27	22			380–2
28	22			383
29	22			384–9
30	22			390–1
31	22			392
32	22			393–4
33	23			395
34	23			396–8
35	23			399
36	23			400–3
37	23			404–5
38A	23			406
38B	23			407
39	23			408–9
40	23			410
41	23			411–2
42	23			413–5
43	23			343
44	23			416–8
45	23			419
46	23			420–5
47	24			427–9
48	24			158,164–5
49	24			430–2
50	24			433–4
51	24			435–9
52	24			440–5
53	24			446
54	25			447–70

	Inquisitions Post Mortem Henry IV (C 137)	Inquisitions Miscellaneous (C 145)		Numbers in this volume
55	26			471–6
56	26			477–84
57	26			485–8
58	27,28			489–527
59		279		-
60	29			528
61	29			529
62	29			530
63			Chanc. Extents for Debts (C 131) 49, no.16	
64			Chanc. Files, Recorda (C 160) 113, no.13	
65			Chanc. Extents for Debts (C 131) 49, no.17	
66	29			531
67	29			[Henry V]
68	29			do.
69	29			532
70	29			533
71	29			534
3 Henry IV 1	30			549
2	30			550–1
3	30			552–3
4			Missing 1821	
5	30			554–7
6	30			558
7	30			559
8	30			560
9	30			561
10	30			562
11	30			563–4
12	30			566
13	30			567
14	30			568
15	30			569
16	30			570–5
17	30			576–7
18	30			578
19	30			579
20	30			580
21	30			581–3

	Inquisitions Post Mortem Henry IV (C 137)	Inquisitions Miscellaneous (C 145)		Numbers in this volume
22	31			584
23	31			586–7
24	31			588–9
25	31			590–3
26	31			594
27	31			595–8
28	31			599–600
29	31			601–8
30	31			609–13
31	32			614–9
32	32			620
33	32			621
34	32			622–4
35	32			625
36	32			626–42
37	32			643–5
38	32			646
39	33			648
40	33			649–50
41	33			107
42	33			651–3
43	33			655
44	33			656–61
45	33			662
46	33			663
47	33			664
48	33			665
49	33			666
50	33			667
51	33			125
52	33			669–70
53			Missing 1821	649
54	33			672
55	33			673
56	33			675
57			Missing 1821	370–1
58		280		
59			Chanc. Files, Recorda (C 260) 114, no. 1	
60		280		
61	33			676
62	33			677
63			Chanc. Files,	

	Inquisitions Post Mortem Henry IV (C 137)	Inquisitions Miscellaneous (C 145)		Numbers in this volume
			Recorda (C 260) 119, no.13 Missing	
64				
65		280		
66		280		
67			Chanc. Extents for Debts (C 131) 50, no.1	
68			Chanc. Extents for Debts (C 131) 50, no.2	
69		280		
70		280		
71	33			678
4 Henry IV 1	34			690–2
2	34			693
3	34			694
4	34			695
5	34			696
6	34			697–8
7	34			699
8	34			700
9	34			701
10	34			702
11	34			703–4
12	34			705–11
13	34			712
14	34			713
15	34			714
16	34			715
17	34			716
18	34			717–8
19	34			719
20	34			721–5
21	35			726–8
22	35			729–30
23	35			731–7
24	35			738–40
25	35			741–3
26	35			744
27	35			745–6
28	35			747–52
29	36			753
30	36			754

		Inquisitions Post Mortem Henry IV (C 137)	Inquisitions Miscellaneous (C 145)		Numbers in this volume
	31	36			755–7
	32	36			758
	33	36			759
	34	36			760–70
	35	36			771
	36	36			772–4
	37	36			775–9
	38	37			780–8
	39	37			789–94
	40	37			795–803
	41	38,39			804–53
	42		281		
	43	40			854
	44	40			855
	45	40			856
	46	40			857
	47	40			671
	48	40			674
	49	40			858
	50			Chanc. Extents for Debts (C 131) 51, no. 1	
	51	40			859
	52	40			860
	53	40			861–4
	54		281		
	55	40			865
	56	40			352
	57	40			866
5 Henry IV	1	41			873
	2	41			874
	3			Missing 1821	
	4	41			720
	5	41			875
	6	41			647
	7	41			876
	8	41			877
	9	41			878
	10	41			879
	11	41			880
	12	41			881–2
	13	41			883–4
	14	41			885
	15	41			887–90

	Inquisitions Post Mortem Henry IV (C 137)	Inquisitions Miscellaneous (C 145)		Numbers in this volume
16	41			891
17	41			892–5
18	41			896
19	42			897–902
20	42			903
21	42			904–7
22	42			908–26
23	42			927
24	42			928
25	43			929–32
26	43			933–5
27	43			936–43
28	43			945–9
29	43			950–4
30	43			955–7
31	44			958
32	44			959–62
33	44			963–6
34	44			967–8
35	44			969
36	44			970–1
37	44			972–3
38	44			974–9
39	44			980–1
40	44			982–5
41	45			986–90
42	45			654
43	45			991
44	45			992
45	45			993
46	45			994
47	45			995
48	45			996
49	45			944
50	45			997
51	45			998
52	45			999
53	45			886
54			Chanc. Extents for Debts (C 131) 52, no. 1	
55			Chanc. Extents for Debts (C 131) 52, no. 2	

	Inquisitions Post Mortem Henry IV (C 137)	Inquisitions Miscellaneous (C 145)		Numbers in this volume
56			Chanc. Extents for Debts (C 131) 52, no.3	
57			Chanc. Extents for Debts (C 131) 52, no.4	
58			Chanc. Extents for Debts (C 131) 52, no.5	
59			Chanc. Extents for Debts (C 131) 52, no.6	
60	45			985
61	45			1000
62		282		
63	45			1001
64	45			1002
65	45			1003–5
6 Henry IV 1	46			1013
2	46			1014
3	46			1015–8
4	46			1019
5	46			1020–2
6	46			1023–9
7	46			1030
8	46			1031
9	46			1032
10	46			1033–4
11	46			1035
12	46			1036
13	46			1037–9
14	46			1041–2
15	47			1043–4
16	47			1045–8
17	47			1049–54
18	47			1055
19	47			1056–9
20	47			1060–2
21	48			1063–83
22	48			1084–91
23	49			1092
24	49			1093
25	49			1094
26	49			1095–8

	Inquisitions Post Mortem Henry IV (C 137)	Inquisitions Miscellaneous (C 145)		Numbers in this volume
27	49			1099–1102
28	49			1103–9
29	49			1110–12
30	49			1113–14
31	49			1115–23
32	50			1124–6
33	50			1127–35
34	50			1136–7
35	50			1138
36	50			1139–40
37	50			1141
38	50			1142–6
39	50			1147–8
40	50			1149
41	50			1150
42			Chanc. Files, Recorda (C 260) 117, no. 5	
43	51			1151–5
44	51			1158–71
45	51			1174
46	51			1175
47	51			1176
48	51			1177–8
49	51			1179
50	51			1180
51	51			1181
52	51			1182
53			Chanc. Extents for Debts (C 131) 53, no. 1	
54		283		
55	51			1185
56	51			977
57	51			1186
58		283		
59	51			1187
60	51			1188

B

CALENDAR

ROBERT WESENHAM

1 HUNTINGDON. Inquisition. Sawtry. 7 Sept. 1400.

He held the manor of Conington with half the advowson of the king in chief of the honour of Huntingdon by knight service, annual value £16 apart from a rent of 40s. which he granted to John Bilney for life on 23 April last.

He died on 9 August last. Thomas his son and heir is aged 13 years and more.

[C 137/1, no.1 missing]
E 149/73, no.2

THOMAS LORD LE DESPENSER

2 Writ 26 Feb. 1400.
SUSSEX. Inquisition. Rotherfield. 15 April.

He held the manor of Rotherfield of the king in chief by knight service. There are the site, annual value nil; 64 a. arable at 3d., 16s.; 80 a. pasture at 2d., 13s.4d.; 56 a. nil because marsh and scrub (*buschaill*); 20 a. meadow of rushes in various places at 8d., 13s.4d.; 1 chase, number of acres unknown, nil because maintaining the enclosure costs annually £6 beyond the profits; 1 watermill 66s.8d.; site of fulling mill, nil because totally destroyed; assize rents of free tenants and villeins £32 payable at the four principal terms by equal parts; various customary works £6 2s.2d., comprising at Candlemas 45s., at Lady Day 7s.6d., at Easter 22s.6d., at Midsummer 15s., and at Michaelmas 32s.2d., from which by the ancient custom of the manor the reeve has 5s. yearly, the beadle 4s.; the custom called 'swonswyne', the tenants rendering £6 13s. at Martinmas; another custom called 'Andrewesreve' at the feast of St. Andrew 50s.; the profits of the fair at the feast of St. Dennis 5s.; view of frankpledge held after Easter and Michaelmas £6; pleas and perquisites of the court nil beyond expenses; a place called Eridge in the aforesaid enclosed chase nil because imparked and occupied by game, which park is called 'Newepark'; another park in the same chase called Hamsell nil because occupied by game. There is a master forester but how much he takes daily is unknown; 1 ranger takes 2d. daily, 60s.8d.; 1 chamberlain, 3 foresters, 2 parkers, 1d. each, £9; 1 forester in the chase in the park on Waterdown 1½d., 45s.[*sic*. Total annual value from E 357/14, m.2: £58 19s.6d.].

William Brenchesle, knight, and his parceners hold a quarter of a knight's fee in Frant by suit of court there.

Thomas le Despenser died on 13 Jan. last. Richard his son and next heir was aged 3 years on 30 Nov. last.

[*Cf. CIM* VII, no.487 (1414)].

C 137/1, no.2
E 152/363

JOHN DE LYLLEBURN, KNIGHT

3 Writ 13 Nov. 1399.
NORTHUMBERLAND. Inquisition. Newcastle upon Tyne castle. 23 April 1400.

He held:

Belford and Easington, half the manors, in his demesne as of fee of the king in chief by knight service, annual values 50s. and 6s.8d., and no more these days because of destruction by the Scots.

Shawdon, the manor with half the vill of Glanton, jointly with Margaret his wife, of Thomas Gray, knight, of the barony of Wark by knight service, annual value 6s.8d., and no more for the same reason.

Lilburn, the manor, of the same Thomas Gray and the same barony, worth nothing annually for the same reason.

Beanley, the manor, in his demesne as of fee of Henry de Percy, earl of Northumberland, of the barony of Earl Patrick by the service of 12 marks yearly, annual value 40s.

He died on 5 Nov. last. Henry his son and next heir is aged 14 years and more.

C 137/1, no.3A

HENRY DE HETON, KNIGHT

4 Writ 28 Jan. 1400.

NORTHUMBERLAND. Inquisition. Alnwick. 23 Feb.

He held in his demesne as of fee:

Chillingham, the manor, of Henry Percy, earl of Northumberland, of the barony of Vescy by knight service, annual value £20.

Hartley, half the vill with the appurtenances called Brierdene, of Richard de Arundell, knight, of the barony of Gaugy by knight service, annual value £20. Long before he died he granted to Henry de Bynkfelde a rent of 26s.8d. from these lands for life, and a similar rent to William Halywell for life.

Tritlington, a certain waste place so called, of Richard de Arundell of the barony of Muschamp, annual value 4 marks.

He died on 1 Nov. last. William his son and heir was aged 6 years and more at Easter last.

5 Writ 10 Feb. 1400.

NORTHUMBERLAND. Inquisition. Newcastle upon Tyne castle. 23 April.

He held in his demesne as of fee:

Brierdene, the manor and half the vill of Hartley, by knight service in accordance with a grant of Edward II by letters patent confirmed by Edward III [*CPR 1317-21*, pp.310-11, 15 Feb. 1319; *1330-4*, p.565] to Thomas de Heton and his heirs male, annual value £20.

Bamburgh, 8 burgages, of the king in burgage by a rent of 8d., annual value 26s.8d.

Chillingham, the manor and castle, of Henry de Percy, earl of Northumberland, of the barony of Vescy by knight service, annual value £20.

Hartley, 1 husbandland, of the lord of Seaton Delaval by knight service, annual value 20s.

Alnwick, 24 a., of Henry de Percy, earl of Northumberland, by a rent of 12d., annual value 40d.

Tritlington, a certain place so called, of Richard de Arundell of the barony of Muschamp in socage, annual value 4 marks.

Doxford, 1 husbandland, of Richard de Arundell of the barony of Gaugy in socage, annual value 6s.8d.

Heathpool. 2 cottages and 1 husbandland, of Lord Darcy of the barony of Muschamp in socage, annual value 6d.

He died on 25 Oct. last. William his son and next heir is aged 6 years and more.

C 137/1, no.4

THOMAS NEWETON

6 CAMBRIDGE. Inquisition. Cambridge. 28 Feb. 1400.

Thomas Neweton, late citizen and mercer of London, held nothing in Cambridge-shire.

He died on 7 Feb. 1399. John Revel of Fowlmere is his kinsman and next heir, being the son of Philip, son of Sarah, daughter of William, brother of Thomas, father of John, his father, aged 26 years and more.

E 149/73, no.3

THOMAS SHELLE, KNIGHT

7 Writ 17 March 1400.

LINCOLN. Inquisition. Louth. 4 April.

He held the manor of Brackenborough, which Thomas Missenden and Isabel his wife gave by a fine of Edward III [CP 25(1) 141/132, no.1] to Edmund Missenden son of Thomas, Juliana his wife, and the heirs of their bodies, with remainder to the right heirs of Thomas. They had issue Bernard who is under age in the king's ward. Edmund died, and Thomas Shelle married Juliana who survives him. He had no other rights in the manor. He died on 21 Jan. [Wednesday after the octave of Hilary] last.

Brackenborough manor, except for 6 a. in Kelstern, is held of the heirs of John Beaumond by knight service, and the heirs hold it of the king in chief, service unknown, annual value £18. The 6 a. are held of the king in chief by knight service, amount unknown, annual value 12d.

Who is his next heir is unknown as he died without heirs of his body.

[Cf. CIM VII, no.53].

C 137/1, no.5, mm.1,2
E 149/74, no.4, m.1

8 Writ, *plenius certiorari*, on petition of Juliana, his widow, that various manors in various counties which she held long before her marriage to Thomas Shelle, both jointly with her former husband, Edmund Missenden, and also in dower, were wrongly taken into the king's hands on account of Thomas's forfeiture, and the king wishes justice to be done. 2 July 1400.

BUCKINGHAM. Inquisition. Aylesbury. 5 July.

He held the manors of Quainton and Great Missenden in right of his wife Juliana, who holds for life and one year more, by the grant of Bernard Brokas, knight, senior, and Walter Cranford, made long before her marriage; and after her death they should descend to the heirs of Edmund Missenden, knight, her former husband. Quainton is held of the prince [of Wales] of the honour of Wallingford by rent of a rose, annual value £20; Great Missenden of the earl of Stafford by a rent of 5s., annual value £20.

He died on 28 Jan. [Wednesday before the Purification].
[*Cf. CPR 1399–1402*, p.154; *CIM* VII, no.62].

C 137/19, no.73

9   Similar writ 8 July 1400.
HAMPSHIRE. Inquisition. Stockbridge. 22 Sept.
He held the manor of Farleigh Wallop jointly with Juliana his wife, [formerly the wife of Edmund Missenden], owing to the minority of Bernard, son and heir of Edmund Mussendene, knight, because Bernard Brocas and Juliana had custody of Edmund's lands by grant of Richard II [*CPR 1391–6*, p.575] until the full age of Bernard, but how or in what form they were granted is unknown. The manor is worth £10 annually, but whether held of the king in chief or of the duchy of Lancaster is also unknown.
Thomas Shelle was beheaded for insurrection on 27 [*sic*] Jan. last.

C 137/1, no.5, mm.3,4

RALPH DE PERCY, KNIGHT

10   Writ 20 Nov. 1399.
DERBY. Inquisition. Chesterfield. 26 Jan. 1400.
He held the manor of Dronfield of the king in chief by knight service, by the grant of Ralph de Crumwell, knight, formerly lord of Tattershall, and Maud his wife, to him and the heirs of his body, with reversion failing such heirs to Ralph de Crumwell and Maud and the heirs of Maud, annual value £7 12s.
He died overseas on 15 Sept. 1397. Ralph Crumwell is dead. It should descend to Maud and her heirs, because Ralph Percy had no heirs of his body. She is aged 50 years and more.

C 137/1, no.6

WILLIAM PERCY

11   Writ 24 Oct. 1399.
YORK. Inquisition. Stokesley in Cleveland. 10 Nov.
Owing to the death of William Percy of Castlelevington and the minority of his son William the manor of Castlelevington was taken into the hands of Richard II. Christina, the widow of the elder William, holds a third part in dower and she still lives. The other two parts remain in the king's hands. William held it in his demesne in fee tail by the grant years ago of Robert Conyers, knight, Thomas de Boynton, knight, and John Conyers, brother of Robert, with remainder if he had no heirs to Margaret his sister and the heirs of her body, and failing them to the said Robert, Thomas and John. It is held of the king in chief by fealty and the service of finding a man with an unbarded horse, armed with acton, pallet, lance and gauntlets of plate, for forty days when there is a war in Scotland. The two parts in the king's hands are worth 10 marks annually.
Also after the death of the elder William the manor of Tanton with its appurtenances, and 8 messuages, 5 tofts, 7 bovates and 7 a. of land in Kildale, and 1 messuage and 5 bovates in Newby were taken into the king's hands. They are held of various lords, Thomas earl of Kent, John Lord Darcy, John Percy of Kildale, and William Mowbray

of Newby, as appears by an inquisition taken after his death [*CIPM* XVII, no. 1079]. The annual values are, Tanton 10 marks, Kildale 20s., and Newby 5 marks.

Afterwards because it was found in the inquisition that his manor and the other premises were held jointly by William and Christina his wife, to them and their heirs, they were released from the king's hands. The two parts of Castlelevington manor should descend to Margaret wife of Thomas Blanfront and her heirs. She is the next heir as sister of William the father and she is aged 30 years and more. William the son died on 8 Oct. last.

[*Cf. CIPM* XVI, nos. 523, 655].

C 137/1, no. 7

ALICE WIDOW OF NICHOLAS HAUT, KNIGHT

12   Writ 20 March 1400.

KENT. Inquisition. Maidstone. 3 April.

Richard Charlys formerly held in his demesne as of fee the manors of Palster, Addington, Little Delce, and Nashenden, and conveyed them to Robert Farynton, clerk, James de Pekham, John Colpeper, and Stephen Norton of Chart, who regranted them to Richard Charlys, Alice his wife, and the heirs and assigns of Richard. He died leaving a son, James Charlys, to whom the reversion descended, but he died under age without heirs. Alice survived. The reversion of the manors passed to Joan, wife of William Rypoun, as aunt and heir of James, sister of Richard Charlys, the father of James. Afterwards William Rypoun and Joan, his wife, by a fine of Richard II [CP 25(1) 111/252, no. 212], granted the reversion of the manors of Palster, Addington and Little Delce, then held by Alice and Nicholas Haut, whom she had married, for the life of Alice, and of the inheritance of Joan, to William Sneyth, William atte Hethe and Richard Janekynes, clerk, and the heirs of Richard. Afterwards Nicholas and Alice Haut attorned to William Sneyth, Hethe and Janekynes, and Hethe and Janekynes quitclaimed to William Sneyth.

William Rypoun, by the name of William Pycher, and Joan his wife, by a fine of 1397 [CP 25(1) 111/248, no. 1007] granted Nashenden manor and 100 a. pasture in Aylesford, Burham, Wouldham, and the vill of St. Margaret by Rochester, to John Frenynghame, William Makynhade, James de Pekham and the heirs of James.

Nashenden manor is held of the king of the castle of Rochester by knight service. The 100 a. are held of Lord de Grey and other lords by gavelkind, services unknown, annual value 10 marks.

Palster manor contains 1 fee, half held of the king in chief of the castle of Leeds by knight service; the other half of the archbishop of Canterbury by knight service, annual value £15.

Addington manor is held of the heir of Roger de Mortuo Mari, late earl of March, of the manor of Swanscombe by knight service, and is in the king's hands owing to his minority; certain lands in Addington and the vill of Ryarsh of Lord Moubray by gavelkind, service unknown, annual value 10 marks; and Little Delce manor of Lord Say of his manor of Patrixbourne by knight service, annual value £4.

Alice died on 11 March last. William son of Nicholas and Alice is next heir, age unknown.

C 137/1, no. 8

JOHN DE BOURGHCHIER, KNIGHT

13 Writ 22 May 1400.

LONDON. Inquisition. 15 June.

He held in his demesne as of fee 1 messuage and 12 shops in the parish of St. Botolph without Bishopsgate, in the suburbs of London, of the king in free burgage as all the city is, annual value £10.

He died on 21 May last. Bartholomew his son and next heir is aged 30 years and more.

14 Writ 22 May 1400.

SUFFOLK. Inquisition. Sudbury. 12 June.

He held in his demesne as of fee 1 messuage, 40 a. arable, 2 a. meadow, and ½ a. wood in Great Wratting and Barnardiston, of the earl of March of his manor of Hundon by a rent of 4s., of Thomas Notebem, knight, of his manor of Great Thurlow, and of Lady Bardolf of her manor of Great Wratting, services unknown, annual value 13s.4d.

Date of death as above. Bartholomew Bourghchier, knight, his son and next heir is of full age.

15 Writ 22 May 1400.

ESSEX. Inquisition. Chelmsford. 3 June.

He held in his demesne as of fee:

Halstead, 20 a. and 40s. assize rent, of the earl of March, a minor in the king's ward, of the honour of Clare, by suit of court at Clare castle every three weeks, annual value with the rent 50s.; and view of frankpledge there, held of the king in chief, rendering 2s. annually by the sheriff of Essex, annual value 40d.

Little Fordham, the manor, of the king of the honour of Boulogne in socage by fealty, from which he granted to John Russh, his esquire, who still lives, an annuity of 8 marks payable at Easter and Michaelmas; annual value beyond the annuity 100s.

Sible Hedingham, 100s. rent at Easter and Michaelmas, of the earl of Oxford, a minor in the king's ward, service unknown.

Ulting, 40 a., of Walter Lord Fitzwalter, service unknown, annual value 20s.

Halstead and Great Maplestead, 40 a. called 'Fitzjohanes', of the earl of Oxford, as before, and of the heirs of John Undercombe, knight, and Margaret formerly the wife of Richard Mewe, and also of the prior of Earl's Colne, for various unknown services, annual value 13s.4d.

Braintree, 1 messuage and 30 a., of the king in chief by a rent of 4d., payable by the sheriff of Essex, annual value 40s.

Colchester, 18s. assize rent payable at Easter and Michaelmas, of the king in free burgage.

Moreton, the manor, of the king in chief by the service of a quarter of a knight's fee, annual value £10.

Great Totham, the manor, of the earl of Stafford, service unknown, annual value £10.

Tolleshunt d'Arcy, 1 messuage and 44 a., of the king of the honour of Dover, by the service of a sixteenth part of a knight's fee, annual value 20s.

Latchingdon, 1 messuage and 100 a. of land and marsh, of the honour of Dover by a rent of 10s., annual value 60s.

Halstead, 1 messuage and 100 a. called 'Hipworthes', of the earl of March, a minor in the king's ward, by a rent of 6d., annual value 66s.8d.

He held in fee tail:

Rettendon, 1 messuage and 100 a., of the bishop of Ely, by the service of a quarter of a knight's fee, annual value 100s.

Woodham Ferrers, 40 a. of the duchy of Lancaster, by a rent of 6d., payable at the turn of Woodham Ferrers, annual value 20s.

Rivenhall and Witham, 1 messuage and 200 a., of lord de Scales, by a rent of 40s., annual value 100s.

Tolleshunt d'Arcy, the manor, of the king of the honour of Boulogne, by a rent of 12d., annual value 20 marks.

He held nothing else in the county, but long before he died he granted to Robert, bishop of London, Richard Waldegrave, knight, William de Wynkefeld, knight, Roger Keterych, and Robert Rikedon, his manors of Stansted, Messing and Langford, to hold to themselves and their heirs in fee simple. All the tenants attorned to them and they still hold.

Date of death as above. Bartholomew de Bourghchier, knight, his son and heir, is aged 32 years and more.

C 137/1, no.9
E 149/74, no.6
E 152/350

KATHERINE WIDOW OF THOMAS DENGAYNE, KNIGHT

16 Writ 15 Jan. 1400.

BEDFORD. Inquisition. Biggleswade. 29 Jan.

Thomas de Stratton, parson of Blatherwycke, and Thomas de Stanes, parson of Upminster, by a fine of Edward III [CP 25(1) 287/45, no.508: licence *CPR 1345–8*, p.246] conveyed the manor of Sandy and the advowson of the chantry of St. Nicholas in the church there, which Roger de Bello Campo then held for life, after this life interest to John Engayne for life, with remainder to his son Thomas, Katherine the wife of Thomas, and the heirs of their bodies, and failing such heirs to the right heirs of John. John is dead, and Thomas died without heirs by Katherine. The right to the manor thus remained in fee simple to Joyce then wife of John de Goldyngton, Elizabeth then wife of Lawrence de Pabenham, knight, and Mary then wife of William Bernak, knight, as sisters and heirs of Thomas, and daughters and heirs of John Engayne. Katherine held it when she died.

By another fine of Edward III [CP 25(1) 288/50, no.780] John and Joyce Goldington and Lawrence and Elizabeth de Pabenham conceded their rights in this manor to Mary and William Bernak, to hold to themselves and their heirs after the death of Katherine, who attorned to them. William Bernak died, and Mary married Thomas la Zouche.

The manor is held of the king in chief, service unknown, annual value 100s.

Katherine died on 31 Dec. last. Mary is aged 50 years and more. John, son of John Courtenay, is next heir by blood to Katherine and is aged 24 years and more.

17 Writ 15 Jan. 1400.

NORTHAMPTON. Inquisition. Kettering. Friday 23 Jan.

She held the manors of Laxton, Blatherwycke and Bulwick, and the advowson of

Blatherwycke. They were conveyed by fines, levied in 1354–5 and shown to the jurors [CP 25(1) 287/45, nos. 501, 508], by Thomas de Stratton and Thomas de Stanes, parsons [as above], to Katherine and Thomas, her husband, the son of John Engayne, knight, and the heirs of their bodies, with remainder to the heirs of John. John died and Thomas died without heirs by Katherine. The reversion therefore remained to Joyce, Elizabeth and Mary [as above] the daughters and heirs of John.

By another fine [CP 25(1) 288/50, no. 780] John and Joyce Goldington and William and Mary Bernak conceded their rights in these manors to Lawrence and Elizabeth Pabenham and the heirs of Elizabeth. They died leaving issue Katherine, married to Thomas de Aylesbury, so that Katherine and Thomas de Aylesbury are now the heirs.

Laxton is held in chief of the crown, service unknown, annual value 100s; Blatherwycke, annual value £7 6s. 8d., and Bulwick, 40s. with the advowson of the former, are held of Thomas Maureward, knight, of his manor of Weldon by knight service, amount unknown.

Date of death and next heir by blood as above. Katherine Aylesbury is aged 28 years and more.

18 Writ 15 Jan. 1400.

HUNTINGDON. Inquisition. Huntingdon. 24 Jan.

When he died Thomas Dengayne, knight, held the manor of Dillington, and it then passed to his sisters Joyce, Elizabeth and Mary, and their husbands [as above]. They granted it to Katherine for life with reversion to themselves.

Katherine also held the manor of Gidding by the grant of Thomas de Stratton and Thomas de Stanes, parsons [as above] by a fine now shown to the jurors [CP 25(1) 287/45, no. 508]. By another fine [CP 25(1) 288/50, no. 780] John and Joyce de Goldyngton and Lawrence and Elizabeth Pabenham conceded their rights in the manor of Dillington to William and Mary Bernak. William died and Mary married Thomas la Zouche, so that Mary and Thomas have the reversion after the death of Katherine.

By the same fine John and Joyce Goldyngton and William and Mary Bernak conceded their rights in the manor of Gidding to Elizabeth and Lawrence Pabenham, whose daughter Katherine is married to Thomas de Aylesbury, and they (Thomas and Katherine de Aylesbury) have the reversion after the death of Katherine Dengayne, to them and the heirs of Katherine de Aylesbury.

The manor of Dillington is held of the abbot of Ramsey, service unknown, annual value £10. Gidding is held of the king in chief, service unknown, annual value 10 marks.

Date of death and next heir by blood as above. Mary is aged 50 years and more, and Katherine wife of Thomas Aylesbury 30 years and more.

19 Writ 15 Jan. 1400.

ESSEX. Inquisition. Witham. 2 Feb.

Thomas Dengayne, knight, was seised in his demesne as of fee of the manor of White Notley, and afterwards it passed to his three sisters and their husbands [as above]. They granted it to Katherine for life with reversion to them and their heirs, and she died seised of it.

She also held Colne Engaine manor with the advowson by the grant of Thomas de Stratton and Thomas de Stanes, parsons [as above], by a fine [CP 25(1) 287/45, no. 501]. By another fine [CP 25(1) 288/50, no. 780] after the death of Thomas Dengayne, John and Joyce de Goldyngton, and William and Mary Bernak, conceded their rights in the manor of White Notley to Lawrence Pabenham and Elizabeth his wife.

The jurors say that Thomas Dengayne, son of John Engayne, and Thomas Dengayne, the brother of Joyce, Elizabeth and Mary, and the husband of Katherine, were one and the same person; and Joyce, Elizabeth and Mary are the heirs of John Engayne.

Lawrence and Elizabeth Pabenham had issue Katherine, and died, so that Katherine, now the wife of Thomas Aylesbury, and Thomas have the reversion of White Notley.

Also by the second fine John and Joyce Goldyngton and Lawrence and Elizabeth Pabenham conceded their rights in the manor of Colne Engaine with the advowson to Mary wife of William Bernak and their heirs. William died and Mary married Thomas la Zouche, so that Thomas la Zouche and Mary are heirs after the death of Katherine.

The manor of Colne Engaine is held of William la Zouche, knight, service unknown, annual value £8. White Notley is held of Thomas Moubray, son and heir of Thomas Moubray, duke of Norfolk, service also unknown, annual value £20.

Date of death and heirs as in last.

C 137/2, no. 10
E 149/72, no. 2

JOHN DE MONTE ACUTO, EARL OF SALISBURY

20   Writ 16 Feb. 1400.

LONDON. Inquisition. 29 March.

He held in his demesne as of fee a tenement called 'Newe Inne' in the parish of St. Benet, Thames Street, in Castle Baynard ward, formerly of John de Beauchamp, knight. It is held of the king in free burgage as is all the city of London, annual value £4. He also held a rent of 1 bow and 6 catapults from a tenement in the parish of St. Dunstan in the East, annual value 20d.

In right of Maud his wife he held a rent of 13 roses from a tenement called 'Romaynsrent' in the parish of St. Mary Aldermary; £10 quitrent from tenements held by Thomas Knolles in St. Antonin's parish; £11 3s. 4d. from tenements held by John Walpole in the parishes of All Hallows, Bread Street, St. Mildred, Bread Street, and St. Mary Aldermary; 5 marks quitrent from a tenement held by Richard Odyham in St. Antonin's parish; and 4 marks quitrent from John Pellyng, citizen and skinner, in All Hallows, Bread Street.

He died on 8 Jan. last. Thomas his son and heir was aged 12 years on 25 March last.

21   Writ 7 April 1400.

SUSSEX. Inquisition. Robertsbridge. 1 May.

By the law and courtesy of England he held a third part of the manor of Bugsell in the dower of Maud his wife, who survives him, assigned by the escheator from this manor and other lands and tenements in Sussex of Alan de Buxhull, knight, senior, her former husband. The other two parts of the manor with other lands of Alan were granted to him by Richard II by letters patent [CPR 1381–5, p. 362], during the minority of Alan de Buxhull, knight, the son and heir, without rendering anything to the king. Afterwards he granted the two parts to William Gobyon, esquire, and Henry Sybbesey of London, draper, until the full age of Alan de Buxhull, knight, the son and heir.

Bugsell manor with 143 a. is held of William Echyngham by homage, fealty, a rent of 4d., and by suit of court at Etchingham every three weeks. A messuage called Bernhurst and 80 a. there are also held of William Echyngham by homage, fealty, a rent of 13s. 4d., and payment of 3d. each 16 weeks for the safeguard of Hastings castle.

At Bugsell 18 a. are held of John Dalyngrugge, knight, as of the manor of Bodiam, by fealty, a rent of 10s.8d., and 3d. each 16 weeks for the keeping of the same castle; 30 a. at Ringden are held of Robert Passhele, as of the manor of Pashley, by a rent of 2s., and 3d. each 16 weeks as before; 20 a. at Haselden are held of John Belhurst of his manor of Bellhurst, by fealty, a rent of 18d., and suit of court every three weeks; a messuage called Socknersh and 150 a. are held of William de Hoo, knight, of his manor of Wartling by knight service; 1 watermill and 12 a. are held of the abbot of Fécamp, by a rent of 4s.1d., and suit at his court of Brede every three weeks.

The manor of Bugsell with all other lands belonging to it, and with a rent of £16, is worth annually £30. The rent is payable at the four terms, the feasts of Michaelmas, Christmas, Easter and Midsummer, and the rent of a third part was paid to John Mountagu, earl of Salisbury, or his servants, before Epiphany, and that of the other two parts was paid to William Gobyon and Henry Sybbesey.

He died on 7 Feb. [*recte* Jan.]. Thomas his son and heir is aged 12 years and more. Henry Pypplesden has held all from the death of John Mountagu to this day, and received all the profits.

> C 137/2, no.11, mm.1–4
> E 152/360

22 Writ, *plenius certiorari*, on petition of Maud his widow, that she held various lands, by inheritance, jointly with John [Aubrey], formerly her husband, and in dower from Alan Buxhull, afterwards her husband, and that all were wrongly taken into the king's hands owing to the forfeiture of the earl, her latest husband. 18 June 1400.

SUSSEX. Inquisition. Robertsbridge. 19 July.

He held a third part of the manor of Bugsell by the law and courtesy of England, in the dower of Maud, late his wife, who survives him, from Alan de Buxhull, knight, senior, late her husband. It is held of William Hoo, knight, and William Echyngham, service unknown, annual value £10.

He died on 7 Jan. last.

> C 137/15, no.69

23 Writ 16 Feb. 1400.

MIDDLESEX. Inquisition. Bow. 8 April.

William de Halden and John Ussher, citizens of London, formerly held in their demesne as of fee the manor of Wick, by the name of all the lands and tenements called 'la Wyke', and sold and confirmed it, with all the lands, tenements, rents, services, meadow and pasture, which they had of the enfeoffment of Adam Fraunceys senior, formerly citizen of London, in the parishes of Hackney and Stepney, by an indenture dated London, 24 Sept. 1357, to Agnes, widow of Adam Fraunceys, for life, with remainder to Maud, daughter of Adam, and the heirs of her body, and failing such heirs to Adam Fraunceys, junior, her brother, and the heirs of his body.

John de Mountagu married Maud, who still lives, and held these lands in her right. Half of the manor is held of the bishop of London, and the other half of the prior of St. John of Jerusalem in England, services unknown, annual value £14 10s.

He died on 7 Jan. last. Thomas his son and heir is aged 12 years and more.

24 Writ 16 Feb. 1400.

SUFFOLK. Inquisition. Boxford. 14 April.

He held the manor of Newton by Sudbury in right of Maud, his wife, who survives him, of the abbess of Malling of her manor of Abbas Hall in Great Cornard by a rent of 4s.4d., annual value 20 marks.

He died on 7 Jan. Thomas his son and heir was aged 12 on 25 March.

25 Writ 16 Feb. 1400.
HERTFORD. Inquisition. St. Albans. 24 April.

John Wroth, junior, William Newerk, chaplain, and Robert Peper formerly held in their demesne as of fee the manor of Shenley, 2 messuages, 352 a. arable, 5 crofts, 17 a. meadow, 80 a. wood and £7 17s. rent in Shenley, Ridge, Parkbury, Aldenham, Watford, North Mimms and St. Albans. These lands and rents, with the services of free tenants and villeins and their families, they had by enfeoffment of John son of Andrew Aubrey, citizen of London, now deceased, and they regranted them to John and Maud, his wife, who survives, and the heirs of their bodies, with remainder to the right heirs of John.

John de Mountagu married Maud, and held the above in right of his wife; the manor of John Salman, service unknown, and the messuages of the abbot of St. Albans, service also unknown, annual value 20 marks. Joan, wife of John Bryan of London, and Joan, wife of Thomas Lichebarwe of London, are cousins and heirs of John Aubrey; Joan Bryan being the daughter of Thomas Hanhampstede, formerly citizen and grocer of London, son of Agnes, one sister and heir of Joan, mother of John Aubrey; and Joan Lichebarwe being the daughter of Alice, daughter of Felicity Pentry, daughter of Isabel, the other daughter and heir of Joan the mother.

John de Mountagu also held the reversion of a messuage called 'le Hyde', 100 a. arable, 2 a. meadow and 20 a. wood in Abbots Langley, of which Richard Fermyn holds two parts for life by the grant of John de Mountagu; and Elizabeth, widow of William de Mountagu, late earl of Salisbury, holds the third part in dower. They are held of the abbot of St. Albans, service unknown, annual value £3.

Date of death and heir as above [no.24].

26 GLOUCESTER. Inquisition. Lechlade. 27 April 1409.

When he died on 5 [*sic*] Jan. 1400 John de Monte Acuto held in fee tail 1 messuage and 1 carucate in Row Earthcott by Bristol, part of the manor of Warblington in Hampshire, which Edward II granted to Ralph de Monte Hermerii, and Thomas and Edward his sons, the king's nephews, and the heirs of their bodies [*CPR 1307–13*, pp.304–5, 29 Dec. 1310]. From them it descended to Margaret, daughter of Thomas, who married John de Monte Acuto senior, brother of William earl of Salisbury, whence it descended to John. It is held of the king by homage and fealty, as is the manor of Warblington.

Heir as above [no.24].

27 ESSEX. Inquisition. Stratford. 30 March 1400.

John Wroth, junior, William Newerk, chaplain, and Robert Peper held in their demesne as of fee 2 messuages, 226 a. arable, 38 a. meadow and £4 7s.6d. rent in West Ham, East Ham, Stratford, and Barking, enfeoffed by John son of Andrew Aubrey, and regranted them to John Aubrey and Maud his wife. John de Monte Acuto afterwards married Maud, and held them in her right. The messuage, parts of the lands and the rent are held of the abbot of Stratford, service unknown, and the rest of Hugh Burnell, knight, service also unknown; annual value 20 marks. Joan Bryan and Joan Lichebarwe are the heirs as above [no.25].

He also held in right of Maud, his wife, 1 messuage, 260 a. arable, 40 a. meadow, 60 a. pasture and 10s. rent in Brook Walden, of the abbot of Walden, service unknown, annual value 60s.

On 20 Sept. 1397 he gave by his indenture to John Brokeman, esquire, for life a tenement called Gosfield, with lands etc. in Gosfield, Bocking, and Finchingfield, to hold by rent of a rose, with reversion to himself and his heirs. It is held of the earl of Oxford, service unknown, annual value 5 marks.

Date of death and heir as above [no. 24].

28   DORSET. Inquisition. Blandford. 26 June 1400.

He held in right of Maud his wife as her dower after the death of Alan de Buxhull, knight, her former husband, a third part of the manor of Bryanston comprising a house called 'Knyghtonchambre' with a granary to the end of the barn; a close called 'Le Flexhey' in the site of the manor; a close called 'Les Rygges'; a close between the manor and the rectory; 72 a. arable of which 16 a. are in 'la Northfelde' near the close of Alice Waryn in 'la Westcombe' with 'la cor', 18 a. from there called 'la Ladylynche' to the end of the town in 'la Southcombe', 22 a. in 'la Combe' in the south part in 'Croftforlange', 10 a. in the east part, and 6 a. in 'Ridelond' and 'la Park'; 10 a. of meadow near the gate of the meadow of the manor; 20 a. scrub in the north part of the wood called 'Bradeley'; pasture for 400 sheep; £4 rent from a tenement called 'Dame Sabyne'; a tenement formerly of Thomas Buysshop; another formerly of John Chapman; a tenement of William Frykes; a tenement of Alice Waryn; and the service of John Cadebury; with a third part of the profits of dovecot, mill, court, attachments of court, ways and wastes, and all other profits, with free entrance and egress. The manor is held of the king in chief by knight service and the third part is valued at 11 marks 4s. 5½d. yearly.

Date of death as above.

[*Cf. CIM* VII, no. 17; *CCR 1399–1402*, pp. 152–4].

C 137/2, no. 11, mm. 5–11
E 149/73, no. 7, mm. 1–4

THOMAS DE TREWYK

29   Writ 6 Feb. 1400.

NORTHUMBERLAND. Inquisition. The king's castle by Newcastle upon Tyne. 15 June 1402.

He held in his demesne as of fee:

Cramlington, 7 husbandlands, of the king in chief of the barony of Gaugy by knight service, annual value 20s.

Whitlow, 2 messuages and 60 a., of the king in chief of the same barony by knight service, annual value 12d.

Hartley, 18 a., of the lord of Seaton Delaval by knight service, annual value 3s. 4d.

South Middleton, 1½ a. of husbandland with 6 a. in Bolam, of the barony of Bolam by a rent of 7s., annual value 3s. 4d.

With Agnes his wife he held the manor of Trewick by the feoffment of Thomas de Fernylaw, Robert de Aukland, and William Broune, chaplains, to them and their heirs. It is held of the barony of Bolam by the service of one unmewed sparrowhawk, annual value 40s.

He died on 24 Oct. 1399. His daughters and heirs are Eleanor, aged 24 years, and Joan 22 years. The lands have been taken into the king's hands.

C 137/2, no.12

GEOFFREY CADEHAY

30   Writ 20 May 1400.

DEVON. Inquisition. Bradninch. 16 Sept.

He held 3 messuages, 3 ferlings in Langley, ½ ferling in Busland and 'Cokereslond', 8 a. in Stickeridge, and 15s.10d. rent in Heath, Cotton and Meadhayes, all parts of the manor of Langley, of the lord of Wellington, of his manor of Uplowman in free socage by a rent of 13s., annual value 44s.

He died on 28 March 1396. Beatrice and Margaret his daughters, aged 30 years and more, and Richard son of Emma, his other daughter, aged 16 years and more, are his heirs.

John Copleston, formerly escheator, took the revenues from the day of Geoffrey's death until 3 Nov. 1398, and Richard Gambon, by grant of Richard II [*CFR 1391–9*, p.283] from 3 Nov. 1398 until the day of the inquisition, both by the hands of Thomas Langelegh, tenant at will, William Langelegh, life tenant, and Richard Wroth, John Ballere and William Churnewall, free tenants in demesne as of fee.

C 137/2, no.13

PHILIPPA WIDOW OF RICHARD SERGEAUX, KNIGHT

31   Writ 18 Oct. 1399.

CORNWALL. Inquisition. Bodmin. 24 Jan. 1400.

She held:

Tremodret, the manor, to herself and the heirs of Richard, of the king of the duchy of Cornwall, of the castle of Launceston by knight service, as 3 fees-morton, annual value £13 6s.8d.

Trevillis, the manor, similarly, of John Herle, knight, of his manor of Tywardreath in socage, annual value £10 2s.

Kilquite, the manor, for life, of the heirs of Richard Sergeaux, by rent of a rose at Midsummer, annual value £46 6s.8d.

Poldu, Lanreath, and Helland, a third part of the manors, in dower, of John de Dynham, knight, of his manor of Cardinham by knight service, as 2½ fees-morton, annual value £10.

She died on 13 Sept. Elizabeth, Philippa, Alice and Joan are the daughters and heirs of Richard and herself. Elizabeth, wife of William Marny, knight, is aged 21 years and more; Philippa, wife of Robert Passele, 18 years and more; Alice, wife of Guy St. Aubyn, 14 years and more; and Joan 7 years and more.

Note by John Syreston, the escheator, that he took all the lands into the king's hands, and fixed a day for holding the court of Tremodret and Trevillis, namely 27 Jan. On that day he sent his clerk, Eurnus Doneythan, to hold the court, but William Bodrugan, bastard, William Janyn of Tregoss, and others unknown entered by force of arms, arrayed for war, insulted and threatened Eurnus, who was unable to hold the court;

and William Janyn held it in the name of William Bodrugan. They levied £8 in rent from the tenants and carried it off.

32 Writ, for fees, 1 April 1400.

CORNWALL. Inquisition. Hellandbridge. 21 June.

She held no fees or advowsons of the king in chief, but of the king of the duchy of Cornwall, of the castle of Launceston, 3½ fees-morton with appurtenances in Tremodret, annual value £10.

33 Writ 18 Oct. 1399.

OXFORD. Inquisition. Chipping Norton. 24 March 1400.

She held in her demesne as of fee of the king in chief, as one knight's fee, the manor of Chipping Norton, annual value £40.

She died on 13 Sept. last. Elizabeth, Philippa, Alice and Joan are her daughters and heirs, aged respectively 30, 28, 14 and 8 years and more.

C 137/4, no.23

RICHARD SERGEAUX, KNIGHT

34 Writ, *plenius certiorari*, as it was found by inquisition before John Copleston that Richard held jointly with Philippa his wife the manor of Tremodret, and also that he held the manor of Kilquite, but it was not stated who has the reversions in default of heirs of Richard and Philippa. 8 July 1400.

CORNWALL. Inquisition. Bodmin. 16 July.

He held in his demesne as of fee the manors of Tremodret and Trevillis and granted them to Otto de Bodrugan, master William Sergeaux, clerk, and John Dreyn, chaplain. They conveyed them to Richard and Philippa his wife, and the heirs of their bodies, with remainder to the right heirs of Richard. They had issue Richard, Elizabeth, Philippa, Alice and Joan. The elder Richard died. Richard the son died under age without issue, and Philippa died. The manors descended to Elizabeth, Philippa, Alice and Joan, as daughters and heirs of Richard and Philippa.

He also held in his demesne as of fee the manor of Kilquite, which he granted to Henry Nanfan and John Pollard for the life of Philippa his wife, and they released their rights in it to Philippa. Thus Richard and Philippa held it, and it descended to the same four daughters.

C 137/3, no.14, mm.1,2

RICHARD SON AND HEIR OF RICHARD SERGEAUX, KNIGHT

35 Writ 1 July 1400.

CORNWALL. Inquisition. Bodmin. 16 July.

Richard Sergeaux, knight, the father, held in his demesne as of fee:

Eathorne, the manor, of the bishop of Exeter in socage of his manor of Penryn, annual value 101s.4d.

Rosenithon, the manor, of Ralph Reskymmer by knight service, annual value £10.

Penarth, 5 messuages and 1 carucate, of John Urban in socage, annual value 43s.4d.

Trefreock, a third part of the manor, of the duchy of Cornwall of the manor of Penmayne in socage; the remainder with half the manor of Pencarrow, of Edward Courteney, earl of Devon, John Rodeney, knight, and John Cheynduyt, by knight service, annual value 20 marks.

Pencarrow, the other half manor, of John Dynham, knight, by knight service, annual value 40s.

Long before he died he held the manors of Predannack, Penhale, Poldu, Helland, Lanreath, Treninick, and Trethevan, and granted them to John Isaac, John Shireston, James Gerveys and Thomas Tremayn, clerk, to hold for his own life, with remainder to Richard his son and his heirs. They are held of John Dynham, knight, by knight service, annual value £40. A third part passed to Philippa his widow in dower, two parts to the younger Richard, who held by the same services as his father and died on 23 June 1396 in his 20th year. His sisters, Elizabeth, wife of William Marny, knight, aged 21 years and more, Philippa, wife of Robert Passele, aged 18 years and more, Alice, wife of Guy de Sancto Albinio, aged 15 years and more, and Joan aged 7 years, are next heirs.

36 Writ 1 July 1400.

OXFORD. Inquisition. Chipping Norton. 12 July.

No lands or tenements were in the king's hands owing to the minority of Richard, son and heir of Richard Sergeaux, knight; but the father held the manor of Chipping Norton to himself, his wife, and the heirs of their bodies. It remained to his wife Philippa. Richard the son died, then Philippa died, and so it descended to Elizabeth, Philippa, Alice and Joan, their daughters and heirs. It is held of the king in chief by knight service, annual value 50 marks.

Richard the son died on 24 June 1396; sisters and heirs as in last.

C 137/3, no.14, mm.3–6

JOAN DAUGHTER OF RICHARD SERGEAUX, KNIGHT

37 Writ 18 Aug. 1400.

OXFORD. Inquisition. Chipping Norton. 31 Aug.

No lands are in the king's hands on account of the deaths of Richard Sergeaux, knight, and Richard his son.

Richard late earl of Arundel held in his demesne as of fee the manor of Chipping Norton, and conveyed it to Richard the father, Philippa his wife, and their heirs. Richard held it, then Philippa, and it descended to their daughters, Elizabeth, Philippa, Alice and Joan. It was taken into the king's hands and the three parts of Philippa, Alice and Joan were retained, whilst the fourth part was released to Elizabeth by virtue of the king's writ. It is held of the king in chief as one knight's fee, annual value £40.

Joan died on 31 July. Elizabeth aged 33, Philippa 19, and Alice 15, are the sisters and heirs of Joan [names of husbands as above, no.35].

38 Writ 18 Aug. 1400.

CORNWALL. Inquisition. Kilquite. 20 Sept.

Richard Sergeaux, knight, held in his demesne as of fee the manor of Rosenithon

C

of the heirs of John Roskymmer, knight, by knight service; and the manor of Eathorne of the bishop of Exeter of the manor of Penryn in socage; annual value together £10.

He held for life the manor of Predannack of the manor of Helston of the duchy of Cornwall in socage; the manor of Penhale of William Tregoes in socage; the manors of Poldu, Helland, Lanreath, Treninick, and half of Pencarrow, of John Dynham, knight, of his manor of Cardinham by knight service; and the manor of Trefreock of John Rodeneye, knight, by knight service; annual value together £40.

They descended to Richard his son by virtue of a feoffment by James Gerveys, John Isaac, Thomas Tremayn, clerk, and John Syreston. Philippa held a third part in dower.

He also held the manors of Tremodret of the castle of Launceston, of the duchy of Cornwall, by knight service, and Trevillis of John Herle, knight, of his manor of Tywardreath in socage, to himself, Philippa his wife, and the heirs of their bodies, annual value £40.

Also for the lives of himself and Philippa he held the manor of Kilquite of John Dynham by knight service, with reversion to his right heirs in fee simple, annual value 20 marks.

All descended to Elizabeth, Philippa, Alice and Joan, as sisters and heirs of the younger Richard, and were taken into the king's hands as of the duchy of Cornwall. Three parts should be in the king's hands, but William Bodrugan, bastard, William Janyn and others entered forcibly, and took, and are still taking, the profits. There is nothing in the king's hands, nor was in the hands of Richard II.

Joan died on 31 July. Elizabeth aged 20, Philippa 19, and Alice 15 [names of husbands as above, no. 35] are her sisters and heirs.

C 137/4, no.24

MARGARET WIFE OF FULK DE PENBRUGGE, KNIGHT

39 Writ 8 Nov. 1399.

BERKSHIRE. Inquisition. Maidenhead. 10 Feb. 1400.

When she died on 10 June 1399 she held:

Shottesbrook, the manor with the advowson of the college there in her demesne as of fee, of the king of the castle of Windsor by the rent of a pair of gilt spurs, or 3s.4d., at Michaelmas, annual value 8 marks.

Cookham, 50 a. in 'Benetfeld' called 'le Hethynnynges', of the king of the manor, which is ancient demesne of the crown, quit of all rent, annual value 20s.

Waltham St. Lawrence, 1 messuage and 2 virgates, of the bishop of Winchester of the manor of Wargrave, by a rent of 18s.5d. and suit of court at Wargrave every 3 weeks, annual value 6s.8d.

William, son of Lawrence Trussell, aged 14 years, is her kinsman and next heir, being the son of Lawrence, son of Warin, brother of William Trussell, father of Margaret. Fulk de Penbrugge has held the lands since the day of her death and received the profits.

C 137/3, no.15

EDWARD DE CLYNTON

40 Writ 18 June 1400.

HERTFORD. Inquisition. Hitchin. 14 Sept.

He held the manor of Pirton and various lands, tenements, rents and services in

Kimpton in fee tail by the grant of Robert Rede, Thomas Darnoll and Richard Reynold, clerks, to his father, John Clynton, knight, deceased, for life, long before his marriage to Elizabeth, with successive remainders to Edward, the heirs male of his body, and the right heirs of John. John died and Edward held them. He died without male heirs. They should descend to William Clynton, knight, his nephew and heir, being the son of William, son of John. They are held of the king of the honour of Pinkney by knight service, annual value £15 15s.8d.

He died on 15 June last. William, his nephew and heir, is aged 28 years and more.

41 Writ 18 June 1400.
KENT. Inquisition. Chiddingstone. 17 Oct.
He held:
Chiddingstone, 30 a. called 'Helderestenement', in gavelkind of Lord Say of his manor of Cudham by fealty, suit of court, 4s.8d. rent, and other services unknown, annual value 2d. an acre; and 20 a. land and 6 a. wood in gavelkind of Reynold Cobeham, knight, by fealty, suit of court, and rent of 4s.8d. at the four principal terms at the manor of Chiddingstone Cobham, each acre being worth annually 2d.

Hever, 1 toft comprising 1 a. land, and 104 a. arable, 40 a. pasture, and 2s.5d. assize rent, by gavelkind. The toft and 100 a. are held of Reynold Cobeham of the manor of Hever by fealty, rent of 16s.4d. at the four terms, 1 cock, 7 hens, 40 eggs and common suit of court at the said manor, the cock and hens at Christmas and the eggs at Easter, half a ploughshare, price 6d. at Michaelmas, and 4 reapers for corn for 1 day in autumn; 4 a. of the manor of Hever Cobham, in gavelkind, by a fealty, a rent of 4d. at the four terms, and common suit of court at the same manor, annual value 2d. an a.; the 40 a. pasture in gavelkind of John Wodekot of the manor of Broxham by a rent of 2s.8d. at the four terms, 2 hens at Christmas, 40 eggs at Easter, 2 reapers for 1 day in autumn, and common suit of court. The toft is worth 4d. annually; 104 a. arable at 2d., 17s.4d;, 40 a. pasture at 1d., 3s.4d.

Brasted and Hever, 5s. annual rent, of the heirs of William atte Seilyerde, and 6s.6d. rent from Richard Staneford for lands there, which the heirs and Richard hold at fee farm of the grant of John de Clynton, father of Edward, payable at the four principal terms.

Chiddingstone, 4 a. meadow in 'la aw. . .e', of the manor of Dartford, service unknown, annual value 4s.

He died on 15 June last. William Clynton, knight, and Richard his brother, and Thomas de Clynton, knight, brother of Edward, are next heirs. William is aged 23 years and more, Richard 18 and more, and Thomas 30 and more.

C 137/3, no.16

BERNARD BROCAS, KNIGHT

42 Writ 22 Feb. 1400.
BUCKINGHAM. Inquisition. Wing. 1 March.
He held at farm for a term of years the manors of Horton and Cheddington by an indenture between John Chitterne and others and himself, dated 2 July 1396, granting them for 8 years from 20 Sept. 1395 for £50 annual rent. They belong to Joan, his widow, for the remainder of the term.

The king by letters patent of 16 Feb. last [*CPR 1399–1401*, p.207] granted to Joan all his forfeited goods and a third part of all his forfeited manors and lands. The manors are held partly of the abbess of Barking, partly of the abbot of Woburn, and partly of the manor of Aston Clinton, services unknown, annual value 40 marks.

He died on 28 Jan. last. William his son and heir is aged 20 years and more.

43 Writ 22 Feb. 1400.

BERKSHIRE. Inquisition. Maidenhead. 19 March.

He held in fee tail:

Clewer, 1 messuage, 1 carucate and 5 a. meadow, annual value 13s.4d., of John Cifrewast by a rent of 25s.8d. and 1 lb. less 1 oz. pepper at Easter and Michaelmas.

Bray, various lands and tenements in the lordship, of the king of the manor of Bray, by a rent of 39s.9½d., annual value 2s.

Cookham, 1 cottage and curtilage, 3 a. arable and 3 a. meadow, of the king of the manor of Cookham, by a rent of 20d., annual value 10s.

Windsor, a tavern and 15 a. arable, of the king of the castle of Windsor, by a rent of 7s.7¾d, annual value 11s.

Dedworth, the manor, of the king by suit of the hundred at the court of the seven hundreds of Cookham and Bray, annual value 66s.8d.

Winkfield and Buntingbury, 112s.¾d. quit rent.

Date of death and heir as above.

44 Writ 22 Feb. 1400.

NORTHAMPTON. Inquisition. Rothwell. 8 March.

By a fine of 1399 made with royal licence [CP 25(1) 178/89, no.188; CPR 1396–9, p.456] he conveyed to William Brocas his son, Sybil, William's wife, and the heirs of their bodies the manor of Weekley, which is held of the king in chief, annual value 20 marks.

Bernard Brocas, knight, his father, by a fine of 1383 [CP 25(1) 289/53, no.95] conveyed to Master Arnold Brocas, clerk, John de Chitterne, clerk, Peter Bolde, William Ermyte, chaplain, and Henry Holte, the manor of Little Weldon called 'Huntesmaner' with other manors and lands to them and the heirs of Peter Bolde. Peter quitclaimed to them. Arnold Brocas, Peter, William Ermyte and Henry are dead. It is held of the king by the service of keeping his deerhounds, annual value 60s.

Date of death and heir as above.

45 Writ 22 Feb. 1400.

DORSET. Inquisition. Evershot. 14 March.

On the day that he was tried and executed Bernard Brocas held in his demesne as of fee the manor of Brimbleby of Hugh Waterton, knight, in the right of Katherine, Hugh's wife, and of the abbot of Sherborne, by knight service, annual value £12.

Date of death and heir [miscalled Bernard Brocas] as above.

[Cf. CIM VII, no.114].

46 Writ, *plenius certiorari*, on petition of Joan his widow concerning their joint holdings. 22 Feb. 1400.

YORK. Inquisition and extent. Denton. 9 March.

He held the manor of Denton in Wharfedale in his demesne as of fee by the grant of Brian Stapilton, William Gascoigne, Arnold Brokas and John Chytarn, clerks, to him, Joan his wife, who survives him, and their heirs. It is held of the archbishop of York of his manor of Otley, service unknown, annual value 40 marks.

He also held jointly with his wife, to them and their heirs, by the grant of Bernard Brocas, his father, certain lands and tenements in Askwith, of Henry earl of Northumberland, of the manor of Spofforth by knight service, annual value 10 marks; and the manor of Ouston, of the same earl of the same manor by knight service, annual value 12 marks.

Date of death and heir as above.

47 Writ, *plenius certiorari*, on petition of Joan his widow, as above. 28 May 1400.

YORK. Inquisition. Denton. 5 June.

He held jointly with Joan the manor of Denton in Wharfedale [as in last], granted by the name of all those lands, tenements, meadows, woods, pastures, rents and services which they had by the grant of Bernard the father.

He also held jointly with Joan, with remainder to the heirs of their bodies, 4 messuages, 100 a. arable, 20 a. meadow and 40s. rent in Askwith, and the manor of Ouston [as in last].

Date of death as above.

48 Writ 22 Feb. 1400.

HAMPSHIRE. Inquisition. Basingstoke. 24 March.

He held in his demesne as of fee the manors of North Fareham and Broxhead, except for 15 a. in Broxhead, of the bishop of Winchester, services unknown, annual values £16 and 40s.

Date of death and heir as above.

Bernard his father by a fine of 1383 [CP 25(1) 289/53, no.95] granted, with other manors in other counties, to Master Arnold Brocas, John de Chitterne and Peter Bolde, clerks, William Hermyte, chaplain, and Henry Holte, and the heirs of Peter, the manors of Beaurepaire and Bradley and 4 messuages, 1 mill, 5 carucates, 12 a. meadow, 30 a. wood and 8 marks rent in Froyle, Basing, Stoke Charity, Southwick, Basingstoke, Hurstbourne and Stratfield Mortimer, not held in chief. Peter released them to the other four. After the deaths of Arnold, William, Peter and Henry, John Chitterne on 17 Aug. 1395 granted them by his charter with other manors to Ralph de Lenham and John Shirlond. They on 22 Aug. following conveyed them to William bishop of Winchester, John bishop of Salisbury, Roger Walden, clerk, John Chitterne, Master John Hengate, and Thomas Hywyk and John Marnham, chaplains. On 2 July 1396 Roger Walden, John Chitterne and John Marnham conveyed to Bernard Brocas the manors of Bradley and Steventon with the other premises mentioned above and other lands and other manors in other counties, for the term of 8 years from 20 Sept. 1396 for £50 rent. They belong to Joan, his widow, for the remainder of the term. On 15 Feb. 1400 the king granted her all Bernard's forfeited goods and a third part of all his manors and other lands [CPR 1399–1401, p.207].

[Cf. CIM VII, nos.128–9].

C 137/3, no.17
E 149/74, no.15
E 152/345

ROBERT PEKENHAM

49 Writ 13 Feb. 1400.

ESSEX. Inquisition. Braintree. 10 March.

He held in his demesne in fee tail, half of all the lands, tenements, rents and services which were formerly held by John de Wauton, knight, and Margaret his wife in Steeple Bumpstead, Sturmer, Birdbrook and Wixoe, to himself and the heirs of his body, by the gift of William de Wauton, parson of Ashdon, and William Warde of Trumpington, clerk, to John de Wauton, knight, and Margaret, grandmother of Robert de Pekenham, by virtue of which grant John de Wauton and Margaret died seised of it, and it descended to Robert as grandson and heir, that is the son of Elizabeth, one of the daughters of John and Margaret. From Robert, who died seised of it without heirs of his body, it descended to Ivo Harleston, his cousin and heir, the son of Margaret, another daughter of John and Margaret, and sister of Elizabeth, mother of Robert Pekenham. The annual value is 10 marks. Half of one messuage and 15 a. of these lands and tenements are held of the king in chief by a rent of 18d. payable by the sheriff. Of whom the rest is held and by what service is unknown.

Similarly he held in his demesne as of fee half a tenement called Downhall in Roydon with other lands, tenements, rents and services, and meadow, in Great Parndon, Little Parndon, and Nazeing, from John and Margaret as the last, of the prior of St. John of Jerusalem in England by a rent of 2s.6½d. payable by equal parts at Easter and Michaelmas, annual value 40s.

John Pekenham, deceased, the father of Robert, held in his demesne as of fee the manor of Whitehall with other lands and tenements in Great Burstead, Little Burstead, Ingrave and Dunton, which he granted to Roger Folyet and John Grafton, clerks, who enfeoffed Nicholas FitzRichard, Nicholas Benyngfeld, clerk, Richard Waltham and others, to hold in fee simple to themselves, their heirs and assigns.

He died on 1 Jan. last. Ivo Harleston is next heir, being the son of Margaret, daughter of John de Wauton and Margaret, and sister of Elizabeth, aged . . . and more.

C 137/4, no.18
E 152/351

WILLIAM SHARESHULL, KNIGHT

50 Writ 22 June 1400.

SHROPSHIRE AND THE ADJACENT MARCH OF WALES. Inquisition. Bridgnorth. 8 July.

Henry Power and William de Broughton by a fine of 1344 [CP 25(1) 287/41, no.326] granted the manor of Boningale to William son of William de Shareshull, knight, [and Joan his wife, in fine] and the heirs of his body. He held it for life and left issue William and Elizabeth. William held it until he died without heirs of his body on 17 May 1400. It is held of the king in chief as an eighth part of a knight's fee, annual value 100s.

Elizabeth had three daughters, Joan, Margaret and Katherine, and died. Of the daughters, Joan had a daughter Joan, married to William Lee; Margaret had two daughters, Isabel and Joyce, and died; Katherine is the wife of Roger Wyllyley. Joan wife of William Lee, Isabel and Joyce, and Katherine are next heirs. Katherine and Joan wife of William are aged 21 years and more. Isabel is 3 years and more, Joyce half a year and more.

51 STAFFORD. Inquisition. Trysull. 10 July 1400.

Henry Power and William de Broughton by a fine of 1344 [as in last] granted the manors of Patshull and Overton to William son of William de Shareshull, Joan his wife, and the heirs of his body. By another fine of 1344 [CP 25(1) 210/15, no. 26] the same Henry Power and William de Broughton, with Thomas Costey, granted the manor of Shareshill to them and the heirs of their bodies. The grantees held the manors for life and had issue William and Elizabeth, and the younger William held them for life.

William the father also held for life to himself and the heirs of his body the manors of Great Saredon and Little Saredon, and two parts of the manors of Coven and Brinsford. They descended to William the son, who held them for life.

He therefore held in his demesne as of fee the manors of Overton, annual value 40s., Great Saredon, 4 marks, Little Saredon, 4 marks, two parts of Coven and Brinsford, 30s., and the manor of Shareshill, £10, of the earl of Stafford, service unknown, except 6 a. called 'Rudyngfeld', 4 a. wood called 'Rudyngfeldesmore' and 1 a. meadow, parts of the manor of Shareshill, of the king in chief by knight service; also the manor of Patshull of the prior of Kenilworth, service unknown, annual value 10 marks.

Date of death and heirs as above.

52 Writ 23 June 1400.
OXFORD. Inquisition. Chipping Norton. 25 Aug.

He held in his demesne as of fee, to himself, his heirs and assigns, by a fine of 1390 [CP 25(1) 289/56, no. 208] the manors of Rousham and Dornford, and also the manors of Patshull, Shareshill, Great Saredon and Little Saredon, and two parts of the manors of Coven and Brinsford, in Staffordshire, and the manor of Boningale in Shropshire, from Richard Fauley, clerk, to William Shareshull and Margaret his wife, with remainder, failing heirs of the body of William, to Richard Harcourt and Margaret his wife, and the heirs of their bodies, and failing them to the right heirs of William. Accordingly William and Margaret Shareshull held these manors. Margaret Shareshull died. Richard and Margaret Harcourt had issue Isabel, and Margaret died. William died seised of the manors of Rousham and Dornford, leaving no heirs of his body, and they should therefore remain to Richard Harcourt.

Rousham is held of the prince [of Wales] of his honour of St. Valéry, service unknown, annual value £10; Dornford of the king of his manor of Wootton by service at the hundred court of Wootton every three weeks, annual value, apart from 5 marks which John Poyle has for life, 66s. 8d.

He died on 17 May. Elizabeth his sister had three daughters; the first, Joan, had a daughter Joan, wife of William Lee, aged 21 years and more; the second, Margaret, married Richard Harcourt and their daughter Isabel is aged 4 years and more; the third, Katherine, aged 21 years and more, is married to Roger Wililey.

C 137/4, no. 19
E 357/14, m. 8

HUGH LA ZOUCH, KNIGHT

53 Writ 23 Oct. 1399.
CAMBRIDGE. Inquisition. Cambridge. 27 Jan. 1400.

He held by the feoffment of William Forde, clerk, John Knyghteleye, Thomas de la Lee, Thomas Skynnere of Shrewsbury, Robert Rikedon, John de la Hide, clerk,

William Halle, clerk, William Corleygh, clerk, Thomas Cru, Robert Russell, Brian de Harleye, Thomas Shabdon, and William de la Lee, to himself and the heirs of his body, the manor of Swavesey with the advowsons of the priory and chapel there, and the manor called 'Zouchesfee' in Fulbourn. Both manors are held of the earl of Richmond: Swavesey in socage, annual value 40 marks; 'Zouchesfee', service unknown, annual value 20 marks.

By the feoffment of Thomas Morys, William Crouch, William Aleyn and Richard Leverer, he held the manor called 'Manersfee' in Fulbourn for life with remainder to John Hyde, parson of Handsworth, William Corlegh, parson of Great Cheverell, John Stratton by Westbury, chaplain, Thomas Lee, Thomas Skynnere, John Borley and William Lee, and their heirs and assigns. It is held of the bishop of Ely by knight service, annual value 10 marks.

He died on 4 July last without heirs of his body. Joyce wife of Hugh Burnell, knight, is his kinswoman and heir, being daughter of John Botourd, son of Joyce, sister of Alan, the father of Hugh, and aged 30 years and more.

54   Writ 23 Oct. 1399.

LEICESTER. Inquisition. Ashby de la Zouch. 17 Dec.

He held the manor of Ashby de la Zouch in his demesne as of fee to himself and the heirs of his body by the feoffment of William Forde, clerk, and others [as in last]. Except for 7½ virgates in Kilwardby, parcel of the manor, it is held of Lord Beaumont, service unknown. The 7½ virgates were held of Richard II in chief of the crown as a quarter of a knight's fee, annual value 57s. 4¾d.

In the manor are 1 capital messuage, annual value nil; 120 a. arable in the common fields, annual value 24s., and no more because one third lies fallow each year; 12 a. meadow in the common fields, 20s.; a park with pasture, nil beyond the sustenance of the game; a dovecot nil because ruinous; a pond nil because unstocked; rents of the town of Ashby, £4 2s. 1¾d. payable by equal parts at St. Thomas the Apostle, Easter and Midsummer; rents of free tenants and villeins, £11 7s. 5½d. payable at Martinmas, Lady Day and Midsummer; 1 watermill and 1 windmill, 53s. 4d.; a common oven 13s. 4d.; tolls of the market every Saturday, with a fair of 5 days at Holy Rood Day, 26s. 8d.; and pleas and perquisites of court 13s. 4d.

Date of death and heir as above.

55   Writ 23 Oct. 1399.

SUSSEX. Inquisition. Midhurst. 5 Apr. 1400.

He held the manors of River and Nutbourne with the advowson of the chapel of River jointly with Joan his wife, who survives him, to them and the heirs of his body, by the gift of William Forde, clerk, and others [as above].

In River there is a capital messuage, annual value nil; 180 a. arable at 3d., 45s.; 10 a. meadow at 10d., 11s. 8d. [sic]; 18 a. several pasture, 4s.; a watermill, 13s. 4d.; a park, nil beyond the keeping of the game and wages of the parker; assize rents of free tenants, villeins and cottars, £10 1¾d. payable at the four terms; and pleas and perquisites of courts, 6s. 8d. It is held of Henry Percy, earl of Northumberland, of the manor of Petworth, service unknown.

In Nutbourne £12 6s. 8d. in rents of free tenants and villeins at the four terms; 3 ruinous watermills, nil; and pleas and perquisites of court, 4s. It is held of the heirs of Robert de Tateshale, as the jurors understand.

He also held to himself and the heirs of his body, by the gift of the same William

Forde, clerk, and others, the advowson of West Chiltington; 100s. 8d. rent from free tenants and villeins there at the four terms, of the king in chief by the service of a quarter of a knight's fee; and pleas and perquisites of court there, annual value 12d. The rent of 100s.8d., except for wards, marriages, reliefs and escheats, he granted long before his death to Thomas Monerpilers for life for the rent of a rose, with reversion to himself and his heirs.

The following knight's fees are held of the manor of River: Stopham, Linch, Barecourt and Yapton, 2½ fees by the heirs of John Darundell, knight; West Marden, ½ fee by Thomas de Arundell; Lurgashall and Coates, 1 fee by Alice Seynt Johan; Rumboldswyke, 1 fee by John Loghteburgh.

Date of death and heir as above.

[Cf. CCR 1399–1402, p.144].

C 137/4, no.20
E 149/72, no.4
E 152/361, 363

MAUD WIDOW OF RICHARD DE STAFFORD, KNIGHT

56 Writ 14 April 1400.

NORTHAMPTON. Inquisition. Rothwell. 23 April.

She held for life of the inheritance of Edmund, bishop of Exeter, son and heir of Richard de Stafford, the manor of Sibbertoft, in fee tail, by the grant of Henry de Tymmore, Richard Lorymer and John Whitynton, clerks, to Richard and Maud and the heirs male of their bodies, with remainder to the right heirs of Richard, father of Edmund, by a fine levied with royal licence [CPR 1370–4, p.151; CP 25(1) 178/84, no.643]. It is held in petty serjeanty by a rent of 53s. 1½d. payable by the sheriff, annual value £12 9s.0½d.

She and Richard her husband died without heirs male, and it should descend to Edmund, who is aged 53 years and more. She died on 30 March last, but who is her heir and of what age is unknown.

57 Writ 14 April 1400.

GLOUCESTER. Inquisition. Winchcombe. 26 April.

She held for life of the inheritance of Edmund, bishop of Exeter, son and heir of Richard de Stafford, in fee tail:

Chipping Campden, half the manor and half the advowson, by the grant of John Whytynton, formerly parson of Naunton, and Richard de Drayton, formerly parson of Seckington, Warwickshire, by a fine [CPR 1377–81, p.272; CP 25(1) 78/78, no.13], to Richard, Maud and their heirs male. They are held of the king in chief as a quarter of a knight's fee, annual value £20.

Aston Subedge, the manor with the advowson, by the grant of Hugh de Hopewas, Henry de Tymmore and Nicholas de Yvyngho, chaplains, by a fine [CP 25(1) 78/72, no. 424]. It is held of the bishop of Worcester, service unknown, annual value £10.

Charingworth, the manor, by the grant of John Goldyng and Maud his wife by a fine [CP 25(1) 78/73, no.434]. It is held of John Lovell, knight, service unknown, annual value £10.

Ullington, the manor, by the grant of Thomas de Hampton, held of Robert Corbet, knight, by knight service, annual value 40s.

They died without heirs male of their bodies, she on 30 March. Edmund the son and heir of Richard is aged 53 years and more.
[*Cf. CIPM* XV, nos.417–8].

C 137/4, no.21
E 149/74, no.9
E 152/355

ELIZABETH WIDOW OF JOHN DE PENBRUGGE, KNIGHT

58 Writ 29 Aug. 1400.

HEREFORD AND THE ADJACENT MARCH OF WALES. Inquisition. Leominster. 9 Sept.
She held jointly with John, formerly her husband:
Boughrood and Eaton Tregoes, the castle and hamlets, with member, namely Trewarne, of the king in chief by a rent of 6d., and if by any other service it is unknown.
Burghill, 1 messuage, 1 carucate, 4 a. meadow, 4 a. wood, and 36s. rent payable at Lady Day and Michaelmas, of the king of the honour of Brecknock, of the inheritance of Humphrey de Bohun, earl of Hereford, by the service of a third part of a knight's fee. They were granted to John and herself and the heirs of John by Robert Whyteney, clerk, and Thomas de Hampton.
Alice widow of Thomas Oldecastell is cousin and next heir of John de Penbrugge, being the daughter of John, brother of Edward, father of John, aged 28 years and more; but who is the next heir of Elizabeth is unknown.
The castle is worth nothing annually. At Boughrood with its member are 1 carucate of demesne lands, 3 a. meadow and 7 a. wood, annual value 40s.; rents of £4 5s. payable at Lady Day and Michaelmas; 2 mills, 1 grinding and 1 fulling, 5 marks; and pleas and perquisites of court, 40s. At Eaton Tregoes are 1 carucate and 10 a. meadow, 60s.; and 33s. 6d. rent payable at the same terms. The holdings at Burghill are valued at 30s. annually, beyond the rent.
She died on 23 Aug. last.

C 137/4, no.22

BRIAN DE CORNEWAILLE, KNIGHT

59 Writ 30 Jan. 1400.

DEVON. Inquisition. Winkleigh. 19 Feb.
He held in his demesne as of fee the manor of King's Nympton with the advowson, of Richard Seymour, knight, of his manor of North Molton by knight service, annual value £20.
He died on 17 Jan. last. Richard his brother and heir is aged 30 years and more.

60 Writ 30 Jan. 1400.

HEREFORD AND THE ADJACENT MARCH OF WALES. Inquisition. Leominster. 19 Feb.
He held in his demesne as of fee various hamlets: Oatcroft, Titley, Cascob, Wapley, Combe and Rodd, with their appurtenances in Lugharness in the Welsh March, with pleas of court and rents. These hamlets are parcels of the castle and town of Stapleton, held of the king in chief of the barony of Burford, annual value £8 5s.

William atte Boure and Maud his wife hold half the manor of Rochford for life, by the grant of Brian, with remainder to his right heirs. It is held of Robert Clifford by the rent of one sparrowhawk, annual value 40s.

Date of death and heir, aged 33 years and more, as above.

61 Writ 30 Jan. 1400.

SHROPSHIRE AND THE ADJACENT MARCH OF WALES. Inquisition. Ludlow. 16 Feb.

He held in his demesne as of fee of the king in chief:

Burford, the manor, parcel of the barony, as 2½ knight's fees, annual value £18.

Overs, the hundred, at fee farm, by a rent of 6s. 8d. payable by the sheriff, annual value 20s.

Stapleton, the castle and vill, with the hamlets of Frodesley and Willey in the Welsh March, with pleas and perquisites of court, as members of the barony of Burford, annual value £12.

Roger Wiggemore has an annual rent of 100s. for life in Leintwardine, Kington, Burrington, and Adforton in Wigmoreland, by the grant of Brian, with reversion to his right heirs. William atte Boure and Maud his wife hold for life an annual rent of 40s. in Whitton, Rockhill and Stokesay, also by the grant of Brian, with reversion to his right heirs.

Date of death and heir, aged 33, as above.

62 Writ 30 Jan. 1400.

WORCESTER. Inquisition. Upton on Severn. 23 Feb.

He held in his demesne as of fee half the manor of Ham, but of whom and by what service is unknown. There are ½ carucate, annual value 13s. 4d.; 4 a. meadow, 13s. 4d.; and assize rents of 20s. payable at Lady Day and Michaelmas; total 46s. 8d. Similarly he held the manor of Carton, of whom and by what service is unknown, annual value 26s. 8d.

William atte Boure and Maud his wife hold for life 1 messuage in Little Sutton, granted by Brian, with reversion to his right heirs. It is held of the earl of March by a rent of 1d., annual value 13s. 4d.

Date of death and heir, aged 30, as above.

63 Writ 30 Jan. 1400.

NORTHAMPTON. Inquisition. Daventry. 24 Feb.

He held in his demesne as of fee 1 messuage, 1 carucate and 4 a. meadow in Thrupp by Daventry, annual value 30s.; and 1 carucate in Welton, annual value 13s. 4d., of whom all are held and by what service is unknown.

On 8 Jan. 1396 by the name of Brian de Cornewaille, knight, lord of Burford and Stapleton, he granted by his charter to William Wysham, knight, Robert Lodelowe, Roger Butley, John Baddeshawe, Nicholas Baker, rector of Burford, John Sturmy, John Sondon, and Robert Gyles their heirs and assigns the manor of Norton by Daventry. It is held of Thomas de Bello Campo, earl of Warwick, by the service of a half a knight's fee, annual value 10 marks.

He died on 7 [sic] January, heir, aged 33, as above.

C 137/5, no. 25
E 149/74, no. 14

GEOFFREY LUCY, KNIGHT

64 Writ 20 Feb. 1400.

BEDFORD. Inquisition. Dunstable. 28 Feb.

He held in his demesne as of fee at Woodcroft in Luton a third part of a messuage, 80 a. arable and 3 a. pasture, annual value 40s., and £4 assize rents, payable at the four principal terms, of the king in chief as a twelfth part of a knight's fee.

He died on 12 Feb. Reynold Lucy, knight, his son and heir, is aged 36 years and more.

65 BUCKINGHAM. Inquisition. Chelmscott. 27 Feb. 1400.

He held the manor of Cublington in his demesne as of fee of the earl of Stafford of the honour of Gloucester by knight service, annual value £10.

Date of death and heir as above.

66 Writ 20 Feb. 1400.

NORTHAMPTON. Inquisition. Northampton. 28 Feb.

He held in his demesne as of fee:

Dallington, the manor, of the abbot of Peterborough by knight service and 20s. rent, annual value £19.

Slapton, the manor, of the earl of Chester by knight service, annual value £10 6½d.

Date of death and heir, aged 40 years and more, as above.

67 Writ 20 Feb. 1400.

HERTFORD. Inquisition. St. Albans. 28 Feb.

He held in his demesne as of fee 1 messuage, 102 a. and 33s.4d. rent in Little Gaddesden, of the rector of Ashridge, as a quarter of a knight's fee, annual value 53s.4d.

He also held the manor of Wigginton of the prince of Wales, of the honour of Berkhampstead, as a quarter of a knight's fee, annual value 65s.3d.

Date of death and heir, aged 40 years and more, as above.

C 137/5, no.26
E 149/74, no.10
E 152/349, 362

ANDREW LOTERELL SENIOR, KNIGHT

68 Writ 6 Oct. 1399.

YORK. Inquisition. Doncaster. 5 May 1400.

He held nothing when he died, but he had held in his demesne as of fee the manor of Hooton Pagnell. He married Hawise, daughter of Philip le Despenser, knight, who survives him, and they had a son Andrew. He gave the manor to Andrew and Joan his wife, and the heirs of their bodies, by licence of Richard II [*CPR 1377–81*, p.318]. It is held of the king in chief by knight service, annual value 20 marks 6s.8d.

He died on 6 Sept. 1399 and his son died on 31 Dec. 1397. Joan, wife of the younger Andrew, being already dead, the manor descended to Geoffrey their son, who is under age. Wardship was granted to Oliver de Staveley by letters patent. He granted it to Henry de Grene, knight [*CPR 1396–9*, pp.329, 332], by whose forfeiture it came into the king's hands. Geoffrey is next heir of Andrew Loterell, junior, and aged 13 years and more. Andrew the son held the manor until he died, then Oliver de Staveley had the profits until Whitsun last, and Henry Grene from Whitsun so long as he lived.

C 137/5, no.27
E 152/345

THOMAS PRESTON, KNIGHT

69 Writ 3 Nov. 1399.

NORTHAMPTON. Inquisition. Rothwell. 18 Nov.

He once held the manor of Gretton of the king in fee farm by a rent of £25 payable at the exchequer and the service of half a knight's fee. He had licence [*CPR 1396-9*, p.338], shown to the escheator, to grant it to Ralph Parles, Henry Hertewell and Lawrence Quynton, and for them to regrant it to him for life, with remainder to Winmer, the son of his son Hugh, Isabel wife of Winmer, and the heirs of their bodies, and failing such heirs the right heirs of Winmer. Its annual value is £12.

He died on Monday in St. Luke last [*sic*, but 18 Oct. was a Saturday in 1399]. Winmer, son of his son Hugh, is heir and aged 17 years and more.

C 137/5, no.28

WILLIAM LECHE OF NEWTON

70 Writ 8 Aug. 1400.

NORFOLK. Inquisition. Swaffham. 14 Oct.

He held the manor of Newton by Castle Acre of the honour of Aumale, by the service of a pair of gilt spurs, price 6d., or 6d. annually at Midsummer, annual value 100s.; and 2 tenements in Cawston and Oulton of Michael de la Pole, earl of Suffolk, of the manor of Cawston, by a rent of 8s. at Michaelmas and Easter, annual value 40s.

He died on 29 July. Katherine wife of John Wesebech, his sister and next heir, is aged 24 years and more.

71 Writ, *plenius certiorari*, as to his status in the manor of Newton. 30 May 1403.

NORFOLK. Inquisition. Hilborough. 5 July.

He held in his demesne in fee tail, to himself and the heirs of his body, the manor of Newton by Castle Acre, by the grant of Richard Holdych by his charter, sealed with his seal and shown to the jurors, dated at Newton on 3 April 1385, to Sybil wife of Nicholas de Leche for life, with remainder to William son of Nicholas and the heirs of his body, and failing such heirs to Katherine, daughter of Nicholas and sister of William, who married John Wysebech, and her heirs.

He also held in his demesne in fee tail, to himself and his heirs by Katherine formerly his wife, 2 tenements in Cawston and Oulton, according to the custom of Cawston manor, by feoffment of Richard Holdych, with remainder to the right heirs of Nicholas.

C 137/5, no.29
E 149/77, no.1

BERTRAM MONBOCHER

72 Writ 12 Oct. 1399.

NOTTINGHAM. Inquisition. Sutton on Trent. 6 Nov.

He held nothing in the county, but long before he died, by a charter of feoffment, he gave to Nicholas Rys, clerk, to hold to himself and his heirs, the manor of Sutton on Trent, which is held of the earl of Richmond, of the honour of Richmond in socage, annual value £10.

He died on 5 Oct. last. Bertram his son and heir is aged 4 years and more.

73 Writ 12 Oct. 1399

NORTHUMBERLAND. Inquisition. Newcastle upon Tyne castle. 18 May 1401.

He held in his demesne as of fee:

Jesmond, a sixth part of the manor with the advowson of the chapel of St. Mary there, and a third part of a watermill called 'Thrysmylne', of the king by the service of a sixth part of a knight's fee, annual value 5 marks.

Shieldfield in the lordship of Byker, 7 a., of Richard de Arundell, knight, in socage, annual value 16s. 8d.

Heaton by Newcastle upon Tyne, 2 husbandlands, of John Musgrave in socage, annual value 10s.

He died on 6 Oct. last. Bertram his son and heir is aged 8 years next Michaelmas.

74 Writ 12 Oct. 1399.

SUSSEX. Inquisition. Ticehurst. 4 Feb. 1400.

He held of the king of the honour of Richmond by knight service:

Hammerden, the manor. There is no chief messuage, but there are 130 a. arable at 4d.; 120 a. wood at 1d.; £10 9s. assize rents, of which 43s. 6d. is payable at Easter and £7 4s. 6d. at Michaelmas; and 1 court, 13s. 4d.

Filsham, the manor, comprising 178 a. of arable at 4d.; 120 a. pasture at 2d.; 4 a. wood at 2d.; and assize rents, £7.

Cortesley, the manor, comprising 16 a. meadow, annual value 16d.; 26s. assize rents, of which 13s. 4d. is payable at Easter and 12s. 8d. at Michaelmas; and a rent of 1800 red herrings from certain tenements at Christmas.

Morley, the manor, in which are 47s. 3d. assize rents payable at Michaelmas.

He died on 3 Oct. last. Bertram his son and heir is aged 4 years and more.

75 Writ, *plenius certiorari*, as to his status in the above manors. 8 June 1401.

SUSSEX. Inquisition. Ticehurst. 28 Aug.

His status in the manors of Hammerden, Filsham, Cortesley and Morley, is to himself and his heirs in fee simple.

76 Writ 12 Oct. 1399.

YORK. Inquisition. Richmond. 6 March 1400.

He held nothing in the county.

He died on 25 Sept. Bertram his son and heir is aged 9 years and more.

C 137/5, no. 30
E 152/345, 363

JOHN FYLILOD

77   Writ 30 Aug. 1400.

SHROPSHIRE. Inquisition. Alveley. 11 Sept.

He held in his demesne as of fee of the king in chief 1 messuage, 1 watermill, 1 carucate, 1 nook of land, 1 a. meadow, 1 a. pasture, 1 a. wood and 30s. rent in Astley and Nordley by the service of finding a horse serjeant with a habergeon (*haubergellus*) to go with the king when he goes with his army into Wales, annual value 48s.4d.

He also held 1 carucate in Romsley of Andrew de Dodmoston, service unknown, annual value 6s.8d.; 1 croft and 1 a. in Alveley of Henry Haggeley, service unknown, annual value 12d.; and 1 nook and 8 a. in Nordley of Roger atte Lee, service unknown, annual value 2s.

He died on 16 July last. Giles Fylilod is his uncle and next heir, being the brother of John his father, and aged 30 years and more.

[Note by Exchequer] 58s. yearly from Friday after [*recte* before] St. Margaret, 23 July to 15 Nov., 16 weeks and 4 days, 18s.8d.

78   Writ 30 Aug. 1400.

WORCESTER. Inquisition. Worcester. 6 Nov.

He held 3 messuages, 40 a. arable and 4 a. meadow in the manor of Kidderminster of William Beauchamp, knight, Lord Abergavenny, in socage by a rent of 12d., annual value 20s.

Date of death and heir as above.

79   Writ 30 Aug. 1400.

WARWICK. Inquisition. Warwick. 13 Nov.

John Meaux, knight, held half the manor of Shrewley in his demesne as of fee of the king in chief, and enfeoffed Nicholas Fylilod, William Fylilod his brother, and the heirs of William. By letters patent of 6 June 1364 [*CPR 1361–4*, p.508] Edward III pardoned the transfer without licence. Nicholas held the half for life and died on 24 Aug. 1382. John, kinsman of William brother of Nicholas, that is the son of John son of William, was then 8 years of age. It was taken into the king's hands and so remained because John did not sue for it after he came of age. It is held of the king in chief by the service of finding an armed man in war for 40 days, annual value 33s.4d.

Date of death, and heir, aged 32 years and more, as above.

NICHOLAS FYLILOD

80   Writ 30 Aug. 1400.

WARWICK. Inquisition. Warwick. 13 Nov.

Jurors and findings as last, adding only: The escheator took the profits from 24 Aug. 1382, when Nicholas died, until Michaelmas following. From then until 10 Nov. 1387, John Horewode had them. Then they were granted by letters patent [*CFR 1383–91*, p.203] to Giles Fililode of Staffordshire on certain conditions. He still holds.

[*Cf. CIPM* XV, no.494].

C 137/6, no.31
E 149/74, no.13

JOAN WIDOW OF RALPH BRACEBRUGG

81   Writ 10 May 1400.

WARWICK. Inquisition. Coleshill. 3 June.

She held the manors of Kingsbury and Plumpton for life by the grant of Nicholas Ryvell, John de Conyngesby, clerk, William de Halughton and Humphrey de Halughton his brother, to Ralph, herself and the heirs of Ralph. They are held of the prince [of Wales] of his manor of Cheylesmore by knight service, amount unknown, annual value £60.

She died on 22 April last. Ralph is son and heir of both Ralph and herself, and was 21 years of age on 1 Feb.

82   WARWICK. Inquisition. Coleshill. 3 June.

Jurors and findings as last, except that the annual value is given as £40 instead of £60.

83   Writ 10 May 1400.

LINCOLN. Inquisition. Bracebridge. 9 June.

She held the manors of Southall in Bracebridge, Buslingthorpe and Wrawby for life, by the grant of Nicholas Ryvell and others [as above, no.81]. The manor of Southall in Bracebridge is held of the king in chief of his manor of Bourne, formerly of the earl of Kent but now in the king's hands, by the service of half a knight's fee, annual value 100s. Buslingthorpe is held of William Ryse of his manor of Ludborough by Fulstow, service unknown, annual value 10 marks. Wrawby is held of Lord Bardolf of his manor of Shelford in Nottinghamshire, service unknown, annual value 5 marks.

She died on 22 April. Her husband died on 11 Aug. 1395, heir as above.

C 137/6, no.32
E 149/74, no.3

JOHN DAVEYS, KNIGHT

84   Writ 15 April 1400.

RUTLAND. Inquisition. Lyndon. 26 April.

He held in his demesne as of fee of the king in chief the manors of Lyndon and Tickencote, as a third part of a knight's fee, annual value 25 marks.

He died on 11 April. John his son and heir is aged 25 years and more.

C 137/6, no.33
E 149/74, no.11

THOMAS ASSHEMAN OF SOMERLEYTON

85   Writ 12 Feb. 1400.

SUFFOLK. Inquisition. Lowestoft. 22 June.

Owing to the madness of Thomas Assheman of Somerleyton 1 messuage, 20 a. arable and 2 a. marsh in Somerleyton and Oulton were taken into the king's hands under Richard II, and so remain. The messuage, 11 a. and the marsh are held of Michael de la Poole, earl of Suffolk, of the hundred of Lothingland in socage by a rent of 12d., annual value 10s. One other acre is held of the heir of Henry Ingelose of the manor of Ashby by a rent of 4d.; and 8 other a. of John Gernegan of the manor of Somerleyton by a rent of 4s.; annual value 3s.4d.

He died on 3 July 1393. John Assheman, son of Walter, brother of John, father of Thomas, is cousin and heir and aged 40 years and more.

C 137/6, no.34

JOHN FROGENHALE

86   Writ 15 June 1400.

KENT. Inquisition. Ospringe. 22 Sept.

He held in his demesne as of fee of the king in chief:

Buckland, the manor and advowson, of the castle of Leeds, as a third part of a knight's fee, annual value £6 17s.7½d.

Luddenham, the manor, of the castle of Dover, paying 10s. every 20 weeks for the guard of the castle, annual value £8 13s.5d.

He died on 14 June last. William his son and next heir is aged 2 years and more.

C 137/6, no.35

WILLIAM RYNGEBORNE

87   Writ 22 March 1400.

HAMPSHIRE. Inquisition. Winchester. 5 April.

He held of the king in chief half the manor of Barton Stacey, half the profits of the hundred, and 1 messuage, 4 a. arable, 3 a. meadow, 6 a. wood., and 1 watermill in Forton, belonging to the half manor, as half a knight's fee, annual value 100s.

He died on 13 March last. William his son and next heir is aged 24 years and more.

C 137/6, no.36

ROBERT SWALWE

88   Writ 11 Feb. 1400.

HAMPSHIRE. Inquisition. Southampton. 28 March.

He held, jointly with Christina his wife, 1 messuage and ½ a. in the town and field of Lymington, of the earl of Devon, service unknown, annual value 9s.3d.

He died on 12 Jan. last. John Swalwe his brother and next heir is aged 22 years and more.

[*Cf. CIM* VII, nos.121–2, 129].

C 137/6, no.37

CLARICE WIDOW OF ROBERT FREVYLL

89   Writ 17 Sept. 1400.

CAMBRIDGE. Inquisition. Cambridge. 20 Sept.

She held a third part of the manor of Little Shelford in dower after the death of Robert

D

Frevyll, her husband. It is held partly of the king in chief as three quarters of a knight's fee, partly of the bishop of Ely as 1½ fees and partly of the earl of Richmond as a quarter of a fee, annual value of the third part £10 and 2 loads of hay, price 6s.

She also held 1 messuage and 16 a. in Little Shelford of the earl of Richmond for life by the grant of Robert Frevyll, service unknown, annual value 13s.4d.

She died on 9 Aug. John Cotill her son and heir is aged 24 years and more.

90   Writ, *melius sciri*, as to whom the holdings should descend. 24 Sept. 1400.
CAMBRIDGE. Inquisition. Cambridge. 27 Sept.

The third part of the manor of Little Shelford and 1 messuage and 16 a. are of the inheritance of Thomas Frevyll, son and heir of Robert. He still lives, aged 40 years and more, and they should descend to him.

C 137/7, no.38
E 149/72, no.7
E 152/344

INGRAM BRUYN, KNIGHT

91   Writ 14 Aug. 1400.
DORSET. Inquisition. Wimborne Minster. 10 Sept.

He held the manor of Ranston in his demesne as of fee of the king in chief as half a knight's fee, annual value 16 marks.

He died on 12 Aug. last. Maurice his son and heir is aged 14 years and more.

92   Writ, for fees, 14 Aug. 1400.
DORSET. Inquisition. Wimborne Minster. 10 Sept.

He held in his demesne as of fee of the king in chief half a knight's fee in Ranston, which is in the king's hands owing to his death.

93   Writ 14 Aug. 1400.
ESSEX. Inquisition. Chelmsford. 3 Sept.

He held the manor of South Ockendon in his demesne as of fee of the countess of Hereford, by the service of 1½ knight's fees, annual value £40.

Date of death and heir as above.

94   Writ, for fees, 14 Aug. 1400.
ESSEX. Inquisition. Chelmsford. 3 Sept.

He held in his demesne as of fee the advowsons of South Ockendon, annual value when it occurs 25 marks; and of the free chapel of St. John the Baptist in Brook Street, annual value of temporalities, when it occurs, 100s.

95   Writ 14 Aug. 1400.
KENT. Inquisition. Deptford. 10 Sept.

He held the manor of Beckenham with the advowson to himself and the heirs male of his body, and failing them to William Marny, knight, and his heirs male. It is held of the king in chief by knight service, annual value 10 marks.

Date of death and heir as above.

96   Writ 14 Aug. 1400.

HAMPSHIRE. Inquisition. Stockbridge. 22 Sept.

He held:

Godshill, 1 close, 20 a. arable, 8 a. meadow and 100 a. heath, of the king in chief, of the manor of Lyndhurst, by the service of rendering yearly 3 arrowshafts or 3d., annual value 32s.8d.

Fordingbridge, the manor, in his demesne as of fee, of the countess of Kent, lady of Bedhampton, as 1 knight's fee, annual value £16 12s.

Rowner, the manor and the advowson, jointly with Elizabeth his wife, who still lives, by the grant of John Martham, parson of Beckenham in Kent, by his indenture dated 24 Feb. 1393, with remainder, in default of heirs male of Ingram to William Marny, son and heir of Robert de Marny, knight, and his heirs male. They are held of the king by a rent of 40s., annual value of the manor £10 and of the advowson when it occurs 10 marks.

Date of death and heir as above.

> C 137/7, no.39
> E 149/74, no.1
> E 152/354

HENRY YEVELE

97   Writ 12 Sept. 1400.

KENT. Inquisition. Wye. 15 Sept.

He held the manors of Trimworth and Fanscombe for life by a grant of Richard II [*CPR 1388–92*, pp.122–3]. Afterwards Richard II granted the advowson of Crundale with the reversion of the two manors after the death of Henry Yevele to the master and chaplains of the college of Maidstone, and the king confirmed this on 6 March 1400 [*CPR 1396–9*, p.27; *1399–1401*, p.230]. The manors should remain to the college in free alms, annual value £20.

He died on 21 Aug. Richard Yevele his kinsman and next heir is aged 30 years and more.

> C 137/7, no.40

JOHN WYTTELBERY

98   Writ 8 May 1400.

NORTHAMPTON. Inquisition. Northampton. 28 Aug.

He held in his demesne as of fee of the king in chief the manor of Horton called 'Wyttelberyesplace', service unknown, annual value £4; and 1 messuage in Blakesley, annual value 26s.8d.

He died on 21 April. Aubrey his son and heir is aged 26 years and more.

99   Rutland. Inquisition. Oakham. 22 July.

He held in his demesne as of fee the manor of Whissendine called 'Wyttelberymaner' of the king in chief of the honour of Huntingdon by knight service, annual value £10; and 3 messuages and 3 virgates in Empingham of Oliver Malyverer, knight, service unknown, annual value 40s. ['3 marks' over erasure in E 149/74].

Date of death and heir as above.

C 137/7, no.41
E 149/74, no.8

JOHN TRAILLY, KNIGHT

100   Writ 7 Aug. 1400.

Cambridge. Inquisition. Cambridge. 19 Aug.

He held in his demesne as of fee of the king in chief 2 messuages, 120 a. and 1 fishery in Quy, as parcel of the manor of Quy, annual value £7 3s.

Long ago he enfeoffed John Warde, clerk, and Ralph Pokelyngton in his manor of Quy, except for those lands and tenements in the manor which were held of the king in chief. Ralph died. John Warde, rector of Northill, conveyed it to Reynold de Grey, lord of Wexford and of Ruthin, Gerard Braybroke, knight, junior, Reynold Ragoun, John Hervy, and John Herteshorn, to hold on certain terms contained in his charter. It is held, except for the above 2 messuages held in chief, of the bishop of Ely, service unknown, annual value 10 marks.

He died on 18 June last. Reynold is his son and heir, aged 22 on 15 July.

101   Writ 7 Aug. 1400.

Bedford. Inquisition. Bedford. 12 Aug.

He held in his demesne as of fee:

Northill, the manor and advowson, of the king in chief by knight service; annual values, manor 20 marks, advowson 40 marks.

Wootton Hoo, the manor, of Robert de Todynham by suit at his court at Bedford every three weeks, annual value nil because he granted an annual rent of £6 from it to John Herteshorn, now deceased, and Alice his wife for the term of their lives.

Ravensden, various lands and tenements, of the heir of Thomas Moubray, duke of Norfolk, a minor in the king's ward, service unknown, annual value 100s.

Long before his death he enfeoffed Gerard de Braybrok, lord of Odell, Gerard de Braybrok, knight, junior, and Edmund Hampden in his manors of Yelden and Chellington, to them, their heirs and assigns, and all the tenants attorned to them. They are held of the earl of Stafford, Yelden by a rent of 13s.4d., annual value 40 marks, Chellington, service unknown, annual value £10.

Also long before his death he enfeoffed by his charter Reynold de Grey, lord of Wexford and Ruthin, Gerard Braybrok, knight, junior, John Warde, rector of Northill, Reynold Ragoun, John Hervy and John Herteshorn in the manor of Carlton, for the life of Joan his wife, who survives, and all the tenants attorned. It is held of Amery de Sancto Amando by knight service, annual value 10 marks.

Date of death and heir as above.

102   Writ, for fees, 7 Aug. 1400.

NORTHAMPTON. Inquisition. Northampton. 14 Aug.

He held in his demesne as of fee the advowson of the church of Woodford by Thrapston in right of patronage there, annual value £10.

Date of death and heir, aged 22 years and more, as above.

C 137/7, no.42
E 149/72, no.1

EDMUND DE DOUNE

103   Writ 28 June 1400.

ESSEX. Inquisition. Maldon. 8 July.

He held in fee tail:

Bradwell juxta Mare, 1 messuage, 1 ruined windmill, 100 a. arable, 4 a. meadow, 2 a. pasture, 40 a. external marsh, 1 broken weir and 10s.4d. rent, of the king in chief as a third part of a knight's fee and by the service of providing 1 lance, price 2s., when the king goes to Wales, annual value 60s.

Down, view of frankpledge yearly in Bradwell on the feast of St. Thomas the Apostle by a rent of 12d. payable by the sheriff, annual value 12d.

Bradwell juxta Mare, 1 messuage, 100 a. arable, 5 a. meadow, 10 a. external marsh, 1 a. wood, 5 old broken weirs and 12s. rent of Joan Lady Swynbourne in scutage (*scuagium*) and fealty, annual value 78s.6d.; 3 a. of John Cook by a rent of 2d., annual value 12d.; 1 messuage, 60 a. arable, 1 a. pasture, 30 a. external marsh and 5s. rent, of Henry Percy, knight, of his manor of Bradwell by a rent of 20s.2d., annual value 35s.10d.; and 30 a. of Bartholomew Bourghchier, knight, by a rent of 7s., annual value 10s.

Asheldham and Steeple, 80 a. arable and 3 a. meadow, of the prior of Stanesgate by a rent of 14s., annual value 26s.8d.; 100 a. of Bartholomew Bourghchier, knight, and John Bodenyk, service unknown, annual value 33s.4d.; and 5 a. of the bishop of Winchester, by a rent of 1 lb. pepper, annual value 20d.

He died on 26 June. John his son and heir is aged 32 years and more.

C 137/7, no.43
E 149/73, no.8

WILLIAM ASTORP, KNIGHT

104   Writ 18 Oct. 1399.

SOMERSET. Inquisition. Wells. 11 March 1400.

Long before he died he held in his demesne as of fee the manor of Camerton with the advowson, and lands and tenements in Doulting, and enfeoffed Alan Benet, rector of Morleigh, William Radewell, rector of Hemyock, John Axhard, rector of Clyst Hydon, and John Wrosell, and gave them seisin that they might give the issues to himself for life, and afterwards re-enfeoff the next and right heirs of the blood of Margaret his wife to herself and her heirs. Robert Palton is her kinsman and next heir.

The manor is held of the bishop of Bath and Wells by knight service, annual value £10; and the lands in Doulting are held of the abbot of Glastonbury, and extend within the said sum of £10.

He died without heirs on 8 Oct.

105 Writ 18 Oct. 1399.

DEVON. Inquisition. Sampford Peverell. 3 Jan. 1400.

He held in his demesne as of fee:

Sampford Peverell, the manor and borough with the advowson, of the king in chief, annual value £30 2s. 0½d.

Boehill and Leonard Moor, certain parcels of land, of Richard Warre of his manor of Burlescombe by knight service, annual value £6 3s.

'Pratteslonde', a parcel so called, of William Aishford of his manor of Ashford by knight service, annual value 22s.

'Preston', the land of, of the heirs of John Welyngton of their manor of Uplowman by knight service, annual value 30s.

Ash Thomas, lands and tenements of John Dauney of his manor of Woodbeer by knight service, annual value 40s.

Sutton, 1 messuage and 1 carucate, of John Dorcestre, annual value 60s.

Colyford, lands and tenements, of the same of his manor of Halberton by knight service, annual value 20s.

Halsewood, a parcel of land so called, of the same of the same manor by knight service, annual value 4s.

Halberton, the hundred, in alternate years, of Lord Despenser of his honour of Gloucester, annual value 6s. 8d.

'Pechecroft', a parcel so called, of John Dorcestre of his manor of Halberton by knight service, annual value 8d.

Aller, the manor, of the king in chief by knight service, annual value £13.

With Margaret his wife, and in her right in his demesne as of fee, he once held the manors of Hemyock and Clyst Hydon and the hundred of Hemyock. They gave them to John Dynham, knight, John Wattecombe, parson of Hemyock, Walter Salterne, parson of Sampford Peverell, and Richard Michel, chaplain. By a fine of 1390 [CP 25(1) 44/66, no. 13] John Dynham and the others granted them to William and Margaret and the heirs of their bodies, failing them to the heirs of the body of Margaret and in default of such heirs with reversion to John Dynham and the others. Margaret died without heirs of her body, and William likewise.

Hemyock manor was held of Edward Courtenay, earl of Devon, of his castle of Plympton by knight service, annual value 38 marks; the hundred of the same earl and castle by knight service, annual value 26s. 8d.

Clyst Hydon manor was held of the same earl of his manor of Okehampton by knight service, annual value £20.

William Astorp also held to himself and his heirs certain lands in Yarnscombe of Robert Chalouner, knight, of his manor of Torrington, annual value 40s.

He died on 8 Oct. He was a bastard and died without heirs. The escheator took his lands into the king's hands.

106 Writ, *plenius certiorari*, as to how and by what service his lands were held. 20 Aug. 1400.

DEVON. Inquisition. Bradninch. 16 Sept.

He held in his demesne as of fee:

Boehill, 15 a. arable, 6 a. meadow, 10 a. wood and alder, and 2s.4d. annual rent, of Richard Warre of his manor of Burlescombe as half a knight's fee and by the service of 1 . . . at Easter.

'Pratteslond', 30 a. arable, 1 a. meadow and 1 a. wood, of William Aisshford, as an eighth part of a knight's fee and by a rent of 4s. at Michaelmas.

Ash Thomas, 40 a. arable and 3 a. wood of John Dauneye of his manor of Woodbeer as a quarter of a knight's fee and . . .8d. rent at Michaelmas.

Colyford, 2 messuages, 1 curtilage . . . 1½ roods of meadow, of John Dorcestre and Margaret his wife in the right of Margaret of the manor of Halberton by the service of . . . part of a knight's fee and 9s. annual rent payable at the four principal terms.

Halsewood, 24 a. wood, and 'Pechecroft', 3 a. arable, held of the manor of Halberton in right of Margaret his wife by a rent of 16d. at Michaelmas.

Yarnscombe, . . . and 40s. rent, of Robert Chalons of his manor of Torrington by knight service.

Halberton, the hundred, in alternate years, of Lord Despenser of his honour of Gloucester.

[Headed] *Nulla inde fiat liberacio absque deliberacione consilii regis, Hill.*

107 Writ, *plura*, 12 July 1402.
DEVON. Inquisition. Crediton. 15 Sept.

He held no more than was stated in the former inquisition, but William Jocens of Trobridge and Joan his wife held of him, in right of Joan, 1 messuage and 1 carucate in Trobridge in the parish of Crediton by knight service, and he held them of Edmund, bishop of Exeter, by homage, fealty, suit of court at the bishop's court at Crediton every 3 weeks, and the service of half a knight's fee.

He was a bastard and died without heirs.

C 137/7, no.44; 33, no.41
E 149/74, no.17

MILES STAPULTON

108 Writ 12 Feb. 1400.
YORK. Inquisition and extent. York. 25 April.

He held to himself and the heirs male of his body, with remainder to the right heirs of Brian de Stapulton, knight, his father:

Wighill, the manor with the hamlet of Easedike, of lord de Moubray by homage and fealty, annual value £10.

Clifford, the manor, of the earl of Kent by homage, annual value £4.

Farlington, two parts of the manor, of the earl of Westmorland by suit of court at Sheriff Hutton, and if by other service the jurors do not know of it, annual value £12.

Little Langton, the manor, of the earl of Richmond, service unknown, annual value £7.

Skelbrooke, a parcel of land, of whom held and by what service is unknown, annual value 5s.

Firby, 1 messuage and 3 a., of whom held unknown, annual value 6s.8d.

Askham Bryan, lands and tenements, of Lord Grey of Rotherfield and Miles de Stapilton, knight, by a rent of 5d., annual value 22s.

Carlton by Snaith and Camblesforth, lands and tenements, of the heir of Brian

Stapulton, knight, his father, by a rent of 13s., annual value £10.
He died on 6 Feb. last. John his son and heir is aged 32 weeks.

109   Writ, *plenius certiorari*, as to his status in the lands, of whom and by what service
they were held. 9 July 1419.
YORK. Inquisition. Clifton. 7 Sept.
    He held to himself and his heirs male Wighill manor with the hamlet of Easedike;
Clifford manor; Farlington, two parts of the manor; Little Langton manor; Skelbrooke,
a parcel of land; Firby, 1 messuage and 3 a.; Askham Bryan, lands etc.; all with
remainder in default of male heirs to the right heirs of his father, Brian de Stapulton,
knight.
    He also held, by the grant of Agnes Arundell, sister and heir of Richard de Boynton,
formerly rector of Binbrook, lands and tenements in Carlton by Snaith and Camblesforth, of the heirs of Brian de Stapulton, knight, deceased, by a rent of 13s.
    The messuage and 3 a. in Firby are held of the heirs of Lord Deincourt and of Miles
de Stapulton, knight, and the parcel in Skelbrooke of Peter del Hay, both services
unknown.

110   Writ 22 Feb. 1400.
SUFFOLK. Inquisition. Kessingland. 5 May.
    He held the manor of Kessingland and 52s.6d. rent in Cretingham and Ashfield of
the king in chief by knight service, to himself and his heirs male, with remainder to
the right heirs of his father, Brian de Stapulton, knight, annual value £8.
    Date of death as above. John his son and heir is aged 33 weeks.

111   Writ 22 Feb. 1400
NORFOLK. Inquisition. Loddon. 7 May.
    He held nothing in Norfolk.
    Date of death and heir as in last.

112   Writ 22 Feb. 1400.
LINCOLN. Inquisition. Horncastle. 11 May.
    He held in his demesne as of fee 3 messuages, 2 cottages and 1 carucate in Baumber,
of Henry son and heir of John de Bello Monte, knight, a minor in the king's ward,
service unknown, annual value £4.
    Date of death and heir, aged 34 weeks, as above.

113   Writ 1 May 1400.
YORK CITY. Inquisition. 17 May.
    He held of the king in burgage as is all the city of York:
    In Bishophill, 4 cottages, annual value 32s.; 4 other cottages, 30s.; 4 cottages, 31s.;
2 cottages, 33s.4d.; the reversion of a messuage and garden held for life by William
de Sheffeld, 40s.; and the reversion of 14 cottages held by William Blenkansopp and
Agnes his wife for the life of Agnes, 40s.
    In Finkle Street, the reversion of 1 messuage, held by the same for the life of Agnes,
annual value 15s.
    In the suburbs outside Micklegate, 4 cottages, 8s.
    Date of death and heir, aged 35 weeks, as above.

114 Writ, *plenius certiorari*, as to his status in the cottages, and who should have them in default of male heirs. 9 July 1419.

YORK CITY. Inquisition. 4 Sept.

He held 14 cottages on Bishophill and 4 others in the suburbs outside the Micklegate, as stated in the writ, with remainder in default of male heirs to the right heirs of his father, Brian de Stapulton, knight.

115 Writ 22 Feb. 1400.

CUMBERLAND. Inquisition. Carlisle. 20 March.

He held to himself and his heirs male with remainder to the right heirs of Brian, his father:

Oughterby, the manor with the hamlet of Bampton, of Thomas de Dacre at a cornage rent of 7s., annual value 100s.

Crosby on Eden, a quarter of the manor, of the bishop of Carlisle by homage and a rent of 11s., annual value 60s.

Cumwhinton, 1 messuage and 12 a., of William de Aglaby, by a cornage rent of 5½d., annual value 5s.

Carlisle, 4 burgages and 3 a., of the king by house-gavel, annual value 16s.

Hornsby, a quarter of the vill, of Thomas de Dacre by homage, annual value 6s. 8d.

Date of death and heir, aged 27 weeks, as above.

C 137/8, no.45
E 152/345, 356–7

ROBERT SHARDELOWE, KNIGHT

116 Writ 11 June 1400.

CAMBRIDGE. Inquisition. Babraham. 18 June.

He held in his demesne as of fee:

Fulbourn, 1 rood, of the king in chief by knight service, annual value 2d.

Shardelowes manor in Fulbourn, of the Earl Marshal and of the tenants of 'Souches' manor in Fulbourn, service unknown, annual value 10 marks.

Fulbourn, 3 roods, of the tenants of Colvyll manor, by knight service, annual value 6d.

He died on 19 July 1399. John his son and heir is aged 1½ years and more.

[The Exchequer copy is the same except for the date, 26 June 1400, but adds]: Margaret his widow held the lands from the Saturday when he died to Michaelmas, and should answer for the profits.

117 Writ 29 June 1400.

ESSEX. Inquisition. Castle Hedingham. 4 Nov.

He held in his demesne as of fee 20 a. arable, 12 a. meadow and 6 a. pasture in Ashen, Birdbrook and Ridgewell, of William Bateman of his manor of Little Sampford by suit of court every 3 weeks, annual value 40s.

Date of death and heir, aged 2½ years and more, as above.

C 137/8, no.46
E 149/72, no.9

HENRY ATTE BROME

118 Writ 18 Nov. 1399.

LONDON. Inquisition. 6 March 1400.

He held in his demesne as of fee a tenement with houses, shops and a plot of land in the parish of St. Michael Bassishaw, of the king in burgage as all the city is, annual value 6 marks.

He died on 1 Nov. 1342. Alice atte Brome is his heir, being the daughter of Ralph his brother, aged 58 years.

After his death Agnes his wife, who held jointly with him for her life, occupied them and took the profits until she married Hugh Jentill. He then held them until he died. Then she married John London, who held them for her life. She died. Then John London married a certain Lucy, and they held them. By his will he left them to Lucy for life, and then to pay for a chaplain to pray for the souls of Lucy and himself in St. Michael's church. After his death the parishioners of that church took possession in accordance with his will, occupied them and took the profits until Simon Standish, chaplain, was inducted into a perpetual chantry. He held the property and took the profits until Robert London and Thomas London, claiming to be the heirs of John London, entered and took possession. They alienated to a certain John Walesby, and he to William Belhome, who now holds and takes the profits.

C 137/8, no.47

THOMAS BASYNGES

119 Writ 3 Aug. 1400

KENT. Inquisition. Kenardington. 11 Aug.

He held in his demesne as of fee the manor of Kenardington, comprising 13½ a. arable; 2 a. meadow; 164 a. pasture; 5 a. 1 rood wood; £6 assize rents from free tenants at Easter and Michaelmas; 33 cocks, price 1½d. each and 82 hens at 2d. at Christmas; 600 eggs at Easter, 2s.; 6 geese at Michaelmas, 3d. each; ½ lb. pepper at Christmas, 5d.; 6 lb. wax at Easter at 5d. the lb.; and the advowson of the church of Kenardington, £10 when it occurs.

A third part of the site of the manor and 37 a. of the said 164 a. are held by the service of a rent of 10s. for the guard of Dover castle. The rest of the site and of the 164 a., and the meadow, wood and rents are held of the archbishop of Canterbury, the abbot of St. Augustine's, Canterbury, and the prior of St. Gregory's, Canterbury, separately by various services. The site is worth nothing annually, each of the 164 a. and 13½ a., 6d., the 2 a. meadow 2s., and the wood nothing because no profit can be taken from the timber.

With Agnes his wife, to them and the heirs of their bodies, he held:

Iffin, the manor, of the prior of St. Gregory's, service unknown, annual value 5 marks.

'Elmeslemersch', the pasture so called, of whom held unknown, annual value nil because waste.

Cockread, the manor, in Romney marsh, of the master of the hospital of Dover, service unknown, annual value £6.

Silwell by Ruckinge, all the lands so called which Reynold de Basynges held, comprising 18 a. arable, held of Henry de Horne, service unknown, annual value 30s.

Stone in the Isle of Oxney, the lands which Walter Alayn held, comprising 25 a., annual value 30s., and 20s. rent from the lands of Stephen de Pysenden in that parish, held of the abbot of St. Augustine's, service unknown.

Redbrook in the parish of Kenardington, 20 a. which John Merscher, senior, held to farm, of the same abbot, service unknown, annual value 40s.

Appledore, 5 a. which Thomas Sedelide held at farm in the town, annual value 7s., of the prior of Dover, service unknown.

Snargate, 20 a. which John Merscher, junior, held, of the same abbot, service unknown, annual value 30s.

Kenardington, various lands in the parish: 10 a. which Thomas Horne held next to the mill, of the archbishop, service unknown, annual value 21s.; 10 a. which John Wille held at farm in 'Lytellarkemede' and 'Bettewildeslonde', of the same abbot, service unknown, annual value 15s.; 2 a. and a windmill standing on them which William Caliot held at farm by 'Pykhelle', of the archbishop and of William Spaket separately, service unknown, annual value 2 a. 2s., the mill nil because ruinous; 8 a. which William Horne held at farm called 'Dygenesland' and 'Boles', of the prior of Dover, service unknown, annual value 8s.; 2 a. which Thomas atte Reche held at farm by 'Kelchesbregge', of the same abbot, service unknown, annual value 5s.; 16 a. called 'Baytones' and 'Boltesland' next to the messuage formerly of Walter Alayn, of the same abbot, service unknown, annual value 12s.; and 40 a. called 'Horsteghe' and 'Kyngesmanland' and other pieces of land which William Benet held at farm, of the archbishop, annual value 38s.

Appledore, all the wood called Park Farm in the parish, annual value 10s., and the pasture there 3s.4d.

He died on 29 July. John his son and heir is aged 24 years and more.

C 137/8, no.48
E 357/14, m.37

THOMAS STANES

120 SURREY. Inquisition *ex officio*. Guildford. 14 Aug. 1400.

He held the manor of Gomshall for life of the king, and he died on 2 Aug.

There are within the moat a hall, 2 chambers, 1 grange, 1 byre and 1 stable, annual value nil; and in the manor 100 a. arable at 4d., a watermill 4 marks, £11 8s. assize rents payable at the four principal terms, 40s. from various customary works, 20 a. underwood at 1d. and view of frankpledge twice yearly, with the perquisites of court every 3 weeks, annual value beyond the fee of the steward 13s.4d. Thomas Clerk atte Hoo has held the whole manor since the day of his death, and has taken the profits.

E 149/74, no.19

ELIZABETH WIDOW OF ROBERT HARYNGDON, KNIGHT

121 SOMERSET. Inquisition. Bridgwater. 28 Aug. 1400.

She held the manor of Huntspill of the king in chief by knight service. Fulk, son and heir of Fulk Fitzwaryn, has the reversion by inheritance, is the next heir, and is under age in the king's ward.

William Cogan, knight, formerly lord of Huntspill, granted and confirmed by his deed now shown to the jurors, dated 20 July 1371, to John Elys, vicar of Meare by Glastonbury, who still lives, an annual rent of 10 quarters of corn for life from his lands in Huntspill, comprising at All Saints 2 qr. wheat and 2 qr. barley and at Candlemas 4 qr. beans and 2 qr. oats, with the carriage of it to a place that the vicar's boat could conveniently reach, and he bound himself and his heirs to warranty by his deed.

In the manor are assize rents of free tenants and villeins at the four feasts, £39 18s.; a close called 'Calvenhey'; a small garden by the court, 2s.; 100 a. meadow in 'Goselese' in separate plots, worth from Candlemas until the hay is cut 8d. per a., after that nil because common; the hay was harvested long before Elizabeth died; in the meadow called Huntspill 'mede' 50 a. meadow from Candlemas to the hay harvest, 6d. an a.; in the field called 'La Harth' 140 a. arable, in that called 'West Yalworth' 10 a., to the north of the court 15 a., in the one to the west 22 a., and in the one called 'Wolsshecrofte' 24 a., all worth 8d. an a.

Robert de Haryngton, late husband of Elizabeth, leased the lands from Michaelmas for the following year to various tenants for 8d. an a. payable at Lammas, which he collected and it is in his hands for the past year. There is a pasture called 'Gossehull', annual value 4s., another south of the court 3s., one called 'Cothampmede' comprising 100 a. at 12d., a dovecot 40d., and pleas and perquisites of the court, with a certain gift on the 2 law-days, 36s.

She died on 19 Aug.

122   SOMERSET. Inquisition. Montacute. 13 Oct. 1400.

She, who elsewhere held of the king in chief, held in dower a third part of the manor of Wigborough, of whom is unknown, annual value 5 marks.

She died on 19 Aug. Fulk son and heir of Fulk Fitzwaryn, in the king's ward, is next heir, aged 15 years and more.

E 149/74, no. 16

THOMAS DUKE OF GLOUCESTER

123   Writ, for fees, 5 Feb. 1400.

ESSEX. Inquisition. Braintree. 20 Dec. 1399 [sic: 1 Henry IV].

He held in his demesne as of fee the advowsons of the churches of Barnston and South Fambridge, annual values when they occur 10 marks and 100s. He held no fees or other advowsons.

124   Writ 4 Nov. 1399.

BUCKINGHAM. Inquisition. Aylesbury. 24 Jan. 1400.

He had an annuity of £20 payable by the sheriff and held nothing else in the county.

He died on 8 Sept. 1397. Anne, wife of Edmund earl of Stafford, and Joan, of full age, 17 and 15 years, and Isabel, aged 13, are his daughters and heirs. From the time of his death Richard II took the annuity by the sheriff.

125   Writ 28 June 1402.

BUCKINGHAM. Inquisition. Stony Stratford. 15 Aug.

He held in his demesne as of fee an annuity of £20 payable by the sheriff, granted to him and his heirs by Richard II by letters patent, on the day of his coronation.

He died on 8 Sept. 1397. His daughters, Anne wife of Edmund earl of Stafford, Joan and Isabel were his heirs. Joan died seised of the annuity because it was taken into the king's hands and then assigned to her. She died on 16 Aug. 1400. Anne and Isabel were her heirs, and it was in the king's hands on account of the minority of Isabel and the deaths of Thomas and Joan. Isabel was professed a nun of the order of Minoresses in the suburbs of London on 23 April last, when she was aged 16 years and more. Anne wife of Edmund earl of Stafford is her heir, aged 20 years and more.

C 137/10; no.50, mm.11,12,24; 11, no.50, m.25; 33, no.51

ELEANOR DUCHESS OF GLOUCESTER

126 Writ 3 Oct. 1399.

LINCOLN. Inquisition. Grantham. 26 Jan. 1400.

She held in her demesne as of fee the manor of Long Bennington of the honour of Richmond, service unknown. There are several buildings, annual value nil; a dovecot, 40d.; 5 carucates with meadow and pasture, £20; £50 annual rent of free tenants and villeins, payable at the four terms, Michaelmas £30, Christmas £7, Easter £7 and Midsummer £6; customary works of villeins, nil beyond the payment which the lord makes to them according to the custom of the manor; perquisites of court held every 3 weeks, beyond expenses of the steward 60s.; and 2 watermills, £4.

She died on 3 Oct. last. Her daughters and heirs are Anne wife of Edmund earl of Stafford, of full age, 17 years and more; Joan, also of full age, 15 years and more; and Isabel, aged 13 on 23 April last.

127 Writ 3 Oct. 1399.

ESSEX. Inquisition. Braintree. 20 Dec.

She held in her demesne as of fee of the king in chief, service unknown:

Pleshey, the castle and manor with the advowson of the chapel in the castle, annual value 100s.

Great Waltham, the manor, annual value £50.

High Easter, the manor with 30s. assize rent from the manors of Hellesdon and Oxnead in Norfolk, annual value, including the 30s., £50; and the court of the honour, annual value £4.

Shenfield, the manor, annual value £20.

Chishall, view of frankpledge, annual value 3s.4d.

She held in her demesne as of fee of William Bourgcher, knight, service unknown, the manor of Wix, annual value £26 13s.4d.

She also held an annuity of £40 10s.10d. payable by the sheriff by halves at Easter and Michaelmas; the office of constable of England, as elder daughter of Humphrey Bohun, earl of Hereford, and her husband held it as of her right all his life; and in her demesne as of fee, in chief, service unknown, the manor of Farnham, annual value 20 marks.

Date of death and heirs as above.

[Exchequer copy] Total extent, apart from fees of the constable, £169 10s.

128 HERTFORD. Inquisition. Bishop's Stortford. 19 Feb. 1400.

She held in her demesne as of fee of the king in chief, service unknown:

Nuthampstead in Barkway, a third part of the manor, annual value 73s.4d.

Hoddesdon, as part of the barony of the county of Essex, view of frankpledge, and court of the honour of Hertford, annual value 17s.4d., namely frankpledge 4s., court 13s.4d.

Farnham in Essex, 40 a. in Hertfordshire as part of the manor.

Date of death and heirs as above.

129 Writ. 3 Oct. 1399.

CAMBRIDGE. Inquisition. Cambridge. 26 Jan. 1400.

She held in her demesne as of fee, of the king in chief, view of frankpledge in Sawston, which should be held once yearly on the morrow of St. Barnabas, annual value 5s.

Date of death and heirs as above.

130 Writ. 3 Oct. 1399.

OXFORD. Inquisition. Oxford. 17 Feb. 1400.

She held in fee tail by a grant of Edward III to William de Bohun and the heirs of his body:

Kirtlington, the manor, of the king in chief as a third part of a knight's fee, annual value 20 marks.

Deddington, the manor, of the king in chief as a third part of 2 fees, annual value 20 marks.

Great Haseley, the manor and advowson, of the honour of Wallingford by knight service, annual value 40 marks.

Pyrton, the manor, similarly held, annual value £16 13s.4d.

By a grant of Richard II [CChR V, p.291, 1384] she held in her demesne as of fee view of frankpledge in Haseley and Pyrton, annual value 40s.

Date of death and heirs as above, except that Anne's age is given as 18, not 17.

131 BERKSHIRE. Inquisition. Abingdon. 23 Feb. 1400.

She held two parts of the manor of Woodspean of the king in chief, service unknown, annual value £6.

Date of death and heirs as above, Anne aged 18.

132 Writ 3 Oct. 1399.

HEREFORD AND THE ADJACENT MARCH OF WALES. Inquisition. Weobley. 25 Feb. 1400.

She held in her demesne as of fee of the king in chief, service unknown, the castle and lordship of Huntington in the Welsh march, annual value 43 marks.

Date of death as above. Anne, Isabel and Joan are her daughters and heirs, ages unknown.

133 Writ of privy seal to John Mauns, escheator. The earl of Stafford and Anne his wife have complained that certain escheators, including the escheator for Herefordshire, have failed to do their office in response to writs of *diem clausit extremum*, because, as they say, they have been told by the council not to perform it without special order. Order to proceed as the law and custom of the realm requires, 7 March 1400.

HEREFORD AND THE ADJACENT MARCH OF WALES. Inquisition. Hereford. 26 April.
Findings exactly as last, with different jurors.

134 Writ 3 Oct. 1399.

GLOUCESTER AND THE ADJACENT MARCH OF WALES. Inquisition. Chipping Sodbury. 16 Feb. 1400.

She held in her demesne as of fee of the king in chief:

Wheatenhurst, the manor, service unknown, annual value £21 7s.

Caldicot castle and Shirenewton, by baron service, annual value 40 marks.

Date of death as above. Her heirs are Anne countess of Stafford, Joan and Isabel, aged 18 years and more, 15 years and more, and, on 23 April last, 13.

135 Writ 3 Oct. 1399.

NOTTINGHAM. Inquisition. Kneesall. 5 March 1400.

She held in her demesne as of fee of the king in chief the manor of Kneesall, service unknown, comprising several ruinous buildings, annual value nil; 180 a. arable with meadow and pasture, £4 13s.4d.; an enclosed park, with herbage, 13s.4d.; a windmill, 6s.8d.; 21s.7½d. assize rents payable equally at Martinmas and Whitsuntide, and £13 19s. payable at the four principal terms; 1 lb. cumin at Martinmas; and 1 lb. pepper at Whitsun.

Date of death and heirs as in last.

136 Writ, for fees, 11 Oct. 1399.

HUNTINGDON. Inquisition. Kimbolton. 29 Jan. 1400.

She held in her demesne as of fee the advowson of the priory of Stonely. The temporalities are valued at 10 marks yearly.

137 CAMBRIDGE. Inquisition. Whittlesford. 14 June 1400.

She held in her demesne as of fee the following knight's fees:

Chippenham, ½ fee held by the abbot of Walden.

Fulbourn, 1 fee held by William Fulbourn.

Thriplow, ½ fee held by John Barynton.

Sawston, 3 fees held by John de Huntyngdon.

138 Writ, for fees, 11 Oct. 1399.

WILTSHIRE. Inquisition. Devizes. 13 Feb. 1400.

She held in her demesne as of fee the advowson of the priory of Monkton Farleigh, the temporalities of which, when they occur, are worth 40 marks annually.

139 Writ, for fees, 11 Oct. 1399.

ESSEX. Inquisition. Braintree. 20 Dec.

She held in her demesne as of fee the following advowsons:

Debden, annual value when it occurs £20.

Shenfield, £8.

Pleshey, free chapel in the castle, 100s.

Great Baddow, free chapel, 20s.
West Thurrock, £13 6s.8d.
Pleshey, college of Holy Trinity, temporalities, £10.
Wix, priory, temporalities, 20 marks.
She held no other advowsons and no knight's fees.

140   HERTFORD. Inquisition. Bishop's Stortford. 19 Feb. 1400.

She held in her demesne as of fee:

Farnham, [Essex], 1 fee formerly held by Walter Arderne.

North Mimms, 1½ fees once held by Thomas de Swanlond and 1½ fees formerly held by William de Kestevene, clerk.

Shenley, ¾ fee formerly held by Richard Salman.

Bushey, 1 fee once held by Geoffrey Jarpevylle and $\frac{1}{10}$ fee once held by Aubrey de Bissheye, both formerly held by Edward prince of Wales.

Hoddesdon, 1 fee once held by Thomas de Bassyngbourne.

Thorley, 1⅕ fees once held by Thomas Chirberge, knight, and ¼ fee once held by the prior of Merton.

Stapleford, 1 fee formerly held by Walter atte Lee.

Ayot, 1 fee formerly held by Richard de Penbrigge, knight.

Enfield, [Middlesex], and Sawbridgeworth, 1 fee formerly held by Jordan de Elsyng and 1 fee formerly held by John Wroth.

Gilston, $\frac{1}{20}$ fee formerly held by John Davy and ½ fee held by John le Deyghere.

Sawbridgeworth, 1 fee formerly held by Hamelin de Martham.

Bishop's Stortford, ½ fee once held by John Boys.

Bollington, [Essex], and Farnham, [Essex], ½ fee and ¼ fee formerly held by Fulk de Baa.

Sawbridgeworth, ½ fee held by Geoffrey de la Mare.

Hyde by Sawbridgeworth, ½ fee held by Geoffrey Josselyn.

Hunsdon, ¼ fee held by John Goldyngton.

Barkway, ½ fee held by Edmund de Lancastre.

Hinxworth and Ashwell, 1 fee formerly held by John Gildesburgh.

Bushey and Digswell, 1 fee formerly held by Alice de Perrers.

Gilston, ½ fee formerly held by the heirs of John de Roos, ½ fee held by William Armurer and $\frac{1}{10}$ fee held by Peter de Goldyngton.

Digswell, ½ fee formerly held by the heirs of William Melksop.

Berden, [Essex], ¼ fee held by the heirs of Lawrence Tany.

141   Writ, for fees, 11 Oct. 1399.

LINCOLN. Inquisition. Grantham. 26 Jan. 1400.

She held in her demesne as of fee:

Holbeach in Holland, 2½ fees in the manor, once held by William son of Hugh de Dacre, knight, which manor was formerly of Thomas de Multon.

Little Ponton, Great Ponton and Ganthorpe in Kesteven, 2½ fees held by John de Haryngton, knight, formerly of Philip de Pauncton, £7 10s.

South Thoresby in Lindsey, 1½ fees held by Thomas de Hethe, knight, in right of Alice his wife, daughter and heir of John de Caltoft, knight, once of John de Segrave.

142   Writ, for fees, 11 Oct. 1399.

SOMERSET. Inquisition. Ilchester. 12 Feb. 1400.

She held in chief ⅓ fee in the manor of Pury, held of her by John Erleigh.

143   Writ, for fees, 11 Oct. 1399.

BUCKINGHAM. Inquisition. Aylesbury. 24 Jan. 1400.

She held in her demesne as of fee the advowson of the abbey of Notley. The temporalities are worth £40 yearly when a vacancy occurs. She held no knight's fees or other advowsons.

144   BEDFORD. Inquisition. Biggleswade. 26 Jan. 1400.

She held in her demesne as of fee the advowsons of Pertenhall, value £8 yearly when it occurs, and of Tilbrook, £10.

145   Writ, for fees, 11 Oct. 1399.

GLOUCESTER AND THE ADJACENT MARCH OF WALES. Extent. Chipping Sodbury. 16 Feb. 1400.

She held no knight's fees but in her demesne as of fee the advowsons of:

Barnsley, which extends at 20 marks yearly.

Shirenewton in the Welsh March, 20 marks.

Caldicot, the free chapel in the castle, 20s.

146   Writ, for fees, 11 Oct. 1399.

KENT. Inquisition. Deptford. 3 Feb. 1400.

She held in her demesne as of fee:

Harbilton in Harrietsham, 1 fee of the honour of Mandeville, formerly held by William de Pympe and John Tistede, annual value when it occurs 75s.

Swingfield, 1 fee once held by William Swynefeld.

Otterden, ¼ and 1/10 fee once held by William de Otrenden.

Sevington, ¼ fee once held by John Satrendon.

Maytham in Rolvenden, 2 fees once held by William Pympe.

Rolvenden, 2 fees once held by Richard atte Lese and the heirs of Henry Aucher.

Benenden, 1 fee once held by Richard atte Lese, knight.

Dodingdale, 1 fee in the manor, 50s.

Rolvenden, ½ fee formerly of Hawise de Mayhamme, once held by William Pympe, and 1 fee once held by Roger de Cassyngtham.

Saynden, ¼ fee held by the heirs of Joce de Otrenden.

Lossenham, ¼ fee once held by Henry Fitzaucher.

Lowden in Rolvenden manor, 3 fees once held by Richard atte Lese, knight.

Knock and Ockley, ½ fee held by the abbot of Robertsbridge.

Staplehurst, ¼ fee held by Robert de Marke, once held by John Somery.

Swingfield, 2½ fees once held by William Aboke.

In the county, 2 fees held by the prior of Bilsington.

E

147   MIDDLESEX. Inquisition. Tottenham. 4 Feb. 1400.

She held in her demesne as of fee:

Greenford and Stickleton, 2 fees held by John de Bealmont and the prioress of Ankerwyke.

Enfield, $\frac{1}{4}$ fee once held by Jordan de Elsyng and John de Rana, 20s.; and $\frac{1}{4}$ fee once held by Jordan de Elsyng and formerly by Thomas Fescamp, 20s.

Northolt and Ickenham, 1 fee less $\frac{1}{20}$ once held by Roger de la Doune, and formerly by Adam Fraunceys.

South Mimms, 1 fee once of Arnold Maundeville, and held by the heirs of Roger Leukenore.

Stickleton, Islington and Hatton by Hounslow, $\frac{1}{2}$ fee held by the heirs of Robert de Norhthampton, and once held by Richard de Norhthampton.

Stickleton, 1 fee once of Hugh de Messinden, and now held by the nuns of Ankerwyke.

Islington, 1 fee held by the heirs of John de Berners.

148   Writ, for fees, 11 Oct. 1399.

OXFORD. Inquisition. Oxford. 17 Feb. 1400.

She held:

Kingham, $\frac{1}{2}$ fee held by the lady of Langley, and $\frac{1}{2}$ fee held by the heirs of John Beaufo.

Wendlebury, 1 fee held by Amery de Sancto Amando.

Stonor, 1 fee formerly held by Edmund de Stonhore.

Latchford, $\frac{1}{2}$ fee held by William Pippard.

Great Haseley, the advowson, £40.

149   Writ, for fees, 11 Oct. 1399.

SUSSEX. Inquisition. Robertsbridge. 1 May 1400.

She held:

Wigsell, 1 fee once held by Thomas Colepeper.

Ore, 1 fee held by Robert de Ore.

150   SURREY. Inquisition. Southwark. 29 April 1400.

She held:

Clapham, Carshalton and Wanborough, 4 fees of the honour of Mandeville, once of Sybil de Boleyn, held by Ralph de Morton and John de Bures.

Horsley manor, 1 fee held by the heirs of John Berners.

151   Writ, for fees, 11 Oct. 1399.

NORTHAMPTON. Inquisition. Northampton. 20 Jan. 1400.

She held:

Northampton, 2 fees, once held by the heirs of Robert de Norhthampton.

Hinton, 2 fees held by Henry de Hynton.

Aynho, $1\frac{1}{2}$ fees held by Ralph Neville.

Aston le Walls, 1 fee once held by Ralph Morton and John Bures.

Culworth, Croughton, and Leckhampstead, 2 fees once held by Hugh de Messynden.

'Compton', 1 fee once held by the heirs of the Earl Marshal.

Hinton in the Hedges, 2 fees once held by William de Hynton, £12.

Aston le Walls, 1 fee once held by John de Sutton.

Hinton by Woodford, 1 fee once held by John de Hinton.

152   [List of knight's fees and advowsons]

BUCKINGHAM: Newton Longville priory and Notley abbey, advowsons.

BEDFORD: Pertenhall and Tilbrook churches, advowsons.

HAMPSHIRE: Fordingbridge church, advowson.

NORTHAMPTON: Hinton, Aynho, Aston le Walls, Culworth, Croughton and Leck-hampstead, 'Compton', Hinton in the Hedges and Hinton by Woodford, knight's fees [as above, no. 151].

OXFORD: Kingham, Wendlebury, Stonor and Latchford, knight's fees, and Great Haseley, advowson [as above, no. 148].

STAFFORD: Spittal Pool, advowson of the chapel.

GLOUCESTER AND THE ADJACENT MARCH OF WALES:

Rendcombe and Hardwicke, 2½ fees held by Thomas de la Mare and Robert de la Mare.

Doynton, 2 fees held by William Tracy.

Charfield, 1 fee held by Robert de Veel.

Eastleach Turville, 1 fee held by the heirs of William Lecch.

Tytherington, 1 fee held by William de Clynton.

Badgeworth and Little Shurdington, 1 fee formerly held by Richard Talbot and 1 fee held by Lord Daudeley.

Eldersfield, [Worcs], 1 fee held by Thomas Berkeley of Coberley.

Chaddesley Corbett, [Worcs], 1 fee once held by William Corbet.

Oxenton and Aston on Carrant, ½ fee once held by Lord Tiptoft.

Kemerton, Aston on Carrant and Boddington, 1 fee once held by William de Bello Campo.

Mangotsfield, ½ fee formerly held by Edmund Blount.

'Bykynton', 1½ fees held by Matthew Gournay.

Kemerton, 1 fee once held by John de Bures.

Dixton and Alderton, 1 fee once held by John de Akelyston.

Little Shurdington, ⅕ fee held by William Cropet.

Dodington, 1 fee held by the heirs of Maud Cantelo.

Shenington, [Oxon], ⅕ fee formerly held by John Pecche, ⅕ fee held by Ralph de Stafford and ⅕ fee once held by Lambert de la More.

Bentham, ½ fee once held by Henry de Harletre.

Lydney, ⅕ fee once held by Robert de Lydon.

Sutton, ⅕ fee once held by Richard de Sutton.

Walcot, [Oxon], ½ fee once held by the heirs of Seman Walcote.

Walton Cardiff, 1 fee once held by Edward de Kerdyff and 1 fee held by the abbot of Tewkesbury.

Reddington, 1 fee once held by Simon Basset.

Crowell, [Oxon], 1⅓ fees once held by Alan de Crawell.

Hethe, [Oxon], ½ fee once held by the heirs of Baldwin de Insula and ⅛ fee once held by Thomas Tey.

Enborne, [Berks.], 1/15 fee once held by Andrew de la Roche.

                                    C 137/10,11, no.50, mm.1–10, 13–24, 26–50
                                    E 149/72, no.5
                                    E 142/355, 356

JOAN DAUGHTER OF ELEANOR DUCHESS OF GLOUCESTER

153 Writ 18 Aug. 1400.

CAMBRIDGE. Inquisition. Cambridge. 20 Sept.

   She held in her demesne as of fee of the king in chief by knight service the court leet of Sawston, held on the morrow of St. Barnabas, value 5s.

   She died on 16 Aug. last. Anne wife of the earl of Stafford and Isabel, a nun of the order of Minoresses in the suburbs of London, between Aldgate and the Tower, are her sisters and heirs. Anne is of full age, 17 years and more. Isabel was 13 on 23 April last.

154 Writ 18 Aug. 1400.

GLOUCESTER AND THE ADJACENT MARCH OF WALES. Inquisition. Thornbury. 13 Sept.

   She held in her demesne as of fee of the king in chief:

   Wheatenhurst, the manor, service unknown, annual value £21 7s.

   Caldicot castle and Shirenewton with their members in the Welsh March, by baron service, annual value £26 13s.4d.

   Date of death and heirs as above.

155 Writ 18 Aug. 1400.

ESSEX. Inquisition. Pleshey. 28 Aug.

   She held in her demesne as of fee of the king in chief:

   Great Waltham, the manor, service unknown, annual value £50.

   Chishall, view of frankpledge, service unknown, annual value 3s.4d.

   Shenfield, 73s.4d. rent from the manor payable at Easter and Michaelmas, service unknown.

   She held of William Bourghchier, knight, the manor of Wix, service unknown, annual value £26 13s.4d.

   Date of death and heirs as above.

156 HERTFORD. Inquisition. Bishop's Stortford. 26 Aug. 1400.

   She held in her demesne as of fee of the king in chief, services unknown:

   Nuthampstead, a third part of the manor, annual value 73s.4d.

   Hoddesdon, view of frankpledge, annual value 4s., and a rent of 12 capons from various tenants there at Christmas, worth 3d. each.

   Date of death and heirs as above.

157 Writ 18 Aug. 1400.

BUCKINGHAM. Inquisition. Aylesbury. 6 Sept.

   She held as part of her portion of the inheritance of Eleanor her mother an annuity of £20 payable by the sheriff, granted by Richard II to Thomas, duke of Gloucester, then earl of Buckingham, and his heirs.

   Date of death and heirs as above.

158 Writ 14 Feb. 1401.

BERKSHIRE. Inquisition. Faringdon. 15 March.

   Richard Talbot, knight, deceased, held half the manor of Shrivenham in his demesne as of fee, and long before his death granted it by his charter to Joan, one of the daughters and heirs of Eleanor, wife of Thomas duke of Gloucester, and her heirs by Gilbert, eldest son of Richard Talbot, or by one of his other sons. She held it when she died without heirs by Gilbert or any other son of Richard. It should revert to Gilbert, who is a minor in the king's ward, as heir of Richard. It is held of the king in chief as one knight's fee, annual value £25 15s.

Date of death and heirs, both aged 16 years and more, as above.

159 Writ, for fees, 24 Aug. 1400.
CAMBRIDGE. Inquisition. Cambridge. 20 Sept.
She held in her demesne as of fee of the king in chief by knight service 1 fee in Fulbourn, held by the heir of John Olyve.

Date of death and heirs as above [no.153].

160 Writ, for fees, 24 Aug. 1400.
GLOUCESTER AND THE ADJACENT MARCH OF WALES. Inquisition. Thornbury. 13 Sept.
She held in her demesne as of fee of the king in chief the advowsons of Barnsley, at alternate presentations, and, in the Welsh March, Shirenewton, extending at £13 6s.8d. each.

Date of death and heirs as above [no.153].

161 Writ, for fees, 24 Aug. 1400.
ESSEX. Inquisition. Pleshey. 25 Sept.
She held in her demesne as of fee the advowsons of:
Wix priory, value of temporalities when vacant £13 6s.8d.
Debden church, annual value when vacant £20.
Shenfield church, £8.
West Thurrock, church or prebend, alternate presentations, £13 6s.8d.

162 Writ, for fees, 24 Aug. 1400.
KENT. Inquisition. Sandhurst. 6 Sept.
She held in her demesne as of fee of the king in chief:
Swingfield, 1 fee held by William Swynefeld.
Maytham in Rolvenden, 2 fees held by William de Pympe.
Rolvenden, 2 fees held by the heirs of Henry Auger and Richard atte Lesse.
Benenden, 1 fee held by Richard atte Lese, knight.
Dodingdale, ½ fee.
Maytham and Rolvenden, ½ fee, formerly of Hawise [de Mayhamme], held by William Pympe.
Rolvenden, 1 fee held by Roger de Cassynham.
Lowden in Rolvenden, 3 fees held by Richard atte Lese, knight.
Swingfield, 2½ fees held by William Aboke.

163 Writ, for fees, 24 Aug. 1400.
NORTHAMPTON. Inquisition. Rothwell. 17 Sept.
She held in her demesne as of fee:
Northampton, 2 fees once held by the heirs of Robert de Norhtampton.
Hinton, 2 fees held by Henry de Hynton.

Aston le Walls, 1 fee held by Ralph de Morton and John Bures.
Culworth, Croughton and Leckhampstead, 2 fees once held by Hugh de Messenden.
'Compton', 1 fee once held by the heirs of the Earl Marshal.
Hinton in the Hedges, 2 fees once held by William de Hynton.
Aston le Walls, 1 fee once held by John de Sutton.
Hinton by Woodford, 1 fee once held by John de Hinton.
Date of death and heirs as above [no.153].

164 Writ 14 Feb. 1401.
WILTSHIRE. Inquisition. Swindon. 16 March.
Richard Talbot, knight, held the manor of Swindon in his demesne as of fee and granted it by charter to Joan, daughter and heir of Eleanor, and her heirs by Gilbert, eldest son of Richard Talbot, or by one of his other sons. She died on 16 Aug. last without heirs of her body. It should revert to Gilbert, who is a minor in the king's ward. It is held of the king in chief of the castle of Dover by a rent of 20s. payable at Easter and Michaelmas by equal parts, annual value £22 7s.
Anne wife of Edmund earl of Stafford and Isabel daughter of Thomas duke of Gloucester are sisters and next heirs of the blood, aged 16 years and more, and 15 years and more.

165 Writ 14 Feb. 1401.
GLOUCESTER. Inquisition. Gloucester. 26 Feb.
Gilbert Talbot, lord of Archenfield, held the manor of Lydney in his demesne as of fee and granted it to Richard Talbot and Ankaret his wife to hold to themselves and the heirs of their bodies. Richard by his charter dated 20 May 1392 granted it to Joan and her heirs by Gilbert, eldest son of Richard Talbot, or by one of his other sons. It is held of the earl of Warwick in socage by a rent of £4, annual value £7.
She died on 16 Aug. without heirs of her body. The manor belongs by right to Ankaret under the grant of Gilbert Talbot. Her sisters, Anne wife of Edmund earl of Stafford and Isabel, are her heirs.

166 [Marginated] A
Portion of Anne, one of the sisters and heirs of Joan, daughter of Eleanor duchess of Gloucester, and wife of Edmund earl of Stafford:
ESSEX: Waltham, manor, £50.
Wix, manor, £26 13s.4d.
Chishall, view of frankpledge, 3s.4d.
HERTFORD: Nuthampstead, a third part of the manor, 73s.4d.
CAMBRIDGE: Sawston, leet of the vill, 5s.
KENT: Swingfield, 1 fee held by William Swynfeld.
Maytham in Rolvenden, 2 fees held by William de Pympe.
Rolvenden, 2 fees held by the heirs of Henry Aucher and Richard atte Lesse, knight.
Benenden, 1 fee held by Richard atte Lese, knight.
Dodingdale manor, held of the earl of Hereford by the service of ½ knight's fee.
Rolvenden and Maytham, ½ fee formerly of Hawise de Mayhamme held by William Pympe.
Rolvenden, 1 fee held by Roger de Cassyngham.
Lowden in Rolvenden, 3 fees held by Richard atte Lese, knight.

Swingfield, 2½ fees held by William Aboke.

ESSEX: West Thurrock, 2nd presentation to prebend, £13 6s.8d.

Debden, advowson, £20.

Wix, priory, advowson, £13 6s.8d.

[Marginated] B

Portion of Isabel, the other sister and heir of Joan, daughter of Eleanor duchess of Gloucester, under age in the king's ward:

GLOUCESTER AND THE WELSH MARCH: Caldicot castle and shirenewton, £26 13s.4d.

Wheatenhurst, manor, £21 7s.

ESSEX: Shenfield, annual rent from the manor, 73s.4d.

BUCKINGHAM: fee from the county, £20.

HERTFORD: Hoddesdon, view of frankpledge, 3s.; and rent of 12 capons, 3s.

NORTHAMPTON: Northampton, 2 fees once held by the heirs of Robert de Northampton.

Hinton, 2 fees held by Henry de Hynton.

Aston, 1 fee held by Ralph de Morton and John Bures.

Culworth, Croughton and Leckhampstead, 2 fees once held by Hugh de Messyngdon.

'Crompton' [sic], 1 fee once held by the heirs of the Earl Marshal.

Hinton in the hedges, 2 fees once held by William de Hynton.

Aston, 1 fee once held by John de Sutton.

Hinton by Woodford, 1 fee once held by John de Hynton.

CAMBRIDGE: Fulbourn, 1 fee held by the heir of John Olyve.

Advowsons:

GLOUCESTER AND THE WELSH MARCH: Barnsley, alternately with the king, £13 6s.8d.

Shirenewton, £13 6s.8d.

ESSEX: Shenfield, £8.

BEDFORD: Pertenhall, £8.

C 137/9, no.49; 24, no.48
E 149/72, no.6
E 152/362, 369

ISABEL DAUGHTER OF ELEANOR DUCHESS OF GLOUCESTER

167 Writ, *quia habitum religionis assumpsit*, 27 April 1402.

BUCKINGHAM. Inquisition. Stony Stratford. 19 May.

No lands are in the king's hands owing to the death of Eleanor, or by the death of Joan one of her daughters, or the minority of Isabel another daughter, who is professed in religion; but there is in the king's hands an annuity of £20 payable by the sheriff, granted by Richard II to Thomas duke of Gloucester.

Isabel was professed in the house of the order of Minoresses in the suburbs of London on 23 April last, when she was aged 16 years. Anne wife of Edmund earl of Stafford, one of the daughters of Eleanor, is next heir, aged 20 years and more.

168 Similar writ, 27 April 1402.

ESSEX. Inquisition. Chelmsford. 12 May.

The manor of Shenfield is in the king's hands owing to the death of Eleanor, the death of Joan her daughter and the minority of Isabel, another daughter. It is held of the king in chief, service unknown, annual value £20.

Profession and heir as above.

169 HERTFORD. Inquisition. Bishop's Stortford. 15 May 1402.

The view of frankpledge of Hoddesdon and a rent of 12 capons from various tenants there at Christmas are in the king's hands for the reason given above. They are held of the king in chief as part of the barony of the county of Essex, annual values 3s.6½d. and 3s.

Profession and heir as above.

170 Similar writ, 27 April 1402.

GLOUCESTER AND THE ADJACENT MARCH OF WALES. Inquisition. Chipping Sodbury. 24 May.

In the king's hands for the reason given above are:

Wheatenhurst, the manor, held of the king in chief, service unknown, annual value £21 7s.

Caldicot castle and Shirenewton in Wales, held of the king in chief by baron service, annual value 40 marks.

Profession and heir as above. Peter Crulle, esquire, has received the issues and profits from the time of the profession of Isabel until the present, title unknown.

171 Similar writ, 27 April 1402.

OXFORD. Inquisition. Oxford. 2 May.

In the king's hands for the above reason are:

Kirtlington and Deddington, the manors, held of the king in fee tail by grant of Edward III to William de Bohun and his heirs; Kirtlington by the service of a third part of a fee, annual value £13 6s.8d.; Deddington by the service of a third part of 2 fees, annual value £13 6s.8d.

Profession and heir as above.

172 Similar writ, 27 April 1402.

HEREFORD AND THE ADJACENT MARCH OF WALES. Inquisition. Hereford. 17 May.

In the king's hands for the above reason are the lordship and castle of Huntington in Wales, held of the king in chief, service unknown, annual value £28 13s.4d.

Profession and heir as above.

173 Similar writ, 27 April 1402.

LINCOLN. Inquisition. Grantham. 16 May.

In the king's hands for the above reason is the manor of Long Bennington comprising various buildings etc., [all as in no.126 above]. It is held of the honour of Richmond by knight service, amount unknown.

Profession and heir as above.

174 Similar writ, 27 April 1402.

NOTTINGHAM. Inquisition. Southwell. 15 May.

In the king's hands for the above reason is the manor of Kneesall, held of the honour of Richmond, service unknown, comprising several very ruinous buildings, annual value nil; 180 a. arable with meadow and pasture, £4 13s.4d.; an enclosed park, herbage 13s.4d.; 1 windmill, 3s.4d.; farm of lands in 'Northlound', 'Southlound' and 'Stywardewong', 21s.7d.; £13 19s. rents of tenants at will; and 1 lb cumin, 2d., and 1 lb. pepper, 12d., in assize rents.

Profession and heir as above.

175   Similar writ, 27 April 1402.
HUNTINGDON. Inquisition. Huntingdon. 31 May.
There are no fees or advowsons in the king's hands for the above reason.

176   CAMBRIDGE. Inquisition. Cambridge. 30 May 1402.
In the king's hands for the above reason is 1 knight's fee in Fulbourn, held by the heirs of John Olyve.

177   Similar writ, 27 April 1402.
SURREY. Inquisition. Bletchingley. 18 May.
In the king's hands for the above reason are 4 knight's fees in Clapham, Carshalton and Wanborough, once held by Sybil de Boleyne of the honour of Mandeville, and held by Ralph Morton and John Bures; and 1 fee in Horsley manor, held by the heirs of John Berners.

178   SUSSEX. Inquisition. Sedlescombe. 3 May 1402.
In the king's hands for the above reason are 1 fee in Wigsell held by Simon de Echyngham and John Colpeper and 1 fee in Ore held by Robert de Ore.

179   Similar writ, 27 April 1402.
BEDFORD. Inquisition. Bedford. 22 May.
In the king's hands for the above reason is the advowson of the church of Pertenhall, annual value when vacant £8.

180   BUCKINGHAM. Inquisition. Stony Stratford. 19 May 1402.
In the king's hands for the above reason is the advowson of the abbey of Notley, annual value of the temporalities when vacant £40.

181   Similar writ, 27 April 1402.
ESSEX. Inquisition. Chelmsford. 12 May.
In the king's hands for the above reason are the advowsons of Shenfield, annual value when vacant £8, Barnston £6 13s.3d., South Fambridge 100s. and Quendon 100s.

182   Similar writ, 27 April 1402.
GLOUCESTER AND THE ADJACENT MARCH OF WALES. Inquisition. Chipping Sodbury. 24 May.
In the king's hands for the above reason are the advowsons of Barnsley, on alternate occasions, extending at £13 6s.8d.; and in Wales, Shirenewton, extending at £13 6s.8d.

183   Similar writ, 27 April 1402.

OXFORD. Inquisition. Oxford. 2 May.

In the king's hands for the above reason are:

Kingham, ½ fee held by the lady of Langley and ½ fee held by the heirs of John Beaufo.

Wendlebury, 1 fee held by Amery de Sancto Amando.

Stonor, 1 fee held by Edmund de Stonhore.

Latchford, ½ fee held by William Pippard.

184   Similar writ, 27 April 1402.

LINCOLN. Extent of fees in the king's hands. Grantham. 16 May.

Holbeach in Holland, manor, 2½ fees held by Thomas Fitzwilliam of Dacre, knight, annual value when vacant £40.

Little Ponton, Great Ponton and Ganthorpe in Kesteven, 2½ fees held by the heirs of John de Haryngton, formerly of Philip de Paunton, £10.

South Thoresby in Lindsey, 1½ fees held by Thomas de Chaworth, knight, formerly of John de Caltoft, £10.

185   Similar writ, 27 April 1402.

MIDDLESEX. Inquisition. Westminster. 31 May.

In the king's hands for the above reason are:

Greenford and Stickleton, 2 fees held by John de Bealmond and the prioress of Ankerwyke.

South Mimms, 1 fee once of Arnold de Maundevill, held by the heirs of Roger de Leukenore.

Stickleton, 1 fee once of Hugh de Messyngden, now held by the nuns of Ankerwyke.

Islington manor, 1 fee held by the heirs of John Berners.

186   HERTFORD. Inquisition. Bishop's Stortford. 15 May 1402.

There is nothing in the king's hands for the above reason.

187   Similar writ, 27 April 1402.

NORTHAMPTON. Inquisition. Northampton. 20 May.

The following are in the king's hands for the above reason:

Northampton, 2 fees held by the heirs of Robert de Norhampton.

Hinton, 2 fees held by Henry de Hynton.

Aston, 1 fee held by Ralph de Morton and John Bures.

Culworth, Croughton and Leckhampstead, 2 fees once held by Hugh de Missenden.

'Compton', 1 fee once held by the heirs of the Earl Marshal.

Hinton in the Hedges, 2 fees once held by William de Hynton.

Aston, 1 fee once held by John de Sutton.

Hinton by Woodford, 1 fee once held by John de Hynton.

188   Similar writ, 27 April 1402.

KENT. Inquisition. Yalding. 29 May.

In the king's hands for the reasons given above are:

Harbilton in Harrietsham by Ospringe, ¾ fee of the honour of Mandeville held by William Pympe and John Tystede.

Otterden, ¼ and 1/10 fee held by William de Otrenden.

Saynden, ¼ fee held by the heirs of Joce de Otrenden.

Sevington, ¼ fee held by John Satrinden.

Lossenham, ¼ fee which Henry Fitzauchere held by Rolvenden.

Knock and Ockley, ½ fee held by the abbot of Robertsbridge.

Staplehurst, ¼ fee formerly of Robert de Marle, held by John Somery.

2 fees in the county held by the prior of Bilsington.

189 Similar writ, 27 April 1402.

SOMERSET. Inquisition. Yeovil. 9 June.

In the king's hands for the reasons given above is ⅓ fee in the manor of Pury, held by John Erleygh.

C 137/11, no.50, m.32; 12, no.51
E 149/78, no.9
E 152/374, 375

AUBREY DE VEER, EARL OF OXFORD

190 Writ 26 April 1400.

SUFFOLK. Inquisition. Hoxne. 25 May.

He held the manor of Mendham called Walsham Hall in his demesne as of fee of the king in chief by knight service, annual value 16 marks.

Formerly he held the manor of Cockfield with the appurtenances called Earls Hall in his demesne as of fee, but long before he died, by his charter dated 13 May 1397, he enfeoffed Richard Waldegrave, knight, Thomas Cogeshale, William Skrene, Robert Neuport and William Tasburgh, clerk, to them, their heirs and assigns. It is held of the abbot of Bury St. Edmunds as of his manor of Cockfield, service unknown, annual value 20 marks.

He died on 23 April. Richard his son and heir was aged 14 at the Annunciation [recte Assumption, 15 Aug.]

191 Writ 26 April 1400.

CAMBRIDGE. Inquisition. Cambridge. 29 May.

He held in his demesne in fee tail of the king in chief by knight service the manors of Castle Camps, annual value £21 6s. 8d., and Saxton, annual value 20 marks, with the advowson of Camps, and 60s. rent from 'Souches Melles' in Newnham by Cambridge.

He held in his demesne as of fee of the earl of March, service unknown, the manor of Swaffham Bulbeck and the advowson of Horseheath. The manor is valued at £10 yearly beyond a rent of 100s., payable in equal parts at Easter and Michaelmas, which on 20 May 1398 he granted by his indented charter to Michael Stancomb, esquire, for life, and it is held accordingly.

He held the following knight's fees:

Balsham, 1 fee held by John Sleford.

Swaffham Prior, 1 fee held by John Shadworth.

Burwell, 1 fee held by Payn Typtot.

Olmstead, ½ fee held by William Skryne.

Nosterfield, ⅛ fee held by John Hunte.

Papworth, 1 fee held by the heirs of John Dengayne.

Silverley, 2 fees held by the prior of St. John of Jerusalem.

Ashley, 1 fee held by the heir of John Honeman.

Horseheath, 1 fee held by the heir of John de Lyndebury, and 12 parts [sic] of 1 fee held by William Aylyngton.

He held no more, but by his charter dated 24 Aug. 1396 he gave to Richard Waldegrave, knight, and others [as above no. 190] the manors of Dullingham called Beauchamps Hall and Poyntz Hall with other lands and tenements there called Baas and Chalers and all his other lands in the same place to hold to themselves, their heirs and assigns. They are not held of the king, but of whom, by what service, and of what value they are is unknown.

Date of death and heir, aged 14 on 15 Aug. last, as above.

192 Writ 26 April 1400.

BEDFORD. Inquisition. Woburn. 14 May.

He held no lands, but the advowson of the patronage of Woburn abbey, annual value nil.

Date of death and heir as above.

193 BUCKINGHAM. Inquisition. Aylesbury. 15 May 1400.

He held in his demesne in fee tail:

Calverton, the manor, of the king in chief, service unknown, annual value £10.

Whitchurch, the manor, of the earl of Stafford by knight service, annual value £40.

He formerly held in his demesne as of fee the manor of Aston Sandford, but on 20 March 1397 he enfeoffed to themselves, their heirs and assigns, Richard Waldegrave, knight, and others [as above, no. 190]. Of whom it is held and by what service is unknown; annual value £10.

He held the advowson of Calverton, annual value £10.

Date of death and heir as above.

194 Writ 26 April 1400.

MIDDLESEX. Inquisition. Westminster. 1 July.

He formerly held the manor of Kensington in his demesne as of fee as the heir of Robert de Veer, late duke of Ireland, which with other lands he granted by his indenture, shown to the jurors, to Philippa duchess of Ireland, to hold in dower, and which she granted by her indenture, also shown to the jurors, dated 1 Aug. 1398, to himself, Walter le Frezwater, Richard Walegrave, knight, William Skrene, Clement Spice, Robert Nyweport and William Tasseburgh, clerk, to hold for her life, paying her a rent of £33 at Easter and Michaelmas by equal parts, with reversion to him and his heirs. Therefore he had no status in the manor except jointly with the others.

Date of death as above. Richard de Veer, knight, his son and heir, is aged 17 years and more.

195 KENT. Inquisition. Wye. 1 June 1400.

He held the manor of Badlesmere with the advowson in fee tail of various lords by various tenures: the site of the manor, 240 a. arable, pasture and wood, and 40s. rent of the king and the earl of Stafford by knight service, that is the site, 220 a. and the rent of the king of the castle of Dover, rendering 20s. 1d. for the guard of the castle, and the remaining 20 a. of the earl of Stafford of the castle of Tonbridge, annual value together 100s.; and 400 a. arable and pasture by gavelkind of various lords, and by rendering a total of £6 17s. 5½d. in rents, annual value beyond these 60s.

Date of death as above, age of heir given as 17.

196 ESSEX. Inquisition. Braintree. 30 June 1400.

He held in fee tail of the king in chief by knight service:

Castle Hedingham, the castle and manor, as parcel of the earldom of Oxford. Long before his death he granted to William . . . by letters patent the office of parker of the park of Castle Hedingham with the herbage of a meadow called 'Parkersmedowe' next to the mill, and all the wood called 'Wyndfeldwode', and sufficient herbage for six great beasts, one heifer, one colt and six pigs in the same park, and a house called Lodge without the burden of repairs. The castle and manor are worth £20 yearly beyond annuities and the fees of various officials.

Sible Hedingham, two parts of the manor called Prayors, with two parts of Bourehall belonging to it. Long before his death he granted to John Swanheld, his servant, who still lives, the keeping of his warren and fisheries in his lordship of Castle Hedingham, Sible Hedingham, Great Yeldham and Little Yeldham for life with a fee of 2d. daily, payable yearly from the manor of Prayors in Sible Hedingham, with livery appropriate to his rank yearly from the earl's wardrobe, 2 cartloads of hay and pasture for his horse in the summer in the same manor. The two parts are worth £8 yearly beyond the rent. Philippa duchess of Ireland holds the third part of the manor of Prayors with the third of Bourehall in dower since the death of Robert duke of Ireland, with reversion to the heirs of the earl after her death.

Little Yeldham, the manor. Long before his death he granted to Alice Bene, who still lives, a rent of 40s. for life from this manor. Its annual value beyond the rent is £12.

Steeple Bumpstead, the manor, annual value £20.

He held in his demesne as of fee:

Doddinghurst and Stansted Mountfichet, the manors, of the king in chief. Doddinghurst is worth 20 marks yearly. Long before his death he granted to Roger Eston, who still lives, a rent of 40s. for life from the manor of Stansted, apart from which the manor is worth 20 marks yearly. Likewise he granted to Robert Smyth, his servant, who still lives, the office of parker of the park of Doddinghurst, and the keeping of the same with his warren in Fingrith and Doddinghurst for life, taking from that manor by the bailiff and farmer there every 12 weeks a quarter of corn, 6s. 8d. yearly for his shoes, and linen cloth for his clothing. He was also granted a house called 'le Logge' in the same park for his lodging, pasture for three cows, one horse and six pigs, and dead wood for his fire, all for his life.

Eyston Hall, the manor, of the earl of March, who is under age in the king's ward, service unknown. Long before he died he granted to John Aylemere, John Bavyngton and Richard Payn, his servants, . . . annually for life from this manor. Apart from this it is worth 40s. annually.

Fingrith, the manor, held in fee tail by the service of acting as queen's chamberlain on the day of her coronation, annual value £20.

Beaumont cum Moze, the manor, annual value, apart from a rent payable to the abbey of St. Osyth, 40s.

Bowers Gifford, 52 a. fallow and marsh, annual value 8 marks.

Tilbury juxta Clare, the manor, which he granted for life to John Bray, who still lives, at a rent of £15. By what service it is held is unknown.

Office of the stewardship of all the king's forests in Essex, service unknown, annual value nil.

He held for life of the king in chief by grants of Richard II [*CPR 1377–81*, pp. 112, 371; *1388–92*, p. 375]:

Hadleigh, the castle, manor and watermill, with reversion to the king and his heirs, service unknown, annual value 20 marks.

Rayleigh, the honour, town, fair and market, with the profits and herbage of the park there, and the manor of Eastwood, with reversion to Edmund duke of York, the king's uncle, and his heirs male, service unknown; annual values, Rayleigh 20 marks, Eastwood £20.

Rochford, the hundred, with reversion to the king and his heirs, service unknown, annual value £10.

Thundersley, the manor, with 26s. 8d. rent from the marsh called 'Westwykmersche' in South Benfleet, with reversion to the duke of York and his heirs male; the manor of the honour of Rayleigh, service unknown, the marsh of the prior of Merton by a yearly rent of 73s. 4d. Beyond another rent of 26s. 8d. they are worth £10 yearly.

Long before he died he granted by his letters patent to John Brerele, esquire, for life, with reversion to himself and his heirs, a tenement called 'Watelyst' in Sible Hedingham. It is held of William Coggeshale, knight, service unknown, annual value 40s.

Similarly he gave and confirmed by his charter to Richard Waldegrave, knight, and others [as above, no. 190] his manors of Grays Thurrock and Langdon Hills, with all his lands and tenements, rents and services in Dunton, Bulphan, East Horndon, West Horndon, Laindon, Basildon and Ramsden, to hold to themselves and their heirs in fee simple, and they held them all his life.

Date of death as above. Richard his son and heir was aged 14 on 15 August.

197 Writ 26 April 1400.

ESSEX. Inquisition. Newport. 3 July.

He held for life the manor of Newport with Birchanger hamlet, by the grant of Edward formerly prince of Wales and duke of Cornwall. Edward III held it after the death of Edmund earl of Cornwall, and granted it to the prince of Wales and his successors for ever, annexed to the duchy of Cornwall. The prince granted it to Aubrey de Veer for life, and it now belongs by right of inheritance to Henry prince of Wales, who is aged 14 years and more. It is held of the king in chief, service unknown, annual value £20.

Date of death and heir, aged 14 years and more, as above.

198 Writ, for fees, 17 Dec. 1400.

ESSEX. Inquisition. Braintree. 26 Sept. 1401.

He held:

Castle Hedingham, ½ fee held by Edward Pychard and ½ fee held by Thomas Baret.

Stevington and Ashdon, 1 fee held by Philip de Keditone.

Leyton, ½ fee held by the abbot of Stratford.

Langdon Hills, ½ fee called Whitehall in Dunton, held by Joan countess of Hertford [*recte* Hereford].

Basildon, Dunton and Laindon, ½ fee held by Ralph de Gynges.

Basildon, 1 fee held by Guy de Bertelysdene.

Aythorpe Roding, 2 fees held by William Bourgchier.

Basildon, Dunton and Laindon, ½ fee held by Henry de Bello Campo.
Margaret Roding, 2 fees held by Thomas de Leyghes.
Finchingfield, 1 fee held by Robert Jehull.
Ramsey, ½ fee for reasonable aid from the villeinage of Ramsey [sic].
Ray Wick, ½ fee held by John Ryly.
Canfield, ½ fee held by William Fitz Adam.
Belchamp, ½ fee held by Geoffrey Mychell and ½ fee held by Robert Offyngton.
Ashen, ¼ fee held by Richard Moselyng.
Little Bromley, 1 fee held by the heirs of John de Brabham.
Little Henny, 1 fee held by the heirs of Thomas de Grey.
Tolleshunt Knights, 1 fee held by John Boys.
Virley, 2 fees held by Robert Neweport.
Tolleshunt Major, ½ fee held by the abbot of Coggeshall.
Rivenhall, ¼ fee held by Robert Archer.
Beaumont, 2 fees, 1½ held by John Armysthorp and ½ by the earl himself.
Hempstead, ½ fee held by John Whynselowe.
Dovercourt and Colne, 2 fees held by the countess of Norfolk and John Ynglysthorp.
He also held the following advowsons extending at the amounts shown:
Downham, £10.
Doddinghurst, 100s.
Beaumont at the third turn, 100s.
Tilbury juxta Clare, 10 marks.
Hatfield Broad Oak, priory temporalities, 40 marks.
Thremhall, priory temporalities, 20 marks.
Blackmore, priory temporalities, £10.
Castle Hedingham, free chapel of the castle, 2 marks.
Farnham, chapel, 10 marks.

199 Writ, for fees, 1 May 1400.
HERTFORD. Inquisition. Buntingford. 25 May.
  He held:
  Bengeo, 1 fee held by the heirs of William FitzGeoffrey and Henry de Sandeford.
  Bramfield and Bengeo by Hertford, 1 fee held by William Kevell, Thomas Moryce
and the prior of Royston.
  Beauchamps, formerly Affledwick, 1 fee held by John Bouchamp.
  Meesden, 1 fee held by the countess of Pembroke.
  Bengeo, 1 fee held by John de Goldyngton.
  Thorley, ½ fee held by John de Goldyngton.
  Cockenach, ½ fee held by John Moryce and ¼ fee held by the prior of Royston.
  He died on 23 April.

200 Writ, for fees, 1 May 1400.
OXFORD. Inquisition. Oxford. 12 May.
  He held no knight's fees or advowsons.

201 Writ, for fees, 1 May 1400.
NORFOLK. Inquisition. Happisburgh. 26 May.

He held:

Loddon, 1 fee held of him by the abbot of Langley.

Ketteringham, 1 fee held by the heirs of John de Arganton, knight.

202   BERKSHIRE. Inquisition. Abingdon. 10 May 1400.

He held no knight's fees or advowsons.

203   BERKSHIRE. Inquisition *ex officio*. Ilsley. 23 June 1400.

He died about the quindene of Easter, namely 23 April last, holding the manors of Langley and Bradley of the king in chief by knight service, annual value £10. Edward Bole is the farmer of the manors for 10 years by an indenture between the earl and himself, at a yearly rent of 19½ marks.

204   Calendar of the lands and tenements which Aubrey de Veer, late earl of Oxford, held of the king in chief.

[Essex] Castle Hedingham, castle and manor, £20.

Sible Hedingham, two parts of the manor called Prayors with two parts of Bourehall, £8.

Little Yeldham, manor, £12.

Tilbury juxta Clare, manor, rents from £15.

Bowers Gifford, 52 a. fallow land and marsh, 5 marks.

[Cambs] Castle Camps, £21 6s.8d.

Total £79 13s.4d.

[Kent] Badlesmere, except 400 a. arable and pasture in gavelkind, 100s.

[Essex] Steeple Bumpstead, £20.

Beaumont, 40s.

Eyston Hall, 40s.

[Bucks] Calverton, £10.

Whitchurch, £40.

Total [£79 0s.0d.]

. . ., 20 marks.

[Berks, Langley and Bradley], £10.

. . ., 20 marks.

. . ., £20.

. . ., 20 marks

[Suffolk, Mendham], 16 marks.

[Total £80 13s.4d.] . . .

C 137/13, no.52
E 149/72, no.8
E 152/352, 362
E 357/14, m.42d.

WILLIAM SON OF JOHN DE IPSTONES, KNIGHT

205   Writ 6 Feb. 1400.

NORTHAMPTON. Inquisition. Rothwell. 15 March.

He held in his demesne as of fee of the king in chief by knight service 3 messuages and 3 virgates in Weston by Welland, annual value 40s.

He died in London on 17 Oct. 1399. His daughters Christina and Alice, aged 6 years and 2 years, are next heirs.

206   Writ 6 Feb. 1400.

STAFFORD. Inquisition. Stafford. 1 May.

He held the manor of Cresswell by Tillington jointly with Maud his wife, who survives him, by a grant to them and their heirs by Robert de More and William Deye, chaplains. It is held of Thomas de Eyton, service unknown, annual value 100s.

He died on 15 Oct. Christina and Alice his daughters and heirs are aged 6 years and more and 3 years and more.

C 137/14, no.53

ELEANOR WIDOW OF GILES DAUBENEY, KNIGHT

207   Writ 8 Aug. 1400.

BEDFORD. Inquisition. Bedford. 12 Aug.

She held a third part of the manor of Kempston, jointly enfeoffed with Giles her husband in fee tail to them and the heirs of their bodies, by a grant made with the king's licence from John de Galmyngton, clerk, and John Mauleverer. It is held of the king in chief by knight service of the honour of Huntingdon, annual value £20.

She died on 6 Aug. last. Giles Daubeney, knight, son of Giles and Eleanor, his heir, is aged 28 years and more.

208   Writ 8 Aug. 1400.

NOTTINGHAM. Inquisition. Newark. 21 Aug.

She held for life in dower of the inheritance of Giles Daubeney, knight, son and heir of Giles, a third part of half a pasture called 'le Southdike' by Broadholme and a third part of a wood there called 'Southehallewode' as part of the manor of South Ingleby. They are held of Lord de Roos by knight service of the castle of Belvoir, annual value of the pasture 13s., and of the wood nil beyond its upkeep because there is no underwood.

She died on 6 Aug. last.

209   Writ 8 Aug. 1400.

LINCOLN. Inquisition. Saxilby. 31 Aug.

She held in dower a third part of the manor of Ingleby of the inheritance of Giles Daubeney, knight, the son. It is held of the Lord de Roos of his castle of Belvoir by knight service, annual value £6.

Date of death as above.

210   Writ 8 Aug. 1400.

SOMERSET. Inquisition. Ilminster. 18 Aug.

She held in dower of the king in chief by knight service, of the inheritance of Giles Daubeney, knight, the son, 2 messuages, 2 gardens, half a dovecot, 51 a. arable, 16

F

a. meadow, 20 a. underwood, a third part of a copse, 5 a. pasture and £49 12s. rent in South Petherton, Barrington, Southarp and Chillington, annual value apart from the rent 117s.10d.

Date of death as above.

211 Writ 8 Aug. 1400.

CORNWALL. Inquisition. Lostwithiel. 3 Sept.

She held in dower of the inheritance of Giles Daubeney, knight, the son, a third part of the manor of Fawton, of the prince as duke of Cornwall in chief of his castle of Launceston by knight service, as a third part of half a fee, annual value £8.

Date of death as above.

C 137/14, no.54
E 149/72, no.3

EMMA WIFE OF RICHARD CRAUCESTRE

212 Writ 30 May 1400.

NORTHUMBERLAND. Inquisition. Morpeth. 23 June.

She held in her demesne as of fee:

Dilston, the manor with the advowson of the chantry of St. Mary Magdalen there, of the king in chief by knight service, annual value 20 marks.

Corbridge, 1 messuage and 80 a., of the king in petty serjeanty by a yearly rent of 10s. payable through the sheriff, annual value 40s.; and 1 burgage there of Henry Percy, earl of Northumberland, in socage. It is of no value, being burnt and destroyed by the Scots.

She died on 21 May last. William Gray, son of William Gray deceased, her son, is next heir, aged 6 years and more. The lands are in the hands of her husband, Richard Crawcestre, by the courtesy of England.

C 137/14, no.55

THOMAS SON AND HEIR OF THOMAS MAUNDEVILLE, KNIGHT

213 Writ 18 Aug. 1400.

ESSEX. Inquisition. Chelmsford. 3 Sept.

The manor of Elmstead came into the king's hands by the death of Thomas Maundeville, knight, and because of the minority of Thomas his son, likewise deceased, and so remains. It is held of the king of the honour of Rayleigh, service unknown, annual value £19 11s.

Thomas Maundeville, knight, once held in his demesne as of fee the manor of Stapleford Tawney with the advowson, and granted it to Thomas Lampet for life for an annual rent of £20 payable at Easter and Michaelmas. This rent is similarly in the king's hands. The manor is held of the same honour, service unknown.

The manors of Black Notley, Broomfield and Chatham, owing to the same death and minority, came into the hands of the countess of Hereford of whom they are held, services unknown, annual values £10 13s.4d., £12 and £9 6s.8d.

He died on 6 Aug. last. Joan wife of John Barry and Alice wife of Helmyng Leget his sisters and heirs are of full age, both 22 years and more.

214 HERTFORD. Inquisition. Bishop's Stortford. 26 Aug. 1400.

Nothing came into the king's hands owing to the death of Thomas Maundeville, knight, and the minority of Thomas his heir, but the manor of Eastwick with the advowson came into the hands of the countess of Kent, being held of her, service unknown, annual value £10.

Date of death and heirs as above.

C 137/14, no.56
E 152/347

CHRISTINA KENTCOMBE

215 Writ 30 Oct. 1399.

DORSET. Inquisition. Dorchester. 28 Feb. 1400.

She held for life jointly with John Kentcombe, her late husband:

Lower Kingcombe, 1 messuage, 31 a. arable and 4 a. meadow, of Humphrey de Stafford, knight, in right of Elizabeth his wife, by knight service, annual value 2 marks.

Toller Porcorum, 1 messuage, 1 watermill, 1 carucate and 40s. rent, of John Lyle, knight, by knight service, annual value with the rent 100s.

They were held by the grant of Guy de Briane, knight, senior, deceased, with reversion to himself and his heirs. Guy is dead, and they should descend to Philippa wife of Henry Lescrop, knight, and Elizabeth wife of Robert son of John Lovell, knight, as grand-daughters and heirs, that is daughters of Guy de Briane, son of Guy senior, knight. Philippa is aged 21 years and more. Elizabeth, in the king's ward on account of other lands and tenements, is aged 16.

Christina was a bastard and died without heirs of her body on 31 Dec. last. John Elys held the lands and took the profits from her death until Christmas last, title unknown.

Writ to the escheator, reciting the above findings and ordering him to make division between Philippa and Elizabeth in the presence of Robert, son of John Lovell, and Elizabeth his wife, or their attornies, retaining Elizabeth's portion in the king's hands. 28 May 1401.

C 137/14, no.57
E 149/74, no.21

JOHN WARRE

216 Writ 23 Dec. 1399.

SOMERSET. Inquisition. Bedminster. 20 May 1400.

He held in his demesne as of fee of the king in chief as of the castle of Bristol, 1 messuage and 1 carucate in Knowle, by a rent of 4s. payable at the castle, annual value 20s.

He died on 5 Oct. 1340. Simon Warre, son of William brother of John, is heir, aged

36 years and more. After the death of John they were held by one Robert Gyene, who intruded without title, until they were taken into the king's hands with other premises for his debts to Edward III; and they are still in the king's hands.

C 137/14, no.58

THOMAS BLOUNT, KNIGHT

217 Writ 18 Feb. 1400.

HAMPSHIRE. Inquisition. Southampton. 28 March.

He held in the right of Joan his wife:

Battramsley, 28s. rent, of the king in chief by a rent of 10s. at the manor of Lyndhurst.

Pilley, 13s. rent, of the king in chief of the same manor, service unknown.

Brookley, 1 messuage and 1 carucate, of John Wroth, knight, by a rent of 1d., annual value 2 marks.

Crowe, 15s. rent, by a rent of 10s. at the manor of Ringwood.

Wallop, 1 messuage and half a carucate, of John Denham by a rent of 20s., annual value 40s.

He died on 12 Jan. Hugh his brother and heir is aged 30 years and more.

218 WILTSHIRE. Inquisition. Salisbury. 26 Feb. 1400.

He held in the right of Joan his wife:

Laverstock, 1 messuage, 40 a. arable and 8 a. meadow, of the king by the service of 4 catapults yearly at Michaelmas, annual value 13s.4d.; the manor, of the abbess of Wilton at fee farm by a rent of £10, annual value 40s.; and 1 dovecot, 3 tofts, 8 a. and 1 fulling mill, of the prior of Ivychurch by a rent of 16s.8d., annual value 20s.

Woodfalls, 1 messuage and 1 carucate, of the bishop of Winchester by a rent of 2s., annual value 40s.

Bathampton, Rolleston and Wylye, £10 rent, of the abbess of Wilton, service unknown.

Salisbury, £4 rent, of the bishop of Salisbury, service unknown.

Date of death and heir as above. His wife survives him.

C 137/14, no.59

ROBERT CHYRCHE

219 Writ 8 April 1400.

ESSEX. Inquisition. Chipping Ongar. 22 June.

He held in his demesne as of fee half a messuage, 240 a. arable, meadow, pasture and wood and 13s.4d. rent in Great Parndon, formerly of John Chirche, his father, deceased. The half messuage, 60 a. and half the rent are held of the king in chief of the honour of Boulogne by suit at the court of the honour every three weeks; the rest is held of the countess of Hereford and of the abbot of Beeleigh, services unknown, annual value 43s.4d.

He died on 7 April last. Joan daughter of John Chirche, wife of Richard Maister, his sister and heir, is aged 32 years and more.

C 137/14, no.60

JOHN SON AND HEIR OF RALPH TYLE

220 Writ 8 Nov. 1399.

Essex. Inquisition. Chipping Ongar. 18 Nov.

Owing to the death of Ralph Tyne who held by the courtesy of England in the right of Alice, formerly his wife, and on account of the minority of his son and heir John, 1 messuage, 270 a. arable, 10 a. meadow, 40 a. wood and 100s. rent in Little Laver and Fyfield, and a rent of 17 capons at the feast of St. Stephen were taken into the hands of Richard II and remain in the king's hands. Forty of the 270 a. and 40 a. wood are held of the king in chief, service unknown; 40 a. are held of the abbot of Waltham Holy Cross by a rent of 9s.8d. payable at Easter and Michaelmas by equal parts; the messuage and the rest are held of Maud FitzRichard by a rent of 17s.6d. payable similarly; total annual value £10 4s.4d.

John son of Ralph died on 4 Nov. last. Thomas Enefeld is next heir, being uncle of Alice, formerly wife of Ralph, and aged 40 years and more.

C 137/14, no.61
E 152/353

ROBERT GREY OF ROTHERFIELD, KNIGHT

221 Writ, for fees, 10 Feb. 1400.

York. Inquisition. Bedale. 1 June.

He held in fee and in right:

Linton in Craven, the advowson, annual value 10 marks.

Bedale and Melsonby, half the advowsons in turn with Miles de Stapilton, knight, co-parcener of Robert, who holds the other halves, annual values £40 and £10.

Bedale, Aiskew, Cowling, Firby, Burrill, Mesonby, North Cowton, South Cowton, Scorton, Morton, Ovington, Dalton, Didderston, Preston under Scar, Uckerby, Great Langton, Hesselton, Leeming, Hunderthwaite, Briscoe, Askham Bryan, and elsewhere in the liberty of Richmond, 2¼ knight's fees, worth annually when a vacancy occurs 5s.

Stillingfleet, Moreby and Dringhoe, 1 fee, 12d.

Upton, ½ fee, 6d.

C 137/14, no.62, mm.3,4

RICHARD GREY, KNIGHT

222 Writ 17 April 1400. [Writs had been issued on 5 Dec. 1399, *CFR 1399–1405*, p.77].

Warwick. Inquisition. Coventry. 19 Feb. 1400.

He held the manor of Olton in the lordship of Solihull for life by the grant of Robert

Grey of Rotherfield, knight, his father, with remainder to the heirs of Robert. It is held of John Dodyngselles, knight, in chief of the barony of Itchington by knight service, annual value £10.

He died on 9 Dec. 1399. Joan wife of John Deyncourt, knight, daughter of Robert Grey of Rotherfield, is heir, aged 13 years and more.

C 137/14, no.62, mm.1,2

ROGER UNDERWODE

223   Writ 2 July 1400.

ESSEX. Inquisition. Billericay. 15 Sept.

He held on the day of his outlawry for felony 5 a. in Great Burstead in right of Joan his wife, also deceased. They were taken into the hands of Richard II and remain in the king's hands. They are held of the abbot of Stratford by a rent of 3d. payable by equal parts at Easter and Michaelmas; annual value 13s.4d.

He died on 31 Oct. 1396. Laura, now the wife of Richard Bregge, daughter and heir of Joan, is aged 30 years and more.

C 137/15, no.63

JOHN MARTYN OF PETWORTH

224   Writ 12 May 1400.

SUSSEX. Inquisition. Petworth. 17 Sept.

Owing to the madness of John Martyn, 2 messuages, 12½ a. 1 rood of meadow in Petworth came into and remain in the king's hands. They are held of John Mot of his manor of Burton by the rent of a red rose at Midsummer; annual value 9s.

He died on 28 April 1394. Idonea Martyn, wife of Richard Ratford, Joan Martyn, wife of John Shepehierd, Rose Martyn and Alice Martyn are next heirs, aged 50, 46, 44 and 40 years.

C 137/15, no.64

EDWARD TREGOOS

225   Writ 23 Aug. 1400.

SUSSEX. Inquisition. Pulborough. 26 Aug.

He held in his demesne as of fee the manor of Goring with its members of Highdown, Dedisham, East Preston and Walderton, of the prince of Wales of the honour of Wallingford by knight service, annual value 50 marks.

He also held the manors of Wiggenholt, Barkham, Ham and Greatham, and lands in Parham and Cootham, but of whom and by what service is unknown. The annual values are 100s., 100s., 50s., 100s., and 2 marks.

He died on 4 Aug. last. John Tregos is his uncle and heir, being the son of Henry, father of Robert, father of Edward, and aged 30 years and more.

226   SUSSEX. Two more inquisitions of the same place and date, with all details as above, but with different jurors.

227 Sussex. Inquisition. Goring. 27 Aug.

All other details as above.

228 Sussex. Two more inquisitions of the same place and date, with all details as above, but with different jurors.

229 Writ, *plenius certiorari*, because his status in the lands was not stated, 4 Sept. 1400.

Sussex. Inquisition. Wiggenholt. 10 Sept.

He held in his demesne as of fee:

Wiggenholt, the manor, of the bailiff of Warminghurst in socage of the manor of Ecclesden by the service of attending the court of the bailiwick every 3 weeks.

Barkham, Ham and Greatham, the manors, and lands and tenements in Cootham, of the earl of Arundel by knight service.

Parham, various lands and tenements, part of the manor of Goring, of the prince of Wales of the honour of Wallingford by knight service.

C 137/15, no.65

ISABEL WIFE OF NICHOLAS RUGGELEY

230 Writ 8 Nov. 1399

Stafford, Inquisition. Stafford. 17 Nov.

She held in her demesne as of fee 1 messuage and 1 virgate in Cannock, the king's bailiwick of Cheslyn Hay and another bailiwick called 'Truwynnesbayly' in the forest of Cannock, all of the king in chief by a rent of 20d. payable at Michaelmas by the sheriff, annual value 13s.4d.

She died on 28 Oct. last. John Salwey, her son and heir, is aged 30 years and more.

C 137/15, no.66

THOMAS SON OF THOMAS CHARLTON OF APLEY

231 Shropshire. [Inquisition by William Banastre, escheator 1399–1400. The first part, concerning the manors of Harcourt, held of the king in chief by knight service, annual value 60s., and Aston Eyre, held of Richard earl of Arundel, service unknown, annual value 100s., is torn off, as is the edge of the later part. Some details are given in the inquisitions on John de Charlton, brother of the elder Thomas (*CIPM* XV, no.329), and on the elder Thomas himself (*CIPM* XVI, no.304), and in the close rolls (*CCR 1402–5*, pp.22–3, 51–2)].

He also held the manor of Great Wytheford. One half has an annual value of 10 marks, and the other half is held of the earl of Arundel. These lands were held by Thomas the father when he died. After his death the custody of his lands and the marriage without disparagement of his heir, the younger Thomas Charleton, were granted, for a payment of £50, to John de Harleston, clerk, Thomas de Overton, clerk, and John Bonette [*CPR 1381–5*, p.484, 22 June 1388], to the use of Richard earl of Arundel until the full age of the heir, or of the next heir if he died under age, and so from heir to heir. They held them from the death of the elder Thomas until 15 Feb.

1389 to the use of the earl. Then they sold the custody of the lands and marriage of the heir to John de Knightley, and so they remain in the king's hands in the keeping of the said John de Knightley.

Thomas de Charlton the father long before he died granted by his indenture to John Attewode, knight, the manor of Apley; one quarter of the manor of Preston on the Weald Moors; 4 messuages, 1 toft, 60 a. arable and 10 a. meadow in Wellington; 1 messuage and 1 virgate in Wappenshall; 1 messuage and 1 carucate in Kinnersley; and 1 carucate in Haughton and Trilwardyn; to hold to himself for life and to his executors for one year after his death. He died on 20 Nov. 1391. After one year they came into the king's hands owing to the minority of Thomas the son, and the king by letters patent dated 8 Feb. 1392 [*CPR 1391–6*, pp.23–4] granted them all to John Knyghteley from the end of the executors' year during the minority of the heir, on payment of 32 marks. They are still held by him of Hugh Burnell, service unknown, annual value 100s.

Thomas Charlton the younger died on 31 Jan. 1399. Helen his sister and Thomas son of Anne, another sister, were next heirs. Helen was aged 12 years. She died on 3 July 1400. Thomas son of Anne is next heir, aged 5 years.

C 137/15, no.67

RICHARD DE KYRKBRYDE, KNIGHT

232 Writ, *plenius certiorari*, as it was found by inquisition under Richard II [*CIPM* XVII, no.1174] that he held a third part of the lordship of Kirklinton with other premises in Kirkandrews and Inglewood, and also jointly with his wife Agnes in Dockray, Wigton etc., but his status and other details were not given. 18 Feb. 1400.
CUMBERLAND. Inquisition. Carlisle. 20 March.

He held in his demesne as of fee of the king in chief:

Kirklinton, a third part of the lordship, by a cornage rent of 16s.¾d., annual value 20s.

Kirkandrews, 4 messuages and 200 a. by a cornage rent of 13s., annual value 40s.

Braithwaite, a purpresture or encroachment so called in the forest of Inglewood, by a rent of 106s.8d. payable through the warden of the forest, annual value 40s.

To himself, Agnes his wife and the heirs male of their bodies, by a grant of John de Curwen, vicar of Bromfield, and John de Aykenhed, rector of Moresby, he held half the manor of Kirkbride of Henry Percy, earl of Northumberland, of his manor of Wigton by a cornage rent of 4s., annual value 100s.; and in Anthorn, 2 messuages, 20 a., 1 cottage and 26s.8d. rent of Nicholas Whitrig of his manor of Whitrigg by a cornage rent of 5d., annual value 26s.8d.

With Joan his first wife, to them and the heirs male of their bodies, by a grant of Adam de Crosseby, Alan de Arkilby, Walter de Welles, and William de Kirkeby, chaplain, he held the manor of Dovenby of Henry Percy, earl of Northumberland, of his manor of Papcastle by a cornage rent of 6s.8d. and 8d. for a watchman of the sea, annual value £10; two parts of the manor of Dundraw of the same earl of his manor of Wigton by a cornage rent of 2s., annual value £4; and 2 messuages and 20 a. in the same place of the same earl of his manor of Wigton by a cornage rent of 2s., annual value 20s.

Elizabeth wife of Hugh de Curwen is daughter and heir of Richard and Joan his first wife and is of full age, 21 years and more.

He also died seised of a free tenure of 4 messuages, 1 cottage, 30 a. arable, and 8

a. meadow in Dundraw, by the grant of John de Curwen, vicar of Bromfield, Robert de Louthre, vicar of Wigton, and William de Skrynanhouse, for life with remainder to his daughter Elizabeth and the heirs of her body. It is held of the same earl of his manor of Wigton by a cornage rent of 18d., annual value 16s.

By the said grant of John de Curwen and John de Aykenhed he held with Agnes his wife, to them and the heirs male of their bodies, 15s.9d. fee farm rent in Wigton, 26 messuages and 200 a. in Dockray and Moorhouse, and 5 a. meadow in Oulton, of the same earl by a rent of 3s.4d., annual value £6 13s.4d.

In his demesne as of fee he held 1 messuage and 100 a. called Lawrenceholm of the same earl of his manor of Wigton, by a cornage rent of 12d., annual value 10s. Helen daughter of Henry Grymbald held of him 1 cottage with curtilage by fealty and a rent of 10s. at Martinmas.

Also held of him were:

Anthorn, 1 messuage and 24 a. by William de Wykes by homage and a rent of 6½d; 1 messuage and 12 a. by William Blakman by homage and 2s.2½d. rent; 1 messuage and 1 a. by Thomas de . . . by 1½d. rent; and ½ a. ½ rood by Nicholas de Whitrig, chaplain, by fealty and 1½d. rent.

Dundraw, 1 free tenement by Alice Lumbard by 1d. rent at Martinmas; 1 a. by Joan Coke by a rent of 2s. and 3d. cornage; 1 messuage by a rent of 5s. and 3d. cornage, 1 messuage by a rent of 12d., 1 messuage and 20 a. by a rent of a pair of spurs every third year, and 1 messuage and 10 a. by a rent of 2s. at Martinmas, all by Amand Mounceux; 1 tenement by Adam de Bromfeld by a rent of 10d. at Martinmas; and 1 messuage by William de Whitrig by a rent of 16d.

He died on 4 April 1399. Richard son and heir of Richard and Agnes is aged 9 years.

233 Similar writ, *plenius certiorari*, for the lands held jointly with Agnes in Wigton and Dockray. 23 Feb. 1400.

CUMBERLAND. Inquisition. Carlisle. 20 March.

He died seised with Agnes his wife, who still lives, to them and the heirs of their bodies, of 15s.9d. rent from free tenants in Wigton, and 26 messuages and 200 a. arable and meadow in Dockray and Moorhouse, with 5 a. meadow in Oulton, by the grant of John de Curwen, vicar of Bromfield, and John de Aykhed, rector of Moresby, held of Henry Percy, earl of Northumberland, of his manor of Wigton by a cornage rent of 3s.4d., annual value £6 13s.4d.

He held no other lands in the county jointly with his wife.

C 137/15, no.68

PHILIP BRYEN

234 Writ, *melius sciri*, enquiring who are the other heirs, as it was stated in the inquisition taken on 14 Feb. 1388 [*CIPM* XVI, no.352] that Philippa, one of the daughters and heirs of Guy Bryen junior, brother of Philip, was one heir of Philip, aged 9 years and more, but who were the other heirs was not known. 4 Dec. 1399.

SOMERSET. Inquisition. Queen Camel. 17 Jan. 1400.

Elizabeth, wife of Robert son of John Lovell, and Philippa, wife of Henry Skrop, knight, daughters of Guy de Bryen junior, brother of Philip, are his neices and heirs. Elizabeth is aged 16 years and more. There are no other heirs.

C 137/15, no.70

MARGARET DUCHESS OF NORFOLK

235 Writ 28 Nov. 1399.

BUCKINGHAM. Inquisition. Wing. 30 Dec.

She held in her demesne in fee tail to herself and the heirs of her body the manor of Penn under a fine of 1344 [CP 25(1) 287/41, no.339] by which William de Neuton, parson of Seagrave, William de Loughton, parson of Witherley, and John de Repyndon, parson of Cold Overton, enfeoffed John de Segrave and Margaret his wife, to themselves and the heirs of their bodies with remainder to the right heirs of John. Hence it descended to Thomas de Mowbray, late duke of Norfolk, as the son of Elizabeth, daughter of John de Segrave and Margaret, and then to the son and heir of the duke, Thomas de Moubray, knight, who is still living. It is not held of the king in chief, but of whom and by what service is unknown; annual value £10.

She died on 24 March last. The duke was then 33 years of age, and he died on 22 September. Thomas Moubray, knight, is son and heir of the duke, and kinsman of John de Segrave and Margaret, and their heir. He was 14 years of age on 17 Sept. last.

236 Writ 11 Feb. 1400.

SUSSEX. Inquisition. Steyning. 9 March.

She held in her demesne as of fee in chief of Richard II the lordship of Bosham with the manor of Stoughton, by the grant of Edward II to Thomas de Brotherton, formerly earl of Norfolk and marshal of England, and the heirs of his body. It descended to Margaret as daughter and heir. She died seised of it on 24 March last, and from her the right to it descended to Thomas de Moubray, late duke of Norfolk, as son of Elizabeth her daughter, and from him to Thomas de Moubray, knight, his son, who still lives. The annual values are Bosham £113 15s.5¾d. and Stoughton £14 9d., but how they are held is unknown.

Date of death, age and death of the duke, and heir as above.

237 WORCESTER. Inquisition on various matters relating to the office of escheator. Droitwich. 30 May 1399.

Margaret duchess of Norfolk died on 23 March last holding the manor of North Piddle, which comprises 1 carucate, annual value 60s., 20 a. meadow 40s., and assize rents of £4 6s.4d. payable at the four terms by equal parts.

Thomas Stourdy, chaplain, outlawed in the county court at Stafford on 12 May 1399 for various felonies at the suit of the king, had in the county 15 sheep worth 15s., 6 . . . worth 30d., 1 heifer 5s., and 1 silver spoon 12d.

238 Writ 18 Nov. 1399.

WORCESTER. Inquisition. Upton upon Severn. 29 Jan. 1400.

She held to herself, the heirs of her body, and the heirs of John de Segrave, knight, her late husband, in her demesne in fee tail, the manor of North Piddle by the said fine of 1344 [no.235], and it descended accordingly. Of whom it is held and by what service is unknown. There are £4 6s.4d. assize rents payable by equal parts at Lady Day and Michaelmas, 1 carucate worth 60s., and 20 a. meadow 40s., total annual value £9 6s.4d.

Date of death and heir as above.

239 Writ 18 Nov. 1399.

SHROPSHIRE. Inquisition. Much Wenlock. 26 Nov.

She held as above, by the fine of 1344, the manors of Stottesdon and Kingswood, and they descended accordingly. Stottesdon is held of the king in chief by knight service, amount unknown, annual value £20. Kingswood is not held of the king, but of whom and by what service is unknown, annual value 100s.

Date of death and heir as above.

240 Writ, for fees, 18 Nov. 1399.

SHROPSHIRE. Inquisition. Much Wenlock. 26 Nov.

She held no knight's fees or advowsons in the county or the adjacent March of Wales.

241 Writ 18 Nov. 1399.

DERBY. Inquisition. Derby. 16 Jan. 1400.

She held in her demesne in fee tail jointly enfeoffed with John de Segrave, knight, her late husband, by a fine similar to that mentioned above [CP 25(1) 287/41, no.341], and descending in the same way, the castle and manor of Bretby, the manors of Rosliston and Coton, and 12 messuages, 14 bovates and £10 rent in Repton, Linton, Milton, Willington, Ashbourne and 'Howes'. Of whom they are held and by what service is unknown. The annual values are Bretby £25, Rosliston £15 6½d., Coton £13 10s.½d. and the 12 messuages etc. £4 6s.8d.

Dates of death and heir as above.

242 Writ 18 Nov. 1399.

LONDON. Inquisition. 14 Dec.

She held in her demesne in fee tail, as daughter and heir of Thomas de Brotherton, by the grant of Edward II [as above, no.236], 1 messuage and a vacant place at the Broken Wharf in the parish of St. Mary Somerset, with chambers, shops and other buildings annexed to it. It is held of the king in burgage, as all London is, annual value £10.

Dates of death and heir as above.

243 Writ 18 Nov. 1399.

WARWICK. Inquisition. Kineton. 31 Dec.

She held in her demesne in fee tail by one of the said fines [no.235] the manors of Aspley, Alspath, Flecknoe and Thurlaston, and they descended accordingly. They are not held of the king, but of whom and by what service is unknown. The annual values are 100s., £4, £10 and 100s.

Dates of death and heir as above.

244 Writ, for fees, 18 Nov. 1399.

WARWICK. Inquisition. Kineton. 31 Dec.

She held no fees or advowsons in Warwickshire.

245　LEICESTER. Inquisition. Loughborough. 5 Feb. 1400.

She held in her demesne in fee tail by the second fine [no. 241] the manors of Seagrave, Sileby, Mountsorell, Great Dalby, Witherley and Cold Overton, and 30 messuages, 30 virgates and 100s. rent in Cotes, Thurnby, Smisby [Derb], Wymeswold, Hoby, Thorpe Satchville, Twyford, Thurmaston, Thorp Busard [Notts] and Melton Mowbray, and they descended accordingly. They are not held of the king, but of whom and by what service is unknown. The annual values are Seagrave £40 11s. 10d., Sileby £40, Mountsorell £7, Great Dalby 40s., Witherley £10, Overton £34, and the 30 messuages etc. £10.

She also held the hundred of Goscote in fee tail under a similar fine [CP 25(1) 287/41, no. 349] of the king in chief by a rent of 100s. payable at the exchequer, annual value 40s.

Dates of death and heir as above.

246　LEICESTER. Inquisition. Loughborough. 5 Feb. 1400.

She held a quarter of a knight's fee in Ingarsby; and the advowsons of Seagrave, Sileby and Kegworth, which extend when they occur at £10, 20 marks and £10.

247　Writ 28 Nov. 1399.

CAMBRIDGE. Inquisition. Cambridge. 20 Jan. 1400.

She held in her demesne in fee tail as daughter and heir of Thomas de Brotherton by the grant of Edward II [as above, no. 236] the manor of Kennett and Kentford. Of whom it is held and by what service is unknown; annual value 20 marks.

Dates of death and heir as above.

248　Writ, for fees, 28 Nov. 1399.

CAMBRIDGE. Inquisition. Cambridge. 20 Jan. 1400.

She held in her demesne in fee tail:
Boxworth, ½ fee held by John Drabon.
Cheveley, 1 fee held by Gilbert Pecche.
Fulbourn, 1 fee held by Walter de Maners.
Trumpington, ½ fee held by Walter de Busshey.

249　CAMBRIDGE. Inquisition *ex officio*. Cambridge. 13 March 1400.

Long before she died she granted to John Longe of Kennett the manor of Kennett and Kentford for a term of years for an annual rent, amount unknown. From 24 March 1399 until 20 Jan. 1400 Edmund Oldhalle and John Longe occupied the manor and took the profits, title unknown, and they are answerable for them.

250　HUNTINGDON. Inquisition. Huntingdon. 24 Jan. 1400.

She held in her demesne in fee tail by one of the said fines [no. 245] the manor of Fen Stanton. It descended accordingly, and is held of the king in chief, service unknown, annual value 200 marks.

Dates of death and heir as above.

251　HUNTINGDON. Inquisition *ex officio*. Huntingdon. 6 March 1400.

She held the manor of Fen Stanton of the king in chief. She died on 24 March, from which date William Shortewade, bailiff there, has taken the profits to the use of Walter

Fitzpiers, clerk, title unknown. Shortewade and Fitzpiers are answerable to the king for the profits.

252 Writ 28 Nov. 1399.
YORK. Inquisition. Coxwold by Newburgh. 10 Jan. 1400.
She held in her demesne in fee tail by one of the said fines [no. 235] the manor of Dinnington, and it descended accordingly. It is not held of the king, but of whom is unknown; annual value £8.
She held in her demesne as of fee the manor of Thwaite, also not of the king, but of whom is unknown; annual value 40s.
Dates of death and heir as above

253 Writ 28 Nov. 1399
ESSEX. Inquisition. Chelmsford. 24 Jan. 1400.
She held in fee tail by the grant of Edward II to Thomas de Brotherton [as above, no. 236] the manors of Chesterford, Dovercourt and Romford. Chesterford is held of the king in chief, service unknown, annual value £30; Dovercourt is held of the earl of Oxford as 1 knight's fee, 43 marks; 15 a. in Romford are held of Adam Karlyl by a rent of 3s., 1 a. of John Love by a rent of 4d., and of whom the rest is held is unknown, annual value £10.
Date of death and heir as above.

254 ESSEX. Inquisition. Chelmsford. 9 Feb. 1400.
She held the following knight's fees in her demesne in fee tail:
Boxworth, Cambridgeshire, ½ fee.
Ketteringham, Norfolk, 1 fee.
Cheveley, Cambridgeshire, 1 fee.
Fulbourn, Cambridgeshire, 1 fee.
Trumpington, Cambridgeshire, ½ fee.
Chesterford, $\frac{1}{20}$ fee.
There are no other fees or advowsons in this county which they can extend.

255 HERTFORD. Inquisition. Buntingford. 6 Feb. 1400.
She held in fee tail by the grant of Edward II to Thomas de Brotherton, Mary his wife, and his heirs [as above, no. 236; only in this inquisition and no. 258 is Mary mentioned] the manor of Weston. It is held of the king in chief of the county of Norfolk, annual value £20.
Dates of death and heir as above.

256 HERTFORD. Inquisition. Buntingford. 5 Feb. 1400.
She held the following in fee tail:
Offley, 5 fees, and 4 fees once held by Roger Bernard.
In the county, 1 fee once held by Roger FitzNicholas.
Weston, ½ fee; ½ fee; ½ fee once held by Henry Roucestr; $\frac{1}{10}$ fee once held by Walter de Norton; $\frac{1}{10}$ fee once held by Robert FitzPagan; $\frac{1}{20}$ fee once held by John FitzEustace; and 1 fee once held by Richard de Boya.
Willian, $\frac{1}{10}$ fee.

Weston, ½ fee once held by John de Burgo.
Hinxworth, ⅕ fee.
Everton, Bedfordshire, 1 fee.
Stagenhoe, Bedfordshire, 1 fee.
Stratton, Millow and Dunton, Bedfordshire, 1 fee.
Clothall, Bedfordshire, ¹⁄₁₀ fee.
There are no other fees or advowsons which they can extend.

257 Writ 18 Nov. 1399.
NORFOLK. Inquisition. Norwich. 22 Dec. 1399.
    She held in fee tail by the grant of Edward II to Thomas de Brotherton [as above, no.236] the manors of Forncett, Lopham, Dickleburgh, Suffield, Ditchingham, Earsham, Hanworth, Halvergate, Framingham, South Walsham and Harleston with the half hundred of Earsham.
    Forncett, annual value £70 3s. 7½d., Suffield, £35, Ditchingham, £46 18s., Earsham, £50 10s. 10½d., Hanworth, £60, Halvergate, £50 6s. 11½d., Framingham, £32 8s. 10d., and South Walsham, £52 14s. 7d., are held of the king in chief, service unknown. Lopham, £50 8s. 4d., is held of the abbot of St. Giles, service unknown. Dickleburgh, £12, and Harleston and the half hundred of Earsham, £30 3d., are not held of the king in chief but of whom is unknown.
    She also held a third part of the manor of Loddon, formerly of her husband, John de Segrave, knight, for life. It descended to Thomas de Moubray, the duke.
    Dates of death and heir as above.

258 SUFFOLK. Inquisition. Ipswich. 29 Dec. 1399.
    She held in fee tail by the grant of Edward II to Thomas de Brotherton and Mary his wife [as above, no.236, and see no.255] the castle and manor of Framlingham, the manors of Walton, Earl Soham and Kennett, the manor and borough of Bungay, the manors of Earl Stonham, Dunningworth, Kelsale, Staverton, Hollesley and Hoo, the hundred of Loes, and £18 rent from Cratfield, Stow Park and Berwick.
    Framlingham, annual value £80, Walton £80 17s. 4d., Earl Soham, £28, Bungay, £70 5s. 1d., Staverton, £36 16s. 3¼d., and Hoo with the hundred, £33 1s. ½d., are held of the king in chief. Kennett, £28 1d., Earl Stonham, £46 17s. 4½d., Dunningworth, £16 8s. 6d., Hollesley, £40 17s. 7¼d., and Kelsale, £60, are not held of the king but of whom is unknown.
    She also held in her demesne in fee tail by one of the said fines [above, no.235] the manor of Peasenhall. It is not held of the king but of whom is unknown; annual value £18.
    Dates of death and heir as above.

259 Writ, for fees, 18 Nov. 1399.
GLOUCESTER AND THE ADJACENT MARCH OF WALES. Extent. Newent. 9 Feb. 1400.
    She held in her demesne in fee tail:
    Llanvair Discoed, 1 fee held by Ralph de Monte Hermerii.
    Mathern, 1 fee held by Bogo de Knovyll.
    Penhow, 1 fee held by Ralph Seymor.
    Portskewett and Harpson, 1 fee held by Matthew Beneland.
    Crick, ½ fee held by William Derneford.

Dinham, ½ fee held by Andrew de Bello Campo.
Maesycwmmer, ½ fee held by Amery Lucy.
Itton, ½ fee held by Henry de Bendevyll.
St. Arvans, ¼ fee held by Leysannus ap Morgan.
Llanmartin, ¼ fee held by Walter de Kemeys.
Henrhiw, ¼ fee held by Roger Seymor and William Adam.
St. Wormet, ¼ fee held by John de Bleccher.
Tidenham, ¼ fee held by Walter Waldyng.
She also held in her demesne in fee tail the advowsons of:
St. Mary's priory, Chepstow, extending at 20 marks.
The free chapel on the Severn in the lordship of Tidenham in the March of Wales,
£10.
The church of Lancaut, 40d.

260 Writ 18 Nov. 1399.
GLOUCESTER AND THE ADJACENT MARCH OF WALES. Inquisition. Newent. 9 Feb.
1400.
She held in fee tail by the grant of Edward II to Thomas de Brotherton [as above,
no.236], the castle and manor of Chepstow and the manor of Tidenham. They are held
of the king in chief by knight service, amount unknown; annual value £207.
Dates of death and heir as above.

261 GLOUCESTER AND THE ADJACENT MARCH OF WALES. Inquisition. Thornbury.
24 . . . 1400–01 (2 Henry IV).
She held the castle and manor of Chepstow and the manor of Tidenham in the March
of Wales. She died on 24 March 1399. Since then Hugh Waterton, knight, has held
them by the king's grant [CPR 1399–1401, p.123].

262 GLOUCESTER. Inquisition *ex officio*. Winchcombe. 1 Oct. 1401.
John Newman of Winchcombe had there when he was outlawed 6 oxen worth 60s.,
6 pigs 10s., 1 bed 10s., and 2 brass pots 8s.
John Spaldyng on the day that he was outlawed had at Cirencester half a dozen full
provender vessels worth 10s., 3 candlesticks, 6 brass pots, 2 pairs of andirons, 1 iron
'vern' and 1 fire-pike. worth 6s.8d., and 8 pairs of shoes 40d.
William Rye when he was outlawed had 1 stack of barley in a granary worth 40s.
Margaret duchess of Norfolk died on 24 March 1399 holding the castle and manor
of Chepstow and the manor of Tidenham. Hugh Waterton, knight, has held them by
the king's grant all the time that Robert Somervyle has been escheator.

263 GLOUCESTER. Inquisition *ex officio*. Newent 28 Nov. 1402.
Thomas Weston who was outlawed in Gloucestershire at the suit of John Barndesley
on a plea of trespass had various goods and chattels worth 6s.8d.
Margaret duchess of Norfolk died holding, as in last. Hugh Waterton, knight, has
occupied them and taken the profits all the time that Robert Whytyngton has been
escheator.

C 137/18, no.72
E 149/71, no.12
E 152/345-6, 355, 359

THOMAS MOUBRAY, DUKE OF NORFOLK

264   Writ 26 Nov. 1399.

CALAIS. Inquisition. 27 Jan. 1400.

He held in his demesne as of fee of the king in chief a square plot in the parish of St. Nicholas towards the church of St. Nicholas on the north. Part is built up with certain houses on it; part lies vacant. It is held by a rent of £[3] and the provision of a watchman for the guard of the city; annual value 12 marks. It is taken into the king's hands.

He died on 22 September last. Thomas Moubray, knight, his son and heir, was 14 on 17 Sept. last.

265   Writ 18 Nov. 1399.

HEREFORD AND THE ADJACENT MARCH OF WALES. Inquisition. Hereford. 31 Jan. 1400.

He held in his demesne as of fee the castle of Swansea and the lordship of Gower with the manor and lordship of Kilvey in Wales of Richard II in chief by knight service, annual value 700 marks; but some time before he died John Skydmore, the escheator of Richard II, occupied them, title unknown.

Date of death and heir, aged 14 years and more, as above.

266   Writ 18 Nov. 1399.

RUTLAND. Inquisition. Uppingham. 12 Jan. 1400.

He held in his demesne as of fee 1 toft and 2 virgates in Alesthorpe next Burley, not of the king, but of whom is unknown, annual value 10s.

Date of death and heir as above [no. 264].

267   Writ, *plenius certiorari*, requiring return of whom the manor of Wing is held. 1 June 1400.

BUCKINGHAM. Inquisition. Wing. 10 July.

The manor of Wing is not held of the king in chief, but of whom and by what service is unknown.

268   Writ 18 Nov. 1399.

LONDON. Inquisition. 14 Dec.

He held in his demesne in fee tail by the grant of Edward II to Thomas Brotherton [as above no. 236] 1 messuage with a vacant plot in the parish of St. Mary Somerset, with shops, chambers and other buildings annexed. It is held of the king in burgage as is all London, annual value £10.

He was aged 33 years and 26 weeks on 22 Sept. when he died. Thomas Moubray, knight, is his son and heir, as well as heir of Margaret duchess of Norfolk, and was 14 on 17 Sept. last.

269   Writ 18 Nov. 1399.

WARWICK. Inquisition. Kineton. 31 Dec.

He held in his demesne as of fee the manors of Aspley, Alspath, Flecknoe and Thurlaston, to himself and the heirs of his body by the grant of William Neuton and others by one of the said fines [above, no. 235]. They descended to Thomas as son of

Elizabeth, daughter of John de Segrave, and thence to Thomas de Moubray, knight, his son. They are not held of the king in chief, but of whom and by what service is unknown; annual values, Aspley 100s., Alspath 40s., Flecknoe £10 and Thurlaston 100s.

He also held in his demesne as of fee:

Caludon, the manor, of the king as of the manor of Cheylesmore, by the service of a pair of gilt spurs or 12d. yearly, annual value £26. From the manor he granted by letters patent £20 rent to Thomas de Clynton for life, and this was confirmed by the king [*CPR 1399-1401*, p.28, 15 Oct. 1399].

Forde, Aspley and Ullenhall, 1 carucate, of whom and by what service is unknown, annual value 26s.8d.

He granted to Richard de Burgh, esquire, who still lives, the manor of Weston by Cherington with the profits for life. It is held of the earl of Ormonde, service unknown; annual value 20 marks.

On 15 Feb. 1392 by his indenture he granted to Robert bishop of London, Walter bishop of Dublin [*recte* Durham], William bishop of Winchester, William [*recte* Richard] bishop of Chichester, Henry earl of Derby, Edward earl of Rutland, John de Lovell, John Devereux, and William Beauchamp, their heirs and assigns, the manor of Kineton on certain conditions not known. It is held of the king by a rent of £12 payable at the exchequer by equal parts at Easter and Michaelmas; annual value payable at the same terms £26.

By letters patent of 14 Sept. 1387 he let the manor at £26 farm to Robert Dalby and Hugh Dalby, who are still alive, for their lives.

Date of death and heir, aged 14 on 17 Sept., as above.

270 Writ 28 Nov. 1399.

CAMBRIDGE. Inquisition. Cambridge. 20 Jan. 1400.

He held in his demesne in fee tail the manor of Kennett and Kentford under the grant of Edward II to Thomas de Brotherton [above, no.236]. Of whom it is held is unknown; annual value 20 marks.

He held no more, but on 15 Feb. 1392 he granted to Robert bishop of London and others [as above, no.269, Walter bishop of Dublin again given for Durham, but Richard bishop of Chichester correctly] the manor of Cherry Hinton and 26s. rent from Ickleton, on certain conditions unknown. They are not held of the king, but of whom and by what service is unknown; annual value £30 13s.4d.

Margaret died on 11 Aug. Thomas was heir, being son of Elizabeth, daughter of Margaret, and was then aged 33 years and more. He died on 22 Sept. Thomas his son and heir was 14 on 17 Sept. last.

271 HUNTINGDON. Inquisition. Huntingdon. 24 Jan. 1400.

He held in his demesne in fee tail in accordance with one of the said fines [above, no.245] the manor of Fen Stanton. It is held of the king in chief, service unknown, annual value 200 marks.

He held no more, but on 15 Feb. 1392 he granted to Robert bishop of London and others [as in no.269 with same errors] the manors of Alconbury, Burton in Lonsdale in Yorkshire, Kineton in Warwickshire, Cherry Hinton in Cambridgeshire, and rents and services in Linslade and Southcott in Buckinghamshire and Stretton in Lincolnshire [*recte* Rutland], with 24s. rent in Northampton.

G

Alconbury is not held of the king, but of whom is unknown; annual value 80 marks.
Dates of death and heirs as in last.

272 Writ 18 Nov. 1399.

NORTHAMPTON. Inquisition. Northampton. 15 Jan. 1400.

He held in his demesne as of fee the manor of Chalcombe and 24s. rent in
Northampton. The manor is held of the bishop of Lincoln of his castle of Banbury
as three quarters of a knight's fee. From it he granted to Hugh Dalby, who still lives,
a rent of £10 for life, payable by equal parts at Easter and Michaelmas on condition
that if it should be one month in arrears after either feast it should be lawful for him
to distrain the whole manor and hold it until the rent be paid. The grant was confirmed
by letters patent of Richard II and the king [*CPR 1396–9*, p. *565*; *1399–1401*, p.*78*].
He also granted Cecily Boule, who still lives, 10 marks annually for life from the same
manor. It is worth 20s. yearly beyond these annuities.

On 15 March 1397 he granted to Thomas Arundell, archbishop of Canterbury,
Richard Metford, bishop of Salisbury, Roger Walden, then treasurer of England,
Edward earl of Rutland, William Farendon, knight, Ralph Selby and Thomas Yokflete,
clerks, William Rees, John Hopcrone, John Lancastre, Thomas Myssenden, Richard
Burgh, Thomas Brunham and Nicholas Blaxhale, to them, their heirs and assigns, with
clause of warranty, the manor of Barton Seagrave and other manors and lands. The
manor is not held of the king, but of whom is unknown; annual value £16.

Long before his death he granted to William Bagot, knight, the manor of Crick for
life, with reversion to himself and his heirs. It is not held of the king, but of whom
is unknown; annual value £20.

Date of death and heir as above.

273 ESSEX. Inquisition. Prittlewell. 13 Jan. 1400.

He held jointly with his wife Elizabeth the manor of Prittlewell by the grant of
Richard earl of Arundel, father of Elizabeth. It is held of the king of the honour of
Rayleigh, by knight service; annual value 20 marks.

Date of death and heir as above.

274 Writ 28 Nov. 1399.

ESSEX. Chelmsford. 24 Jan. 1400.

He held in his demesne in fee tail under the grant of Edward II to Thomas Brotherton
[above, no.236]:

Chesterford, the manor, of the king in chief, service unknown, annual value £30.

Dovercourt, the manor, of the earl of Oxford as one knight's fee, annual value 43
marks.

Romford, the manor; 15 a. of Adam Karlyl by a rent of 3s. and 1 a. of John Love
by a rent of 4d., but of whom the rest is held is unknown; annual value £10.

Jointly with Elizabeth his wife he held the manor of Prittlewell by the grant of
Richard earl of Arundel, father of Elizabeth, to them and the heirs of their bodies.
It is held of the king of the honour of Rayleigh by knight service; annual value 20 marks.

Long before he died he granted to William Halle, his esquire, for life, the manor
of Moreton with reversion to himself and his heirs. Of whom it is held is unknown;
annual value £10.

Dates of death and heir as above.

275 HERTFORD. Inquisition. Buntingford. 6 Feb. 1400.

He held in his demesne in fee tail under the grant of Edward II to Thomas de Brotherton [above, no.236] the manor of Weston. It is held of the king in chief as of the county of Norfolk; annual value £20.

Date of death and heir as above.

276 Writ 18 Nov. 1399.

GLOUCESTER AND THE ADJACENT MARCH OF WALES. Inquisition. Newent. 9 Feb. 1400.

He held in his demesne in fee tail under the grant of Edward II to Thomas de Brotherton [above, no.236] the castle and manor of Chepstow in the Welsh march, and the manor of Tidenham. They are held of the king in chief by knight service; annual value £207.

Date of death and heir as above.

277 Writ 18 Nov. 1399.

NORFOLK. Inquisition. Norwich. 22 Dec.

He held in his demesne in fee tail under the grant of Edward II to Thomas de Brotherton [above, no.236] the manors of Forncett, Lopham, Dickleburgh, Suffield, Ditchingham, Earsham, Hanworth, Halvergate, Framingham, South Walsham, and Harleston with the half hundred of Earsham.

Forncett, annual value £70 3s. 7½d., Suffield, £35, Ditchingham, £46 18s., Earsham, £50 10s. 10½d., Hanworth, £60, Halvergate, £50 6s. 11¼d., Framingham, £32 8s. 10d., and South Walsham, £52 14s. 7d., are held of the king in chief, service unknown.

Lopham is held of the abbot of St. Giles, annual value £50 8s. 4d., service unknown.

Dickleburgh, £12, and Harleston with the half hundred of Earsham, £30 3d., are not held of the king in chief but of whom is unknown.

He also held in his demesne as of fee a third part of the manor of Loddon, but of whom and by what service is unknown; annual value 5 marks.

In right of his wife Elizabeth he held the manor of Kenninghall by the grant of William de Monte Acuto, late earl of Salisbury, to Elizabeth and William her former husband. It is held of the king in chief, service unknown, annual value £72.

Long before his death he granted by letters patent to John Kirkestede, esquire, who still lives, two parts of the manor of Loddon for life with reversion to himself and his heirs. It is not held of the king but of whom is unknown; annual value 10 marks.

Dates of death and heir as before.

278 NORFOLK. Inquisition. Long Stratton. 15 April 1406.

Extent of the manor of Forncett:

Various buildings, annual value nil; fruit of fruit trees, 4d.; herbage in the site of the manor and orchard, 2d., containing in all 2 a. arable; 168 a. 1 rood arable in demesne at 6d., £4 4s. 3d.; 166 a. called 'Caylond' at 1d., 13s. 10d.; 26 a. 1 rood meadow for mowing at 2s. 6d., 65s. 7½d.; 9½ a. meadow at 12d., 9s. 6d., 23 a. 1 rood of wood at 12d., 23s. 3d.; 2 alder groves containing 3 a. called 'Meokker' and 'Waswodeker' at 5d., 15d.; assize rents of free tenants and villeins, £13 16s. 8¾d. at St. Andrew, Easter and Michaelmas, and no more because various lands and tenements are burdened with rents in the hands of the lord by way of escheat, which lands with £7 6s. 8d. from the farm of lands and tenements called 'Wyllyames' in Tacolneston and 12d. from the farm of a quarter of the market of Stratton amount to £14 10s.4d.; 1 windmill now worth nothing and nothing in the last year of Thomas de Mowbray on account of the need for repair, but usually worth 20s.; profits of manor courts, 'Garton' court and 'Knyght' court, £4 17s.10d.; 45 winter works at 3 for 1d., 15d.; 15 summer works at 5 for 2d., 6d.; 135(?) autumn works at 1d., . . .s.7d.; 100½ carrying services (*averagia*) at 1½d., 12s. 6¾d.; 35 boon works in autumn at ½d., 17½d.; 37 carting works at 1d., 3s.1d.; 41 hens at Christmas at 1d., 3s.5d.; 205 eggs at Easter at 4d. per 100, 8d. and ½ farthing; customary monies received for foldage, 12d. at Michaelmas; with service of mowing at Lammas, 5s.4d.; and certain knight's fees and parts, namely 126 208th parts of knight's fees with wards, marriages, rents, reliefs, escheats and all other profits belonging to Forncett manor, of various tenements as appear in the exchequer, which are worth £24 and which were assigned to Elizabeth duchess of Norfolk, by Henry IV in dower with the advowson, which extends at £20 when it occurs.

[Apparent total £70 3s.7½d., as in no.277 above].

279 LEICESTER. Inquisition. Loughborough. 5 Feb. 1400.

He held in his demesne in fee tail by the grant of William de Neuton, parson of Seagrave, William de Loughton, parson of Witherley, and John de Repyndon, parson of Cold Overton, by a fine of 1344 [above, no.241] the manors of Seagrave, Sileby, Mountsorell, Great Dalby, Witherley and Cold Overton, with 30 messuages, 30 virgates and 100s. rent in Cotes, Smisby, Wymeswold, Hoby, Thorpe Satchville, Twyford, Thurmaston, Thorp Busard and Melton Mowbray, parcels of the manors of Seagrave and Sileby. They are not held of the king, but of whom is unknown; annual values, Seagrave £40 11s.10d., Sileby £40, Mountsorell £7, Great Dalby £40, Witherley £10, Cold Overton £33 and the messuages and virgates £10.

He also held by a similar fine [above, no.245] the hundred of Goscote. It is held of the king by the service of 100s. rent; annual value 40s.

He also held of the king in his demesne as of fee the manor of Melton Mowbray by knight service, amount unknown, annual value £33.

On 6 Jan. 1394 he granted to Roger Joddrell for life 16 messuages and 10 virgates in Whetstone, with reversion to himself and his heirs. They are held of Lord Beaumond, service unknown; annual value £8.

Date of death and heir as above.

280 SUFFOLK. Inquisition. Ipswich. 29 Dec. 1399.

He held in fee tail [details as in no.258 above].

281 Writ 28 Nov. 1399.

NOTTINGHAM. Inquisition. Nottingham. 16 Jan. 1400.

He held in his demesne in fee tail to himself and the heirs of his body, for the name, honour, title and style of earl of Nottingham, which Richard II granted him, £20 rent from the castle of Nottingham by the hands of the sheriff.

Date of death and heir as above. Margaret held no lands in the county when she died on 24 March 1399.

282 DERBY. Inquisition. Derby. 16 Jan. 1400.

He held in his demesne in fee tail by the grant of William de Neuton and others by a fine of 1344 [above, no.241] the castle and manor of Bretby and the manors of

Rosliston and Coton, with 12 messuages, 14 bovates and £10 rent in Repton, Linton, Milton, Willington, Ashbourne and 'Howes'. Of whom they are held is unknown; annual values, Bretby £25, Rosliston £15 6½d., Coton £13 10s.½d. and the messuages and bovates £4 6s.8d.

Date of death and heirs as above.

283 Writ 18 Nov. 1399.

SHROPSHIRE. Inquisition. Much Wenlock. 26 Nov.

He held in his demesne in fee tail by the grant of William de Neuton and others under two fines of 1344 [above, nos. 235, 241] the manors of Stottesdon and Kingswood.

Stottesdon was held of Richard II by knight service, amount unknown; annual value £20. Kingswood was not held of the king but of whom is unknown; annual value 100s.

Date of death and heir as above.

284 Writ 24 Nov. 1399.

BEDFORD. Inquisition. Bedford. 31 Dec.

He held in his demesne as of fee of the king in chief of the barony of Bedford:

Bedford, the castle, by the service of being almoner on the day of the coronation. Because it is not built up or enclosed the annual value is 10s. and no more. Long before he died he granted the keeping of it with the profits for life to John Woketon, who is still living.

Haynes, Willington and Stotfold, the manors, annual values £10, 40 marks and £16.

Bromham, ¼ carucate, in the hands of a tenant at will, annual value 60s.

Cople, Cardington, Great Barford, Southill, Maulden, Wootton, Ickwell and Salph End, 37s. rent from the vills.

Bedford, the court baron held every three weeks, annual value 30s.

On 3 Oct. 1397 at the inn of the bishop of Ely in London he granted by his letters patent to William Rees, who still lives, an annuity of 20 marks for life from the manor of Willington, by the hands of the farmers, bailiffs and reeves there, at Easter and Michaelmas by equal parts. Also on 26 May 1388 he granted by letters patent to John Cauley a rent of 10 marks for life from the same manor; similarly to John Tunstal 40s., and to Robert Gousill £20. All are still living.

To William Mareschal, who is still alive, he granted the office of parker of Haynes with agistments and with the wages and fees of the office for life. This was confirmed by the king.

At Epworth in the Isle of Axholm in 1397–8 he granted to John Barkeworth, chaplain, by letters patent the free chapel of Haynes with its appurtenances for life, with reversion to himself and his heirs, to celebrate and support services there for the souls of his ancestors. Time out of mind there have belonged to the said chapel 60 a. arable and 26s.8d. rent from certain lands, and the rents of the prior and convent of Cauldwell in Shelton. Barkeworth still holds these.

Date of death and heir as above.

285 BUCKINGHAM. Inquisition. Wing. 30 Dec. 1399.

He held in his demesne in fee tail by one of the fines of 1344 [above, no. 235] the manor of Penn. It is not held of the king, but of whom is unknown; annual value £10.

He held the manor of Wing in right of Elizabeth his wife by the grant of Richard earl of Arundel, her father, to them and the heirs of their bodies. Of whom it is held and by what service is unknown; annual value £80.

On 15 Feb. 1392 he granted to Robert, bishop of London, and others [as above, no.269] his lands, tenements and services in Linslade and Southcott.

Date of death and heir as above.

286   Writ 18 Nov. 1399.

WORCESTER. Inquisition. Upton on Severn. 29 Jan. 1400.

He held in his demesne in fee tail by one of the fines of 1344 [above, no.235] the manor of North Piddle. It is held of Thomas earl of Warwick, service unknown. There are £4 6s.4d. assize rents payable by equal parts at Lady Day and Michaelmas, 1 carucate 60s., and 20 a. meadow 40s., making an annual value of £9 6s.4d.

Date of death and heir as above.

287   SUSSEX. Inquisition *ex officio*. Horsham. 23 Feb. 1400.

He held in his demesne in fee tail the lordship of Bosham, and the manor of Stoughton belonging to it, with its members.

He died on 22 Sept. John Pelham, knight, has held them since that date and taken the profits.

288   Writ 11 Feb. 1400.

SUSSEX. Inquisition. Steyning. 9 March.

He held in his demesne in fee tail of the king in chief, granted by Richard Hakeluyt and William Moigne to William de Brewosa, senior, and Alice his wife by fines of 1316–17 [CP 25(1)236/47/14 nos. 1465, 1469], from whom they descended to John their son, John his son, John his son, John earl of Nottingham his son, and so to him, Thomas the duke:

Bramber, the castle and manor, annual value £32 17s.; and the manors of Knepp, £7 17s., Shoreham, £19, Horsham, 100s., Bewbush, £6, Findon, £21 6s., Washington, £25 5d., Beeding, £28 5s.4d., West Grinstead, £10, and King's Barn, £18 12s.4d.

Under the grant of Edward II to Thomas de Brotherton [above, no.236] he held the lordship of Bosham with the manor of Stoughton, service unknown; annual values, Bosham £113 15s.5¾d. and Stoughton £14 9d.

Date of death and heir as above.

289   Writ 28 Nov. 1399.

YORK. Inquisition. Coxwold by Newburgh. 10 Jan. 1400.

He held:

Thirsk and Hovingham, the manors, in his demesne as of fee of the king in chief by knight service, amount unknown, annual values £45 and £20.

Dinnington, the manor, in fee tail under the grant by one of the fines of 1344 by William de Neuton and others [above no.235]. It is not held of the king, but of whom is unknown; annual value £8.

Thwaite, the manor, in his demesne as of fee, not of the king, annual value 40s.

Long before he died he granted the manor of Kirkby Malzeard to Richard de Burgh for life, the knight's fees and advowsons and the chase of Nidderdale belonging to it excepted, by rent of a rose at Midsummer. Of whom it is held is unknown; annual value 40 marks.

Also long before he died, by his deed dated 15 Feb. 1392 he granted to Robert bishop of London, and others [as in no.269, with William for Walter bishop of Durham, and Robert for Richard bishop of Chichester] the manor of Burton in Lonsdale to hold with other manors on conditions not known.

Date of death and heir as above.

C 137/16 no.71a
E 149/73, no.1
E 152/345–6, 355, 359, 362

290 Writ, for fees, 18 Nov. 1399.
NORTHAMPTON. Inquisition. Northampton. 15 Jan. 1400.
He held in his demesne as of fee and right:
Grimscote in Cold Higham, Whilton and Staverton, 4 fees.
Crick, 1 fee.
Cold Ashby, Welford, Sulby, Staverton, Whilton and Grimscote, 3 fees.
Cranford, ½ fee.
Grimscote and Cold Higham, ½ fee.
Whilton and West Haddon, 1½ fees.
Crick, ⅓ [*recte* ¾] fee.
'Brunhale', 1½ fees.
Heyford, 1 fee.
Yelvertoft, ⅓ fee.
Chalcombe, the advowson of the priory of, extended at £10 yearly when a vacancy occurs.

291 Writ, for fees, 21 July 1400.
BEDFORD. Inquisition. Bedford. 14 Sept.
He held no knight's fee or advowsons.

292 Writ, for fees, 21 July 1400.
NOTTINGHAM. Inquisition. Nottingham. 3 Nov.
He held in his demesne in fee tail:
Egmanton manor, 1 fee, formerly held by John de Evyle, annual value £30.
Serlby manor with the hamlet of Torworth, ⅓ fee, formerly held by Hugh de Serleby, £15.
Egmanton, Staythorpe, Kelham and Cromwell, 2 fees.
Auckley and Finningley, 1 fee.
The advowsons of Sutton Bonington, annual value 16 marks, and Thorp Bussard, 10 marks.

293 DERBY. Inquisition. Derby. 5 Nov. 1400.
He held no knight's fee or advowsons.

294 Writ, for fees, 18 Nov. 1399.
SHROPSHIRE. Inquisition. Much Wenlock. 26 Nov.
He held no knight's fees or advowsons.

295 Writ, for fees, 18 Nov. 1399.

WARWICK. Inquisition. Kineton. 31 Dec.

He held in fee and right:

Wappenbury, 4½ fees, £20.

Street Ashton, Copston, Brockhurst, Brinklow and Harborough, 2¼ fees, £40.

Newbold on Avon, Cosford, Long Lawford and Little Lawford, 2½ fees, £20.

Walton Deyville, ¼ fee, 60s.

Smite, 2½ fees, £40.

Hampton in Arden, 1 fee, £10.

Chadwick, 1/10 fee, 40s.

Nuthurst and Hopsford, ½ fee, 100s.

Cesters Over, 1 fee, £10.

Newnham Paddox, 1 fee, 100s.

Baddesley Clinton, ¼ fee.

Heselholt, ½ fee.

Blyth, ½ fee.

Bentley, ½ fee.

296 LEICESTER. Inquisition. Loughborough. 5 Feb. 1400.

He held in his fee and right:

Kirby Bellars, 2 fees.

Frisby, ½ fee, 100s.

Oadby, ⅛ fee, 60s.

Ab Kettleby, Kirby Bellars and Burton on the Wolds, 1 fee, £10.

Melton Mowbray, ¼ fee, 100s.

Stathern, ½ fee, 100s.

Eastwell, ½ fee, £6 13s.4d.

Goadby Marwood, ½ fee, £10.

Wyfordby, ½ fee, 100s.

Burton Lazars, ½ fee, £10.

Little Dalby, Welby and Sysonby, 1 fee, £10.

Queniborough, 1 fee, £12.

Cold Newton, 1 fee, 100s.

Hoby, 1 fee, 100s.

Pickwell, 3 fees, £20.

Leesthorpe, ½ fee, 60s.

Bitteswell and Ullesthorpe, 2 fees, £6.

Thrussington and Ratcliff on the Wreak, 1 fee, £11.

Ingarsby, ¼ fee.

The advowsons of Seagrave, £10, Sileby, 20 marks, and Kegworth, £10.

297 Writ, for fees, 18 Nov. 1399.

RUTLAND. Inquisition. Uppingham. 12 Jan. 1400.

He held in his fee and right:

Empingham, 2 fees which William Basynges and Margaret his wife once held.

298 Writ, for fees, 28 Nov. 1399.

CAMBRIDGE. Inquisition. Cambridge. 20 Jan. 1400.

He held in his demesne as of fee:

Boxworth, ½ fee held by John Drabon.
Cheveley, 1 fee held by Gilbert Pecche.
Fulbourn, 1 fee held by Walter de Maners.
Trumpington, ½ fee held by Walter Busshey.

299 Writ, for fees, 18 Nov. 1399.
GLOUCESTER AND THE ADJACENT MARCH OF WALES. Extent. Newent. 9 Feb. 1400.
  He held in his demesne in fee tail:
  Llanvair Discoed, 1 fee held by Ralph de Monte Hermerii.
  Mathern, 1 fee held by Bogo de Knovyll.
  Penhow, 1 fee held by Ralph Seymour.
  Portskewett and Harpson, 1 fee held by Matthew Beneland.
  Crick, ½ fee held by William Derneford.
  Dinham, ½ fee held by Andrew de Bello Campo.
  Maesycwmmer, ½ fee held by Amery Lucy.
  Itton, ½ fee held by Henry de Bendevyll.
  St. Arvans, ¼ fee held by Leisannus ap Morgan.
  Llanmartin, ¼ fee held by Walter de Kemeys.
  Henrhiw, ¼ fee held by Roger Seymour and William Adam.
  St. Wormet, ¼ fee held by John de Bleccher.
  Tidenham, ¼ fee held by Walter Waldyng.
  Chepstow, the advowson of St. Mary's priory, extending at 20 marks.
  Severn, the advowson of the free chapel in the lordship of Tidenham in Wales, 40s.
  Lancaut, the advowson, 40d.

300 Writ, for fees, 18 Nov. 1399.
HEREFORD AND THE ADJACENT MARCH OF WALES. Inquisition. Leominster. 19 Feb.
1400.
  He held the following in his demesne as of fee:
  Penrice, 1 fee held by John Penrys, knight.
  Porteynon, 1 fee held by the same.
  Llangennith, ½ fee held by John de la Mare.
  Webley, ½ fee held by John de la Bere, esquire.
  Penmaen, ¼ fee held by Simon Wyngham.
  Reynoldston, 1 fee held by Richard Vernon, knight.
  Langrove, ½ fee held by Thomas Denys, knight.
  Nicholaston, ½ fee held by Richard Mauncell.
  He also died seised of certain advowsons of churches unknown.

301 Writ, for fees, 28 Nov. 1399.
YORK. Inquisition. Coxwold by Newburgh. 10 Jan. 1400.
  He held:
  Wighill and Easedike, ¼ fee, 10 marks.
  Healaugh and Follifoot, ¾ fee, 100s.
  Bainton, ½ fee, 10 marks.
  Carlton Miniott, Sand Hutton and Isle Beck, ¾ fee, 60s.
  Thirsk, ⅙ fee, 20s.
  Fryton and Howthorpe, ¾ fee, 100s.
  Thirkleby, 1 fee, 100s.

South Holme, ⅛ fee, 20s.

Harlthorpe, ¼ fee, 20s.

Bickerton, ¼ fee, 20s.

Coxwold, ½ fee, 50s.

Yearsley, ¼ fee, 25s.

Oulston, ¼ fee, 25s.

Gilling, Holme and Kirby Knowle, 1 fee, 100s.

Humburton, ¼ fee, 25s.

Carlton Miniott, ⅙ fee, 20s.

Hayton, ½ fee and 1/10 fee, 30s.

Fifteen fees in the following manors and vills: Boltby, Ravensthorpe, Thirlby, Cowesby, Newsham, Ness, Stillingfleet, Riplingham, Brantingham, Hessle, Tranby, Asselby, North Ferriby, Swanland, Willerby, Wolfreton, Bentley, Wyton, Skipwith, Thorpe, Scalby, Foxholes, Brigham, Scarcroft, Sherburn, Fraisthorpe, Etton, Breighton, 'Nothame', Cliffe, Kirkby Moorside, Fadmoor, Gillamoor, 'Lylyngton', Upsall and Thornbrough, 100 marks. The earl of Kent held the lands and tenements from which these fees were derived, of the inheritance of Thomas late lord Wake.

Twelve and a half fees in the following manors and vills: Malton, Brompton, Langton, Sawdon, Sutton, Knapton, Old Malton, Howe, Wykeham, Hayton, Wintringham, Scampston, Sherburn, Thorpe Bassett, Plumpton, Mulwith, Goldsborough, Swindon, South Holme, Wombleton, Muscoates, Barugh, Newsham, Holme upon Spalding-moor, Ferriby, Willerby and Breighton, 100 marks. Ralph de Euyr, knight, and his co-parceners held the lands and tenements from which these fees come, of the inheritance of lord de Vescy.

Kepwick, 1 fee, £20.

Thorp Arch, Tockwith and Long Marston, 3½ fees, 40 marks, the land from which they come held by Thomas de Meteham.

Kilburn, Butterwick and Thornton on the Hill, 3½ fees, 40 marks, of the lands formerly of Robert de Eyvill.

Slingsby, Coulton and Sledmere, 3 fees, 40 marks, of the lands late of Ralph Hastynges.

Scawton and Helmsley, 1 fee, 10 marks.

Brandsby and Stearsby, 1 fee, £10.

Armethorp, 1 fee, £10.

Rigton, ¼ fee, 25s.

Flasby, Eshton, Elslack and Arnford, 1 fee, £10.

Winterburn, ½ fee, 100s.

Hebden, ½ fee, £10.

Bank Newton in Craven, ¼ fee, 25s.

Sedbergh, Elland and Coldcotes, 1 fee, £20.

Burton, 1/20 fee, ½ mark.

Sedbergh, 1½ fees, 100s.

Lawkland, ⅙ fee, 40s.

Clapham, 'Colset', Skutterskelfe and Norby, 2 fees, £40.

Horton in Ribblesdale and Fountains Scale, 1 fee, £10.

Fawber, Grisdale and Horton in Ribblesdale, 2 fees, 40 marks.

Beecroft, ½ fee, 100s.

Thornton, ½ fee, 100s.

Healaugh and Follifoot, ¾ fee, 100s.

Sledmere, 1 fee, £20.

Slingsby, Coulton and Howthorpe, 2 fees, £40.

Scawton, ½ fee, 5 marks.

Harmby, ½ fee, 5 marks.

Brafferton, Cundall and Leckby, 1 fee, 40 marks.

Bainton, ½ fee, 10 marks.

Fryton and Howthorpe, ¾ fee, 100s.

Garton on the Wolds, ¼ fee, 100s.

The advowsons of Byland abbey and Newburgh priory by Coxwold.

302 Writ, for fees, 18 Nov. 1399.

NORFOLK. Inquisition. Norwich. 22 Dec.

He held in fee tail of the king in chief:

Watton, 11 fees held by William de Roos.

Surlingham, Kirby Bedon, Hellesdon, Cringleford and Keswick, 4 fees held by Ralph Dakre.

Narborough, 2 fees held by John Bardolph.

Flordon, 1 fee held by William Boteveyllen.

Newton Flotman and Swainsthorpe, ½ fee held by John de Sweynnysthorpe.

Mundford, ½ fee held by the bishop of Ely.

Hethel and Carleton, ¼ fee held by William Cursoun.

Tacolneston, 1 fee held by Peter de Dovedal.

Haddiscoe, 1 fee held by the heir of FitzOsbert.

Fersfield, 2½ fees held by the heirs of Robert de Bosco.

Billingford, 1 fee held by Ela de Boteler and John Peyton.

Blo Norton, 1 fee held by John de Sancto Moro.

Hethel, $\frac{1}{100}$ fee held by John le Warde.

Shelton, 1 fee held by Robert de Shelton.

Hardwick and Shelton, ¼ fee held by the heirs of Harvey de Shelton.

Forncett, ¼ fee held by the heirs of John de Claveryng.

Ovington, 1 fee held by the heirs of Peter Bozoun.

Fundenhall and Creake, 4½ fees held by the heirs of Robert de Crayk.

Bromholm and Ellingham, ½ fee held by the heirs of Baldwin de Bosco.

Palling, ½ fee held by Simon de Felbrigg.

Hethel, ½ fee held by the heir of Robert de Nevylle and 1 fee held by Peter de la Penne.

Broomsthorpe and Hethersett, ½ fee held by the heirs of Hugh de Pynkeney.

Moulton, ½ fee held by the heirs of Guy le Verdoun.

Swainsthorpe, ½ fee held by the heirs of John Cursoun.

Roughton and Weston Longville, $\frac{1}{10}$ fee held by Clement de Plumstede.

East Harling and Little Massingham, 3 fees held by Simon de Felbrigg.

Ketteringham, 1 fee held by the earl of Oxford.

Watton, 11 fees held by William Roos.

Wacton, Thorpe, Hales, Dickleburgh and Loddon, 3 fees held by John de Segrave of 'Fulestan' (?Folkestone).

Barningham and Erpingham, ½ fee held by Robert Broun.

Stockton, $\frac{1}{20}$ fee held by John Bygot.

West Dereham, ½ fee held by Peter Tameworth.

Bressingham, 8 fees held by John Verdoun.

Starston, 1 fee held by John de Herewastok.

Hethel, $\frac{1}{20}$ fee held by the master of St. Giles, Norwich.

Edgefield, 1½ fees held by the heirs of John de Claveryng.
Roughton and Weston Longville, 5 fees held by the heirs of Thomas de Merton.
Starston, 1 fee held by the heirs of William de Bovile.
Seething, 1¼ fees held by William de Calthorp.
Poringland, ¾ and ⅓ of ¼ fees held by the heirs of John de Claveryng.
Fundenhall and Creake, 4½ fees held by the heirs of Robert de Creyk.
Yaxham, 1 fee held by John Cursoun.
Seething, 1 fee held by the abbot of Langley, the abbot of Sibton, the master of St. Giles, Norwich, and Harvey de Stanhowe.
Pirnhow, 3½ fees held by the heirs of James de Crayk.
Mettingham, 1/35 fee, and Seething, 1/40 fee, held by Robert de Hedyngham.
Roughton and Merton, 1 fee held by Roger de Hales.
Barningham, Witchingham, Smallburgh, Bessingham, Greenesvill, 'Gryngelond', Ketteringham, Fleggburgh and Baconsthorpe, 5¾ and ⅛ fees held by William de Rokele.
Beyton, 1 fee held by William Lyncolne.
Oby, Ingham, Burnham and Fleggburgh, 3 fees held by John Caly.
Moulton, ¼ fee held by Nicholas de Stradsete.
Colney and Carleton, 1 fee held by Elizabeth de Colneye.
Creake and Fundenhall, 4½ fees held by the heirs of Robert Creyk.
Seething, 1/20 fee held by William Calthorp.
Badingham and Seething, 1/40 and ¼ fees held by Robert de Senges.
Cockley Cley, ¼ fee held by the prior of Butley and parceners.
Bixley, 1 fee held by the prioress of Carrow and John de Norwico.
Fritton, 1/20 fee held by Roger Revet.
Shelton, ½ fee held by Isabel widow of John Begot.
Shotesham and Tharston, 15⅓ fees held by Agnes widow of John Mautravers.
Hethel, ¼ fee held by Richard de Goldyngham.
Holkham, Sutton, Gooderstone and Carbrooke, 7½ fees held by the heir of Dennis de Monte Canisio.
Garboldisham, ½ and ⅛ fees held by the heir of Robert de Bosco.
He also held the following advowsons, extending at the amounts shown: Suffield, £20; Westwick, 8 marks; Gillingham, 100s.; Rockland, 100s.; Holverston, 40s.; Aldborough, 12 marks; Starston, 24 marks; Lopham, 20 marks; Forncett, £20; Hethel, 18 marks; Long Stratton, 6 marks; Little Wacton, 40s.; Great Wacton, 6 marks; Fritton, 8 marks; East Harling, 13 marks; Denton, 10 marks, alternate presentations; Weybridge priory, 40s.; Earsham, 24 marks; Ditchingham, 25 marks; Colby, 10 marks; Alby, 10 marks; Alburgh, 15 marks; Winston, 40s.; Windle, 40s.; Ellingham, 40s.; Stockton, 6 marks; Redenhall, 25 marks; Bixley, 40s.; Brockdish, 100s.; Banyngham, £10; St. Lawrence, South Walsham, 20 marks; Poringland, 15s.

303 SUFFOLK. Inquisition. Ipswich. 29 Dec. 1399.
He held in fee tail:
Flixton, 1 fee held by William Boteveylyn.
Bradley, 4 fees held by John son of Thomas Becourt.
Shadingfield, Thorington, Bruisyard, Sweffling and Great Ringstead, 4 fees held by John de Brosyerd.
Scarnestone and Burstall, 3¾ fees held by John Rochford, Bartholomew de Elingham and Alice widow of John Holbrok.
Helmingham, Yoxford, and Middleton, 3½ fees held by John de Thorp, William Swillington and their parceners.

Yoxford, Heveningham, Stickingland and Burgh, $3\frac{1}{2}$ fees held by William Swillyngton and Edmund de Ufford.

Akenham, Whittingham, Clopton and Hasketon, $3\frac{1}{4}$ fees held by Giles Breause.

Gosbeck and Easton, 2 fees held by Richard de Gossebek.

Newton and Wherstead $1\frac{1}{4}$ fees held by Oliver de Todynham.

Wixoe, 1 fee held by John de Wyckelowe.

Monewden, $\frac{1}{2}$ fee held by John Adam.

Hacheston, $\frac{1}{2}$ fee held by Godfrey de Hilton.

Kettleburgh, $\frac{1}{2}$ fee held by the heir of Thomas Ketilbre.

Charsfield, $\frac{1}{4}$ fee held by Nicholas de Weylond.

Chediston and Easton, 1 fee held by Thomas Bavent.

Cookley, $2\frac{1}{4}$ fees held by John de Fresyngfeld, John de Weylond and Thomas Bavent.

Cransford, $\frac{1}{4}$ fee held by Adam Tastard and William de Hoo.

Framlingham, $\frac{1}{10}$ fee held by Simon Taillour; $\frac{1}{4}$ and $\frac{1}{6}$ fee held by Thomas Ketilbere.

Kelsale, $\frac{1}{24}$ fee held by Nicholas de Kelishale.

Martlesham, 3 fees held by Thomas de Verdoun.

Heveningham, $\frac{1}{2}$ fee held by Cecily de Hertford.

Framlingham, $\frac{1}{20}$ fee held by John Austyn.

Saxmundham, 1 fee held by Robert Swan.

Crowfield, 1 fee held by Philip Harneys.

Uggeshall, 4 fees held by Roger FitzOsbert.

Blaxhall, 1 fee held by Thomas de Weylond.

Ramsholt, $\frac{1}{2}$ fee held by William de Rammesholt.

Wantisden, $\frac{1}{4}$ fee held by the prior of Butley.

Glemham, $\frac{1}{4}$ fee held by Richard Philip.

Denham, 1 fee held by John de Denham.

Iken, $\frac{1}{2}$ fee held by Roger Faussebroun.

Carlton Colville, $\frac{1}{2}$ fee held by John de Carleton.

Syleham, $1\frac{1}{2}$ fees held by John de Sancto Moro.

Campsey Ash, $\frac{1}{2}$ fee held by Margery Moysy.

Brampton, $\frac{1}{2}$ fee held by John Randulph.

Theberton, $\frac{1}{2}$ fee held by Emma de Norwico.

Elveden, $\frac{1}{2}$ fee held by the heirs of John de Gelham.

Wilby, Benhall and Norton in Colneis, $3\frac{3}{4}$ fees held by Guy Ferrers.

Colneis, $\frac{1}{2}$ fee held by William Oudyn.

Stonham Aspall, 1 fee held by Roger Aspele.

Ringshall, Baylham, Broke Hall, Darmsden, Kembroke and Levington, 4 fees held by the heirs of Robert de Wornaville(?) and John Rokelane.

Offton, 2 fees held by Richard Loveday.

'Plomesyerd', $\frac{1}{10}$ fee held by John de Peyton.

Colneis, $\frac{1}{2}$ fee held by Alexander de Prato and parceners.

Leiston, $\frac{1}{2}$ fee held by Robert de Skales and William de Caldecote.

Trimley St. Martin, $\frac{1}{2}$ fee held by William Videln.

Caldecott and Gislingham, $\frac{1}{2}$ fee held by Fulk de Goldyngham.

Higham, $\frac{1}{4}$ fee held by John Reymes.

Market Weston, 1 fee held by Hugh Hoville.

Peasenhall, Falkenham, Waldringfield, Sternfield and Farnham, 4 fees held by Nicholas de Segrave and Guy Ferrers.

Aveley, $\frac{2}{3}$ fee held by William Ynge.

Mickfield, $\frac{1}{4}$ fee held by Roger de Aspele.

Stonham, ¼ fee held by John Monye.

Ilketshall, 1 fee held by the heir of Morgan de Ilketishale.

Freston and Holbrook, 1 fee held by Alice Holbrok.

Stonham, ¼ fee held by Robert de Upston.

Layham and Holton St. Mary, 2 fees held by Robert de Reydon and Richard de Brompton.

Sproughton, 1 fee held by Richard Loveday.

Coddenham, 1/20 fee held by the prior of Holy Trinity, Beeston.

Brokes Hall, 1/10 fee held by Alice de Holbrok.

Baylham and Colneis, 1 fee held by John de Rothinge.

Ilketshall, 1/20 fee held by William Rous and 1/20 fee held by Walter Telle and his parceners.

Barrow, 2½ fees held by Katherine Gyfford.

Boxford, 1/40 fee held by John de Boytesford.

Ufford, 1/10 fee held by William Aumbergull.

'Bradewater', ¼ fee; Sternfield, ½ fee; Burgate ⅓ fee; and Langeston, ⅐ fee; held by John de Langeston, annual value £6 13s.4d.

Offton, 2 fees held by Robert de Stotevylle.

Grimston and Blowfield, 1½ fees held by John Beumond.

Colneis, ½ fee held by the lord of 'Stampes'.

Norton, 1 fee held by Wakelyn de Norton.

Colneis, ¼ fee held by Maud de Langenho.

Ufford, 1 fee held by Robert de Ufford.

Iken, ½ fee held by William Sturmyn.

Barton and Herringswell, ½ fee held by the heir of Stephen Berton.

Tunstall by Nettlestead, ½ fee held by John Typtot.

He also held the following advowsons, extending at the amounts shown: Dodnash priory, £20; Theberton chapel, 40 marks; Shadingfield, 6 marks; Bungay priory, £40; Iken, 10 marks; Bromeswell, 5 marks; Kelsale, £20; Tunstall, 40 marks; Eyke, 15 marks; and Clopton, 25 marks.

304 Writ, for fees, 21 July 1400.

SUSSEX. Extent. Bramber. 22 Aug.

He held as parcels of the honour of Bramber;

Broadwater, the manor, held by Thomas Camoys, knight, extending at £40.

Sompting and Ewhurst, the manor, 2½ fees.

Coombes, 4 fees held by John Halsham.

Lancing, lands and tenements, held by Richard Rademelde, 2 fees.

Michelgrove and Heene, the manor, 1 fee held by John Muchelgrove and Thomas earl of Arundel .

Sheepcombe, 5 virgates held by Maud Joop, ¼ fee.

Clapham, the manor, 2 fees held by Thomas Seyntoweyn.

Sullington, the manor, 2 fees held by Thomas earl of Arundel.

Westmeston, the manor, 4 fees held by John Brewes, knight.

West Grinstead, the manor, 1 fee held by Thomas Moubray, knight, and a tenement held by John Clothale as ¼ fee, 6s.8d.

Morley and Woodmancote, the manor, 4 fees held by William Percy.

Kingston by Sea, 4 fees held by Thomas Skelton and Joan his wife.

Horton, the manor, 1¾ fees held by Philip Mabank.

Washington and Findon, 2 virgates held by John Arundell as $\frac{1}{10}$ fee.

Colstaple and 'Langeford', 2 virgates held by Thomas earl of Arundel as $\frac{1}{10}$ fee.

Little Bookham in Surrey, the manor, held by William Heron, knight, as 1 fee.

Wappingthorn and Wowood, the manors, held by Ralph Codyngton and Henry Codyngton, extending at £7 10s.

Shipley, 1 virgate held by John Preston as $\frac{1}{20}$ fee.

Annington, 1 tenement held by Stephen prior of Sele in free alms by the service of $\frac{2}{3}$ fee; and 1 tenement held by John Roberd as $\frac{1}{3}$ fee.

Southwick, 9 virgates held by the prior of Reigate in free alms, 46s., rendering 18s. for scutage when levied at 40s.

Erringham, 4 virgates held by John Brewes, knight, as $\frac{1}{5}$ fee.

Hazelholt, 2 virgates held by John Colepeper, 10s.

Lower Beeding, 4 virgates held by Alice widow of Edward St. John as $\frac{1}{5}$ fee; 1 virgate held by Richard Bernard and Beatrice his wife as $\frac{1}{20}$ fee; 1 fee held by Henry Palmere, William Epsle, Joan his wife, and others; and 1 virgate held by Robert Palmere and others as $\frac{1}{20}$ fee.

Ham, 2 virgates held by Lucy Michell and others as $\frac{1}{10}$ fee, 2s.; and 1 virgate of 'Swetman' lands held by Robert Jourdan and others as $\frac{1}{20}$ fee.

'Stanford', 1 virgate held by Stephen prior of Sele as $\frac{1}{20}$ fee; and 1 virgate held by John Asshbrennere and others as $\frac{1}{20}$ fee.

Slaugham, $\frac{1}{2}$ virgate, holder unknown, $\frac{1}{40}$ fee.

'Stanford', $\frac{1}{2}$ virgate of 'Becchele' lands held by John Becchele as $\frac{1}{40}$ fee.

Findon, Westmeston and Shipley, 1 tenement held by John Brewes, knight, as 1 fee.

Findon, 1 virgate of 'Fraunceys' lands held by Agnes atte Wolde as $\frac{1}{20}$ fee; and 1 virgate held by Richard Fauconer as $\frac{1}{20}$ fee.

Washington, 1 virgate held by John Cambray as $\frac{1}{20}$ fee.

Westmeston, 1 virgate held by John Brewes as $\frac{1}{20}$ fee.

Shipley, 1 virgate held by the prior of the hospital of St. John as $\frac{1}{20}$ fee.

Findon, 2 virgates, holder unknown, $\frac{1}{10}$ fee.

Horsham, $\frac{1}{2}$ virgate held by Roger Terry as $\frac{1}{40}$ fee.

'La Felde', 5 virgates held by Thomas earl of Arundel as $\frac{1}{4}$ fee.

Horsham, 1 virgate held by the prioress of Rusper as $\frac{1}{20}$ fee.

Weston, 1 virgate held by John Bonewyk as $\frac{1}{20}$ fee.

Ifield, 1 virgate held by Thomas Blast and others as $\frac{1}{20}$ fee.

Grinstead, 1 virgate held by John Need as $\frac{1}{20}$ fee.

Byne, 4 virgates held by Joan widow of James de Byne as $\frac{1}{5}$ fee.

Wyckham, 4 virgates held by Hugh Quecheche, Richard atte Sonde and Simon Benfeld as $\frac{1}{5}$ fee.

Steyning, 3 virgates held by Hugh Quechche, paying 6s. for scutage when levied at 40s.; 3 virgates held by the same Hugh and others, 17s.6d., paying 7s. for scutage when levied at 40s.; 'La Combe', 2 virgates held by Thomas earl of Arundel as $\frac{1}{10}$ fee; 1 other virgate, holder unknown, $\frac{1}{20}$ fee,; 1 virgate of the lands of 'le Frye', once held by William Lychepoule, holder unknown, $\frac{1}{20}$ fee,; and 2 a. once of John Erysshe of the lands of 'Sage', amount and value unknown.

Horsham, $\frac{1}{2}$ virgate of 'Cobat' lands held by Henry Frenssh as $\frac{1}{40}$ fee,

Westmeston, 3 virgates of 'Lyones' lands held by Henry Tuttebury, 15s.; paying 6s. for scutage when levied at 40s.

Buddington, 2 virgates held by the abbess of Godstow in free alms as $\frac{1}{10}$ fee.

Steyning, $1\frac{1}{2}$ virgates held by Hugh Queche and John Atteberne as $\frac{1}{5}$ fee.

Shipley, 1½ virgates held by William Epsley, junior, as ⅕ fee.

Storrington by Thornwick, 2 virgates held by Thomas Chambre, John Colomeres and William Panethorne as 1/10 fee.

West Grinstead, the advowson belonging to the barony of Bramber, 20 marks.

St. Leonard, advowson of the free chapel in the forest, also belonging to the barony, 40s.

305 Writ, and writ for fees, both dated 28 Nov. 1399.

LINCOLN. Inquisition. Gainsborough. 12 Jan. 1400.

He held in his demesne as of fee the manor of Epworth in the Isle of Axholme, except for certain lands which he had granted by his various letters patent for the lives of the grantees with reversion to himself and his heirs: to Thomas Joynour of Epworth, 1 messuage and 1 bovate by rent of a rose at Midsummer, annual value 13s.4d.; to John Salman, 1 messuage and 2 bovates in Low Burnham, 26s.8d.; to William de Byntre, 1 messuage, 15 a. arable, and 1 a. meadow in Epworth, 30s.; to Hugh Cooke, 1 toft called 'Sulbyplace', 1 croft called 'Lubbancroft' and 1 croft called 'Pipercroft' by rent of a rose, 7s.; to Robert Gobyn, 1 messuage, 1½ bovates and 1½ a. meadow in Epworth, 26s.8d.; to Ralph de Brumham, 40s. rent from various tenants in Haxey; to John de Disworth, 40s. rent in East Ferry, Gunthorpe and East Kinnard's Ferry; and to Richard Lynne, the passage of Kinnard's Ferry, annual value 10 marks.

Long before his death he granted to John de Brunham and his heirs for ever 10s.6d. out of the 16s. assize rent which he paid in Belton and Butterwick in the isle, in exchange for 15 a. in Belton to enlarge his park of Belgraves in the isle, annual value 20s.; and to Nicholas atte Wode, deceased, and Alice his wife for their lives with reversion to himself and his heirs, 8 messuages and ½ bovate in Epworth, annual value 7s.

The manor is held of the king in chief by knight service, and is worth annually, apart from the above grants, £70.

Long before he died he granted certain annuities for life: to Edward de Clynton, £20 by equal parts at Easter and Michaelmas; to Thomas de Brunham, for his service for works in Gower and other business, 40 marks by his charter shown to the jurors; and to William Fouler, his receiver in the Isle of Axholm, 10 marks.

He held no more but long before he died he granted to Hugh de Waterton, knight, his manor of Wroot for life with reversion to himself and his heirs. It is held of the abbot of St. Mary's, York, in socage, amount unknown, annual value 100s.

On 15 Feb. 1392 he granted to Robert, bishop of London, and others [as in no.269 above, with William for Walter bishop of Durham, and Robert for Richard bishop of Chichester] all his lands in Stretton [Rutland] on conditions unknown to the jurors, annual value 60s.

He held the following knight's fees extending at the amounts shown:

Gainsborough, 2 fees, 100 marks.

Scawby and Sturton by Scawby, ½ fee, £4.

Haxey, Butterwick and Kelfield, ½ fee, £4

Burnham, 1 fee, 10 marks.

Haxey, ¼ fee, 60s.

Westwoodside, 1/10 fee, £4.

Beltoft and Butterwick, ⅔ fee, 100s.

Beltoft, 1/15 fee, 60s.

Belton, 1/12 fee, 60s.

Owston, 1/20 fee, 40s.

Belton, 1/20 fee, 40s.

Amcotts, Althorpe and Garthorpe, $\frac{1}{12}$ fee, 60s.
Blyborough, 1 fee, 20 marks.
Burton by Lincoln and West Ferry, $\frac{1}{2}$ fee, 100s.
South Ferriby, 1 fee, £10.
Yawthorpe, 1 fee, 100s.
Date of death and heir as above.

C 47/9, no.38
C 137/17, no.71b, mm.1–30
E 149/73, no.1
E 152/355, 358

ELIZABETH WIDOW OF THOMAS DUKE OF NORFOLK

306 BUCKINGHAM. Assignment of dower in the manors of Linslade and Southcott, in the presence of John Symmes, farmer of the manors, and William Bedeford and William Bollenhurst, attorneys of Thomas son and heir of Thomas duke of Norfolk:

Rents of free tenants: from the abbot of Woburn 4d.; John Capp 23d.; Roger Wedon 2s.; and John Archere 4s.8d. Total 8s.11d., or a third part of 26s.7d.

Rents of tenants by court roll: from Alan Hemroke 8s.8d.; Thomas Arnore 18s.; John Symmes 5s.; John Cook 8s.2d.; Milleward 8s.2d.; and Richard Mariet 5d. Total 48s.5d., or a third part of £7 5s.4d.; with all their customary works.

Also 1 a. of wood lying next to the field called 'Gosecroft' on the south side, that is a third part of 3 a.; and a third part of the profit of the leet after Michaelmas at Linslade, as it occurs yearly.

307 HEREFORD AND THE ADJACENT MARCH OF WALES. Assignment of dower in the lordship of Gower. 6 July 1400.

English Gower (*Anglashrie, Anglissher*), the county, annual value £22 7s.4$\frac{3}{4}$d.

Pennard, the manor, £24 6s.$\frac{1}{4}$d.

Kittlehill, the manor, 78s.7$\frac{1}{2}$d.

Loughor, the castle and lordship, £7 11s.3$\frac{1}{2}$d.

Llandimore, a third part of the manor, being the ancient dower of Cecily de Turbervile, with 34s.8d. of the third part of the lands formerly of Richard Scorlak in the lord's hands by escheat, of which John Dalamare, chaplain, holds 1 tenement, annual rent 10s.; David Baugh 1 tenement, 5s.; Juliana Carowe 1 tenement, 9s.; William Davy 1 tenement, 6s.; John Bouer $\frac{1}{2}$ a. meadow, 12d.; Jankyn ap David ap Jevan 1 a. meadow, 3s.; and William Ferrour 1 curtilage, 8d. So the third part of the whole manor is worth yearly £13 11s.9$\frac{1}{2}$d.

Kilvey, a third part of a coal mine, £30.

Clyne, a third part of the forest, 8s.10$\frac{1}{2}$d.

Swansea, 2 cornmills, one called 'Brynmelles', £6 13s.4d.; 1 fulling mill, 25s.6d.; 1 garden called 'le Orchard', 13s.4d.; and also the following burgages of which:

In West Street Master John Fairewode holds 2$\frac{1}{2}$; Henry Hatley 2$\frac{1}{2}$; John Jacob 1; John Fairewode 1; John Horton 1$\frac{1}{2}$; David ap William $\frac{1}{4}$; and Robert ap Thomas 1; all at 12d. each, 9s.9d.

In St. Mary Street John Horton holds $\frac{1}{4}$; Jevan ap Cradoc 1; Robert Jurdan 1; John Wynmerd $\frac{1}{2}$; Henry Key and Daukyn Ph'ot $\frac{1}{4}$; Thomas ap Ries $\frac{1}{2}$; Robert Jurdan $\frac{1}{2}$; Robert Firly $\frac{1}{2}$; William Dalamare 1$\frac{1}{2}$; John Bailly $\frac{1}{2}$; John Fairewode 1; Jevan ap Cradoc

H

½; Walter Taillour ½; Thomas Carrou 1; Walter Walle 1; John Horton 1; Philip Sutton ¾; Thomas Sengulton ¼; John Blake 1; John de Neeth 1; Stephen Walsshe ½; Henry Key ½; Jevan Key ¼; Jevan ap Cradoc ½; and Thomas Sengulton ⅓.

In High Street Thomas ap Rees holds ⅔; William Dalamare ½; John Baker, 'berman', ½; William Knoille ½; Thomas Sengulton ½; John Dier, chaplain, ½; Thomas ap Rees ½; Isabel Stackpoll ½; Agnes Doudeney ½; William Dalamare 1½; Thomas Sengulton 1; Thomas Malifaunt ½; Philip Scotton ½; John Sayr ½; William Dalamare ½; Thomas Meredith ½; Richard Will ½; Alice Marsh ½; Agnes Doudeney ½; John Somery ½; John Dier, chaplain, ½; Robert Perkyn ½; Thomas Henry 1; Joan Sweyn ½; Heytteley ½; Thomas ap Rees ½; and William Willi ½.

In Fisher Street Robert Perkyn holds 1; Thomas Cornys ½; Thomas Mallifaunt 1; John Horton ½; John Neeth ¼; Robert Filios(?) ¼; Philip Hoper ¼; John Taillour ¼; David ap Gr[iffith] ½; John Horton 1 and also ½; Henry Poret 1; Henry Key ½; John Horton ¼; Helen Key ⅔; Thomas ap Rees 1; Richard Ric[ard]½; Christina Hobbe 1; John Mauncel ½; John Horton ½; Robert Perkyn 1 and 1; John Touker, fisherman ('visher') ½; William Athelard ½; Daukyn Key ½; Henry Key ½; William Bars ½; Richard Mannyn 1; Thomas Charles ½; Thomas Osbarn ⅓; Thomas Sengulton ½; Roger ap Ll[ewellyn] 1; Walter Willi ½; Jevan ap Henry 1; Helen Key ⅔; Roger ap Ll[ewellyn] 1; Richard Ricard ½; Thomas Sengulton 1; William Willi ½; Jevan ap Robert ½; John Dier ½; William Dalmare ½; and John Fairewode 2.

In High Street, at end of the street on the east next to the water of 'Dovereyn', Robert Knepin and Thomas Malifaunt hold ⅔; David Fouleyn ⅓; John Mores ¼; John Horton ¼; and Thomas Malifaunt ½.

Total burgage rents: all at 12d., 73s.5d.

Also a third part of the perquisites of the hundred of Swansea, £4 8s.10½d.

A third part of the fisheries, 106s.8d.

A third part of the revenue from market tolls and a third part of burgage rents (*chenser*), 26s.8d.

One weir called 'Stremeweris' held by Robert Perkyn and John Poket, 12d.

Two parcels of pasture called 'Ilond' and 'Reedmede', 13s.4d.

New rent of Robert ap William ap Madog for 1 messuage and 7 a., 6d.

Increased rent of Felicity Baker for ½ burgage, 2s.6d.

New rent of John Horton for a weir called 'le Hose', 2s.

A quarter burgage formerly of Maurice Smyth, 4s.

One weir held by Thomas Seman, 12d.

Two cellars next to the bailiff's bridge, 8s.2d.

Four shops above the cellars 16s.

Two rooms built over the shops, 6s.

One garden held by Nicholas Harold, 12d.

Twenty acres of hilly pasture at 'Portmanmede', 6s.8d.

One empty place formerly of Henry Conewey, usually 4s. but now nil because vacant and lying waste.

One other empty place by the smithy of Maurice Smyth, nil.

One place formerly of Thomas Gr[iffith], usually 3d., now nil.

One weir called 'Purchasewere' and 'Ole Newere', usually 16d., now vacant, nil.

One pool by 'Blakestone', usually 20d., now vacant, nil.

One burgage formerly of John Trewman; 1 formerly of John Constable; ¼ in 'Stretesend' formerly of Thomas Wrenche; 1 in West Street formerly of Thomas Taillour; and ¼ formerly of Robert Carow; now all vacant and worth nothing.

A third part of 8 a. meadow above the water of Tawe not extended at any value because they belong by ancient custom to the fees of the steward and the receiver.

Certain liberties outside the town of Swansea by the following bounds and limits: the whole way leading from West Street to 'le Skette' and thence to 'le Blakepull' on the north; by the water of 'Blakepull' on the west; by the sea on the south; and by the waters of Tawe on the east.

Total value of dower: £128 13s. 11½d.

Also the following fees:

Porteynon, the manor, which John Penrees, knight, holds as 1 fee.

Nicholaston and 'Mauncellifeld', the manor, which Richard Mauncell holds as ½ fee.

Webley, the manor, which John de la Biere holds as ⅓ fee.

Llangennith, the manor, which John de la Mare holds of John de Penrees, and he of the lord as 1 fee.

'Vorshull' and Fernhill, which John Bounte holds as ¼ fee.

308 LEICESTER. Assignment of dower in the presence of the king's farmers and the next friends of the duke's heir. 24 June 1400.

The former duke's manor of Melton Mowbray is extended at £34. Assigned to Elizabeth are:

Various demesne lands: a holding (*cultura*) of 10 a. in 'Berclyff', 3s. 4d.; a half holding above 'Nethirbrynkes', 3 a. on the south, 4s.; a holding at 'Brigende', 6 a., 2s. 8d.; a meadow at 'Hardynghet', 20d.; 9 selions of fallow above 'Warlow', 4s.; a half of 8 selions on the same to the west, 12d.; a croft called 'Almescroft', 5s. 4d.; a holding which abuts on the water towards 'Priourscroft', 4s.; 1½ a. of a holding in 'Balnesfyld' to the south of the same, which holding contains 3 a. and part of an a., 8d; 3⅓ a. arable on the east side at 'Rywenge', which contains 10 a., 20d.; 2 a. arable lying to the east in a holding under 'Orgerpark', which contains 6a., 14d.; 2 a. meadow lying to the north in 'Beltonmedowe', 8s.; 2 a. and ⅓ of 2 a. on the north behind 'le Emylyn', 8s.; 40 selions of fallow lying to the south with ditches and spurs in the close of 'Framelande', abutting on a headland to the east into 'Loundynges' and from the headland above the lord's wood, and 14 selions of fallow in the same close with ditches and spurs to the north of the said wood, and next to the wood, and one head abutting on the 'Sixtenbywold', the other to the east to 'le Syke' which leads from the end of the wood to 'la Garpe in to Loundeinges', annual value 10s.

Total rents of demesne lands assigned, 55s. 6d.

Assize rents from tenants, 54s. 3d., namely: from the heirs of Lady Segrave 2s.; John Spycer 20s.; Richard Stretton 3s.; Margaret Roskyn 16s.; John Bellers 3d.; John Wydeford 2d.; John Melton 1d.; Walter Roskyn 2s. 1d.; Margery Roskyn [1s.]; John Bapton 8d.; John in the Yerd 1 lb. pepper; James Bellers, knight, 6s.; and Thomas Flethby 3s.

From tenants at will, 70s. 10d., namely: from John Chauene 20s.; John Orger 16d.; Isabel Cartwright 6s.; William C. . . 18d.; John Abbott, junior, 12s.; Thomas Conour 2s.; John Holande 8s.; and tenants of the common farm(?) 20s.

Also 1 chamber in the manor with a solar under, in the hands of the lord and partly ruinous.

Oadby, assize rents of the manor, 7s. 8d., namely: from William Baual 3s. 8d.; William Assheby 2d.; the abbot of Garendon 6d.; John Peek, chaplain, 21d.; John Saxtenby, chaplain, 15d.; and William Gonyld 4d.; 1 virgate formerly occupied by John Joye, and 1 bovate formerly held by John Pacy, lying in waste, 14s. 8d.; a third part of the profits of fairs, markets, portmotes and tolls of the manor in Melton Mowbray by the officials of the duchess each year; a third part of the profit of the agistment of the manor in the meadow called 'Emylyn'; a third part of the free courts, view of frankpledge of the manor, of all the profits, forfeitures and fines of those courts, and of all forfeitures and fines and other profits of the same manor as . . . in all ways or wastes taken by the same officials; and a third part of the demesne wood to the north as appears by the metes and bounds, annual value 2s.

C 137/17, no.71b, mm.31–2; 19, no.79

ROBERT PEKENHAM

309 Writ for proof of age of Ivo Harleston, son of Margaret, one of the daughters of Margaret, wife of John de Wauton, knight; and of Robert Pekenham, son of Elizabeth, the other daughter. Ivo Harleston claims to have been born at Wimbish and baptised in the church of St. Clement there; and Robert Pekenham at Dunton and baptised in the church of St. Mary there. Order to warn master Roger Walden, who was granted the custody of all the lands. 10 Oct. 1399.

[Endorsed]: Ivo was not born in Wimbish, or in Essex. The rest of the writ has been executed. Roger Walden was informed of the place and date.

Essex. Proof of age. Brentwood. 6 Nov.

James Stokwell, aged 50 years and more, being carefully examined, says that Robert was 21 on the feast of St. Margaret the Virgin (20 July) last, having been born in Dunton on that feast in 1378 and baptised in St. Mary's church there. This he well remembers because he saw Ralph Goshalm, now deceased, Nicholas Bonfeld, then rector of the church, and Margaret wife of Richard Palmere raise him from the font.

William Smith and John Rother, each 48 years and more, similarly examined, confirm this. They remember that Joan wife of William Seman was with Elizabeth Pekenham at the birth, carried Robert to the church, and coming from the church told them of it.

Simon Masseleyn, 50 years and more, met the party of godparents in the highway by the church, and they told him.

Nicholas Hynde was then in the service of John Pekenham the father at Dunton, and was sent with the godparents to the church.

John Stace and John Wolk, each 48 years and more, say that Alice wife of John Stace was pregnant with a daughter called Agnes, who was born on the morrow of the said feast and baptised the next day, John Wolk being godfather.

Richard Canon, 48 years and more, remembers that his father, William Canon, was present in the church and held the baby in his arms, and came from the church relating that Robert was the son of John Pekenham.

Gilbert Cok and William Pymmore, each 50 years and more, know his age by inspection of a book of martyrs in the church in which the birth was noted.

Henry Belet and John Wayte, each 49 years and more, were in the chapel of St. Margaret at Burstead by Dunton making offerings in honour of St. Margaret and, returning home, met Joan wife of William Seman carrying the baby.

C 137/19, no.74

IVO HARLESTON

310 Writ for proof of age. He claims to have been born at Cambridge and baptised in St. Clement's church there. Order to inform Roger Walden, who was granted custody of the lands. 26 Oct. 1399.

[Endorsed] The escheator was unable to find and warn Roger.

CAMBRIDGE. Proof of age. Cambridge. 27 Jan. 1400.

The jurors say that Ivo Harleston, son of Margaret, one of the daughters and heirs of Margaret, wife of John de Wauton, knight, was born at Cambridge on Palm Sunday [11 April] 1378 and baptised in St. Clement's church there on the same afternoon; and being separately examined say that they know this for the reasons stated.

John Brygham, aged 55, says that Adam the vicar was with him in his house when he was asked to go to the church to baptise Ivo on that Sunday.

John Wattes, 51, heard on the Monday after Palm Sunday that Margaret was delivered of Ivo, and sent her a gallon of sweet wine.

Stephen Neel, 45, says that Agnes his wife was a servant of Margaret and carried Ivo to the church.

Simon Cardemaker, 60, was in the church and held the bowl for the vicar to wash his hands after the baptism.

Hugh Plowrigh and Richard Outlawe, each 58, on that day went with master Ivo la Zouch, chancellor of Cambridge University, to the church, and after the baptism to the house of the friars minor to hear the preaching of holy scripture.

John Merton and John Skulton, each 53, had a dispute on that day, but settled it in the church at the time of the baptism.

John Pole, 63 was arbitrator in their dispute.

Thomas Caldecote, 59, and Thomas Skynnere, 70, were with Master Ivo Zouch, then chancellor of Cambridge University, in Trinity Hall, when Roger Harleston, the father, sent his servant John Dyne to ask Zouch to be godfather.

John Broun, 48, ran in the afternoon to the house of Thomas Arwe, smith, to heat an iron rod with which the water in the font was heated for the baptism of Ivo in St. Clement's church.

C 137/19, no.75

JOHN SON OF CHRISTINA WIDOW OF JOHN ATTE BERGH

311   Writ for proof of age, 9 Feb. 1400.

WILTSHIRE. Proof of age. Salisbury. 17 Feb.

John Wermenstre, aged 50, duly examined, says that John atte Bergh was 21 on Thursday before St. Thomas the apostle [18 Dec.] last, having been born at Salisbury on Thursday before St. Thomas the apostle [20 Dec.] 1375 and baptised in the church of the hospital of St. Nicholas there on the Friday following; master John Edyngton, master John Stratforde and Lucy wife of Nicholas Taillour raising him from the font. This he remembers because he had then by his first wife an eldest son, William, who died on the same day, and his death is recorded in a missal in that church.

William Bayly, 60, on that Thursday dined with the warden of that hospital, and at dinner was told of the birth.

William Haule, 61, well remembers because Juliana his . . . died and her death is recorded in a missal of the parish church of St. Thomas, Salisbury.

Adam Not. . ., 60, . . . D. . .ary, 65, William Bry. . .ede, 49, Lawrence Skynnere, 57, Robert Warner, 52, Thomas Croullyng, 58, and Robert Dolewyne, 63, remember because on the day that John atte Bergh was born Nicholas Bonham, father of Christina, gave a large dinner at Salisbury. They were present there and at the dinner were told of the birth.

John Skynnere, 55, well remembers because Petronilla his daughter died on the day after John was born.

William Popra. . ., 62, says that his son John was ordained monk in the abbey of Malmesbury on that day, and this was recorded in the chapter book of the abbey.

C 137/19, no.76

ALICE WIFE OF GUY DE ST. AUBYN

312 Writ for proof of age of Alice wife of Guy de St. Aubyn, one of the daughters of Philippa, wife of Richard Sergeaux, knight, in ward of John Cornewaill, who is to be informed. 23 May 1400.

[Endorsed] John was informed by . . . Boneylle and Richard Bailly.

CORNWALL, Proof of age. Hellandbridge. 21 June.

Thomas Meyny, senior, John Bera, Thomas Meyny, junior, William Lychour, Thomas Tregadek, John Stephyn atte Stone, Henry Pakett, John Waterlond, Stephen Degher, Richard Whityng, John John, Henry Seynt Mayban, jurors, say that Alice was born at Colquite in the parish of St. Mabyn and baptised in the church there on 1 Sept. 1384, and is therefore aged 15.

[The statements of the individual jurors are all illegible].

C 137/19, no.77

ROGER SON OF JOHN DEYNCOURT, KNIGHT

313 Writ for proof of age, 7 Aug. 1400.

WARWICK. Proof of age. Coventry. 22 Oct.

Eneas W. . ., aged 53 years and more, duly examined, says that Roger was aged 23 on Thursday in Whitweek [10 June] last. He was born at Kenilworth castle on Thursday in Whitweek [21 May] 1377, and baptised there, while Eneas was in London in the king's chancery, seeking a common pardon for himself, such as the king granted to all his lieges. On returning home he was told that the wife of John Deyncourt had given birth to Roger on that Thursday.

John Beaufitz, Henry Barbour of Cubbington, Nicholas Prentost, Thomas Ellesford and John Northampton, all 44 years and more, say that Roger was 23 because it was commonly said at Coventry at Corpus Christi [19 May] that the wife of John Deyncourt had borne a son, Roger, at Whitsun in the castle. A certain Roger Beauford, brother of the pope [Gregory XI], a prisoner of John duke of Lancaster in the custody of John Deyncourt in the castle, was his godfather.

John Clerk of Stivichall, and William . . . ., each 60 years and more, remember that Edward III died on 21 June following the birth. They were servants of William prior of Kenilworth, who baptised Roger.

John Draper of Fenny Compton and William Gildyng, each 56 years and more, were servants of John Deyncourt and after the churching of John Deyncourt's wife were sent to London to their master, who was awaiting the coronation of the new king.

John Commaunder and John de Barowe, each 63 years and more, were servants of

Edward III at the time of his death and long before. After the burial they returned to their homes at Kenilworth and heard of the birth and baptism.

The escheator warned Agnes, widow and executrix of William Arundell, knight, at Ansty, to be at Coventry for the proof of age on the day stated, by John Werst, Thomas Ferst, Robert More and William Lore, but no one came on her behalf.

C 137/19, no.78

ELIZABETH BRIENE

314 Writ for proof of age, 13 Feb. 1400.

LONDON. Proof of age of Elizabeth Briene, one of the daughters and heirs of Guy de Briene, knight, junior, kinsman and heir of William, tenant in chief of Richard II. Guildhall. 13 March 1400.

Thomas Dodyngton, aged 60 years and more, John Holbech, 62 and more, John Clerc, 50, John Assheley, 50 and more, Geoffrey Sutton, 60, Lawrence Dureham, 55 and more, William Hatton, 55, Richard Pyry, 63, John Barnaby, 50 and more, John Reynald, 56, John Pryme, 58, and Roger Asshelyn, 50 and more, jurors, being duly examined, state that Elizabeth was born in the parish of St. Peter Paul's Wharf in Queenhithe ward on 13 March 1381 and baptised in the church there two days later. Thomas Dodyngton, John Holbech, John Clerc, John Assheley and Geoffrey Sutton remember because Guy de Briene dined with them in a house close to that in which Elizabeth was born, and at the dinner they were well and truly informed.

As to the baptism, Lawrence Dureham, William Hatton and Richard Pyry say that at the request of the father they held wax torches beside the font during all the time of the baptism, and so remembered it. John Barnaby, John Reynald, John Pryme and Roger Asshelyn saw a servant of the father carrying some pots full of wine called 'bastard' to the church and drank of it there.

Therefore they all say that she was 18 on 13 March.

[Inquisition] C 137/19, no.85
[Writ] C 137/19, no.91

THOMASIA ONE OF THE DAUGHTERS AND HEIRS OF RALPH MEYNYLL, KNIGHT

315 Writ for proof of age. Reynold de Bethell says that she is of age and claims her lands. Order to inform Thomas Fraunceys, clerk, Roger Bradbourn and Thomas Hyntes, executors of William Meynyll, knight, who had the wardship. 24 Jan. 1400.

DERBY. Proof of age. Derby. 19 Feb.

The jurors say that she was born at Derby and baptised in St. Peter's church there on 6 Jan. 1386 and is now aged 14 years and more. Carefully examined as to how they know this, they replied separately:

Edmund de Timley, aged 55 years and more, sold a grey horse to Ralph her father on that 6 Jan., and Ralph told him that his wife had borne a daughter, Thomasia, on that day.

William Payn, 45 and more, remembers because Magota his wife was midwife at the birth.

John Spencer, 44 and more, says that in that year Robert, his elder brother, who would have been his father William's heir if he had lived, went to Scotland and died there, and so he (John) had his father's inheritance.

Richard Castell, 42 and more, married Emma his wife in the same church of St. Peter and was standing at the door when Thomasia was brought in and baptised.

Robert Cupper, 45 and more, says that Joan his wife, who is still alive, was at Thomasia's birth.

Peter Swerde, 60 and more, carried the basin and ewer to the church, and after the baptism washed the hands of the godfather and godmothers.

William Powse, 58 and more, says that a dispute had arisen between William de la Dale and John Mulder, both of Derby, and they reached an agreement before the priest in the church after the baptism.

Robert Hodgrey, 43 and more, had a daughter Elizabeth of the same age as Thomasia and baptised after her in that church on the same day.

Ralph Bower, 49 and more, had a son John who died on the day that Thomasia was born, and the death was recorded in a missal in the church.

Peter Cryche, 54 and more, was sent to inform one godfather and two godmothers by order of Ralph Meynyll, knight, Thomasia's father on that 6 Jan.

Richard Hewstre, 50 and more, rode to London to get various colours for his art on that day. Ralph asked him to buy various fowl for him, if they were for sale there, and told him that his wife had a daughter Thomasia on that day.

John de Rasyn, 54 and more, went with Ralph the father to the church and made a note in a book within a week of the baptism.

C 137/19, no.86

BEATRIX, SISTER AND HEIR OF ROBERT, SON AND HEIR OF JOHN DE HAULEY, KNIGHT

316 LINCOLN. Inquisition for proof of age. Louth. 5 April 1400.

The jurors say that she was born at Riby and baptised in the parish church there on the feast of St. Peter in Cathedra [22 Feb.], and was aged 16 on that feast last past, and this they remember for the following reasons:

John Milley of Woodthorpe, aged 44, and John Milysaunt of Withern, 50, say that on the day of the birth John Rudham, clerk, was staying with Robert Hauley, grandfather of Beatrix, and on the Monday following was presented to the church of St. Mary Mablethorpe.

Roger Mabylson, 50, and John Brygge, 46, both of Mablethorpe, say that on that day John Rothewell, clerk, was retained by Robert the grandfather to hold his courts in Riby or elsewhere in the county.

John Westerne of Mablethorpe, 48, and John Genel of Middlethorpe, 50, say that at that time Simon Wryght was building a new house in Riby and was seen by many people to be caught by a gust of the north wind and blown to the ground, breaking two bones in his right side.

John de Skrevelby, 60, and Benet Rogerson, 54, both of Laceby, say that on that day John Cook was put in the stocks there on suspicion of robbery and, having escaped, was seen by many people to break his shin bone whilst running away.

John Wower of Laceby, 45, and Robert Warner of Mablethorpe, 41, say that William Warner, father of Robert, was blind and fell into a well at that time and was almost drowned.

Philip Jonson of Mablethorpe, 40, and John Yonge of Theddlethorpe, 50, say that at that time there was a tempest, the sea broke over the shore at North Coates, and a great part of the country was submerged.

C 137/19, no.87

RALPH DE BRACEBRUGGE, KNIGHT

317 Writ, *melius sciri*, stating that an inquisition held by Alan Waldeyve, escheator of Richard II, [*CIPM* XVII, no.605] found that Nicholas Ryvell and John de Conyngesby, clerks, William de Halughton and Humphrey de Halughton, by their charter, conveyed to Ralph de Bracebrigge, knight, and Joan his wife the manors of Kingsbury and Plumpton, and all the other lands which they had of his grant, to them and the heirs of Ralph, and that Ralph died on 20 Oct. 1395. Joan survived him and held them of the king in chief of his manor of Cheylesmore. John son of Ralph died under age, and Ralph, brother of John and son of the elder Ralph, is next heir and under age. But William de Lodyngton, the king's attorney in the Common Bench, says that Ralph was alone seised of these lands in his demesne as of fee, and that Joan had no status in them as the inquisition supposed. 3 Dec. 1399.

WARWICK. Inquisition. Coventry. 12 Dec.

He held in his demesne as of fee of the king of his manor of Cheylesmore by knight service, amount unknown, the manors of Kingsbury and Plumpton, annual value £40. He died seised alone of these on 20 Oct. 1395. Joan his wife was not jointly seised in any way, and had no status in them. John was his son and heir, and died without heirs of his body about three years ago. Ralph, brother of John and son of the elder Ralph, was 20 years of age on 2 Feb. last and is next heir.

Robert Goushill and the aforesaid Joan, now his wife, have held ever since the death of Ralph de Bracebrugge, knight, but by what title or claim is unknown.

C 137/19, no.88

ROGER STANLAKE

318 Commission to John Roche, John Drayton, Hugh Wolf, William Fauconer and the escheator in Oxfordshire and Berkshire to inquire what Roger Stanlake, an idiot, holds. 24 Dec. 1399 [*CPR 1399–1401*, p.214].

BERKSHIRE. Inquisition before John Roche, John Drayton, Hugh Wolf and the escheator. Abingdon. 6 April 1400.

Richard Stanlake held various lands in Sutton Courtenay, which descended to his son Roger. They are held of Edward Courtenay, earl of Devon, but their value and how or to whom they were sold or alienated is not at present known.

319 OXFORD. Inquisition before the same. Oxford. 5 April 1400.

Richard Stanlake, father of Roger, died seised in his demesne as of fee of various lands and tenements in Witney, held of the king in chief, annual value 40s. They descended to Roger, and John Mareys, who had custody of Roger, sold them to various men 30 years and more past.

320 OXFORD. Inquisition. Same place and date and before the same commissioners, but with different jurors.

Richard Stanlake the father held 1 messuage and 2 virgates in Carswell of the abbot of Eynsham by a rent of 13s.4d., annual value beyond the rent . . . ; 1 parcel of meadow in the same place; 1 messuage in Witney in 'Crondonstrete', which John Bush 'cop'lus'(?) now occupies, annual value 6s.8d.; 1 messuage and 3 virgates in Littlemore which William Bernard now occupies, 53s.4d.; 1 messuage with adjoining lands in Cowley, 40s.; and a fair called 'Sanford hith', 53s.4d. Of whom and by what service the lands in Witney, Littlemore and Cowley are held is unknown.

He also held 1 croft in Cogges called 'Hillescroft' of the lord of Cogges by a rent of 8s., annual value beyond the rent 6s.8d.

After the death of Richard all descended to Roger his son by right of inheritance. John Mareys of Wiltshire sold them to various people, but by what right is unknown.

C 137/19, no.89

THOMAS HOLBROOK

321A DEVON. Inquisition. Bradninch. 21 April 1400.

Thomas Holbrook held certain lands and tenements in his demesne as of fee in Clyst Gerred of John earl of Salisbury of his manor of Wonford by knight service, annual value 10s.

He died on 18 March. Thomas son of Robert Ramesey, his next heir, is aged 6 years and more.

JOHN SON OF WILLIAM BLEES

321B Writ to escheator in Herefordshire for proof of age. He claims to have been born at Staunton on Wye and baptised there, and asks for the lands of his inheritance, which are in the king's hands owing to the minority of the earl of March. 25 Aug. 1400.

C 137/19, no.90

WILLIAM EYR

322 Writ, *melius sciri*, concerning lands in Reperry, Bodmin, Cannalidgey, 'Pengwannawoles, Pengwennawartha', Ruthdower, Treliver and Tregamere, which were taken into the hands of Richard II on account of the outlawry of William Eyr. 20 July 1400.

CORNWALL. Inquisition. Mousehole. 3 Dec. 1400.

William Tregoos held all the lands named in the writ in his demesne as of fee, and gave them to William Eyr for life and six years more, and so he held them when he was outlawed. The reversion after the reserved term of years was to William Tregoos and his heirs. They comprise:

Reperry, Tregamere and Treliver, 6 messuages and 2 a. held of the prince of Wales and duke of Cornwall of his castle of Launceston, of the duchy of Cornwall, in socage by a rent of 3s.4d.

Bodmin, 2 messuages held of the prior of Bodmin by a rent of 3s.4d. with suit of court at Bodmin every three weeks.

Cannalidgey, 4 messuages and 2 a. held of Robert Hill of the manor of Halton by a rent of 6s.

'Pengwannawoles, Pengwennawartha' and Ruthdower, 6 messuages and 4 a. held of John de Pomeray, knight, of his manor of Tregony by a rent of 3s.4d.

Total annual value 60s.

William Eyr held no more in Cornwall when he was outlawed or afterwards. He died on 31 Oct. 1394. Isabel Eyr, wife of Thomas Mon and daughter of Richard Eyr, brother of William, is next heir and aged 24 years. William Tregoos is still alive.

323   Further writ, *melius sciri*, why two parts of the manors of Pengwedna and Reperry were taken into the king's hands under Richard II, and what was their value, 4 July 1401.

Return that the two parts were taken by William Burleston, late escheator, by the name of all the lands of William Eyr in Reperry, Bodmin, Cannalidgey, 'Pengwanna-woles, Pengwennawartha', Ruthdower, Treliver and Tregamere, because of his out-lawry. They were held for life and six years more by the grant of William Tregoos, who is still alive, with reversion to himself and his heirs. They are still in the king's hands, annual value 60s.

C 137/19, no.92

JOHN SON OF THOMAS GARWYNTON OF WELL

324   KENT. Inquisition *ex officio*. Ashford. 11 Nov. 1399.

He held in chief of Richard II as half a knight's fee half the manor of Stour by Ashford of the castle of Dover, annual value £4.

He died on 25 Sept. 1397. William, son of Thomas Garwynton, brother of John, the next heir, is aged 1 year and more. John Brode, formerly escheator, has taken the issues.

C 137/19, no.93

RICHARD SCORLAG, JUNIOR

325   GOWER. Inquisition before William Stradlyng, knight, steward of Gower, and John Bouer, escheator. 15 June 1400.

Recites a privy seal writ of 31 May 1400 inquiring, the lordship of Gower being in the king's hands owing to the minority of Thomas Mowbray, whether Richard Maunsell is next heir in tail of Richard Scorlag, junior; and since it is said that he held in fee tail certain lands in Llanrhidian which Richard Scorlag, senior, similarly held in fee tail before him, inquiring also when he died, and what is the age of Richard Maunsell.

The lordship of Gower is in the king's hands owing to the minority of Thomas son and heir of Thomas Moubray. The younger Scorlag held 1 mill, annual value 40s., and lands and tenements, 60s., in Llanrhidian. He died on 25 July 1390. Richard Maunsell, the next heir, is aged 24 years and more.

Thomas de Bello Campo, earl of Warwick, lord of Gower, took the profits owing to the minority from the death of Scorlag until 27 Jan. 1397. Then Thomas Mowbray, marshal of England, lord of Gower, took them until Michelmas last. Since then the king has had them by the receiver of Gower.

E 149/74, no.20

HENRY GRENE, KNIGHT

326 Writ, *plenius certiorari*, to William Westbury and the escheator and sheriff, on the petition of Ralph Grene. 26 May 1400.

HAMPSHIRE. Inquisition before William Westbury and the escheator. Andover. 12 July.

Henry Grene, knight, son of Henry Grene, knight, held the manor of Grately with the advowson for life by the courtesy of England, in right of Maud, late his wife, with remainder to their children. She held it by inheritance after the death of her father, Thomas Mauduyt, knight. It is held of the earl of Hereford, annual value £10.

He died on 29 July 1399. Ralph son of Henry and Maud, the next heir, is aged 22 years and more.

327 WILTSHIRE. Inquisition before William Westbury and the escheator and sheriff. Warminster. 10 July 1400.

He held for life in right of Maud his wife, heir of Thomas Mauduyt, knight, with remainder to the children of Maud and himself:

Warminster, the manor and hundred, annual value £50;

Westbury, a manor called 'Le Mauduytes', £10;

Ditteridge, half the manor, 40s.; all of the king by knight service.

Fiddington by Market Lavington, half the manor, 50s., of the bishop of Salisbury.

Date of death and heir as above.

328 Similar writ to John Hervy and the escheator and sheriff. 26 May 1400.

BEDFORD. Inquisition before the escheator and sheriff. Woburn. 24 July.

He held in fee tail to himself and the heirs male of his body by the grant of Henry Grene, senior:

Chalton, the manor and chapel, with lands in Toddington, extent unknown, of the Earl Marshal, service unknown, annual value 100s.

Colworth, the manor, with lands in Great Catsey Wood, Souldrop, Sharnbrook and Felmersham, of Thomas Grene, knight, by knight service, annual value 40s.

He held nothing in right of his wife Maud or in any other way. Date of death and heir as above.

329 BUCKINGHAM. Inquisition before the same. Wavendon. 23 July 1400.

He held in fee tail to himself and the heirs male of his body by the grant of Henry Grene, senior:

Great Woolstone and Wavendon, the manors, with lands and tenements in Emberton, Filgrave, Olney, Chicheley and North Crawley, of Thomas Grene, knight, by knight service; annual values, Great Woolstone 100s., Wavendon 40s., the lands etc. 8 marks.

Date of death and heir as above.

330   Similar writ to Edmund Forde and the sheriff and escheator. 26 May 1400.
GLOUCESTER AND THE ADJACENT MARCH OF WALES. Inquisition before Edmund
Forde and the escheator. Chipping Sodbury. 19 July.

In the March of Wales he held half the manor of Mathern by the courtesy of England
in right of Maud late his wife, who held by inheritance after the death of Thomas
Mauduyt, knight, her father. It is held of the lordship of Chepstow, which is in the
king's hands, service unknown, annual value 10 marks, with remainder to the children
of Maud and himself.

Date of death and heir as above.

331   Similar writ to John Baryngton and the escheator and sheriff. 26 May 1400.
ESSEX. Inquisition before John Baryngton and the escheator. White Roding. 31 July.

The manor of White Roding with the advowson was held in their demesne as of fee
by John Olneye, Nicholas de Cogenho and John Cook of Comberton. By a fine of
1364 [CP 25(1) 288/47 no.633] they granted it to William de Quenton, knight, and
Isabel his wife for their lives with remainder to Henry son of Henry Grene of Isham
and the heirs of his body. So he held it in fee tail, of the king in petty serjeanty by
the keeping of a sparrowhawk when the king is pleased to come to these parts, annual
value £10.

Date of death and heir as above.

332   Similar writ to John Styvecle and the escheator and sheriff. 26 May 1400.
CAMBRIDGE. Inquisition before the escheator and sheriff. Comberton. 12 July.

By the same fine as in the last he held of the king in chief by knight service the manor
of Comberton called Merks, annual value £20 marks.

Date of death and heir as above.

333   HUNTINGDON. Inquisition before the same. Alconbury. 9 July 1400.

He held the manor of Buckworth with the advowson by the courtesy of England
in right of Maud his wife, who held by inheritance after the death of her father Thomas
Mauduyt, knight, with remainder to their children. It is held of lord la Zouche, service
unknown, annual value 20 marks.

Date of death and heir as above.

334   Similar writ to Thomas Cotyngham and the escheator and sheriff. 26 May 1400.
NORTHAMPTON. Inquisition before Thomas Cotyngham and the escheator and sheriff.
Thrapston. 1 July.

He held in fee tail to himself and the heirs male of his body by the grant of Henry
Grene, his father:

Drayton, the manor, of the king in chief by knight service, annual value 100s.

Lowick, the manor and advowson, of the earl of Stafford by knight service, annual
value 10 marks.

Harringworth, 9 messuages, 1 toft, 3 virgates and 12 a. meadow, of lord la Zouche,
service unknown, annual value 40s.

Great Houghton, $\frac{1}{9}$ of the manor, 4 messuages, 1 carucate, $3\frac{1}{2}$ virgates, 2 a., $1\frac{1}{2}$ roods
meadow and 6s.8d. rent, of Thomas Grene, knight, service unknown, annual value
£4.

Cotes, the manor, with lands, tenements, rents and services in the vills and hamlets of Raunds, Ringstead, Little Addington, Irthlingborough, Stanwick, Chelveston, Hargrave, Cotes Bydon, Middle Cotes and Mill Cotes belonging to it, of Thomas Grene, knight, by the service of 1 fee, annual value £10.

Date of death and heir as above

C 137/20, no.1
E 149/72, no.10

RICHARD HURST

335 Writ 12 Oct. 1400.

SUSSEX. Inquisition. Hailsham. 25 Oct.

With Margaret his wife, who survives him, he held the manor of Pebsham of the abbot of Robertsbridge, service unknown, annual value £20.

He died on 21 Jan. last. Margaret and Philippa, his daughters and next heirs, are aged 9 years and more and 3 years and more.

C 137/21, no.1

WILLIAM WHYTE OF WILDEN

336 Writ 5 Feb. 1401.

BEDFORD. Inquisition. Wilden. 20 April.

He held in his demesne as of fee 1 messuage, 1 croft of 2 a. and another of 27½ a. in Wilden, of the king of the honour of Peverel, annual value 4s.

He died on 16 May 1393. Thomas his son and heir was 28 on 25 Jan. last. The king has held the lands since William's death and received the profits by the hands of the escheators.

C 137/21, no.2

WILLIAM SON OF ROGER DE HERON, KNIGHT

337 Writ 18 Nov. 1400.

CAMBRIDGE. Inquisition. Cambridge. 12 Jan. 1401.

He held nothing in Cambridgeshire. He died on 10 Nov. William his son and heir is aged a quarter of a year.

C 137/21, no.3
E 149/75, no.6

THOMAS ROMESY

338 Writ 10 Dec. 1400.

WILTSHIRE. Inquisition. Martin. 16 Dec.

He held:

South Damerham, 1 messuage, 60 a. and 8s. rent, of John Lord Lovel, service unknown, annual value 38s.

East Martin, 1 messuage and 1 virgate by a rent of a rose, of William Peytefyn, annual value 6s.8d.

South Damerham, 1 messuage and 40 a., of Walter Romesy, knight, service unknown, annual value 6s.8d.

Martin, 1 messuage and ½ virgate, of William Peytefyn, by a rent of 2s.6d., annual value 6s.6d.

He died on 19 July last. Thomas his son and heir is aged 10 years.

339 HAMPSHIRE. Inquisition *ex officio*. Farnham. 8 Dec. 1400.

He held half the manor of Farnham of the king in chief, service unknown, annual value 100s.; and 1 messuage and ½ carucate in Farnham of the bishop of Winchester by a rent of 25s.3d., annual value 40s.

Date of death and heir as above.

340 Writ 10 Dec. 1400.

HAMPSHIRE. Inquisition. Winchester. 10 Jan.1401.

He held half the manor of Farnham of the king in chief, service unknown, annual value £8.

He died on 26 July [Monday after St. James, *recte* before St. James, 19 July]. Heir as above.

C 137/21, no.4

ALICE WIFE OF MALCOM DE LA MARE

341 Writ 20 Oct. 1400.

SHROPSHIRE. Inquisition. Shrewsbury. 18 Nov.

She held nothing of the king in chief when she died. Who is the next heir and how old is unknown.

342 Writ 8 Oct. 1400.

WORCESTER. Inquisition. Worcester. 6 Nov.

Malcolm de la Mare and Alice held for the life of Alice the second part of the manor of Kidderminster of John Beauchamp of Holt, knight, Joan his wife, and the heirs of John, with reversion to them, by assignment of Walter Ramesey. After the death of Joan and the forfeiture of John by judgment of parliament, the reversion came into the king's hands. Richard II by letters patent [*CPR 1388–92*, p.80, 10 July 1389], shown to the jurors, granted the reversion with a third part of the manor and the manor or priory of Astley to John de Hermesthorp and William Wenlok, clerks, John Catesby, Henry Bruyn, Robert Burguillon and John Meysy, their heirs and assigns.

Malcolm and Alice de la Mare attorned to John de Hermesthorp and the others. They granted the third part and the reversion of the second to Nicholas Hillyng, knight, and Thomas Aldebury, clerk, by the king's licence [*CPR 1388–92*, p.307, 19 Sept. 1390], also shown to the jurors. Alice attorned to them and so held it when she died, with reversion to Hillyng and Aldebury. The three parts are held of the king in chief as 1 knight's fee. The annual value of the second part is £10.

Alice died on 28 June. Agnes wife of John Bysshop is niece and heir, being the daughter of Robert, brother of Alice, and aged 40 years and more.

343　Commission to Philip Holgot, Roger Partrych, Henry Moton, John Gomond and the sheriff. 7 July 1400 [*CPR 1399–1401*, p.346].

HEREFORD. Inquisition before Philip Holgot, Henry Moton and John Gomond. Hereford. 10 Jan. 1401.

She held in fee tail:

Little Hereford, the manor, of the king of the honour of Brecon by knight service, annual value 80 marks.

Yatton, the manor, of the earl of March by knight service, annual value £10.

She died on 27 June 1400 leaving no heirs of her body. She came from Yorkshire, and who is next heir is unknown.

> C 137/21, no.5
> C 137/23, no.43
> C 137/33, no.68

RICHARD WELDE

344　Writ, *melius sciri*, inquiring what he held of Robert earl of Oxford on the day that he died. 5 May 1401.

ESSEX. Inquisition. Hatfield Broad Oak. 6 July.

He held the manor called Longbarns in Beauchamp Roding with the advowson of Beauchamp Roding in his demesne in fee tail by the service of one knight's fee. Owing to the forfeiture of Robert de Veer, late earl of Oxford, it is held of the king in chief; annual values, manor £12 6s.2d., advowson 106s.8d.

He died on 3 May 1392. Elizabeth his daughter, wife of Lewis Mewes, is heir and was 15 years of age on 29 June last. Roger Marchall, deceased, has held the manor since Richard's death by grant of Richard II [*CPR 1391–6*, p.497, 15 Aug. 1394].

> C 137/21, no.6
> E 149/76, no.7

WILLIAM HOLM

345　Writ 28 May 1401.

HAMPSHIRE. Inquisition. Winchester. 4 June.

William Holm held in his demesne as of fee 2 tenements, 2 cottages, 2 curtilages and 4 tenter yards (*tentoria*) in Winchester, which descended to William his son, who was born an idiot. They were therefore taken into the king's hands under Richard II and are still so held. They are held of the king in chief by a yearly rent of 1d.; annual value 5 marks.

He died on 20 May last. Thomas Smyth, his next heir, is aged 40 years and more.

346　Writ, *melius sciri*, as to who is the heir, as there is information that Thomas Smyth is not the next heir and was inadvertently so named by the escheator and jurors. 8 July 1401.

HAMPSHIRE. Inquisition. Winchester. 13 July.

Isabel who was the wife of Henry Rende is heir, being the daughter of John, brother of William Holm, father of William, and aged 40 years and more.

C 137/21, no.7

JOAN DAUGHTER OF THOMAS SON OF THOMAS GARDENER OF GISSING

347 Writ 20 April 1401.

NORFOLK. Inquisition. Norwich. 10 May.

Owing to the death of Thomas Gardener of Gissing and the minority of Joan, daughter of Thomas son of Thomas, his grand-daughter and heir, the manor of Gissing and 30 a. were taken into the king's hands under Richard II and so remain. Two parts of the manor are held of William Beauchamp of the stewardship (*senescallicia*) of Bury, by the service of two knight's fees, and the third part of the abbot of Bury St. Edmunds, service unknown. The 30 a. are held of the manor of Winfarthing, which is in the king's hands owing to the minority of Edward Hastyngs, service unknown. Annual value together £20.

She died on 15 Dec. 1391. Robert, son of Robert Butveleyn of Flordon and Katherine his wife, sister of Cecily, mother of Joan, is next heir and aged 22 years and more.

C 137/21, no.8
E 149/77, no.20

JOHN SYBYLE

348 Writ 23 Nov. 1400.

CAMBRIDGE. Inquisition. Cambridge. 18 Jan. 1401.

He held of the king in chief 1 toft and 40 acres in Great Wilbraham. He was outlawed in Essex on a plea of trespass at the suit of Margaret countess of Norfolk, and his lands were taken into the king's hands and so remain; annual value 13s.4d.

He died on 20 Nov. 1393. William his son and next heir was 21 on 8 Dec. last. The escheator has taken the issues and profits since the outlawry.

C 137/21, no.9

PHILIP POPHAM

349 Writ 30 Dec. 1400.

HAMPSHIRE. Inquisition. Odiham. 22 Jan. 1401.

He held by knight service:

Barton Stacey, half the manor, of the king in chief in his demesne as of fee, annual value 11 marks.

Dummer, the manor, of the honour of Wallingford, which Philip his father held, jointly with Elizabeth his wife, to them and the heirs of their bodies, by the grant of John Wygmour, annual value 5 marks.

He died on 18 Nov. Philip his son and heir is aged 1 year 9 months.

I

350 Writ 30 Dec. 1400.

BERKSHIRE. Inquisition. Wantage. 19 Feb. 1401.

William Waryn, clerk, granted to Philip Popham, son of Philip Popham, knight, Elizabeth his wife, and the heirs of the body of the younger Philip, an annual rent of 10 marks from the manor of Lyford, payable at Easter and Michaelmas, with the right to distrain if in arrears by 15 days, and then to hold until the rent is satisfied. It is held of the abbot of Abingdon by knight service and a payment of 6s. 8d. every 17 weeks for the guard of Windsor.

He died on 18 Nov. Philip his son and heir is aged 1 year 10 months.

C 137/21, no. 10
E 152/369, no. 1

THOMAS FOULEHURST

351 SHROPSHIRE. Inquisition. Newport. 5 March 1401.

He held in his demesne as of fee of the king two parts of the manor of Pickthorn by a rent of 16d. payable annually by the sheriff, annual value 60s. 7d.

He died on 15 Dec. last. Thomas his son and heir is aged 2 years and more.

352 SHROPSHIRE. Inquisition. Bridgnorth. 29 Dec. 1402.

He held only two parts of the manor of Pickthorn, as stated in the inquisition before Robert de Thormes, formerly escheator; but long before his death he held in his demesne as of fee two parts of the manor of Cressage, in which he enfeoffed John Ostage and Roger Jallok, chaplains, on condition that after his death they paid his debts and enfeoffed his heir when he reached full age. The latter two parts are held of the earl of March of his manor of Stanton Lacy, service unknown; annual value 20 marks.

He died on 13 Dec. 1400. Thomas his son and next heir is aged 7 years and more.

C 137/40, no. 56
E 152/370, no. 3, and 372.

JOHN HUNTER

353 Writ 30 Jan. 1401.

CUMBERLAND. Inquisition. Carlisle. 5 March

He held in his demesne as of fee of the king in chief in socage 1 carucate and 3 a. meadow in Salkeld by a rent of 6s. 8d. payable at the exchequer of Carlisle by the sheriff at Michaelmas, annual value 20s.

He died on 3 Sept. 1400. Isabel and Cecily, his daughters and heirs, are of full age, 14 years and more.

C 137/21, no. 12

ELEANOR DE BRIDWYK

354 Writ 20 March 1400.

STAFFORD. Inquisition. Penkridge. 21 Oct. 1400.

She held nothing in the county.

She died on 3 Oct. 1399. Elizabeth wife of Thomas Fylkyn, her daughter and heir, is aged 28 years and more.

355 SHROPSHIRE. Inquisition. Shifnal. 11 Oct.

She held in her demesne as of fee of the king in chief half the manor of Bridwick by a rent of 2s.6d., annual value 20s.

Date of death and heir as above.

C 137/21, no.13
E 149/77, no.5

MARY WIFE OF THOMAS LA ZOUCHE

356 Writ 26 May 1401.

ESSEX. Inquisition. Halstead. 9 June.

She held in her demesne as of fee the manor of Colne Engaine with the advowson of William le Zouche, service unknown, annual values, manor £8, advowson 100s.

She died on 19 May last. John Bernak, knight, her son and heir, is aged 28 years and more.

357 Writ 26 May 1401.

LEICESTER. Inquisition. Hallaton. 7 June.

She held in her demesne as of fee of the king in chief the manor of Hallaton of the honour of Peverel as half a knight's fee, annual value 11 marks.

Date of death and heir as above.

358 Writ 26 May 1401.

BEDFORD. Inquisition. Biggleswade. 10 June.

She held in her demesne as of fee of the king in chief the manor of Sandy and the advowson of the chantry at the altar of St. Nicholas there as half a knight's fee; annual values, manor 100s., chantry 40s.

Date of death and heir as above.

359 Writ 26 May 1401.

HUNTINGDON. Inquisition. Huntingdon. 4 June.

She held in her demesne as of fee the manor of Dillington of the abbot of Ramsey, service unknown, annual value £10.

Date of death and heir, John son and heir of William Bernak and Mary, as above.

C 137/21, no.15
E 149/75, no.2

WILLIAM THRELKELD OF OUSBY

360 Writ 30 Jan. 1401.

CUMBERLAND. Inquisition. Penrith. 22 March.

He held in fee tail to himself and the heirs male of his body two parts of half the manor of Ousby by the grant of John Crofton by licence of Edward III, with remainder to the right heirs of William Threlkeld, knight, his father. It is held of the king in chief by knight service as a twentieth part of a fee, and 7s. 2d. cornage rent payable at the exchequer of Carlisle by the sheriff; annual value 17s. 7d.

He died on 3 Nov. last without heirs male of his body. William de Threlkeld of Crosby, knight, is cousin and next heir of his father William de Threlkeld, knight, being the son of John the son of the elder William. He is aged 40 years and more and the manor should remain to him.

C 137/21, no. 16

AGNES WIDOW OF THEOBALD GORGES, KNIGHT

361   Writ 17 Nov. 1400.

SOMERSET. Inquisition. Ilchester. 25 Nov.

She held in dower of the inheritance of Thomas Gorges, brother and heir of Bartholomew, son and heir of Theobald, a third part of the manor of Wraxall, of the earl of Devon by knight service, annual value 20 marks.

She died on 15 Nov. last.

362   DORSET. Inquisition. Dorchester. 24 Nov. 1400.

She held in dower as above:

Sturminster Marshall, 7 cottages and a third part of 2 watermills. They are held with the two parts of the manor, formerly held by Theobald, of the king by the service of rendering him a pair of gilt spurs or 6d. each time that he visits the forest of Purbeck. Annual value of her dower there payable by equal parts at Candlemas, Whitsun and All Saints, £6.

Upper Kingcombe, 1 messuage of Robert Lovell and Elizabeth his wife of the manor of Rampisham by knight service, annual value 13s. 4d.

Date of death as above.

363   Writ 17 Nov. 1400.

DEVON, Inquisition. Exeter. 27 Nov.

She held in dower as above a third part of the manor of Braunton. It is held with the other two parts of the king in chief by the service of rendering him three barbed arrows whenever he goes hunting in Exmoor forest, and by fealty. Annual value of the third part £6 13s. 4d.

She died on 18 Nov. last. Thomas Gorges brother and heir of Bartholomew is aged 28 years and more.

364   Writ 17 Nov. 1400.

HAMPSHIRE. Inquisition. Southampton. 12 Jan. 1401.

She held in dower as above a third part of the manor of Knighton in the Isle of Wight of the lordship of Carisbroke castle by knight service, annual value 10 marks.

She died on 15 Nov. last.

C 137/21, no. 17
E 149/77, no. 21
E 152/371

AGNES WIDOW OF NICHOLAS THURMOND

365 Writ, *melius sciri*, stating that she is said to have held lands of the inheritance of William, son of William Botreaux, knight, who died in the king's ward. 8 March 1401.

SOMERSET. Inquisition. Frome. 26 March.

She held the manor of Luckington of Lord Audeleygh of his manor of Nether Stowey, annual value 4 marks; and 1 toft and 80 a. called Page House of the prior of St. John of Jerusalem, annual value 20s.; all for life, services unknown, by the grant of William atte Huyde, John Swynsfford, William Nypered and Peter le Vyse, with remainder to William, son and heir of William de Botreaux, knight, under age and in the king's ward on account of other lands held in chief, and lately deceased.

She died on 2 March last.

366 Writ 26 March 1401.

SOMERSET. Inquisition. Milborne Port. 7 June.

She held for life by the grant of John Iryssh, William atte Hyde, John Swyneford, William Nyppere and Peter le Wyse, with reversion to William de la Bere [sic], his heirs and assigns, the feoffment being shown to the jurors.

Luckington, the manor of Lord Audelegh, of his manor of Nether Stowey, service unknown, annual value £10.

Page House, 1 toft so called, of the prior of St. John of Jerusalem in England, service unknown, annual value 40s.

Mells, 2 tenements, of the abbot of Glastonbury, service unknown, annual value 13s.4d.

She died on 2 March last. William de la Bere is heir and aged 30 years and more.

C 137/21, no.18
E 149/77, no.12

HENRY ATTE WAYE

367 Writ 1 Nov. 1398.

Further writ ordering return to chancery of inquisitions already taken. 12 Nov. 1399.

DEVON. Inquisition. Exeter. 12 July 1399.

Henry atte Waye, an idiot from birth, held in his demesne as of fee 1 messuage, 1 ferling and 40 a. of moorland heath in Waytown in the tithing of Gorhuish in the parish of Inwardleigh, annual value 2s.; and 1 messuage and ½ ferling in Stockbeare in the tithing of Jacobstowe, annual value 12d.

John Aston, formerly escheator, took them into the king's hands and so they remain. The premises in Waytown are held of Thomas Crydye of his manor of Gorhuish by knight service, and those in Stockbeare of Nicholas Bromforde of his manor of Broomford by knight service.

He died 23 Sept. John Rede is next heir, being son of Susan, daughter of William atte Waye, brother of Henry, and aged 30 years and more.

C 137/22, no.19

ROBERT CHARLES, KNIGHT

368 Writ 5 March 1401.

NORFOLK. Inquisition. Loddon. 12 March.

He held in his demesne as of fee of the abbot of Langley, Henry Ingelose and the prioress of Campsey Ash lands and tenements in Loddon, Sisland, Thurton, Hardley, Chedgrave, Norton Subcourse, Heckingham, Mundham and Thwaite, services unknown, annual value 16 marks 6s. 8d.

With Anne his wife and Walter Doreward, who still lives, he held 1 messuage and 80 a. land of alders and rushes (*alnea et juncar*) in Thurton, annual value 13s. 4d.; and 1 watermill of no annual value; all held of Edward Hastynges, knight, of his manor of Bergh Apton by a rent of 17s.

He died on 21 Feb. Thomas his son and heir is aged 23 years and more.

369 Writ 5 March 1401.

SUFFOLK. Inquisition. Framlingham. 19 March.

He held to himself and the heirs of his body, of the king in chief by knight service, the manor of Kettleburgh with the advowsons of Kettleburgh and Easton, annual value £35; and £10 annual rent from the prior (*prier*) of Wangford for various tenements in Stoven, Wangford and Uggeshall, paid at St. Andrew's day, Easter, Midsummer and Michaelmas, and held of the abbot of Langley, service unknown.

Date of death and heir as above.

C 137/22, no.20
E 149/77, no.2

RICHARD RADEMELDE

370 Writ 6 July 1401.

SUSSEX. Inquisition. Bramber. 13 Oct.

He held in his demesne as of fee:

Lancing, two parts of the manor, of Thomas Moubray, son and heir of Thomas late duke of Norfolk, who is under age in the king's ward, of his honour of Bramber, by knight service, annual value £4 17s. 8d.

Albourne, two parts of the manor, of the bishop of Chichester of his manor of Streatham by knight service, annual value 60s. 4d.

Beverington, two parts of the manor, annual value £6 13s. 4d.

He died on 6 Nov. last. Ralph Rademelde is his brother and heir.

371 Writ, *melius sciri*, inquiring of whom the two parts of Beverington manor mentioned in the above inquisition are held. 1 Nov. 1401.

SUSSEX. Inquisition. Bramber. 18 Nov.

The two parts are held of Thomas West, knight, of his manor of Blatchington, service unknown, except for 14 a. which are held of the king of the honour of the Eagle, part of the duchy of Lancaster, by the service of 6s. 8d. for the guard of Pevensey castle.

C 137/22, no.21

RICHARD SON OF WILLIAM GAMBON

372 Writ 31 Jan. 1401.

CAMBRIDGE. Inquisition. Cambridge. 4 Feb.

No lands are in the king's hands on account of the death of William Gambon and the minority of Richard.

Richard held in his demesne as of fee the manor of Wendy, and 1 tenement and 90 a. in Wendy and Kneesworth, by the grant of John West to himself, his heirs and assigns. The manor is held of the earl of Westmorland of the honour of Richmond in socage by suit of court once yearly at the customary place, annual value 100s. The tenement and 90 a. are held of William FitzRauff by rent of 6s. 8d., annual value 33s. 4d.

He died on 25 Sept. last. By Margaret his wife, who survives him, he had issue Richard, aged one quarter year, his next heir.

C 137/22, no.22
E 149/75, no.5

ANNE WIFE OF WILLIAM HAUSTEDE

373 Writ 26 Jan. 1401.

NORTHAMPTON. Inquisition. Towcester. 9 Feb.

She held in dower a third part of the manor of Deanshanger, and 2 cottages, and 3 a., annual value 40s. All, together with the two parts of the manor which John Cope holds, are held of the king in chief as a fortieth part of a knight's fee. The reversion belongs to John Cope and his heirs by letters patent of Richard II confirmed by the king [*CPR 1396–9*, p.210; *1399–1401*, pp.18,63], which were shown to the escheator and jurors.

She died on 9 Dec. last.

C 137/22, no.23

ROGER FRANKELAYN

374 Writ 12 Dec. 1400.

YORK. Inquisition. Market Weighton. 21 March 1401.

He held 1 messuage and 3 bovates in Market Weighton of Stephen le Scrope, knight, son of Richard le Scrope, knight, by a rent of 2s., annual values, messuage 40d., land 10s.

He died on 24 Nov. last. William Frankelayn, chaplain, his son and heir, is aged 30 years and more.

C 137/22, no.24
E 149/76, no.2

ROBERT COYNE

375   Writ 18 Nov. 1400.

SHROPSHIRE. Inquisition. Market Drayton. 13 Dec.

He held by the courtesy of England after the death of Hugelina his wife, who held in her demesne as of fee:

Langley, a third part of the manor with the advowson, of the king in chief by knight service as a twelfth part of a knight's fee, annual value 51s.9d.

E [sic], the manor, of the lord of Woodcote by rent of a rose, annual value 41s.7d.

Shrewsbury, a burgage with garden, of the king in free burgage, annual value 6s.3d.

Leighton and Garmston, various lands and tenements, of the lady of Leighton, service unknown, annual vaue 46s.9d.

Brockton, certain lands and tenements, of the king in chief, service unknown, annual value 13d.

He held in his demesne as of fee:

Garmston, lands and tenements called 'Dounctonesplace', of the lady of Leighton, service unknown, annual value 21s.11d.; various lands and tenements of the inheritance of Thomas Cresset, deceased, of the same lady, service unknown, annual value 49s.7d.; and a pasture called 'Banasteresclos', of William Banastre by a rent of 13s.4d., annual value beyond the rent 12d.

He died on 12 Oct. last. Robert his son and heir is aged 8 years and more.

376   STAFFORD. Inquisition. Tyrley. 13 Dec. 1400.

He held in his demesne as of fee:

Weston Coyney, the manor, of the earl of Arundel by a rent of 6s.8d., annual value 106s.

Holme, the manor, of the lord of Careswall, service unknown, annual value 46s.2d.

Bucknall Marsh, various lands and tenements, of John Delves, service unknown, annual value 18s.9d.

'Smytheslond' in Halfhide, a toft and lands so called, with other adjacent lands, of the lord of Alton, service unknown, annual value 29s.3d.

Date of death and heir as above.

HUGELINA WIFE OF ROBERT COYNE

377   Writ 18 Nov. 1400.

SHROPSHIRE. Inquisition. Market Drayton. 13 Dec.

She held in her demesne as of fee a third part of the manor of Langley with the advowson, the manor of E [sic], lands in Leighton and Garmston, a burgage and garden in Shrewsbury and lands in Brockton [as described in no.375 above]. She married Robert Coyne and had issue Robert, both of whom survived her, and so Robert Coyne the elder held them by the courtesy of England.

She died on 4 Sept. last. Robert her son and heir is aged 8 years and more.

378 STAFFORD. Inquisition. Tyrley. 13 Dec. 1400.

She held nothing in the county. Date of death and heir as above.

C 137/22, no.25

RICHARD THOMER ESQUIRE

379 Writ 18 June 1401.

SOMERSET. Inquisition. Milborne Port. 28 June.

He held to himself and his heirs by his wife Alice 1 messuage, 60 a., 10 a. meadow, 8 a. wood and 31 a. pasture in Henstridge of the manor of Henstridge by knight service, which manor is in the king's hands by the forfeiture of John earl of Salisbury, annual value £4; and 1 messuage and 30 a. in Yenston of Amice widow of Stephen Derby, knight, by rent of a rose, annual value 40s.

He died on 19 Oct. John his son and heir is aged 8 years and more.

C 137/22, no.26

WILLIAM BARDE

380 YORK. Inquisition. Osgodby by Scarborough. 2 Sept. 1400.

He held in his demesne as of fee two parts of the manor of Osgodby by Scarborough, and the reversion of the third part which Margaret widow of Robert Barde, his father, holds in dower. It is held of the king in chief of the honour of Aumale by homage and fealty, annual value 40s.

He died on 28 May last. Robert his son and heir was aged 14 on 25 April.

Writ to assign dower to Agnes his widow in the presence of Roger de Stapilton, who has the wardship by letters patent, and the attorneys of Agnes. 11 Nov. 1401.

381 Writ 10 July 1401.

YORK. Inquisition. York castle. 12 Oct.

He held in his demesne as of fee two parts of the manor of Osgodby near Scarborough of the king of the honour of Aumale by homage and fealty, annual value 33s.4d.

He died on 28 May 1400. Robert Barde his son and heir was 15 on 23 April last. The king has received the issues and profits from the day of William's death by the hands of the escheators.

C 137/22, no.27
E 149/73, no.4

MARGARET BARDE

382 Writ 6 July 1401.

YORK. Inquisition. York castle. 12 Oct.

She held a third part of the manor of Osgodby in dower for life after the death of Robert Barde, her husband, with reversion to Robert, son of William, son of the said

Robert. It is held of the king of the honour of Aumale by homage and fealty; annual value 16s.8d.

She also held for life the manor of West Lutton by demise of her husband, with reversion as above. It is held of other than the king, service unknown, annual value 40s.

She died on 16 June. Robert, son of William Barde, son of Robert, is her heir, and was aged 15 on 23 April last.

C 137/22, no.27

JOHN CLEMENT OF LITTLE CARLTON

383 Writ 6 May 1401.

LINCOLN. Inquisition. Saltfleetby. 8 Oct. 1401.

Owing to his outlawry 60s. rent from a third part of the manor of Manby was taken into the king's hands. He held it in dower of Sybil his wife, who still lives. The third part of the manor is held of the earl of Richmond in socage, the amount of which, and how much the third part is worth beyond the rent, is unknown.

Who is heir and of what age is likewise unknown. He died on 15 Sept. 1396.

C 137/22, no.28

ROBERT DE PALTON

384 Writ 1 Dec. 1400.

OXFORD. Inquisition. Woodstock. 20 Dec.

He held in his demesne as of fee the manor of Shipton on Cherwell called 'Paltonescourt' and 10 virgates with the advowson, of John Lord Lovell by knight service as one fee, annual value £10. Also in Shipton he held 1 messuage of the manor, formerly of Richard Fouks, annual value 2 marks.

He died on 18 Aug. William his brother and heir is aged 21 years and more.

385 Writ 5 Sept. 1400.

HAMPSHIRE. Inquisition. Lymington. 2 Nov.

He held nothing in the county.

He died on 17 Aug. last. William his brother and heir was aged 20 on 8 Sept. last.

386 Writ 1 Dec. 1400.

HAMPSHIRE. Inquisition. Winchester. 24 Jan. 1401.

He held the manor of Ower in his demesne as of fee of William Asthorp, knight, as a quarter of a fee, annual value 5 marks.

He died on 18 Aug. William his brother and heir is 21 years and 17 weeks old.

387 WILTSHIRE. Inquisition. Salisbury. 27 Sept. 1400.

He held nothing in the county.

Date of death and heir as above [no.385].

388   Writ 1 Dec. 1400.

WILTSHIRE. Inquisition. Hindon. 10 March 1401.

He held:

Lake, the manor, of John de Monte Acuto, earl of Salisbury, by knight service, forfeited to the king, annual value £10.

Oare, the manor, of the lord of Camerton, in socage, annual value £4.

Draycot Fitz Payne, 100s. rent, of Lord Berkeley by knight service.

Calcote, 3 messuages, 3 virgates and 1 meadow of 8 a., of the honour of Wallingford by knight service, annual value 20s.

Chicklade, 1 messuage, 1 carucate and 20s. rent, of Lord Berkeley by knight service; annual value of the messuage and carucate 20s.

He died without heirs of his body on 18 Aug. last. William his brother and heir is aged 21 years and more.

389   Writ 5 Sept. 1400.

SOMERSET. Inquisition. Bruton. 24 Sept. 1400.

He held in his demesne as of fee:

Camerton, the manor with the advowson, of the bishop of Bath and Wells by knight service, annual value 10 marks.

Doulting, 1 carucate, of the abbot of Glastonbury by knight service, annual value 5 marks.

Holcombe and 'Dounhous', 2 tofts, 5 a. and 7 enclosed pastures, of John Doune in socage, annual value 18s.

'Haywode', 1 tenement, 33 a. and 7 a. meadow, of the earl of Ormonde by knight service, annual value 40s.

Date of death and heir as in last.

C 137/22, no.29
E 149/74, no.18

WILLIAM PALTON

390   Writ for proof of age, 17 Sept. 1401.

SOMERSET. Proof of age. Wells. 8 Oct.

[*3 names illegible*] and Abel Kendale, all aged 60 years and more, duly examined, state that William brother and heir of Robert Palton was born at Paulton and baptised in the chapel there on 8 Sept. 1379. He was therefore 22 on 8 Sept. last. They remember because they were at dinner with Elizabeth FitzRoger, lady of Chewton Mendip, when she was told of the birth and asked to be godmother.

Richard Michell, Thomas Sambrook, Richard Walbrond and Hugh Walbrond, all aged 50 years and more, on that day were together when they heard that John Harewell, then bishop of Bath and Wells, had a new bell made at Wells weighing eight thousand (?) pounds. William was therefore 22 on the date stated.

John Toner, Robert Ives, Henry Vykarys and John Cokhull, all aged 40 years and more, were together coming to Farmborough, when they met William Erlyngham coming from Bristol to Paulton to raise William from the font. He was therefore 22 on 8 Sept. last.

C 137/22, no.29, mm.12,13

RICHARD SON OF JOHN BROUNYNG

391   Writ 20 Oct. 1400.

GLOUCESTER. Inquisition. Gloucester. 2 Nov.

Richard, kinsman and heir of Thomas Rodberugh, died under age in the king's ward. He held in his demesne as of fee:

Harford, 1 messuage, 3 virgates of hilly land and 3 a. meadow, by knight service of William late earl of Stafford, who died in the king's ward. They are now held of Edmund earl of Stafford; annual value 13s.4d.

Rodborough, the manor, by knight service of the late king, of the manor of Minchinhampton, which belonged to the alien abbess of Caen. The late king granted it to the duke of Gloucester to hold during the war with France, but it is now held of the king in socage of the said manor by a rent of 20s. and by the service of carrying the money of the abbess from Minchinhampton to Southampton; annual value 73s.4d.

Thropp, 8 messuages, 1 carucate of hilly land, 2 watermills, 5 a. meadow, 3 a. wood and 30s. rent, of Roger de Mortimer, late earl of March, lately found to be held by knight service but really of the king in socage by the service of assisting at the holding of the hallmote of the earl at Bisley when reasonably summoned. They are now held of Edward Charlton and Eleanor his wife, countess of March, in her right; annual value £4.

Ebley, 3 messuages, 3 half virgates and 13s.4d. rent, of Reynold Cobham and Eleanor his wife, in her right, of the manor of Stonehouse by a rent of 2s., annual value 40s.

Notgrove, 4 messuages, 3 carucates of hilly land, 4 a. meadow, 20 a. pasture and 10s. rent, of Tideman, bishop of Worcester, by homage and fealty, annual value £4.

He died without heirs of his body on 1 May. Cecily his sister and heir is aged 13 years and more.

C 137/22, no.30

THOMAS DAYVILLE OF SOUTH CAVE

392   Writ 24 Feb. 1401.

Further writ of same date, ordering release of the lands to William Hungate, to whom the king has granted them [*CPR 1399–1401*, p.441].

YORK. Inquisition. Pocklington. 19 March.

He held in his demesne in fee tail:

South Cave, the manor, with appurtenances in Swanland and elsewhere, of Thomas de Moubray, under age in the king's ward, who holds in chief by knight service, annual value 20 marks.

Burland in Eastrington, the manor, and other lands and tenements in Burland, of the bishop of Durham by a rent of 30s., annual value beyond the rent £3.

Howden, lands and tenements, of the same bishop in burgage, annual value 13s.4d.

Spaldington, 40s. rent from the lands and tenements of Peter de Hay, payable by equal parts at Whitsun and Martinmas.

'Endewode' in Howdenshire, lands and tenements, of the same bishop, service unknown, annual value 12s.

He died on 1 Feb. last. Thomas his son and heir is aged 17 years.

C 137/22. no.31

JOHN RODENEY, KNIGHT

393   Writ 14 Jan. 1401.

SOMERSET. Inquisition. Keynsham. 10 Feb.

He held by knight service by the grant of John Lupeyate, parson of Backwell, John Horne, parson of Weston, Robert vicar of Westbury and Thomas Balon, to him, Katherine his wife, and the heirs of their bodies:

Backwell, the manor and advowson, of Lord Despenser, who is under age in the king's ward, annual value 6 marks.

Saltford, the manor and advowson, of the same, annual value 10 marks.

Twerton, the manor, of the same, annual value 10 marks.

Rodney Stoke, the manor, half of the bishop of Bath and Wells and half of the same lord, annual value £10.

Draycott and Cheddar, 2 messuages and 2 virgates, of Peter de Courteney, knight, annual value 20s.

He also held the manor of Lamyatt, half of the king as earl of Derby by knight service and 13s.4d. rent; part of the bishop of Bath and Wells of his manor of Creech by knight service; and the rest of the prior of St. John of Jerusalem of his manor of Evercreech; annual value £10. Also 6 messuages and 6 virgates in the hamlet of Hallatrow of Lord Despenser by knight service, annual value 40s.; and the manor of Dinder of the bishop of Bath and Wells by knight service, which manor Richard Virgo, Edith his wife and Isabel his daughter held by the grant of John Rodeney for a rent of 10 marks, with reversion to himself.

He died on 19 Dec. Walter his son and heir is aged 30 years and more.

394   Writ, *plenius certiorari*, as to the status of Lord Despenser in Rodeney's lands. 6 April 1401.

SOMERSET. Inquisition. Somerton. 2 May.

He held in fee tail the manors of Backwell, Saltford and Twerton and half the manor of Rodney Stoke by knight service of Lord le Despenser who is under age in the king's ward.

Thomas le Despenser, knight, who forfeited to the king, held the services owed by John Rodeney as parcel of the county of Gloucester by the grant of Edward I to Gilbert, sometime earl of Gloucester, his wife Joan and their heirs. They had three daughters, Eleanor, Elizabeth and Joan. Hugh le Despenser, son of the earl of Winchester, married Eleanor. The services were divided and those which Rodeney held were allocated to Eleanor and Hugh. They had two sons, Hugh and Edward, and after their deaths Hugh held them, and he died without heirs of his body. Then Edward held them and his son was Thomas le Despenser, who held as parcel of the honour of Gloucester. Thus this Thomas, who forfeited to the king, father of the present Lord Despenser, who is in the king's ward, held the services of the late John Rodeney in fee tail as parcel of the county of Gloucester.

C 137/22, no.32
E 149/77, no.13

ISABEL WIFE OF WILLIAM SEYNT JOHN

395 Writ 3 May 1401.

NORTHAMPTON. Inquisition. Moreton Pinkney. 11 May.

She held the manor of Moreton Pinkney for life of the king in chief as one quarter of a knight's fee, annual value 10 marks. Henry Grene, knight, gave it by royal licence to Giles de St. John, Isabel [his mother], and the heirs of the body of Giles. Isabel survived him and so held it.

She also held in her demesne as of fee a third part of the manors of Stoke Bruerne, Shutlanger and Alderton with the advowsons of Stoke Bruerne and Alderton on the third vacancy. They are held of Reynold de Grey of Ruthin, service unknown, annual value 10 marks.

She died on 28 April [30 April in E 149/77, no.4]. Margery wife of William Harwedon and daughter of Giles de St. John is heir, that is daughter of Giles, son of Isabel, and aged 30 years and more [34 in E 149/77, no.4].

C 137/23, no.33
E 149/77, no.4

THOMAS LOVELL, ESQUIRE

396 Writ 18 Sept. 1401.

KENT. Inquisition. Sittingbourne. 22 Sept.

He held the manor of Milsted for life by the courtesy of England, of the inheritance of his wife Joan, one of the daughters and heirs of Thomas Hageschawe, knight. It is held of the king in chief by homage; annual value £4.

He died on 11 Sept. Thomas his son and heir is aged 13 years and more.

397 Writ 18 Sept. 1401.

SOMERSET. Inquisition. Bruton. 2 Oct.

He held by the courtesy of England of the inheritance of Joan his wife:

Milton Clevedon by Bruton, the manor, of Richard de Sancto Mauro, knight, of his manor of Castle Cary, as two knight's fees, annual value £20.

East Wanstrow, one quarter of the manor, of John Dename, knight, by knight service, amount unknown, annual value 10 marks.

Date of death and heir as above. The marriage of Thomas the son belongs to Richard de Sancto Moro, as appears by a document shown to the jurors, and not to John Dename.

398 SOMERSET. Inquisition. Bruton. 25 June 1403.

He held, it is said, the manor of Milsted in Kent of the king in chief.

He held nothing of the king in chief in his demesne as of fee in Somerset and Dorset, but he held by the courtesy of England of the inheritance of Joan his wife:

Milton Clevedon by Bruton, the manor, of Richard de Sancto Mauro, knight, annual value £7.

Wanstrow, a quarter of the manor, of John Denham, knight, annual value 53s.4d.

Clevedon, a rent of £10 from the manor, of Lord le Despenser.

Date of death and heir, aged 15 years and more, as above. Since Thomas's death Richard de Sancto Mauro has taken the issues and profits of Milton Clevedon, John Denham those of Wanstrow, and John Bluet the £10 rent.

C 137/23, no.34
E 149/79, no.11

JOAN WIFE OF ROGER DE LA LEE

399 Writ 26 Oct. 1400.

SHROPSHIRE. Inquisition. Shrewsbury. 17 Nov.

She held in her demesne as of fee:

Langley, a third part of the manor, with the advowson of the chapel of Ruckley, of the king in chief as one third of a quarter of a knight's fee, annual value 40s.

'Le Lee', 1 messuage and 1 carucate of Robert Lee of Roden by a rent of 1d., annual value 26s.8d.

Hadnall, 1 messuage and 1 virgate, of the same by a rent of 1d., annual value 10s.

Leighton, 3 messuages and 3 virgates, of the abbot of Shrewsbury by a rent of 6s.8d., annual value 30s.; and 1 messuage and 1 nook, of Thomas earl of Arundel by a rent of 2s., annual value 10s.

Shrewsbury, 1 burgage, of the king in free burgage, annual value 2s.

She died on 18 Sept. Petronilla, wife of Robert Lee of Roden her daughter and heir is aged 22 years and more. Robert and Petronilla have no issue.

[Note on E 149/77, no.6] £6 8s.8d. yearly from 18 Sept. to 15 Nov., 8 weeks 3 days, 20s.10½d.

C 137/23, no.35
E 149/77, no.6

ROBERT TURK, KNIGHT

400 Writ 24 Jan. 1401.

CAMBRIDGE. Inquisition. Royston. 1 Feb.

He held 1 messuage and 10 a. in Orwell of John Beauford, marquess of Dorset, by a rent of 2s., annual value 8s.

He died on 27 Dec. last. Joan his daughter and heir is aged 26 years and more.

401 Writ 3 Jan. 1401.

BEDFORD. Inquisition. Luton. 8 Jan.

He held in his demesne as of fee:

Woodcroft in Luton parish, 1 messuage and 100 a., of the king in chief by knight service, annual value 40s., and no more because the land lies on the hills untilled and uncultivated.

Biscot, 1 messuage and 100 a., of Baldwin Bereford, knight, by a rent of 7 marks, annual value 5s.

Luton, 2 messuages and 100 a., service unknown, annual value £4.

He died on 27 Dec. Joan wife of John Waleys, his daughter and heir, is aged 26 years and more.

402 Writ 3 Jan. 1401.
HERTFORD. Inquisition. Buntingford. 12 Jan.
He held:

Aspenden, 1 messuage, 76 a. and 2 a. meadow [1 tenement called 'Taryes', 80 a. and 2 a. pasture in E 149/76] by a rent of 22d. and attendance at the sheriff's tourn twice yearly, annual value 4 marks; and 4 a. in the field called 'Le Legh' in the parish by a rent of 1d.; annual value 16d.

Wakeley, the manor and advowson, 300 a. and 15 a. meadow [and a rent of 40d. in E 149/76], of William FitzRauff by a rent of 14s., annual value 10 marks.

Ardeley, 100 a., 10 a. wood and 1 a. meadow [and a rent of 13s.4d. in E 149/76], of the manor of Ardeley by a rent of 16s. and suit of court every 3 weeks, annual value 6 marks.

Cottered, 40 a. and 2 a. meadow, of Andrew Bures and Ralph Cheny by a rent of 16s., annual value 20s.

Hitchin, 11 cottages and 15 a. [40 a. in E 149/76], of the manor of Hitchin by a rent of 4s. and suit of court every 3 weeks, annual value 2 marks.

Flamstead, 1 toft and 30 a., of the prior of Dunstable of the manor of Flamstead by a rent of 5s.6d., 1 lamb, 1 lb. cumin and suit of court every 3 weeks, annual value 6s.8d.

He was true patron of a chapel called Biggin in Hitchin [and a chantry near Hitchin in E 149/76].

Date of death and heir as above.

403 Writ 3 Jan. 1401.
LONDON. Inquisition. 9 Jan.
He held nothing in London.
He died on 28 December between 6 and 7 a.m. Heir as above.

C 137/23, no.36
E 149/76, no.8

KATHERINE DE NOTYNGHAM

404 Writ 6 March 1401.
BERKSHIRE. Inquisition [?East] Ilsley. 10 May.

She died on 6 Feb. last, holding for life 1 messuage, 1 carucate, 2 a. meadow, 30s. rent, pasture for 8 oxen going with the herd of the abbot of Reading, and the pasture called Northbrook, several pasture for 300 sheep on the Down, and pasture for all manner of beasts on the common Down without rendering pannage, all belonging to the messuage and lands with other appurtenances in Blewbury; with reversion to William son and heir of William Venour, formerly citizen and grocer of London, to whom Alexander Meryng and Agnes his wife granted the reversion by a fine of 1381–2 [CP 25(1) 12/75, no.13]. They are held of the king in chief as a quarter of a fee and by a rent of 6d. payable at the hundred of Moreton at Michaelmas; annual value 5 marks.

No heir is known.

405   Writ, *plenius certiorari*, reciting the findings of the above inquisition, and stating that by the fine mentioned in it Alexander Meryng and Agnes his wife granted the reversion to William Venour, Stephen Haynes, Roger Asshebournham, John Caldewell, clerk, and Philip Cradelee, and the heirs of William; that Stephen, Roger, John and Philip are dead, and the holdings should descend to William Venour, junior, who is of full age. Order to inquire if this is so. 14 June 1401.

BERKSHIRE. Inquisition. East Ilsley. 18 June.

She died on 6 Feb. She held for life exactly as in the last, except that the reversion was to William Venour, Stephen Haym, Roger Ashebournham, John Caldewell, clerk, and Philip Caradelee, and the heirs of William Venour. William, Stephen, Roger, John and Philip are dead, and the reversion should be to William son of William Venour, who is aged 30 years and more.

No heir is known.

C 137/23, no.37
E 152/369, no.3

THOMAS SON AND HEIR OF WILLIAM MARCHE, KNIGHT

406   Writ 10 Nov. 1400.

NORFOLK. Inquisition. Attleborough. 18 Nov.

Owing to the death of William Marche, knight, who held of the king in chief, and the minority of Thomas his son and heir, the manors of Stanhoe, and Crowshall in Attleborough, and 1 tenement called 'Kyngeshalle' and 100 a. in Stanhoe were taken into the king's hands and so remain.

The site of the manor of Stanhoe is held of Hugh Bavent by a rent of 4d.; 100 a., part of the manor, are held of the prior of Castle Acre by 3s. rent; 40 a. are held of the heirs of William Sharneborne by 20d. rent; 11 a. of the abbot of North Creake by 12d. rent; 12 a. of William Calthorp, knight, by 2s. rent; 20 a. of Henry bishop of Norwich by 12d. rent; and 100 a. of William de Souche knight by 4s. rent; annual value 7 marks.

Crowshall manor is held of Lady Cromwell of her manor of Plassing Hall by a rent of a pair of gilt spurs or 6d., annual value £10.

The tenement called 'Kyngeshalle' and 100 a. are held of the king in chief by the service of keeping a brachet, annual value 40s.

Thomas Marche died on 19 May 1400. John Marche his brother and heir was aged 13 years and more at his death. Joan wife of Thomas Chipstead is sister and heir of John Marche and aged 17 years and more.

JOHN BROTHER AND HEIR OF THOMAS MARCHE

407   Writ 15 Nov. 1400.

NORFOLK. Inquisition. Wymondham. 20 Nov.

The lands etc. listed in the last inquisition are in the king's hands owing to the death of Thomas Marche and the minority of John his brother and heir.

K

John died on 15 Oct. Joan wife of Thomas Chipsted, his sister and heir, is aged 17 years and more.

C 137/23, nos.38,38b
E 149/76, nos.11,12

MAURICE BERKELEY, KNIGHT

408 Writ 15 Oct. 1400.

WILTSHIRE. Inquisition. Amesbury. 16 Dec.

He held to himself and his heirs male with remainder to Thomas de Berkeley, Lord Berkeley, the manors of Brigmerston and Milston with the advowson of Milston, of the same Lord Berkeley by a yearly rent of 1 barbed arrow, annual value 10 marks.

He held to himself and his heirs that manor of Brigmerston which was formerly of Stephen de Brightmerston, of the above manor of Brigmerston, service unknown, annual value 5 marks; and the manor of Milston 'Gogeon' of the same manor of Brigmerston, service unknown, annual value 50s.

He died on 2 Oct. Joan his wife is pregnant. Failing Joan's child, Isabel daughter of Maurice Berkeley, aunt of Maurice, would be heir, aged 50 years and more.

409 Writ 12 Oct. 1400.

GLOUCESTER. Inquisition. Chipping Sodbury. 8 Nov.

He held:

Rockhampton, lands which were formerly parts of the manor: rents, services, feedings and a pasture called 'Shepardynde', annual value 4 marks; a parcel called 'le Lese' of about 20 a., another called 'Twentyacres', and a third called 'Nynetenacres', worth 8 marks with the advowson of the church there; making by estimation one sixth of the manor, in his demesne as of fee of the king in chief, service unknown.

King's Weston, Aylburton and Rockhampton, the manors, jointly with Joan his wife, who survives, by the feoffment under royal licence [*CPR 1399–1401*, p.288] by John Berkeleigh and John Denham, knights, Thomas Stowell and Thomas Mulleward, chaplain, to them and the heirs of their bodies, with remainder to the right heirs of Maurice; annual values, King's Weston £40, Aylburton 50 marks, Rockhampton, excluding the parcels mentioned above, 40 marks; held of the king in chief, services unknown.

Uley and Bradley, the manors, of Thomas Lord Berkeley, service unknown, annual values 20 marks and 10 marks.

Stoke Gifford and Walle, the manors, to himself and the heirs male of his body, with remainder in default of such heirs to Thomas de Berkelegh, of the bishop of Worcester, service unknown, annual value 20 marks.

Date of death and heirs as above.

C 137/23, no.39
E 152/355, no.9

JOHN ROCHES, KNIGHT

410 Writ 8 Oct. 1400.

WILTSHIRE. Inquisition. Marlborough. 27 Oct.

He once held in his demesne as of fee among others the manors of Wroughton and Winterslow, the latter of the king in chief, service unknown; lands, tenements, meadows, feedings, pastures, rents, services and woods in Bromham, Berwick Bassett and West Chisenbury; and a lordship in Hardenhuish, with 18s. rent and other profits and services of the lordship.

By the name of John Roches, knight, he granted these premises with 2 marks rent from John Cokkulbergh for lands and tenements which he held for life in 'Browton' [recte Brinkworth] by his grant and with reversion to himself; 5 marks rent from Nicholas Webbe for lands which he held for life in Broughton Gifford, by similar grant, and the reversions of the lands; and the reversion of all the lands and tenements which Robert Kent, now deceased, similarly held for life by like grant in Chelworth; to master William Byde and Stephen Botiller, their heirs and assigns, by his charter shown to the jurors, and dated 2 July 1377. They had seisin and the tenants attorned to them.

By their charter dated 4 Feb. 1378, likewise shown to the jurors, they granted to John Roches, Willelma his wife and the heirs of their bodies, with remainder failing such heirs to his right heirs, the said manors, lordship, rents and other holdings and reversions, including the rents of John Cokkulbergh in Brinkworth and of Nicholas Webbe in Broughton Gifford, the reversions of these lands and of the lands of Robert Kent in Chelworth and Crudwell. By livery of seisin and the attornment of the tenants John and Willelma duly held them. Then on 1 March 1390 John, disregarding the issue he and Willelma then had, gave by his charter to Maud widow of Robert de la Mare, knight, Lawrence Bren, William Storton, William Weston and the heirs of the body of Maud, with reversion, failing such heirs, to his own right heirs, all the above lands and all his lands in Calne, Compton Bassett, Cherhill, Devizes, Chelworth, Berwick Bassett, Eastcott, Crudwell, Winterbourne Bassett, Richardson, Chiseldon, West Chisenbury, Alderbury and Hardenhuish, with all his holdings in the lordship, and the reversions of the lands in Horton and Shaw by Melksham which John and Willelma secured by a fine of Richard II [CP 25(1) 256/54, no.12]. By this gift the feoffees were seised of them and still hold.

John and Willelma formerly secured to themselves and the heirs of their bodies the manor of Whaddon from Thomas Gorges, senior. It is held of the duchy of Lancaster of the manor of Trowbridge, service unknown.

All except the manor of Winterslow are held of other than the king, but of whom is unknown.

Hence he held nothing but the manor of Whaddon when he died and that jointly with his wife, who still lives.

He died on 20 Sept. 1401 [2 Henry IV, recte 1400]. Robert son and heir of both John and Willelma is aged 11 years and more.

Richard II in parliament in 1398 [Rot.Parl. III, p.369] pardoned and released his lieges for alienation without licence among other offences. By virtue of this the king has no rights in the manor of Winterslow or in any of the above lands and tenements owing to the death of John Roches, the minority of the heir or any alienation.

[Many readings doubtful].

C 137/23, no.40

JOAN HESILRYG

411 YORK. Inquisition. York. 22 Jan. 1401.
Joan wife of Donald Hesilryg, knight, held the manor of Hemlington of Thomas

late earl of Kent at farm for life by a rent of 10 marks, with reversion to the earl who forfeited it, annual value 20 marks.

She also held for life in Cottingham 2 messuages, 6 bovates, 12 a. meadow and 1 piece of land. Edmund de Brygham and John de Spayne, junior, were enfeoffed in fee simple on condition that she held for life with reversion to the same earl and his heirs, annual value £10.

She died on 18 Dec. last.

412 Writ 30 Jan. 1401.

NORTHUMBERLAND. Inquisition. Newcastle upon Tyne castle. 7 April.

Robert de Esselyngton once held the manor of Eslington and half the vills of Whittingham, Thrunton and Barton in his demesne as of fee, and he married Elizabeth. They had issue George, Elizabeth and Isabel. When he died the manors descended to George his son and heir. He died and they passed to Elizabeth and Isabel, his sisters and heirs, as shown by the inquisition on him [*CIPM* IX, no.454].

Then Elizabeth, Robert's widow, married John Heron, knight, and after the death of George she was dowered in the chancery of Edward III of a third part with remainder to Elizabeth and Isabel.

Isabel granted to Donald Hesilrygge one half of two parts of the manor of Eslington and half of two parts of half the vills by a fine of Edward III [CP 25(1) 181/13, no.132; see also nos.117, 119, 120, 133] with the reversion of half of the third parts which Elizabeth her mother held in dower. Donald granted them to Thomas Surtes, knight, Hugh Westwyk, Edmund Hesilrygge, and their heirs and assigns. John Heron attorned to them. They granted them by their charter to Donald, Joan his wife, and the heirs of Donald.

Elizabeth died, and her holdings came to Isabel as sister and heir. She by a fine of Edward III conveyed them to Donald and Joan and the heirs of Donald [CP 25(1) 181/13, no.133]. Again John Heron attorned to them.

John Warton holds lands and tenements in Framlington of Donald and Joan of their manor of Eslington by a rent of 40d. yearly, with reversion to John Midylham and Eleanor his wife, and the heirs of Eleanor after the death of John.

Elizabeth wife of John Heron died. The third part of the manor and of the half vills then came to Joan for life after the death of Donald for the reasons already given. Donald died without heirs of his body and William Hesilrygge was his brother and heir, and to him Thomas Hesilrygge was son and heir, aged 30 years and more.

Joan died holding the above manor of the king in chief by a rent of 6 marks payable by the sheriff, and 16s. to the castle of Bamburgh for the service of carting logs (*truncagium*). The half vills of Whittingham, Thrunton and Barton are held of the king by a rent of 40d. payable by the sheriff, annual value 40s. and no more these days because of destruction by the Scots.

She died on 21 Dec. 1400. John Warton is next heir and aged 30 years and more.

C 137/23, no.41
E 149/76, no.3

ROBERT TAUK

413 Writ 27 July 1401.

WILTSHIRE. Inquisition. Salisbury. 6 Aug.

He held by the courtesy of England of the inheritance of his late wife Elizabeth 1 messuage, 18 a. and 2 a. meadow in West Dean, of Miles Stabiltone, knight, and Henry Popham, services unknown, annual value 5s.4d.

He died on 9 April. Thomas son of Robert and Elizabeth is heir of Elizabeth and aged 21 years and more.

414 Writ 6 May 1401.

HAMPSHIRE. Inquisition. Winchester. 4 July.

He held by the courtesy of England in the right and inheritance of Elizabeth late his wife:

West Tytherley, half the manor with the advowson, of the king in chief in grand serjeanty, annual value £10.

East Dean, the manor, of the lord of the manor of East Tytherley, service unknown, annual value £6.

Stanbridge, 1 messuage, 40 a., 6 a. meadow and a fishery in the river Test beginning at 'le blakedyche' and leading to 'le Muxemede', of Thomas Kenne, service unknown, annual value 13s.4d.

Romsey, various tenements, of the abbess of Romsey in socage, annual value 40s.

Southampton, various tenements, of the king in burgage, annual value 20s.

Date of death and heir as above.

415 Writ 12 July 1401.

SUSSEX. Inquisition. Chichester. 22 July.

He held in his demesne as of fee:

Chichester, 1 cottage outside the East Gate, annual value 2s.; 1 tenement in East Street next the tenement of William Neel, nil because totally waste; 1 messuage in North Street next St. Olave's church on the north, nil because ruinous; 1 messuage there formerly of William atte Hoke, 2s.; 1 toft formerly of John Pleystowe, 4d.; 1 cottage opposite the church of St. Peter the Great, 2s.; and 1 croft outside the North Gate in the liberty called 'Honycroft', containing 15 a. at 8d., 10s.; all held of the king in free burgage by a rent of 15s.3d. at Hockday and suit of court in the city each fortnight, with relief after the death of each tenant, and similarly whenever there is an alienation according to the custom of the city.

Westhampnett, the manor, of which the site is worth nothing yearly; 2 gardens of 1½ a., 2s.; 1 dovecot, 5s.; 95 a. at 4d.; 16 a. of separate pasture at 4d.; and 1 watermill, nil; held of lord de Seynt Johan of his manor of Halnaker by a rent of 13s.4d. and suit of court every three weeks. Also in Hampnett 1 messuage, nil because totally waste; a dovecot, 3s.4d.; a garden of 1½ a., 2s.; and 100 a. at 6d.; held of the same lord by knight service; and of the prior of Boxgrove 1 toft and 21 a. by a rent of 14s. and 1 lb. pepper at the 4 terms, worth nothing beyond the rent.

He was accustomed to render for those lands to the bishop of Exeter 5s. and to the prior of Shulbrede 6s., but for which parcels is unknown.

Eartham, 1 messuage, annual value nil because ruinous; a garden of ½ a., 12d.; 36 a. at 3d.; and 4 a. pasture at 3d.; of the earl of Arundel of his manor of Bignor, service unknown.

He died on 9 April. Thomas his son and heir was aged 20 years and more on 1 Aug.

C 137/23, no.42

E 149/77, no.14

PHILIP LE DESPENSER, KNIGHT

416   Writ 8 Aug. 1401.

YORK. Inquisition. Hessle. 3 Sept.

He held in his demesne as of fee:

Cowden in Holderness, 7 messuages, 10 tofts, 24 bovates, and 1 toft in which a windmill was formerly built, of Thomas de Lancastre, knight, steward of England, of the honour of Aumale by knight service, annual value £8.

Great Cowden, 2 tofts, 1 bovate and 12d. rent, of the archbishop of York by foreign service, annual value 10s.

Paull, 3 tofts, 4 bovates and 4s.6d. assize rent.

Paull Holme, 1 messuage and 1 bovate.

Keyingham, 12 a. pasture called 'Petilandes'.

Keyingham and Ottringham in Holderness, 1 piece of 10 a. called 'Aldercroft' and 1 toft and 12 a., all held of the same Thomas of the honour of Aumale by knight service, annual value 8 marks.

Hedon, 16d. assize rent, of the same.

Dringhoe, 4 tofts, 9 bovates and 2d. rent; and Dunnington, 6 tofts, 24 bovates and a court held once yearly at Michaelmas; of the master of St. John of Jerusalem in England by a rent of 5s., annual value £7 6s.8d.

Swinefleet, 3 tofts, with ½a. in Reedness with appurtenances in Swinefleet, of Thomas Reednesse, knight, by a rent of 2d., annual value 26s.8d.

Parlington, the manor, of the king as of the crown by the service of a quarter of a knight's fee, annual value £12.

He died on 4 Aug. last. Philip his son and heir is aged 36 years and more.

Writ to give seisin, 14 Sept. 1401.

417   Writ 8 Aug. 1401.

ESSEX. Inquisition. Toppesfield. 10 Sept.

He held in his demesne as of fee the manor of Camoys in Toppesfield of the earl of March of the honour of Clare, the earl being under age in the king's ward, service unknown, annual value £10.

Date of death and heir as above.

418   Writ 8 Aug. 1401.

LINCOLN. Inquisition. Boston. 27 Aug.

Henry de Beamys, knight, once held in his demesne as of fee the manor of Great Limber, and, except for 12s. rent and the services due from the tenement of Nicholas de Lymbergh, clerk, granted it by licence of Richard II [*CPR 1381–5*, p. 562] to Philip le Despenser, senior, Philip le Despenser his son, and James de Roos, knights, by his charter dated at Limber on 3 June 1383. The royal licence and his charter were shown to the jurors. It was ancient demesne held of the king, service unknown, annual value 100s.

He died at Goxhill on 4 Aug., heir as above.

C 137/23, no.44
E 149/75, no.8

CONSTANCE WIFE OF PETER DE MAULEY THE SIXTH

419 Writ 21 June 1401.

YORK. Inquisition. Malton. 12 July.

She held in dower, of the king in chief by knight service by the assignment of Thomas de Percy, earl of Worcester, guardian of the lands and heir of Peter de Mauley, son of Peter son of Peter VI, her husband:

Bainton, the manor, with its members in Bainton, Neswick, Kilnwick, Applegarth and Hunmanby, annual value 100 marks.

Akenberg, the manor, 40s.

Lythe, the advowson, 10 marks; Hinderwell, the advowson, 66s.8d.; and a third part of the advowson of Bainton, annual value of the whole being £20.

She held in fee tail:

Seaton in Cleveland, the manor, by the grant of William Ak, parson of Lockington, John Braythewelle, parson of Hinderwell, Robert Lorimer and William de Malton to Peter de Mauley and Constance then his wife, and the heirs male of their bodies, with remainder to the right heirs of Peter. Therefore it should remain to Peter, son of Peter, son of Peter. It is held of John de Darcy, knight, of his manor of Whorlton, annual value 100s.

Healaugh and Reeth in Swaledale, half the manor, by a fine of 1375 [CP 25(1) 277/137 no.43] to Peter and Constance his wife, with remainder to the heirs male of his body and his right heirs. It should descend as above. It is held of Ralph earl of Westmorland of the castle and manor of Richmond by knight service, annual value £20.

Bransholme, the castle and manor, Sutton on Hull, the manor, and the six advowsons of the chantries of 6 chaplains celebrating in the chapel of Sutton in Holderness, by virtue of a grant by Richard Ravenser, Robert Lorimer and Thomas de Beverley to Thomas de Sutton, knight, and Agnes his wife, and the heirs male of their bodies, with remainder in tail male to Peter de Mauley and Constance his wife, and Peter de Mauley his son and Margery his wife, with reversion to the right heirs of Thomas de Sutton. Thomas and Agnes died without heirs male of their bodies. Peter and Margery had issue Peter to whom the manors and advowsons should descend. The castle and manor of Bransholme are held of Robert Hilton, knight, service unknown, annual value 40s. The manor of Sutton on Hull and the advowsons are held of Thomas of Lancastre, steward of England, of the manor of Burstwick and of the lordship of Holderness, services unknown; annual values, manor £40, chantries each 5 marks.

Constance died on 9 June. John Godard her son and heir is aged 14 years and more.

C 137/23, no.45
E 152/364

BALDWIN FREVYLL, KNIGHT

420 Writ, ordering return of inquisition already taken by the late escheator. 2 May 1401.

SURREY. Inquisition. Southwark. 19 Oct. 1400.

He held nothing that could be taken into the king's hands. Long before his death he gave by charter to Thomas de Hulton, clerk, Thomas de Stoke, William de Lee of Stotfold, William de Boule, Alan Waldeeyef and John de Yoxhale his manors of Lea Marston and Stratford by Tamworth in Warwickshire, Gunthorpe and Lowdham in Nottinghamshire, and Ashtead in Surrey.

He also gave them the reversion of all his lands which Joyce his mother, Thomas de Stoke, William de Boule, John Chamberleyn, Roger Botyler, Thomas de Preston and John de London held of his inheritance for their lives, as dower, or by any other title.

Ashtead manor is not held of the king in chief but of the earl of Arundel of his castle of Reigate by a rent of 13s.4d.

He died on 4 Oct. Baldwin his son and heir was aged 5 years on Midsummer day.

421   Writ 14 Oct. 1400

SURREY. Inquisition. East Clandon. 25 Nov.

He held the manor of Ashtead of the king in chief as one knight's fee. There are 1 hall, various chambers and 1 garden, annual value nil; 1 byre and 1 stable, also nil; a dovecot, 2s.; 300 a. at 6d.; £9 13s.4d. rents of free tenants and villeins, that is 48s.4d. at each of the four principal terms.

He died on 6 Oct. Baldwin his son and heir was aged 2 years at Midsummer last.

422   Writ 14 Oct. 1400.

WARWICK. Inquisition. Coleshill. 26 Oct.

He held the castle of Tamworth in his demesne as of fee of the king in chief by knight service, annual value £10.

Henry Caytewayte, William de Boule and others held two parts of the manor of Middleton and the manor of Wyken by Coventry in their demesne as of fee and by a charter granted them to Baldwin Frevill and Joan his wife and the heirs of their bodies, with remainder to Joyce, widow of Baldwin, father of Baldwin Frevill, and the right heirs of the younger Baldwin. Joan died without heirs and Baldwin married Maud and had issue Baldwin. The elder Baldwin is dead and the manors should to to Adam de Peshale, knight, and Joyce, now his wife.

Wyken manor is held of the prior of Coventry, service unknown, annual value £10. The two parts of Middleton manor are held of the dean of Tamworth, annual value 100s.

He died on 4 Oct. Baldwin his son and heir is aged 4 years.

423   Writ, ordering an inquisition if not already held. 10 Dec. 1400. [Endorsement] that before the arrival of the writ the escheator had taken the inquisition, a copy of which is attached. He gave the inquisition to William Slepe, [escheator in Shropshire], at Warwick on 5 December to be delivered to the chancery without delay, and Slepe swore that he would so deliver it.

WARWICK. Inquisition. Coleshill. A copy of the last.

424   WARWICK. Inquisition. Coventry. 21 Jan. 1401.

He held in his demesne as of fee:

Tamworth, the castle with its members, of the king in chief by knight service, annual value £12.

Stipershill, the court with the warren, of the king in chief, service unknown, annual value £3.

Middleton, two parts of the manor, of the college of Tamworth, service unknown, annual value 40 marks.

Lea Marston and Stratford by Tamworth, the manors, of whom held and by what service unknown, annual value £20.

Wyken, the manor, of the prior of Coventry, service unknown, annual value £12.

Date of death as above. Baldwin his son and heir was aged 2 on Midsummer day last.

Adam de Pershale, knight, has entered the manors of Middleton and Wyken, title unknown.

425   Writ, *plura*, 5 Feb. 1401.

WARWICK. Inquisition. Tamworth. 10 March.

He held the castle of Tamworth and the court of Stipershill [as in no.424].

He held a third part of Middleton, which he purchased from John Hillary, of the college of Tamworth, service unknown. William Boule and Henry Caytewayte, clerks, held the manors of Lea Marston and Stratford by Tamworth, and a third part of Middleton, described as all the lands, tenements, rents and services in Middleton formerly of John Dymmok, and granted them to Baldwin Frevill, Joan his wife, and the heirs of their bodies, and, failing such heirs, to Joyce formerly wife of Baldwin Frevill, knight, for life, and the right heirs of Baldwin Frevill, the grandfather.

The same William Boule and Henry Caytewayte, clerks, gave them also the manor of Wyken by Coventry, except the lands which William de Repyndon, Ralph Baudy, William de Sewale, junior, Richard Benet, John Carter, John Aleynson, William Anable, junior, John Burbage and William Anable, senior, separately held in the same, until the manor of Lea Marston should be quit of a rent of 20 marks which Eleanor de Launde has and takes from it. Whenever it should be freed from the annuity by the death of Eleanor or otherwise the manor of Wyken, except those lands, should remain to Adam de Peshale, knight, and Joyce for the life of Joyce, and they should also have the excepted lands of William de Repyndon and the others named, to Baldwin and Joan and the heirs of their bodies until the manor of Stratford be freed from a rent of 7 marks which Adam de Breton, clerk, has. When it is so freed by the death of Adam de Breton or otherwise, it shall remain, except the above, to Adam and Joyce for her life, and after her death to Baldwin Frevill and his heirs.

Adam de Breton and Eleanor de la Launde are dead. Joan died without heirs of herself and Baldwin. Then Baldwin married Maud, and had a son also called Baldwin and died.

The above manors and third parts should remain to Adam de Peshale, knight, for the life of Joyce, now his wife. Wyken is held of the abbey of Combe, service unknown, annual value £10; the third part of Middleton manor of the dean of Tamworth, service unknown, annual value 10 marks; and the manors of Lea Marston and Stratford of the castle of Tamworth, service unknown, annual value £10.

He died on 4 Oct. Baldwin his son and next heir was aged 4 at Midsummer last.

Baldwin Frevill, knight, the father, gave by charter to John Buttort and Richard Fyton, knights, Henry Caytewayt and William Boule, clerks, William Purfrey and Henry Standych his manor of Shortley by Coventry on condition that they enfeoffed Baldwin and Joyce and the heirs and assigns of Baldwin. John Byttort, Richard Fyton and Henry Standych died. The others granted the manor to Roger de Aston, parson of Weston under Lizard, John Styward and others, their heirs and assigns contrary to the above condition. In virtue of this alienation the king entered by his escheator, in right of the heir of Baldwin, in the king's ward. It is held of the prior of Coventry, service unknown, annual value 10 marks.

426 Writ 14 Oct. 1401.

NOTTINGHAM. Inquisition. Nottingham. 8 Nov.

He held nothing which could be taken into the king's hands.

Date of death and heir, aged 5 years at Midsummer, as above.

C 137/23, no.46
E 149/77, no.17
E 152/363

ISABEL WIDOW OF WALTER FAUCONBERGE

427 YORK. Inquisition. Stamford Bridge. 15 June 1401.

She held the manor of Rise with 2½ carucates in Withernwick belonging to it; 2 carucates in Catwick; 6 carucates in Catfoss; 2 carucates and 3 bovates in Dringhoe; 1 carucate in Ulrome; 3 carucates in Marton; ½ carucate in South Frodingham; 1 carucate in Bilton; 2 carucates in North Skirlaugh; 2 bovates in Hornsea Burton; 3 carucates in Withernwick and Great Hatfield; and 6 carucates in Bewholme; all of Thomas of Lancastre of the honour of Aumale by knight service and suit of court every 3 weeks at the wapentake of Holderness, and 9s. yearly for the guard of Skipsea castle.

She also held the manor of Eastburn, except 2 messuages and 2 bovates there, under a fine of 1360 [CP 25(1) 275/124, no.40] between Walter de Faukonberge and Isabel, and William Tykton and Hugh Swattok, chaplains, by which Eastburn and Rise were granted to Walter and Isabel in tail male with remainder to the right heirs of Walter. All the premises except the manor of Eastburn are parcels of the manor of Rise in demesne or in service.

Eastburn manor is held of the king in chief by knight service, annual value 15 marks payable by equal parts at Easter and Michaelmas. Rise is worth 24 marks, payable by equal parts at Whitsun and Martinmas, and the lands in Withernwick £10 yearly payable at the same terms.

Walter died without male issue by Isabel. The reversion therefore descended to Thomas Faukonberge, knight, son and heir of Walter. Afterwards in the quindene of Midsummer 1372 a fine [not found] was levied between John de Neville, knight, and Thomas son of Walter, by which Thomas granted his estate in these manors to John, and Isabel attorned to him. He died and the reversion descended to Ralph Neville, earl of Westmorland, his son and heir, now aged 30 years and more.

Isabel died on 19 May. John Bygot, knight, son and heir of John Bygot, knight, brother of Isabel, is next heir and aged 26 years and more.

428 Writ 23 May 1401.

YORK. Inquisition. Thirsk. 27 June.

She held for life:

High Worsall in the liberty of Allerton, the manor, with remainder to John Sayer and John son of John Laurensson, kinsmen and heirs of Thomas de Seton, knight. It is held of Walter bishop of Durham of his manor of Northallerton, in right of his church of St. Cuthbert, Durham, by knight service, annual value 40s.

South Kilvington, 6 messuages and 11 bovates of arable and meadow, with remainder as above, of Stephen le Scrope, knight, of his manor of Upsall, service unknown, annual value 6 marks.

Pockthorpe, the manor, with remainder as above, of Henry Percy, earl of Northumberland, as of his manor of Spofforth, service unknown, annual value 20s.

South Otterington, half the manor, with remainder to Elizabeth who was wife of Adam Bekwith and her heirs, of the abbot of Byland in right of his church of St. Mary, service unknown, annual value 100s.

John Sayer is aged 5 years and more; John son of John Laurencesone 17 and more. Date of death and heir as above.

429   YORK. Inquisition. Thirsk. 27 June 1401.

She held in dower a third part of the castle and manor of Skelton in Cleveland and a third part of the manor of Marske, parcel of the manor of Skelton, with reversion to Henry Percy, earl of Northumberland, for the life of Thomas Fauconberge, knight, who is still living, by a grant of Thomas, made with licence of Edward III [*CPR 1370–4. p.295*], by which he gave two parts of the manor and castle of Skelton and of the manor of Marske, with reversion of the remaining parts after the death of Isabel, to the earl and John de Felton, knight. Isabel attorned for the third parts. Afterwards the earl and John de Felton conveyed them to Thomas de Tweng, clerk, Roger Lascels, knight, and Robert Lyon, vicar of Marske in Cleveland, for the life of Thomas Fauconberge by royal licence. Thomas Tweng and Roger Lascels died. The two parts and the reversion of the third therefore remained to Robert Lyon. He conveyed them by his charter to the earl, William Latymer, Nicholas de Carreu, Michael de Ravendale, clerk, John Lasyngby of Rounton and John Capon for the said term, again with licence of Edward III [*CPR 1374–7, p.177*]. All are dead except the earl, to whom they should remain for the said term. They are held of the king in chief of the crown by knight service. The third part is worth 10 marks yearly.

Date of death and heir as above.

Writ to give seisin, 4 July 1401 [*CFR XII, pp.112–3*].

C 137/24, no.47
E 149/75, no.7
E 152/364, 365

ISABEL WIDOW OF JOHN DE SUTTON

430   Writ 6 Feb. 1401.

WORCESTER. Inquisition. Worcester. 19 Feb.

She held the vill of Dudley to herself and her heirs male, of the king as parcel of the castle of Dudley in Staffordshire, which is held of the king in chief as half a barony, by the grant of Stephen Swetmon of Dudley and John Colleshull, chaplain, to Isabel and John de Sutton, formerly her husband, and the heirs male of their bodies, by a fine made with licence of Edward III [*CPR 1340–3, p.1*; CP 25(1) 287/40, no.284], annual value £22.

She died on 10 April 1397. John de Sutton is next heir, being son of John, son of John, son of Isabel and John, and aged 21 years 3 weeks and more. John Beauford, earl of Somerset, has occupied the vill since the death of Isabel and taken the profits by the grant of Richard II [*CPR 1396–9, p.109*].

431 Writ 6 Feb. 1401.

STAFFORD. Inquisition. Wolverhampton. 17 Feb.

She held to herself and her heirs male by the grant of Stephen Swetmon of Dudley and John Colleshull by a fine [as above]:

Dudley castle, with the manors of Sedgley, Kingswinford and Rowley Regis as members of the castle, of the king in chief by the service of half a barony; annual values, castle nil, Sedgley £60, Kingswinford £4 beyond £11 10s. payable at the exchequer at Easter and Michaelmas as fee farm, Rowley Regis 10 marks.

Tipton, 1 toft, 1 carucate, 6 a. meadow and 6 a. pasture, of John Hervyle by a rent of 12d.

She also held by the grant of Nicholas, rector of Kingswinford, to John and herself for their lives, with remainder to Thomas their son for life and the right heirs of John, the manors of Himley, annual value 8 marks, Swindon 100s., and Upper Penn 12 marks. They are held as members of the castle of Dudley.

Date of death, heir, and holding by the earl of Somerset as above.

432A Writ 6 Feb. 1401.

GLOUCESTER AND THE ADJACENT MARCH OF WALES. Inquisition. Cardiff. 16 Feb.

She held for life in Glamorgan and Morgannok the castle of Dinas Powis and half the manors and advowson of Dinas Powis and Llanedarn, of Thomas late Lord Despenser as half a knight's fee, by the grant of John de Sutton, knight, and Joan his wife, by a fine levied in the county court of Glamorgan of Edward le Despenser, father of Thomas, at Cardiff on 6 Oct. 1365, to Isabel and Richard de Duddeley, her former husband, and Richard their son for their lives, with reversion to John and Joan and the heirs of John; annual values, castle nil, half manors £13 14s., half advowsons nil.

Date of death and heir as above. Thomas late Lord le Despenser held and took the profits from the death of Isabel until 13 Jan. 1400 when he died. Robert Poyns, formerly escheator, then held until 1 Nov. last, and Robert Somervyle, escheator, since 1 Nov.

432B Writ to the escheator of Lincolnshire for proof of age, on petition of John, son of John, son of John, son of John Sutton, who claims to have been born at Gedney and baptised there. The earl of Somerset who has the wardship should be informed. 13 Feb. 1401.

C 137/24, no.49
E 149/77, no.8

THOMAS GRAY, KNIGHT

433 Writ 18 Dec. 1400.

NORTHUMBERLAND. Inquisition. Morpeth. 1 June 1401.

He held:

Wark, the castle and manor, jointly with Joan his wife who survives, to them and the heirs of their bodies, with remainder to his right heirs, of the king in chief by knight service, annual value nil owing to destruction by the Scots.

Bamburgh, 1 messuage and 26 a. called 'Straideland' lying in the fields, from which it was the custom for the tenants to supply ploughshares at the castle of Bamburgh, and for which he renders 4s.6d. payable by the sheriff of Northumberland. They are held of the king by this service, annual value 10s. Also 3 burgages of the king in chief in free burgage at a rent of 4s., annual value nil these days because of destruction by the Scots.

Middleton, 3 vills by, in his demesne as of fee of Henry Percy, earl of Northumberland, of the barony of Beanley by knight service, a rent of 5 marks, the rent called 'truncagium', 39s.5¼d. for carting to Bamburgh castle, and 7s.6d. for the rent called 'Cudbertferry' on the Aln, payable by the sheriff, annual value nil for the same reason.

Doddington, the site of the manor, in his demesne as of fee of the same earl of the barony of Alnwick by knight service and a rent of 13s.4d. for the guard of the castle, annual value nil for the same reason.

Ewart, the manor, of the same earl and barony by knight service and a rent of 13s.4d. for castle guard, annual value nil.

Howick, the manor, of the same barony by knight service, annual value 20 marks.

Hawkhill, the manor, of the same barony by knight service, annual value 10 marks.

Alnwick, a messuage and lands in the fields, of the same earl by a rent of 12d., annual value 8s.

Reaveley, half the manor, of the heirs of Alan de Heton, knight, of the manor of Ingram by knight service, annual value nil for the same reason.

Earle, half the manor, of the duchy of Lancaster of the barony of Stamford by knight service, annual value nil for the same reason.

Hebron, the manor, of Richard Arundel, knight, of the barony of Muschamp by knight service, annual value nil for the same reason.

Pressen, certain lands, of the same knight and barony by knight service, annual value nil for the same reason.

Coldmartin, a third part of the manor, of John Folbur of the manor of Fowberry by knight service, annual value nil for the same reason.

'Le Lofthe. . .', 1 husbandland with two cottages with a place so-called, of Lord Darcy of the barony of Muschamp, annual value nil for the same reason.

Yeavering, 1 husbandland, of Richard de Arundel of the same barony in socage, annual value nil for the same reason.

Biddlestone, 3 husbandlands, of Lord Lowick in socage, annual value nil.

Kilham, 1 husbandland and cottage, of Richard Arundel of the manor of Kilham in socage by a rent of 2d., annual value nil.

He died on 25 Nov. last. Thomas Gray, knight, his son and heir, is aged 18 years and more.

434 Writ 18 Dec. 1400.

NEWCASTLE UPON TYNE. Inquisition. 15 Feb. 1401.

He held in his demesne as of fee 4 tenements outside Pilgrim Street Gate; 2 tenements in Broad Chare; 1 tenement on Sandhill where Thomas Candeler lives; 1 tenement in 'Nethirsyde' in which Ellis Porter lives; 1 cellar under the tenement of John de Careton on the 'Nethirflesshwerrawe'; 2 waste tenements in 'Nere Marketyate'; 46s.8d. rent from the tenement of Sampson Hardyng in Pilgrim Street; 20s. rent from the tenement of John Caretone in the 'Netherflesshwer Rawe'; 26s. rent from 2 tenements in Pandon held by William de Norham; 6s.8d. rent from a tenement of the prior of Tynemouth in 'Beremarketgate' in which William Litster lives; and 6s.8d. rent from a tenement of William de Fulthorp, knight, in Skinner Gate.

They are held of the king in free burgage, rendering 2s. rent which is part of the £100 fee farm of Newcastle upon Tyne. Beyond the rents they are worth 36s. annually.

He died on 7 Dec. [Thursday after St. Andrew; no.433 gives before St. Andrew].
Thomas Gray, knight, his son and heir, is aged 19 years.

C 137/24, no.50

THOMAS LATYMER, KNIGHT

435 Writ 20 Sept. 1401.
SOMERSET. Inquisition. Wells. 6 Oct.
  He held the manor of West Chelwood in his demesne as of fee of the king in chief
by the service of a quarter of a knight's fee, annual value 10 marks.
  He died on 14 Sept. Edward Latymer, esquire, his brother and heir, is aged 50 years
and more.

436 Writ 20 Sept. 1401
LEICESTER. Inquisition. Market Harborough. 27 Sept.
  He held in his demesne as of fee a third part of half the manor of Gumley, of Thomas
de Burton, knight, as a twentieth part of a knight's fee, annual value 33s.4d.; and a
third part of the manor of Church Langton with the advowson at the third vacancy,
of Thomas de Asteley, knight, as a twentieth part of a knight's fee, annual value 54s.
  Jointly with Anne his wife, who survives, he held to them and his heirs by a grant
of John de Mydelton, parson of Chipping Warden, and Thomas Cleydon, chaplain:
  Smeeton Westerby, a third part of the manor, of Richard Turvyll, service unknown,
annual value 5 marks.
  Foxton, a third part of the manor, of Thomas de Burton, knight, service unknown,
annual value 4 marks.
  Date of death and heir, aged 40 years and more, as above.

437 Writ 20 Sept. 1401.
STAFFORD. Inquisition. Lichfield. 11 Nov.
  In right of Anne his wife, formerly the wife of John Beysyn, who held jointly by
royal licence for her life, he held:
  Ashley, two parts of the manor with the advowson, of the king in chief by knight
service, annual value £6.
  Water Eaton, 60s. rent from various lands and tenements, of the earl of Stafford,
service unknown.
  Date of death and heir, aged 44 years and more, as above.

438 Writ 20 Sept. 1401.
SHROPSHIRE. Inquisition. Shrewsbury. 16 Oct.
  He held two parts of the manor of Broseley in his demesne as of fee in right of Anne
his wife, who held jointly with John Beysyn, her former husband, by the grant of
Walter de Walton, parson of Billingsley, and John Child of Knightley. The are held
of the prior of Wenlock by the service of being steward to the prior, annual value 100s.
  Date of death and heir, aged 40 years and more, as above.

439 Writ 20 Sept. 1401.

NORTHAMPTON. Inquisition. Northampton. 9 Oct.

He held in his demesne as of fee:

Chipping Warden, the manor, advowson and hundred, of the king in chief by a rent of 75s. to the castle of Rockingham, annual value £40 [36 marks].

Upton by Northampton, 1 toft and 24 a., of Richard Clendon of Upton, service unknown, annual value 20s., which 20s. he granted to William Kyrkeby for life.

Duston by Northampton, three quarters of a virgate, anciently valued at 5s., of John Grey, service unknown.

Northampton, a meadow in a place called 'Kyngeshale', of the king in free burgage, annual value 40s.

Little Bowden, a third part of the manor, of the king of the ancient demesne of the crown, annual value 26s.8d.

Desborough and Rushton, a third part of half the manor, of the prior of St. John of Jerusalem in England of the manor of Harrington as a twentieth part of a knight's fee, annual value 13s.4d. [a third part of a quarter of the manor].

Carlton, a third part of the manor, of Reynold Lucy, knight, by the rent of a sparrowhawk, annual value 10s.

Great Weldon, a quarter of the manor, of John Knyvet by rent of a pair of spurs, value 3d., annual value 6s. [a third part of a quarter of the manor].

Sulby, 5s. rent from the revenues of the abbot there payable at Easter.

Dingley, 3 a. fallow and a little wood called 'Loughtlond', of the prior of St. John of Jerusalem in England, service unknown, annual value 2s.

He also held jointly with Anne his wife, who survives him, to them and his heirs:

Braybrooke, the castle and advowson, of the prince of Wales of the honour of Berkhampstead by knight service, by the grant of William Northwode, parson of Anderby, and John de Mydelton, parson of Chipping Warden, by a charter shown to the jurors, annual value 40 marks.

Rothwell, the manor called 'Latymeresfee', of the earl of Stafford, service unknown, by the grant of John de Mydelton, parson of Wardon, and Thomas Cleydon, chaplain, annual value 10 marks.

Watford, £4 rent payable by the prior of Daventry at Easter and Michaelmas, of John Isbury by a rent of 2s., by the same grant.

Chipping Warden, 1 carucate, 3 a. arable and 2 a. meadow and pasture, formerly of Robert Brewode and Maud his wife, of Henry bishop of Lincoln, of his castle of Banbury, service unknown, by the same grant, annual value 28s.

Little Bowden, a third part of half the manor, of Thomas Maureward, knight, by the grant of Thomas de Burton, knight, service unknown, annual value 26s.8d.

Burdon's Hall, the manor, of the king of the honour of Peverel by suit of court at Duston twice yearly, by the grant of Richard Rideware and Emma his wife by a fine of Richard II [not found] shown to the jurors, annual value 20s.

Trafford, the manor, of Thomas Percy, knight, as a twentieth part of a knight's fee, by a grant of John Pulton and John Waryner of Kirton in Lindsey, shown to the jurors, to them and Ustard Saumon of Gainsborough, now deceased, and the heirs of Thomas, annual value 40s. [60s.].

Date of death and heir, aged 40 years and more, as above.

[Small variations in E 149/77, no.18 in square brackets.]

C 137/24, no.51
E 149/77, no.18
E 152/372, 376

RALPH CHEYNY, KNIGHT

440 Writ 16 Nov. 1400.

WILTSHIRE. Inquisition. Westbury. 2 Dec.

He held by the courtesy of England in right of Joan his late wife, daughter of John Pavely, knight:

Brook, the manor, with half the profits of the hundred of Westbury, half the profits of the portmote, fair and markets there, and £6 rent from the manors of Westbury and Huntenhull, of the king in chief as half a knight's fee, annual value £20 13s.4d.

Imber, half a messuage and 2 carucates, of the prior of Bradenstoke by a rent of 12s.6d., annual value 20s.

Hilperton, half the manor and the advowson, of the earl of March as a quarter fee; annual values, half manor 40s., advowson £10.

Ditteridge, 1 messuage and 1 carucate, of the bishop of Bath and Wells, service unknown, annual value 40s.

He died on 11 Nov. last. William his son and heir, and heir of Joan his wife, is aged 26 years and more.

441 Writ 16 Nov. 1400.

CAMBRIDGE. Inquisition. Cambridge. 27 Nov.

He held in his demesne as of fee two parts of the manor of Cheyneys with its appurtenances in Steeple Morden, Clapton and Bassingbourn, and the reversion of the third part which Katherine widow of Edmund Cheyny, knight, the brother to whom Ralph was heir, holds in dower. The whole is held of the king of the honour of Boulogne as half a knight's fee, annual value of the two parts £12.

Date of death and heir as above.

442 Writ 16 Nov. 1400.

LINCOLN. Inquisition. Louth. 29 Nov.

He held the manor of Tothill with the advowson in his demesne as of fee of the earl of Chester of the honour of Chester by knight service, annual value £40; also a croft in Tothill containing 40 a. pasture, of Roger Swelyngton of the manor of Castle Carlton in socage by fealty and a rent of 10½d., annual value 20s.

Date of death and heir as above.

443 Writ 16 Nov. 1400.

HERTFORD. Inquisition. Buntingford. 29 Nov.

He held in his demesne as of fee:

Cottered, the manor called Chenyes; of which 60 a. are held of the king in chief of the honour of Boulogne as a quarter of a knight's fee; annual value 60s.; 1 messuage and 1 croft containing 1 a. of Henry Bateman by a rent of 12d., annual value 3s.4d.; and 1 tenement and 11 a. of Andrew Bures by a rent of 21d., annual value 2s.

Reyndels and Longcroft in Cottered, 9½ a., of the same William [sic] Bateman by a rent of 2½d., annual value 18d.

Cottered, 2 a., of William FitzRauf by rent of 1 lb. of cumin, annual value 6d.; 20 a. and 1 grove of wood containing 1½ a., of John Clerk by a rent of 5s., annual value 6d.

Holbrook in Cottered, 9 a., of John parson of Cottered in right of the church by a rent of 4s., annual value 6d.

Date of death and heir as above.

444 Writ 16 Nov. 1400.

SOMERSET. Inquisition. Ilchester. 25 Nov.

He held nothing in the county. Date of death and heir as above.

445 DORSET. Inquisition. Abbotsbury. 26 Nov.

He held nothing of the king in chief, but Thomas de Gorges held in his demesne as of fee the manor of Litton Cheney with the advowson, and gave it to Ralph de Gorges, Eleanor his wife, and the heirs of their bodies. They had issue Elizabeth, Eleanor and Joan, and died and their holdings were divided. This manor and advowson were allotted to Elizabeth as her share, and she had issue Robert de Asshton, and died, and they descended to him, and he died without heirs of his body. Then they descended to Maurice Russell, knight, and Ralph Cheyny, knight; Maurice being the son of Ralph son of Eleanor, sister of Elizabeth, and Ralph being the son of Joan, the other sister of Elizabeth, mother of Robert. They divided the manor and advowson, so that Ralph Cheyny held half the manor with alternate presentations to the church when he died.

The whole is held of Richard Stucle of his manor of Chewton by knight service. In Cheyny's half are 80 a. arable of which two parts can be sown yearly, worth 10d. an a., and after reaping nothing, and the third part is fallow and common and worth nothing; 30 a. meadow in several places from Candlemas to Lammas worth 3s. an a.; 100 a. pasture from Christmas to 8 Sept., agistment 60s.; assize rents of free tenants and villeins payable at the four principal terms, 60s.; and pleas and perquisites of the court of the half manor, 5s.

Date of death and heir as above.

C 137/24, no.52
E 149/75, no.4

WARIN LERCEDEKENE, KNIGHT

446 Writ 10 Dec. 1400.

DEVON. Inquisition. Newton Abbot. 10 Jan. 1401.

He held 1 messuage and 3 ferlings in 'Visham' in his demesne as of fee by knight service as of the manor of Dartington, annual value 26s. 8d. The manor is in the king's hands since and because of the death of John earl of Huntingdon.

He held jointly with Elizabeth his wife by the gift of Matthew Gurnay, Thomas Tryvet and Baldwin Malet, knights, and John Hull, to them and the heirs of their bodies with remainder to his right heirs:

Haccombe, the manor and advowson with the advowson of a chantry, of Edward earl of Devon of the honour of Okehampton by homage, fealty and the service of a third part of a knight's fee, annual value £9 5s.

Ringmore, the manor, of the same earl and honour as . . . part of a knight's fee, annual value £11.

Combeinteignhead, the manor, of John Brightlegh of his manor of Stokeinteignhead by homage, fealty and the service of a quarter of a knight's fee, annual value, 78s.

South Tawton, the manor, of Thomas earl of Warwick by the service of one knight's fee, annual value £10.

L

George Nympton, the advowson, at alternate presentations . . . [2 lines illegible].
He died on 21 Sept. last. Eleanor, Margery and Philippa are his daughters and heirs
. . .

C 137/24, no.53
E 357/14, m.17v.

PHILIPPA WIDOW OF JOHN DE HASTYNGES

447 Writ 8 Oct. 1400.
BUCKINGHAM. Inquisition. Wing. 3 Nov.
   She held 1 toft and 40 a. in Ashendon in dower after the death of John, son of John
de Hastynges, earl of Pembroke, her husband, of the inheritance of John son of John,
with reversion to Reynold Grey of Ruthin his heir, he being the son of Reynold, son
of Elizabeth, sister of John, father of Lawrence, father of John, father of John. He
is aged 30 years and more. It is not held of the king, but of whom and by what service
is unknown; annual value 13s.4d.
   She died on 25 Sept. Edmund, son of Roger earl of March, brother of Philippa, her
nephew and next heir is aged 9 years and more.

448 Writ 8 Oct. 1400.
NOTTINGHAM. Inquisition. Sturton le Steeple. 14 Nov.
   Oswaldbeck soke, after the death of John de Hastynges, earl of Pembroke, by a
decision of the council of Edward III and because of the minority of John, his son
and heir, came into the hands of Richard II. After the death of the heir under age in
the king's ward, it was released to Reynold Lord Grey of Ruthin as next heir, being
the son of Elizabeth [etc. as above]. By a fine of Richard II [CP 25(1) 390/59, no.17]
shown to the jurors, Reynold conveyed it to Robert bishop of London, John bishop
of Hereford, Robert de Haryngton, Gerard de Braybrook, senior and junior, and John
Bagot, knights, who are still living, and John de Roos of Helmsley and Philip Okore,
knights, deceased.
   Richard earl of Arundel married Philippa and sued for reasonable dower from the
lands of her late husband, as well as from the lands which Anne widow of John earl
of Pembroke, and Mary de Sancto Paulo, widow of Aymer de Valencia sometime earl
of Pembroke, held in dower of the same inheritance.
   In the presence of Reynold and with the consent of the bishops and other feoffees
the then escheator assigned this soke to Philippa as part of her dower. It is held of the
king in chief as a tenth part of a knight's fee, annual value 40 marks, and the reversion
is to the above feoffees.
   Date of death and heir as above.

449 Writ 8 Oct. 1400.
LINCOLN. Inquisition. Grantham. 13 Nov.
   The manors of Belchford, Donnington on Bain, Goulceby and Waddington
descended to Reynold Lord Grey of Ruthin [as in last], and he conveyed Donnington,
Goulceby and Waddington manors with 10 messuages, 2 carucates and 20 a. meadow
in those places and in Alkborough to the same feoffees by the same fine. The four
manors were similarly assigned in dower to Philippa. The reversion of Belchford manor

is to Reynold Grey of Ruthin, aged 30 years and more. It is not held of the king, but of whom and by what service is unknown; annual value 20s. The reversion of the other three manors is to the feoffees. They are held of the king in chief by the service of a tenth part of a knight's fee; annual value £4 6s. 8d.

Date of death and heir as above.

450   Writ 8 Oct. 1400.

HERTFORD. Inquisition. Waltham Cross.

Ten marks rent from the manors of Stanstead Abbots and Stanstead Bury descended to Reynold Lord Grey of Ruthin [as in no. 448 above]. He by another fine of Richard II [CP 25(1) 290/59, no. 16] conveyed this and other property to John Hull, Robert bishop of London, John bishop of Hereford, Robert de Haryngton, Gerard Braybroke, senior and junior, and John Bagot, knights, who are still alive, and John de Roos of Helmsley and Philip Okore, knights, deceased, and the heirs of John Hull. The fine and a quitclaim of his rights to the other feoffees by charter of John Hull were shown to the jurors.

A third part of the rent was assigned as above [no. 448] to Philippa in dower with reversion to the feoffees. It is not held of anyone because it is not a rent in service.

Date of death and heir as above.

451   Writ 8 Oct. 1400.

ESSEX. Inquisition. Chelmsford. 12 Nov.

The manors of Vange, East Haningfield, West Haningfield and Fordham descended to Reynold Grey of Ruthin [as in no. 448] and he by the same fine conveyed East and West Hanningfield and Fordham to Robert bishop of London and the other feoffees [as in no. 448]. The four manors were assigned to Philippa in dower with reversion of the last three to the feoffees and of Vange to Reynold Grey. Vange is not held of the king, but of whom and by what service is unknown; annual value £4. The other three manors are held of the king in chief as half a knight's fee; annual values, East Hanningfield £20, West Hanningfield £10, Fordham £16.

Date of death and heir as above.

452   Writ 8 Oct. 1400.

BEDFORD. Inquisition. Woburn. 4 Nov.

She held half a knight's fee in Potton in dower after the death of her husband, John son of John earl of Pembroke, which half fee William Latymer once held. The reversion is to Reynold Grey of Ruthin, being the son of Reynold, son of Elizabeth [as in no. 447] aged 30 years and more.

The half fee with the manor of Blunham, which belongs to it, is held of the abbot of Bury St. Edmunds, service unknown. It is worth nothing except when a casual vacancy occurs. There has been none since the death of Philippa.

Date of death and heir as above.

453   Writ 8 Oct. 1400.

MIDDLESEX. Inquisition. Parish of St. Clement Danes outside Temple Bar. 12 Nov.

The manor of Tottenham called 'Penbrokesmanere' descended to Reynold Grey de Ruthin [as in no. 448]. He conveyed it by a fine [CP 25(1) 151/81, no. 155], shown to the jurors, to Roger de Walden and Guy Mone, clerks, John Walden, esquire, brother of Roger, Thomas Wastle, vicar of Clavering, Richard Scot, clerk, Richard Stucle and Henry Bruyn. A third part of the manor was assigned to Philippa in dower with reversion to these feoffees. It is held of the king of the honour of Huntingdon as a sixth part of a knight's fee, annual value £6 13s.4d.

Date of death and heir as above.

454 Writ 8 Oct. 1400.

LONDON. Inquisition. 12 Nov.

She held 1 messuage and 6 shops with 6 solars above them in the parish of St. Mary at Hill in Billingsgate ward in dower after the death of John her husband, with reversion to Reynold Grey of Ruthin, as above. They are held of the king in free burgage as is all the city of London, annual value 66s.8d. Reynold is aged 30 years and more.

Date of death and heir [described as Edmund son of Edmund *recte* Roger] as above.

455 Writ 8 Oct. 1400.

SOMERSET. Inquisition. Queen Camel. 8 Nov.

The manors of Odcombe, Middle Marston and Little Marston descended to Reynold Grey of Ruthin [as in no.448]. He conveyed them by a fine [above, no.450] to John Hull and the other feoffees. The former escheator assigned them in dower to Philippa with reversion to these feoffees. They are held of the countess of Kent of her manor of Queen Camel, service unknown; annual values, Odcombe 5 marks, Middle Marston 100s., Little Marston £12.

Date of death and heir as above.

456 Writ 8 Oct. 1400.

KENT. Inquisition. Rochester. 8 Nov.

John earl of Pembroke held the manor of Newington Lucies in fee tail, with remainder in default of male heirs to Geoffrey Lucy, knight. After the death of John de Hastynges the son, Geoffrey Lucy granted it to Reynold his son and Margaret his wife and the heirs of their bodies by royal licence. [*CPR 1391–6*, p.376].

Richard earl of Arundel married Philippa widow of John and sought reasonable dower. The escheator assigned her a third part of the manor with reversion to Reynold Lucy. It is held of Humphrey, the king's son, of his manor of Middleton by knight service, annual value 33s.4d.

Date of death and heir [described as Edmund son of Edmund *recte* Roger], as above.

457 KENT. Inquisition. Rochester. 8 Nov. 1400.

The manors of Hartley, Cleyndon and Luddesdown descended to Reynold Grey of Ruthin [as in no.448]. By one fine [above, no.488] he conveyed the manor of Hartley to Robert bishop of London and the other feoffees, and by another fine [above, no. 450] he conveyed the manor of Cleyndon to John Hull and the other feoffees. The three manors were assigned to Philippa in dower by the escheator. The reversions of Hartley and Cleyndon manors are to the respective feoffees, and that of Luddesdown to Reynold Grey of Ruthin, aged 30 years and more.

Hartley is held of the king in chief of the fee (*scutum*) of Pembroke by knight service, annual value £6; Cleyndon of the prior and convent of Rochester of their manor of Darenth, service unknown, annual value 60s.; and Luddesdown of the earl of March of his manor of Swanscombe by homage and a rent of 38s., annual value £7.

Date of death and heir as above [no.454].

458 Writ 8 Oct. 1400.

NORTHAMPTON. Inquisition. Northampton. 6 Nov.

The manors of Towcester and Yardley Hastings and the advowson of Yardley Hastings descended to Reynold Grey of Ruthin [as in no. 448]. He conveyed Towcester by a fine [above no. 450] to John Hull and the other feoffees. Yardley Hastings manor and advowson were assigned by the escheator to Philippa in dower, with reversion of the manor to the feoffees and of the advowson to Reynold Grey.

Towcester is held of the earl of Stafford of the honour of Gloucester as a quarter of a knight's fee, annual value 40 marks. Yardley Hastings manor and advowson are held of the king in chief of the honour of Huntingdon by a rent of one unmewed sparrowhawk, or 2s. The advowson is worth nothing, because there has been no vacancy since the death of Philippa.

Date of death and heir as above [no. 454].

459 Writ 8 Oct. 1400.

WORCESTER. Inquisition. Worcester. 6 Nov.

The manor of Inkberrow descended to Reynold Grey of Ruthin [as in no. 448]. He conveyed it by a fine [above, no. 450] to John Hull and the other feoffees. The fine and release by John Hull were shown to the jurors. A third part of the manor was assigned to Philippa in dower with reversion to the feoffees. It is held of the prior of Hereford, service unknown, annual value 100s.

Date of death and heir as above [no. 454].

460 Writ 8 Oct. 1400.

CAMBRIDGE. Inquisition. Cambridge. 30 Oct.

The manor of Great Shelford descended to Reynold Grey of Ruthin [as in no. 448]. He conveyed a third part by a fine to Robert bishop of London and the other feoffees and two parts to John Hull and the other feoffees by two fines mentioned [above, nos. 448, 450]. John Hull released to his co-feoffees. The manor was assigned in dower to Philippa by the then escheator. A third part is held of the king in chief in petty serjeanty, two parts of the bishop of Ely by rent of a sparrowhawk or 2s., annual value of the whole 12 marks. The reversions are to the respective feoffees.

Date of death and heir as above [no. 454].

461 Writ 8 Oct. 1400.

BERKSHIRE. Inquisition. Newbury. 5 Nov.

The manor of Benham descended to Reynold Grey of Ruthin [as in no. 448], and he by a fine shown to the jurors conveyed it to Robert bishop of London and the other feoffees [as in no. 448]. It was assigned in dower to Philippa with reversion to the feoffees.

Date of death and heir as above [no. 454].

462 Writ 8 Oct. 1400.

SURREY. Inquisition. Paddington. 10 Nov.

The manors of Westcott and Paddington and 1 messuage in Southwark descended to Reynold Grey of Ruthin [as in no.448]. By one fine [above, no.450] he conveyed the manor of Westcott and the messuage in Southwark to John Hull and the other feoffees, and by another [above, no.448] he conveyed the manor of Paddington to Robert bishop of London and the other feoffees. They were all assigned in dower to Philippa. Westcott is held of the duchy of Lancaster of the honour of the Eagle by fealty, Paddington of the king in chief as a quarter of a knight's fee, and the messuage of the bishop of Winchester, service unknown; annual values, Westcott £10, Paddington 66s.8d., the messuage 12d.

Date of death and heir as above [no.454].

463 Writ 8 Oct. 1400.

HEREFORD AND THE ADJACENT MARCH OF WALES. Inquisition. Hereford. 8 Nov.

The castle, town and lordship of Abergavenny in Wales descended to Reynold Lord Grey of Ruthin [as in no.448]. He by a fine [licence, *CPR 1388–92*, p.514; fine not found] conveyed them to William Bagot and William Fenys, knights, John Pycard and William Wenlock, esquires, John Olney, Nicholas Salwey, clerk, Robert de Warrewyk, clerk, John de Styvecle and Henry Bruyn, who are still alive, and Henry Grene, knight, deceased. Henry Bruyn released to the others. The escheator assigned a third part of the castle, town and lordship to Philippa in dower.

William Fenys, Nicholas Salewey and Robert de Warrewyk quitclaimed their rights in the two parts with the reversion of the third part held by Philippa to Henry Grene, William Bagot and the other feoffees. They conveyed the two parts with the reversion of the third by a fine made with royal licence [*CPR 1391–6*, pp.697–8; CP 25(1) 83/50, no.66] to Thomas archbishop of York, Thomas de Percy and Payn Typetot, knights, Robert Pobelowe, clerk, Thomas Reed of Wales and John Tauk for the life of Joan wife of William Beauchamp, knight, with reversion after her death to Henry Grene and the other remaining feoffees. Philippa attorned to the archbishop and the others.

The archbishop and the others transferred to William Beauchamp and Joan two parts and the reversion of the third part which Thomas Poynings alias St. John and Philippa then his wife held at that time. So she held a third part.

The castle, town and lordship are held of the king in chief as one knight's fee and by a rent of 1d., annual value £26 13s.4d.

Date of death and heir as above [Edmund correctly given as son of Roger].

464 Writ 8 Oct. 1400.

WARWICK. Inquisition. Coventry. 5 Nov.

The manor of Fillongley descended to Reynold Grey of Ruthin [as in no.448]. He by a fine [above, no.450] granted it to John Hull and the other feoffees. The escheator allotted it to Philippa in dower with reversion to the trustees. Half is held of the honour of Leicester of the duchy of Lancaster as a third part of a knight's fee, and the other half of the heirs of Philip Marmion, service unknown, annual value £10.

Date of death and heir as above [no.463].

465 LEICESTER. Inquisition. Hinckley. 8 Nov.

The manors of Burbage and Barwell, 4 messuages, 80 a. and 40s. rent in Dadlington, and the advowsons of Burbage, Leire and Shackerstone descended to Reynold Grey of Ruthin [as in no.448]. He by a fine [above, no.450] conveyed them to John Hull and the other feoffees. The manor of Barwell, the holdings in Dadlington and the advowsons of Burbage, Leire and Shackerstone were assigned to Philippa in dower with reversion to the feoffees. They are all held of the prior of Coventry, service unknown, annual value 20 marks.

Date of death and heir as above [no.463].

466   Writ 8 Oct. 1400.

HAMPSHIRE. Inquisition. Lymington. 2 Nov.

She held in dower of the king in chief, service unknown, and of no value except when a vacancy occurs:

Thruxton, 1 fee once held by John de Cornewaille.

Snoddington, Hook and Houghton, 1½ fees held by Ingram Berenger.

No tenant has died since the death of Philippa. The reversion is to Reynold Grey of Ruthin, aged 30 years and more.

Date of death and heir as above [no.463].

467   Writ 8 Oct. 1400.

YORK. Inquisition. Coxwold. 12 Feb. 1401.

She held a third part of the manor of Ravensthorpe with Boltby in dower after the death of her husband, with remainder to Beatrice Lady de Roos of Helmsley, because Reynold de Grey of Ruthin, knight, kinsman and heir of the late earl [as in no.448] after the death of John son of the late earl and before Philippa was dowered granted the whole manor to Beatrice for life, and all the tenants attorned to her. It is held of Alice countess of Kent of her manor of Kirkby Moorside by knight service, annual value of the third part 106s.8d.

Date of death and heir as above [no.463].

468   Writ 8 Oct. 1400.

YORK CITY. Inquisition. 25 Nov.

She held a third part of a tenement in Bishophill in dower after the death of her husband, with remainder to Beatrice Lady Roos of Helmsley for life, because Reynold Grey of Ruthin, the heir, granted it to Beatrice [as in no.467] and all the tenants attorned to her. It is held of the king in chief in free burgage, annual value 6s.8d.

Date of death and heir as above [no.463].

469   Writ 8 Oct. 1400.

NORFOLK. Inquisition. Bergh Apton by Brooke. 23 Nov.

She held in dower:

Gooderstone, the manor, of the king in chief, service unknown, annual value 40 marks.

Saxthorpe, the manor, of the king in chief, service unknown, annual value 20 marks.

Winfarthing, the manor, of the barony of Monchensy as 1 fee, annual value £20.

Sutton, the manor, with the advowsons of Sutton and Brumstead, of Lord Mowbray of the manor of Forncett as 2½ knight's fees, annual value £50.

Hockham, the manor, of the same lord of the same manor by a rent of 9d. for castle ward, annual value £20.

Ashill, a third part of the manor called Uphall with the advowson, of the king in chief by the service of napery at the coronation, annual value 40s.

Tibenham, the manor, of the abbot of Bury St. Edmunds in socage by a rent of 1d., annual value 20s.

She died on 25 Sept. Edward de Hastynges, knight, aged 19 years and more, in the king's ward, is next heir. He is kinsman and heir of the earl of Pembroke, being the brother of Hugh de Hastynges, son of Hugh, knight, son of Hugh, knight, younger brother of John, elder son of Hugh, knight, brother of John, Knight, father of Lawrence, father of John.

Edmund, son of Roger earl of March, brother of Philippa, her next heir in blood, is aged 9 years and more.

470 Writ 7 Oct. 1400.
SUFFOLK. Inquisition. Wickham Market. 17 Dec.

The manor of Otley descended to Reynold Grey of Ruthin [as in no.448]. He by a fine [above, no.450] conveyed it to John Hull and the other feoffees, and Hull released it to them. The escheator assigned it to Philippa in dower and she held it with reversion to the feoffees. It is held of Roger earl of March in socage of the honour of Gloucester, annual value £20.

Date of death as above. Roger son of Edmund [*recte* Edmund son of Roger] earl of March, her brother and next heir, is aged 9 years and more.

C 137/25, no.54
E 149/74, no.7, 76, no.1
E 152/360, 362, 367

RICHARD DE SANCTO MAURO, KNIGHT

471 Writ 17 May 1401.
DORSET. Inquisition. Maiden Newton. 26 May.

He held the manor of Winfrith Eagle of the king in chief as a quarter of a knight's fee, by the gift of John Derby, Walter de Polton and John de Westbury, chaplains, to Nicholas de Sancto Mauro and Muriel his wife, and the heirs of their bodies, with remainder to the right heirs of Muriel, by a fine of Edward III [CP 25(1) 287/45, no.541] shown to the jurors. Richard was their son and heir. The manor is worth £23 6s.8d. annually.

He died on 15 May last. Richard his son and heir is aged 23 years and more.

472 Writ 17 May 1401.
LONDON. Inquisition. 8 June.

He held in his demesne as of fee of the king in free burgage a great house with garden and four shops in the parish of St. Peter the Poor, by the house of the Austin friars. When occupied and rented the house is worth 5 marks annually, but it has long been unoccupied and unrented and worth nothing. The 4 shops and garden are valued at 40s. annually.

Date of death as above. Richard de Sancto Mauro, knight, his son and heir, is aged 24 years and more.

473 Writ 17 May 1401.
WILTSHIRE. Inquisition. Westbury. 26 May.

He held in his demesne as of fee:

Wittenham, the manor, with the advowson of Rowley, of the heir of Thomas le Despenser of the honour of Gloucester by knight service, amount unknown, annual value 100s.

Langham, the manor, of Humphrey Stafford, knight, of his manor of Southwick, service unknown, annual value 109s.8d.

He also held in right of Ela, his wife, who is of full age and still lives:

Westbury, half the manor, a quarter of the hundred and of the portmote of the manor, and the advowson of the chantry of St. Mary in the church there, of the king in chief by knight service, amount unknown, annual value £34 5s.6½d.

Hilperton, a quarter of the manor and of the advowson, of the duchy of Lancaster of the castle of Trowbridge by knight service, amount unknown, annual value 53s.4¾d.

Imber, a quarter of the manor, of the prior of Bradenstoke, service unknown, annual value 26s.8d.

Luckington, a third part of the manor, in dower, of Walter de la Pole, knight, and Elizabeth his wife, in right of Elizabeth, service unknown, annual value 74s.9d.

Date of death and heir as above.

474 Writ 17 May 1401.

DEVON. Inquisition. North Molton. 1 June.

He held the manor of North Molton with the advowsons of North Molton and Black Torrington with Ela his wife of the king in chief by knight service, by the gift of John Chitterne and John Bromflet, clerks, by their deed and by licence of Richard II [*CPR 1377–81*, p.215], both shown to the jurors, to them, Edmund Seyntlou, clerk, and William de Brithlegh, deceased, and the heirs male of their bodies, with remainder to the right heirs of Richard.

There are 1 capital messuage, annual value nil; 3 cornmills, value 30s. payable by equal parts at the four principal terms; 4 carucates, 40s.; 800 a. gorse and heath at ¼d. an a.; assize rents and rents of villein holdings, £31 6s.1¼d. at the four principal terms; assize rents of burgage tenants, 106s.3¼d. at Michaelmas; a rent of 100s. called 'le yene' at Michaelmas; pleas of courts of the manor, borough and hundred of North Molton, 33s.4d. by common estimation; and the advowsons of North Molton, 40 marks, and Black Torrington, 20 marks.

Date of death and heir as above [no.471].

475 Writ 17 May 1401.

GLOUCESTER. Inquisition. Clifton. 27 May.

He held:

[Meysey Hampton], the manor and advowson with all the knight's fees belonging to the manor, of the earl of Stafford by knight service, amount unknown, annual value £26 8s.10d. He gave them to his son Richard, Alana his son's wife, and the heirs of their bodies, with remainder to his own right heirs. Richard the son still lives and has male issue.

Clifton, third part of the manor with the advowson and knight's fees, of the heir of Thomas le Despenser of the honour of Gloucester, annual value 60s.2d.

Winterbourne, . . ., of Thomas de Bradeston, son and heir of Edumund de Bradeston, knight, in dower of Ela his wife, who survives him, from Thomas de Bradeston, her former husband, annual value £6 13s.4d.

Tytherington, 10 a. meadow, . . . 2s.; and Horton, 2 messuages with orchards and gardens of no annual value, 259 a. arable at 2d., 20 a. meadow at 12d., 60 a. pasture at 4d., and 6½ a. wood nil; of Walter Pole, knight, and Elizabeth his wife, of the inheritance of Elizabeth, by fealty.

Breadstone, the manor with the advowson of the chantry of the chapel of St. Michael there, annual value £7 6s.

Bulley, the manor, by fealty, annual value . . .

Stinchcombe, the manor, annual value . . .

Arlingham, 1 messuage with yards and garden adjacent, annual value . . ., 86 a. arable at 2d., 10 a. meadow at 2s., and 10 a. pasture at . . .

Date of death and heir as above [no.471].

476 Writ 17 May 1401.

SOMERSET. Inquisition. Bruton. 26 May.

He held:

Castle Cary, Marsh with the borough of Wincanton, South Barrow and North Barrow, the manors, and the advowsons of Ansford and North Barrow, to himself and the heirs of his body, of the king in chief by knight service, by the grant of John Derby, Walter Polton and John de Westbury, chaplains, to Nicholas de Seymour and Muriel his wife, his father and mother, and the heirs of their bodies, with remainder to the right heirs of Muriel by a fine of 1358 [CP 25(1) 287/45, no.541]. Richard was the son and heir of Nicholas and Muriel. The annual values are: Castle Cary manor with the advowson of Ansford and all the knight's fees belonging to it, £126 17s.10d., of which the rents of the tenants of the manor at the four terms amount to £100; Marsh manor with the borough of Wincanton, £28 10s.5d., out of which the rents of tenants amount to £20; South Barrow, £7 16s.11d.; and North Barrow manor with the advowson, £11 3s.1d. The last two manors were granted by Richard to John Bull for rents of £7 16s.11d. and £11 3s.1d. payable at the four terms.

Bratton Seymour, the manor, of the king in chief by knight service, to himself, his heirs and assigns, annual value £6 4s.2d.

Road, the manor and advowson, of Walter Rodeney, knight, by knight service, to himself and his heirs, annual value £27 15s.10d., including rents of £24 16s.3d. payable at Easter and Michealmas.

Stoke Lane, the manor, of the heir of the earl of Salisbury by knight service, to himself and his heirs, annual value £8 19s.10d. Except for 18 a. wood of no annual value, he granted it to Stephen Forester and Richard Artowe at Michaelmas 1395 for 8 years at a rent of £8 19s.10d. payable at the four terms.

Shepton Montague, certain lands and tenements, to himself and his heirs, of the heir of the earl of Salisbury by fealty in free marriage [sic]: 3 messuages with curtilages and 1 virgate, annual value 20s.; 336 a. arable at ½d.; 8 a meadow at 12d.; and 24 a. arable at 4d.; all granted at Easter 1400 to John Gane for 20 years for a rent of 26s.8d. payable at the four terms.

Charlton Mackrell and Charlton Adam, certain lands and tenements, in fee simple to himself, his heirs and assigns, of Nicholas Poulet by a rent of 12d.: 2 messuages with curtilage and garden, annual value nil; 203 a. arable at 2d.; 8 a. meadow at 20d.; and 12 a. pasture at 8d.; all of which by a charter dated 20 Sept. 1383 he granted to Walter Sylvayn, esquire, who still lives, for life, for a rent of 33s.4d. payable at Easter and Michaelmas.

He held jointly with Ela his wife, who survives him:

Prestleigh, the manor, and Blackford, half the manor, of Elizabeth Palton of her manor of Croscombe by knight service, amount unknown, to them for the life of Ela, by the gift and demise of John Manyngford, John Fantleroy and John Bray, as appears by their charter shown to the jurors. The half manor is divided into four parts: East Hall, held of the heir of John Fitzrichard by knight service, amount unknown; 'Whyteley', of the heir of Thomas Courtenay by a rent of 6s.8d.; 'Thystelham', of the heir of the earl of Salisbury by a rent of 3s.4d.; 'Brycestenement', of Thomas Barthy by a rent of 20s. Long before this grant he was seised in his demesne as of fee of Prestleigh manor and half the manor of Blackford and conceded them to John Manyngford, John Fantleroy and John Bray for the life of Ela, as appears by his charter also shown to the jurors. Annual values, Presteleigh £8, the half of Blackford £6 9s.2d.

Shepton Montague and Knowle by Bruton, lands called 'Botevylestenement' comprising 1 messuage with curtilage, annual value nil; 80 a. arable at 1d.; 5 a. meadow at 2s.; 16½ a. pasture at 12d.; 1 a. wood nil; and 4 a. wood called 'Schortwode' nil; to them and their heirs of the heir of the earl of Salisbury by fealty, by the grant by charter of Richard Wayte, John Gregory, Walter Hyspynell and John Bakehous.

Blackford by Compton Pauncefoot, the manor, of Reynold Cobham, service unknown, from Hamo Fitzrichard by a fine of 1393 [CP 25(1) 201/32, no.1], annual value £4 5s.4d.

North Woolston and South Woolston, a rent of 100s.8d. from 12 messuages, 51 a., and 4 a. meadow, payable at the four principal terms, of Reynold Cobham, service unknown, granted by the same fine. The 12 messuages etc. are held by the following tenants for life, with remainder to Richard and Ela and his heirs: Nicholas Cadbury and John his son, Agnes Wylkes, Robert Lyff and Joan his wife, Richard Forester and Margery his wife, Richard Love and Margery his wife, John Faukes, junior, and Maud his wife, John Miles and Margery his wife, John de Houpere and Alice his wife, Richard Toukere and Alice his wife, Nicholas Sugge and Joan his wife, John Plente and Juliana his wife, John Goulde and Joan his wife, and John Faukes, senior.

Bratton Lyndes, a rent of 13s.4d. payable at Easter and Michaelmas, granted to them by John Swan for his life, as appears by his deed shown to the jurors.

Date of death and heir as above [no.471].

C 137/26, no.55
E 149/77, no.11

ELIZABETH WIDOW OF NICHOLAS AUDELEY, KNIGHT

477 WILTSHIRE. Inquisition. Heytesbury. 18 Nov. 1400.

She held half the manors of Broughton Gifford and Ashton Gifford with the advowson of Codford by a grant of Adam de Fulford and William Peek, chaplains, to Nicholas, Elizabeth herself and the heirs of their bodies, with remainder to the right heirs of Nicholas. He died without heirs of his body.

Roger Hillary and Margaret his wife granted the reversion of half of the above halves, which should have come to Margaret after the death of Elizabeth, by a fine of 1391 [CP 25(1) 289/56, no.225] to Robert bishop of London, Reynold Grey of Ruthin, knight, John Markham, Hugh de Holes, and John de Woderove, now deceased, and the heirs of Hugh. They should now remain to the bishop, the other feoffees and the heirs of Hugh.

Margaret and John Tochet, knight, are next heirs of Nicholas, Margaret, aged 50 years, being his sister, and John, aged 26, son of John, son of Joan, his other sister.

The half manor of Broughton Gifford is held of the heirs of John Combe, service unknown, annual value 20 marks. The half of Ashton Gifford is held of the lord of Boyton, service unknown, annual value £10, the advowson 20 marks.

Elizabeth died on 27 Oct. John [*recte* Henry] Beaumond, under age in the king's ward, is next heir, being the son of John, son of John, son of John, brother of Elizabeth.

478 Writ 30 Oct. 1400.

GLOUCESTER. Inquisition. Gloucester. 1 Nov.

She held jointly with Nicholas half the manor of Badgeworth, by the grant of Adam de Fulford and William de Peek, the reversion being conveyed by the same fine of 1391 [above, no.477].

Date of death, heirs of Nicholas and her heir as above, the age of John Tochet being given as 28 years and more, and of Henry Beaumond [correctly named] as 19 on 25 July last.

479 Writ 29 Oct. 1400.

DEVON. Inquisition. Exeter. 16 Nov.

She held the manors of West Raddon, Newton Tracey by Barnstaple, and George Nympton, a quarter of the manor of Kilmington, and 6s. rent in East Anstey and West Anstey, with the advowson of Newton Tracey, to herself and the heirs of Nicholas by the grant of Adam de Fulford and William Peek, the reversion being conveyed by the fine of 1391 [above, no.477]. West Raddon is held of the heir of the earl of March, who is under age in the king's ward, by knight service, annual value £8 6d.; Newton Tracey with the advowson, of the heir of John de Welynton, who is under age in the ward of John Wroth, knight, by knight service, annual values, manor £4 10s., advowson 100s.; George Nympton of Robert Chalonner, knight, by knight service, annual value 33s.4d.; the quarter of Kilmington of Edward earl of Devon by knight service, annual value 26s.8d.; and the rent of Robert Cruwys by knight service.

Date of death, heirs of Nicholas, Margaret being aged 51 years and more, and her heir Henry Beaumond, aged 12 years, as above.

480 Writ 29 Oct. 1400.

LONDON. Inquisition. 22 Dec.

She held of the king in free burgage, to herself and the heirs of Nicholas and herself, one messuage in the parish of St. Gregory by St. Paul's, by the grant of William de Bello Campo, brother of the earl of Warwick, to them, the heirs of their bodies, and the right heirs of Nicholas, annual value 10 marks.

Also in free burgage, as all London is, she held one tenement in Shoe Lane in the parish of St. Bride in the suburbs, by the grant of Richard Rodbord, parson of Monnington on Wye, and William Peek, chaplain, to them, the heirs of their bodies, and the right heirs of Nicholas, annual value 50s.

Nicholas, in his testament enrolled in the hustings and shown to the jurors, left the reversion to Elizabeth, William Nasshe and John Mareschall, his executors, to be sold after the death of Elizabeth and himself, the resulting money to be used to augment the services in the abbey of Hilton at the discretion and order of the executors. The reversion is therefore to them to dispose of in accord with his will.

Date of death and heir of Elizabeth, aged 17 years and more, as above.

481   Writ 29 Oct. 1400.

SOMERSET. Inquisition. Bridgwater. 17 Oct. 1400.

She held in fee tail by the gift made with royal licence [*CPR 1385–9*, p. 239] of Richard Rodberd and William Peek, chaplains, to Nicholas, Elizabeth herself, and the heirs of their bodies, with remainder to his right heirs:

Nether Stowey, Downend and Puriton, the manors, of the king in chief by the service of half a barony. Nether Stowey is valued in assize rents, arable, meadow and pasture in demesne, which were anciently let to farm, at 40 marks yearly payable at the four principal terms; Downend similarly at 60s.; and Puriton £20.

Wollavington, the manor, of the abbot of Glastonbury by a rent of 1d., and worth annually in assize rents, arable, meadow, and pasture in demesne £24.

Stockland Bristol, the manor; a third part of the heir of Thomas Tryvet by suit of court, a third part of the master of St. Mark, Bristol, by suit of court, and a third part of the prior of Stogursey by the rent of a rose; and Crandon, the manor, of the same heir of Thomas Tryvet by a rent of 2s. The two are worth 20 marks in assize rents payable at the four terms, including demesne arable, meadow and pasture anciently let to farm.

Honibre, the manor, of Joan Lady Moune, service unknown. The manor and demesne lands are let to farm, assize rents of free and customary tenants including the farm, £20.

Woolston, 1 messuage and 40 a. arable, of the heir of John de Bello Campo, of the manor of Downend by suit of court, annual value 40s.

Nicholas died without heirs. John Tochet and Margaret who was the wife of Roger Hillary, knight, deceased, are next heirs. By a fine of 1393 [CP 25(1) 290/57, no.293] shown to the jurors, William de Stretehay, now deceased, Thomas de Thikenes, Philip Stretehay and Richard de Snede recognised half the manors of Nether Stowey, Downend, Puriton, Woolavington, Stockland Bristol, Crandon and Honibre, with the messuage and 40 a. in Woolston to be the right of Margaret, and Roger and Margaret agreed for themselves and the heirs of Margaret that these lands, which Elizabeth widow of Nicholas Audeley held for life of the inheritance of Margaret, should after the death of Margaret go to John Tochet, son of John Tochet of Markeaton, knight, Thomas Tochet, parson of Mackworth, John Cokayn the uncle, John Tochet son of Richard Tochet of Mackworth, William Pakeman and the heirs of John son of John.

Date of death, heirs of Nicholas, John Tochet being aged 29 years and more and Margaret aged 49, and of Elizabeth, Henry Beaumond aged 17 years and more, as above.

482   Writ 29 Oct. 1400.

STAFFORD. Inquisition. Tyrley. 12 Dec.

She held in dower from her late husband:

Audley and Balterley, a third part of the manors, and the manors of Endon and Over Longsdon, except for 30s. rent in Over Longsdon, Heighley, Balterley and Audley, with reversion except for the 30s. rent to John Tochet, knight, and Margaret who was the wife of Roger Hillary, knight, as next heirs of Nicholas, who held them in fee simple and died without heirs of his body.

Alstonfield, a third part of one third of the manor, by assignment of Nicholas de Stafford, knight, deceased, which third part he held for life by the grant of Nicholas Audeley with reversion to himself and his heirs. The third part belongs after the death of Elizabeth to John Tochet and Margaret as above.

Betley, the vill except for two parts of the fishponds and stanks, a third part of the park of Heighley, a third part of the manor of Horton, and 30s. rent in Heighley, Balterley, Audley and Over Longsdon, with reversion to John Tochet, son of John, son of Joan, sister of Nicholas, Margaret wife of Roger, the second sister, and Fulk Fitzwaryn, son of Fulk, son of Margaret, the third [half] sister of Nicholas, who died without heirs of his body, by virtue of a gift in tail by John de Kynardeseye. He gave them to Nicholas de Audeley, grandfather of Nicholas, and Joan his wife, and the heirs of the body of Nicholas. After their deaths James de Audeley, knight, son and heir of Nicholas, held them, and after his death Nicholas his son and heir.

By a fine of 1393 [CP 25(1) 290/57, no.294] Roger Hillary, knight, and Margaret his wife granted the reversion of the half manor of Endon, a third part of the manor of Betley, half the manor of Audley and half of one third of the manor of Balterley, which Elizabeth held in dower and which after her death should come to them and the heirs of Margaret, to William Stretehay, now deceased, Thomas Thikenes, Philip Stretehay and Richard Snede, and the heirs of Thomas Thikenes, for the life of Margaret, and after her death to John Tochet, knight, of Markeaton, Thomas Tochet, parson of Mackworth, John Cokayn the uncle, John Tochet, son of Richard Tochet of Mackworth, William Pakeman, and the heirs of John son of John.

Audley and Balterley are held of the lady of Alton in socage, annual values, third part of Audley £16, third part of Balterley 13s.4d.; Endon of the earl of Stafford in socage, annual value £6(?); Over Longsdon of the heir of John de Horton in socage, annual value 50s.; third part of Betley of the heir of William de Betteley, annual value £6; and Horton of the earl of Stafford in socage, annual value 60s.

Date of death, heirs of Nicholas, John Tochet being 28 years and more and Margaret 50, and of Elizabeth, Henry Beaumond 16 years and more, as above.

483 SHROPSHIRE. Inquisition. Market Drayton. 13 Dec. 1400.

She held:

Ford and Newport, the manors, with various tenements in Muchel Aston by the grant of William Peeke and Adam de Fulford [above, no.477].

Edgmond, the manor, to Nicholas and herself, the heirs of their bodies and the right heirs of Nicholas by the grant of Richard Rodbert, parson of Monnington on Wye, and Roger de la Nasshe, parson of Peterstone, with remainder failing such heirs to James de Audeley of Heighley, knight, and his heirs.

Red Castle, the castle and manor so called, in dower of Nicholas, with remainder to John Tochet, Margaret wife of Roger Hillary, knight, and Fulk Fitzwaryn [as in no.482].

By a fine of 1391 Roger and Margaret Hillary granted the reversion of half the manors of Ford and Newport and a third part of that of Edgmond to Robert bishop of London and other feoffees and the heirs of Hugh de Holes [as in no.477]; and by a fine of 1393 they granted the reversion of a third part of Red Castle to William Stretehay and other feoffees and the heirs of John son of John Tochet [as in no.482].

Ford, Newport and Edgmond are held of the king in socage; Red Castle of the heir of John Harcourt by a rent of 1d.; and the tenements in Church Aston of the king of the manor of Edgmond in socage; annual values, Ford £63, Newport £10, Edgmond £20, Red Castle £23 and Church Aston £4.

Date of death, heirs of Nicholas, John Tochet being 28 years, Margaret 50 years, and Fulk Fitzwaryn 11 on 3 May, and of Elizabeth, Henry Beaumond, 16 years and more, as above.

Writs to the escheator of Shropshire and Staffordshire to partition the lands equally between John Tochet and Margaret Hillary. 7 Feb. 1401.

484 Writ 29 Oct. 1400.
HEREFORD AND THE ADJACENT MARCH OF WALES. Inquisition. Hereford. 27 Nov.
   She held jointly with her husband:
   Newport in Cemais in Wales, the castle, vill, manor and lordship, by the gift of James de Audeley to them and the heirs of Nicholas, of the king by knight service, annual value £60. An agreement was made between William de Valence, former earl of Pembroke, and William Martyn, lord of the castle, lord of Newport in Cemais, by which William Martyn granted for himself and his heirs that the tenants of this lordship should make suit at the county court of Pembroke, and so it is held. In the lordship are the manor of Newcastle in Cemais with 1 messuage, 5 carucates, 1 mill, 3s.10d. rent, 250 a. wood and 5 a. meadow in Eglwyswrw, half of 5s. rent in Cilrhedyn, 1 messuage, 4 carucates, 1 mill and 3 a. meadow in Fagwyr Goch, and 3 carucates, 1 mill, 11s.9d. rent and 20 a. wood in Fishguard, by the grant of William Peek, Richard Bene and Thomas Kalne, chaplains [licence, *CPR 1388–92*, p.500, 4 Nov. 1391].
   Monnington on Wye and Dilwyn, the manors, by the grant of James de Audeley to them and the heirs of their bodies, with reversion failing such heirs to him; Monnington of Thomas earl of Warwick of the honour of Colwyn by knight service, annual value £. . ., Dilwyn of the duchy of Lancaster by knight service, annual value £24.
   James de Audeley married Joan, who died. Then he married Isabel, and they had issue Margaret, and he died. Nicholas died.
   John Tochet, knight, son of John Tochet, Margaret widow of Roger Hillary, and Fulk Fitzwaryn, son of Fulk, son of Margaret, daughter of James by his second wife Isabel, are the heirs of James.
   By a fine of 1391 the reversion of the third part of the manors of Dilwyn and Monnington on Wye was conveyed by Roger and Margaret Hillary to Robert bishop of London, the other feoffees, and the heirs of Hugh de Holes [as in no.477], and by a fine of 1393 the castle, vill, commote and lordship of Newport in Cemais, with 2 messuages, 3 mills, 12 carucates, 8 a. meadow, 270 a. wood and 20s. 1d. rent in Eglwyswrw, Red Walls, Cilrhedyn and Fishguard, and a third part of the castle, manor, vill, hundred and lordship of Llandovery, and the commote of Perfedd and Hirfryn were conveyed to Nicholas and Margaret for the life of Margaret with remainder to John Tochet, son of John and others [as in no.481].
   Margaret is aged 50 years and more, Fulk Fitzwaryn 11.
   Date of death as above. Henry Beaumond, her next heir, as above, is aged 16 years and more.

C 137/26, no.56
E 149/77, no.9
E 152/355, 370
E 357/14, m.32

ALICE WIDOW OF AUBREY DE VEER, EARL OF OXFORD

485 Writ 29 April 1401.
ESSEX. Inquisition. Halstead. 9 June.
   She held in dower:

Steeple Bumpstead, the manor, of the inheritance of Richard de Veer, son of the earl, of the king in chief, service unknown, annual value 20 marks.

Beaumont cum Moze, the manor, of the king in chief, service unknown, annual value beyond a rent of £10 granted to the abbot and convent of St. Osyth 66s.8d.

Stansted Mountfichet, a rent of 16s.4d. from the manor.

Eyston Hall, the manor, but Aubrey de Veer granted by charter to John Baryngton, John Aillemer and Richard Payn, his servants, 2d. each daily from it, payable by the farmer at Easter and Michaelmas. It is held of the earl of March, who is in the king's ward, service unknown, annual value beyond the grants 40s.

She died on 29 April last. Richard her son and heir was 16 on 15 Aug. last.

486 Writ 1 May 1401.

LONDON. Inquisition. 6 May.

She held in her demesne as of fee of the king in free burgage, as all London is, a house in the parish of St. Augustine on the wall within Bishopsgate, annual value 8 marks.

Date of death and heir, aged 15 on 15 Aug., as above.

487 Writ 29 April 1401.

KENT. Inquisition. Ospringe. 18 May

She held in dower of Aubrey, of the king, of the castle of Dover as three quarters of a knight's fee and by payment of 23s.10d. annually for the ward of the castle:

Badlesmere, the manor and advowson, and in the vill 198 a. at 3d., 49s.6d.; 40 a. pasture at 2d., 6s.8d.; 24 a. of great wood, worth nothing beyond the services because it cannot be felled; 42s. assize rents from various tenants at the four terms; 5 cocks at 1½d. and 31 hens at 2d., from various tenants at Christmas, 5s.9½d.; and 280 eggs from various tenants at Easter at 5d. the 100, 14d.

She also held there in gavelkind 400 a. of land and pasture at 3d., 100s. and no more because burdened with £7 3s.6d. payable annually to various lords of fees; and 3 a. of seasonable wood worth nothing because felled in the last two years, but when able to be felled worth 3s.

Date of death as above. Richard de Veer, knight, aged 18 years and more, and John his brother, aged 12 years and more, are her sons and heirs.

488 Writ 29 April 1401.

BUCKINGHAM. Inquisition. Stony Stratford. 6 June.

She held in dower for life:

Whitchurch, the manor, of Edmund earl of Stafford by knight service, annual value £30.

Calverton, the manor and advowson, of the king in chief by a rent of 33s.4d., annual value of the manor £10.

Date of death as above. Richard de Veer, her next heir, is aged 16 years and more.

C 137/26, no.57

E 149/75, no.3

THOMAS DE BELLO CAMPO, EARL OF WARWICK

489 Writ 8 June 1401.

SURREY. Inquisition. Guildford. 14 Oct.

He held to himself and the heirs male of his body the advowson of Cranleigh, granted with the king's licence by a fine of 1361 [*CPR 1361–4*, p.105; CP 25(1) 288/46, no.596] between Thomas de Bello Campo, earl of Warwick, and John de Bukyngham and others, to him and his son Thomas and the heirs male of his body. It is not held of the king, but of whom and by what service is unknown; annual value nil.

He died on 8 April. Richard his son and heir was 19 on 25 Jan.

490 Writ 12 April 1401.

BERKSHIRE. Inquisition. Faringdon. 27 July.

He held in his demesne as of fee the advowson of Compton Beauchamp, not of the king in chief, but of whom and by what service is unknown; annual value 10s.

Date of death and heir as above.

491 Writ 12 April 1401.

BUCKINGHAM. Inquisition. Stony Stratford. 6 June.

He held to himself and the heirs male of his body the manors of Hanslope and Quarrendon under a fine of 1344 made with royal licence [*CPR 1343–5*, pp.251–2; CP 25(1) 287/41, no. 332]. By this John de Melbourne and Roger de Ledbury, clerks, conveyed them to Thomas de Bello Campo, earl of Warwick, and Katherine his wife, Guy their son and the heirs male of his body, and failing such heirs to Thomas his brother and the heirs male of his body. Thomas and Katherine died, and Guy died without heirs. Hanslope is held of the king by the service of being one of the chamberlains of the exchequer, annual value £60. Quarrendon is not held of the king, but of whom and by what service is unknown; annual value £26.

He held the offices of chamberlain and usher of the exchequer by the grant of John de Bukyngham and others by a fine of 1361 [above, no.489]. They are held of the king in chief by the service of the offices, value nil this year.

Richard II granted on 27 April 1383 [*CPR 1381–5*, p.270] that his executors should hold his lands for one year after his death without rendering anything to the king, and spending the profits in accordance with his will.

Date of death and heir as above.

492 Writ 12 April 1401.

CALAIS. Inquisition. 15 July.

He held in his demesne as of fee 3 messuages of the king by the service of 4s.2d. rent and the provision of 3 watchmen for the safeguard of the town, annual value 10 marks.

Date of death and heir as above.

493 Writ 12 April 1401.

RUTLAND. Inquisition. Uppingham. 9 June.

He held the manors of Barrowden and Greetham and the hundred of Wrangdike under a fine of 1344 [CP 25(1) 192/6, no.36] by which John de Melbourne and Roger de Ledbury, clerks, conveyed them to Thomas de Bello Campo for life and to his sons,

M

Rembrinus, now deceased, for life, and Guy and Thomas and their heirs male in turn. Guy died without heirs male. They are held of the king in chief by knight service, amount unknown; annual values, Barrowden £20, Greetham 40 marks, the hundred beyond the fee of the steward 10 marks.

He also held to himself and his heirs male by the grant of John de Bukyngham and others under a fine of 1361 [above, no.489] the manor of Preston and Uppingham of the king in chief by knight service, amount unknown, annual value 40 marks.

Grant of Richard II [as in no. 491]; date of death and heir as above.

494 Writ 12 April 1401.

Essex. Inquisition. Stratford. 3 May.

He held one knight's fee in Westbarrow with the advowsons of North Fambridge and Stambridge by the grant of John de Bukyngham and others by a fine of 1361 (above, no.489), of the king in chief by knight service, amount unknown; the fee worth nothing this year, the advowsons 6s.8d. and 6s.

Thomas Aldebury, clerk, held in his demesne as of fee the manor of Walthamstow Tony and by a fine of 1400 [CP 25(1) 290/59 no.8], shown to the jurors, granted it to Thomas earl of Warwick and Margaret his wife and the heirs of their bodies. It is held of the king of the honour of Boulogne, service unknown, annual value 40 marks.

Nicholas Lillyng, knight, Roger Tangele, clerk, and Thomas Aldebury held in their demesne as of fee the manor of Walthamstow Francis, and by their charter granted it to Thomas and Margaret and the heirs of their bodies. It is also held of the king of the same honour, service unknown, annual value £10.

Date of death and heir as above.

495 Writ 12 April 1401.

Cambridge. Inquisition. Newmarket. 30 May.

He held of the king in chief:

Kirtling, the manor, conveyed by John de Melburn and Roger de Ledbury, clerks, by a fine of 1344 [CP 25(1) 287/41, no.334] to the earl, Guy his son, and the heirs male of the body of Guy, with remainder to Thomas his brother and the heirs male of his body. It is held by knight service, annual value £30.

Long Stanton, 10 marks rent, conveyed by John Bokyngham and others by a fine of 1361 [above no.489].

Grant of Richard II [as in no.491]; date of death and heir as above.

496 Writ 12 April 1401.

Wiltshire. Inquisition. Devizes. 9 June.

He held:

Cherhill, the manor, conveyed by John de Melbourn and Roger de Ledbury, clerks, by a fine [above, no.495], of the king in chief as half a knight's fee, annual value £40.

Woodborough, half a knight's fee, conveyed by John Bukyngham and others by a fine of 1361 [above, no.489], of the king in chief, with the advowson; values, fee nil this year, advowson 10s.

Hinton, the manor, in his demesne as of fee, of whom and by what service is unknown; annual value 100s.

Grant of Richard II [as in no.491]; date of death and heir as above.

497 Writ 12 April 1401.

HERTFORD. Inquisition. St. Albans. 4 June.

He held the manor of Flamstead, conveyed by John de Mellebourn and Roger de Ledebury, clerks, by a fine of 1344 [above, no.495], of the king by the service of keeping the highway called Watling Street between Redbourn and Markyate; annual value £40.

Grant of Richard II [as in no.491]; date of death and heir as above.

498 Writ 12 April 1401.

GLOUCESTER. Inquisition. Chipping Campden. 14 June.

He held the manors of Chedworth and Lydney and the advowson of the church of Notgrove, conveyed by John de Bukyngham and others by a fine of 1361 [above, no.489], the manors of the earl of Gloucester, and the advowson of the earl of Essex, services unknown.

At Chedworth is a capital messuage, annual value nil; 4 a. meadow, 4s.; underwood, 20s.; assize rents from free and customary tenants payable at Michaelmas and Lady Day by equal parts, £12; and pleas and perquisites of courts, 2s. In Lydney there are no buildings, but 2 a. underwood, 2s.; assize rents of free and customary tenants, £4; and pleas and perquisites of the court, 6s.8d.

Edmund de Brugge, Richard Bromley, clerk, and Robert Russell held the manor of Childs Wickham by Evesham, and by their charter shown to the jurors conveyed it to Thomas, earl of Warwick and lord of Gower, and Margaret his wife, who survives, and the heirs of their bodies. It is held of the earl of Gloucester, service unknown, annual value £20.

Grant of Richard II [as in no.492], date of death and heir as above.

499 Writ 12 April 1401.

LEICESTER. Inquisition. Leicester. 11 June.

Philippa widow of Guy de Bello Campo held the manor of Kibworth Beauchamp for life by the grant of Thomas de Bello Campo, senior, with reversion to Thomas the father and his heirs. He granted the reversion by a fine of 1383 [CP 25(1) 289/53, no.79] to John Say, Richard de Pyryngton, clerk, and Richard de Brumlegh. They by another fine of 1383 [CP 25(1) 289/53, no.81] granted it to Thomas, Margaret his wife and the heirs of their bodies. Philippa died and they held the manor. The tenure is of the king in chief by the service of napery at the coronation of the queen; annual value £50. The fines and royal licence for the grant were shown to the jurors.

Date of death and heir as above.

500 Writ 12 April 1401.

NORFOLK. Inquisition. Watton. 8 June.

He held the advowson of Shouldham priory of the king in chief, service unknown, by a grant of John de Bukyngham and others by a fine of 1361 [above, no.489], annual value 10s.

Philippa widow of Guy de Bello Campo held the manors of Saham Toney, Necton and Little Cressingham with the hundreds of Wayland and Grimshoe for life, by the grant of Thomas de Bello Campo the father, with reversion to Thomas. By fines of 1383 [above, no.499] he granted the reversion to John Say, Richard de Pyryngton and Richard de Brumlegh, clerk, and they to him, Margaret his wife and the heirs of their bodies. Philippa died and so they held them, all of the king in chief, services unknown;

annual values, Saham Toney £20, Necton £10, Little Cressingham 10 marks, the two hundreds 100s.

Thomas Aldebury, clerk, held the manor of Panworth in Ashill and by a fine of 1400 [above, no.494] granted it to Thomas, Margaret his wife and the heirs of their bodies. It is held of the earl of March of the honour of Clare, service unknown, annual value £10.

Date of death and heir as above.

501   Writ 12 April 1401.
LONDON. Inquisition. 11 May.

With Margaret his wife he held a mansion in Old Dean's Lane with 6 houses, 16 shops, 1 toft and the rent of 16 shops in the parish of St. Sepulchre, which Stephen Sutton, valet of the chamber of the earl, held for life.

Hugh Segrave, knight, Richard de Pirryngton and John Hermesthorp granted these to them and the heirs of their bodies by their charter shown to the jurors. Sutton attorned to them. They are held of the king in free burgage, as is all the city, annual value £12.

Date of death and heir as above.

502   Writ 12 April 1401.
WORCESTER. Inquisition. Evesham. 31 May.

He held in his demesne as of fee:

Fickenappletree, half the manor, of William de Bello Campo, knight, service unknown, annual value 40s.

Grafton Flyford, 1 messuage and 1 carucate called Hill Court, and in Hadzor a wood called 'Ovewode' of the abbot of Westminster, service unknown, annual value 30s.

Droitwich and Upwich, 2 salt vats and salt houses, 11¾ saltwater pans (*duas salinas et bullerias, xj et iij quartr' plumborum aque salse*) and a rent of 26s. 8d., of the king in socage, annual value of the saltpans and salt vats 20s.

He held to himself and his heirs male by a grant of John de Bokyngham, bishop of Lincoln, and others, by a fine of 1361 [above, no.489]:

Worcester, the castle and shrievalty, with the hundred and members, the manors of Elmley Lovett, Yardley, Syntley and Abberley, and half a knight's fee in Redmarley. The castle, shrievalty, hundred and members, and the manors of Elmley Lovett, Syntley and Abberley are held of the king in chief by knight service as half a fee. The castle with a parcel of meadow called 'Castelsu' is worth 40s. yearly, the shrievalty with the hundred and profits of a brine-pit (*puteus acque salse*) called 'Shyreveshole' in Droitwich, belonging to the shrievalty, 60s., the manor of Elmley Lovett 20 marks, the manors of Syntley and Abberley £20, and the half fee nil this year. Yardley manor is held of the abbot of Pershore, service unknown, annual value £10.

By the grant of John de Melborne and Roger de Ledbury, clerks, by a fine of 1344 [above, no.491] he held the manor of Shrawley in fee tail as a quarter of a knight's fee, annual value 20 marks.

He held in his demesne half the manor of Perry by Worcester with a watermill called 'Frogmille' under the bank of the moat of Worcester castle, annual value £6.

Hugh de Segrave and Henry de Ardern, knights, and Richard de Pyryngton and John Harewode, clerks, held in their demesne as of fee the castle of Elmley and the manor of Elmley Castle, the manors of Wadborough, Stoulton, Salwarpe and Kersoe, as members and parts of the castle and manor of Elmley, and 14 saltpans and 20 marks rent in Droitwich, and gave them by their charter to the earl and Margaret and the heirs of their bodies. The manor of Salwarpe with the saltpans and rent are held of the prior of Coventry, service unknown, annual value £40. The rest are held of the bishop of Worcester, service unknown, annual value 100 marks.

Edmund Brugge, John Aleyn and Richard de Tenedbury held 14 saltpans (*salinas*) in Droitwich and Upwich in their demesne as of fee, and of their salt house 14 saltwater pans (*et de bullaria sua xiv plumborum aque salse*) in Droitwich . . . Upwich, and by their charter shown to the jurors, gave them to the earl, Margaret his wife and the heirs of their bodies. The saltpans and salt house are held of Eleanor [*recte* Elizabeth?] countess of Kent, service unknown, annual value 4 marks.

William Cokeseye and William Spernore, esquires, and Roger Tangeley and Richard Bromley, clerks, held in their demesne as of fee the manors of Bewdley, Grafton, Earls Croome, and Ribbesford with Brook and Lindon belonging to it, and 12 cottages, 8 messuages and £10 rent in Worcester, and granted them to the earl, Margaret and the heirs of their bodies by their charter shown to the jurors. Bewdley is held of the abbot of Pershore, service unknown, annual value 20 marks; Grafton of the abbot of Westminster, service unknown, 20 marks; Earls Croome of the bishop of Worcester, service unknown, £10; Ribbesford of the earl of March, 20 marks; the cottages, 20s., and the messuages, £4, of the king in chief in socage.

Long before he died the earl granted the following manors, not held in chief, for the lives of the grantees with reversion to himself and his heirs as appears by his charters shown to the jurors: Wyre Piddle and Little Comberton to Robert Huggeford for a rent of £6 payable in equal parts at Easter and Michaelmas; Great Comberton to William Parys for rent of a rose at Midsummer; and Hadzor to Nicholas Lyllyng, knight, for rent of a red rose at Midsummer. In virtue of the earl's charters Robert Huggeford, William Parys and Nicholas Lyllyng were seised of these manors and so remained for the rest of the earl's life.

The castle of Worcester, the shrievalty and hundred, the manors of Elmley Lovett, Yardley, Syntley and Abberley, and the half fee were parcel of the lands which Richard II granted on 27 April 1383 that his executors should hold for one year after his death without rendering anything to the king [as in no. 491].

Date of death and heir as above.

503 Writ 12 April 1401.

HAMPSHIRE. Inquisition. Lymington. 30 June.

He held 2 messuages in Southampton and the office of weigher (*pesagerie*) there of the king in socage, annual value £10.

Date of death and heir as above.

504 Writ 12 April 1401.

NORTHAMPTON. Inquisition. Northampton. 6 June.

William de Herle, knight, and Thomas de Radeclyf, parson of Olney, by a fine of 1339 [CP 25(1) 177/75, no. 181] conveyed the manor of Moulton to Ralph de Basset of Drayton Bassett and Joan his wife for their lives, with successive remainders to Ralph de Basset the son and Joan, daughter of Thomas de Beauchamp, earl of Warwick, and the heirs of their bodies, the male heirs of Ralph de Basset, Ralph de Stafford for life, Richard de Stafford for life, Ralph son of Ralph de Stafford and his heirs male, Richard son of Richard and his heirs male, and finally to Thomas son of Thomas de Bello Campo the earl, and his heirs male. Thus he held it, of the king in chief as half a knight's fee.

Long before his death he granted by letters patent shown to the jurors to John Longevyll, esquire, 10 marks yearly for life; and to William Gyn custody of the warren of Moulton for life. Apart from these grants the annual value of the manor is £27.

By the grant of John de Melbourne and Roger de Ledebury by a fine of 1344 [above, no.491] he held the manor of Potterspury of the honour of Tutbury as one knight's fee, annual value £20.

Long before his death he gave the manor of Cosgrove, not held of the king in chief, to Nicholas Lyllyng for life to hold by the rent of a rose at Midsummer, with reversion to himself and his heirs.

Potterspury is part of the lands included in the grant of Richard II of 1383 [above, no.491].

Date of death and heir as above.

505   NORTHAMPTON. Inquisition. Moulton. 8 June. Jurors as in last.

He held in his demesne as of fee:

Potterspury, the manor, of the earl of Hereford, of the honour of Gloucester, as one knight's fee, annual value 37 marks.

Moulton by Northampton, the manor, of Reynold Grey of Ruthin of his manor of Yardley Hastings as half a knight's fee. Long before he died he granted to Nicholas Lyllyng, knight, all the houses in the lower manor of the manor of Moulton with warren, produce, pasture of 'firses', 4 fishponds, and herbage in the wood called 'le Tofft' for life for a rent of 10 marks; and to John Lungevill, esquire, 10 marks rent from the manor for life, with reversion to himself and his heirs. The annual value beyond this rent is £18 4s.

He also held the reversion of the manor of Cosgrove and a rent of a red rose from the manor, which he gave to Nicholas Lyllyng for life with reversion to himself, annual value £20. It is held of the earl of his manor of Hanslope by a rent of one unmewed sparrowhawk or 2s.

Date of death and heir as above.

506   Writ 12 April 1401.

HEREFORD AND THE ADJACENT MARCH OF WALES. Inquisition. Hereford. 2 July.

He held the castle of Painscastle and the manors of Elfael and Aberedw in the March by the grant of John de Melbourne and Roger de Ledebury, clerks, by the fine of 1344 [above, no.495].

The castle and site of the buildings and the manor of Elfael are worth nothing yearly, the manor of Aberedw 10 marks. At Elfael there are 1 carucate worth 12s. yearly, let to farm payable at Michaelmas; 10 marks assize rents from the burgesses of Painscastle payable at Lady Day and Michaelmas; 6 a. meadow, 6s.; 3 forests, namely New forest, Old forest and Richard's forest, worth £20 between the Invention of the Holy Cross and Michaelmas, and nothing thereafter; 3 pastures worth 10 marks from the Invention of the Holy Cross to All Saints Day, and nothing thereafter because common until Lady Day; 1 forest called Colwyn worth 10 marks between Hockday and Michaelmas, afterwards nil because common to all tenants and residents from Michaelmas to Candlemas; a pasture called 'Utradgogh' worth 26s. 8d. and so let to farm payable at all Saints Day; assize rents this year of £13 6s. 8d. called rent of St. Andrew, payable at Candlemas; courts monthly and three-weekly, 10 marks, and a hundred court every three weeks, 40s.; £13 6s. 8d. rents at Midsummer; the custom called 'kylfmayr', £12 equally at Lady Day and Michaelmas; the custom called 'cowegeld' each third year, £4 15s. when it occurs, on May Day and was so paid in 1400; and 2 fairs on the eves of St. Barnabas and St. Simon and St. Jude, £6.

They are held in right of the earldom of Warwick of the king in chief by knight service.

Date of death and heir as above.

507 Writ 12 April 1401.

DEVON. Inquisition. North Tawton. 6 Aug.

He held the manor of South Tawton of the king in chief, service unknown, by the grant of John de Melbourn and Roger de Ledebury, clerks, by a fine of 1344 [CP 25(1) 287/41, no.333], to Thomas earl of Warwick for life with successive remainders to Thomas his son for life, Guy, brother of Thomas and his heirs male, Rembrinus his brother and his heirs male and the heirs male of Thomas. There are 40 a. wood with pasture, annual value 2s.; 100s. 1d. rent of assize payable at the four terms by equal parts; and pleas and perquisites of court, by estimation 18s.

Date of death and heir as above.

508 Writ 12 April 1401.

STAFFORD. Inquisition. Tamworth. 15 Aug.

Ralph Basset of Drayton Bassett, knight, gave all his lands in Walsall by the name of the manor of Walsall to William de Herle, knight, and Thomas de Radeclyve, parson of Olney, and their heirs by a fine of 1339 [CP 25(1) 287/40, no.255], and they conveyed them to Ralph Basset for life with successive remainders to his son Ralph and Joan his wife, daughter of Thomas earl of Warwick, and the heirs of their bodies, the male heirs of Ralph Basset, senior, Ralph de Stafford for life, Richard de Stafford for life, Ralph son of Ralph de Stafford and his heirs male, Richard son of Richard and his heirs male, and finally Thomas de Bello Campo, the earl, and his heirs male. Sir Thomas held it of the king in chief at fee farm, paying annually £4, annual value £20.

Thomas de Aldebury, clerk, held in his demesne as of fee the manor of Drayton Bassett, and 10 marks rent in Tamworth, and by a fine of 1400 [above, no.494] conveyed it to the earl, Margaret his wife and their heirs. It is held of the heir of Ralph Basset of Weldon of his manor of Great Weldon, service unknown, annual value £40.

Long before he died by his charter shown to the jurors he granted to William Spernore the manors of Perry and Barr, not held of the king in chief, to hold for life by rent of a rose at Midsummer, with reversion to the earl and his heirs.

Date of death and heir as above.

509 Writ 12 April 1401.

WARWICK. Inquisition. Warwick. 6 June.

He held in his demesne as of fee:

Warwick, 6 messuages, formerly of Richard Heye, chaplain, and others, annual value 20s; 24 a. arable and 2 a. meadow, formerly of Robert Sotemay, 13s.4d.; and 2 a. quarry [sic], one formerly of William Aleyn and the other of Richard Greyne and John Mountford, 12d.; all held of the king in burgage; and 1 cottage, formerly of John Brewster, not held of the king, but of whom and by what service is unknown, annual value nil.

Stratford on Avon, 1 messuage, worth 10s., in his hands by purchase of William Selot, the lord's villein, held of John Prat and William Wenlok of the manor of Shottery, service unknown.

By the grant of John de Melbourn and Roger de Ledebury, clerks, by a fine of 1344 [above, no.495] he held Warwick castle and the manors of Warwick, Brailes, Claverdon, Tanworth, Sutton Coldfield, Berkswell and Lighthorne, extending as follows:

Warwick, the castle, annual value nil; site of the manor nil; 300 a. arable, 40s.; 40 a. meadow, 40s.; an old park called Wedgnock, worth in the maintenance of the game £13 6s.8d; a several pasture called Packmores, 20s.; a watermill, £6 13s.4d.; a several pasture on the banks of the Avon, 66s.8d.; assize rents, £35 6d., payable at Lady Day and Michaelmas by equal parts; and pleas and perquisites of court with view of frankpledge, 60s.

Brailes, site of the manor, nil; a dovecot, 5s.; pasture by the manor, 5s.; 4 carucates, 8 marks; 60 a. meadow, 60s.; underwood, nil this year because destroyed by the duke of Norfolk; assize rents, £33 9s.2d., payable as above; customary works at St. Andrew's day, 20s.10d., and at Whitsun, 16s.8d.; a watermill, 20s.; pleas and perquisites of court with view of frankpledge, 40s.; and market tolls, 20s.

Claverdon, site of the manor, nil; a park, beyond the keeping of the game 6s.8d.; 1 carucate, 13s.4d.; 30 a. meadow, 20s.; rents of tenants, £12 1s.6d., payable as above; and pleas and perquisites of court with view of frankpledge, 6s.8d.

Tanworth, site of the manor, nil; the close there, 40d.; 2 carucates, 40s.; underwood, nil this year; 10 a. meadow at 6d.; assize rents, £10, payable as above; and pleas and perquisites of court, 6s.8d.

Sutton Coldfield, site of the manor, nil; a dovecot, nil this year because not stocked; 200 a. waste land, 10s.; 15 a. meadow, 15s.; a park, beyond the keeping of the game 40s.; a fishpond and pond, 20s.; a watermill, 40s.; rents of tenants, £10, payable as above; and pleas and perquisites of court with view of frankpledge, 20s.

Berkswell, site of the manor, nil; 200 a. arable, 26s.8d.; 20 a. meadow, 20s.; a park, beyond the keeping of the game 13s.4d.; underwood, 20s.; and assize rents, £29, payable as above.

Lighthorne, site of the manor, nil; a dovecot, 3s.4d.; 3 carucates, 60s.; 30 a. meadow, 30s.; assize rents, £20, payable as above; and pleas and perquisites of court, 6s.8d.

The castle and manors are held of the king in chief by a tenth part of the service of an earl.

He also held the manors of Budbrooke and Grove Park to himself and his heirs, by the grant of John Hastang to Thomas his father, himself and his heirs male. Extents: .

Budbrooke, site of the manor, nil; 3 carucates, 60s.; 20 a. meadow, 20s.; assize rents, £8, payable as above; and pleas and perquisites of court, 10s.

Grove Park, site of the manor, nil; and 1 carucate and 1 parcel of pasture, 33s.4d.

These two manors are held of John de Beynton of Maxstoke, knight, service unknown.

By the grant of John Bokyngham and others by a fine of 1361 [above, no.489] he held the manor of Barford and one knight's fee in Alcester of the king in chief, Barford as half a knight's fee; annual value, Barford 100s., Alcester nil.

On 12 Sept. 1392 he granted to Walter Power, esquire, £10 yearly in time of peace and £20 in war from the manors of Budbrooke, Grove Park and Haseley, payable by equal parts at Midsummer and Christmas. Richard II confirmed this on 4 July 1394 [CPR 1391–6, pp.465–6]. The rent was in arrears by 100s. when the earl died on 8 April last.

Thomas Aldebury held in his demesne as of fee the manor of Ladbrooks in Tanworth and by a fine of 1400 [above, no.494] conveyed it to the earl, Margaret his wife and their heirs. It is held of the king of the honour of Peverel as a tenth part of a fee, annual value 100s.

Long before he died he gave the manor of Ashorne, not held in chief, to John Danyell for life to hold by the rent of a rose at Midsummer, with reversion to himself and his heirs.

He also held in his demesne in fee tail under the fine of 1361 [above, no.489] 40 marks rent in Moreton Morrell. Afterwards he purchased the manor of Moreton Morrell to hold to himself and his heirs. From this manor the above rent was customarily levied as rent in service, half from the holding of Nicholas Pype and half from that of Roger Tiryon. Later he enfeoffed Nicholas Lyllyng, knight, and others to hold to themselves and their heirs, without other payment than the 40 marks rent. This rent belongs to Richard his son and heir.

Grant of Richard II [as in no.491]; and date of death and heir as above.

C 137/27, no.58
E 149/75, no.2
E 152/369, no.4

THOMAS DE BELLO CAMPO, EARL OF WARWICK

510 Writ, for fees, 15 July 1402.
SURREY. Inquisition. Shere. 24 Jan. 1403.
No fees but only the advowson of Cranleigh, extended at 20 marks, which was taken into the king's hands owing to the death of the earl.

511 Writ, for fees, 15 July 1402.
STAFFORD. Inquisition. Walsall. 15 Jan. 1403.
Taken into the king's hands owing to his death was half a fee in Chillington, held by the heir of John Gyffard, annual value 20 marks.

No advowsons or other fees were so taken because all belonged to the manor of Drayton Bassett, of which he and his wife Margaret, who still lives, were jointly seised, by the grant of Thomas Aldebury, clerk, by a fine of 1400 [CP 25(1) 290/59, no.8].

512 Writ, for fees, 12 Jan. 1403.
DORSET. Inquisition. Dorchester. 28 Jan.
Taken into the king's hands was 1 knight's fee in Upper Melcombe and Nether Melcombe, held by the heirs of Ralph Basset and John Serne, annual value £40. There were no advowsons.

513 Writ, for fees, 15 July 1402.
ESSEX. Inquisition. Chelmsford. 20 Feb.
No fees were taken but the advowson of North Fambridge, which extends at 100s.

514 Writ, for fees, 15 July 1402.
HERTFORD. Inquisition. St. Albans. 3 March 1403.
He held no fees, but the advowsons of Flamstead, extending at £20, and a free chapel in the manor there, 40s.

515 Writ, for fees, 15 July 1402.

WORCESTER. Inquisition. Worcester. 27 July 1403.

The following fees were taken into the king's hands, extending at the amounts shown:

Crowle, 1 fee held by the preceptor of St. Wolstan's, Worcester, and John Froxmere, 100s.

Eckington, ⅓ fee held by Henry Greyndour, 33s.4d.

Fairfield, 1 fee held by the heir of Thomas Botiller of Sudeley, knight, £20.

Little Kyre, ½ fee held by Roger [le Mortymer], 40s.

Redmarley Oliver, 1 fee held by Hugh Cheyne, knight and John Meysy, 66s.8d.

Waresley, ½ fee held by the heir of Robert de Clare, 40s.

Barrow, ½ fee held by the heir of William de Berewe, 20s.

Norchard. ¼ fee held by John Blount, 13s.4d.

Woodmanton by Grafton, part fee held by the heir of Robert de More, . . .

Eastham, 1 fee held by William Lyngorn, clerk, and others, £20.

Shelsley Beauchamp, 1 fee held by William Wysham, knight, £10.

And the following advowsons:

Little Comberton, 6 marks.

Great Comberton, 20 marks.

Shrawley, . . .

Elmley Lovett, £10.

Abberley, 100s.

Hadzor, 10 marks.

Witton St. Mary, 5 marks.

Upton Warren, 10 marks.

St. Peter by Worcester castle, free chapel, 15s.

Droitwich, chantry, £11 13s.4d.

He also held jointly with his wife [by the grant] of Henry de [Ardern], knight, Richard de Peryngton and John Harewode, clerks, William Cokesey and William Spernore, esquires, and Roger Tangely and Richard Bromley, clerks, . . . to them and the heirs of their bodies . . .

516 Writ, for fees, 15 July 1402.

RUTLAND. Inquisition. Oakham. 3 Oct.

The following were taken into the king's hands:

Wing, 1 fee held by the abbot of Thorney, £10.

Ridlington, 1 fee held by John Holand, knight, £10.

Glaston, 1 fee held by the heir of Robert de Haryngton, knight, 20 marks.

Lyndon, ½ fee held by the heir of John Davys, knight, 10 marks.

Martinsthorpe, ½ fee held by John Seyton, 100s.

Barrow and Wenton, 1 fee held by Robert Sherard in right of his wife, and by the prioress and nuns of Stamford, £10.

Manton, ⅕ fee held by John Lylford, 10 marks.

Cottesmore, 1 fee held by John Daprichecourt, knight, £12.

Pilton, ¼ fee held by John Uffynton, 100s.

North Luffenham, 1/40 fee held by the heir of John Basset, 2s.

Barrowden, 1/40 fee held by the heir of Robert Nevyle, 2s.

And the following advowsons:

Cottesmore, £20.

Barrowden, 20 marks.
South Luffenham, £10.
Preston, 100s.

517 Writ, for fees, 15 July 1402.
OXFORD. Inquisition. Banbury. 28 Nov.
The following were taken into the king's hands:
Drayton, ½ fee held by the heir of Richard de Ardern, £10.
Sibford, 1 fee held by the heir of Thomas de Brocton and Robert [*sic*, no surname], £15.
Chadlington, 1 fee held by the heirs of Richard de Boyvill and Nicholas de Aston, £20.

518 Writ, for fees, 15 July 1402.
BUCKINGHAM. Inquisition. Aylesbury. 1 Nov.
In Hanslope the following were taken into the king's hands:
½ fee held by John Bosno, £10.
1 fee held by William Brampton in right of his wife, 20 marks.
¼ fee held by Thomas Knyght, clerk, 40s.
¼ fee held by the heir of Robert Mancell, 40s.
¼ fee held by the heir of Richard Newenham, clerk, 26s.8d.
$\frac{1}{40}$ fee held by the heir of John Fraunceys, 5s.
$\frac{1}{40}$ fee held by the heir of Richard Hoese, 5s.
⅛ fee held by Walter Dastyn, 20s.
And the following advowsons:
Hanslope, 70 marks.
Quarrendon, a chantry in the church, 60s.
Hanslope, a chantry, 40s.
Castlethorpe, a chantry, 40s.

519 Writ, for fees, 15 July 1402.
BERKSHIRE. Inquisition. Remenham. 6 Nov.
The following were taken into the king's hands:
Aston Upthorpe and Winterbourne, 1 fee held by the heirs of Gilbert son of John de Ellesfeld, £20.
Compton Beauchamp, ½ fee held by the heirs of Peter de Eketon, £10.
Swallowfield and Shinfield, ½ fee held by the heir of John de Sancto Johanne of Langham, £20.
Beech Hill and Garston, $\frac{1}{10}$ fee held by the heirs of John Blount, 40s.
Ashampstead and Basildon, 1 fee held by the heir of Ralph de Knyveton, £20.
Remenham, 1 fee held by the heir of Peter de Monte Forti, £10.
Also the advowson of Compton Beauchamp, 10 marks.

520 Writ, for fees, 15 July 1402.
NORTHAMPTON. Inquisition. Brackley. 12 Oct.
The following were taken into the king's hands:
Norton by Daventry, 1½ fees held by the heir of Geoffrey de Cornewayle and the heir of John Golafre, £20.

Muscott, ¼ fee held by the heir of Philip Gerveys, 60s.
Strixton, ¼ fee held by the heir of Richard Preiers, 10 marks.
Yardley Gobion, ¼ fee held by the heir of Henry Gobyon, 20s.
Easton Maudit, 1 fee held by the heir of Lawrence Trussell, 100s.
Ashton, ¼ fee held by the heir of John Hardershull, £10.
Southwick and Perio, 1 fee held by the heir of Peter de Monte Forti, 20 marks.

521   Writ, for fees, 15 July 1402.
CAMBRIDGE. Inquisition. Cambridge. 4 Nov.
The following were taken into the king's hands:
Brinkley, ½ fee held by the heirs of John Mouhon and Andrew Mouhon, 60s.
Whittlesford, ¼ fee held by Edmund de Thorp, knight, in right of his wife, 40 marks.
And the following advowsons:
Kirtling, 20 marks.
Brinkley, 10 marks.

522   Writ, for fees, 15 July 1402.
GLOUCESTER. Inquisition. Newent. 1 Dec.
The following were taken into the king's hands:
Weston, ½ fee held by William Reymund, £10.
Sezincote, ½ fee held by the abbot of Bruern, 60s.
Dorsington, ½ fee held by the heir of Henry de Preyers, £10.
Dry Marston, ½ fee held by the prior of Little Malvern, 100s.
Poulton, 1 fee held by William Beaumont, £20.
Purton on Severn, ¼ fee held by the heirs of John ap Adam, 100s.
Compton Greenfield, ½ fee held by the heir of Maurice de Berkeley, £10.
Over, 1 fee held by John de Berkeley, knight, £10.
Westcote by Stow on the Wold, ½ fee held by Giles Mallory, knight, £10.
Bromsberrow, 1 fee held by Hugh Waterton, knight, £10.
Also the advowson of Notgrove, 100s.

523   Writ, for fees, 15 July 1402.
HEREFORD AND THE ADJACENT MARCH OF WALES. Inquisition. Hereford. 9 Dec.
The following were taken into the king's hands:
Stoke Edith and Upper Sapey, 1 fee held by the heir of Roger de Mortuo Mari, £15.
Westhide, 1 fee held by John son of Walter Helion, 100s.; and ½ fee held by the heirs
of John le Brut, Thomas Rauley and the abbot of Gloucester, £10.
Chadnor, 1 fee held by the heir of Thomas de Chabbenore, 20s.
Winforton, 1 fee held by the heir of Roger de Mortuo Mari, uncle of Roger de
Mortuo Mari, junior, knight, 100s.
Eyton, 1 fee held by the heir of John de Penbrugge, 40s.

524   Writ, for fees, 15 July 1402.
HAMPSHIRE. Inquisition. Andover. 16 Sept.
The following were taken into the king's hands:
'Wynkeleye', ½ fee held by the heirs of Sir Edward Kendale, £10.
Shalden, 1 fee held by the heir of Sir John de Hampton, £20.

525 Writ, for fees, 15 July 1402.

WILTSHIRE. Inquisition. . . . . 18 Sept.

The following were taken into the king's hands:

Lydiard, 1 fee held by William de Bray, knight, £20.

Combe, ⅕ fee held by the heir of John Tony, 40s.

Tidcombe, 1/10 fee held by the heir of Peter Oliver, 20s.

Woodborough, ½ fee held by the heir of Adam de la Ryvere, 10 marks.

Costow, 1 fee held by the abbot of Stanley, £20.

Britford, 1 fee held by the heir of Thomas de Seint Omer, £20.

And the advowsons of the free chapel of Cherhill, 40s., and of Woodborough, 10 marks.

526 Writ, for fees, 1 Nov. 1402.

SUSSEX. Inquisition. Angmering. 12 Jan. 1403.

The following was taken into the king's hands:

Rumboldswyke, 1 fee which the heirs of John de Foxle, and Walter de Wik held, £10.

527 Writ, for fees, 15 July 1402.

WARWICK. Inquisition. Warwick. 4 Nov.

The following were taken into the king's hands:

Farnborough, 1 fee held by Thomas de Raleigh, £20.

Seckington and Wilnecote, 1 fee held by Thomas Burdet, £20.

Dosthill, ½ fee held by John Burdet, knight, £10.

Baddesley, 1 fee held by the heir of John Harecourt, £10.

Mancetter, ½ fee held by William de Bello Campo, knight, £10.

Amington, 1 fee held by William de Clyndon, knight, £20.

Curdworth, ½ fee held by Helen de Ardern, 100s.

Moxhull, ½ fee held by Helen de Ardern, 100s.

Wiggins Hill, ¼ fee held by the heir of Ralph Wylyngton, 40s.

Whitacre, ¼ fee held by the heir of John Pecche, 60s.

Elmdon, ½ fee held by the same, 100s.

Waver Marston, ¼ fee held by the heir of Hugh de Hereberd, 60s.

Whittington, 1 fee held by William lord of Atterley, £20.

Great Packington, 1 fee held by the prior of Kenilworth, 100s.

Sheldon, ½ fee held by Richard Arundel, knight, £15.

Corley, ½ fee held by William de Bello Campo, knight, £10.

Baxterley, ⅙ fee held by the heir of John de Harecourt, 60s.

Longdon, 1/20 fee held by the abbot of Westminster, 40s.

Chelmscote, ½ fee held by Thomas Holand, £10.

Shotteswell, 1¼ fees held by Baldwin Bereford, knight, and John Beauchamp of Holt, knight, £20.

Ratley and Upton, 1 fee, 1/10 fee and ¼ fee held by John Maynwarying, the heir of Hugh de Upton and John de Upton, £13.

Brailes, ⅙ and ¼ fee held by the heir of John Segrave and the heir of John Mountfort, 70s.

Barton, ¼ fee held by William Ranes and John de Clynton, 40s.

Compton Wyniates, ½ fee held by Edmund Compton, £10.

Charlecote, ½ fee held by the heir of John de Mountfort, 100s.

Fenny Compton, $\frac{1}{2}$ fee held by the heir of Thomas de Ardern, 100s.

Bedsworth, $\frac{1}{4}$ fee held by Thomas Archer, 40s.

Monkspath, 1 fee held by William Mountfort, £10.

Wormleighton, 1 fee held by the heir of John Harecourt, £20.

Pillerton Hersey, 1 fee held by John de Thornebery, knight, £20.

Walton Deyville, 1 fee held by Mabel [*recte* Maud] widow of John Lestraunge, knight, £20.

Walton Mauduit, $\frac{1}{20}$ fee held by the same Mabel [*recte* Maud], 10s.

Winterton, $\frac{1}{2}$ fee held by the heir of Lord le Despenser, 100s.

Whitchurch, 1 fee held by the heir of Peter de Monte Forti, £20.

Wellesbourne, 1 fee held by the same, £20.

Weston and Barcheston, $\frac{1}{2}$ fee held by William de Bello Campo, knight, and Edward Benstede, knight, and Joan his wife in right of Joan, £10.

Mollington, $\frac{1}{2}$ fee held by the prior of Kenilworth, £10.

Halford, $\frac{1}{4}$ fee held by the heir of John Fosse, £10.

Cherington, $\frac{3}{4}$ fee held by Thomas Lucy, £10.

Compton Verney, 1 fee held by Richard Northlond, knight, in right of his wife, £20.

Willoughby, $\frac{1}{2}$ and $\frac{1}{5}$ fee held by the master of the hospital of St. John of Oxford, and the heir of Thomas de Ardern, £10.

Napton on the Hill, $\frac{1}{5}$ fee held by the heir of Ralph Basset of Sapcote, 40s.

Grandborough, $\frac{1}{10}$ fee held by the heir of Robert son of Adam de Napton, 20s.

Shuckburgh, 2 parts and $\frac{1}{3}$ fee held by John Catesby and the prioress of Wroxall, £10.

Harborough, 1 fee held by William Hathewyk, £20.

Birdingbury, $\frac{1}{2}$ fee held by John Olney of Weston, £10.

Marton, $\frac{1}{2}$ fee held by William de Bello Campo, knight, £15.

Hill Wootton, 1 fee held by William de Clynton, knight, £20.

Shiten Hodnell, $\frac{1}{6}$ fee held by the abbot of Combe, 40s.

Hodnell Gurmunt, $\frac{1}{5}$ fee held by John Harryes, 40s.

Hodnell Bruiz, $\frac{1}{3}$ fee held by the prioress of Nuneaton, 60s.

Rugby, $\frac{1}{2}$ fee held by Edmund earl of Stafford, £10.

Binley, $\frac{1}{20}$ fee held by the abbot of Combe, 20s.

Astley and Milverton, 1 fee held by the heir of Nicholas de Asteley, £20.

Marston, 1 fee held by the same, £10.

Hunningham, $\frac{1}{4}$ fee held by Edward Metteley in right of his wife, 100s.

Radbourne, $\frac{1}{10}$ fee held by John Catesby, 20s.

Walcot, $\frac{1}{5}$ fee held by the dean and chapter of St. Mary's, Warwick, 40s.

Frankton and Kenilworth, $\frac{1}{2}$ fee held by Thomas de Molyngton, £15.

Baginton, $\frac{1}{2}$ fee held by William Bagot, knight, £10.

Holme, $\frac{1}{6}$ fee held by the abbot of Rocester, 20s.

Bedworth and Willey, 1 fee held by William de Beauchamp, £15.

Little Lawford, $\frac{1}{5}$ fee held by the abbot of Combe, the abbot of Pipewell and the heir of Geoffrey Crofte, £10.

Barnacle and Shilton, $\frac{1}{2}$ fee held by John Beauchamp of Holt, knight, and Roger Grisley in right of his wife, £10.

Ladbroke, 1 fee and $\frac{1}{4}$ fee held by John Catesby and the master of the hospital of St. John of Oxford, £15.

Woodcote, $\frac{1}{6}$ fee held by Thomas Hubaud, 40s.

Coundon, $\frac{1}{16}$ fee held by William de Bello Campo, knight, 10s.

Radford and Fulready, ½ fee held by the prior of Kenilworth, £10.

Brandon, ½ fee held by Richard de Arundell, knight, £10.

Thurlaston, 1 fee held by the heir of Thomas duke of Norfolk, £20.

Draycote and Bourton on Dunsmore, 1 fee held by Guy bishop of St. Davids and others, £20.

Lillington, 1 fee held by the prior of Kenilworth, £20.

Ashow and Caldecote, ½ fee held by the prior of Kenilworth and William Allesley, £10.

Cawston, ½ fee held by the abbot of Pipewell, £10.

Avon Dassett and Hunscote, 1 fee and ½ fee held by the heir of John Pecche and by Thomas de Erdyngton, £30.

Exhall, ¼ fee held by William Corbyson of Kenilworth, 40s.

Upton, 1 fee held by Thomas de Molyngton in right of his wife, £20.

Billesley, 1 fee held by the same, £10.

Coughton, ½ fee held by Guy Spyney, 100s.

Spernall, 1 fee held by the heir of Nicholas Durnashale, £10.

Alcester, ½ fee held by William de Bello Campo of Powick, knight, 100s.

Preston Bagot and Kington, 1 fee held by the master of the hospital of St. John of Jerusalem in England, £10.

Snitterfield, 1 fee held by William de Bello Campo, knight, £20.

Fulbrook, ⅓ fee held by William Vaux, Thomas Knyght, clerk, and others, 100s.

Hatton and Beausale, 1/16 fee held by the heir of Richard Abovebrook and Richard Ask, 20s.

Studley Hay and Studley Pandonger, ¼ and 1/42 fee held by William de Beauchamp, knight, 105s.

Wilmcote, 1 fee held by John Lyle, £10.

Luddington, ¼ fee held by John Wyard in right of his wife, 100s.

Loxley, 1 fee held by the prior of Kenilworth, £15.

Stretton on Fosse, ½ fee held by Margaret widow of Roger Hillary, £10.

And the following advowsons:

Warwick, deanery of the college of the Blessed Virgin Mary, held by Thomas Yonge, clerk, extending at £20 when it occurs; and five prebends there held by Robert Mile, William Brugge, Thomas Knyght, Robert Roule, and Richard Bromley, clerks, each extending at 100s.

Warwick, priory of St. Sepulchre, 10 marks.

Warwick, hospital of St. John, 100s.

Warwick, hospital of St. Michael, 40s.

Lighthorne church, 20 marks.

Berkswell church, £20.

Sutton Coldfield, 20 marks.

Wedgnock, free chapel called Cuckow church, 40s.

C 137/28, no.58
C 47/9, no.40

HUGH HASTYNGES, KNIGHT

528   Writ 25 June 1401.

HAMPSHIRE. Inquisition. Barton Stacey. 10 Aug.

He held in his demesne as of fee in chief of Edward III by knight service 2 a. in Sutton

Scotney lying in the open field called 'Hentechele' between the lands of William White on both sides, annual value 11d.

He died on 29 July 1347. Edward Hastynges, knight, is his kinsman and heir, namely brother of Hugh, esquire, son of Hugh, knight, son of Hugh, knight, brother of John son of Hugh Hastynges. On 12 May last he was aged 19 years.

The escheators have held the lands since his death and accounted for the revenues.

C 137/29, no.60

WILLIAM HERTHILL

529 Writ for proof of age, stating that he was in ward of Roger Sapurton, who should be warned. 28 Feb. 1401.

[Endorsed] He was warned by John Northfolk and John Norreys.

WARWICK. Proof of age. Tamworth. 10 March.

Duly examined the jurors say that William Herthill, kinsman and heir of Richard Herthill, knight, was born at Baginton and baptised there on 25 Jan. 1380, and so is aged 21 years and more.

Thomas Mydelmore, aged 50 years and more, was present in the church at the baptism, and his son Thomas was then married to Joan there.

Robert de Aston, 53 and more, Adam Seyntcler, 48 and more, William Hawe, 46 and more, and Thomas Waryng, 44 and more, were at Warwick on that 25 Jan. before the king's justices, when Giles Herthill, knight, the father, was told of the birth.

Roger Whatcroft, 50 and more, was married to Joan his wife in that church on that 25 Jan.

Thomas Codyngton, 52 and more, remembers because his house was burnt down on that day, and those who came to help told him that Giles Herthill, knight, had a son by Katherine his wife on that day.

Robert atte Grene, 51 and more, John atte Merssh, 48 and more, Richard atte Byrches, 44 and more, Henry Barkere of Tamworth, 49 and more, and John Notehurst, 53 and more, began a pilgrimage to the court of Rome on the day that William was born and baptised.

C 137/29, no.61

THOMAS SURTEYS, KNIGHT, SON AND HEIR OF ALEXANDER SURTEYS

530 Writ for proof of age, stating that he was in ward of Margaret Surteys, his mother, who should be warned. 20 July 1401.

NORTHUMBERLAND. Proof of age. Newcastle upon Tyne castle. 28 Oct.

John Corbet, aged 54, Adam de Seeton, 53, William Holgrave, 60, William Hydewyn, 62, Robert de Hedle, 49, and Robert de Belyngham, 48, duly examined, say that Thomas was 21 years of age on Monday 18 April. This they know because they were at Durham for an inquisition with the sheriff about the death of John Boukyn of Gateshead when William Bowes, knight, came and told them that Alexander Surteys had a son born, and baptised in the church of Dinsdale on Tees, and that Thomas S [sic] was godfather, and he and others were there; and by the date of the inquisition in the custody of the coroner, William de Chestre, they are sure of his age.

William Benet, 48, Robert Heburn, 51, William de Wodeburn, 43, John Prestewyk, 47, John Bekynton, 55, and John Yongare, 45, say that Alice wife of William Benet was in Alexander's house at Dinsdale on Tees when Thomas was born, and afterwards in church where she was godmother. William Bent and a certain John Pykdene took Thomas Surteys to Silton in Yorkshire to be in the care of a nurse there on the morrow of Trinity, when he was aged 6 weeks. Also they say that John de Dalton, chaplain of Alexander, wrote the name and date of Thomas's birth in a missal in the church, and this writing proves his age. It is also proved by the inquisition on Alexander in Northumberland [*CIPM* XV, no.411].

C 137/29, no.62

NICHOLAS SPENSER

531   Writ 12 March 1401.

LONDON. Inquisition. 29 March.

Nicholas Spenser, formerly citizen of London, held in his demesne as of fee a tenement called 'le Welhous', 4 shops with solars above in Bowyers Row in the parish of St. Martin Ludgate, and 2 shops with solars outside Ludgate in the same parish, all of the king in free burgage, annual value £10.

He died on 9 Sept. last. John Gerard is next heir, being the son of John, son of Nicholas Gerard, brother of Robert Horner, father of Thomas, father of Maud, mother of Nicholas Spenser, and aged 42 years and more.

C 137/29, no.66

JOAN WIDOW OF JOHN SON OF THOMAS BLANCHARD

532   Writ to assign dower 22 Oct. 1400 [*CCR 1399–1402*, p.220].

WILTSHIRE. Assignment of dower in the presence of John Blanchard, son and heir of John and Joan, under age in the king's ward, Nicholas Blanchard and William Heyder, attorneys and next friends of John son of John, and Walter Tylly now husband of Joan, who was granted custody of all the lands. 28 Nov.

Cutteridge: the hall and lower chamber to the south end of the same; the lower chamber east at the north end of the same hall; the east end of the kitchen, about half of the same house [i.e. kitchen ?]; the east grange on the south side of the mansion with granary under one roof, with a little stable there for two horses; a little room next to the stable; half the garden on the east side; 1 messuage with curtilage and half the dovecot called 'Hugones'; 1 a. arable in the common field called 'Hugonesacre'; 1 croft of arable called 'Brodecroft' in the common field; 1 a. arable called 'Cokkecroft'; 1 a. arable called 'Hugonescroft'; 1 parcel of arable called 'Langebre. . .'; 1 a. meadow and 1 a. pasture called 'Ecroftes'; 1 parcel of meadow called 'la More', and 1 parcel of meadow called meadow at 'Strethende'; 1 a. meadow called 'Cokkesmede'; 1 parcel of pasture called 'Petresclose'; 1 parcel of pasture called 'Southgroves'; 1 grove of wood and underwood; and rent and services from the lands which William Heyder holds at will. This is about a third part of the lands which John Blanchard her former husband held in his demesne as of fee.

Also £8 17s. 9d. of the farm of the manor of Barford St. Martin with the bailiwick of the forest called 'la S. . .' [torn off] in Grovely Wood which John Blanchard granted to Bernard Brocas and others, [a third part of] £26 13s.4d., the farm which John Blanchard had.

C 137/29, no.69

MARGARET WIDOW OF WILLIAM LUCY, KNIGHT

533 HEREFORD. Assignment of dower in the absence of the next heir who did not wish to be present. Leominster. 19 Sept. 1401.

Richard's Castle lordship: 1 meadow called 'Parkmedowe' with the second crop of the same; 2 other meadows called 'Astemedowe' and 'Shawemedowe'; all lands, tenements, meadows, pastures, rents and services in Batchcott, Rochford and Overton; all lands called 'Masoneslondes'; 1 pasture or close called 'Hakelettes close'; assize rent of 3d. yearly in 'Hylle' and Halton; all rents and dayworks of tenants of the manor of Richard's Castle, namely by custom certain mowings of corn; and 2 woods called 'Evenes' and 'Sonheld'.

C 137/29, no.70

JOAN WIDOW OF THOMAS QUATREMAYNS

534 OXFORD. Assignment of dower in the presence of Richard Quatremayns, John Middelwod, John Shereman, Robert Chapman, Richard atte More and the individual tenants of the manor. 7 Sept. 1400.

From the manor called 'Quatremaynsplace' of North Weston, and all lands etc.:

In the capital messuage 1 high chamber at the end of the hall towards the east, with 1 drawing chamber and adjacent latrine, 2 low chambers under the high chamber, 1 called 'wolhous' and the other 'norcerye', with a latrine in the latter; 1 little stable attached to the high chamber in the internal part of the manor; 1 house under one roof, having 3 doors, attached to the said stable in the interior of the manor, which house has 3 workshops called 'pressynghous', 'larderhous' and 'malthous' and one high chamber over the 'larderhous' and 'malthous' with free ingress and egress by the doors of the hall; 2 bays of a long house under one roof covered with straw next to the 'pressinghous'; a third part of the profits of the dovecot with free ingress and egress; 2 bays of the great barn to the south with the portico annexed; a third part of 'Rekheys' next to the said barn; 2 bays in the great sheepfold towards the west; and 1 bay in the piggery to the north.

And a third part of the following: the croft called 'Dykedecroft' containing 2½ a. to the east; the croft called 'Frankeleynescroft' 2 a. to the east; the great garden with 'le Assheheys' to the south; the curtilage called 'Orchard' to the north; the croft called 'Brodecroft' to the north; 'Cotageheys' to the south; the pond with fishery; and 'Moryeveheys'.

And rents of free tenants, 30s. 1½d.: Hugh Swon, 8s. 10d.; Nicholas Sherewynd, 7½d.; John Baylly, 10s.8d; John Carpenter, 10s.

Fifty-three a. arable lying in the following furlongs: ½ a. in 'Nethermersshacr' next to land of John Hamelden on the north; 1 a. in 'Netherhachet' to the south of John Knyghtwyne; ½ a. in 'Overhachet' to the north of William Baldyndon; 1 'havedlond' in 'Mersshydych'; 2 a. in 'Behyndelangedon' to the south of Roger Pope; ½ a. in

'Uponlangedon' next to John Carpenter on the west; 1 a. in 'Lepesdon' next to Roger
Pope on the east; ½ a. in the same next to the rector of Thame; 1 a. called 'Thornyacre'
towards 'Lepersonhul'; 1 a. in the same furlong to the west of Walter Seykyn; 1 a.
called 'Pykedacre' in 'Pykede' to the south of Roger Pope; 1 a. called 'Langelond' in
'Langdongrene' to the west of the said Roger; 1 a. in 'Goselond' to the south of the
said Roger, and ½ a. to the south of William Wace; ½ a. in 'Ryhamfeld' on the north
of William Baldyndon; 1 a. in 'Hangelond' to the east of 'Frameseworth land'; 2 a.
in 'Brodeweye to the west of Roger Pope, and ½ a. in the same field next to Nicholas
Gater; ½ a. in 'Northsandfurlong'; ½ a. in 'Thamemanland' to the north of Walter
Seykyn; 2 a. in 'Stonycroft' to the west of John Hamelden; 1 a. in 'Oversand' to the
west of Thomas Pede; 1 a. in the 'Quocche'; 1 a. in 'Efurlong' to the west of Thomas
Pede, and 1 a. in the same between the lands of Thomas Pope on both sides; 1 a. in
'Otefurlong' to the south of John Middelwod; 1 a. in 'Gosylake' to the east of William
Baldyndon, and ½ a. in the same to the west of William Knyghtwyne; ½ a. in 'Morefur-
long' to the west of Walter Seykyn; 1 a. in 'Quychefurlong' to the east of John
Hamelden; 1 a. in 'Milleway' next to Roger Pope; 2 a. in 'Hammefurlong' to the north
of John Weston; 1 a. in 'Brokefurlong' to the west of Roger Pope; 1 a. in 'Tyshull'
to the east of Roger Pope, and ½ a. in the same to the south of John Carpenter; 1½ a.
in 'Behynderyggewey' to the west of Richard Elys; 1 a. in 'Myllyngesford' to the south
of William Baldyndon; 1 a. in 'Malybrok' called 'Hedacre' next to Roger Pope, and
½ a. in the same to the south of John Weston; 2½ a. in 'Mussefurlong' to the south of
Roger Pope; 1 a. in 'Whethull' to the west of John Weston; ½ a. in 'Brodewey' to the
west of John Weston, 1 a. in the same to the east of Thomas Pede, and 1½ a. to the
west of Alice Colles; 3 a. in the furlong next the gate of the manor on the way to Thame
to the north of 2 spinneys called 'Hawethornes', and ½ a. in the same next to the road
to Thame, 1 a. outside (*extra*); ½ a. on 'le Stampe' next to Thomas Pede to the north,
1 a. on the same to the south of 'Fermelond', and ½ a. to the south of John Wotton;
½ a. to the north of John Wotton; ½ a. to the south of Roger Pope; ½ a. to the north
of 'Fermelond' [last 4 items repeated]; 1 a. to the north of Richard Elys, 1 a. outside
(*extra*); ½ a. by the road to Thame called 'Cristemershull'; ½ a. 'Behynde Assheheys'
to the north of Richard Elys, 1 a. in the same furlong lying next to 'Dykedecrofte',
1 a. outside (*extra*), and 2 roods in the same with a third part of the water called
'Wateryngplace'.

Also assigned to Joan: 10 a. meadow, of which 2 a. are called 'the Fereyte', 2 a. the
'Mylletene', and 1 a. lies in the 'Lynchetene', a third part of 'Bolehok' extending
lengthwise to east and west, 1½ roods lie in 'Brodedole' on the west, 1 a. in 'Astmede'
to the west, 1 a. in the meadow called 'Fourtene' extending lengthwise to north and
south, and 2 a. lie by 'le Bryggeacre'.

In Thame, a third part of the rent of 2 burgages which Thomas Quatremayns held
of the bishop of Lincoln by the service of 1d. rent and suit of court twice yearly.

In Henley upon Thames, in the capital messuage of Thomas there called
'Gobyonsplace', 1 high chamber at the end of the hall to the north, 2 low chambers
attached to the hall, another high chamber next to the first high chamber, with a kitchen
under; 1 garden next to the kitchen with free egress and ingress by the doors of the
hall; 1 vacant place on the north of the kitchen; thus by metes and bounds marked
and defined.

Henley upon Thames, 3 a. arable in the fields which Thomas Clobber holds, of
which 3 roods lie in a field called 'Aldefeld' to the south of Thomas Clobber, 3 roods
in the same field between the lands of Thomas on both sides, 3 in a field called 'Drayerys'
between his lands on both sides, and 3 more in the same between his lands on the north;

and in 1 a. called 'Medeacre' a third part of 'sexti Horstoke'; and 4d. rent of certain tenants.

In Rotherfield Greys, a third part of the formerly built up place called 'Ardernes' to the south; 27 a. 1 rood of fallow land scattered in various crofts: 2 a. in 'Parkcroft' to the east with bounds annexed, 5 a. in 'Huydecroft' with bounds to the east, 2 a. in 'Crokydcroft' next 'Huydecroft' with bounds, 1 a. in 'Crokydcroft' by 'Brodefeld' to the east with bounds, 2½ a. in a croft next to 'Ardernesplace' to the south with bounds, 3 a. in 'Longecroft' to the north with bounds; 2 a. in 'Rethermerefeld' to the east with bounds; 2 a. in 'Shepecroft' with bounds; ⅓ a. in 'Heyronescroft' to the east with bounds; 7 a. in 'Brodefeld' to the south with bounds; 2 a. arable lengthwise by the ditch of the meadow called 'Retherfeldsmede'; and 1 rood of meadow to the east in the meadow of Rotherfield Greys.

In Standlake 19s.9d. rent from free tenants: from Thomas Fyssher 16s., and from Robert Besyly 3s.9d.

C 137/29, no.71

THOMAS DE ASSELE, KNIGHT

535   YORK. Inquisition *ex officio*. York castle. 28 Jan. 1401.

He held in his demesne as of fee of the king in chief by knight service the manor of Bingley, extending in Bingley, Priesthorpe, Eldwick, Lees, Hainworth, Cottingley, Marley, Cullingworth, Micklethwaite, Gilstead and 'Birstford', annual value £13 6s. 8d.

He died on 2 Nov. last. Thomas his son and heir is aged 22 years and more.

C 137/29, no.72
E 152/364, no.2

RALPH BASSET, KNIGHT

536   STAFFORD. Inquisition *ex officio*. Stafford. 10 Aug. 1401.

Ralph Basset of Drayton Bassett, knight held in his demesne in fee simple of the king in chief by knight service:

Walsall, half the manor, with 1 messuage, 120 a., 20 a. meadow, 4 a. pasture and 10 a. wood which Ralph Basset, knight, his grandfather, acquired from Alice Archer; 10 a. called 'Godfordesland' which his grandfather acquired from Richard Hillori, parson of Wolstanton; 12d. rent from lands and tenements held by Adam de Wytton there and in Wyrley; 2 messuages, 1 toft and ½ virgate which John Petyt and Adam Tailour once held there, which he gave to William Coleson and the heirs of his body, with reversion failing such heirs to himself and his heirs; and 1 messuage and 1 garden lying in 'Russhehalestrete' which he granted to John Flecher of Walsall and Alice his wife and John their son for their lives for a rent of 6s. 8d., which rent and reversion he held at his death. Annual value of all, apart from the reversions, £20.

He died on 5 May 1389 without heirs of his body. Edmund earl of Stafford, son of Hugh, son of Ralph, son of Margaret, sister of Ralph Basset, father of Ralph, father of Ralph, is heir, aged 23 years and more.

Thomas de Bello Campo, formerly earl of Warwick, by colour of a fine of 1339 to Ralph Basset by William Heerle, knight, and others [CP 25(1) 287/40, no.255] intruded upon the half manor, lands and tenements over the royal possession, which pertained to the king owing to the successive minorities of Thomas and William, late earls of Stafford, and Edmund now earl of Stafford, who were all in the king's ward, and took the issues and profits, until the death of Thomas earl of Warwick on 8 April. For the issues he is answerable to the king.

C 137/29, no.73

THOMAS DE NORMANTON

537   LINCOLN. Inquisition *ex officio*. Navenby. 30 Oct. 1400.

He once held in his demesne as of fee the manor of Normanton and lands in Swarby comprising by estimate 1 messuage, 40 a. arable and 10 a. meadow. He had three daughters, Margaret, Isabel and Elizabeth. After his death they entered and divided his lands. Margaret took half the manor of Normanton, Isabel the other half, and Elizabeth the lands in Swarby.

Roger Punchard dispossessed Margaret without a judgment and all her life she claimed against him. He died leaving a son, Ralph, an idiot. Margaret entered her part, and a certain brother Brian Gray and Eustacia mother of Ralph ejected her in the name of Ralph. She died without heirs of her body.

Elizabeth, whilst still under age, married William Nicolson, also under age, and they both still under age alienated Elizabeth's lands in Swarby to Roger Punchard. He died holding them.

Elizabeth had three daughters, who are still alive, Nicola married to Peter Bayllyf, Joan married to John Camyn of Cowick, and Avelina. Elizabeth died, and Isabel is dead, and the daughters of Elizabeth, sister of Margaret, are therefore her heirs.

All is held by Ralph, the idiot, and should belong to the king on account of his madness. The manor is held of Thomas Bardolf, service unknown, annual value of the half 20s. The lands in Swarby are held of Walter Pedwardyn, knight, service unknown, annual value 10s.

C 137/29, no.74

JOHN SON OF WILLIAM HOOD

538   DEVON. Inquisition. Herton. 29 Aug. 1401.

John Hood, son of William Hood of Northcott, is an idiot from birth. He held 1 messuage and 1 ferling in Northcott, which he gave to William Hood and William his son in fee simple.

William the father died. William the son has held it for 9 years past and still holds and occupies it; annual value 40d. John Hood is still alive.

C 137/29, no.75

JOAN COKE

539   DEVON. Inquisition. Great Torrington. 27 Aug. 1401.

Joan Coke was an idiot from birth. She held 1 messuage and 10 a. in the tithing of Torrington, which she gave to Thomas Somer, his heirs and assigns. Thomas is dead.

Joan his widow has occupied and taken the profits from the beginning of Lent last, on behalf of Joan his daughter and heir; annual value 2s.

C 137/29, no.76

RALPH HASTYNGES, KNIGHT

540 Writs, ordering the inquisition below to be sent into chancery, 20 and 22 June 1401.
[Endorsed] The escheator received the writs at Richmond on 2 July and despatched them with the inquisition on the following day.

Another writ, ordering release of the lands, 15 Oct. 1401 [CCR 1399–1402, p.428]. YORK. Inquisition ex officio. Slingsby. 23 June.
Ralph de Hastynges, knight, of Slingsby held in his demesne as of fee of Thomas, son and heir of Thomas duke of Norfolk, of his manor of Thirsk by knight service, the castle and manor of Slingsby with its members in Slingsby, Coulton and Howthorpe. The castle and manor of Slingsby are worth £16 annually, payable, by equal parts at Martinmas and Whitsun, Coulton 40s., and Howthorpe £8, both payable at the same terms.
He died on 27 Oct. 1397. Richard de Hastynges, knight, his son and heir, will be 20 years of age on 24 Aug. next.

C137/29, no.78
E 149/76, no.5

WILLIAM WYNGEFELD, KNIGHT

541 NORTHAMPTON. Inquisition ex officio. Peterborough. 18 Nov. 1400.
William Wyngefeld, knight, held 16 marks rent in Paston, Milton, Borough Fen and Castor and a wood of 3 a. in Paston, annual value 7s.6d., with reversion after his death to Robert Veer, late duke of Ireland, and his heirs. By his forfeiture they should belong to the king.
William died on 25 May 1399. Aubrey de Veer and Alice his wife held them from that date until 12 Nov. 1399. Since then John Holand of Paston has held by letters patent [CPR 1399–1401, p.78] shown to the escheator and jurors.

542 RUTLAND. Inquisition ex officio. Oakham. 20 Nov. 1400.
He held the manor of Market Overton, annual value £20, with reversion to Robert Veer, as above.
Maud countess of Oxford has occupied it since his death, and taken the profits. Date of death as above.

543 NORTHAMPTON. Inquisition ex officio. Peterborough. 23 April 1404.
He held with reversion to Robert Veer, late duke of Ireland, who forfeited to Richard II, and his heirs:
Paston, 10 a. separately enclosed, namely 2 a. wood and the rest untilled pasture; the covering of the 2 a. wood would sell altogether at 5 marks beyond the cost of the

enclosure; and 1 garden called 'le Moreyerd' with ash trees growing in it, total value of trees for felling 2 marks.

Milton, 2 a. wood called 'Blackmanneswode', the crop being worth 100s. for sale beyond the cost of the enclosure.

They are in the hands of John Holand of Paston, title unknown.

He once held 1 a. wood called 'Grumbaldeswode' in Milton, now worth nothing because Thomas Gerard of Milton took away all the timber to his own use and the king's loss of 40s., title unknown. Similarly he once held a garden in Paston called 'le Welleyerd' with ash trees, worth nothing because John Holand has removed them, title unknown, with loss to the king of 40s.

E 149/77, no.3

ISABEL WIDOW OF EDMUND DE DRAYTON

544 SHROPSHIRE. Inquisition *ex officio*. Shrewsbury. 31 May 1401.

She held for life certain lands jointly with Edmund her husband in Market Drayton, Eyton and Eaton. He was outlawed for felony. She died on 20 April last. They descended to Richard, brother and heir of Edmund, who was also outlawed. They are worth 40s. annually and are so let to farm, payable at Easter and Michaelmas.

E 149/77, no.7

RICHARD LENYET

545 WORCESTER. Inquisition *ex officio*. Worcester. 6 Nov. 1400.

Richard Lenyet, who inherited a messuage and 30 a. in Tenbury, is an idiot from birth. They are held of the manor of Tenbury, service unknown, annual value 3s.4d.

On 10 July 1400 at Pershore, a horse worth 20s. was the cause of the death of William Smyth of Pershore.

On 10 April 1400 in the Severn by Worcester castle a boat worth 6s.8d. caused the death of John, son of John Carpenter of Clevelode.

E 149/77, no.19

WILLIAM DANGULEM, KNIGHT

546 DORSET. Inquisition *ex officio*. Shaftesbury. 29 Aug. 1402.

He held the manor and advowson of Stour Provost for life by the grant of Richard II, annual value £23 6s.4½d.

He died on 26 Aug. last.

E 149/79, no.12

WALTER BROMWICH

547 HEREFORD. Inquisition. Hereford. 11 March 1401.

Edmund de Mortuo Mari, late earl of March, gave to Walter Bromwich an annual rent of 20 marks from the manor of Mansell Lacy for life.

He died on 9 Feb. last. The rent should revert to Edmund, son and heir of Roger late earl of March, who is under age in the king's ward. Edward de Charleton and Eleanor his wife hold the manor in dower since the death of Roger, her late husband.

E 149/76, no.9

JOHN SEWARD

548 WILTSHIRE. Inquisition. Salisbury. 6 Aug. 1401.

John Seward of Winterslow held in his demesne as of fee of the king in chief 1 messuage, 32 a. and 8 a. wood in Winterslow; the reversion of 15 a. arable and pasture for 30 sheep in Winterslow 'South' which Alice Dodenammes holds in dower; and the reversion of a toft, 4½ a. and 1 rood which John Willy holds for a term of years in the same, of the king in chief by a rent of 5s. 2d. and suit of the hundred of Amesbury every 3 weeks; annual value of all nil.

He died on 21 Dec. 1394. Richard Godeman is next heir, being the son of John Godeman, son of Edith, sister of John Seward, and aged 39 years and more.

E 149/77, no.15

RICHARD MAUDELEYN, CLERK

549 Writ 5 May 1402.

SURREY. Inquisition. Southwark. 20 Sept.

He held nothing in Surrey.

He died on 28 Jan. 1400. Who is his next heir is unknown.

C 137/30, no.1

JOHN LYNFORD

550 Writ 7 Oct. 1401.

BUCKINGHAM. Inquisition. Newport Pagnell. 17 Oct.

He held the manor of Sherington in his demesne as of fee of the king in chief as a third part of a knight's fee, annual value 100s.

He died on 3 Aug. John his son and heir is aged 28 years and more.

551 Writ 7 Oct. 1401.

RUTLAND. Inquisition. Oakham. 14 Oct.

He held in right of Katherine his wife, who survives him:

Manton, the manor called 'Luffewykmaner', of the earl of Warwick by the rent of one sparrowhawk or 2s., annual value 8 marks.

Ridlington, Glaston, Langham and Normanton, 4 marks rent, of the same earl of his manor of Morcott by suit of court twice yearly at Morcott.

He died on 3 Aug. John, son of John and Katherine, his heir, is aged 32 years and more.

C 137/30, no.2

WILLIAM SPERNORE

552 Writ 5 Oct. 1401.

WARWICK. Inquisition. Henley in Arden. 22 Oct.

He held the manor of Spernall for life, of Richard, son and heir of Thomas late earl of Warwick, under age in the king's ward, of the castle of Warwick as half a knight's fee, with reversion to Walter Holt as son and heir of Eleanor, daughter of Nicholas Dirnasall, annual value £6 13s.4d.

He died on 30 Sept. Walter Holt was aged 19 years and more on 18 July. Margaret is William's daughter and next heir, aged 16 years and more.

553 Writ 5 Oct. 1401.

STAFFORD. Inquisition. Walsall. 28 Nov.

He held nothing of the king in chief, but Thomas de Bello Campo, earl of Warwick, after his marriage to Margaret, who survives him, granted his manors of Perry and Barr to William for life for the rent of a rose at Midsummer, with reversion to himself and his heirs. Richard de Bello Campo, knight, the son of Thomas, is heir, aged 19 years on 25 January. They are not held of the king in chief but of whom and by what service is unknown; annual values, Perry 100s., Barr 5 marks.

He died on 25 Sept. Margaret and Joyce his daughters and heirs are aged 17 years and 10 years, and more.

C 137/30, no.3
E 152/376, no.1

WILLIAM FIENLES, KNIGHT

554 Writ 22 Jan. 1402.

OXFORD. Inquisition. Oxford. 28 Jan.

He held nothing in the county.

He died on 19 Jan. Roger his son and heir is aged 16 years and more.

555 BERKSHIRE. Inquisition. Twyford. 26 Jan. 1402.

He held in his demesne as of fee of the king in chief a bailiwick in the forest of Windsor called 'le Twychene' by a rent of 10s. to the castle of Windsor, annual value 24s.6d.

Date of death and heir as above.

556 Writ 22 Jan. 1402.

HAMPSHIRE. Inquisition. Romsey. 27 Feb.

He held nothing in the county.

Date of death and heir as above.

557 Writ 22 Jan. 1402.
SUSSEX. Inquisition. Hailsham. 27 Feb.
 He held nothing in the county.
 Date of death and heir as above.

C 137/30, no. 5
E 152/375, 378

JOHN ALISAUNDRE OF OUSBY

558 Writ 27 Nov. 1401.
CUMBERLAND. Inquisition. Penrith. 10 Jan. 1402.
 He held in his demesne as of fee of the king in chief 1 tenement and 12 a. arable and meadow with one eighth of the lordship of the town of Ousby, as a twenty-fourth part of a knight's fee, at a cornage rent of 6d. and also 22½d. at the exchequer of Carlisle for socage, annual value 4s.
 He died on 25 April 1400. Robert his son and next heir is aged 30 years and more. William de Louthre and Robert de Mulcastre, knight, formerly escheators, held the lands and took the profits, because held of the king in chief.

C 137/30, no. 6

JOHN MARSSHTON

559 Writ 22 April 1402.
SHROPSHIRE. Inquisition. Shrewsbury. 30 March.
 He held in his demesne of fee:
 Little Sutton, 2 messuages, 1½ virgates and 3 a. meadow, of the king in socage by rent of 4s. 6d. payable by the sheriff in equal parts at Easter and Michaelmas and suit of court at the hundred of Munslow once yearly, annual value 10s.
 Corfton, 4 a. arable, of Hugh Burnell, knight, Lord Burnell, of the manor, service unknown, annual value 4d.
 He died on 12 March. Thomas his son and heir is aged 30 years and more.

C 137/30, no. 7

JOHN PATENEY, CLERK

560 Writ 30 Oct. 1401.
SURREY. Inquisition. Southwark. 19 Nov.
 He held in his demesne as of fee in Mitcham 1 a. of the earl of Stafford, who is under age in the king's ward, by a rent of 2d., annual value 8d.; a parcel of meadow, comprising 3 roods and 1 swath, of whom is unknown, annual value 8d.; 5 a. arable of the prior of Merton by a rent of 2½d., annual value 8d.; 4½ a. of the prior of Christ Church, Canterbury, by a rent of 3d., annual value 6d. the a.; and 1 toft and 1 a. of John Dymmok, esquire, by a rent of 4d., annual value 6d.
 He died on 4 Nov. 1400. Who is his heir is unknown.

C 137/30, no. 8

MARGARET WIFE OF JOHN DE PEKEBRYGGE, KNIGHT

561 Writ 12 Feb. 1402.

HUNTINGDON. Inquisition. Huntingdon. 5 April.

She held two parts of a toft, 40 a. arable, 4 a. meadow and 6 a. wood in Washingley of the king in chief as two parts of one fortieth of a knight's fee by a rent of 13s.4d., annual value nil beyond the rent.

She died on 7 Aug. last. John son and heir of John and Margaret was 15 years of age on 30 Jan.

C 137/30, no.9
E 149/78, no.6

ELIZABETH WIFE OF THOMAS BEKERYNG, KNIGHT

562 Writ 28 May 1402.

BUCKINGHAM. Inquisition. Aylesbury. 6 June.

She held in her demesne as of fee of the king in chief by knight service, amount unknown:

Burnham, one third of two parts of the manor called Huntercombe.

Beaconsfield, a third part of the advowson, annual value with the above 20s.

Eton, one third of two parts of the manor, annual value 20s.

She died on 22 April last. John Rous her son and heir is aged 24 years and more.

C 137/30, no.10
E 149/78, no.5

ROBERT ASSHEFELDE

563 Commission to Roger Drury, knight, Thomas Derham, Richard Alred, Thomas Hethe and Henry Notyngham to enquire about the concealment of divers wards and marriages in Norfolk and Suffolk, which should pertain to the king. 4 Feb. 1402 [*CPR 1401–5*, p.68].

SUFFOLK. Inquisition before Roger Drury, knight, Richard Alfred [*sic*] and Thomas Hethe. Henhow. 12 April.

He held in his demesne as of fee the manor of Little Haugh of the king in chief by knight service, and enfeoffed by the king's licence [*CPR 1399–1401*, p.387, 25 Nov. 1400] John Ixworth, Walter Ixworth and John Berton, clerks, and others, and he took the profits before and after the enfeoffment all his life.

Roger Drury, knight, who held and still holds 1½ a. of meadow in Thurston of that manor by fealty and a rent of 13d. yearly, and John Bayle of Hessett, senior, who also held and still holds certain lands and tenements by a rent of 6d. and other lands, never attorned for these services; and so Robert Asshfelde died seised in his demesne as of fee of the manor and services.

The above feoffment was made on condition of enfeoffing Robert, grandson and heir of Robert, when he became 21, thus by fraud and collusion excluding the king from the wardship and marriage of Robert. Annual value £20.

He died on 18 Aug. 1401. Robert the heir, son of John, son of Robert, was aged

12 years and more at that time, and was taken into the ward of Roger Davy, and so remains.

He also held in his demesne as of fee half the advowson of the priory of Ixworth and 1d, rent of the king in chief by knight service, annual value 4d.

[*Cf. CIM* VII, no.208].

564 Writ 20 April 1402.

SUFFOLK. Inquisition. Henhow. 10 May.

He held in his demesne as of fee:

Little Haugh, the manor, of the king in chief by knight service of the barony of Hatch Beauchamp in Somerset as a twenty-fifth part of a knight's fee, annual value £20.

Stowlangtoft, the manor and advowson, with lands and tenements in Stowlangtoft, Yoxford, Langham, Bardwell, Winston, 'Belyngham', Hepworth, Weston, Walsham, Hunston, and Great and Little Ashfield, of the abbot of Bury St. Edmunds by knight service, annual value £20.

Stanton, 1 tenement called 'Mekelfeldis' with the advowson of half the church, of the tenants of the manor of Horsford by knight service, annual value 5 marks; another tenement there called 'Nicholis de Stanton' and another called 'Toroldys' of the said abbot, service unknown, annual value 40s.

Date of death and heir, aged 14 years and more, as above.

565 NORFOLK. Inquisition. Wimbotsham. 2 Jan. 1404.

Robert de Asshfeld of Suffolk held in his demesne as of fee the manor called 'Dersynghamsmanere' in the vills of Beechamwell and Barton Bendish of James Byllyngford, service unknown, annual value 10 marks; and the manor called 'Josysmanere' in Shingham of the earl of March of the honour of Clare, service likewise unknown, annual value 5 marks.

Date of death and heir, aged 14 at the time of the elder Robert's death, as above. John Berton, clerk, has held and taken the profits since his death, title unknown.

C 137/30, no.11

C 137/45, no.68

JOHN PONTON

566 Writ 16 Feb. 1402.

DEVON. Inquisition. Exeter. 5 April.

John Ponton of Exeter, outlawed in London on 19 July 1395 at the suit of Robert Skyres, executor of William Horbury, clerk, in a plea of debt, held in his demesne as of fee 2 messuages and 2 gardens in Exeter in Paul Street; 4 shops and a cellar in Smith Street; 1 messuage, 1 garden and 4 shops outside the south gate; 1 messuage inside the gate; 3 cottages and a garden outside the east gate; and 1 messuage outside the north gate; all held of the king in free burgage, as is all the city of Exeter, annual value 30s.

He granted them all by his charter on 9 June 1396 to Adam Skut of Exeter, his heirs and assigns.

He died on 19(?) July 1396 [eve of St. Margaret, Saturday, 20 Richard II, but Saturday was 15 or 22 July]. Richard his brother and next heir is aged 40 years and more.

John Copleston, escheator, and the other escheators have held the premises since the outlawry and taken the profits. At present all are ruinous and empty and no one is occupying or taking the profits.

C 137/30, no.12

JOHN PAULYN OF HUNMANBY

567   Writ 12 Sept. 1402.
YORK. Inquisition. Kilham. 30 Sept.
He held in his demesne as of fee of the king in chief 2 messuages, 4½ tofts and 11¼ bovates in Hunmanby and 4½ bovates in Fowthorp in Hunmanby by knight service, annual values, messuages and tofts 12s., bovates 45s.; and one other bovate and messuage in Hunmanby of Thomas Prendergest by knight service, annual value 6s.
He died on 10 Aug. last. William his son and heir is aged 40 years and more.

C 137/30, no.13

RICHARD MALBYSSH

568   Writ 1 May 1402.
YORK. Inquisition. York. 12 July.
He held in his demesne in fee tail to himself and his heirs male by the grant of John Fairefax, clerk, the manors of Acaster Malbis, Copmanthorpe and Scawton, annual values £30, £10 and £10. Of whom Copmanthorpe is held is unknown: the others are of Richard Fairefax by knight service.
He died on 1 Nov. last. William his son and heir is aged 9 years and more.

C 137/30, no.14

JOHN FRESSHEVYLE OF PALTERTON

569   Writ 8 Oct. 1382.
Copy of inquisition, 29 Oct. 1382 [*CIPM* XV, no.766].

Writ, reciting the above, reporting the assertion that Beatrice widow of John Fresshevyle, pregnant when he died, had borne another daughter. 1 July 1402.

DERBY. Inquisition. Chesterfield. 15 Aug.
Beatrice widow of John, son of John Frechevyll, was pregnant when he died, and gave birth to Isabel, another daughter and heir, now aged 19 years and more.

C 137/30, no.15

RALPH DEYNCOURT

570   Writ 14 Feb. 1402.
BUCKINGHAM. Inquisition. Wooburn. 25 Feb.
The manor of Wooburn was taken into the king's hands owing to the death of William

Deyncourt, who held in chief of Richard II, and the minority of Ralph his son and heir, who died in the king's ward. It is held of Henry bishop of Lincoln as one knight's fee, annual value £16.

Ralph died on 7 Nov. 1384. John Deyncourt, knight, his brother and heir, is aged 20 years and more.

571   Writ 14 Feb. 1402.

NOTTINGHAM. Inquisition. Bingham. 21 Feb.

The manor of Granby was taken into the king's hands for the above reasons. It was held in chief of Richard II by knight service, annual value £34.

Date of death and heir as above.

572   DERBY. Inquisition. Bolsover. 18 Feb. 1402.

Ralph Deyncourt, a minor in the king's ward, held the manor of Holmesfield in his demesne as of fee of the king in chief by foreign service, annual value £15 payable at Martinmas and Midsummer; but William Deyncourt, his father, long before he died, granted Ralph de Nevel, knight, John Ferefax, Richard de Duthap, Matthew de Torkesey, Robert de Wyclyff, clerk, and John Deyncourt of Whaley, their heirs and assigns a rent of 100 marks from this manor and other lands and tenements in other counties, as appears by his charter.

Ralph also held the manor of Elmton in his demesne as of fee of the king in chief by foreign service, annual value £6.

Date of death and heir as above.

573   Writ 14 Feb. 1402.

DERBY. Inquisition. Bolsover. 23 Feb.

The following manors were taken into the king's hands for the above [no. 570] reasons:

Holmesfield, held of the king in chief by foreign service, value in gavelage rents payable at Martinmas and Midsummer £15.

Elmton, held of the king in chief by foreign service, annual value in rents, services and gavelage £6.

Date of death and heir as above.

574   Writ 14 Feb. 1402.

NORTHAMPTON. Inquisition. Welford. 24 Feb.

Taken into the king's hands for the above reasons were 17 virgates of land and meadow in Duddington by Collyweston, held of the duchy of Lancaster of the inheritance of the earldom of Lincoln by a rent of one unmewed sparrowhawk, annual value £10.

Date of death and heir as above.

575   Writ 14 Feb. 1402.

LINCOLN. Inquisition. Sleaford. 15 July.

The manors of Blankney and Branston were taken into the king's hands for the above reasons. Richard II granted them to John Nevyl of Raby, knight, to hold until the

full age of Ralph or the next heir. They are held of the king by barony, annual value
£42.

Date of death and heir as above.

C 137/30, no.16
E 149/79, no.4

BALDWIN DE RADYNGTON, KNIGHT

576   Writ 17 Nov. 1401.
SOMERSET. Inquisition. North Newton. 1 Dec.

He held for life by the courtesy of England with reversion to William Wroth, esquire,
the son and heir of Maud his wife, in North Newton 1 messuage, 100 a., 20 a. meadow,
6 a. wood and 6 a. pasture; and in Exton 1 messuage and 20 a. meadow. They are held
of the king in chief as a quarter of a knight's fee, annual value 100s.

William Wroth is aged 28 years and more. Emma atte Wode, Baldwin's sister and
next heir, is aged 40 years and more.

He died on 16 Nov. last.

577   Writ 17 Nov. 1401.
MIDDLESEX. Inquisition. Enfield. 5 Dec.

He held for life by the grant of Robert Rynge, William Hweler and others the manor
of Durrants in Enfield, with remainder to William Wroth, esquire, son and heir of
his wife. It is held of the countess of Hereford by knight service, annual value 10 marks.

He died on 16 Nov. last. Emma atte Wode, his sister and next heir, is aged 40 years
and more.

C 137/30, no.17

JOHN FREMAN

578   Writ 8 June 1402.
LINCOLN. Inquisition. Lincoln. 22 June.

Because of the outlawry of John Freman at the suit of John Rasyn, clerk, in a plea
of debt on 19 Nov. 1386, 1 waste messuage and 3 bovates in Faldingworth came into
the hands of Richard II. They are held by knight service in fee tail of the fee of Hay,
which Thomas de Holand, late earl of Kent, forfeited to the king; annual value 13s.4d.

He died on 8 Dec. 1398. Richard Neny is his heir, being the son and heir of Joan,
his daughter, and was aged 22 on 14 Sept. 1399.

C 137/30, no.18

THOMAS SON OF AGNES WIDOW OF HENRY SEGERE
OF YEOVIL

579   Writ 16 June 1402.
SOMERSET. Inquisition. Yeovil. 22 Sept. 1402.

Owing to the madness of Thomas, son of Agnes, widow of Henry Segere, a half
messuage in Yeovil is in the king's hands. It is held of the rector of Yeovil by a rent
of ¼d. and suit at the rector's court, annual value 4s.

He died on 7 July 1401. Margery wife of William Jolyf, his aunt and heir, is aged 30 years and more. John Jolyf and Margery and John Wylby have held it since the death of Henry and Agnes, for all the life of Thomas, and still do so.

C 137/30, no.19

CECILY DAUGHTER OF WILLIAM COOK OF EPWORTH

580   Writ 26 Oct. 1401.

LINCOLN. Inquisition. Belton in the Isle of Axholme. 2 Nov.

She held in her demesne as of fee:

Belton and Epworth, 4 messuages, 7 tofts, 1 bovate, 15½ a., 1 bovate, 1 a. and 2 parts of a toft, of the king in chief by the service of a twentieth part of a knight's fee, annual value 6s.8d.

Epworth, 7 a. meadow, of Lord Mowebray of his manor of Epworth in socage by a rent of 2s. payable at Easter and Michaelmas, annual value 12d.

She died on 24 May. Thomas del Both of Selby is next heir, being the son of Hugh, son of Robert, son of Adam, brother of Robert Ruddok, father of John, father of William Cook, father of Cecily, and aged 40 years and more.

C 137/30, no.20
E 149/79, no.3

ADOMAR DE ATHELLES, KNIGHT

581   Writ 19 April 1402.

NORTHUMBERLAND. Inquisition. Morpeth. 26 April.

John Lescrop, knight, and Elizabeth his wife held in their demesne as of fee the manor of Ponteland in right of Elizabeth, and granted it to Adomar Dathell, knight, for life with reversion to themselves and her heirs by a fine of 1392 [CP 25(1) 181/14, no.26]. It is held of the king by knight service as of his manor of Mitford, annual value 20 marks.

He died on 13 April. Elizabeth, daughter of David de Strabolgi, formerly earl of Atholl, son of David, brother of Adomar, is his next heir, and aged 30 years and more.

582   Writ 19 April 1402.

NEWCASTLE UPON TYNE. Inquisition. 27 April.

He held nothing in the city.

He died on 13 April. Elizabeth wife of John le Scrope, knight, is his cousin and next heir, being daughter of David earl of Atholl, son of David, brother of Adomar, and aged 30 years and more.

583   Writ 19 April 1402.

YORK. Inquisition. Selby. 24 April.

He held for life £30 rent payable in equal parts at Whitsun and Martinmas from lands and tenements held of the king in chief in Thixendale, Auburn, Foston on the Wolds, Scorborough, Argam, Beverley, Filey, Beswick, Nafferton, Lowthorpe, Thwing,

Kilham and Burnby, by the grant of John Conyers, Gilbert Elvette, William de Mitford, and Thomas Clerc of Wold Newton, with successive remainders to John Lescrop, knight, and Elizabeth his wife, the heirs of the body of Elizabeth by Thomas de Percy, knight, the younger, formerly her husband, and her heirs by the said John Lescrop, as appears by a fine shown to the jurors [CP 25(1) 278/146, no.59]. Of whom the rent is held is unknown.

He died on 13 April last. Elizabeth, wife of John Lescrop and daughter of David Strabolgy deceased, late earl of Atholl, is his cousin and heir and aged 36 years and more.

C 137/30, no.21

WILLIAM SALESBURY *alias* WILLIAM GILBERT

584 Writ 12 Feb. 1402.

CALAIS. Inquisition. 20 June.

He held in his demesne as of fee of the king in chief 4 tenements in the parish of St. Mary by a rent of 14s. and the service of providing 4 watchmen for the defence of the city, annual value £10.

He died on 16 April 1393. Joan wife of John Ramessey of Calais, shearman, is his kinswoman and heir, aged 34 years and more.

From his death for five years Richard Cliderowe occupied all the tenements and took the profits, title unknown. After that he sold 2 to the duke of Norfolk, and 1 to John Ramessey. The fourth he still occupies.

585 Writ, *melius sciri*, as it was found by an inquisition before John Neuport, escheator, on 18 July 1394 that William Salesbury *alias* Gilbert held in his demesne as of fee all his lands in Calais and left no will, and that Joan, wife of John Ramesey, daughter of Alice Middelton, daughter of Margaret, sister of William, was one heir, and John Gilbert, son of Constance the other sister, was the other heir; and afterwards by another inquisition by Lawrence Wotton on 20 June last it was found as above [no.584]; and John Ramesey and Joan have petitioned that John Gilbert died in the lifetime of William, and that Joan was the sole heir and so remains; order to enquire when he died and how Joan is his kinswoman and heir. 22 Oct. 1402.

CALAIS. Inquisition. 27 Nov.

John Gilbert, son of Constance, one sister of William Salesburi *alias* Gilbert, died on 12 March 1392 on his journey to Rome with the said William Gilbert. Joan wife of John Ramsey is his kinswoman and sole heir, namely the daughter of Alice, daughter of Margaret, the other sister of William.

C 137/31, no.22
C 137/40, no.42

JOHN DEYNCOURT, KNIGHT

586 Writ 13 Feb. 1402.

ESSEX. Inquisition. Brentwood. 2 March.

He died on 3 Nov. 1393 holding in his demesne as of fee the reversion of the manor

o

of Upminster after the death of Lora widow of William Morewode. The reversion of this manor, then called the manor of Gaynes in Upminster, was formerly held by William de Wyndesore, knight, by grant of Richard II [*CPR 1377–80*, p.503] to him and his heirs after the death of Lora, who held it for life and died on 4 Nov. 1393.

Joan Southerey, daughter of Alice Perrers, John Corson, knight, John Wymbyssh and Agnes his wife, and William Trendyll, clerk, have occupied the manor and taken the profits since the death of Alice de Perrers, 16 Dec. 1399. Roger son and next heir of John Deyncourt is under age in the king's ward.

587 ESSEX. Inquisition *ex officio*. Brentwood. 2 May 1403 [*recte* 1405: in 1403 2 May was not a Saturday and Helmyng Leget was not escheator].

He died seised of the manor of Upminster, all details as in last with the following additions:

The manor is held of the king, service unknown, annual value £10.

Alice de Perrers and Peter Wyndesore occupied it from 3 Nov. 1393 until 16 Dec. 1399. John Corson, knight, Joan Southerey, daughter of Alice Perrers, John Wymbyssh and Agnes his wife, and William Trendyll, clerk, have occupied it since 16 Dec. 1399. Alice de Perrers, Peter Wyndesore, John Corson, knight, Joan Sotherey, John Wymbyssh and Agnes, and William Trendell are answerable to the king for the profits, and refuse to give satisfaction to the escheator for the king.

C 137/31, no.23
E 149/81, no.7

JOHN FITZWARYN

588 Writ 5 Jan. 1402.

SHROPSHIRE. Inquisition. Munslow. 7 Feb.

He held in his demesne as of fee in chief of Reynold Grey, lord of Ruthin, cousin and heir of Hugh Hastynge, knight, the manor of Aston in Munslow in Corvedale by the service of a quarter of a knight's fee, annual value 53s.4d.

He died on 22 Dec. William his son and heir is aged 30 years and more.

589 Writ 2 Jan. 1402.

BERKSHIRE. Inquisition. Appleton. 12 Jan.

He held by the courtesy of England in right of Margaret his late wife, daughter of Giles de la Mote, sister and heir of Thomas de la Motte, two parts of the manor of Appleton with the advowson. They are held of the king by the service of a quarter of a knight's fee, annual value 10 marks.

He died on 21 Dec. last. William son and heir of John and Margaret is aged 30 years and more.

C 137/31, no.24
E 149/79, no.7
E 152/375, no.2

THOMAS POYLE, KNIGHT

590   Writ 1 Jan. 1402.

SURREY. Inquisition. Guildford. 23 Jan.

He held in his demesne as of fee:

Guildford, 2 watermills, annual value 50s. each, 100s.; assize rents in Guildford, Stoke next Guildford, and Chiddingfold, 100s.; view of frankpledge on Monday after Martinmas, and the court every 3 weeks, annual value beyond the stipend of the steward, 12d.; and 6 a. meadow in Stoke next Guildford at 12d., 6s.; all of the king in chief as half a knight's fee.

Tongham in the hundred of Farnham, 1 hall and 1 grange worth nothing yearly, and 1 grove containing 1 a. worth nothing beyond the cost of the enclosure; 24 a. arable at 6d., 12s.; 60 a. pasture at 2d., 10s.; of the bishop of Winchester of his manor of Farnham, service unknown; and 12 a. arable at 6d., 6s., of the abbot of Chertsey of his manor of Ash, service unknown.

He died on 19 Dec. John Poyle, knight, his brother and heir, is aged 40 years and more. John Wyldes, miller, has occupied the watermills and the lands in Tongham and taken all the profits since the death of Thomas Poyle.

591   Writ, *plura*, 10 Feb. 1402.

SURREY. Inquisition. Guildford. 8 March.

He held 10s. rent from a fulling mill which Robert Vynt holds for life, and half an acre in Hartington of William Weston in 'La Bury' sometime held by Mabel Poyle, rendering 3d. annually at the four principal terms.

592   Writ 14 March 1402.

BERKSHIRE. Inquisition. Abingdon. 18 March.

He held various lands and tenements in Chilton of the abbot of Abingdon by the service of half a knight's fee, annual value 9 marks.

Date of death and heir as above.

593   Writ 1 Jan. 1402.

OXFORD. Inquisition. Oxford. 10 Jan.

He held the manor of Hampton Poyle with the advowson in his demesne as of fee of the king in chief as half a knight's fee, annual value 10 marks.

Date of death and heir as above.

C 137/31, no.25
E 152/375, nos.1, 5

WILLIAM HERTHILL

594   Writ 8 July 1402.

Writ from the escheator to the sheriff to have 12 free and lawful men at Tamworth on 10 Aug. 24 July.

WARWICK. Inquisition. Tamworth. 10 Aug.

He held in his demesne as of fee of the king in chief as a quarter of a knight's fee two parts of half the manor of Newton Regis, and the reversion of the third part which

Mary widow of Richard Herthill holds in dower; annual values, the site of the half manor nil, 2 untilled carucates with adjacent meadow 26s.8d., and assize rents of 4 marks 3s.4d. payable by equal parts at Michaelmas, St. Andrew, Lady Day and Midsummer.

The manor of Pooley was held in their demesne as of fee by Thomas de Asteley, knight, Ralph Baddesley, Robert de Mapull, John Chaloner and William de Hethecote, chaplains, and they by their charter gave it to Richard Herthill, knight, and Alice then his wife, and the heirs of their bodies. They had issue Giles and Elizabeth. Giles married Katherine daughter of John Walche, and they had issue William Herthill. Alice, Giles and Richard died. The manor was then taken into the king's hands until 21 March 1401, when William proved his age and received his grandfather's lands. The manor is held of the heir of Baldwin Frevyll, knight, a minor in the king's ward, by the service of an unmewed osprey. Annual values: the manor nil, 2 carucates 26s.8d., 40 a. meadow nil this year because they were mown and the hay carted before the death of William Herthill, and assize rents 20s. payable by equal parts at Michaelmas and Lady Day.

He died on 22 June. Elizabeth daughter of Richard and Alice and wife of John Fraunceys of Ingleby, his aunt and heir, is aged 60 years and more.

C 137/31, no.26

ROBERT WALTON

595 Writ to the chancellor of the county palatine of Lancaster ordering an inquisition by James de Radclyf, late escheator, to be sent to the chancery. 6 Jan. 1402.

LANCASHIRE. Inquisition. Wigan. 12 July 1400.

He held of the king in chief as of the crown:

West Derby, 3 bovates, as a twentieth part of a knight's fee by a rent of 6s.8d., and they were held of him by John de Thengwall in his demesne as of fee by knight service and a rent of 6s.8d.

Walton, 4 bovates now part of the manor of Walton, by the serjeanty of administering the king's bailiwick in the wapentake of Derbyshire, annual value 20s.; and the manor, in his demesne as of fee by knight service, except the 4 bovates, annual value 20 marks.

Much Woolton, 20 a., in his demesne as of fee of the prior of St. John of Jerusalem in Smithfield in socage, annual value 6s.8d. beyond the deduction of 10s.

He also held a place in Derby called Newsham of the king in chief of the duchy of Lancaster, annual value 4s.

He died on 15 March 1400. John his son and heir is aged 20 years and more.

596 Writ to the chancellor of the county palatine of Lancaster, 6 Feb. 1401 [CFR XII, p.120].

LANCASHIRE. Inquisition. Upholland. 18 Jan. 1402.

Long before his death he held the manor of Walton of the king in chief by knight service. It is also said to be held of John de Lovell, knight, in socage by a rent of 60s.

Robert Walton granted it to John de Walton, chaplain, and Richard de Halsale, their heirs and assigns. They granted it to Henry le Norreys of Speke and Robert Molyneux of Melling, their heirs and assigns. Henry by his charter released it to Robert Molyneux who then held it alone. He granted it to Helen daughter of Robert de Walton and the heirs of her body, with remainder to Margaret her sister and the heirs of her body, and failing them to remain as is fully set out in the charter. The annual value is 20 marks.

Robert did not hold it or any other lands in Lancashire when he died on 29 March 1400. Helen is next heir by virtue of the charter and aged 28 years.

597   Commission to William Gascoigne and John Cokayn to enquire what lands etc. Robert Walton held. 27 June 1402 [*CPR 1401–5*, p.131].

Order of Gascoigne and Cokayn to the sheriff of Lancashire to have 24 knights or other worthy men at Lancaster on Saturday 24 March as jurors. 18 March 1403.

Writ to Gascoigne and Cokayn, enclosing the above inquisition [no.595] to assist their inquiry. Lancaster. 20 March 1403.

Order to sheriff of Lancashire to have jurors at Lancaster for an enquiry before Gascoigne and Cokayn on Saturday next, 24 March. 20 March 1403.

Jurors sworn for the king to enquire about the articles contained in the writ attached to this panel.
Ralph de Radclif, knight
Nicholas de Longford, knight
John de Assheton, knight—juror
John de Dalton, knight—juror
Gilbert de Haydok, knight
Alan de Penyngton, knight
John de Radclif, knight
Thomas Flemmyng, knight
Ralph de Langeton
John de Bothe—juror
John de Radclif of Chadderton
Henry de Eccleston—juror
Ralph de Clayton—juror
Robert del Holt—juror
Richard de Rixton
Ellis de Entwisell
John de Loughton of Hindley—juror
John Laurence of Poulton—juror
John de Croft of Claughton
Hugh Warde—juror
William de Harleton—juror
Richard Botiller of Kirkland
John de Oxclif
John de Thorneton
Roger de Etheleston, senior
William de Heton—juror
Ralph de Kerden—juror
Mainpernors: John Kent, Robert Romayn, Henry Pyke, Roger Rose
    [Headed] 'Der'.

LANCASHIRE. Inquisition before Gascoigne and Cokayn. Lancaster 24 March.

John de Thengwall held in his demesne as of fee 3 bovates in Derby of Robert de Walton by knight service and 6s. 8d. yearly, and Robert held them of the king in chief of the crown as a twentieth part of a knight's fee and by 6s. 8d. rent; annual value 6s. 8d.

Robert Walton also held a place in Derby in this county called Newsham in his demesne as of fee of the king of the duchy of Lancaster in socage, service unknown, annual value 4s. He held no more, but long before he died he had held the manor of Walton in Derbyshire in this county and certain lands in Walton and Much Woolton. By his charter dated at Walton manor, 8 Jan. 1398, he enfeoffed John de Walton, chaplain, and Richard de Halsale, their heirs and assigns on condition that they should regrant according to his will.

Afterwards he told them that his will was that after his death they should enfeoff Helen his daughter and the heirs of her body. If she should die without heirs the lands should pass to her sister Margaret and her heirs. Failing such heirs they should pass in turn to Henry de Walton, Henry le Noreys of Speke and Margaret the bastard daughter of Robert and their heirs. John de Walton and Richard de Halsale thus held these lands for the whole of Robert's life, and afterwards supposing that they might become too poor and weak to maintain their status in various pledges which they had given, as might easily happen, enfeoffed Henry Noreys of Speke, John de Irland and Robert Molyneux of Melling, their heirs and assigns, on condition that they should fulfil the will of Robert de Walton.

They were accordingly seised, and afterwards Henry le Noreys released all his rights therein to John de Irland and Robert de Molyneux. They then enfeoffed Helen and her heirs, with successive remainders failing such heirs to Margaret her sister and her heirs, Henry le Noreys and his heirs, Margaret the bastard daughter of Robert de Walton and her heirs, and the right heirs of Robert de Walton.

The manor of Walton and the other holdings there are held of the king in chief of the crown in socage and a rent of 60s., annual value 20 marks. The lands in Much Woolton are held of the prior of St. John of Jerusalem in England in socage and a rent of 6s. 8d., annual value 10s.

Robert Walton died on 15 March 1400. John his son and heir was then aged 20. He then, under age, claimed the manor and other lands. These were held by John de Walton, chaplain, and Richard de Halsale until they enfeoffed Henry le Noreys, John de Irland and Robert Molyneux. From then Robert Molyneux and Helen the daughter of Robert took the profits until she married Robert de Fasacreley. Then they held until 12 July 1400. Since then Nicholas de Atherton, knight, has held and taken the profits, title unknown.

EMMA WIDOW OF ROBERT WALTON

598 LANCASHIRE. Assignment of dower. Walton. 22 March 1402. Thomas More, escheator, in accordance with a writ under the seal of the duchy, took the oath of Emma not to marry without royal licence, in the presence of Nicholas de Atherton, knight, who has a grant of the wardship and marriage of John son and heir of Robert, and John de Irland, knight, and John de Bykerstath, next friends and attorneys of John, and assigned reasonable dower to Emma:

One grange with orchards and 'le Hallefeld' as divided; half a place called 'le Branderth' in the east part next to Derby, and the little 'hygh' at the end of the orchard; 1 a. meadow lying next to 'Balleacre' with a parcel called 'le Leghs' and ½ a. called

'Bewedons halfacre'; 1 toft by 'le Shepcote'; and messuages, lands and tenements held at will by rent by John de Bewedon for 9s., Thomas de Ellale 4s., Ellis Colle 25s., Henry le Palmere 6s., Simon de Stawebrygley 4s., Thomas Bawelond 4s., Eleanor Boydell 16d. and John de Shexl 4s.

The rents and services of Ellis del Hall, 10s.4d.; Richard Halsale, 5s.; John de Walton, chaplain, 7d.; John de Laylondshyre, 2s.9½d.; John Bullok 'Cestr', 2s.; William de Walhull, 2s.; John Barton, 12d.; Thomas Walsall, 20d.; John Bullok, 9¼d.; Thomas Gybson, 9½d.; Thomas Merton, 2½d.; Richard Raven, 2d.; and John Bouk, 17d.

A third part of: the 'Frerfeild' lying in the middle of the 'Frerfeild'; the marsh with common pasture; the mill; a place called 'Colathewayt'; and the lands which John Fotour holds at will, 5½d.

All to hold as dower of all the lands of Robert de Walton in the county, which were taken because of the minority of John his son and heir.

C 137/31, no.27

JOHN LYNCOLN, CLERK

599 Writ 24 Feb. 1402.

KENT. Inquisition. Boughton under Blean. 20 March.

He held for life by the grant of Richard lord Ponynges, with reversion to Richard himself and his heirs 1 ruinous messuage, annual value nil; 16 a., 16s.; and 24s.6d. rent in Boughton under Blean, Preston by Faversham, Sheldwich, Molash and Selling by Chilham.

He died on 16 Nov. 1393 and who is next heir is unknown. The premises were taken into the king's hands and so remain because Robert de Ponynges, son and heir of Richard, who held certain lands in chief, is under age in the king's ward. These premises are held in gavelkind of the abbot of Faversham and others by fealty and other services.

600A KENT. Inquisition. Boughton under Blean. 30 March 1394.

He held 1 messuage, 16 a. and 34s.6d. rent in Boughton under Blean, Preston by Faversham, Sheldwich, Molash and Selling by Chilham of the manor of Westwood as above.

Date of death and heir, aged 14 years and more, as above.

600B Writ, enquiring why the chantry or free chapel of Westwood with its possessions was taken into the king's hands. 5 Nov. 1394.

[Endorsed] The chantry was taken into the king's hands because its possessions had been granted as above to John Lyncoln.

Another writ, *melius sciri*, reciting the above findings, and ordering enquiry as to the annual value of the lands and of whom they are held. 8 Nov. 1402.

KENT Inquisition. Ospringe. 15 Nov.

He held the premises in question for life of the abbot of Faversham of the manor of Westwood in gavelkind by fealty and suit of court at Faversham, annual value 16s.

Robert son of Richard Ponynges is the heir to whom the reversion belongs.

C 137/31, no.28

HUGH LE DESPENSER, KNIGHT

601 Writ 21 Oct. 1401.

LEICESTER. Inquisition. Leicester. 6 Nov.

He held in his demesne as of fee 6 messuages, 6 tofts and 6 virgates in Rothley of the prior of St. John of Jerusalem in England in socage, annual value 21s.4d.

He died on 14 Oct. Anne wife of Edward Boteler, knight, his sister and heir, is aged 30 years and more.

602 Writ 21 Oct. 1401.

STAFFORD. Inquisition. Stafford. 19 Jan. 1402.

He held in his demesne as of fee 1 messuage and 1½ virgates in Cooksland and Seighford of Thomas Harecourt, knight, of his manor of Ellenhall, service unknown, annual value 13s.4d.

Date of death and heir, aged 32 years and more, as above.

603 Writ 21 Oct. 1401.

LINCOLN. Inquisition. Stamford. 27 Oct.

He held in his demesne as of fee the manor of Bonby of the king in petty serjeanty by the service of carrying a white rod before the king at Christmas if he should be in Lincolnshire, annual value £8.

Date of death and heir, aged 30 years and more, as above.

604 Writ 21 Oct. 1401.

WARWICK. Inquisition. Tamworth. 15 Nov.

He held in his demesne as of fee the manor of Solihull, the advowson of the church and of the chantry called Holywell there, 1 messuage called 'Gryffyns' with 120 a., 16 a. meadow and 10 a. wood in Solihull, which were of Richard Caldeford, chaplain. They are held of John Dodyngsels, knight, service unknown; annual values, manor £20, church £40 but not vacant, chantry 20s. also not vacant, messuage etc. 100s. He also held £8 rent from free men and villeins in Sheldon, of the lord of the manor of Brandon, payable at Easter and Michaelmas, service unknown.

Date of death and heir, aged 32 years and more, as above.

605 Writ 21 Oct. 1401.

NORTHAMPTON. Inquisition. Bulwick. 3 Nov. 1401.

He held jointly with Sybil his wife, who survives him, the manor and advowson of Collyweston by the grant of Henry le Despenser, bishop of Norwich, Thomas Freseby and William Lodebrok, to them and the heirs of Hugh. It is held of John Dodyngsels, knight, service unknown, annual value 5 marks.

Date of death and heir, aged 32 years and more, as above.

606 Writ 21 Oct. 1401.

YORK. Inquisition. Howden. 6 Nov.

Henry le Despenser, bishop of Norwich, Thomas de Frysseby and William de Lodbrook formerly held in their demesne as of fee the manor of Hotham with its members and appurtenances in Hotham, Everthorpe, Drewton and Bursea with the advowson of the church of Hotham. All the tenements in Hotham and Drewton are held of the bishop of Durham by a rent of 6s., annual value 20 marks; 1 mill and 1 croft called 'Northolme', part of the holdings in North Cave of Stephen Lescrop, knight, by a rent of 11s.4d., annual value 13s.8d.; 2 messuages and 8 bovates in North Cave of Walter Faukonberge by a rent of 2s., annual value 40s.; all the holdings in Everthorpe of Alexander de Lounde by a rent of 1 lb. pepper, annual value 3s.; and those in Bursea of Marmaduke Constable by knight service, annual value 20s.

The said feoffees, by their charter shown to the jurors and dated 3 April 1385 at Collyweston, gave all the premises to Hugh le Despenser, now deceased, and Sybil his wife, to hold to them and the heirs of Hugh for ever.

Date of death and heir, aged 36 years and more, as above.

607 Writ 21 Oct. 1401.

BUCKINGHAM. Inquisition. Aylesbury. 18 Nov.

He held nothing in the county.

Date of death and heir, aged 30 years and more, as above.

608 Writ 21 Oct. 1401.

BEDFORD. Inquisition. Bedford. 21 Nov.

He held nothing in the county.

Date of death and heir, aged 32 years and more, as above.

C 137/31, no.29
E 149/78, no.7

ANNE WIDOW OF THOMAS LATIMER BOCHARD

609 Writ 4 Aug. 1402.

LEICESTER. Inquisition. Market Harborough. 28 Aug.

Anne widow of Thomas Latimer Bochard ['Bochard' is interlined each time that the name occurs] held in dower by assignment of Edward Latimer Bochard, brother and heir of Thomas, half the manors of Gumley and Church Langton with the advowson of Langton at alternate presentations, of William [sic] de Asteley, knight, by knight service, annual value 100s.

She also held for life, jointly with Thomas and his heirs, of his inheritance, the manors of Foxton and Smeeton Westerby of William Burton by knight service, annual value £4; and the manor of Norton, of the earl of Warwick, service unknown, annual value 7s.

She died on 17 July. Edward Latymer Bochard, heir of Thomas, is aged 40 years and more.

610 Writ 4 Aug. 1402.

NORTHAMPTON. Inquisition. Northampton. 4 Aug. 1402 [*sic*].

She held jointly with her husband to them and his heirs:

Braybrooke, the castle, of the prince of Wales of the honour of Berkhampstead as half a knight's fee, annual value £20; and 'Westhallfee' manor with the advowson, of the prior of St. John of Jerusalem in England by a rent of 12d., annual value 10 marks.

Rothwell, the manor called 'Latymersfee', of the earl of Stafford, service unknown, annual value 10 marks.

Watford, £4 rent by the hands of the prior of Daventry, of John Isbury of Watford by a rent of 2s.

Little Bowden, half the manor.

She held the following for life in dower by assignment of Edward Latymer Bochard, her husband's brother:

Little Bowden, the other half of the manor, both halves of the prince of Wales of the honour of Berkhampstead, annual value 52s.

Upton by Northampton, 1 toft and 24 a., of Richard Clendon of Upton, service unknown, [no value given].

Duston, three-quarters of a virgate, of John de Grey of Rotherfield, service unknown, annual value 5s.

Northampton, a meadow called 'Kingeshale', of the king in free burgage as of the office of reeve of the town, annual value 40s.

Desborough and Rushton, a third part of the manors, of the prior of St. John of Jerusalem in England of the manor of Harrington, service unknown, annual value 13s.4d.

Carlton, a third part of the manor, of Reynold Lucy, knight, by a rent of an unmewed sparrowhawk, annual value 10s.

Great Weldon, one quarter of the manor, of John Knyvet, service unknown, annual value 6s.

Sulby, 5s. rent from the tenants of the abbot of Sulby at Michaelmas.

Dingley, 3 a. unploughed arable and a wood called 'Loughlond', of the prior of St. John of Jerusalem in England, service unknown, annual value 2s.

Date of death and heir of Thomas as above.

611 Writ 6 Aug. 1402.

STAFFORD. Inquisition. Penkridge. 17 Aug.

She held in dower of the inheritance of John Beysyn, her late husband, by a grant to him and his heirs by Walter de Walton, parson of Billingsley, and John de Childe of Knightley:

Longnor, a third part of the manor.

Ashley, two parts of the manor.

Water Eaton, 2 carucates, 12 a. meadow and 5 marks rent.

Robert Daunsere, formerly parson of Eccleshall, held the reversion of all these premises in his demesne as of fee. By a fine of 1389 [CP 25(1) 289/55, no.190] shown to the jurors he granted that the two parts of Ashley and the 2 carucates, 12 a. meadow and 5 marks rent which Thomas and Anne held for the life of Anne of the inheritance of Robert and which after the death of Anne should revert to John de Middleton, parson of Chipping Warden, William Northwode, parson of Anderby, Thomas de Cleydon and the heirs of John, should remain to Thomas Latymer for his life if he should survive Anne, and that the third part of Longnor which they held in the dower of Anne and which ought to revert to the heirs of Robert after their deaths should remain with the other premises to Agnes widow of John de Morhall for life, with successive remainders to Thomas Crew and Juliana his wife, and the heirs of the body of Juliana by John Clopton formerly her husband, her heirs by Thomas Crewe, and the right heirs of Agnes.

The manor of Longnor is held of the earl of Stafford, service unknown, annual value of the third part 16s.8d.; the two parts of Ashley of the king in chief as half a knight's fee, the messuage there being worth nothing annually, the garden 2s., 10 a. meadow 10s. but nothing this year because mown during the lifetime of Anne, 2 carucates 60s., assize rents of free tenants £6 and pleas and perquisites of court 5s.

The 2 carucates, 12 a. meadow and 5 marks rent in Water Eaton are held of the lord of Stretton by a rent of 3s.4d.; the carucates are worth 26s.8d. but nothing this year because lying fallow, and the 12 a. meadow 12s. but nothing this year because already mown.

She died on 17 July last. Agnes sister and heir of John Beysyn is aged 60 years and more.

612 Writ 6 Aug. 1402.

SHROPSHIRE. Inquisition. Much Wenlock. 18 Aug.

She held in dower of the inheritance of John Beysyn, sometime her husband, a third part of the manors of Billingsley, Millichope, Wrickton and Walkerslowe, and of 3 messuages, 2 carucates, 4 a. meadow, 4 a. wood and 52s. rent in Lower Poston, Upper Poston and Thonglands.

She also held for life of the same inheritance two parts of the manor of Broseley by the grant of Walter de Walton, parson of Billingsley, and John de Chylde of Knighteley, to John Beysyn and Anne and his heirs.

Robert Daunsere, formerly parson of Eccleshall, held all these premises in his demesne as of fee. By the fine of 1389 [above, no.611] he granted that the two parts of Broseley manor which Thomas Latymer and Anne held for the life of Anne of Robert's inheritance and which should revert after the death of Anne to John de Middleton, parson of Chipping Warden, William Northwode, parson of Anderby, Thomas de Cleydon and the heirs of John should remain to Thomas Latymer for his life, if he survived Anne, and that these two parts of Broseley with the rest of the premises, which they held in the dower of Anne, should remain after their deaths to Agnes widow of John Morhall for life, with successive remainders to Thomas Crewe and Juliana his wife, the heirs of the body of Juliana by John Clopton, formerly her husband, her heirs by Thomas Crewe, and the right heirs of Agnes.

The manor of Billingsley is held of the abbot of Séez overseas, service unknown, annual value of the third part 40s.; Millichope of the prior of Wenlock by a rent of 30s., annual value of the third part 30s.; Wrickton of the king in chief by the keeping of a goshawk for half a year, annual value of the third part 20s.; Walkerslowe similarly by the keeping of a goshawk for the king for half a year, annual value of the third part 20s.; the 3 messuages, 2 carucates, 4 a. meadow, 4 a. wood and 52s. rent of Hugh Burnell, knight, service unknown, annual value of the third part beyond the rent, which is payable by equal parts at Lady Day and Michaelmas, 26s.8d.; and the two parts of Broseley of the prior of Wenlock by the service of being steward of the prior. There are 1 messuage, annual value nil; a garden with dovecot, 3s.4d.; a wood of which the underwood is worth 3s.4d.; 2 carucates, 40s.; 1 a. meadow, 2s.; rents of free tenants and villeins, 100s. payable by equal parts at Lady Day and Michaelmas; and perquisites of court, 2s.

Date of death and heir of John Beysyn as above [no.611]

613 Writ 18 Nov. 1402.

SOMERSET. Inquisition. Ilchester. 28 Nov.

She held in dower of the inheritance of Edward Latymer, brother and heir of Thomas, a third part of the manor of West Chelwood of the king in chief by knight service, annual value 44s. 5¼d.

Date of death as above.

C 137/31, no.30
E 149/78, no.8

ELIZABETH WIDOW OF HENRY GREY OF WILTON

614 BUCKINGHAM. Inquisition. Olney. 28 March 1402.

She held two parts of a quarter of the manor of Olney in dower of Henry Grey, of the king in chief as a tenth part of a knight's fee, annual value 6 marks.

She died on 9 Jan. 1402. Richard her son and heir is aged 12 years and more.

615 BUCKINGHAM. Inquisition. Olney. 10 April.

She held two parts of a quarter of the manor of Olney, as above.

Date of death as above. Richard son and heir of Henry Grey of Eton [sic] and Elizabeth is aged 12 years and more. One third of the two parts belongs by right to Joan wife of Ralph Basset of Drayton Bassett.

616 Writ 6 Feb. 1402.

GLOUCESTER AND THE ADJACENT MARCH OF WALES. Inquisition. Newent. 4 April.

She held in her demesne in fee tail of the king of the duchy of Lancaster the manor of Dingestow otherwise called Llanddingat in the Welsh March as half a knight's fee by the feoffment of Reynold Grey of Wilton, knight, to Henry his son and Elizabeth and the heirs of their bodies, annual value £12.

She died on 10 Jan. Richard her son and heir is aged 10 years and more.

617 Writ 1 Feb. 1402.

DERBY. Inquisition. Higham. 21 March.

Her late husband, Henry Grey, enfeoffed John de Broghton, junior, John rector of Shirland, Richard Boteler of Gilling, Robert de Alfreton, chaplain, Henry de Babyngton and others in the manor of Shirland with other lands. They assigned the manor to her in dower with reversion to themselves.

618 Writ 6 Feb. 1402.

HUNTINGDON. Inquisition. Huntingdon. 12 April.

She held in fee tail of the earl of Oxford as a third part of a knight's fee by the grant of Reynold Grey, knight, to Henry his son and Elizabeth and the heirs of their bodies ther manor of Yelling, annual value 100s.

She held the manor of Toseland at farm to herself and her executors, of the king by letters patent [*CPR 1399–1402*, p.243] until the full age of Richard her son and heir.

She died on 10 Jan. Richard is aged 10 years and more.

619   Writ 6 Feb. 1402.

ESSEX. Inquisition. Chelmsford. 21 Feb.

She held in her demesne as of fee jointly with Henry Grey to them and their heirs by the grant of Reynold Grey, father of Henry, with reversion failing such heirs to the right heirs of Reynold:

Snoreham, the manor, of the prior of Christ Church, Canterbury, service unknown, annual value 100s.

Debden, the manor called Weildbarns, of the countess of Hereford, service unknown, annual value 10 marks.

Danbury, the manor called Herons otherwise the manor of Danbury, of the same countess, annual value 100s.

Axfleet Marsh, the manor in Canewdon, of the king of the honour of Rayleigh, service unknown, annual value 100s.

In dower of Henry Gray she held:

Purleigh, the manor, of the king in chief by knight service, annual value £17; and 1 messuage, 102 a. and 23 a. marsh called 'Lachyngdonebernes' [now Purleigh Barns] of the earl of March, service unknown, annual value 29s.8d.

Great Leighs, the land called Lowleys, of the countess of Hereford, service unknown, annual value 30s.

She also held to farm during the minority of Richard her son and heir by letters patent [*CPR 1399–1401*, p.243] certain lands in the marshes by Maldon called Sayers and South House of the dean and chapter of St. Martin le Grand, London, by a rent of 4s., annual value 40s.

She died on 10 Jan. Richard is aged 10 years and more.

C 137/32, no.31
E 149/78, no.3

NICHOLAS DE LONGFORD, KNIGHT

620   Writ 10 Oct. 1401.

DERBY. Inquisition. Derby. 24 Oct.

He held in his demesne as of fee:

Killamarsh, half the vill, of the king in chief of the honour of Peverel by the service of finding a horse worth 5s. with a sack and a 'prik' when there is war in Wales, annual value 100s.

Thurvaston, half the vill, of the king by the payment of 8 marks at Easter and Michaelmas. This rent Richard II granted to master Richard Swyfte, carpenter, for life, and he still lives. Annual value nil beyond the rent.

Longford, the manor, of the bishop of Coventry and Lichfield by knight service, annual value £20.

Hathersage, the manor, of Robert de Swylynton, knight, of the manor of Crich by knight service, annual value 10 marks.

Barlborough and Whitwell, a quarter of the manor, of John Dercy, knight, service unknown, annual value 100s.

Morton, half the manor, of John Lord Deincourt, service unknown, annual value 10 marks.

Hasland, one sixth of the manor, of Maud widow of Ralph de Crumwell, knight, of the manor of Dronfield by a rent of 5s., annual value 20s.

Boythorpe, three quarters of the manor, of the countess of Kent, service unknown, annual value 40s.

Edensor, three quarters of a messuage and 2 bovates, of the heirs of Godfrey Foljambe, service unknown, annual value 10s.

Stanton, three quarters of 2 messuages and 2 bovates, of Thomas Foljambe, service unknown, annual value 10s.

Chatsworth in the Peak, three quarters of 1 bovate, of William de Ingewardoby, service unknown, annual value 3s.4d.

He died on 31 Aug. Nicholas de Longeford, knight, his son and heir is aged 28 years and more.

C 137/32, no.32

WILLIAM GRYVELL OF CHIPPING CAMPDEN

621 Writ 4 Sept. 1402.

GLOUCESTER. Inquisition. Cheltenham. 27 Sept.

He held in his demesne as of fee:

Meon, the manor, of the king in chief by knight service, annual value 100s.

Milcote in Warwickshire, 3 a. parcel of the manor which are in Gloucestershire, of the king in chief by knight service, annual value 12d.

Chipping Campden, 2 virgates of Edmund Stafford, bishop of Exeter, and Edward Lodlowe in socage, annual value 40s.

Mickleton, 8 messuages and 1 virgate of Thomas abbot of Eynsham in socage, annual value 10s.

Pebworth, 2 virgates, and 13s.4d. rent, of Robert Corbet, knight, senior, in socage, annual value 40d.

Ullington, 5s. rent, of the same Robert in socage, annual value 40d.

He died on 1 Oct.1401. Lewis his son and heir is aged 30 years and more.

Joan his widow has received the issues of Meon and of the 3 a. in Milcote since his death, right unknown. Lewis has held all the rest.

C 137/32, no.33

THOMAS UGHTREDE, KNIGHT

622 Writ, ordering return to chancery of an inquisition already taken *ex officio*. 8 May 1402.

YORK. Inquisition *ex officio*. Middleton. 12 April 1402.

He held in his demesne in fee tail:

Kilnwick Percy near Pocklington, the manor, by knight service of William Lord Latimer, under age in the king's ward, annual value 100s.

Scagglethorpe, Colton and Laund, the manors, and lands and tenements in Moor Monkton, by knight service of Thomas Lord de Moubray, under age in the king's ward, annual value £10.

Towthorpe, the manor, by knight service of Lord de Moubray annual value 100s.

He died on 18 Nov. Thomas son of his deceased son William, his next heir, is aged 18 years and more and married to Margaret daughter of John Godarde, knight.

623   Writ 1 May 1402.
YORK. Inquisition. Pocklington. 27 May.
He held the manors of Kexby, Kilnwick Percy, Hook, Scagglethorpe, Colton and Laund with certain lands and tenements in Moor Monkton, and rents of £15 14s. 10½d. from the manor of Leppington. On 8 Sept. 1398 he gave them to Robert Twyer, knight, master Adam Fenrother, rector of Catton, Walter Rudestan of Hayton and William Conestable of Catfoss; and on the following Sunday they demised them to him to hold at their will, and so he held them, and not by any other status as was said.
Kexby is held of the earl of Westmorland by fealty, annual value 50 marks; Kilnwick Percy of William Lord Latimer, under age in the king's ward, annual value 100s.; Hook of the abbot of St. Mary's, York, by fealty, annual value 10 marks; and the other manors of Lord de Moubray, under age in the king's ward, annual value £10.
Date of death and heir as above.

624   Writ, *melius sciri*, as to how the manor of Kilnwick Percy was entailed, as to his estate in the other manors, and what tenements he held in Moor Monkton. 20 June 1402.
YORK. Inquisition. York castle. 22 Sept.
Robert de Scardeburgh, knight, John Dayvill, John Lascels and William de Rykhall, chaplain, held in their demesne as of fee the manors of Kilnwick Percy near Pocklington, Towthorpe, Scagglethorpe, Colton and Laund and certain lands and tenements in Moor Monkton. They granted them by their charter of 1346–7 to Thomas Ughtred, knight, father of Thomas, and Margaret his wife and the heirs male of Thomas. Thomas held them as heir of his father and mother. The tenements in Moor Monkton comprise 12 messuages, 24 bovates and 20 a. meadow, which together are called the manor of Moor Monkton.

C 137/32, no.34

ISABEL WIFE OF JOHN WADE

625   Writ 29 Jan. 1402.
MIDDLESEX. Inquisition. Westminster. 5 July.
She held nothing in Middlesex, but William Olneye, formerly citizen and fishmonger of London, and Isabel then his wife, holding in fee simple in right of Isabel, by their charter dated at Halliwick on 25 March 1369, shown to the jurors, granted the manor of Halliwick to Adam de Berden, parson of St. Mary at Hill, London.
William Olneye died. Isabel by her deed dated at London on 23 Oct. 1375, also shown to the jurors and enrolled in chancery, released it to Adam and his heirs. So he held it in his demesne as of fee, and by his deed dated at Halliwick on 5 April 1377 granted it to John Wade, citizen and fishmonger of London, who is still living, and Isabel then his wife, to them, the heirs of their bodies and their right heirs. They held for her life and she died without heirs by him on 9 June 1400.
He at Halliwick on 20 June 1400, by his charter also shown to the jurors, granted it to Henry Webbe and John Duk, clerks, John Warner, John Wakelegh, citizen and

at that time alderman of London, and John Ferrour, their heirs and assigns; and they by charter conveyed it to John Cokayn, Henry Pounfreyt, Richard Forester, William Tristour and John Lamburn, their heirs and assigns. John Wade, Henry Webbe and his co-feoffees, and John Cokayn and his co-feoffees separately held the manor from the death of Isabel. Of whom it is held and by what service is unknown; annual value 20 marks.

John son of William Olneye and Isabel, next heir in blood to Isabel, is aged 30 years and more.

C 137/32, no.35

EDMUND DUKE OF YORK

626 Writ 4 Aug. 1402.

MIDDLESEX. Inquisition. Westminster. 19 Sept.

Edward III granted to him and his heirs male 1,000 marks yearly payable at the exchequer by equal parts at Easter and Michaelmas. This was confirmed by Richard II and Henry IV by letters patent, and he died seised of it. Richard II created him duke of York, and by letters patent, confirmed by Henry IV, granted him and his heirs male £1,000 yearly payable similarly. The letters patent of Richard II were shown to the jurors. [*CChR* V, p.174; *Rep. on Dignity of a Peer*, v, p.54; *CPR 1377–81*, pp.84–5; *1385–9*, p.62; *1399–1401*, pp.134–5].

He died on 1 Aug. Edward earl of Rutland and Cork and now duke of York, his son and heir, is aged 29 years and more.

627 Writ 4 Aug. 1402.

LONDON. Inquisition. 19 Sept.

He held nothing in London.

Date of death and heir, aged 26 years and more, as above.

628 Writ 4 Aug. 1402.

BUCKINGHAM. Inquisition. Wendover. 19 Sept.

He held the manor of Wendover in his demesne in fee tail of the king in chief by knight service with wardships and marriages, reliefs, escheats, knight's fees, advowsons of churches and chapels and other profits, liberties and benefits, with view of frankpledge, by the grant of Richard II to himself and his heirs male [*CPR 1385–9*, p.300], confirmed by the king, annual value £72.

Date of death and heir, aged 30 years and more, as above.

629 RUTLAND. Inquisition. 'Bradcroft'. 31 Aug. 1402.

He held in his demesne in fee tail of the king in chief by the grant of Edward III [*CPR 1374–7*, pp.474–5] to himself, Isabel his wife and his heirs male, with remainder to the king and his heirs, 1 cottage, 53 a. arable, and 11 a. meadow, in Great Hambleton, and 42 a. arable and 2 a. meadow in Ryhall, annual value 40s. They are called 'Penbrokelandes' and are members and parcel of the castle of Fotheringhay.

He also held in fee tail 1 mill called 'Bradcroftmilnes' and 13 a. meadow parcel of the castle of the lordship of Stamford, annual value 20s.

Date of death and heir, aged 28 years and more, as above.

630   Writ 4 Aug. 1402.

NORTHAMPTON. Inquisition. Oundle. 26 Aug.

He held the castle and manor of Fotheringhay with their members of Nassington, Yarwell and Southwick, in his demesne as of fee of the king in chief by knight service by the grant of Edward III [*CPR 1374–7*, pp.474–5] to himself, Isabel and their heirs male, with reversion to the king and his heirs; annual values, Fotheringhay £36, the members £26 13s.4d.

Date of death and heir, aged 28 years and more, as above.

631   Writ 4 Aug. 1402.

CAMBRIDGE. Inquisition. Royston. 20 Sept.

He held an annuity of £20 payable by the sheriff in his demesne as of fee to himself and his heirs by the grant of Edward III [*CPR 1377–82*, pp.84–5], service unknown; also of the king in chief by the grant of Richard II to himself and his heirs male 40s. rent in Bourn in the lordship of Cambridge as parcel of the manor of Anstey in Hertfordshire.

Date of death and heir, aged 28 years and more, as above.

632   HUNTINGDON. Inquisition. Huntingdon. 22 Sept. 1402.

He held nothing in the county.

Date of death and heir, aged 28 years and more, as above.

633   Writ 4 Aug. 1402.

GLOUCESTER. Inquisition. Tetbury. 29 Aug.

He held 6 tenements in Doughton and Charlton by Tetbury in his demesne in fee tail by the grant of Edward III confirmed by letters patent of the king shown to the jurors [*CPR 1374–7*, pp.74–5; *1399–1401*, pp.134–5]. They are members of the manor of Vastern in Wiltshire, held of the king in chief, service unknown, annual value 40s.

Date of death and heir, aged 30 years and more, as above.

634   Writ 4 Aug. 1402.

LINCOLN. Inquisition. Stamford. 23 Aug..

Edward III by letters patent of 8 May 1363 [*CChR* V, p.178] granted to him and his heirs male the castle manor and vill of Stamford and the manor and vill of Grantham, with remainder to the king and his heirs. They are held of the king in chief, service unknown; annual values, Stamford £20, Grantham £44.

Date of death and heir, aged 28 years and more, as above.

635   LINCOLN. Inquisition with a different jury. Stamford. 23 Aug. 1402.

Same presentment concerning Stamford, but no mention of Grantham.

636   Writ 4 Aug. 1402.

NORFOLK. Inquisition. East Rudham. 2 Sept.

He held in his demesne as of fee of the king in chief the castle of Castle Rising with the advowsons of Castle Rising and South Wootton, which Richard II granted to Thomas duke of Gloucester and his heirs male and which after the death of Thomas the present king granted to him with advowsons, knight's fees etc. [*CPR 1399–1401*,

P

p.144], services unknown; annual values, the castle 80 marks, Castle Rising church
. . .½ marks, South Wootton church 100s.

Date of death and heir, aged 24 years and more, as above.

637 Writ 4 Aug. 1402.

HERTFORD. Inquisition. Buntingford. 7 Sept.

He held of the king in chief with remainder to him in default of male heirs, services
unknown:

Anstey, the castle and manor, by the grant of Edward III [CPR 1374–7, pp.474–
5] to him, Isabel then his wife and his heirs male, annual value 40 marks.

Hitchin, the manor, with the reversion of all the lands which Elizabeth widow of
Edward Kendale holds in dower there, by the grant of Richard II [CPR 1385–9, p.292]
to him and his heirs male; annual values, Hitchin 80 marks, the reversion when it occurs
20 marks.

Date of death and heir, aged 30 years and more, as above.

638 Writ 4 Aug. 1402.

WILTSHIRE. Inquisition. Wootton Bassett. 6 Sept.

He held of the king in chief in fee tail by the grant of Edward III, confirmed by
the king by letters patent shown to the jurors [CPR 1377–81, pp.84–5; 1399–1401,
pp.134–5], the manors of Vastern, with its members of Wootton Bassett and Winterbourne Bassett manors, annual value 100 marks; Tockenham, annual value £10;
Compton Bassett, annual value £30; Somerford Keynes, annual value £24; and Chelworth with the keeping of the forest of Braydon belonging to it, annual value 20 marks;
all services unknown.

Similarly by the grant of Richard II, confirmed by the king, by letters patent shown
to the jurors [CPR 1388–92, p.377], he held Sevenhampton manor with the hundreds
of Highworth and Cricklade, annual value £40 beyond an annuity of 40 marks granted
to John de Foderynghey for life by Richard II. The services are all likewise unknown.

Date of death and heir, aged 30 years and more, as above.

639 Writ 4 Aug. 1402.

ESSEX. Inquisition. Rayleigh. 14 Sept.

Richard II granted him on 3 Feb. 1391 the reversion of the honour, vill, fair and
market of Rayleigh, with the herbage of the park of Rayleigh, and the manors of
Thundersley and Eastwood all of which Aubrey de Veer, knight, held for life by the
grant of the same king, to him and his heirs male, as part of his grant of £1,000 yearly
made when he was created duke of York [CPR 1388–92, p.377]. The honour, vill etc.
of Rayleigh are held of the king, service unknown, annual value £7; the manor of
Eastwood of the king in chief, service unknown, £48 7s. 3¾d; Thundersley of the honour
of Rayleigh, service unknown, 20 marks.

He held the park of Rayleigh to himself and his heirs male by the grant of Henry
IV [CPR 1399–1401, p.354], except that part which was reserved for Joan de Bohun,
countess of Hereford, with the game both there and in the parks of Hadleigh and
Thundersley by the grant of Richard II [CPR 1391–6, p.648]. The park is held of the
king in chief, service unknown, annual value beyond the sustenance of the game 40s.

He also held in chief for life, service unknown, by the same grant of Henry IV the
castle and lordship of Hadleigh, except the part reserved for the countess of Hereford.

He also held a certain marsh (*wagessum*) in the lordship of Hadleigh, status and service unknown, annual value 100s.

John Calston held the bailiwick of the hundred of Rochford by the grant of Henry IV [*CPR 1399–1401*, p.154], and the duke did not hold it when he died.

Date of death and heir, aged 30 years and more, as above.

640 Writ, *plenius certiorari*, concerning the marsh about which the jurors did not know. 2 Oct. 1402.

ESSEX. Inquisition. Rayleigh. 12 Oct.

He had no status in a marsh called Ray but held it and took the profits without any title from the death of Aubrey de Veer, earl of Oxford, until his own death; annual value £10 13s.4d.

He also held the manor of Rayleigh with the view of frankpledge without title from the death of Aubrey de Veer until his own death. The manor is held of the king, service unknown, annual value £8.

Aubrey de Veer had various stock in the manor of Eastwood: 10 cows and a bull, worth 10s. each; 200 ewes and 10 rams, 15d. each; 16 horses for the plough, 16s.; 2 carriage-horses, 40s.; 8 ganders, 2s.8d.; 6 hens and a cock, 14d.; one cart bound with iron and another not so bound, 6s.8d.; 2 ploughs with all their equipment, 10s.; 1 iron bushel pot bound with iron, 8d.; 1 winnowing-fan, 1 peck and 1 seed basket, 18d.; 100 a. sown with corn at 5s.; and 100 a. sown with oats at 2s.

All the stock belonged to Richard II and was held without title or royal grant.

641 Writ 4 Aug. 1402.

YORK. Inquisition. Doncaster. 3 Sept.

By the grant of Edward III [*CChR* V, p.174; *Rep. on Dignity of a Peer*, v. p.54] he held in his demesne in fee tail to himself and his heirs male of the king in chief by the service of two knight's fees:

Conisbrough, the castle, manor, vill and lordship and all its members, annual value beyond the wages of foresters, warreners, reeves, bailiffs and other officers and the repair of the castle and charges issuing from it £40.

Wakefield, the manor and vill with the lordship, and its members with the castle and vill of Great Sandal and the vills of Holmfirth and Sowerby, annual value beyond the fees of steward, foresters, warreners, reeves, bailiffs and other officers £100.

Hatfield, the manor, with the vills of Thorne and Fishlake with their members, parks, warrens, chases and appurtenances, annual value beyond the maintenance of the steward, parkers and bailiffs £80.

By the grant of Richard II by letters patent shown to the jurors [*CPR 1385–9*, p.62] he held in fee tail £400 from the customs of Kingston upon Hull and £100 from the issues of Yorkshire, payable by the sheriff, as part of the annuity of £1,000 granted, when he was created duke of York in 1391, with the assent of the lords and the community of the realm in parliament.

Date of death and heir, aged 28 years and more, as above.

642 Writ 4 Aug. 1402.

NORTHUMBERLAND. Inquisition. Newcastle upon Tyne castle. 24 Aug.

On 27 May 1398 the duke by his charter shown to the jurors granted to Edward earl of Rutland and Cork, his son, for life the lordship of Tynedale with all the lands, rents, lordships, franchises and liberties, paying £166 13s.4d. annually by equal parts at Martinmas and Whitsun. He held it until taken into the king's hands on the death of the duke. It is worth nothing these days beyond the rent because devastated by the Scots. It is held of the king in chief by knight service. The lord has chancellor, justices, bailiffs and other officers, holding pleas of the crown and all manner of other pleas, and has so held them from time immemorial

Date of death and heir, aged 30 years and more, as above.

C 137/32, no.36
E 149/78, no.4
E 152/373, 377

REYNOLD TRAILLY

643   Writ 27 Nov. 1401.

CAMBRIDGE. Inquisition. Cambridge. 20 Dec.

He held in his demesne as of fee of the king in chief 100 a. and a fishery, parcel of the manor of Quy, annual value £7 3s.

John Trailly, his father, long before his death granted by charter to John Warde, clerk, and Ralph de Pokelyngton the manor of Quy, except for the above. Ralph died. John Warde, rector of Northill, granted it to Reynold Grey, lord of Wexford and Ruthin, Gerard Braibrok, knight, junior, Reynold Ragon, John Hervy and John Hertishorn. Reynold released his rights to them. It is held of the bishop of Ely, service unknown, annual value 10 marks.

He died on 18 Oct. Margery wife of William Huggeford, knight, is his kinswoman and heir, being the daughter of Katherine, daughter of Walter, father of John, father of John knight, father of Reynold, and aged 30 years and more.

644   Writ 27 Nov. 1401.

BEDFORD. Inquisition. Bedford. 16 Dec.

He held in his demesne as of fee:

Northill, 1 a., of the king in chief by knight service, parcel of the manor, which with the advowson, except the 1 a., he granted by his charter to Gerard Braybrok, knight, junior, Thomas Peyvre, Edmund Hampden, John Hervy, John Warde, parson of Northill, John Herteshorn and their heirs by the king's licence [*CPR 1399–1401*, p.523], and the tenants attorned to them. The 1 a. is worth 6d. yearly.

Ravensden, the manor, annual value 33s.4d. and no more because long before his death he granted John Herteshorn, esquire, by his charter, a rent of 5 marks from it for life. It is held of Lord Moubray, in the king's ward, service unknown.

He also held a rent of a rose from the manor of Wootton Hoo, and 2 a. wood and half the escheats, reliefs, wardships, marriages and profits of court, with the reversion of the manor, which William Mabely holds for life and 2 years more, by the grant of John Traylly, knight, for the rent of a rose. The wood has no annual value because William Mabely will have the thorn and hazel with the boughs of trees there (*habebit omnes spunas et corulos cum ramis arborum in dicto bosco crescent'*).

The half of the escheats, relief etc. are worth 4d. yearly. Long before his grant to William Mabely, John Traylly, knight, the father, granted by charter to John Harteshorn and Alice his wife, now deceased, a rent of £6 from the manor for their lives. The manor is held of Robert Todenham, service unknown.

Long before he died he granted to Reynold Grey, lord of Wexford and Ruthin, Gerard Braybrok, knight, junior, John Warde, rector of Northill, Reynold Ragoun, John Hervy and John Herteshorn all his rights in the manor of Carlton, which they held for the life of Joan widow of John Trailly by the grant of John Trailly father of Reynold; and also long before his death he granted to Gerard Braybrok, lord of Odell, and Gerard Braybrok, junior, knights, Edmund Hampden and their heirs his rights in the manors of Yelden and Chellington, which they had for 20 years by the grant of John Traylly.

Date of death and heir as above.

645 NORTHAMPTON. Inquisition. Thrapston. 26 Jan. 1402.

He held nothing in the county.
Date of death and heir as above.

C 137/32, no.37
E 149/78, no.2

JOHN SYWARD

646 Writ 10 Feb. 1402.

DORSET. Inquisition. Melcombe Regis. 2 March.

He held in his demesne as of fee;

Winterborne Clenston, the manor, of the lady of Mari. . .yon, service unknown, annual value £10.

Shilvinghampton, 8s. rent, of the abbess of Shaftesbury, service unknown.

Swyre, 1 messuage and 100 a., of . . . Swyre, annual value 32s.

Frome Vauchurch, half the manor and the advowson, of Edward Charleton in dower of his wife Eleanor, formerly wife of Roger earl of March, of the manor of Wigmore, assigned to Eleanor in dower, service unknown, annual value . . .

Horiford and Sutton Poyntz, 1 messuage and 1 carucate, of Alice de Bryene, service unknown, annual value 10 marks.

Cheselbourne Ford, half the manor, of . . ., service unknown, annual value £4.

Cheselbourne, 1 messuage and 1 carucate, of the abbess of Shaftesbury, service unknown, annual value £4.

Fiddleford, 20s. rent . . .

Bagber, 1 messuage, 3 a. and 12d. rent, of the lady of Bagber, service unknown, annual value with the rent 3s.

Winterborne Nicholaston, 1 messuage and 40 a., of Roger Seymour of Somerset, service unknown, annual value 20s.

Winterborne Monkton, 1 messuage and 40 a., of the abbot of Bindon, annual value 40s.

Whatcombe, 1 messuage, 1 carucate . . ., service unknown, annual value 20s.

The premises belonged to William de Wynterburn, father of Katherine, mother of John Syward, and his heirs. John Syward enfeoffed William Canyngton, Robert Penn, knight, John Bryt, Thomas Hobbes and John Jurdan, and they re-enfeoffed him and the heirs of his body, with remainder to the right heirs of William Wynterburn. He died without heirs of his body.

John Heryng, son of Walter Heryng, son of Alice, sister of William, is the next heir of William Winterburn and aged 28 years and more.

He also held jointly with Joan his wife, who survives, the manor of Stinsford, 15 a. in Kingston Maureward, 100 . . . in Fordington, . . . 13s.4d., and £14 rent in Muckleford, by the gift of William Canyngton, Robert Penn, Ralph Bryt and John . . . to them and the heirs of their bodies . . .
[14 lines illegible]
. . . and the manor of Fordington is held of the lord of Fordington, service unknown.

He died on 7 Feb. Who is next heir on his father's side is unknown. On his mother's side it is the above named John Heryng, aged 28 years and more.

647 DORSET. Inquisition. Dorchester. 20 July 1404.

Maud wife of Thomas Brocas and Alice wife of John Sturmyn, daughters of William Syward, are next heirs of John Syward on his father's side and aged 26 years and more and 25 years and more.

C 137/32, no.38
C 137/41, no.6

WILLIAM CLAVILL

648 Writ, stating that he held in chief of the heir of Roger de Mortimer, earl of March. 5 May 1401.

DORSET. Inquisition. Wareham. 31 Oct.

He held nothing in his demesne as of fee or in service of the heir of Roger de Mortimer, late earl of March, in the king's ward, or of anyone else; but William Baret and Joan his wife held in their demesne as of fee in right of Joan 1 messuage, 3 carucates, 7 a. meadow, 6 a. wood, and rents of 20s., 1 lb. pepper and ½ lb. wax in Afflington. By a fine of 1317 [CP 25(1) 49/30, no.112] they granted these holdings to Ralph de la Hyde and Eleanor his wife and the heirs of their bodies, with successive remainders failing such heirs to John de la Hyde and Edith his wife and the heirs of their bodies, and Henry de la Hyde and his heirs.

So Ralph and Eleanor held them, and after their deaths the holdings passed to Ralph their son and heir, who married Alice daughter of William Filole and died without heirs. The premises descended to Joan and Edith, daughters of Ralph and Eleanor and sisters of the younger Ralph, by virtue of the fine. Joan died without heirs of her body, and Edith married William Clavill and they had issue and she died without heirs [*sic*]. William held them by the courtesy of England, and against him Alice daughter of William Filole brought a writ of dower demanding a third part as the assignment of Ralph, son of Ralph, her late husband, and she recovered it against William Clavyle.

She still lives. Afterwards William held two parts by the courtesy of England with the reversion of the third part after the death of Alice. After his death they remain to John Stoklond as grandson and heir of John de la Hyde and Edith his wife, being the son of Eleanor, daughter of John and Edith. This John Stoklond's estate William Bonevyle, knight, has.

They are held by knight service of Edward de Charleton, knight, and Eleanor his wife as her dower of the inheritance of Roger de Mortimer, late earl of March, her former husband, annual value of the two parts 100s.

By another fine of 1317 [CP 25(1) 49/30, no.115] Henry de la Hyde granted to William Baret and Joan his wife 1 messuage, 1 mill, 2 carucates, 25 a. meadow, 400 a. heath, and rents of 30s. and 1 lb. pepper in Moreton, Hurst, Woolgarston and

Knitson, to hold of him for their lives by the rent of a rose at Midsummer, with successive remainders to Ralph de la Hyde and Eleanor his wife and the heirs of their bodies, John de la Hyde and Edith his wife and the heirs of their bodies, and Henry de la Hyde and his heirs. After the death of William Baret and Joan the lands descended to Ralph and Eleanor, and so as above, to Edith and William Clayvile. They now remain to John Stoklond as above.

The premises in Moreton and Hurst are held of Elizabeth countess of Salisbury by knight service, annual value of two parts 6 marks; those in Woolgarston of the prior of Christchurch by knight service, two parts 11s.; those in Knitson of John Rempston by knight service, two parts 13s.4d.

William Clavill also held for life jointly with Edith his late wife, who was the daughter of Ralph de la Hyde, the manors of Ferne by Wimborne St. Giles, comprising 1 messuage, 1 carucate, 6 a. meadow and 10 a. wood, and of Hyde in Tarrant Hinton by Pimperne, comprising 1 messuage, 1 carucate, 1 a. meadow and 60 a. pasture. By two fines of 1358 [CP 25(1) 50/43, nos. 231, 236] William Fillol granted them to William Clavyle, senior, for life, with successive remainders to William Clavyle, junior, and Edith his wife, the heirs of the body of Edith, and the right heirs of William Clavyle, senior. Now they remain to Peter Clayvile, brother of William, senior, and he is aged 18 years and more.

Hyde is held of the abbess of Shaftesbury by knight service and Ferne of Thomas Wake of his manor of Wimborne St. Giles by knight service, annual value together 10 marks.

He was a bastard and died without heirs of his body on 2 April last.

C 137/33, no.39

JOHN DE CHERLETON OF POWYS, KNIGHT

649 Writ 28 Oct. 1401.

LONDON. Inquisition. 12 Nov.

He held 1 messuage in the parish of St. Sepulchre in his demesne as of fee of the king in free burgage, as all the city is held, annual value 6 marks.

He died on 19 Oct. last. Edward Cherleton, knight, his brother and heir, is aged 28 years and more.

650 Writ 23 Oct. 1401.

SHROPSHIRE AND THE ADJACENT MARCH OF WALES. Inquisition. Shrewsbury. 3 Nov.

He held in his demesne as of fee of the king in chief in the March:

Welshpool, the castle, annual value nil; the manor, 1 grange(?) annual value 10s., and a park with no underwood and pasture worth nothing beyond the sustenance of the game; the borough, with fairs at St. Leonard, St. Augustine and the Decollation of St. John the Baptist with casual revenues never exceeding 66s. 8d. annually, a weekly market annual value 40s., assize rents £10, 2 carucates nil this year because lying fallow and unused, the pasture is common, 20 a. meadow annual value 40s., and pleas and perquisites of the court 20s.; all held as a sixtieth part of a barony.

Buttington, the manor, 1 messuage, 1 carucate annual value nil because fallow, the pasture is common, and 20 a. meadow 40s., and a hamlet called Trewern parcel of the manor with assize rents of £10, and pleas and perquisites of court of the manor 10s.; all held as a fiftieth part of a barony.

Talgarth, the manor, 1 messuage nil, 1 carucate 6s. 8d. but nil this year because fallow, the pasture is common, and 20 a. meadow 20s.; held as a . . . part of a barony.

Mathrafal, the manor, 1 messuage nil, 1 carucate . . . pasture nil because fallow and common, 20 a. meadow 20s. but they were mown in the lifetime of John Cherlton, underwood nil beyond the sustenance of the game, and pasture in the wood 2s.; held as an eightieth part of a barony.

Tafolwern, the manor, 1 messuage nil, and 1 chase nil beyond the sustenance of the game; held as a twentieth part of a barony.

Ystrad Marchall and Llanerchydol, the commotes, assize rents £20, a rent called 'porthiantgaia', that is winter feeding, payable at All Saints £4, and pleas and perquisites of court 30s., held as a sixtieth part of a barony.

Cyfeiliog, the commote, assize rents £20, rents of 4 quarters of oat flour at Candlemas, rent of 40 hens at Christmas at 1d., and pleas and perquisites of court 30s.; held as a fiftieth part of a barony.

Caereinion, the commote, assize rents £20, rent called winter feeding (*pittura*) £8, and pleas and perquisites of court £4; held as a tenth part of a barony.

Arwystly, Mechain Uwchoed and Mechain Iscoed, assize rents £40, 40 hens at Christmas at 1d., and pleas and perquisites of court 40s.; held as a fortieth part of a barony.

Deuddwr and Teirtref, assize rents £30, 100 hens at 1d., rent called winter feeding at All Saints £4, and pleas and perquisites of court 40s.; held as a fiftieth part of a barony.

Mechain Uwchoed and Iscoed, rents of £34 at Lady Day and Michaelmas, winter feeding 100s., and pleas and perquisites of court 20s.; held as a fortieth part of a barony.

Mochnant, assize rents £24, winter feeding £4, and pleas and perquisites of court 30s.; held as an eightieth part of a barony.

Llangurig, the lordship, assize rents 100s., and pleas and perquisites of court 20s.; held as a sixth part of a knight's fee.

Plas Dinas, the lordship, assize rents 100s., and pleas and perquisites of court 26s. 8d.; held as an eighth part of a knight's fee.

Llanidloes, the market town, assize rents 100s., 2 fairs at St. Lawrence and Midsummer with casual revenue not exceeding 40s., a market every Saturday with casual revenues not exceeding 40s., and pleas and perquisites of court 16s.; held as an eightieth part of a barony.

Machynlleth, the market town, assize rents 100s., 2 fairs at St. John before the Latin Gate and St. Margaret with casual revenue not exceeding 40s., a market every Wednesday 40s., and pleas and perquisites of court 40s.; held as an eightieth part of a barony.

Llanfyllin, the market town, assize rents 40s., 2 fairs at St. Philip and St. James and St. Simon and St. Jude 30s., and pleas and perquisites of court 20s.; held as a hundredth part of a barony.

In the county he held in his demesne as of fee:

Pontesbury, the manor, assize rents £40, wood value of underwood nil, the pasture is common, and pleas and perquisites of court 40s.; held as a twentieth part of a knight's fee.

Charlton, the castle nil; the manor, 1 carucate nil this year because fallow, and assize rents £6; all of Thomas abbot of Shrewsbury, service unknown.

Lydham, the manor, 1 messuage nil, 1 carucate nil this year because fallow, pasture common, assize rents 100s., and pleas and perquisites of court 16s.; of John bishop of Hereford, service unknown.

Aston, 1 messuage and 1 virgate 6s.8d.; of the abbot of Shrewsbury by a rent of a pair of shoes.

Withington, 1 messuage and 1 virgate 10s.; of William Clifford, service unknown.

Isombridge, ½ a. meadow 6d.; of Isabel Eynesford, service unknown.

Uppington, 1 messuage and 1 virgate 5s.; of Hugh [Burnell], knight, service unknown.

[E 136/189/7] Total annual revenues: from the March £298 13s.; from Shropshire £54 18s.2d.

He died without heirs of his body on 19 Oct. Edward his brother and next heir is aged 30 years and more.

C 137/33, no.40
E 136/189/7
E 149/79, no.2

IDONEA WIFE OF JOHN POULET

651 SOMERSET. Inquisition *ex officio*. Montacute. 13 Oct. 1400.

She held:

Compton Durville, lands and tenements of the king in chief by knight service, annual value £4.

Cudworth, the manor, of John Chidyok of his manor of 'Cholbargh', service unknown, annual value £10.

Oath, lands and tenements, of Matthew de Gurnay, knight, by knight service, annual value 5 marks.

Seavington St. Mary, lands and tenements, of Cecily widow of Thomas Bonevyle, service unknown, annual value 5 marks.

Seavington Dennis, 5 a. of Humphrey de Stafford, knight, by knight service, annual value 5s.

Charlton Mackrell, lands and tenements of the earl of March, service unknown, annual value 53s.4d.

Walscombe, lands and tenements, of John Chidyok, service unknown, annual value 30s.

Ludney, lands and tenements, of John Chidyok, service unknown, annual value 35s.

She died on 15 Sept. John son of Idonea and John and next heir of both is aged 1½ years.

652 Writ, *plura*, 16 June 1401.

SOMERSET. Inquisition. Bridgwater. 14 Oct.

She held:

Chard, 1 messuage and 1 fulling mill, of the bishop of Bath and Wells by knight service, annual value 8s.

Dinnington, 1 toft with garden, 8 a. and 2 a. meadow, of the heir of [Alexander de] la Lynde by knight service, annual value 5s.

Charlton Adam, advowson of the chantry in the chapel of the Holy Spirit at the 4th presentation.

The custody of these in addition to all those found in the other inquisition belongs to the king owing to the minority of the heir.

653 Writ, *melius sciri*, as it was found by inquisition that she held in Chard and Dinnington as above, but her status and right were not stated, nor of whom the latter was held. 16 Nov. 1403.

SOMERSET. Inquisition. . . . 23 Jan. 1404.

She had no status or right in the messuage and fulling mill in Chard. The toft, garden, 8 a. and 2 a. meadow in Dinnington were held by John Kayl in his demesne as of fee and granted to John Beynyn for life in 1376–7 without rent, with reversion to John Kayl and his heirs. John Beynyn held them. John Kayl had issue John and Idonea. John Kayl the father died and they descended to the son. He died without heirs of his body, and so the reversion descended to Idonea as sister. Idonea died. John Beynyn still holds and takes the profits. They are held of Alexander de la Lynde of his manor of Dinnington by a rent of 4d. at Michaelmas.

654 DORSET. Inquisition *ex officio*. Beaminster. 11 Oct. 1400.

She held 1 tenement in Loscombe which belongs to the king because elsewhere she held of the king in chief and because her heir John is under age. Its annual value is 16s.

She died on 2 Sept.

C 137/33, no.42
C 137/45, no.42
E 149/77, no.10

THOMAS ATTE HALL OF SOUTH CLIFFE

655 Writ, *plenius certiorari*; as an inquisition taken before John Godard, late escheator of Richard II, [*CIM* V, no.171] found that a messuage and 2 bovates in South Cliffe in the parish of North Cave, which William Nelotson held on the day that he was outlawed, were taken into the king's hands by Thomas Graa, escheator, and were held for 3 years and more, and were held of Thomas atte Hall of South Cliffe, order to enquire whether Thomas is dead or not, who is next heir, and by what service they are held. 24 Nov. 1401.

YORK. Inquisition. Kilham. 30 Sept. 1402.

He has been dead for 14 years and more but the jurors do not know on what day he died. Alice who was the wife of William de Ake of Lockington, his daughter and heir, is aged 40 years and more.

William Nelotson held of him on the day that he, William, was outlawed 1 messuage and 2 bovates in South Cliffe in the parish of North Cave by fealty, and by what other service is unknown.

C 137/33, no.43

THOMAS SON AND HEIR OF JOHN SEYNTOWEYN

656 Writ 8 Aug. 1402.

HEREFORD AND THE ADJACENT MARCH OF WALES. Inquisition. Hereford. 18 June 1403.

He held the manors of Burlingjobb, Walton and Womaston and 57s. rent in Presteigne, all in the March of Wales; and 1 toft, 50 a., 2 a. meadow, 6 a. wood and 5s. rent in Garnstone and two parts of the manor of Burton, all in Herefordshire, with the reversion of the third part which Richard Lyngayne and Isabel, formerly the wife of John Seyntoweyn, brother of Thomas, now hold in the dower of Isabel. He held as kinsman and male heir of Ralph de St. Audoen, knight, being the son of John, son of John, son of Ralph, who held in fee tail to himself and the heirs male of his body.

The premises, except those mentioned below, are held of Henry Percy, earl of Northumberland, Henry Percy the son, William Beauchampe, Lord Abergavenny, Hugh de Burnell, knight, and Thomas Overton, clerk, of the honour of Radnor by knight service, annual value £14 13s.4d. The 57s. rent in Presteigne is held of the same in socage of the same honour, service unknown, annual value nil because the tenements have been burnt and destroyed by the Welsh rebels. Six of the 50 a. in Garnstone are held of Richard Sarnesfeld by 12d. rent, 4 of the 6 a. wood are held of John Bradley by a rent of 20d.

He died on 22 June last. Patrick Seyntoweyn, son of Ralph, is next heir male and aged 40 years and more.

657 Writ, *plenius certiorari*, reciting last inquisition, which does not say what estate Thomas had in the toft etc., and whether he died without heirs male, and ordering inquiry into how Patrick is kinsman and next heir, whether Burlingjobb, Walton and Womaston are one manor or several, and what estate he had in the toft etc. 10 Sept. 1403.

HEREFORD AND THE ADJACENT MARCH OF WALES. Inquisition. Hereford. 16 Feb. 1404.

They say that Burlingjobb and Womaston are one manor, not separate, and that Walton is one manor. John is brother of Thomas Seyntoweyn, son of John, son of John, son of John, son of Ralph junior, son of Ralph senior. His predecessors died seised of the manors from time immemorial. They descended from father to son, from Ralph to Ralph to John to John to John and so to Thomas. Patrick is the next heir of Thomas, being the son of Ralph junior, father of John, father of John.

658 Writ 8 Aug. 1402.

SUSSEX. Inquisition. Clapham. 18 Aug.

The manor of Clapham by the death of John Seyntowayn, who held of the heir of Thomas duke of Norfolk, under age in the king's ward, by knight service, and owing to the minority of Thomas Seyntowayn, who died under age, came into the king's hands and so remains. It is held of the heir of the duke of the honour of Bramber. There are the site of the manor, annual value nil; 1 dovecot, 6s.8d.; assize rents and farms, £6 13s.4d. payable by equal parts at the four principal terms; 140 a. at 3d.; 30 a. wood at 1d.; and pasture for 300 sheep, 6s.8d. He also held 1 messuage there called 'le Compe' of the same Thomas son of the duke of the manor of Findon in socage, annual value 5s. Stephen prior of Sele has occupied the manor since the death of Thomas.

He also held 11 a. in the meadow of Arundel at 7d. of the earl of Arundel in socage; 20s. assize rents in Burgham and 2s. assize rent in Kirdford of the bishop of Chichester in socage; and the manor of Ilsham of the same bishop, service unknown. In the manor are 1 site, annual value nil; assize rents, 5s.5d. by equal parts at Christmas and Midsummer; 40 a. arable at 4d.; and 20 a. meadow at 8d. The bishop has occupied the manor since the death of Thomas.

Date of death and heir as above (no.656).

659   Writ, *plenius certiorari*, reciting the last inquisition and saying that Patrick was not the heir, but that Joan sister of Thomas was and Thomas son of Joan now is. Order to inquire. 24 Feb. 1410.

SUSSEX. Inquisition. Bramber. 4 March.

Patrick, named in the inquisition, was not the heir on 22 June 1402, but Joan sister of Thomas then was, Thomas Dounton, son of Joan, is now next heir and aged 11 years and more.

C 137/33, no.44, mm. 1–4, 9–12
E 149/79, no.1

JOAN WIFE OF THOMAS DOUNTON

660   Writ 7 Feb. 1404.

HEREFORD AND THE ADJACENT MARCH OF WALES. Inquisition. Weobley. 16 July 1406.

Joan wife of Roger Dounton, rightly called Joan wife of Thomas Dounton, sister and heir of Thomas Seyntoweyn, brother and heir of John Seyntoweyn, held:

In the Welsh March: the manor of Burlingjobb and Walton, the manor of Womaston, and two parts of 57s. rent in Presteigne with the reversion of the third part which Richard Lyngayn and Isabel his wife, formerly the wife of John Seyntoweyn, now hold in the dower of Isabel.

In Herefordshire: two parts of the manor of Burton, and the reversion of the third part similarly held by Richard Lyngayn and Isabel in dower; and two parts of a toft, 50 a., 2 a. meadow, 6 a. wood and 5s. rent in Garnstone, with the reversion of the third part held by the same in dower.

The manor of Burlingjobb and Walton, the manor of Womaston, two parts of Burton, and of the toft, 44 of the 50 a., 2 a. meadow and 2 out of 6 a. wood in Garnstone, are held of the heir of Roger de Mortuo Mari, earl of March, who is in the king's ward, of the honour of Radnor by knight service, annual value 22 marks. The two parts of 57s. rent with the third part are held of the same in socage of the honour of Radnor, service unknown, annual value 20s. and no more because of waste and arson by the Welsh rebels. Six of the 50 a. in Garnstone are held of Richard Sarnesfeld by a rent of 12d. and 4 of the 6 a. of wood there are held of John Bradeley by a rent of 20d.

She died on 20 May 1403. Thomas her son and heir is aged 7 years.

661   Writ, *plenius certiorari*, enquiring what estate she held in the manor of Burton, by what name the heir of the earl of March is known, and what estate she had in the rent in Presteigne. 26 May 1408.

HEREFORD AND THE ADJACENT MARCH OF WALES. Inquisition. Hereford. 23 June.

Robert de St. Audoen held the manor of Burton in his demesne as of fee and granted it by charter to Ralph de St. Audoen and Alice his wife and their heirs. They had issue John, who had issue John, Thomas and Joan. John had issue Isabel. She received two parts with reversion of the third part held by Isabel her mother, and died without heirs. Thomas as uncle and heir then held the two parts until he died. Then Joan entered as sister and heir of Thomas, and held it to herself and her heirs.

The heir of the earl of March is called Edmund de Mortuo Mari. By what service she held the 57s. rent in Presteigne is unknown.

C 137/33, no.44, mm.5–8

JOHN SON AND HEIR OF NICHOLAS ATTE BROOKE

662 Writ for proof of age, 6 March 1402.

HAMPSHIRE. Proof of age. Winchester. 21 March.

John Abraham, aged 60 years, says that John atte Brooke was 22 years of age on 26 Jan. last [Sunday before Candlemas] because he was born at Rotherwick on 30 Jan. [Sunday before Candlemas 1379] and baptised in the church there on the same day, and he was there because he was godfather.

William Pope, 50, says that John is 22 years and more, and he knows because he was riding by Rotherwick on that day, met John Abraham and asked him where he was coming from; he answered that he was coming from the church after the baptism.

John Shupevere, 50, saw the baptism in the church.

John Parnel, 40, also saw the baptism in the church.

John Smyth, 60, was in the church to make an agreement between Thomas atte Churche and William Wyfold, and saw the baptism.

Richard Grigge, 40 and more, came to Rotherwick on that Sunday to dine with John his brother, and heard mass and saw the baptism.

John Mesurlyn, 60, was at the church, paid John Syfurwast, esquire, 12s. rent and saw the baptism.

Richard Elys, John Camere, John Dount, John atte Mere and Thomas Gregory were together practising archery opposite the church at the time of the baptism, and afterwards dined with the father.

C 137/33, no.45

THOMAS SON OF EDMUND WALDEYVE

663 Writ for proof of age, stating that he was in the ward of Alan Waldeyeve, who should be warned. 12 May 1402.

WARWICK. Proof of age. Warwick. 25 Sept.

The jurors say that Thomas son of Edmund Waldeyve and Margery, and heir of Margery, was aged 21 on 13 Jan., having been born at Mollington on 13 Jan. 1380 before 9 o'clock and baptised in Mollington church on the same day.

Peter Lyndraper, aged 60 years, was at the church on that day and saw the baptism.

Richard Coke, 40, spoke with the chaplain who baptised Thomas on that day.

Thomas Crosse, 47, knows because his eldest son John died on that day at Mollington.

William Reve received his inheritance at Mollington on that day on the death of his father.

Thomas Cartere had a son, Thomas, born on that day.

Thomas Cateson, 50, was present in the church at the baptism.

John Bokyngham, 50, was disseised of his free tenement in Mollington on that day.

Thomas Davy, 50, saw the child being carried to the church in a woman's arms on that day.

Richard Magot, 50, received a great sum of money at Mollington on that day.

John Gunson saw Thomas in the hands of the priest at the baptism.

John Marchall, 40, raised a newly built chamber in Mollington on that day.

William Correbrygge was at Mollington on that day and spoke with Edmund the father, who told him.

C 137/33, no.46

ALICE DAUGHTER OF GODFREY FOLJAMBE, KNIGHT

664 NOTTINGHAM. Proof of age. Cotham. 29 Oct. 1401.

William Gentyll of Cotham, aged 50 years and more, says that Alice is aged 14 years and more, because she was born at Cotham and baptised in All Saints' church there on 27 June 1387. He knows because Thomas Grace, vicar of Cotham, was instituted on 6 June 1387, at which time Alice's mother was pregnant, and she bore Alice on 27 June next, and Alice was baptised on the same day.

John de Dover of Cotham, 50 and more, knows because on 2 Aug. 1387 his son Richard was born at Cotham and baptised in the church there, and Alice was born before that.

William Wylche of Cotham, 40 and more, knows because on 28 June 1387 Adam de Eyleston, kinsman of Alice, bought a horse for 100s. from John de Leek, knight, Alice's grandfather, and he was present and saw her.

John de Kneton of Cotham, 30 and more, was staying with Godfrey Foljambe, knight, Alice's father, at Cotham on the Thursday on which she was born.

Thomas Jonson of Elston, 60 and more, paid Robert de Goushill £20 at Cotham and saw her then.

William Vycarman of Elston, 60 and more, says that . . . at Cotham . . . John Moore bought from John Leek, Alice's grandfather, 100 . . . on 18 Sept. 1387, before which day Alice was born.

William Palmer, 40 and more, knows because his son John was born at Elston on 9 Sept. 1387 and Alice was born before that.

John Coke of Hawton, 40 and more, was in the church and saw the baptism of Alice.

Richard Wylche of Hawton, 40 and more, [bought from] William Leek 20 quarters of pease for the use of Godfrey Foljambe, knight, Alice's father, at Screveton on 13 Aug. 1387, and she was born before that day and he saw her then.

William del Hay of Hawton, 40 and more, bought a horse from Roger de Upton, chaplain of John Leek, Alice's grandfather, at Cotham on 12 Aug. 1387 and saw her then.

John Vausour of Hawton, 34 and more, married Alice daughter of William Weston at Cotham on 7 Aug. 1387, and Alice was born before that and he saw her.

John Roberdson of Elston, 40 and more, built a new chamber at Elston on 9 Sept. 1387, and Isabel his wife was Alice's nurse on that day and for a long time afterwards, and he saw her in her cradle.

C 137/33, no.47

JOHN SON AND HEIR OF HENRY CONQUEST OF HOUGHTON CONQUEST

665 Writ for proof of age, 8 April 1402.

[Endorsed] Thomas Mewe, who had the wardship, was warned to be at the church of Houghton Conquest on 18 May by Richard Colles, Henry Manton, Thomas Curson and William Eyr of Houghton Conquest.

BEDFORD. Inquisition and proof of age by 12 good and lawful men all aged 42 years and more. Houghton Conquest. 18 May.

John Richer says that John Conquest is aged 21 years and more because, as he knows, he was born at Houghton Conquest and baptised in the church there on Thursday 30 June 1379 [*sic*]. Within a quarter of a year after the birth Henry Conquest enfeoffed the rector of Houghton Conquest in all his lands in Houghton Conquest on certain conditions after seisin. Richer was witness of the seisin, and at the dinner afterwards was present with other neighbours, and this was before 7 July 1382 (*citra festum translacionis Sancte Thome martiris citra annum sextum*).

Thomas atte Hall of Wootton within a fortnight of the birth married Alice daughter of William Bernevyll.

Richard Doncesson, William Catesson, William Straunge and Thomas Querndon on 10 June 1381 set out on a pilgrimage to Canterbury, and when they returned to Houghton Conquest six days later they found all their houses and barns in Chapel End there accidentally burnt down.

William atte Dene on the day of the birth and baptism was living in Houghton Conquest, and on that day Maud his wife, now deceased, gave birth to his eldest son William, now chaplain of Cardington.

John Lyllyngston remembers because in that year he and Elizabeth his wife took certain lands for life by indenture from Henry Conquest in Houghton Conquest, and by the date of the indenture he knows and proves the age.

John Typper says that in the year that John was born his father Robert Typper of Wootton died and Henry Conquest allowed him to enter his father's lands.

William Barker and William Weston were in the church on the day of the churching of the mother of John Conquest, and afterwards at the feast with Henry Conquest the father. William Barker was staying with William rector of Marston Moretaine, who was godfather. William Weston was with the rector as bailiff and rode to the feast. There William Barker was a servant in the kitchen and served William Weston in the hall.

C 137/33, no.48

JOHN SON AND HEIR OF HENRY HELION

666 Writ for proof of age, because he claims to be of full age although found to be under age by the inquisitions taken after the death of his father [*CIPM* XVII, nos.66–8; three inquisitions of which two said 5 years and more, and one (evidently correctly) 12 years and more, Oct. and Nov. 1391, June 1392]. He is in the ward of John Clerk, vicar of Chrishall, by the grant of John Dorward and Roger Walden, to whom Richard II granted the wardship. The king, by the information of John Dorward and others of the council, and also by inspection of his person in his own presence, believes that he is of age. 6 Nov. 1401.

ESSEX. Inquisition. Saffron Walden. 1 Dec.

John Basset, aged 52 years and more, says that John Helion was aged 21 years and more on 24 Feb. last because he was born at Chrishall on 14 Feb. 1379 and baptised in the church there. Master John Dunwich, rector of Borley, John Basset of Chrishall and Amice prioress of Ickleton raised him from the font on St. Valentine's day. This he knows because he had a daughter Isabel baptised there on the following day.

Thomas Heynes, John Elis and Robert Lawney, all 49 years and more, were in the church on the day of the baptism for the burial of Margaret wife of John de Wawton, knight.

John Parker, 50, Roger Serle, 52, John Pite, 49, and John Lavenham, 60, were in the field of Henry Helion called 'Pirifeld' measuring, and saw the godparents coming from the church on that day.

William Selonge and Richard Serle, both aged 56, dined with the rector on that day, and he told them of it at dinner.

John Morice and William Serle, both 52 and more, were at the house of John Birle, then constable there, about the building of a new barn by John Birle, and heard of the birth.

C 137/33, no.49

THOMAS SON AND HEIR OF THOMAS RALEGH

667 Writ for proof of age, requiring the warning of Agnes widow of Thomas Ralegh the father, William Fry, Robert Fry and Thomas Kyngesland, who had the wardship, to attend. 15 Dec. 1401.

[Endorsed] They were warned by John Tymbrell, William Baily, Henry atte Ford and Henry Devyll.

WARWICK. Proof of age. Warwick. 26 Dec.

The jurors say that Thomas was 21 on Friday 4 Feb. last because he was born on Friday 3 Feb. 1380 [Friday after Candlemas in each case] at Farnborough and baptised in the church there before 9 o'clock.

Richard Waldeyeve, aged 60, had a wooden cross made and raised in the church on that day in honour of the Trinity and for the health of his soul.

John Wodelowe, 40, was building a house at Farnborough and his right arm was injured by a sudden fall of timber from the house.

Eneas de Baddeby, 45, knows because his eldest son Thomas died at Farnborough on that day.

John Harreys, 60, received a large part of his inheritance because his father died on that day.

Thomas Vyncent, 40, had a son baptised in the same font on that day and named Richard.

John Drapere, 41, married Joan his wife in that church on that day.

Roger Bulston, 50, was disseised of his free tenement in Farnborough on that day.

John Broun, 40, had a new chamber built in Farnborough at that time.

John Rody, 40, built a new house then.

Thomas Gregory, . . ., was in the church and saw the baptism.

John Tewe, . . ., saw a woman carrying Thomas from the church after the baptism.

John Faukener, 46, was in the church and saw the baptism.

C 137/33, no.50

ALAN SON AND HEIR OF ALAN DE BUXHULL, KNIGHT

668 Writ, *plenius certiorari*. An inquisition of 6 Dec. 1381 [*recte* 14 Nov. 1381, *CIPM* XV, nos.459–60] found that Alan de Buxhull, knight, held certain lands and that his heirs were his daughters, Elizabeth wife of Roger Lynde and Amice, late the wife of John Beverley; and they being of full age the lands, apart from the dower of his widow Maud, were released to them; but Maud was pregnant and afterwards gave birth to Alan, whereupon the lands were resumed into the king's hands until he should be of full age. Order to inquire whether he is still alive, and if so of what age. 19 March 1402.

DORSET. Inquisition. Sturminster Marshall. 13 July.

Alan, son of Alan de Buxhull, knight, is still living, is next heir and is aged 21½ years and more.

669 Similar writ, 19 March 1402.

SUSSEX. Inquisition. East Grinstead. 23 May.

Alan, son of Alan de Buxhull, knight, is alive and is next heir to Alan. He was born on 20 Jan. 1382 and is therefore aged 21 years and more [*sic*].

670 Writ for proof of age, ordering that Maud, widow of John de Monte Acuto, earl of Salisbury, [his mother], and William Gobyon, esquire, and Henry Sybbesey, draper of London, who are holding two parts of the manor of Bugsell during the minority, be warned. 19 Aug. 1402.

[Endorsed]: They were warned by John Pychard and William Est and were present and raised no objections.

LONDON. Proof of age. Guildhall. 12 Sept.

The jurors say that he was born in the parish of St. Helen Bishopsgate on 22 June 1381 [5 Richard II, *recte* 1382, 6 Richard II], and this they know for the following reasons:

John Bechesworth, aged 55 years and more, Richard Carpenter, 56 and more, and Nicholas Preston, 55 and more, on that day saw Nicholas Dagworth, on behalf of Thomas duke of Gloucester, John Fordehome, bishop of Ely, and Isabel the king's daughter, raise him from the font [but Isabel died in 1379, Thomas was not duke of Gloucester until 1385, and Fordham was not provided to Ely until 1388].

Hugh Trap, 60 and more, Thomas Holt, 58 and more, William Wycombe, 50 and more, Robert Powair, 50 and more, Richard Tutford, 60 and more, and Robert Bridport, 50 and more, at the request of the father held six lighted wax torches by the font throughout the time of the baptism.

Robert Stanley, 50 and more, William Marwe, 60 and more, and Richard Loundres, 54 and more, saw a servant of Alan the father carrying jugs of sweet wine called 'bastard' and 'Romeney' to the church, and they were present and well and truly drank of it.

C 137/33, no.52

671 Similar writ, 28 June 1403.

LONDON. Proof of age. Guildhall. 10 July.

The jurors say that he was born in the parish of St. Helen Bishopsgate on 22 June 1382 and baptised in St. Helen's church.

John Bechesworth, aged 56 years and more, Richard Carpenter, 57 and more, and Adam Gace, 4. . . and more, know this because in their presence Nicholas Dagworth and the others [as in last] raised him from the font.

Hugh Trap, 61 and more, Thomas Holt, 59 and more, William Wycombe, 51 and more, Robert Power, 51 and more, Richard Tutford, 61 and more, and Robert Bridport, 51 and more, held blazing torches throughout the baptism ceremony.

Robert Stanley, 51 and more, William Marewe, 60 and more, and Richard Loundres, 55 and more, saw a servant of Alan's father carrying jugs of sweet wine called 'Romeney' to the church, and they were present and drank of it.

C 137/40, no.47

JOHN SON AND HEIR OF RICHARD VYLERS KINSMAN AND HEIR OF SIMON PAKEMAN

672 Writ for proof of age, 24 April 1402.

LEICESTER. Proof of age. Leicester. 18 May.

Thomas Pachet, aged 50 years, says that John was born at Brooksby and baptised in the church there on 6 May (feast of St. John before the Latin Gate) 1380, and was therefore 21 on the last occurrence of that feast. He knows because Richard his brother was born on that day, and the other jurors know for the following reasons:

John Bret, 48, was sent to Sproxton to John Brabazon, knight, to ask him to be godfather.

William Swayn, 46, married Cecily daughter of Richard Ardern on that day.

William Redley, 41, was present in the church and went to the rectory to fetch salt for the baptism.

John Forster, 49, because his daughter Margaret was born and baptised in the same church on that day.

John Neel, 41, bought 2 a. in the meadow of Brooksby from John Poutrell on that day, and he knows by the date of the charter.

William atte Persones, 61, took seisin of a messuage in Rearsby on that day by the grant by charter of Thomas Nevyll.

Robert de Broughton, 46, buried Ralph his father in the church of Rearsby on that day.

John Poutnell, 42, because his daughter Juliana married James Cotiler of Leicester on that day.

Richard Fraunceys, 41, because Stephen Longulers died on that day and was buried in the church of Brooksby.

John Rontour, 42, because on that day Reynold his son fell into a well in Muston and died, and lay there for three days.

John Brunne, 49, knows because in that year the house of Richard Munceux in Bescoby was totally destroyed by fire.

C 137/33, no.54

WILLIAM SON AND HEIR OF JOHN SYBYLE

673 Writ for proof of age, 5 Nov. 1401.

CAMBRIDGE. Proof of age. Cambridge. 19 Nov.

The jurors say that he was born on 8 Dec. 1379 at Horseheath and baptised there, and this they remember for the following reasons:

John Pelter was in the church to hear mass and saw the baptism.

Stephen Fitzwilliam was going from the church to his house and met William being carried to the church in a woman's arms.

John Webbe said that his wife had a son John who was baptised immediately after William.

William Hamond says that on that day the parish chaplain sat at table with him at 9 o'clock and told him of the birth.

John Millere says that at dawn on that day he was with John Sybyle the father who told him that his wife had a son.

John Norffolk was a servant of John Sybyle and carried the basin and ewer to the church.

Henry Smyth was a farmer for John Sybyle, took his farm to Horseheath, paid him, and there saw William carried from the church after baptism.

John Lynton was in the church and held the book beside the chaplain at the baptism.

William Bodeneye said that Joan his wife was with the mother all through the night.

John Longe was in the church reading the third morning lesson and heard William crying at the font.

John Hikkeson and John Foster say that they had a dispute, and on that day John Sybyle the father caused them to reach an agreement in his house, when William was brought back from the baptism.

674 Writ for proof of age, 1 Dec. 1402.

CAMBRIDGE. Inquisition. Cambridge. 6 Jan. 1403.

Same as the above except that the ages of the jurors are given: John Pelter 52, Stephen Fitzwilliam 45, John Webbe 48, William Hamond 58, John Myllere 49, John Norffolk 45, Henry Smyth . . ., John Lynton 43, William Bodeneye 48, John Longe 49, John Hikkeson 47 and John Foster 51.

C 137/33, no.55
C 137/40, no.48

CHRISTOPHER SON AND HEIR OF CHRISTOPHER DE MORICEBY, KNIGHT

675 Writ for proof of age, ordering James de Pykeryng, executor of James de Pykeryng, knight, who had the wardship, to be summoned to attend. 27 Nov. 1401.

[Endorsed] He was summoned by Richard Ryot and William Fox and was present.

CUMBERLAND AND WESTMORLAND. Proof of age. Penrith. 7 Jan. 1402.

The jurors say that Christopher is aged 21 years 6 weeks and more, because he was born at Winderwath and baptised in the free chapel there on Monday 12 Nov. 1380, and this they know for the following reasons:

William del Legh, knight, aged 40 years and more, heard mass in that chapel on that day.

John de Skelton, 40 and more, because on the Monday of the birth the house of Thomas Burgh, chaplain, caught fire, and he came by the chapel to put it out, and there people told him of the birth.

Richard de Beaulieu, 60 and more, bought a horse from Richard Corsoun at the chapel on that day and saw the baptism.

Richard de Louther, 40 and more, had a brother called Richard [sic] who was baptised there immediately after Christopher.

William de Osmonderlawe, 40 and more, went to the chapel on that Monday to bury Margery his sister, and saw the baptism.

Thomas de Raghton, 40 and more, was thrown from his horse outside the chapel and broke his arm on his way to mass, and several people told him of the baptism.

John De Dalston, 40 and more, coming to the chapel to hear mass accidentally broke his right ankle on that day.

Richard Skelton, 50 and more, was at the chapel for the wedding of John Roos and Maud daughter of Richard Englissh on that day and saw the baptism.

Bertram Coldthird, 60 and more, because on that day John Storme was killed by Thomas Dykson at Winderwath. Dykson fled to the park of Whinfell and Bertram pursued him for the felony and was told of the birth.

William de Hudelston, 40 and more, because on that Monday the bell tower of the chapel was blown down by a high wind.

Robert de Grydesdale, 60 and more, because on that day the mill of Winderwath was destroyed by the flooding of the river Eden, and it was common talk that Christopher was born.

John de Brakanthwayt, 40 and more, because on that Monday William his brother was drowned in the river Eden by the chapel, and he came there and heard of the birth.

C 137/33, no. 56

ANKARET WIFE OF THOMAS NEVYLL, KNIGHT, AND WIDOW OF RICHARD TALBOT, KNIGHT

676 WILTSHIRE. Assignment of dower in the presence of William Fauconer and Robert Clerk, attorneys of Gilbert son and heir of Richard Talbot . . . 4 Feb. 1402.

Swindon, 1 chamber in the south part of the manor, with the chamber under and the close attached; 2 places in a barn in the east and 2 places in a byre in the north, with free ingress and egress; a third part of a meadow at the west end; 16 a. at 'Lodelawe', 3 a. in 'Eldeorchard', 3 a. at 'Chalcrofte', 2 a. at 'Coursdyche' and 2 a. at 'Droppe', all in the 'Middelfeld'; 8 a. at 'Langelond', 1½ a. at 'Middelwatendon' and 3½ a. at 'Over Watenden', all in 'le Estfeld'; 6 a. at 'Langelond', 1½ a. in 'Northwestefurlong' and 9½ a. in 'Eldemede', all in 'le Northfeld'; 8 a. meadow in 'Newenham', and 2 a. meadow in 'le More' to the north.

Rents and services of tenants there: John Debenham 8s., John Cadon 8s., Robert Purr . . ., John Boundy 11s.2d., John Admond 8s.4d.; and in the borough and portmote rents of Thomas Whyteman 5s.6d., Thomas Boundy 18d., John Pyrton 7s.2d., William Turke 2s.6d., John Debenham 2s.6d., . . . Whyteman 18d., John Godard 4s.2d., William Wytyll 6s., Agnes Coriour 3s.2d., Thomas Brome 3s. and Thomas atte Forde 2s.6d.

C 137/33, no. 61

JOHN SON AND HEIR OF ROBERT DE WALTON

677 [LANCASHIRE. Proof of age. *Several lines missing*].

Robert de Bradshagh, aged 40 years and more, says that John de Walton was born on 7 Dec. 1379 and baptised in the church of Walton on the same day by William del Halle, the vicar. John del Vikers was godfather and Denise de Andernes godmother.

Robert was attending the church on that day and saw John raised from the font, and so he knows that he is aged 21 years and more. The following jurors know the same because:

John de Sotheworth, 40 and more, was at the church for a loveday between William Robynson and . . . of Kirdale when John was baptised.

John del Twys, 40 and more, was at the church to hear mass before going to buy fish at Bootle, and was present at the baptism.

Robert de Eld. . . was at the church to hear news from Ireland of the Earl Edmund [of March].

Henry de Penketh, 40 and more, was at the church to buy corn from Robert Wilkynson.

Humphrey de Twys, 40 and more, was at the church to hear mass before going to Kirkdale to buy two oxen from Robert Wilkynson of Kirdale.

William de Laghok, 40 and more, was at the church to hear mass before going to Litherland to see a corpse and wreck on the seashore.

John del Hey, 40 and more, was at the church to see John del Hethe.

John de Andern. . ., 40 and more, was at the church for a cockfight between John de Sikes and Robert del Heth.

John de Bugard, 40 and more, was at the church . . . to see a man at Liverpool.

C 137/33, no.62

JOAN WIDOW OF EDMUND INGALDESTHORP

678   YORK. Assignment of dower in the presence of John Nevill, knight, husband of Isabel, daughter and heir of Edmund. Menethorpe.

Assigned in dower from all the lands of Edmund:

Menethorpe: One third of a third part of the lands which he held jointly with Richard Waterton and Constance his wife, annual value 13s.4d.; all the houses at the . . . end of the hall of the chief messuage of 'Swynton' with free ingress and egress; a 'baye' with the 'auteshote' at the east end of the great barn called 'Cornebarne'; a 'baye' at the north end called 'la Heybarne'; a house called 'le smythyhous'; and a house called 'le stables' to the north with free ingress and egress.

Part of the demesne lands: 5 a. in 'Wynnykfild' to the north; 7 a. at the 'crossebuttys' in 2 pieces of 4 a. and 3 a.; 6 a. on 'Sparoweclyff' to the north; 3 a. and 'yenge' at 'Brokebank' to the north; 4 a. and 'yenge' at 'Brokewell'; 2 a. at 'Longe Gelowe'; 2 a. at 'Shorte Gelowe'; 1 a. at 'Glyntre'; 5 a. together above 'Mowsewre' to the south; 3 a. together above 'Longebarnestoke'; 2 a. in 'le Halthe'; 2 a. in 'le Clyff'; 2 a. meadow at 'Overwynshley' to the south; and ½ a. meadow at 'Kylnerthbrigges' to the east; which lands William Culburn holds by a rent of 17s.4d.

Rents: 2½d. from a messuage and land which John Hunte holds; 2s.10d. from a messuage of Alice Lawton; 2½d. from a messuage of Robert Mersser; 18d. from the heir of William Busshell; 20s. from . . . bovates held by Roger Colburn; 7s. from 1 messuage and ½ bovate held by John Godley; and . . . a. of wood lying together at the east end of 'Shawe'.

C 137/33, no.63

JOHN WODEFORD, ESQUIRE

679   LEICESTER. Inquisition ex officio. Waltham on the Wolds. 6 April 1402.

He held in his demesne as of fee 6 messuages and 6 virgates in Wyfordby of Thomas, son and heir of Thomas late duke of Norfolk, under age in the king's ward, service unknown, annual value 36s.8d.; and 1 messuage and 2 a. in Melton Mowbray and Sysonby of the same, service unknown, annual value 3s.4d.

He died on 17 Aug. 1401. Robert his son and heir will be 18 years of age on 21 May next.

C 137/33, no.64
E 149/79, no.16

ROBERT BADERON

680 GLOUCESTER. Inquisition *ex officio*. Newnham. 26 May 1402.

He held in his demesne as of fee 1 messuage and 1 carucate in Awre, which King John granted to Walter de Aura, senior, his ancestor, for his homage and service, by the name of 2 virgates, 6 a. and 1 meadow called 'Hundomor', by the service of 1 mark yearly, annual value 20s.

He died on 3 Nov. 1376. His widow Joan claimed a third part in dower and held it until she died on 26 June 1396. Maud and Joan, his daughters and next heirs, were aged 18 years and more and 17 years and more when he died. They held two parts. Maud married John Felde. John, Maud and Joan took the profits of the two parts without royal licence until 9 Feb. 1397 when Joan died without heirs. John Felde and Maud then held two parts and since the death of Robert's widow they have also held the other part, comprising 16 a. arable and 2 a. meadow. They are holding it all without royal licence, title unknown.

C 137/33, no.65
E 152/373, no.2

HENRY DE AURE

681 GLOUCESTER. Inquisition *ex officio*. Newnham. 26 May 1402.

He held 10 tenements in St. Briavels and an office in the forest of Dean called 'Forstereswyke' of the king in chief of the castle of St. Briavels by the duty of serving for 40 days in that castle in time of war, annual value 7s.

He died on 13 Oct. 1401. Richard his son and heir is aged 21 years and more.

C 137/33, no.66
E 152/373, no.1

WILLIAM ASTON

682 GLOUCESTER. Inquisition *ex officio*. Gloucester. 16 March 1402.

William Aston of Aston Ingham has been an idiot since 9 Jan. 1400. He holds a tenement called 'Astonescourt' in Ley by Westbury, annual value 26s.8d.

He and Alice his wife have taken the profits during this time.

C 137/33, no.67

WILLIAM DE FERRARIIS

683 Writ, *plenius certiorari*, reciting that Edward III on 3 March 1337 granted [*CPR 1334–8*, p.418] the reversion of the manor of Walton upon Trent, after the death of Isabel the queen mother, who then held it, to Henry de Ferrariis and his heirs, and an inquisition by Philip Lutteley, escheator, on 6 Sept. 1358 [*CIPM* X, pp.358–9] found that Queen Isabel held it for life and that the reversion belonged to William son and heir of Henry de Ferrariis; order to enquire when he died, etc. 1 Dec. 1401.

DERBY. Inquisition. Repton. 13 Feb. 1402.

William de Ferrariis died on 8 Jan. 1371. The William de Ferrariis who is still living is the next heir male to the manor and advowson of Walton upon Trent, being the son of Henry, son of the first William, and aged 28 years and more.

Godfrey Foljambe, knight, occupied the manor and took the profits from the death of William until Christmas 1376, title unknown. Then Richard Hampton, esquire, held it until 12 April 1385 by grant for life by letters patent [*CPR 1377–81*, p.77], and Thomas Sy and William Gold since 12 April 1385 by letters patent [*CPR 1381–5*, p.547], with John Delwe and Henry Coton, clerk, but the title of the last two is unknown.

C 137/33, no.69

JOHN POKESWELL

684 SOMERSET. Inquisition *ex officio*. Ilchester. 23 Jan. 1402.

He held by the courtesy of England in right of the inheritance of Eleanor, sometime his wife:

Woolmersdon, a third part of half the manor, of the manor of Nether Stowey by knight service. Stowey was in the king's hands by reason of the death of Lady Daudele. John Tochet, knight, has now secured it in right of his inheritance. Annual value of the third part, 33s.4d.

Uphill and Christon, a quarter of the manor, of the manor of Blagdon, annual value 60s.; and a fifth part of a rent of 40d. from 1 messuage and 40 a. arable, meadow and pasture in West Lydford, of the manor of West Lydford. All the fees of the manors of Blagdon and West Lydford were in the king's hands owing to the forfeiture of the earl of Huntingdon, or by his death and the minority of the heir; and now by the king's grant [*CPR 1399–1401*, pp.274, 397, 457] these fees and manors are held by the abbot of St. Mary Graces; and of these manors John and Eleanor held all their lands, rent and revenues in Uphill, Christon and West Lydford, by priority of all other lords of whom they held elsewhere in the county, in right of Eleanor.

Bedminster, a third part of the manor, of Thomas Beauchamp, knight, of the manor of White Lackington by knight service, annual value 50s.

Compton Durville, a third part of the manor, of Baldwin Malet, knight, of the manor of Sutton Mallet by knight service, annual value 4 marks.

Cossington, a third part of a toft and a third part of a carucate, of John Brente, lord of that manor, by knight service, annual value 15s.

West Chilton, 1 carucate called 'Chaldecote', of the manor by knight service, of the heir of Thomas Tryvet, knight, not in the king's hands at the time of John Pokeswell's death, annual value 40s.

Huntspill, 1 messuage and a third part of a carucate in the manor, in the hands of the earl of Somerset with knight's fees until the full age of Fulk Fitzwaryn, by the king's grant, annual value 20s.

Burnham, 1 carucate, of the bishop of Winchester of that manor by knight service, annual value 40s.

Churchill, 1 toft and 1 virgate called 'Lyncombe', of Ellis Fitzpayn of that manor in socage, annual value 5s.

He died on 13 Dec. 1400. John the son and next heir of both Eleanor and John is aged 17 years and more.

C 137/33, no.70

LAWRENCE BROMHILL

685 Exchequer writ of *certiorari* as to the value of the lands he held which are in the king's hands. 10 Dec. 1401 [Enrolled, E 368/174, *brevia retornata*, m.17].
HEREFORD. Inquisition. Hereford. 14 Jan. 1402.

The jurors are totally ignorant of what lands he held; so far as they know he had none in Herefordshire or the adjacent March of Wales.

686 HEREFORD. Another inquisition of same place and date but with different jurors.

The jurors are totally ignorant, as in last.

E 149/76, no.10

ELIZABETH WIDOW OF HENRY SUTHILL AND FORMERLY WIFE OF ROBERT DE STODHOWE

687 YORK. Inquisition *ex officio*. Wombwell. 7 May 1402.

She held for life, with remainder to Robert de Stodehowe, son and heir of Robert de Stodehowe, who is under age in the king's ward because of lands elsewhere in Burnby by Pocklington held in chief by knight service:

Wombwell, 3 messuages, 2½ bovates and 11s. rent, of John de Annesley, knight, in socage, annual value 40s.

Studdah in Richmond, the manor, of Stephen Lescrope, knight, in socage, annual value 40s.

Hudswell, 1 cottage and 60 a., of the abbot of St. Agatha's in socage, annual value 17s.

Huby, 1 messuage and 1 furlong (*cultura*), of other than the king, annual value 7s.
Birdsall, ½ carucate, of whom and by what service is unknown, annual value 7s.

She died about 1 May 1401. Robert her son and heir is aged 19 years and more.

Hugh Wombwell has occupied the premises in Wombwell since the day of her death, Cuthbert Barbour of Richmond those in Hudswell, Robert Stonlap the manor of

Studdah, and Robert Stodehowe the land in Birdsall. They have taken the profits and are answerable to the king.

E 149/78, no.8

SIMON MUCHELL

688 WILTSHIRE. Inquisition *ex officio*. Amesbury. 4 Nov. 1401.

He held in his demesne as of fee of the king in chief by knight service 1 messuage and 1½ virgates in Milton Lilborne.

He died on 28 May last. Thomas his son and heir is aged 17 years.

E 149/79, no.13

THOMAS BOYVYLE KNIGHT

689 WARWICK. Inquisition *ex officio*. Little Packington. 1 Feb. 1402.

He held in his demesne as of fee a third part of the manor of Little Packington called 'Boyvilespart' of Lord Beaumont, who is under age in the king's ward, of the honour of Winchester by knight service, annual value 26s.8d.

He died on 11 Dec. 1401. John his son and next heir is aged 10 on 24 June. The custody of the lands and the marriage belong to the king owing to the minority of Lord Beaumont.

E 149/79, no.17

JOHN GREY

690 Writ 10 Sept. 1403.

LEICESTER. Inquisition. Leicester. 21 Sept.

He held half a messuage and half of 4 carucates in Harston of the king of the duchy of Lancaster as a twenty-fourth part of a knight's fee, annual value 30s.

He died on 26 Aug. Isabel wife of John Walshe, aged 23 years and more, and Alice wife of John Leyke, aged 19 years and more, are his daughters and heirs.

691 Writ 10 Sept. 1403.

NOTTINGHAM. Inquisition. Nottingham. 24 Sept.

He died seised in his demesne as of fee of the manor of Hickling, held of the earl of Kent by suit of court twice yearly at Plumtree, annual value 8 marks.

Jointly with Emma his wife, who survives, he held in his demesne for life the manor of Langford of Lord Moubray, service unknown, annual value £20.

He died on 6 Sept. last. Isabel wife of John Walshe of Leicestershire, aged 26 years and more, and Alice wife of John Leek, esquire, aged 21 years and more, are his daughters and next heirs.

692 DERBY. Inquisition. Sandiacre. 13 Oct. 1403.

He held in his demesne as of fee:

Sutton Scarsdale, the manor, of the king of the duchy of Lancaster as a quarter of a fee, annual value 10 marks.

Sandiacre, the manor, of the king in chief by a rent of 33s.4d., annual value £10; and a place called 'le Conyngar', of Richard Grey, lord of Codnor, service unknown, annual value 30s.

Kirk Hallam, the manor, for life jointly with Emma his wife, who survives, of the abbot of Dale Abbey and others, service unknown, annual value 8 marks.

Date of death and heirs as above [no.691].

C 137/34, no.1
E 152/389

JOHN CALEMAN OF HORSEHEATH

693 Writ 3 Feb. 1403.

CAMBRIDGE. Inquisition. Cambridge. 10 Feb.

He held in his demesne as of fee 1 messuage, 30 a. arable, 1½ a. meadow and 1 a. pasture in Shudy Camps, Nosterfield and Horseheath, in chief by the service of a twentieth part of a knight's fee, annual value 13s.4d.

He died on 12 Feb. 1402. Robert Warner and Elizabeth wife of John Hatholf are his heirs; Robert being the son of Agnes, his daughter, aged 21 years and more; and Elizabeth his other daughter, aged 30 years and more.

C 137/34, no.2

RICHARD LESCROP, KNIGHT

694 Writ 5 June 1403.

LEICESTER. Inquisition. Leicester. 26 Sept.

He held a rent of 9s.3d. in Medbourne with the advowson, of the king in chief by a rent of 2d. payable by the sheriff at Easter. The church is worth 20 marks annually.

He died on 30 May. Roger Lescrope, knight, his son and heir, is aged 30 years and more.

C 137/34, no.3

THOMAS BARENTYN

695 Writ 11 Dec. 1402.

OXFORD. Inquisition. Tetsworth. 21 Dec. 1402.

He held the manor of Chalgrove of the prince [of Wales] by knight service, annual value 40 marks.

He died on 22 June 1400. Reynold his son and next heir is aged 20¾ years. Thomas Harcourt and Joan his wife have held the manor meanwhile and taken the profits, title unknown.

C 137/34, no.4
E 152/385, no.1

JAMES DE ROOS, KNIGHT

696 Writ 28 Feb. 1403.

YORK. Inquisition. Beverley. 23 April

He held in his demesne as of fee a third part of the manor of Hunmanby of the king in chief by the service of a ninth part of a barony, annual value £8 13s.4d.

He died at Gedney in Lincolnshire on 12 Feb. last. Robert his son and heir was aged 13 years on 1 Nov. last.

697A Writ 28 Feb. 1403.

LINCOLN. Inquisition. Boston. 18 April.

He held nothing in the county.

Date of death and heir as above.

697B LINCOLN. Inquisition with 5 of the same jurors. Gedney. 3 Oct. 1403.

He held nothing in the county.

C 137/34, no.5
E 149/83, no.5
E 152/380, no.4

ROGER FORSTER OF WELLINGTON

698 Writ 29 July 1403.

SHROPSHIRE. Inquisition. Shrewsbury. 10 Sept.

In Wellington he held 1 nook comprising ¼ carucate of the king in chief by the serjeanty of keeping the hedges in the forest of Wrekin, annual value 4s.; 1 messuage, 2 burgages and 1 cottage of the king in free burgage by a rent of 2s. payable by the sheriff at Michaelmas, annual value 6s.; and 1 messuage, formerly of John Dagon, of Lord Burnell, service unknown, annual value 10s.

He died on 21 July. Roger his son and next heir is aged 26 years and more.

C 137/34, no.6
E 149/82, no.2

PETER BOYS

699 Writ, stating that he was outlawed for failing to appear before the justices of the Bench of Richard II to answer Thomas Halghewell on a plea of transgression. 6 July 1403.

DEVON. Inquisition. Kingsbridge, 3 Sept.

Owing to the outlawry of Peter Boys 1 messuage and 1 ferling in North Yarnscombe in Stokenham were taken into the king's hands and so remain. They are held of Richard Ayschford and Alice his wife by fealty and a rent of 11s. He held them jointly with

Emmota his wife long before his outlawry to them and the heirs of their bodies, with remainder to Richard and Alice, annual value 2s. Emmota died long before and Peter granted the holding to his son John long before the outlawry. Peter died on 23 Nov. 1391. John his son and heir is aged 40 years and more.

C 137/34, no.7

THOMAS STRETE

700   Writ 25 June 1403.

HAMPSHIRE. Inquisition. Godshill. 10 Sept. 1403.

He held 2 messuages with curtilages in Newport in the Isle of Wight of the king in chief, annual value 6s.8d.

He was a bastard and died without heirs on 15 July 1390.

William Fursy and Joan his wife have occupied and taken the profits since his death, title unknown.

C 137/34, no.8
E 152/387

WALTER DEVEREUX, KNIGHT

701   Writ 24 April 1403.

HEREFORD. Inquisition. Hereford. 16 June.

He held the manor of Weobley in his demesne as of fee with Agnes his wife who survives him. It was held in her right in fee tail to herself and the heirs of her body as part of a barony, but how large a part is unknown, annual value £40.

He died on 25 July 1402. Walter his son and next heir was aged 15 years about Christmas last.

C 137/34, no.9

THOMAS BOKYNGHAM, SENIOR

702   Writ 1 July 1403.

SUSSEX. Inquisition. Bramber. 2 Aug.

He held nothing in the county, but long before he died he was outlawed, and on the day of his outlawry he held 1 messuage and 1 shop in New Shoreham and 8 a. in Old Shoreham, the messuage of Lord Ponynges by a rent of 4s., the shop of the prior of Sele by a rent of 12d., and the 8 a. of the abbot of Battle and the prioress of Rusper, services unknown; total annual value 5s.10d. They were taken into the king's hands owing to the outlawry, and so remain.

He died on 24 Dec. 1398. Robert his son and heir is aged 30 years and more.

C 137/34, no.10

ISABEL DAUGHTER AND HEIR OF WILLIAM BLOUNT

703 Writ 1 Sept. 1403.

GLOUCESTER. Inquisition. Thornbury. 4 Sept.

She held two parts of the manor of Bitton of the king in chief by knight service, amount unknown; and also 1 messuage and ½ virgate there of John Deverose, knight, and Joan his wife, by a rent of 5s.; annual values, £20 and 2s.

She died on 22 Aug. last. John Blount, her father's brother and her next heir, is aged 26 years and more.

704 Writ 10 Sept. 1403. Worcester.

GLOUCESTER. Inquisition with jurors as in last. Thornbury. 12 Sept.

In the king's hands owing to the death of William Blount, who held them in his demesne as of fee, and because of the minority of Isabel his daughter, who died in the king's ward, are two parts of half [*sic*] the manor of Bitton, and 1 messuage and ½ virgate there. The part of the manor is held of the king in chief as a quarter of a knight's fee, annual value £20, and the other lands of John Deverose, knight, and Joan his wife by a rent of 5s., annual value beyond that 2s.

William died on 28 April 1399 and Isabel on 22 Aug. last; heir as above.

C 137/34, no. 11

HUGH SHIRLEY, KNIGHT

705 Writ 28 July 1403.

SUFFOLK. Inquisition. Barnham. 24 Aug.

He held nothing in Suffolk.

He died on 21 July 1403. Ralph his son and heir was aged 13 on 23 April last.

706 Writ 28 July 1403.

NOTTINGHAM. Inquisition. Nottingham. 17 Sept.

He held in his demesne as of fee of the king in chief a rent of 13s. 4d. in Bunny, service unknown.

Date of death and heir, aged 12 years and more, as above.

707 DERBY. Inquisition *ex officio*. Derby. 21 Aug. 1403.

He held in his demesne as of fee of the king in chief of the duchy of Lancaster by knight service:

Shirley, the manor, annual value £20 [*sic*].

Hoon, the manor, annual value 10 marks.

Date of death and heir, aged 12 years and more, as above.

Robert del Heygh of Cheshire, who adhered to Henry Percy, the traitor, held in his demesne as of fee 1 messuage in Chaddesden, now forfeited to the king, annual value 12s. 4d.

John de Assheburn of Cheshire, who similarly rebelled, held in his demesne as of fee two parts of a messuage in Spondon, also forfeited, annual value 15s.

708 Writ 7 Sept. 1403.

DERBY. Inquisition. Callow. 22 Sept.

He held of the king in chief of the duchy of Lancaster by knight service:

Shirley, the manor, annual value £10 [sic].

Hoon, the manor, annual value 10 marks.

Hollington, 6 marks rent, service unknown.

Wyaston, 1 messuage, service unknown, annual value 3s.

Yeaveley, the manor, service unknown, annual value 46s. 8d.

Cromford, 1 messuage, service unknown, annual value 20s.

Date of death and heir, aged 12 years and more, as above.

709 Writ 28 July 1403.

STAFFORD. Inquisition. Stafford. 25 Oct.

He held nothing in the county.

Date of death and heir, aged 15 years and more, as above.

710 Writ 28 July 1403.

LEICESTER. Inquisition. Leicester. 3 Sept.

He held nothing in the county.

Date of death and heir, aged 12 years and more, as above.

711 WARWICK. Inquisition. Nuneaton. 15 Sept. 1403.

He held the manor of Ettington in his demesne as of fee of the king of the duchy of Lancaster, service unknown, annual value 20 marks.

Date of death and heir, aged 12 years on 23 April, as above.

C 137/34, no. 12
E 149/82, no. 1
E 152/390, no. 4

WILLIAM PYRYE

712 Writ 6 Nov. 1402.

WORCESTER. Inquisition. Droitwich. 13 Nov.

Roger, parson of Merton, held a watermill called 'Mertonmulle' in Salwarpe by Droitwich in his demesne as of fee, and granted it to Nicholas de Pyrie and Agnes his wife for their lives, with remainder to Walter, son of Nicholas, and his heirs. So they held it and died, and Walter held it and had issue Walter atte Pyrie, who was outlawed for felony. It descended to him and he had issue another William, and it descended to him. During the life of William the father it was taken into the hands of Edward III on account of the outlawry. No other lands were in the king's hands for that reason.

A new mill has been built on the site, and the mill and site are held of the earl of Warwick by a rent of 6s. 8d., annual value 2s.

William son of Walter died on 16 Feb. 1399.

William, son of William the son and next heir of William son of Walter, is aged 30 years and more.

C 137/34, no.13

JOHN CRADDELEY

713   Writ 24 May 1403.
NOTTINGHAM. Inquisition. Nottingham. 18 June.
   He held in his demesne as of fee:
   Ratcliffe on Soar and Kingston on Soar, 1 messuage, 2 cottages and 9 bovates of arable and meadow, of the king, in socage in petty serjeanty, annual value 26s.8d.
   Thrumpton, 1 messuage and 3 bovates of arable and meadow, of Nicholas de Stapulford by a rent of 1 lb. cumin, annual value 21s.
   He died about 14 Sept. 1391. Robert his son and heir is aged 22 years and more.
   Richard Denton of Leicestershire and Thomas West of Northamptonshire have taken the profits of all the premises, title unknown.

C 137/34, no.14

ROBERT URSWYK, KNIGHT

714   Writ 27 May 1403.
YORK. Inquisition. Northallerton. 24 Aug.
   He held jointly with his wife Joan 20 marks rent from Langbargh wapentake at Easter and Michaelmas in accordance with a grant of Thomas Longley, clerk, to them, their heirs male, their heirs general and the right heirs of Robert, to be received from Thomas de Fauconberge, knight, who holds the wapentake of the king in chief at fee farm, as appears by their charter shown to the jurors. The grant was made by licence of Richard II [*CPR 1396–9*, p.402], and they attorned to Thomas. The rent is held of the king in chief by knight service and is worth nothing beyond the rent itself.
   He died on 27 Sept. 1402. Robert de Urswyk, knight, his son and heir, is aged 30 years and more.

C 137/34, no.15
E 152/380, no.7

THOMAS DE METHAM, KNIGHT

715   Writ 7 Sept. 1403.
YORK. Inquisition. Howden. 19 Sept.
   He held nothing in the county because by letters patent dated 20 Nov. 1401 [*CPR 1401–5*, p.14] the king gave him licence to enfeoff Alexander de Metham, knight, his son, in 8 messuages and 17 bovates in Southburn and Tibthorpe, held of the king in chief, to hold to himself and his heirs without interference by the king, his heirs or their officers. He accordingly made the grant by his charter dated 8 March 1402, and his son was seised of them.

Thomas died on 28 Aug. 1403. Alexander his son and heir is aged 21 years and more.

C 137/34, no.16
E 152/380, no.6

JOHN HERVYLE

716   Writ 20 Feb. 1403.
STAFFORD. Inquisition. Walsall. 13 March.
He held the manor of Wednesbury of the king by the grant of Henry de Tymmore, parson of Elford, and John de Tymmore to himself, Alice his wife and the heirs of their bodies, by licence of Edward III [*CPR 1364–7*, p.165]. It is held by a rent of 20s. payable by the sheriff at Michaelmas; annual value £10.
Alice died, and John died on 16 Feb. Henry their son and heir is aged 30 years and more.

C 137/34, no.17
E 152/390, no.2

ANNE WIFE OF JAMES BERNERS, KNIGHT

717   Writ 17 May 1403.
SURREY. Inquisition. Leatherhead. 21 May.
She held the manor of West Horsley for life by the grant of Henry IV [*CPR 1399–1401*, pp.82–3] with remainder to Richard son of James Berners and his heirs. It is held of the king in chief of Windsor castle by the service of half a knight's fee and 6s. 8d. every 24 weeks; annual value 40 marks.
She died on 14 April. Richard son of James, her heir, is aged 21 years and 12 weeks.

718   Writ, *plura*, 29 June 1403.
SURREY. Inquisition. West Horsley. 21 Aug.
She did hold more, namely the advowson of West Horsley, the park and warren with the manor. They are held of the king in chief of the castle of Windsor, as is the manor, by fealty and rendering 6s. 8d. every 24 weeks; annual value 100s.
Heir, aged 21 years and more, as above.

C 137/34, no.18
E 149/82, no.4

JOHN APPLER

719   Writ 14 July 1403.
LINCOLN. Inquisition. Spalding. 16 Oct.
He was outlawed at the suit of John Ravenser, parson of Algarkirk. In consequence 1 messuage and ½ a. in Whaplode were taken into the king's hands and so remain. They are held of John Porter of Whaplode of his manor of Hagbeach Hall, service unknown; annual value 2s. and no more because burdened with a rent of 3s. to the manor.

He died on 4 Oct. 1400. William Medawe of Whaplode, his heir, is aged 30 years and more.

720   Writ 8 April 1404.
LINCOLN. Inquisition. Spalding. 20 April.
As last, except that the outlawry is said to be in a plea of debt and the heir is described as William de Medowe of Whaplode, nephew and heir, being the son of Margaret, sister of John.

C 137/34, no.19
C 137/41, no.41

ROBERT SCALES, KNIGHT

721   Writ 11 Jan. 1403.
CAMBRIDGE. Inquisition. Cambridge. 10 Feb.
He held in his demesne as of fee of the king in chief two parts of the manor of Haslingfield, and the reversion of the third part which Joan his mother holds in dower of Roger Scales, knight, his father, service unknown; annual value of the two parts £20, the one part £10.
He died on 7 Dec. Robert his son and heir is aged 6 years and more.

722   Writ 28 Jan 1403.
HERTFORD. Inquisition. Barkway. 7 Feb.
He held nothing in the county.
Date of death and heir as above.

723   Writ 11 Jan 1403.
ESSEX. Inquisition. Braintree. 10 Feb.
In Rivenhall he held 19s.3d. assize rent from the lands of Robert Leynham, 3s.4d. from those of John Whelere and 3s.4d. from those of Alice Davy; and the reversion of 3s.4d. from those of John Whelere and Alice Davy which Joan his mother, widow of Roger Scales, holds for life in dower. All are payable at Easter and Michaelmas, and held of the honour of Boulogne, services unknown.
Date of death and heir as above.

724   Writ 11 Jan. 1403.
NORFOLK. Inquisition. Stoke Ferry. 19 Feb.
He held in his demesne as of fee the reversion of the manors of Scales Hall in Middleton, Islington, Howe and Raynham of the king in chief of the honour of Haughley and by ward of the castle of Dover, services unknown; and also the reversion of the manor of Castle Hall in Middleton of the earl of March of the honour of Clare by the service of a pair of gilt spurs. All are held for life by Joan his mother, being jointly enfeoffed with Roger her late husband; annual values, Scales Hall £10, Islington £10 10s.2d., Howe £13 6s. 8d., Raynham £10 11d., Castle Hall 10 marks 14d.
Date of death and heir as above.

R

725 SUFFOLK. Inquisition. Baylham. 21 Feb. 1403.
He held nothing in the county.
Date of death and heir as above.

C 137/34, no.20
E 149/81, no.4
E 152/381

GERARD DE BRAYBROOK, KNIGHT

726 Writ 4 Feb. 1403.
BEDFORD. Inquisition. Turvey. 2 March.
John de Wodhull, son of John de Wodhull, knight, baron of Wodhull, held the manors of Odell and Langford, and enfeoffed Thomas de Reynes and Lawrence de Pabenham, knights, John Curteys and William de Wodhull. They by a fine of 1376 shown to the jurors [CP 25(1) 288/50 no.786, licence *CPR 1374–7*, p.275] granted them to Gerard Braybrook, knight, and Isabel his wife for their lives with remainder to Nicholas de Wodhull and his heirs. Isabel died and Gerard held them. They should remain to Nicholas de Wodhull. Both are held of the king in chief by knight service; annual values, Odell £20, Langford £30.
He died on 1 Feb. last. Gerard Braybrook, knight, his son and heir, is aged 30 years and more. Nicholas Wodhull is aged 50 years and more.

727 Writ 4 Feb. 1403.
NORTHAMPTON. Inquisition. Earls Barton. 19 Feb.
He died on 1 Feb. holding nothing of the king, but Robert Braybrok, bishop of London, William Thirnyng, John Hervy and John Bonham held the castle and manor of Castle Ashby with their appurtenances, except the advowson, in their demesne as of fee, with 3 messuages and 60 a. in Chadstone. They granted them to Gerard Braybrok, knight, and Isabel his wife for their lives, with successive remainders to Reynold Braybrok, knight, and Joan for their lives, Gerard Braybrok, knight, junior, and his heirs male, Reynold Braybrok and his heirs male, and the right heirs of Gerard Braybrok, senior.
Isabel died in the lifetime of Gerard Braybrok. Gerard then held the premises for life, with remainder to Reynold and Joan for their lives. They are held of Reynold Grey of Ruthin, services unknown; annual values, Castle Ashby 37 marks, Chadstone 40s.
Gerard Braybroke, knight, his son and heir, is aged 30 years and more.

728 Writ, *plenius certiorari*, questioning the omission of Gerard Braybrok, junior, from the list of feofees, in the above inquisition, the naming of Bonham in place of John Boun, and the omission of certain conditions of the grant. 12 March 1403.
NORTHAMPTON. Inquisition. Northampton. 23 March.
He died on 1 Feb. 1403 holding nothing of the king in chief but Robert bishop of London, Gerard Braybroke, knight, junior, William Thirnyng, John Hervy and John Boun held the castle and manor of Castle Ashby and Chadstone in their demesne as of fee. These they granted to Gerard Braybroke, knight, senior, and Isabel for their lives. If they should die within 10 years their executors were to hold them for the

remainder of the term. So they held. By another deed the feoffees granted that after the 10 years the lands should remain to Reynold Braybroke, knight, and Joan and their heirs male, on condition that if John, son and heir of John Hemenale, knight, should die without lawful heirs of his body, the remainder to the heirs of Reynold and Joan should cease and they should hold for life. If they died without heirs male or John son of Robert Hemenale died without lawful heirs of his body, after their deaths the remainder should be successively to the heirs male of Gerard de Braybrook, knight, senior, the heirs male of Reynold, and the right heirs of Gerard, senior.

Gerard de Braybroke, senior, and Isabel attorned to Reynold and Joan. Isabel died during the life of Gerard. John son of Robert de Hemenhale died without heirs of his body. The ten years is ended. Therefore Gerard held for life with remainder to Reynold and Joan.

The manors are held of Reynold Grey of Ruthin, Castle Ashby by suit each month at his court at Earls Barton called 'Baronsmote', annual value £20, and Chadstone by suit at his hundred of Wymersley every three weeks, annual value 100s.

Heir as above.

C 137/35, no.21
E 149/80, no.4

ALICE WIDOW OF WILLIAM STERRE

729   Writ 8 March 1402.

CALAIS. Inquisition. 12 May.

She held of the king a tenement in the street called 'Mesondeustrete' on the west, between the tenement of John Kekerard to the north and the cottage of James Wales to the south. It came to her by inheritance from her parents, and is held by the service of providing a watchman for the defence of the city, as appears by a charter of Edward III. Beyond the cost of the watchman it is worth 20s. yearly.

She died at Bordeaux 16 or 17 years ago. There was no other heir than Robert Parker, her uncle, that is brother of her mother, aged 60 years and more. He held it and let it to farm for three years; then John Bonde entered it by virtue of a charter of Richard II and held it for 13 years, profiting to the extent of £13.

730   Writ, *melius sciri*, asking what was her status and how Robert Parker was the heir. 12 Oct. 1402.

CALAIS. Inquisition. 8 Jan. 1403.

She held of Richard II, by the service of providing a watchman for the defence of the city, a house with garden in the street called 'le Mesondieux' between the tenement once of John Kykerard to the north and the cottage once of James Wale to the south. It was of the inheritance of Alice Sterre, her mother, in fee simple, granted to William Sterre and Alice by a charter of Edward III, to them and their heirs. William died and Alice the mother held it for her life; then Alice the daughter entered as next heir and held it until banished from Calais for 6 years for various offences. She died at Bordeaux. After her banishment Robert Parker, her uncle, brother of her mother, occupied it, let it, provided the watchman, and took the profits in the name of the younger Alice during her life. After her death, as next heir he took the profits for 3 years and more. He is next heir and aged 60 years and more.

C 137/35, no.22

GILES DAUBENEY, KNIGHT

731 Writ 24 Aug. 1403.
CORNWALL. Inquisition. Liskeard. 13 Sept.
    He formerly held in his demesne as of fee two parts of the manors of Trenay, Fawton, Polruan and Essa, with the reversion of the remaining third part which Eleanor widow of Giles Daubeney, knight, his father, held in dower. By his charter shown to the jurors, dated 27 July 1396, he granted them to John Hulle, John Wadham, Thomas Daubeney, William Daubeney, William Lynne, Robert Kylby and William Goldyngton and their heirs and assigns. Eleanor attorned to them for the third part. They are held of the prince of Wales of the castle of Launceston of the duchy of Cornwall by knight service as a half fee-morton, annual value £24.
    He died on 22 Aug. 1403. John his son and heir is aged 9 years and more.

732 Writ 24 Aug. 1403.
BEDFORD. Inquisition. Kempston. 3 Sept.
    He held a third part of the manor of Kempston in his demesne as of fee of the king in chief of the honour of Huntingdon by the service of one third of half a knight's fee, annual value £20.
    Date of death and heir as above.

733 Writ 24 Aug. 1403.
SOMERSET. Inquisition. Ilminster. 12 Sept.
    He held the manor and hundred of South Petherton, with the hamlets of Barrington, Chillington and Southarp, in his demesne as of fee of the king in chief as one knight's fee. By his indenture shown to the jurors, dated South Petherton 20 Nov. 1397 and licensed by letters patent, dated 16 Nov. 1397 [CPR 1396–9, p.263], he granted to William Daubeney a rent of 10 marks for life from the premises, payable at the four terms, with the provision that if it should be in arrears by 15 days he might enter and retain the premises until satisfied of it. Giles gave William 3s.4d. as seisin of the rent. Annual value 110 marks.
    He also held the rent of a rose from a messuage, 100 a., 10 a. meadow and 60 a. heath in Kilmersdon, which William Nywebury and Alice his wife hold for life by the grant of Giles Daubeney, his father, by a fine of 1363 [CP 25(1) 200/26, no.75] shown to the jurors, with reversion to Giles Daubeney and his heirs.
    Date of death and heir as above.

734 Writ 24 Aug. 1403.
LINCOLN. Inquisition. Lincoln. 8 Sept.
    He held of the inheritance of Giles Daubeney, knight, his father, the manor of South Ingleby with its members in Saxilby and Broxholme and the advowson of Broxholme, of lord de Roos of the castle of Belvoir by knight service, annual value £22.
    Date of death and heir as above.

735 Writ 24 Aug. 1403.
NOTTINGHAM. Inquisition. Broadholme. 13 Sept.

He held of the inheritance of Giles Daubeny, knight, his father, 100 a. fallow, 200 a. pasture and 60 a. wood in Thorney, with 13s.4d. assize rent in Broadholme, as part of a knight's fee, of the manor of South Ingleby in Lincolnshire, of Lord de Roos of his castle of Belvoir, annual value 40s.

Date of death and heir as above.

736 Writ, for fees, 24 Sept. 1403.
LINCOLN. Extent. Lincoln. 6 Oct.

He held the advowson of Broxholme, parcel of the manor of South Ingleby, which he held with appurtenances in Saxilby and Broxholme of the Lord de Roos of his castle of Belvoir by knight service, value when vacant 10 marks.

C 137/35, no.23
E 149/81, no.2

NICHOLAS MOLYNS

737 SOMERSET. Memorandum.

It was found by inquisition at Crewkerne by Richard Micheldevere on 21 Nov. 1387 [*CIPM* XVI, no.602] that John Molyns had amongst other holdings in his demesne as of fee of the inheritance of Giles Daubeney, who held of the king in chief and was under age in the king's ward, 1 messuage, 2 watermills, 1 dovecot, 30 a. arable, 8 a. meadow, 3 a. pasture and 10s. rent in South Petherton, held of the manor of South Petherton by knight service, and a rent of £4; and that Nicholas Molyns was his son and heir, aged 7 years and more.

It was found by another inquisition at Ilchester on 15 March 1403 before John Savage, escheator, that Nicholas was then aged 22 years [below, no.858].

On 25 May 1403 Nicholas, present in person in chancery, protested that the premises were not held of Giles Daubeney as found in the inquisition, and his protestation was admitted in court and his fealty accepted. All the premises descended and were released to him.

Writ to John Savage, formerly escheator, ordering him to send to the chancery the assignment of dower made by him to Margaret widow of Giles Daubeney. 13 March 1410.

C 137/35, no.23, mm.13, 14

MAUD CANTELO

738 Writ 29 Dec. 1402.
WILTSHIRE. Inquisition. Calne. 3 Feb. 1403.

She held the manor of Heddington for life with remainder to the heirs of Robert Cauntelo, her late husband. It is held of the earl of Hereford as a fortieth part of a knight's fee, annual value £8, of which £6 2s.8d. is from service rents payable at the four principal terms.

She died on 17 Dec. Elizabeth wife of Richard Cheddre, daughter of Robert, son of Maud, is next heir and aged 23 years and more.

739 Writ 29 Dec. 1402.
GLOUCESTER. Inquisition. Chipping Sodbury. 12 Jan. 1403.

She held in her demesne as of fee:

Dursley and Newington Bagpath, the manor with the park, of the king in chief as half a knight's fee, annual value £21 9s.4d., of which £20 8s.6d. is in service rents payable at the four principal terms.

Leonard Stanley, 1 messuage, 1 carucate, 10 a. meadow, 5 a. wood and 100s. in rent; of the king in chief as a quarter of a fee. The rents are payable at Easter and Michaelmas. The rest is worth 53s.4d. annually.

Dodington, the manor, of the earl of Stafford of his manor of Thornbury, service unknown, annual value £11 8s., of which £10 13s.4d. is service rents payable at the four usual terms.

Date of death and heir as above.

740 Writ, *plenius certiorari*, as to the heirs of Robert Cantelowe. 5 Feb. 1403.
WILTSHIRE. Inquisition. Calne. 8 Feb.

Elizabeth wife of Robert Cheddre is the heir of Robert Cauntelo, namely daughter of Robert, son of Robert.

C 137/35, no.23

HUGH QUECCHE

741 SURREY. Inquisition. Reigate. 8 Jan. 1403.

He held by the courtesy of England after the death of Elizabeth his wife 2 tenements called Woodplace and Boxers in Coulsdon, of the abbot of Chertsey, service unknown, annual values 40s. and 26s.8d.

He also held in his demesne as of fee:

Chipstead, the manor in Chipstead, Merstham and Nutfield, of the king in chief by knight service, annual value 10 marks.

Chipstead and Woodmansterne, 1 tenement called Eyehurst, of the manor of Woodmansterne, service unknown, annual value 53s.4d.

Coulsdon and Waddington, 1 tenement called Kenley, of the abbot of Chertsey, service unknown, annual value 33s.4d.

Merstham, part of a grove containing about ½ a., of the prior of Canterbury, annual value nil because large timber.

He died on 1 Nov. Joan his daughter and heir is aged 26 years and more.

742 Writ, *melius sciri*, as to the heirs of Elizabeth his wife. 17 Feb. 1404.
SURREY. Inquisition. Leatherhead. 12 March.

Joan wife of John Norton esquire, daughter of Hugh Quecche and Elizabeth, is her heir and aged 28 years and more.

743 Writ 11 Dec. 1402.

SUSSEX. Inquisition. Steyning. 29 Dec.

He held in his demesne as of fee:

Steyning, a tenement called 'Gervayses' and 3 virgates, of the honour of the castle of Bramber by knight service, in the king's hands owing to the minority of Thomas Mowbray, annual value 26s. 8d.; 3 virgates once of Thomas Testard, of the same honour by knight service, annual value nil; certain lands and tenements once of Ralph atte Berne, of the same honour by knight service, annual value 6s. 8d.; 1 a. formerly of Robert Bokyngham, of the same honour by a rent of 18d. at Michaelmas payable at the manor of King's Barn, annual value beyond that nil; and 1 tenement and 5 virgates called Nash formerly of William atte Watere, of the abbot of Fécamp of his manor of Steyning by knight service. The manor is in the king's hands during the war, and from this holding Juliana widow of William atte Watere has 13 marks for life, annual value beyond this nil.

Wyckham, certain lands formerly of Agnes Pikard, jointly with Richard Bokyngham of the honour of Bramber by knight service, annual value 2s.

Chailey, lands, of William Heron, knight, lord Say, of his manor of Streat, service unknown, annual value 20s.

Bolney, a tenement called 'Bolkes', of whom held and by what service is unknown; annual value 13s. 4d.

Hickstead, 3½ a. meadow, of the prior of St. John of Jerusalem in England of his manor of Saddlescombe, service unknown, annual value 3s. 4d.

Ovingdean, 53s. 4d. assize rents, of whom held and by what service is unknown.

In fee tail he held a tenement and 120 a. called Pickwell in Cuckfield of the manor of Hurstpierpoint by knight service, annual value 40s.

Date of death and heir, aged 25 years and more, as above.

C 137/35, no.25
E 149/82, no.3

CLARICE DAUGHTER AND HEIR OF WALTER BOUKER

744 Writ 3 July 1403.

DEVON. Inquisition. Buckfastleigh. 25 Sept.

Owing to the idiocy of Clarice daughter and heir of Walter Bouker half a messuage and half a ferling in Dean Prior were in the hands of Richard II and of the king. With the other halves they are held of the prior of Plympton of his manor of Dean Prior by a rent of 3s. 10d., annual value of the halves 12d.

She died on 8 April without heirs of her body. William Tolchet is her nephew and heir, being the son of Margaret her sister, and aged 40 years and more.

C 137/35, no.26

ALICE WIFE OF JOHN MANERS, KNIGHT

745 Writ 2 Jan. 1403.

NORTHUMBERLAND. Inquisition. Newcastle upon Tyne castle. 29 Jan.

She held in her demesne as of fee:

Seaton Delaval, Callerton and North Dissington, two parts of the manors, and two parts of a quarter of the manor of Hartley, and a quarter of the same manor in service [*sic*], of the king in chief by homage, fealty, suit of the county court every six weeks. and by 1⅙ knight's fees and other services, annual value of the two parts £22 and no more these days because of destruction by the Scots; and also the reversion of the remaining third part of the first three manors and of a quarter of Hartley, which Joan widow of Henry de la Vale, knight, holds in dower.

Holywell, two parts of a messuage and 12 a., of the barony of Bywell by suit of court thrice annually and other services, annual value 16d.; and the reversion of the third part which Joan holds in dower.

Seaton, fealty, suit of court, mill and 26s.8d. rent from the lands of Stephen le Scrop, knight, William de Vescy and William de Halywell in Holywell, of the same barony, annual value 28s.

Joan widow of Henry de la Vale also holds for life the manors of Dukesfield and Branton, a rent of 8 marks from the manor of Branton, and half the manor of Biddlestone by a fine of 1372 [CP 25(1) 181/13, no. 154], with remainder after her death to William de Whitchestre, son and heir of Alice, annual value £15 and no more because of destruction by the Scots. They are held of others than the king, but of whom is unknown.

She died on 26 Dec. last. William Whitchestre her son and heir is aged 30 years and more.

746 Writ 2 Jan. 1403.
NEWCASTLE UPON TYNE. Inquisition. 26 April.

She held in her demesne as of fee two parts of 16s. rent from a tenement of the prior of Tynemouth in Newcastle. Richard Goldesburgh, knight, and Joan his wife held the third part in right of the dower of Joan, with reversion to Alice. It is a quitrent held of no one.

Date of death and heir as above.

C 137/35, no.27

HUGH MORTYMER, KNIGHT

747 Writ 1 Aug. 1403.
BEDFORD. Inquisition. Luton. 20 Aug.

He held in his demesne as of fee of the king in chief a third part of the manor of Luton with the hundred of Flitt and the leet there, the third part of the manor as a third part of half a knight's fee, the hundred and leet by a rent of 60s. payable by the sheriff at Midsummer, annual value £43.

He also held in Luton 1 horse-mill and 1 garden of Hugh de Stoppusley by a rent of 2s., annual value 13s.4d.; 1 cottage of John Roulond and William Asshe by a rent of 14d. and 2 boon works in the autumn, annual value 3s.4d.; and 2 a. and 1 rood of meadow of John Waleys by a rent of 3s., annual value 3s.4d.

He died on 21 July last. John Cressy, senior, is next heir, being the son of Maud, daughter of Joan, daughter of Hugh, father of Henry his father, and aged 24 years and more.

Writ to assign dower to Petronilla his widow. 17 Sept. 1403.

748 Exchequer writ, ordering the escheator to make a full extent of the third part of the manor and of the hundred, as in the above, and to have it before the barons of the exchequer on the quindene of Martinmas next, with the above inquisition, now in the escheator's bag of particulars in the keeping of the king's remembrancer. 26 Oct. 1403.

[*Cf.* View of account of the escheator, E 368/176, mm. 265–6].

BEDFORD. Inquisition. Luton. 12 Nov. 1403.

He held a third part of the manor of Luton, annual value £28, comprising assize rents at Easter and Michaelmas £12 16s. 8d., demesne land and mill at the four terms £13 13s. 4d. and perquisites of court 30s.

The hundred of Flitt with the leets and profits of the hundred is worth £15 yearly, comprising rent of the hundred called 'Wauheselver' at Martinmas 14s. 5d., rent called 'Deseneselver' at Easter 43s. 4d., 'Shirefshot' at Candlemas and Midsummer £6 8d., and perquisites of court £6 1s. 7d.

749 Writ, *melius sciri*, as to his status in the mill, garden, etc. mentioned in the above inquisition [no. 747]. 12 March 1404.

BEDFORD. Inquisition. Luton. 4 April.

The horse-mill, cottage etc., are all held in his demesne as of fee.

750 Writ 1 Aug. 1403.

SHROPSHIRE AND THE ADJACENT MARCH OF WALES. Inquisition. Much Wenlock. 8 Sept.

He held in his demesne as of fee of the king in chief by knight service the manor of Quatt, annual value £9.

Long before he died he enfeoffed Roger Hay and Hugh Carpenter, clerks, Richard Crateford, chaplain, now deceased, and Richard Leghton in fee simple in the manor of Chelmarsh and other holdings in Chelmarsh and the hamlets of Lye Hall, Bromlow, Meadow Town, and Medlicott. Crateford and Leghton released them to Hay and Carpenter who still hold.

Date of death and heir as above [no. 747].

751 Writ 1 Aug. 1403.

GLOUCESTER AND THE ADJACENT MARCH OF WALES. Inquisition. Thornbury. 4 Sept.

He held in Magor in the March in his demesne as of fee of the king in chief by knight service, amount unknown, 1 messuage, 1 dovecot, 6½ a. arable, 6 a. pasture and 5 marks rent from various tenants, annual value nil because burnt and wasted by Owen de Glyndourdy and other traitors in his company, but they were worth £4 yearly.

He died on 21 July. Edmund Rodeberegh, his next heir, is aged 38 years and more.

752 Writ, *plenius certiorari*, as to how Edmund Redebergh is heir. 12 Oct. 1403.

GLOUCESTER AND THE ADJACENT MARCH OF WALES. Inquisition. Thornbury. 12 Nov.

Edmund Rodebergh is the heir and full age, but how he is heir is completely unknown.

C 137/35, no. 28
E 149/81, no. 1

CHRISTINA BROYE

753 Writ 15 May 1403.

HEREFORD. Inquisition. Hereford. 22 Sept.

John Couley and Richard Ruydyng, chaplains, by their charter by licence of Richard II [*CPR 1388–92*, p.128] granted 1 manor of 6½ virgates in Aylton with the advowson of the chapel to Robert Broye and Christina his wife for their lives, with successive remainders to John Warde, Isabel his wife and the heirs of the body of Isabel, and Thomas Walleweyn son of Richard Walleweyn, his heirs and assigns. So she held it in fee tail of the king by the serjeanty of following at her own costs in his army in Herefordshire whenever he comes there, and outside the county at the king's costs of 12d. a day, and by 24s. rent; annual value 66s. 8d.

She died on 9 May. Isabel wife of John Warde, her daughter and heir, is aged 40 years and more.

C 137/36, no.29
E 149/81, no.9

ROBERT SOTIRLEE

754 Writ 24 Jan. 1403.

SUFFOLK. Inquisition. Blythburgh. 19 April.

He held the manor of Uggeshall with the advowson to himself and the heirs male of his body by the grant of William Joce of Helmingham and William del Hill, formerly parson of Sotterley, with remainder failing such heirs to Walter de Soterle and the heirs male of his body. It is held of Thomas Earl Marshal, who is in the king's ward, of Framlingham castle by the service of 4 knight's fees; annual value 20 marks.

He died on 6 July 1402 without male or other heirs. It should remain to Walter Soterle, who is aged 40 years and more.

C 137/36, no.30
E 149/81, no.13

JOHN SON AND HEIR OF JOHN DE FELTON, KNIGHT

755 Writ 12 Feb. 1403.

NORTHAMPTON. Inquisition. Chipping Warden. 12 March.

No lands came into the hands of Richard II by the death of John de Felton, knight, father of John de Felton, or on account of the minority of the latter, nor are any so held. John de Felton the father long before his death, by his charter shown to the jurors, enfeoffed William Hatleseye, Richard Elyngham, John Goodeman and Richard Mersk, chaplains, in the manor of Hinton by Woodford. They granted it by charter to William de Hylton, lord of Hilton, Thomas Heryngton, John Stotesbury, John Faukener of Byfield and Peter Mersk, parson of Kildale, their heirs and assigns. It is held of the earl of Stafford by knight service, amount unknown, annual value 100s.

John de Felton the son died on 31 Jan. John son and heir of Walter Faucomberge, knight, and Joan late his wife, sister of John de Felton the father, is heir and aged 30 years and more.

756 Writ 12 Feb. 1403.

NORTHUMBERLAND. Inquisition. Newcastle upon Tyne castle. 26 March.

John de Felton, junior, held two parts of the manor of Edlingham to himself and the heirs of his body by a fine of 1315–16 [CP 25(1) 285/30, no. 125), by which William de Felton recognised the right of Robert de Felton, and Robert granted the manor to William for life with remainder to William son of William and the heirs of his body. There is a castle, annual value nil. In the two parts are 132 a. by the short hundred, 80 a. meadow and two parts of a watermill. They are worth 40s. yearly and no more because of destruction by the Scots. The manor is held of Henry Percy, earl of Northumberland, of his barony of Beanley by the rent of one unmewed sparrowhawk, or 6d. at Midsummer.

He also held two parts of Lemmington Hall, 1 shieling called Rughley, 2 parts of 7 husbandlands and 8 cottages, 1 tenement in Newton, certain lands and tenements in Lemmington, and two parts of 7s. 6d. rent in Bolton, annual value 40d., but of whom they are held is unknown.

He held in his demesne in fee tail:

Black Heddon, two parts of the manor, of Ralph de Nevyl, earl of Westmorland, of his barony of Bywell by knight service, annual value £4.

South Dotland, two parts of the manor, of Henry Percy, earl of Northumberland, of the barony of Prudhoe by knight service, annual value 2s. and no more because of destruction by the Scots.

Steel in Redesdale, two parts of a place so-called, of the manor of Otterburn by the service of 1 grain of pepper at Christmas; and two parts of certain lands and tenements in Thirston of the barony of Mitford by a rent of 18d., annual value 13s. 4d.

Nafferton and Nafferton Hall, two parts of lands there, of the king in chief by knight service, annual value £4.

He died on 31 Jan. Elizabeth daughter of John Felton and wife of Edmund Hastynges, knight, is the heir of John the son by virtue of the grant to William de Felton, father of John, knight, and his heirs, she being the daughter of John, knight, son of William, to whom the grant in fee tail was made.

757 Writ, *melius sciri*, as it was not stated of whom certain lands are held and how Elizabeth is heir. 9 April 1403.

NORTHUMBERLAND. Inquisition. Newcastle upon Tyne castle. 25 April.

The shieling called Rughley is held of Henry Percy, earl of Northumberland, of his barony of Vescy in socage; two parts of 7 husbandlands and 8 cottages, 1 tenement in Newton and the lands in Lemmington of the same Henry Percy in socage as hamlets of Edlingham; the two parts of Lemmington Hall of the prior of St. John of Jerusalem in England in socage; two parts of 7s. 6d. rent in Bolton of the hospital of St. Thomas of Bolton in socage; and the place called Steel in Redesdale of Henry Percy the son in right of Gilbert Umfravyle, who is in the king's ward, of the manor of Otterburn by the service of 1 grain of pepper.

Elizabeth, daughter of John de Felton, knight, is the sister and heir of John the son, and heir of John de Felton, and holds by right of the gift of William de Felton to William the father of John de Felton, knight. She is aged 23 years and more.

C 137/36, no. 31

E 152/384, nos. 1, 2

JOHN CLEY, CLERK

758   Writ 20 June 1403.

SUFFOLK. Inquisition. Otley. 28 June.

William Bardolf, knight, lord of Wormegay, by his charter of 1380–81 granted to John Clay, clerk, the manor of King's Hall in Clopton with the advowson of Debach for life, with reversion to himself and his heirs, and the tenants attorned. William Bardolf died. John Clay assigned to Agnes widow of William Bardolf half the manor in dower, as it is of such tenure that widows should have half in dower by custom from time out of mind. So John Clay held half the manor with the advowson of Debach, and the reversion of the other half. After his death they belong to Thomas Bardolf, knight, son of William Bardolf. The half with the reversion is worth 66s. 8d. annually, the advowson nothing. The whole manor and the advowson are held of the king in chief as a quarter of a knight's fee.

Thomas Bardolf is aged 30 years and more. John Clay died on 22 April last. Thomas his brother and next heir was aged 40 years and more when John died.

C 137/36, no. 32
E 152/388, no. 2

JOHN FILOLL

759   Writ 27 March 1403.

DORSET. Inquisition. Dorchester. 23 April.

He held:

Langton Matravers in Purbeck, the manor, of John Fauntleroy and Joan his wife by a fine of 1398 [CP 25(1) 51/52, no. 124] by which they granted it to John Filoll for life, with remainder to William Filoll and Joan his wife and the heirs of their bodies, to hold of John and Joan Fauntleroy and the heirs of Joan, by the rent of a rose, with reversion failing such heirs to William and Joan Filoll to John and Joan and the heirs of Joan Fauntleroy; annual value £10.

Stockley in Bere Regis, 2 virgates, jointly with Alice his wife, who survives, and the heirs of their bodies, with remainder to his right heirs, of Robert Turbervylle, knight, by the service of a pair of spurs, price 6d.; annual value 26s. 8d.

Southcombe, Winterborne Muston, Winterborne Zelston, Mapperton and Morden, £24 rent from the manors, which are held by William Filoll and Joan his wife and the heirs of their bodies in fee tail.

He died on 12 March last. William his son and heir is aged 23 years and more.

C 137/36, no. 33

REYNOLD COBEHAM, SENIOR, KNIGHT

760   Writ 16 July 1403.

NORTHAMPTON. Inquisition. Brackley. 4 Aug.

He held a third part of the manor of Aynho in the dower of Eleanor his wife from her former husband John Darundell. It is held of the heirs of Humphrey de Bohun, earl of Essex, by knight service, annual value £10.

He died on 6 July last. Reynold his son and heir was 21 on 11 Nov. last.

The exchequer copy [E 149/81, no.10], originally dated 27 Sept., has the date and other details changed to agree with the above. Only the names of the jurors remain different.

761 Writ 16 July 1403.
HERTFORD. Inquisition. Hitchin. 25 Sept.
   He held nothing in the county.
   Date of death and heir as above.

762 Writ 16 July 1403.
CALAIS. Inquisition. 7 Aug.
   He held in hs demesne as of fee of the king in chief a house in the parish of St. Nicholas on a corner beside the road to the castle, by the service of providing two watchmen for the defence of the town, annual value 4 marks.
   Date of death and heir, aged 21, as above.

763 Writ 16 July 1403.
WILTSHIRE. Inquisition. Salisbury. 4 Aug.
   He held the manor of Langley Burrell of the duchy of Lancaster in his demesne as of fee of the manor of Trowbridge by knight service, annual value £20.
   In right of Eleanor his wife who survives him he held:
   Sherrington and Codford, the manors, and half the manors of Elston and Stapleford, of the king in chief by knight service.
   Boyton, Corton, Winterbourne Stoke and Coate, the manors with the advowson of Boyton, of the earl of Salisbury by knight service, amount unknown.
   Hill Deverill, the manor, of the earl of March by knight service.
   Great Somerford, the manor and advowson, of the heir of Lord Tiptoft by knight service.
   Date of death and heir as above.

764 Writ 16 July 1403.
SUSSEX. Inquisition. Horsham. 19 Sept.
   He held 19s.4¼d. rent in Hartfield of the bishop of Winchester of his manor of Withyham called Monken Court by a rent of 12d.; and 4s. fee farm from a tenement called Plawhatch in East Grinstead.
   In right of Eleanor his wife, as dower of John de Arundell, knight, her former husband he held:
   Old Shoreham, a third part of the manor, of Lord Moubray of the honour of Bramber by knight service, amount and annual value unknown.
   Cudlow and Chancton, a third part of the manors, of the earl of Arundel, service and annual value unknown.
   Date of death and heir as above.

765 Writ 16 July 1403.
SOMERSET. Inquisition. Yeovil. 31 July.
   He held in right of Eleanor his wife the manors of Cucklington and Stoke Trister with the advowsons, and the office of chief forester of Selwood, of the king in chief

by knight service; annual values Cucklington £10, Stoke Trister £10, office of chief forester 10s.

Also in right of the inheritance of Eleanor he held the manor of Hendford and 57s. rent in Yeovil of the heir of the earl of March, who is in the king's ward, of the honour of Gloucester by knight service, annual value of the manor £20.

Date of death and heir as above.

766 Writ 16 July 1403.

DORSET. Inquisition. Sturminster Marshall. 26 July.

He held by the right of inheritance of his wife Eleanor, who survives him:

Morden, the manor, of the king in chief by a rent of 8s. payable by the sheriff, annual value 10 marks.

Witchampton, the manor, of the heir of the earl of March, in the king's ward, by knight service, annual value £10.

Lytchett Matravers, the manor, of the heir of the same earl by knight service, annual value 10 marks.

Philipston, the manor, of the abbess of Wilton by a rent of 25 quarters of salt, annual value £4.

Langton Matravers, the manor, of the heir of the earl of Salisbury, in the king's ward, by petty serjeanty, annual value 10 marks.

Wimborne St. Giles, the manor, of the heir of the earl of March by knight service, annual value 53s.4d.

Worth Matravers, the manor, of the earl of Hereford by knight service, annual value £10.

Frome Whitfield, the manor, of the same earl by knight service, annual value 20 marks.

Loders, the manor, of the abbot of Forde by knight service, annual value 100s.

Wootton Fitzpaine in Marshwood, the manor, of the heir of Henry Lourty by knight service, annual value £10.

Eggardon, Woolcombe and West Moors, 2 carucates, 40 a. meadow, 100 a. pasture and 10 a. wood, of the abbot of Forde by knight service, annual value 5 marks.

Winterborne St. Martin, ½ toft, 60 a. arable and 20 a. pasture, of Roger Saymour, kinsman and heir of Bello Campo [sic], by knight service, annual value 10s.

Date of death and heir as above.

767 Writ 16 July 1403.

GLOUCESTER. Inquisition. Tetbury. 3 Sept.

He held:

Stonehouse, the manor, in right of his wife Eleanor who survives, of the bishop of Winchester, service unknown, annual value £30.

Minchinhampton, 1 toft, 1 dovecote, 1 carucate, 12 a. meadow and 100s. rent, of Hugh Waterton, knight, and Katherine his wife of their manor of Minchinhampton by the service of 43s.3½d., suit of court every three weeks and other customs, annual value nil beyond the rent.

Shurdington, 1 messuage, 1 virgate and 100s. rent, of Thomas Lord Furnivall and Ankaret his wife by a rent of 6d., annual value £4.

Date of death and heir as above.

768 Writ 16 July 1403.

KENT. Inquisition. Rochester. 16 Aug.

He held in his demesne as of fee:

Aldington by Maidstone, the manor, of the king of the castle of Rochester by a rent of 14s. for the guard of the castle payable on St. Andrew's day, annual value 60s.

Hever, a tenement so-called, in gavelkind of the archbishop of Canterbury of his manor of Bexley, the abbot of St. Augustine's, Canterbury, of his manor of Plumstead, Elizabeth lady le Despenser and John Chaloner, service unknown, annual value 12d.

Hulberry, the manor, with the advowson of Lullingstone, of the prior of Leeds of his manor of Leeds by suit of court there at Michaelmas, annual value 40s.

East Shelve and Boardfield, the manor, part of the king of the castle of Dover by the service of 3s. 4d. every 24 weeks for the guard of the castle, annual value 40s.; the rest of the abbot of Faversham, John Champeyne and others in gavelkind, for various unknown services, annual value £8.

Westwell, a tenement so-called in Westwell, of Thomas Swynbourn, knight, in gavelkind of his manor of Boughton Aluph, and of others whose names and the services are unknown, annual value 40s.

Westerham, a tenement called 'La Serne', in gavelkind of the abbot of Westminster of this manor, service unknown; from it the prior and convent of Tonbridge take 2s., and the heirs of Roger Leukenore 14s.; annual value beyond these rents 20s.

Austin, the manor, in gavelkind of the archbishop of Canterbury, lord la Zouche, William son of Nicholas Oryel, knight, of his castle of Eynsford, Alan Seintjoust of his castle of Lullingstone, and others whose names and the services are unknown, annual value 66s. 8d.

Chiddingstone, the manor, in gavelkind of the archbishop of Canterbury, John de Frenyngham, John Chaloner, Philip Sencler, knight, and Margaret his wife in right of Margaret, as of their manor of Penshurst, and of others whose names and the services are unknown, annual value 100s.

Bowzell, the manor, in gavelkind of the archbishop of Canterbury, John de Frenyngham, George Modell, Reynold de Pekham, and others whose names and the services are unknown, annual value 40s.

Sherenden, the manor, in gavelkind of Hugh de Bures of his manor of Halstead by a rent of 2s. 6d. and 4 ploughshares yearly at various terms, annual value 100s.

Brookland, the manor, in gavelkind of the abbot of Westminster of his manor of Stangrove, service unknown, annual value 53s. 4d.

Newage, Boardfield, Cooling, Cliffe, Stoke, Hoo, Bromley, Frindisbury, Wouldham, High Halstow, Newhythe and Hadlow, 1 messuage, 40 a., 20 a. meadow, 40 a. marsh and 100s. rent, of Lord Grey of Codnor, Reynold Braybrok, knight, and others whose names and the services are unknown, annual value £10.

Elmley, pasture in the isle, in gavelkind of Stephen le Scrop, knight, of his manor of Northwood Sheppey, service unknown. For this pasture and the manor of Sherenden 40 marks is owed yearly to the master and brothers of Magdalen College, Cobham, annual value nil beyond this rent.

Date of death and heir as above.

769 KENT. Inquisition. Canterbury. 13 Sept. 1403.

He held in fee tail the manor of West Cliffe by Dover by a grant of Edward III dated at Reading, 7 Feb. 1347 [*CPR 1345–8*, p.250].

On 28 April 1403 John Ungerham, chaplain, as attorney of Reynold son of Reynold, as ordered by Reynold's writ, gave seisin of the manor to Thomas Guynes, attorney of Reynold Curteys and Margaret his wife, daughter of Reynold son of Reynold, in accordance with a charter of Reynold to them. This was done by virtue of a letter of attorney of Reynold Curteys and Margaret given to Thomas Guynes for receiving seisin, both letters to be publicly shown and read on the Saturday of the grant. But they were not then and there publicly shown and read; and John Saghere, then farmer of the manor, and Richard Litelbery, Robert atte Wode, John Norman and Eustace Lyon, tenants of the manor, were present at the time of the seisin, and they, after livery of seisin, were asked by the attorneys to place themselves from that time in all respects towards Reynold Curteys and Margaret as formerly they had been to Reynold son of Reynold, this in the name of the lord without any other attornment by the delivery of any money or other things, or any payment of rent or farm from that day to this.

They do not know whether this manner of seisin is full seisin, and seek the judgment of the king's council.

The manor is held of the king in chief as one knight's fee. There are the site with ruinous barn and other damaged buildings, annual value nil; 120 a. at 6d., 40s. [sic]; 305 a. pasture at 2½d., £4 [sic]; £8 rent from various tenants at the four terms; and perquisites of court and view of frankpledge, worth nothing beyond the costs of the bailiff.

He also held other lands and tenements of the manor of Postling in right of Eleanor his wife in dower of her former husband, John Arundel, knight, with remainder to John, son and heir of John, son of John Arundel and Eleanor.

Date of death and heir as above.

770 SURREY. Inquisition. Reigate. 20 Sept. 1403.

He held:

Oxted, the manor, of the king in chief of the honour of Boulogne by knight service, annual value £20.

Starborough otherwise Prinkham, the manor with three messuages in Billeshurst, Haxted and Stonehurst, in fee tail of the abbot of Battle of his manor of Limpsfield by a rent of 63s.4d. and suit of court every three weeks. William atte Forde by a rent of 40d., John Haderesham by a rent of 2s., the heir of Ralph atte Helle by a rent of 12d., John Olyver by a rent of 10s., the abbot of Hyde by a rent of 28s.8d. and 1 lb. cumin at his manor of Felcourt, and of the prior of St. John of Jerusalem in England by a rent of 2d; annual value of this manor and messuages £20.

Southwark, a house, in fee tail of the prior of Southwark, service unknown, annual value 20s.

He held in right of Eleanor his wife in dower from John de Arundell, knight, her former husband, a third part of each of the following manors:

Buckland, of lord le Despenser by knight service . . .

West Betchworth, of the same lord by knight service, annual value 13s.4d.

Walton on the Hill, of the earl of Stafford by a rent . . .

Bletchingley, . . . annual value £7.

Colley, of the earl of Arundel by knight service, annual value 13s.1d.

Date of death and heir as above.

C 137/36, no.34
E 149/81, no.10
E 152/391, no.3

ROGER MORTEMER, ESQUIRE

771 Writ. 5 Jan. 1403.

WORCESTER. Inquisition. Worcester. 18 Jan.

He held in his demesne in fee tail by a fine of Richard II [CP 25(1) 260/25, no.47] the manors of Martley and Great Kyre by the grant of Thomas Belue and Hugh Manne to John de Herle, knight, and Elizabeth his wife, with successive remainders failing male heirs to Roger Mortemer, Maud his wife and the heirs of their bodies, and the right heirs of Elizabeth Herle. John and Elizabeth died without heirs, and Maud died. Roger therefore held them; Martley of the king in chief, service unknown, annual value £20, comprising £18 in rents payable at the four feasts, and 1 carucate and 10 a. of demesne, annual value 40s.; Great Kyre of the barony of Burford, service unknown, annual value 20s.

He died on 13 Dec. last. John son and heir of Roger and Maud is aged 11 years and more.

C 137/36, no.35
E 149/82, no.5

ROGER HILLARY, KNIGHT

772 Writ 4 May 1403.

LEICESTER. Inquisition. Leicester. 17 Sept.

Jointly with Margaret his wife, who survives him, he held 6 messuages, 2 carucates and 32 a. meadow in Snarestone and 15 a. meadow in Barrow on Soar by the grant of Hugh parson of Stretton on Fosse and William de Strethay to them and the heirs of the body of Roger, with remainder failing such heirs to John, son of Saer de Rochefort, knight, junior, and his heirs male. Snarestone is held of the heirs of John Charnels by the rent of a rose, annual value 40s.; Barrow on Soar of Thomas de Erdyngton, also by rent of a rose, annual value 18s.

He died without heirs of his body on 13 June 1400, and Margaret has taken the profits since his death.

John son of Saer, son of Joan, sister of Roger, and Elizabeth wife of John Russell, knight, daughter of Elizabeth, the other sister of Roger, are next heirs, John aged 40 years and more and Elizabeth 50 years and more.

773 WARWICK. Inquisition. Nuneaton. 15 Sept. 1403.

Jointly with Margaret his wife he held the manor and advowson of Stretton on Fosse, 5 messuages and 2 carucates in Warton, 20 a. arable, 6 a. meadow and 14s. rent in Erdington, 1 messuage, 2 a. arable and 2 a. meadow in Sutton Coldfield, 6s. rent in Witton, and 5s. rent in Aston by the grant of Hugh parson of Stretton on Fosse and William de Stretehay, as in last.

Stretton on Fosse manor and advowson are held of the earl of Warwick by a rent of 1d., annual value 60s.; Warton of the same by rent of a rose, annual value 20s.; Erdington of Lord Burnell by rent of 1d., annual value 22s.; Sutton Coldfield of the earl of Warwick by rent of 1d., annual value 20d.; the rent in Witton of Philip de Pirye by rent of a rose; and that in Aston of the heir of John de Buttourt by rent of 1d.

Margaret has held them and taken the profits since his death.

Date of death and heirs as above.

S

774 Writ 4 May 1403.

STAFFORD. Inquisition. Wolverhampton. 13 Sept.

He held of the king in chief in grand serjeanty 1 messuage, 8 a., 14 a. meadow, 4 a. pasture, 4 a. wood, 3s.4d. rent and the office of keeper of the enclosure of Ashwood in Kingswinford, by the service of finding a man to keep the enclosure, by the gift of John de Sutton, formerly lord of Dudley, to him and his heirs by Margaret his wife, with reversion failing such heirs to John de Sutton and his heirs.

He died without such heirs. John de Sutton is dead, and John de Sutton, knight, son of John de Sutton, knight, his son, is heir and aged 24 years and more. Thomas Yonge has held since his death and taken the profits, annual value 3s.2d.

He held jointly with Margaret his wife, by the grant by their indented charter shown to the jurors of Hugh, sometime parson of Stretton on Fosse, and William de Strethay to them and the heirs of Roger, with remainder failing such heirs to John son of Saer de Rochefort, knight, junior, and the heirs of his body:

Rushall, 1 carucate and 10 a. meadow, of John Grubber by a rent of 1d., annual value 18s.

Bescot, the manor; Bloxwich, 1 messuage, 2 carucates, 20 a. meadow, 4 a. wood and 20 a. pasture; Goscote, 20s. rent from various free tenants payable at Michaelmas and Lady Day; Shelfield, 1 messuage, 1 carucate, 20 a. meadow, 3 a. wood, 20 a. pasture and 10s. rent from free tenants; all of the earl of Warwick as of his manor of Walsall by a rent of 2d., annual value 10 marks.

Aldridge, the manor, of the heir of Robert de Stapilton by a rent of 3s.4d. at Michaelmas, annual value 60s.

Great Barr, 1 messuage, 1 carucate, 10 a. meadow and 22 a. wood, of the same heir by a rent of 11s., annual value 10s.

Perry Barr and Hamstead, 1 messuage, ½ carucate, 10 a. meadow, 4 a. wood, 10 a. pasture and 20s. rent from free tenants, of the heir of Philip de Pirie by a rent of 1d., annual value 40s.

West Bromwich, 2 messuages, 20 a., 3 a. meadow, 2a. pasture and 10s. rent, of the heir of Eleanor de Alrewas by a rent of 5s., annual value 20s.; and 1 messuage, 12 a. arable and 2 a. meadow, of the heir of John Devros, by a rent of 12d., annual value 6s.8d.

Essington, 1 messuage, 2 carucates, 10 a. meadow, 10 a. pasture and 10 a. wood, of John de Sutton of the barony of Dudley by rent of a rose, annual value 40s.

White Sich, 1 messuage and 1 carucate, of the dean of Wolverhampton by rent of a rose, annual value 20s.

Fisherwick, the manor, of the bishop of Chester by knight service, annual value 60s.

Wednesbury, 6 messuages, 1 watermill, 3 carucates, 10 a. meadow and 10s. rent, of John de Harnevill, by a rent of 1d., annual value 60s.

Seisdon, Upper Penn, Trysull and Wombourne, 1 messuage and 20s. rent from various tenants, of John de Sutton of the barony of Dudley by a white rose, annual value 20s.6d.

Huntington, 1 cottage, of the heir of Henry de Pilatenhale by a rose, annual value 12d.

Tipton, 9s. rent from free tenants, of Lord Burnell by a rose, annual value 9s.

Perry Barr, 1 virgate, of the heir of Richard de Barre by 1 grain of cumin (?), annual value 9s.

Handsworth, 10 a., of the heir of John Buttort, by rent of 1d., annual value 40d.

Bentley, 1 carucate, of the heir of John Bentilegh by a rose, annual value 20s.

Cannock and Wyrley, 3 messuages and 10 a., of Nicholas de Ruggeley by rent of a rose, annual value 10s.

Darlaston, 1 messuage and 3 a., of John de Derlaston by a rose, annual value 2s.

Date of death and heirs as above. Margaret has held and taken the profits since his death.

> C 137/36, no.36
> E 152/390, no.5

MAUD WIDOW OF ROGER CLIFFORD, KNIGHT

775 Writ 12 March 1403.

NORTHUMBERLAND. Inquisition. Hart. 20 May.

She held the manor of Hart with Hartlepool of the king in chief by homage and fealty, jointly enfeoffed with Roger her late husband, to them and the heirs of Roger. The manor comprises 204 a. arable in demesne, 24 a. foreshore and 33 a. meadow in demesne with orchards, which are all let this year to various tenants at will paying together £10 at Whitsun and Martinmas; and several pasture let this year for 13s.4d. payable at the same terms.

The annual value of the vill of Hartlepool is £10. She also held the port there which includes the waters of Tees to the south of the town and northwards along the coast to Blackhall. It is customary to take from ships mooring within these bounds, with boats laden or unladen 8d., and without boats 4d. She took 6s. weekly from the market at Hartlepool on Tuesdays and Fridays, and from each shop in the market place for stallage ½d., and for each packhorse stand ½d. She had a fair twice yearly at St. Lawrence and the Invention of the Holy Cross, taking from each shop and from each packhorse stand ½d. which usually amounted to £10 yearly for 12 years past; but now it is worth nothing because destroyed by Ralph Lumley and his tenants and servants, Robert Browne, William de Stable, John Denton, William Ward and others, during her lifetime, and by Marmaduke Lumley, his tenants and servants, because they did not wish to allow customs or tolls to be collected within these bounds, but prevented and still prevent it by force of arms, and are buying and selling there without paying customs or tolls.

There are various free tenants of the manors: Ralph de Nevyll, earl of Westmorland, holds free of the manor the vill of Elwick by homage and fealty and no other service; John de Lumley, under age in the king's ward, holds free of the same manor the vill of Stranton by homage, fealty, and 1 pair of gilt spurs or 12d., 1 lb. pepper and 1d. at Martinmas; Ralph Baron Greystoke, knight, holds similarly the vill of Brierton by homage, fealty and 15d. rent at Martinmas; William Fulthorp, knight, holds 4 husbandlands in Morleston by homage, fealty and 12d. rent, and 3 husbandlands in Throston by homage, fealty and 1d. at Martinmas; Gerard Heron holds 1 carucate in North Hart by homage, fealty and no other service; Richard de Nelston holds the vill of Nelson by homage, fealty and no more; Ralph Bulmer holds the vill of Thorpe Bulmer by homage, fealty, wardship and marriage; William Gower of Eldon holds 1 messuage and 4 bovates in Eldon by homage, fealty and a rent of 2d.; and Alan Lombard holds 6 burgages in the vill of Hartlepool by fealty and a pair of gilt spurs at Martinmas.

In the manor of Hart are 25 husbandlands which are leased this year to various tenants at 10s., and for the customary works of each 18d. at Martinmas; also 35 cottages worth 12d. each, 1 windmill leased this year for 40s., and 1 pasture leased for 6s.8d.

She died on 28 Feb. John Clifford, under age in the king's ward, is the next heir of Roger, being the son of Thomas, knight, son of Roger, and aged 13 years and more.

776 Writ 12 March 1403.
YORK. Inquisition. Skipton. 28 May.
She held a third part of the manor of Skipton in dower for life after the death of Roger her husband, of the king in chief by knight service as part of Skipton manor, annual value £28.
Date of death and heir as above.

777 Writ 12 March 1403.
LONDON. Inquisition 31 May.
She held 1 tenement in the parish of St. Dunstan in the West in the suburbs of London jointly with Roger, to them and the heirs of Roger. It is held of the king in free burgage and a rent of 1d. payable at the exchequer at Michaelmas by the sheriffs, annual value 10 marks.
Date of death and heir, aged 14 years and more, as above.

778 Writ 12 March 1403.
CUMBERLAND. Inquisition. Penrith. 5 June.
She held for life:
Skelton, a third part of one third of the manor, in dower, of the king in chief by a cornage rent of 8½d. and ⅓ of ½d. payable at the exchequer at Carlisle on 15 Aug., annual value 60s.
Carlisle, 1 burgage, by grant of the reversion to Roger and herself and the heirs of Roger by Richard de Cardieux and Joan his wife, both now deceased, to hold after their deaths. It is held of the king in free burgage by a rent of 4d. at Michaelmas, annual value 6s.8d.
Date of death and heir, aged 13 years and more, as above.

779 WESTMORLAND. Inquisition. Appleby. 17 May 1403.
She held jointly with Roger her husband to them and his heirs the castle and manor of Brougham, which are usually worth 100s. yearly, but now nothing because all lying totally waste after destruction by the Scots. All the profits this year do not suffice for the repair and custody of the castle.
She also held in dower of Roger, all with the above castle and manor being held of the king of the crown by knight service:
Winton, the manor, annual value £20.
Mallerstang, 1 byre in the manor of Kirkby Stephen called Southwaite, annual value 20s.
Brough, 10 byres in the manor at 'Knolhowe', Skirrygill, Calva, Oldpark Gill, Swinestone, Mouthlock, Thorny Gale, Borren, Seavy Rigg and Strice Gill, annual value 100s.
Oldpark Gill, the park, annual value 40s., and Heggerscale, 1 byre so called, annual value 70s.9d., both in the manor of Brough.
King's Meaburn, the manor, annual value 10 marks.

Whinfell, forest, moor and pasture outside the close of the forest to the south, annual value 10s.; a third part of the forest to the north, tenements and 40 a. there called Blaunchelande, Whinhowe and Barrockbank, and 5 messuages with arable and meadow called Woodside in the forest, annual value 5 marks.

Temple Sowerby, 1 messuage and 16 a. arable and meadow, and in Clifton 1 messuage and 16 a. arable and meadow, annual value 12s.; and also in Clifton a third part of 22 quarters 6 bushels of oats from the manor in the spring, annual value 7s.

Rents from the following free tenants at Easter and Michaelmas with services and fees:

William de Fulthorp and his heirs, 17s. 8d. for the manor of Kaber, held by homage, fealty and that rent, annual value £4.

Thomas de Blenkansopp and his heirs, 6s. for the manor of Hillbeck, similarly held, and extending at 100s.

William Stirkland and his heirs, 7s. 5d. for half the manor of Waitby, similarly held, extending at 60s.

Ralph Baron Greystoke, 25s. 6d. for rents and services from the manors of Dufton, Bolton, Brampton and Yanwath, similarly held, extending at £20.

John son of William de Lancastre and his heirs, 21s. 8d. for the manor of Milburn, similarly held, extending at 100s.

Robert de Sandford and his heirs, 3s. 4d. for the manor of Sandford, similarly held, extending at 40s.

The abbot of Shap and Gilbert Curwen, 10s. 10d. for the manor of Shap, similarly held, extending at £10.

John Derwentwater and his heirs, 13s. 6d. for the manor of Ormside, similarly held, extending at 100s.

Robert Thornburgh and Isabel his wife, 17s. 8d. for the manors of Warcop and Waitby, similarly held in right of Isabel, extending at £10.

William Whapelote and Helen his wife, in her right, and Adam Bacon, 13s. 8d. for the manor of Hilton, similarly held, extending at 20s.

William Whapelode, 2s. for lands and tenements in Appleby called 'Ribillandes', similarly held, extending at 20s.

Thomas son of William de Warthecopp and Margaret his wife, 6s. 10d. for the manor of Colby, similarly held, extending at 60s.

William Fulthorp and his heirs, 6s. 8d. for pasture between Mousegill and Belah, similarly held, extending at £4.

John son of William de Lancastre, £4 for rents and services in the manor of Milburn, similarly held, extending at £4.

William de Wherton, 6s. for the manor of Wharton, similarly held, extending at 100s.

William de Styrkland, 6d. for lands and tenements in Soulby, similarly held, extending at 10s.

Richard de Rystewald and William de Qwerton, 5s. for lands and tenements in Tebay, similarly held, extending at 20s.

Robert de Leton, 6d. for lands and tenements in Rookby, similarly held, extending at 2s.

William Judde, 1d. for lands and tenements in Clibburn, similarly held, extending at 6s. 8d.

A third part of the profits of the sheriffdom of Westmorland, extending at 6s. 8d.

Brougham, the advowson, extending at 5 marks.
Date of death and heir, aged 13 years and more, as above.

C 137/36, no.37
E 149/81, no.5
E 152/380, no.3; 383, no.2; 384, no.3

JOAN WIDOW OF RALPH BASSET OF DRAYTON BASSETT, KNIGHT

780 Writ 17 Nov. 1402.
LONDON. Inquisition. 12 May 1403.
   She held nothing in London.

781 Writ 17 Nov. 1402.
LINCOLN. Inquisition. Lincoln. 29 Jan. 1403.
   She held a third part of the manor of Greetwell in dower of the honour of Tickhill by a rent of 3s.4d., annual value 5 marks.
   She died on 9 Nov. last. The third part should descend to Edmund earl of Stafford as heir of Ralph, being the son of Hugh earl of Stafford, son of Ralph, son of Margaret, sister of Ralph, father of Ralph, father of Ralph Basset, and aged 25 years and more.

782 Writ 17 Nov. 1402.
NORFOLK. Inquisition. Wiveton. 2 Dec.
   She held a third part of the manor of Sheringham in dower for life of the king in chief, service unknown, annual value £13 6s.8d.
   She died on 20 [sic] Nov. It should descend to Edmund earl of Stafford as above.

783 Writ 16 Nov. 1402.
STAFFORD. Inquisition. Walsall. 18 Dec.
   Ralph Basset of Drayton Bassett held in his demesne as of fee the manors of Pattingham and Drayton Bassett, and gave them to Ralph de Olneye and Robert de Birlyngham, chaplains. By a fine of 1340 [CP 25(1) 210/14, no.56] they were conveyed to Ralph and his heirs male, with successive remainders to Ralph, son of Ralph, son of Ralph Basset of Drayton Bassett, and the heirs of his body, Ralph de Stafford, knight, for life, Richard de Stafford, knight, for life, Ralph son of Ralph de Stafford and his heirs male, Richard son of Richard de Stafford and his heirs male, and Thomas de Bello Campo, earl of Warwick, and his heirs.
   The Staffords died without heirs male. Ralph, son of Ralph, son of Ralph Basset, married Joan and died without heirs. The manors were then taken into the king's hands. Pattingham was allotted to Joan in dower. Drayton Bassett remains in the king's hands because Richard de Bello Campo, son of Thomas, son of the earl of Warwick, is a minor who will be 21 on 25 Jan. next. Pattingham is held of the barony of Dudley, service unknown, annual value 20 marks.
   Joan died on 9 Nov.

784 Writ 17 Nov. 1402.

SURREY. Inquisition. Southwark. 28 Jan. 1403.

Ralph Basset of Drayton Bassett held in his demesne as of fee 2 messuages and 8 shops in Southwark and enfeoffed Thomas Aston, knight, John Leyr, clerk, and John Chercheman, citizen of London, on condition that they should alienate and appropriate with the king's licence and that of the lords of the other fees to the master of Bethlehem outside Bishopsgate, but this condition was broken, no alienation was made, and they have kept and taken the profits from the death of Ralph. Joan was dowered with a third part, held of the abbot of Bermondsey, service unknown, worth 46s. 8d. annually.

She died on 9 Nov., and the third part should descend to Edmund earl of Stafford as next heir, as above.

785 Writ 13 Nov. 1402.

NOTTINGHAM. Inquisition. Nottingham. 20 Nov.

She held for life by the grant of Walter Skyrlowe, bishop of Durham, Richard Scrope, late bishop of Chester, Richard Scrope and Thomas de Aston, knights, and John de Leyre, John Broun and John Outhorpe, clerks, the manor of Ratcliffe on Soar with reversion to Walter Skyrlowe and the others. It is held of the king in chief, service unknown, annual value £20.

She also held in dower a third part of the manor of Colston Bassett by assignment of the same feoffees, with reversion to them. It is held of the king in chief, service unknown, annual value £10.

She died on 9 Nov. last. Heirs unknown.

786 Writ 13 Nov. 1402.

LEICESTER. Inquisition. Loughborough. 20 Nov.

She held for life by the grant of Walter Skyrlawe, bishop of Durham, and the other feoffees, as in the last, with reversion to them:

Barrow on Soar, a quarter of the manor, of the king in chief by knight service, annual value £10.

Ragdale and Willowes, a third part of the manor, and Ratcliffe on the Wreak, a third part of the manor, of the heirs of Ralph Basset of Weldon by knight service, annual value £7 6s. 8d.

Long Whatton, a third part of 12 virgates, of Henry Lord Beaumont by knight service, annual value 40s.

She died on 9 Nov. and had no heirs.

787 Writ 16 Nov. 1402.

BUCKINGHAM. Inquisition. Stony Stratford. 23 Nov.

Ralph Basset held the manor of Olney and granted it with others to William Herle, knight, and Thomas Radeclyve, parson of Olney. By a fine of 1339 [CP 25(1) 287/40, no. 255] between Ralph Basset of Drayton Bassett, Ralph son of Ralph, son of the first Ralph, and Joan his wife, daughter of Thomas de Bello Campo, earl of Warwick, and Simon Pakeman as guardian of the young Ralph, on the one side, and William Herle and Thomas de Radeclyve on the other, the manors of Walsall in Staffordshire, Olney in Buckinghamshire and Long Buckby in Northamptonshire were settled on Ralph Basset of Drayton Bassett for life, with successive remainders to Ralph his grandson and Joan daughter of the earl of Warwick, wife of Ralph, and the heirs of their bodies, the heirs male of Ralph Basset the grandfather, Ralph Stafford for life, Richard de Stafford for life, Ralph son of Ralph Stafford and his heirs male, Richard son of Richard de Stafford and his heirs male, Thomas de Bello Campo, son of the earl of Warwick, and his heirs male, and the heirs of the earl.

Accordingly Ralph Basset of Drayton Bassett held Olney for life and so died. Ralph his son died in the lifetime of his father. Then, therefore, Ralph the grandson and Joan daughter of Thomas de Bello Campo held it. Meanwhile Ralph de Stafford and Richard de Stafford and both their sons died without heirs. Joan also died without heirs male of her body. Then Ralph the grandson married Joan, the subject of this inquisition. He died without heirs of his body and the manor was accordingly taken into the king's hands. In the chancery of Richard II it was assigned to Joan in dower, the other lands descending to Thomas son of Thomas de Bello Campo in accordance with the fine.

Henry Grey of Wilton took possession of one quarter of Olney, title unknown. Owing to the minority of his son Richard two parts of the quarter are in the king's hands. Joan having died, the third part descends to Thomas son of Thomas de Bello Campo under the fine. He was 21 years of age on 25 Jan.

The manor is held of the king in chief by knight service, annual value of three quarters £45, of a third part of a quarter £4 10s.4d. [sic].

She also held a third part of the manor of Sherington in dower from Henry Grey, with reversion to Richard Grey. It is held of the king in chief as a twentieth part of a knight's fee, annual value 40s.

She died on 9 Nov.

788 Writ 20 Feb. 1403.

DEVON. Inquisition. Exeter. 5 March.

She held in dower a third part of the manor of Tawstock and a third part of the advowson, of the inheritance of Fulk Fitzwaryn, son and heir of Fulk Fitzwaryn, knight, under age in the king's ward, whereby the other two parts are in the king's hands. The third part is worth annually £26 6s.8d. The whole manor with the advowson is held of the king in chief as an eighteenth part of a barony as parcel of the barony of Barnstaple. Ralph Basset died without heirs of his body, holding in fee tail with reversion to Fulk by a fine of 1370 [CP 25(1) 44/60, no.381] between Thomas Daudeley and James Daudeley of Heighley, knight, the reversion which Ralph Basset held for life being given successively to Thomas Daudeley and the heirs of his body, Roland brother of Thomas and his heirs, and James brother of the same and his heirs, and the right heirs of Thomas, and so to Fulk, as son of Fulk, son of Margaret, sister of Thomas. Thomas, Roland and James, like Ralph, died without heirs, and so it descended to Fulk.

She died on 18 [sic] Nov. 1402.

C 137/37, no.38
E 149/80, no.1
E 152/390, no.2

AGNES WIDOW OF WILLIAM BARDOLF, KNIGHT, LORD OF WORMEGAY

789 Writ 15 June 1403.

BUCKINGHAM . Inquisition. Aylesbury. 27 June.

She held in dower with reversion to Thomas Bardolf, son and heir of William, of whom and by what service is unknown.

Wendover, 10 a., annual value 12d.

Wendover, Aston Clinton, Bledlow and Hulcott, 36s. 11d. rent.

Wendover and Bledlow, 2 sparrowhawks rent, annual value nil.

Birchmore and Eaton Bray in Bedfordshire, 7 hides.

Wendover, 1 fee and a tenth part of a fee, annual value nil.

She died on 12 June. Thomas Bardolf, knight, the son and heir, is aged 30 years and more.

790 Writ 15 June 1403.

LINCOLN. Inquisition. Caythorpe. 30 June.

She held in dower of the king in chief, service unknown, a third part of the manor of Ruskington of the inheritance of Thomas Bardolf, knight, son and heir of William, annual value £6 13s.4d.

Date of death and heir as above.

791 Writ 15 June 1403.

HERTFORD. Inquisition. Hertford. 28 June.

William Bardolph held the manor of Crowbury in his demesne as of fee and granted it by charter to John Cleye, clerk, John Grene, clerk, Robert Alisaundre, Nicholas Horseth and their heirs and assigns, and the tenants attorned to them. William died and Agnes recovered one third by writ of dower, and the tenants attorned to her. The reversion is to John Cleye and the other feoffees. The third is worth 30s.4d. annually and is held of Edward de Benstede, knight, service unknown.

He also held the manor of Bardolphs in Watton at Stone with the advowson of the free chapel of St. Mary there, and by his charter by licence of Edward III granted it to Robert Bardolf, knight, for life with reversion to himself and his heirs. William and Robert died. It was taken into the king's hands. The chancery assigned a third part to Agnes in dower with reversion to Thomas Bardolf, knight, the son, and also in dower the next presentation to the chapel. The third part is worth 66s.8d. yearly, the presentation nil. The whole is held of the king in chief as a quarter of a knight's fee.

Date of death and heir as above.

792 Writ 15 June 1403.

SUSSEX. Inquisition. Lewes. 7 July.

William Bardolf, knight, held in his demesne as of fee the manor of Birling and £12 assize rent in Berwick. By his charter dated at Birling on 12 June 1377 he granted them by royal licence [*CPR 1374–7*, p.404] to Nicholas de Carreu, Robert Bardolf, Adam Wigmore and Robert son of William Alesaundre for the life of Agnes, with reversion to himself and his heirs. All the tenants attorned to them. William Bardolf and Adam Wigmore died. The others by charter dated 20 March 1389 granted them to Agnes for life, and again all the tenants attorned to her. They are held of the king in chief of the crown as one knight's fee, annual value £16 8s.10d.

He also held in his demesne as of fee the manor of Barcombe with its appurtenances in Barcombe, Fletching and Lewes, and granted it by his charter to John Cleye and John Grene, clerks, William Walcote and Nicholas Horseth. After his death Agnes recovered a third part in dower. John Cleye and the others granted the manor with reversion of the third part to John Wigenhalle, his heirs and assigns. He by his charter conveyed it to John le Leek, clerk, Albin de Enderby, Ellis de Middelton, Ralph

Adderle, John Grene, clerk, Nicholas Horseth, John Antrouse, Richard Gegge, Thomas Somerheld, and John Garnoun, and Agnes attorned to them. The third part is held of the earl of Arundel, service unknown, annual value £4 8d.

Date of death and heir as above.

793 Writ 15 June 1403.
NORFOLK. Inquisition. Shouldham. 4 July.

She held in dower the manors of Wormegay, Stow Bardolph, Fareswell in Fincham, Cantley and Strumpshaw, of the inheritance of Thomas Bardolf, knight, son and heir of William Bardolf, knight, and with reversion to him, by assignment in the chancery of Richard II.

William Bardolf held the manor of North Runcton in his demesne as of fee, and by his charter dated 12 June 1377 granted it with royal licence [*CPR 1374-7*, p.404] to Nicholas de Careu, Robert Bardolf, Adam Wygmore and Robert son of William Alisaundre, for the life of Agnes, with reversion to himself and his heirs. William Bardolf and Adam Wygmore died. The others by their charter dated 20 March 1389 granted it to Agnes for life, and the tenants attorned to her.

William also held in his demesne as of fee the manor of Caister in Fleggburgh by Yarmouth and enfeoffed William Bardolf, knight, his son, and his heirs. William the father died and the son assigned a third part to Agnes in dower for life with reversion to himself.

She also held the following knight's fees, assigned in dower in the chancery of Richard II, with reversion to Thomas Bardolf, knight, her son and heir, extending at the amounts shown:

Watlington, Tottenhill, Setchey, Shouldham Thorpe and Langham, 1 fee held by Lawrence Trussebute and others, 60s.

Wreningham, Ashwellthorpe, Neyland, Hapton and Fundenhall, 1 fee held by Edmund de Thorp, knight, 60s.

Foston and Shouldham Thorpe, ¼ fee held by John de Fyncham and others, 10s.

Watlington, ¼ fee held by Lawrence Trussebute and others, 10s.

Thorpland, East Winch, Gayton, and Wallington, 1 fee held by William Hunte and others, 60s.

Stradsett, Watlington, Basil, Ryston, Fordham, Roxham, Saham Toney and Syderstone, 2 fees held by the heirs of Elizabeth Stratesete, 100s.

Fincham, West Dreham, Roxham and Fordham, 1 fee held by John de Fyncham and others, 30s.

Barton Bendish, Eastmoor, Bacton, Beachamwell and Mattishall Burgh, 1 fee held by Thomas Lovell, £4.

Yaxham, Shipdham, Mattishall, Reymerston, Letton and Bradenham, ¼ fee held by Thomas de Estoft, 100s.

East Lexham, Litcham, Kempstone, Great Dunham, Swaffham, Great Setchey and Little Setchey in South Lynn, 1 fee held by Osbert de Mundeforth and others, 150s.

Great Ellingham, 2 fees held by the heirs of Robert Mortimer, 100s.

East Tuddenham and North Tuddenham, 1 fee held by Robert Kokefeld, knight, and others, 60s.

Grimston, Wootton and Hillington, ¼ fee held by the heirs of John Norman, 20s.

Morley, Wicklewood, Wymondham, Deopham, Hackford and Crownthorpe, ½ fee held by John atte Crosse and others, 100s.

Terrington, ½ fee and ¼ fee held by John Howard, knight, and others, 10s.; ¼ fee held by John Howard, 20s.; ⅛ fee held by Robert Braunche, 13s.4d.; and ⅛ fee held by John Marschall, 13s.4d.

Tilney, ⅛ fee held by Philip de Tylney, 20s.

Tilney, Clenchwarton, and Wiggenhall St. Mary the Virgin, ¾ fee and ½ of ¼ fee held by Edmund Noon, knight, and others, 100s.

Narborough, 2 fees held by William de Narburgh and others, £6 13s.4d.

Hempton, Waterden, Barsham, Whissonsett, Pudding Norton, Toftrees and Stanfield, 1 fee held by the prior of Hempton and others, 60s.

Larling, Rushford, Shadwell and Foulden, ¾ fee held by Edmund Gonvill, 40s.

Caston, Rockland, Toftrees, Thompson, Briston, Beckerton, Roudham, Shipdam and Buckenham, 1 fee held by Katherine lady of Caston, 40s.

Holkham, ¼ fee held by Richard Smyth, 3s.4d.

Cockthorpe and Field Dalling, ¼ fee held by Vincent de Ball', 13s.4d.

Blakeney, Glandford, Wiveton, Irmingland and Langham, 1 fee held by Thomas Estlee, knight, 30s.

Hindringham, Roughton and Felbrigg, ¾ fee held by Edward de Shelston, knight, 20s.

Hindringham, ¼ fee held by William Wylleby and others, 20s.

North Burlingham, South Burlingham, Beighton, Buckenham, Moulton, Freethorpe and Tunstall, 1 fee held by Stephen Raghwyse and others, 30s.

Raveningham, 1 fee held by the prior of St. Olave, 40s.

Hindringham, ¼ fee held by Rose Nowers and others, 13s.4d.

Wiggenhall St. Germans and Islington, 1 fee held by Edmund de Raynham, 66s.8d.

She also held for life in dower all the rents, services and other fees of William Bardolf and all the suits of court owed by his manors, the honour of Wormegay or the other manors which she held for life, and also the advowsons of: Wormegay priory, extending at 6s.8d.; Westbrigg, 3s.4d.; Whinbergh, 5s.; Garvestone, 6s.; Cantley, 10s.; North Runcton, the first presentation, 6s.8d.

The manors of Wormegay, Stow Bardolph, Fareswell in Fincham, and North Runcton, with the fees and advowsons of Wormegay, Westbrigg, Whinbergh, Garvestone and North Runcton, are held of the king in chief by the service of one third of the barony of Wormegay. The manors of Cantley, Strumpshaw, and Caister in Fleggburgh, with the advowson of Cantley, are held of the king in chief as one fee of the barony of Gurnay. Annual values: Wormegay manor £10; Stow Bardolph £13; Fareswell £6 13s.4d.; Strumpshaw 60s.; Cantley £10; North Runcton £8; Caister 100s.

Date of death and heir as above.

794 SUFFOLK. Inquisition. Otley. 28 June 1403.

William Bardolf, knight, lord of Wormegay, by his charter [licence *CPR 1381–5*, p.376] granted the manor of King's Hall in Clopton to John Cleye, clerk, for life with reversion to himself and his heirs, and Cleye assigned half the manor in dower to Agnes. The tenure is such that widows should have half in dower by custom time out of mind. The reversion belongs to Thomas Bardolf, knight, son and heir of William Bardolf, because John Cleye died in the lifetime of Agnes. The half is held of the king in chief as an eighth part of a knight's fee, annual value 66s.8d.

Date of death and heir as above.

C 137/37, no.39
E 149/81, no.3
E 152/388, no.1

AMERY DE SANCTO AMANDO, KNIGHT

795 Writ 15 June 1402.

DEVON. Inquisition. Ipplepen. 30 June.

He held the manor of Ipplepen jointly with his wife. By a fine of 1394 [CP 25(1) 45/68, no.151, licence *CPR 1391–6*, p.333] he and Eleanor his wife granted the manor to Henry Ingepenne and Richard Parkere, and they regranted it to them in tail male, with successive remainders to Amery his son and Joan his son's wife in tail male, the heirs of Amery and Eleanor, and the right heirs of Amery. It is held of the king in chief by the service of a third part of a knight's fee, annual value £30.

He died on 13 June holding jointly with Eleanor. Amery the son died without male heirs. Ida, wife of Thomas West, daughter of Amery, aged 10 years and more on 6 May, and Gerard Braybrook, son of Eleanor, his other daughter, aged 10 years and more, are his heirs.

796 Writ 15 June 1402.

DERBY. Inquisition. Repton. 3 Oct.

He held in his demesne as of fee the manor of Catton on Trent and granted it to Henry Ingepenne, William Tuderley and Philip Shipiere. Afterwards by a fine of 1402 [CP 25(1) 290/59, no.50] shown to the jurors they regranted it to him and Eleanor his wife for their lives with remainder to Thomas Pevere, Geoffrey Ippelpenne, Henry Durneford, clerk, Edmund Daunvers and the heirs of Edmund. They did not hold it in his lifetime, but after his death Eleanor entered and holds it of the king in chief of the duchy of Lancaster, service unknown, annual value 10 marks.

He died on 14 June, heirs as above.

797 Writ 26 Nov. 1402.

WILTSHIRE. Inquisition. Ludgershall. 4 Dec.

He held in his demesne as of fee the manors of Netheravon and Haxton. He granted them to Henry Ingepenne and others, and they regranted them by the fine of 1402 [above, no.796]. He did not hold them during his life, but Eleanor entered after his death. They are held of the king in chief of the duchy of Lancaster, annual value £16.

He died on 14 June, heirs as above.

798 BERKSHIRE. Inquisition *ex officio*. Grandpont. 3 July 1402.

He held the manor of Basildon in his demesne as of fee by the service of one knight's fee, annual value £24.

He died on 14 June last. Gerard son of Eleanor, his daughter, and Ida his other daughter are his next heirs, Gerard unmarried and 10 years of age, Ida married to Thomas son of Thomas West, knight, and aged 11 years.

799 Writ, stating that William Hilton, late escheator, was removed before he held an inquisition. 17 Jan. 1403.

BERKSHIRE. Inquisition, in the presence of John Hull and Hugh Hals, justices of assize, in virtue of letters of privy seal. Grandpont. 19 Feb.

He held in his demesne as of fee:

Basildon, the manor, which Amery his father gave to William de Mulsho, William de Haule, William de Forde, John de Evesham and John Froylle. They granted it to

Amery the father for life with successive remainders to the son, Ida his wife and the heirs of their bodies, and to the right heirs of the father. Amery the father held it, and after his death Amery the son and Ida held it. They had issue Eleanor, who had issue Gerard Braybrook, who still lives. Ida died and Amery married Eleanor and had issue Ida, who is now married to Thomas son of Thomas West, knight. Amery the son died and the manor descended to Gerard de Braybrook and Ida, his other daughter. It is held of the king in chief by knight service, annual value £24.

Woodhay and Ilsley, the manors, which he granted to Robert Shotesbrok, his heirs and assigns. By a fine of 1402 [CP 25(1) 290/59, no. 38] shown to the jurors, Shotesbrok regranted it to Amery and Eleanor for their lives with remainder to John Chitterne, clerk, Thomas Pevere, Edmund Daunvers, Richard Parker of Malmesbury, Henry Ingepenne and the heirs of Edmund, so he died holding jointly with Eleanor.

St. Helen's by Abingdon and Eaton by Cumnor, the manors, with 1 messuage, 1 carucate and £7 annual rent in Chilton and Sutton. These he granted to Henry Ingepenne, William Tuderle and Philip Shipiere, and by a fine of 5 May 1402 [CP 25(1) 290/59, no. 50] they regranted the manor of St. Helen's and the lands etc. with the reversion of the manor of Eaton, which Margaret widow of John Evesham held for life with reversion to them, to Amery and Eleanor his wife for their lives, with remainder to Thomas Pevere, Geoffrey Ippelpenne, Henry Durneford, clerk, and Edmund Daunvers and the heirs of Edmund. Amery and Eleanor never held them during his lifetime, but after his death Eleanor entered St. Helen's and the lands and has taken the profits.

Basildon, annual value £20, Woodhay 10 marks, and Ilsley £40, are held of the inheritance of the earl of Hereford, St. Helen's 7s., Eaton nil, and the messuage etc. in Chilton and Sutton £7, of the abbot of Abingdon, except Sutton which is held of the earl of Devon, all services unknown.

Amery died on 14 June last. Ida his daughter and heir was aged 10 on 6 May last. Gerard Braybrok, his grandson and other heir, is aged 10 years and more.

800   Writs 15 June and 26 Nov. 1402.

GLOUCESTER. Inquisition. Cirencester. 18 Dec.

He held in his demesne as of fee the manors of South Cerney and Cerney Wick. He conveyed them to Henry Ingepenne and others and they regranted them by a fine of 1402 [as above, no. 796]. Amery and Eleanor were not seised of them, but after Amery's death Eleanor entered and now holds them and takes the profits. They are held of the earl of Hereford, service unknown, annual value 20 marks.

Date of death, 14 June, and heirs as above.

801   OXFORD. Inquisition. Oxford. 19 Feb. 1403.

He held in his demesne as of fee:

Bloxham and Alkerton, the manors, the hundred of Bloxham, and a third part of the manor of Adderbury, except 1 a. in Bloxham, and granted them to Robert Shotesbroke, who regranted them to Amery and Eleanor for their lives [as above, no. 799]. So he died holding jointly with Eleanor who survives him.

Bloxham, the 1 a. excepted above, of the king in chief, service unknown.

Pudlicote and Chilson, the manors. He granted them to Henry Ingepenne and others and they regranted to Amery and Eleanor by a fine of 1402 [as above, no. 796]. Eleanor entered after his death.

Annual values: Bloxham manor and hundred 20 marks, the 1 a. there 2d., Alkerton

30s. and the third part of Adderbury 10 marks, all held of the king in chief service unknown; Pudlicote and Chilson £10, held of the king as of the duchy of Lancaster.

Date of death and heirs as above.

802   Writ 15 June 1402.

BUCKINGHAM. Inquisition. Stony Stratford. 15 Feb.

He held in his demesne as of fee the manor of Grendon Underwood and its appurtenances, and 1 messuage, 2 carucates, 20 a. meadow, 40 a. pasture in Grendon and Edgcott, with knight's fees and the advowson of Grendon. He granted them to Henry Ingepenne and Roger Lansant, their heirs and assigns. They regranted them to Amery and Eleanor his wife for their lives, and afterwards by their charter shown to the jurors, in order to enhance his status therein, gave and granted them to him, the heirs of his body and his right heirs. So he was seised of them in fee tail jointly with Eleanor who survives him.

The annual value is 20 marks. The manor of Grendon with a messuage and close in Edgcott are held of the prince [of Wales] of the earldom of Cornwall, the other lands of the earl of Stafford, services unknown.

Date of death and heirs as above.

803   BEDFORD. Inquisition. Shefford. 13 Feb. 1403.

He held in his demesne as of fee:

Harlington, the manor. Amery his father held it and granted it to William de Mulsho, William de Haule, William de Forde, John de Evsham and John Froyll. They granted it to Amery the father for life with remainders, and so it descended to Gerard de Braybrooke and Ida [as above, no.799].

Cotton End, the manor, and he granted it to Thomas Daunteseye, Henry Ingepenne and Philip Shypyer. By a fine of 1400 [CP 25(1) 6/73, no.8] they granted it to Amery and Eleanor for life, with remainder to his heirs male, the heirs of their son Amery, and his right heirs. Ida is his daughter and heir.

Houghton Conquest, Millbrook, Ampthill and Grange by Millbrook, the manors, with 6 messuages, 3 carucates, 80 a. meadow, 20 a. wood and 100s. rent in Priestley and Steppingley, and granted them to Robert Shotisbrooke, and he by a fine conveyed them to Amery and Eleanor [as above, no.799]. So he died jointly enfeoffed with Eleanor.

Annual values: Harlington £20, Cotton End £15, Millbrook, Ampthill and Grange 40 marks, Houghton Conquest and the other lands £10. Harlington, Cotton End, Millbrook, Ampthill and Grange are held of the king in chief by knight service; Houghton Conquest of Lord Latymer, service unknown; Priestley and Steppingley of Lord Mowbray.

Date of death and heirs as above.

C 137/37, no.40
E 149/79, no.6
E 152/386, no.1

EDMUND EARL OF STAFFORD

804   Writ 9 Aug. 1403.

NORTHAMPTON. Inquisition. Rothwell. 26 Sept.

He held the manor of Woodford near Byfield by inheritance from Ralph Basset of

Drayton Bassett, as kinsman and heir, being the son of Hugh, son of Ralph, son of Margaret, sister of Ralph, father of Ralph, father of Ralph, father of Ralph Basset. It is held of John Lovell, knight, service unknown, annual value 100s.

He died on 21 July last. Humphrey his son and heir was aged 1 year on 15 August last.

805   Writ 9 Aug. 1403.

HEREFORD AND THE ADJACENT MARCH OF WALES. Inquisition. Hereford. 2 Oct.

He held in the right and inheritance of Anne his wife the castle and lordship of Huntington in the March of the king in chief, service unknown, annual value £28 13s.4d.

Date of death and heir as above.

806   Writ 9 Aug. 1403.

WILTSHIRE. Inquisition. Collingbourne Abbots. 1 Oct.

He held in his demesne as of fee:

Wexcombe, the manor, with the hundred of Kinwardstone; the manor of Orcheston St. Mary with view [of frankpledge]; the manor of Knook with view of frankpledge; and the borough of Great Bedwyn; all in chief at fee farm, rendering £31 10s. yearly at the exchequer by the sheriff, and worth yearly beyond this and beyond another rent of 100s. granted to Geoffrey Blake for life from the manor of Orcheston by letters patent of the earl, 100s.

Stanton St. Quintin, Smallbrook and Littleton Drew, the leets, annual values, 3s.4d., 12d. and 12d.

Lopshill, 6s.8d. rent; and Hyde by Damerham, 33s.4d. rent.

He also held of the king in chief in the dower of Anne his wife the manor of Burbage, assigned to her from all the lands in various counties, in Ireland and in Calais of Thomas late earl of Stafford, her former husband, service unknown, annual value 100s.

Date of death and heir as above.

807   Writ 22 Sept. 1403.

HAMPSHIRE. Inquisition. Winchester. 11 Oct.

He held in the dower of his wife from all the lands of Thomas late earl of Stafford, her former husband:

Petersfield, the town, with a market every Saturday and two fairs each year at the feasts of St. Peter and St. Andrew, annual value £6 10s.; and 4 hamlets belonging to the town, namely Mapledurham, Weston, Nursted and Sheet, annual value with pleas and perquisites of court at Petersfield £7 3s.4d.; all of the king in chief of the honour of Gloucester by knight service.

Corhampton, the manor, of Lord St. John by knight service, annual value 106s.8d.

Fordingbridge, a rent of 16d. from tenements in the glebe of the church.

Date of death and heir as above.

808   Writ 9 Aug. 1403.

SURREY. Inquisition. Bletchingley. 24 Sept.

He held in his demesne as of fee of the king in chief:

Bletchingley, the manor, lordship and town, of the honour of Clare by knight service and a rent of 5s. called 'parkselver' payable by the sheriff; annual value, beyond the profits of the park to the south which is worth 100s., and also beyond a rent of 10 marks granted to Nicholas Bradshawe for life by letters patent of the earl after his marriage to Anne, £9.

Titsey, 68 a. arable and 72 a. pasture, of the honour of Clare by knight service, annual value 18s.9d.

Camberwell, certain lands, tenements and rents, service unknown, annual value, beyond a rent of 5 marks granted to William Carleton for life by letters patent of the earl after his marriage, 20s.

Ockham, the manor, service unknown, annual value £6.

He also held a tenement in Southwark of the abbot of Bermondsey, service unknown, annual value 46s.8d.

Date of death and heir as above.

809 SUSSEX. Inquisition. Horsham. 22 Sept. 1403.

He held nothing of the king in chief or of anyone else in his demesne as of fee or in service.

Date of death and heir as above.

810 Writ 9 Aug. 1403.

WARWICK. Inquisition. Rugby. 21 Sept.

He held in the dower of his wife from the lands of Thomas earl of Stafford, her late husband:

Tysoe, the manor, of the king in chief, service unknown, comprising site of the manor, annual value nil; demesne lands, meadow and pasture 100s.; assize rents from both free and customary tenants, payable equally at the four principal terms, £21 13s.4d. and pleas and perquisites of court 3s.4d.

Wootton Wawen, £4 rent from the manor which after his marriage he granted by his letters patent to Roger Bradshawe and Elizabeth his wife for their lives. Of whom it is held is unknown.

He also held in his demesne as of fee the manor of Whatcote, annual value, beyond a rent of £10 granted to Ralph de Stafford for life by Hugh earl of Stafford, father of Edmund, 66s.8d. of whom it is held is unknown.

Date of death and heir as above.

811 Writ 9 Aug. 1403.

CORNWALL. Inquisition. Trevigro. 18 Sept.

He held in his demesne as of fee 2 parts of the manor of Calliland of the castle of Trematon by knight service, annual value £10.

Date of death and heir as above.

812 Writ 9 Aug. 1403.

NOTTINGHAM. Inquisition. Carlton on Trent. 24 Aug.

He held of the king in chief in right of the inheritance of Anne his wife the manor of Kneesall, service unknown. There are several quite ruinous buildings, annual value nil; 180 a. arable with meadow and pasture £4 13s.4d.; 1 enclosed park, of which the herbage is worth 13s.4d.; 1 windmill, 6s.8d.; assize rents payable at Martinmas and

Whitsun, 21s.7d.; rents of another kind payable at Martinmas, Easter, Whitsun and Michaelmas, £3 19s.; 1 lb. cumin at Martinmas and 1 lb. pepper at Whitsun.

Date of death and heir as above.

813 Writ 9 Aug. 1403.

NORFOLK. Inquisition. Holt. 20 Sept.

He held in the dower of his wife of the inheritance of Thomas late earl of Stafford, of the king in chief, services unknown:

Wells, the manor, comprising 1 capital messuage, annual value nil, herbage there 12d., 160 a. arable by the short hundred at 6d., 70s., 5 a. meadow at 20d., 8s.4d., farm of lands in the hands of the lord by escheat, 6s.8d., assize rents, £7 13s.1d. payable by equal parts at St. Andrew, Easter, Midsummer and Michaelmas, 10 hens at Christmas, 10d., 60 winter and summer works at ½d., 2s.6d., 40 autumn works at 1d., 40d. and pleas and perquisites of court with a leet once yearly, 40s.

Wiveton, 20 a. arable at 6d., 10s., 40 a. pasture at 2d., 6s.8d., farm of escheated lands, 21d., 1 a. meadow, 20d., assize rents by equal parts at Easter and Michaelmas, 15s., 5 hens at Christmas at 1d., 5d., 10 winter and summer works at ½d., 5d., 15 autumn works at 1d., 15d., and pleas and perquisites of court with half a leet once yearly, 13s.4d.

Long before he died he granted the manor of Sheringham by a charter, date unknown, to Edmund bishop of Exeter, Thomas Stanley, Nicholas Bubbewyth and others, and all the tenants attorned to them. It is held of the king in chief, service unknown, annual value £40.

Date of death and heir as above.

814 SUFFOLK. Inquisition. Gazeley. 11 Sept. 1403.

He held in the dower of Anne his wife, assigned to her in the chancery of Richard II from the inheritance of Thomas late earl of Stafford, her former husband:

Desning, the manor, of the king in chief of the honour of Gloucester, service unknown. There are 1 capital messuage, annual value nil, herbage there, 2s., 200 a. arable by the short hundred at 6d., 100s., 186 a. pasture at 2d., 31s., 7 a. mowable meadow at 20d., 11s.8d., 2 parks, agistment nil beyond the sustenance of the game and enclosure for pigs; 1 windmill, 13s.4d.; 1 fulling mill in Cavenham, 20s.; 1 rabbit warren, 60s.; 1 pond called 'Cavenham ponde' with bed of rushes, 40s.; £6 in assize rents by equal parts at Michaelmas and Easter; farm of escheated lands, 13s.4d. at the same terms; various services and customs, 6s.8d.; and pleas and perquisites of court with a leet once a year, 100s.

Gazeley, 14 a. arable, of John atte Lane, service unknown, annual value at 4d., 4s.8d.

Haverhill, the manor called Castle Hall, of the king in chief of the honour of Gloucester. There are the site, annual value nil; herbage there, 8d.; 50 a. arable at 6d., 25s.; 50 a. pasture at 2d., 8s.4d.; 5 a. mowable meadow at 20d., 8s.4d.; 10 a. pasture at 4d., 40d.; assize rents, 40s.; escheated lands, 4s.; a wood of 5 roods, with underwood every tenth year worth 5s.; and pleas and perquisites of court, 13s.4d.

Date of death and heir as above.

815 Writ 9 Aug. 1403.

GLOUCESTER AND THE ADJACENT MARCH OF WALES. Inquisition. Thornbury. 21 Sept.

In the dower of Anne his wife from the lands of Thomas late earl of Stafford, her former husband, he held of the king of the honour of Gloucester, services unknown:

T

Thornbury, the manor and borough, with its members, Oldbury, Kington, Morton, Falfield and Marsh, annual value £98 19s. 5d.

Oldland, view of frankpledge held twice yearly at Easter and Michaelmas, 13s. 4d.

Gloucester, a rent of 10s. with a court every 3 weeks, perquisites 6s. 8d.

Rendcomb, the manor, with lands and tenements in North Cerney, 104s. 8d.

In right of the inheritance of Anne he held the manor of Wheatenhurst of the king in chief, service unknown, annual value £21 7s.

In the same right he held the castle of Caldicot and Shirenewton in the March of Wales of the king by baron service, annual value £26 13s. 4d.

In his demesne as of fee of the king in chief, service unknown, he held the castle and vill of Newport and the lordship of the county of Wenllwch, with its members in Stow, Rhymney, Dowlais, Pencarn, Dyffryn and Ebbw, with the manor, lordship and forest of Machen annexed to the lordship of Wenllwch, which were worth yearly before the insurrection of Owen de Glyndourdy £215 17s., but now nothing because all burnt, destroyed, wasted and made nought by Owen and the other rebels in his company.

Date of death and heir as above.

816 Writ 9 Aug. 1403.

Essex. Inquisition. Chelmsford. 10 Sept.

He held in right of the inheritance of Anne his wife of the king in chief:

Pleshey, the castle and manor, service unknown, annual value 100s.

Great Waltham, the manor, annual value £50.

High Easter, the manor, with 30s. rent from the manors of Hellesdon and Oxnead in Norfolk, annual value with the rents £50.

Shenfield, the manor, service unknown, annual value £20.

Chishall, view of frankpledge, annual value 3s. 4d.

High Easter, court of the honour, annual value £4.

An annuity of £40 10s. 10d. by the sheriff by equal parts at Easter and Michaelmas; and the office of constable of England.

Farnham, the manor, service unknown, annual value £13 6s. 8d.

Also of her inheritance, of William Bourgcher, knight, the manor of Wix, service unknown, annual value £26 13s. 4d.

And in the dower of Anne:

Chipping Ongar, the manor, of the king in chief of the honour of Boulogne by knight service, annual value £6 13s. 4d.

Horseham, the manor, with its appurtenances in Haverhill, of the earl of March by knight service, annual value £4 17s.

In his demesne as of fee he held the hundred of Ongar, pleas and perquisites of the court of which are worth 53s. 4d. yearly.

Date of death and heir as above.

817 Hertford. Inquisition. Bishop's Stortford. 11 Sept. 1403.

He held of the king in chief in right of the inheritance of Anne his wife, service unknown:

Nuthampstead in Barkway, a third part of the manor, annual value 73s. 4d.

Hoddesdon, view of frankpledge, and Hertford, the court of the honour, parcel of the barony of Essex, annual values 4s. and 13s. 4d., together 17s. 4d.

Hoddesdon, a rent of 12 capons at Christmas.

Farnham in Essex, 40 a. parcel of that manor, annual value 13s.4d.
Date of death and heir as above.

818 Writ 9 Aug. 1403.
LINCOLN. Inquisition. Lincoln. 18 Sept.
He held in his demesne as of fee the manor of Greetwell of the honour of Tickhill, service unknown, annual value 20 marks.

In right of the inheritance of Anne his wife he held the manor of Long Bennington of the honour of Richmond, service unknown. There are several buildings [as in no. 126 above].
Date of death and heir as above.

819 Writ 9 Aug. 1403.
HUNTINGDON. Inquisition. Papworth St. Agnes. 19 Sept.
He held in his demesne as of fee of the king of the honour of Gloucester the leet of Stilton, Wood Walton, Folksworth, Winwick and Sawtry, held yearly at Easter at Sawtry, annual value 17s.4d.
Date of death and heir as above.

820 CAMBRIDGE. Inquisition. Caxton. 18 Sept.
He held of the king in chief in right of Anne his wife a view of frankpledge in Sawston, held on 12 June [morrow of St. Barnabas], annual value 5s.
Date of death and heir as above.

821 Writ 9 Aug. 1403.
BEDFORD. Inquisition. Bedford. 22 Sept.
He held in his demesne as of fee:

Biddenham, a court held every 3 weeks, with view of frankpledge of Biddenham, Turvey, Holcot, and Roxhill, held twice yearly at Biddenham at Easter and Michaelmas, annual value 13s.6d.; the leet of Roxton, held twice yearly at the same terms, 2s.; and the leet of Pavenham and Battlesden held twice yearly in those vills, 4s.6d.

Yelden, a rent of 13s.4d. from the lands of John Trailly, knight, payable at Hockday, and 1d. rent from the same knight's lands in Chellington.

Ralph Basset of Drayton Bassett, knight, held in his demesne as of fee 20 a. in Turvey in the park of Newton Blossomville, of John Trailly, knight, annual value 6s.8d.; 5 a. in the same park of the king in chief by knight service, annual value 20d.; and 50 a. in Turvey, parcel of the manor of Newton Blossomville, of Gerard Braybrok, knight, annual value 8s.4d. These he granted to Elizabeth Beauchamp for life. He died and she granted her rights in them to Nicholas Bradeshawe. Edmund earl of Stafford, cousin and heir of Ralph, namely son of Hugh, son of Ralph, son of Margaret, daughter of Ralph, father of Ralph, father of the Ralph de Basset lately deceased, confirmed them to Nicholas, and granted them for the life of Nicholas, with reversion to Edmund for life, and then to Humphrey his son, and the heirs of Edmund.
Date of death and heir as above.

822 BUCKINGHAM. Inquisition. Olney. 24 Sept. 1403.

He held in his demesne as of fee of the king in chief:

Little Brickhill, the manor, of Dover castle by a rent of 10s. yearly, annual value £7 1s.

Horwood, a rent of 9½d. and a nail of cloves from the tenants at Martinmas.

Great Horwood, a court every 3 weeks with 2 leets at Great Kimble at Easter and Michaelmas.

Great Missenden, 2 leets.

Singleborough, 2 leets.

Horwood, 1 leet at Michaelmas.

Lamport, Lenborough, Bourton and Maid's Moreton, 2 leets at Easter and Michaelmas.

Broughton, Wavendon, Great Woolstone, North Crawley and Milton Keynes, leets twice yearly at Broughton.

Bow Brickhill, 1 leet twice yearly.

Edgcott, 1 leet at Michaelmas.

Annual value of all these courts together, 42s.6d.

He also held in the dower of Anne his wife from all the lands of Thomas late earl of Stafford, her former husband:

Easington, the manor, of the king in chief of the honour of Gloucester, annual value 73s.4d.

Ludgershall, a yearly rent of 13s.4d. payable at Martinmas.

Bletchley, a rent of 2s. from the manor at Hocktide.

Of the right of inheritance of Anne he had £20 from the issues of the county by the sheriff by equal parts at Easter and Michaelmas.

Ralph Basset of Drayton Bassett, knight, held the manor of Newton Blossomville of Henry Grey, lord of Shirland, annual value 100s.; and lands and tenements called Butlers and Wakes in Clifton Reynes, Butlers of the king in chief by knight service, and Wakes of Reynold Grey of Ruthin by knight service, annual value of the two together 100s. Ralph granted the lands and tenements to Elizabeth Beauchamp for life, and so they came to Nicholas Bradeshawe for life with reversion to Edmund earl of Stafford [as in no.821 above].

John Billyng holds 50 a. arable, 8 a. meadow and 10s. rent in Sherington for life of the lands of Ralph Basset with reversion to Edmund and his heirs. These are held of John Lynford, service unknown, annual value 20s.

Date of death and heir as above.

823 Writ 9 Aug. 1403.

KENT. Inquisition. Tonbridge. 19 Sept.

He held in his demesne as of fee the castle and vill of Tonbridge, although a third part was assigned in dower to Anne as widow of Thomas de Stafford; and the manor of Dachurst, with 75s.3½d. at various terms from the manor of Hadlow.

In the dower of Anne he also held the manor of Hadlow except for the 75s.3½d. rent. This manor with Dachurst is held of the archbishop of Canterbury by homage and the service of being his steward on the day of his enthronement. Together they are worth £20 annually an no more, because the manor of Dachurst is burdened with a rent of 100 marks payable to the prior and convent of Tonbridge and 3s.10d. to the prior of Rochester.

He also held in his demesne as of fee:

Yalding, the manor, of the king of the honour of Clare as half a knight's fee, comprising the site with various ruined buildings, annual value nil; 371 a. arable at 4d., £6 3s.8d.; 122 a. pasture at 2d., 20s.4d.; 31 a. meadow at 6d. when it can be mown, 15s.6d.; a watermill at Twyford Bridge belonging to this manor, 20s.; £18 11½d. in assize rents payable at the four terms; 97½ hens at 1½d. at Christmas, 12s.2d.; 367 eggs at 4d. a 100 at Easter, 14¾d.; and customs and services, 46s.8d.

Agnes Frevyle has an annuity of 100s. granted by Edmund in writing, for her life long before his death.

Edenbridge, a tenement, of the abbot and convent of St. Peter, Westminster, by rent of a pair of gilt spurs worth 6d., annual value £8.

Brasted, the reversion of the manor, which John de Farnyngham holds for life by the grant of Hugh de Stafford by a rent of 40 marks. Thomas Stafford, after his marriage to Anne, waived the rent for the life of John de Farnyngham, who is still alive. The manor is held of the archbishop of Canterbury by homage and the service of being his butler on the day of his enthronement.

Date of death and heir as above.

824 BUCKINGHAM. Inquisition. Olney. 24 Sept. 1403.

He held:

Great Kimble, 3 fees formerly held of him by the earl of Oxford.

Whitchurch, 1 fee held by Elizabeth Loterell.

Cublington, 2 fees held by Geoffrey Lucy.

Little Marlow and Singleborough, ½ fee held by Joan Crumbewell, extending at 100s.

Buckingham, 2 fees held by John Frome.

Hillesden, ½ fee formerly held by the earl of Oxford.

Dorton, 1 fee formerly held by John Bernyngham.

Wotton Underwood, 2 fees formerly held by Roger le Warde and Richard Greneville.

Broughton, 1 fee formerly held by the earl of Oxford.

North Crawley, 1 fee held by Lord le Burnell.

Bletchley, ½ fee held by Reynold de Grey, 25s.

Bow Brickhill and Caldecott, 1 fee held by John Wodevyle.

Bradwell, ½ fee held by Thomas de Bradwelle, £10.

Great Missenden, ½ fee formerly held by Hugh de Pleisy and Henry Huse, £10.

Dorton, Wotton Underwood and Chilton, 1½ fees held by Thomas le Peyvre, William le Souch and John de Bello Campo, £30.

Great Horwood, Oakley and Newton, 1 fee held by the prior of Newton Longville.

He also held in the dower of Anne his wife the advowson of Newton Longville priory, temporalities when they occur £10; and in the right and inheritance of Anne the advowson of Notley abbey, temporalities £40.

825 Writ 9 Aug. 1403.

SHROPSHIRE AND THE ADJACENT MARCH OF WALES. Inquisition. Shrewsbury. 15 Sept.

He held in his demesne as of fee of the king in chief by knight service:

Caus, the castle, annual value nil; and 3 parts of the lordship of Caus comprising the manor, annual value nil; a dovecot, nil because ruinous; 2 carucates of demesne, 26s.8d. pasture in the park below the castle, 10s.; and 4 a. meadow 6s.

Worthen, the free borough, assize rents of burgesses, £4 13s.5d.; and 1 watermill 23s.4d.

Minsterley, the hamlet, 1 watermill, 13s.4d.; 3 a. meadow, 4s.6d.; assize rents of free tenants and others, £8 18s.2d.; a rent of 4 collars for greyhounds at St. Nicholas, 8d.; 2 lb. pepper, 20d.; 2 lb. cumin, 3d. at Christmas and Easter; 1 barbed arrow at St. Nicholas, 1d.; agistment in the park, 13s.4d.; and pannage when it occurs, 8s.

Forden, the hamlet in the March, 1 carucate of non-arable demesne pasture, 12s.; and 1 watermill, 17s.

Over Gorther, the hamlet, assize rents of free tenants and villeins at Lady Day and Michaelmas, 30s.1½d.; and 2 quarters of great corn at Michaelmas, 6s.8d.

Nether Gorther, the hamlet, assize rents, 48s.11d.; and 3 quarters of corn at Michaelmas, 10s.

Bacheldre, the hamlet, 13s. assize rents of free tenants at Lady Day and Michaelmas.

Wallop, the hamlet, 1 carucate of demesne, 40d.; assize rents, 2s.; with 3 parts of the free chase of Hogstowe, of which the pasture £4; and 2 other pastures called Hayes and the Breiddin, 40s.

Hope, the hamlet, 60s.

Adstone, the hamlet, 27s.6d., with pleas and perquisites of court and other franchises by the law and custom of the March, 60s.

He also held 10 messuages in Bridgnorth of the king in free burgage, annual value 10s., and 30s. rent there; and 4 messuages and 10s. rent in Astley Abbotts by Bridgnorth of the abbot and convent of Shrewsbury by a rent of 28s.8d., annual value 3s.4d.

Thomas de Stafford, after his marriage to Anne, granted to Nicholas de Bradeshawe a rent of 20 marks for life from the lordship of Caus, and the office of constable of Caus castle. He still lives, but he granted the constableship to William Bromshulf, and Edmund confirmed it to him for his life. Edmund also granted a rent of 10 marks for life from the manor of Caus to John Cook for life by letters patent.

Date of death and heir as above.

826 SHROPSHIRE. Inquisition. Shrewsbury. 29 Nov. 1403.

He held the castle of Caus and three parts of the lordship as appears in another inquisition returned to the chancery. William Bromshulf, constable of the castle, has held them since the death of the earl with the pleas and perquisites of the court on the spoken order of the king, and is taking the profits for the safe keeping of the castle.

827 Writ 9 Aug. 1403.

LONDON. Inquisition. 27 Sept.

He held in the dower of Anne his wife from the lands of Thomas late earl of Stafford, her former husband, £5 1s.4d. quitrents, comprising 26s.8d. from a tenement called 'le Beaurepair' in All Hallows the Less parish now held by Walter Kyng, 20s. from a tenement there held by the same, 24s. from a tenement opposite the church door held by Thomas Pygot, 6s.8d. from a tenement called 'le Horn' held by Margery Wotton, and 24s. from a tenement in Gowers Lane held by John Brikles. The rents are held of the king in burgage, as is all London.

Date of death and heir as above.

828 Writ 9 Aug. 1403.

NORTHAMPTON. Inquisition. Rothwell. 26 Sept. 1403. [The chancery and Exchequer copies have different lists of jurors].

He held in his demesne as of fee:

Rothwell, the manor and hundred, except for a rent of £4 18s. 10¾d. which he held in the dower of Anne his wife, formerly wife of Thomas Stafford, annual value £21 5s.4d., including this rent and beyond the following rents granted for life: 10 marks to Henry Sewell by Thomas by letters patent before he married Anne; and 100s. to John Holt, £10 to Thomas Lawrence and 10 marks to Elizabeth Beauchamp, all by Edmund after his marriage to Anne.

Aldwincle, Thrapston, Woodford, Wylwen Cotes, Lowick, Ringstead, Raunds, Mill Cotes and Denford, the leets held at Denford at Easter and Michaelmas.

Little Addington, Finedon, Burton Latimer, Cranford and Barton Seagrave, the leets, held at Barton at Easter and Michaelmas.

Southwick, Perio, Tansor, Glapthorn and Cotterstock, the leets, held at Cotterstock at Easter and Michaelmas.

Stanion, the leet, held there twice yearly.

Gloucester, the court called the court of the honour of Gloucester held every three weeks in the precinct of these vills.

Annual value of all these courts together, 52s.8d.

He also held the manor of Glapthorn in the dower of Anne, annual value £7 10s. With all the above it is held of the king in chief of the honour of Gloucester.

He also held in his demesne as of fee:

Moulton, 1 messuage, 2 virgates, 8 a. meadow and 2s. rent, of whom is unknown, annual value 20s.

Draughton, 1 messuage, 3½ virgates, 20 a. meadow and 1 curtilage and 4 cottages, formerly of Henry Ysonde, annual value 56s.8d.; and rents from the lands of William Lavendon, 18d.; from those of William Abovetheton, 18d.; from a messuage once held by Walter Ram, 6d.; and from a messuage of Stephen Holand, 6½d.; all payable by equal parts at Michaelmas, St. Thomas, Palm Sunday and Midsummer; of whom they are held is unknown.

After the death of John Vyncent of Rothwell, who held for life with reversion to Ralph Basset of Drayton Bassett, whose heir Edmund was, he held the reversion of the manor of Thorpe Lubenham; 1 toft and 2 carucates in Arthingworth; 6 messuages and 6 virgates in Hackleton; 2 messuages, 2 virgates and 10 a. wood in Horton; and 3s. rent from Piddington. Of whom these are held is unknown; annual value together 10 marks.

After the death of Ralph Basset he also held as his next heir the manor of Woodford by Byfield, of John Lovell, knight, service unknown, annual value 100s.; and the reversion of the manor of Whiston, held for life by Nicholas Bradshawe, of whom and by what service is unknown, annual value 20 marks.

Date of death and heir as above.

829 Writ 9 Aug. 1403.

STAFFORD. Inquisition. Wolverhampton. 17 Sept.

He held in his demesne as of fee:

Stafford, the castle; Bradley, the manor and advowson, with its members of Billington, Tillington, Woollaston, Shredicote, Longnor, Stretton, Dunston, Coppenhall and Forebridge; and two parts of the manor of Hyde Lea; all of the king in chief by knight service, comprising:

Stafford, the castle, annual value nil; 2 carucates of demesne, 40s.; 10 a. meadow, 13s.4d.; 1 park, pasture 24s.; and pannage when it falls due, 24s.

Bradley, 1 toft, 12d.; 1 carucate in demesne, 20s.; and 2 a. meadow, 3s.

Forebridge, pasture, 10s.; a marsh called 'le Pytelpole', nil; pasture called 'Thenes-dych', 6s. 8d.; assize rents of free tenants and others in all these places, £39 6s. 6½d. and 6 barbed arrows at Lady Day and Michaelmas; and view of frankpledge twice yearly at Forebridge, and pleas and perquisites of court held every 3 weeks, 40s.

Hydes Lea, 2 parts of the manor: 2 parts of a carucate of demesne, 13s. 4d., 4 a. meadow, 4s. 8d.; 2 fishponds, nil; and 2 parts of a park, pasture 8s.

Madeley under Lyme, site, nil; 2 carucates, 30s.; 12 a. meadow, 19s.; 1 watermill, 20s.; 1 fulling mill, nil because totally ruinous; 2 parks, pasture of the larger 10s. and of the lesser called 'le Deshed', 20s.; underwood in 2 parks, 20s.; in the larger park a turbary, 13s. 4d.; and several pasture called 'Netherstede', 30s.; in the manor of Madeley with the hamlet of Radwood assize rents from free tenants and others, £17 13s. 4d. at the four terms; 4 fishponds with fisheries, 13s. 4d.; and view of frankpledge twice yearly, with pleas and perquisites of court every 3 weeks, 40s.

Stafford, 1 fishpond below the town called 'Kyngespole' with a watermill at the head of the fishpond, of the king in chief at a fee farm of 2 marks payable at the exchequer by the sheriff, annual value beyond this 20s.; 3 messuages and 3 tofts, 6s. 8d.; and the reversion of 1 messuage, held of the king in free burgage, which Elizabeth widow of Nicholas de Stafford, knight, holds for life by the grant of Hugh late earl of Stafford, 6s. 8d.

Coton Hill next Stafford, 1 toft with 1 carucate, of the prior of St. Thomas by Stafford, service unknown, annual value 13s. 4d.

Burton, 1 messuage, annual value 2s.

Derrington and Stallbrook, reversion of the hamlets which Giles del Hyde holds for life by the grant of Hugh, late earl, of the lord of Wem by knight service, annual value 100s.

Norton in the Moors, the manor, of the king in chief, service unknown; with the hamlet of Grotton and certain lands in Norton, of Lord Audeley of his manor of Endon, service unknown; annual value of all £16.

Stafford, the reversion of a tenement after the death of John de Clyfton and Isabel his wife, who still lives, of the king in free burgage, annual value 40s.

Rowley Regis, 1 messuage, of the castle of Stafford, service unknown, annual value 40s.

After he married Anne, Edmund granted to Nicholas Bradshaw for life an enclosed pasture called 'le Halgh' held of the castle of Stafford, annual value 66s. 8d.; and from the castle and lordship he granted for life to Henry Swan for his good counsel 26s. 8d.; to Nicholas Leveson 26s. 8d.; and to Adam de Eggeley, William Smert, Nicholas Parker, John Clerkesham, and John Prees, yeomen of his chamber, 5 marks each.

He also made the following grants for life: to John Delves, esquire, 20 marks from the manor of Norton in the Moors; to Thomas de Greneway, esquire, 10 marks from the lordship of Norton; to John de Thikenes and William Howton, esquires, 100s. from the manor of Madeley; to Thomas Arblaster, esquire, 100s. from the castle of Stafford; to John Hampton, esquire, 10 marks from the lordship of Stafford; to Hugh Calclogh, esquire, 10 marks from the manor of Madeley; and to Agnes de la Chambre 20s. from the castle of Stafford.

The following lands, tenements, advowsons and reversions descended after the death of Ralph Basset to Edmund as his kinsman and heir, since Ralph held them in his demesne as of fee:

Tamworth, 6 marks rent, of the king in chief in free burgage, held for life by John de Clyfton by the grant of Ralph Basset of Drayton Bassett.

Lichfield, 1 messuage, of the bishop of Chester, service unknown, annual value 6s.8d.

Pattingham, 1 messuage, annual value 3s.4d.

Walsall, 1 place(?) of land, woods and pasture of rushes (*scirpis*) called Clayhanger, which Ralph Basset, knight, bought from William Coleson, annual value 20s.(?); 1 carucate between the vill and the park called 'les Wastes' which Ralph bought from someone of Walsall, annual value 10s.; and a piece of land called 'le Conyngger', 6s.8d.

Drayton Bassett, advowson of the chantry of five chaplains in the church celebrating for the souls of Ralph Basset and his heirs, in his demesne as of fee, of whom unknown.

Walsall, 3 parcels containing 1½ carucates in the park, bought of William Coleson, Thomas Hexstall and John Hogyn, in his right as of fee, of whom unknown, annual value 26s.8d.

Drayton Bassett, 8 tofts, 2 carucates and 40 a. wood called 'Jonesclos', bought from John atte Lee, of the manor in his right as of fee, service unknown, annual value 20s.; and 1 messuage there bought from one of his villeins, also held of the manor, service unknown, annual value 3s.

Tamworth, 1 messuage, bought from Magota de Botery, in his right as of fee of the king in free burgage, annual value 3s.4d.

Packington, reversion of the manor, held for life by Thomas de Aston, knight, by the grant of Ralph Basset, of whom unknown, annual value 10 marks.

Fazeley, 10 cottages, bought of Ralph Smyth, in his right as of fee of the manor of Drayton Bassett, service unknown, annual value 8s.

830 Writ 9 Aug. 1403.

CALAIS. Inquisition. 4 Dec.

He held 5 marks rent from a house in the parish of St. Nicholas next to the highway leading to the castle. Thomas formerly earl of Stafford held it in his demesne as of fee of the king in chief by the service of providing two watchmen, and let it to farm to Henry Tamworth, his heirs and assigns for 100 years from Easter 1391 at a rent of 5 marks sterling.

Date of death and heir as above.

831 HAMPSHIRE. Inquisition. Winchester. 11 Oct. 1403.

He held the following knight's fees of the king of the honour of Gloucester, extending at the amounts shown:

Mapledurham, ¼ fee held by the heirs of Henry Merkanne, 15s.; and ⅛ fee held by the heirs of Richard Burton, 15s.8d.

Penton Mewsey, 1 fee once held by John de Acton, 40s.

Stanbridge Earls, 1 fee once held by Thomas Daunvers and Agnes his wife, 40s.

Houghton by Stockbridge, 1 fee formerly held by John Hoghton, 40s.

Fordingbridge, the advowson, in the dower of Anne his wife, £40.

832 Writ, for fees, 9 Aug. 1403.

CORNWALL. Inquisition. Trevigro. 18 Sept.

He held in his demesne as of fee the advowson of South Hill, annual value £20 to the profit of the rector there.

833   Writ, for fees, 9 Aug. 1403.

NORFOLK. Inquisition. Holt. 20 Sept.

He held in his demesne as of fee of the king in chief:

Wells, the advowson, annual value £20.

Foulsham, Banham, and Wood Norton, 1 fee formerly held by Thomas de Morlee, knight, Joan widow of Thomas de Felton, knight, and William de Jerberge.

Whitwell, ½ fee held by William Gambon.

Kettlestone, the advowson held in right of Anne his wife, £8.

Date of death and heir as above.

834   SUFFOLK. Inquisition. Gazeley. 11 Sept. 1403.

He held in his demesne as of fee of the honour of Gloucester:

Moulton, 1 fee called Stonehall formerly held by Henry earl of Derby and others; and the advowson of Brettenham; both belonging to the manor of Desning.

Various fees belonging to the manor of Haverhill:

Denston, 1 fee formerly held by William Hore.

Waldingfield, ½ fee held by Thomas Pevere.

Withersfield, 1¼ fees held by William de Clopton and John Deverose, knights.

Aldersfield, ¼ fee held by Mary de Clopton.

Rede, ½ fee held by William Hore.

Annual value of these fees with the advowson, when they occur, £17 10s.

Date of death and heir as above.

835   BEDFORD. Inquisition. Bedford. 22 Sept. 1403.

He held the following:

Roxhill, 1 fee formerly held by the earl of Oxford.

Biddenham and Holcot, 2 fees held by John Trailly.

Turvey, 1 fee held by John Trailly.

Yelden, 1 fee held by John Trailly, £10.

Chellington and Pavenham, 1 fee held by John Trailly.

Potsgrove, 1 fee held by Geoffrey Lucy.

Battlesden, 1 fee held by Thomas Frambaud.

He also held in right of his wife Anne the advowsons of Pertenhall, extending at £8, and Tilbrook, £10.

836   Writ, for fees, 9 Aug. 1403.

SOMERSET. Inquisition. Yeovil. 19 Sept.

He held in the dower of Anne his wife from the lands of Thomas her former husband the advowson of the abbey of St. Mary, Keynsham, of which the temporalities are worth £20 when they occur; and in right of the inheritance of Anne, a third part of a knight's fee in Pury, held by John Erlegh.

837   Writ, for fees, 9 Aug. 1403.

WILTSHIRE. Inquisition. Collingbourne Ducis. 1 Oct.

He held the following, extending at the amounts shown:

Havering, ½ fee held by John Midelton, £10.

Little Bedwyn, ½ fee held by the heirs of William Braybrok, £6 13s.4d.

Stokke, ½ fee held by Thomas Stokke, £10.

Sutton Mandeville, 1 fee held by Thomas West, knight, . . . 8d.

Knook, ½ fee held by John Lovell, knight, 100s.

Charlton by Hungerford, 1 fee held by William Hoppegras, 66s.8d.

Wootton Rivers, 1 fee held by Hugh Craan, 100s.

Middleton, ⅕ fee held by John Lillebon, 66s.8d.

Salterton, ½ fee held by Edward Botiller, £6 6s.8d.

Wilton by Great Bedwyn, 1 fee held by the prior of Mottisfont, £10.

Chirton, 1 fee held by the heirs of William FitzJohn, 60s.

Winterbourne Dauntsey, ½ fee held by John Daunteseye, knight, £10.

. . ., 1 fee formerly held by Maurice de Berkeley, 40s.

Orcheston St. Mary, 1 fee held by Walter de Scoteneye, 40s.

Wolf Hall, 1 fee held by William Sturmy, knight, £10.

Wootton Rivers, ½ fee held by the heirs of John de . . ., £10.

Puthall, ½ fee held by the prior of Easton, 100s.

Tollard Royal, 2 fees formerly held by Robert de Lucy and John de Gouyz, £20.

Woodhay, 1 fee in right of Anne his wife, held by the heirs of Amery de Sancto Amando, 100s.

Netheravon, ¼ fee also held by the heirs of Amery de Sancto Amando, 25s.

He also held in right of his wife the advowson of the priory of Monkton Farleigh, extending at £26 13s.4d. when a vacancy occurs.

838 Writ, for fees, 9 Aug. 1403.

NORTHAMPTON. Inquisition. Rothwell. 26 Sept.

He held the following, extending at the amounts shown:

Thrapston, Ringstead and Denford, ½ fee held by Richard Chamberleyn, Margaret Table and Richard Duffyn, £10.

Mill Cotes, ½ fee held by Richard Chamberleyn, 100s.

Denton, ½ fee held by Thomas Gryffyn, knight, 100s.

Wylwen Cotes, 1/16 fee held by Richard Chamberleyne, 20s.; and 1/40 fee also held by him, 6s.8d.

Barton Seagrave, ¼ fee held by Margaret late countess of Norfolk, 50s.

Woodford, ½ fee held by John Cokerell and Walter Jager, 100s.

Glendon, ⅙ fee held by Andrew Neubotell, 10 marks.

Rothwell, 1 fee held by William la Zouche of Harringworth, £20; ¼ fee held by John Gayton, £8; and ½ fee held by Thomas Latymer, knight, 100s.

Nether Heyford, ⅕ fee held by Richard de Flore, £4.

Pilton, ⅛ fee held by William de Pylton, 75s.

Burton Latimer and Finedon, ¼ fee held by the abbot of Croxton, 40s.

Lowick, ½ fee held by Henry Grene, knight, Thomas Cotyngham and John Tyndale, 100s.

Draughton, ¼ fee held by John Albon, 100s.

Tansor, 1 fee held by Thomas Camoys and others, £10.

Isham, ½ fee held by John Carnell, 20s.

Denford, 1 fee held by Richard Chamberleyn, £10.

Barton Seagrave, Raunds and Cranford, 2 fees held by Richard Cloune and the heirs of John Fossebroke, £12.

Raunds, ½ fee held by John Trayle, knight, 40s.

Addington, 1/20 fee held by Nicholas Pyell, 10s.

Polebrook, Thurning, and Clapton, 1 fee held by the abbot of Peterborough and Roger Mowy, 40s.

He also held in right of Anne his wife of her inheritance:

Northampton, 2 fees held by the heirs of Robert of Norhampton.

Hinton, 2 fees held by Henry de Hynton.

Aynho, 1½ fees held by Ralph Nevyll.

Aston, 1 fee once held by Ralph Moreton and John Bures.

Culworth, Croughton and Leckhamsted, 1 fee once held by Hugh de Myssenden, £10.

'Compton', 1 fee once held by the heirs of the Earl Marshal.

Hinton in the Hedges by Brackley, 2 fees once held by William de Hynton.

Aston le Walls, 1 fee formerly held by John de Sutton.

Hinton by Woodford, 1 fee once held by John de Hynton.

839 Writ, for fees, 9 Aug. 1403.

SURREY. Inquisition. Bletchingley. 24 Sept.

He held the following:

Burpham, ½ fee held by Thomas Wyntershull.

Titsey, 2 fees held by John Ovedale and William Cressewyk.

Titsey and Camberwell, ½ fee formerly held by John Devereux.

Mitcham, ¼ fee held by the prior of Merton.

Camberwell, ¼ fee held by William Vachan.

Mitcham, ¼ fee held by the prioress of Haliwell; and ¼ fee held by the prior of St. Mary Overy.

Bletchingley, ½ fee formerly held by William Venour.

Ockham, 1/20 fee formerly held by Walter Frelond; and 1/20 fee now held by him.

Camberwell, ½ fee held by Henry Bekewell.

Also in right of the inheritance of Anne his wife:

Clapham, Carshalton and Wanborough, 4 fees of the honour of Mandeville, formerly of Sybil de Boleyn, and now held by Ralph de Morton and John de Bures.

Horsley, 1 fee in the manor held by the heirs of John Berners.

He held the advowson of Bletchingley in his demesne as of fee, £10; and that of Ockham in the dower of Anne his wife, 66s. 8d.

840 Writ, for fees, 9 Aug. 1403.

SHROPSHIRE AND THE ADJACENT MARCH OF WALES. Inquisition. Shrewsbury. 15 Sept.

He held the following:

Acton Burnell, 1 fee held by Hugh Lord Burnell.

Wattlesborough, 1 fee held by the heir of Fulk Corbet.

Westbury, 1 fee held by the heir of Richard de Lodelowe, knight.

Whitton and Vennington, ⅕ fee held by John de Witton and his parceners.

Aston Pigott and Great Wollaston, 1 fee held by John Corbet and his parceners.

Hanwood, ⅔ fee held by William de Webbeley and his parceners.

Eyton and Bretchel, ½ fee held by John Iton and his parceners.

Home, ¼ fee held by John de Burton.

Horton, ¼ fee held by William Bowelere and his parceners.

Coton, ¼ fee held by the heir of Thomas Marchall.

Lake, 1/10 fee held by Richard de Lake and his parceners.

Hampton, $\frac{1}{6}$ fee held by the heir of Roger Corbet.

Brockton, $\frac{1}{16}$ fee held by Hugh Mauncell.

Worthen, $\frac{1}{16}$ fee held by William de Worthyn.

Beachfield, $\frac{1}{5}$ fee held by William Taillour and his parceners.

Yockleton, $\frac{1}{16}$ fee held by John Goutheman.

He also held the advowsons of Caus, the free chapel in the castle, extending at 40s.; Worthen, £20; Wentnor, 100s.; and Shelve, 66s.8d.

The fourth presentation to the churches of Worthen, Wentnor and Shelve belongs to the heirs of Robert de Harley.

841 Writ, for fees, 29 Sept. 1403.

SHROPSHIRE AND THE ADJACENT MARCH OF WALES. Inquisition. Bridgnorth. 8 Oct.

Repeats the list of fees as in the last inquisition, adding only the annual values:

Acton Burnell, 10 marks; Wattlesborough, 10 marks; Westbury, 12 marks; Whitton and Vennington, 8 marks; Aston Pigott and Great Wollaston, 106s.8d.; Hanwood, 40s.; Eyton and Bretchel, 50s.; Home, 40s.; Horton, 46s.8d.; Coton, 40s.; Lake, 13s.4d.; Hampton, 20s.; Brockton, 10s.; Worthen, 10s.; Beachfield, 30s.; Yockleton, 13s.4d.

The advowsons are omitted, but the following is added:

Weston and Binweston, 1 fee held by the heirs of John Corbet, 100s.

Walton, $\frac{1}{4}$ fee held by the heirs of Richard Hagre, 33s.4d.

Leigh, $\frac{1}{4}$ fee held by Thomas Corbet, 30s.

He died on 21 July last.

842 Writ, for fees, 9 Aug. 1403.

LINCOLN. Extent. Lincoln. 18 Sept.

He held the following by right of inheritance, extending at the amounts shown:

Bracebridge and Skellingthorpe, 2 fees once held by Hugh Wake, £11.

Little Kyme, 1 fee once held by Philip de Kyme, 100s.

Tathwell, $1\frac{1}{2}$ fees held by William Tathewell, £6; and $\frac{1}{4}$ fee held by Geoffrey de Appulby, 20s.

Thurlby, $\frac{1}{4}$ fee held by William Wastneys, 20s.

Braceborough, $\frac{1}{2}$ fee held by William Wastneys, 50s.

Carlby, 1 fee held by William Wastneys, 100s.

Bassingthorpe, $\frac{1}{3}$ fee held by Robert Bassetwyn, 33s.4d.

Denton, $\frac{1}{3}$ fee held by William FitzAlain, 33s.4d.

Bourne, $\frac{1}{3}$ fee in the hundred held by William Wastneys, 33s.4d.

Haconby, $\frac{1}{5}$ fee held by Robert Bagot, 20s.

North Rauceby, $\frac{1}{2}$ fee held by the prior of St. John of Jerusalem in England, 50s.

And in the right and inheritance of Anne his wife:

Holbeach in Holland, $2\frac{1}{2}$ fees in the manor once held by William son of Hugh Dakre, knight, the manor having once been held by Thomas Multon, £40.

Great Ponton, Little Ponton and Ganthorpe in Kesteven, $2\frac{1}{2}$ fees held by John de Haryngton, knight, and once by Philip de Paunton, £10.

South Thoresby by Belleau in Lindsey, $1\frac{1}{2}$ fees held by Thomas Chaworth, knight, and once by John de Caltoft, knight, £10.

843 Writ, for fees, 9 Aug. 1403.

WARWICK. Inquisition. Rugby. 21 Sept.

He held the following, extending at the amounts shown:

Barton, ¼ fee formerly held by Edmund Wayte, 25s.

Little Wolford, ½ fee held by William Ingram, 50s.

Great Wolford, 1 fee held by William Ingram, 100s.

Burmington, ½ fee and ¼ of ½ fee held by Humphrey de Stafford, 62s.

Compton Scorpion, 1 fee held by Thomas Burdet and Geoffrey Noreys, 100s.

Willington, ½ fee held by Robert Holeweye, 50s.

Compton Wynyates, ¼ fee held by Edmund de Compton, Thomas Hayron and Thomas Aveton, 25s.

Temple Tysoe, ½ fee held by the prior of St. John of Jerusalem in England, 50s.

Westcote, ½ fee held by the master of St. John's, Oxford, 50s.

Bubbenhall, 1 fee held by the heirs of John Beauchamp of Holt, 100s.

Ruin Clifford, ½ fee held by Alice Power, 50s.

Idlicote, 1 fee held by the prior of Kenilworth, 100s.

Norton Lindsey, 1 fee held by the earl of Warwick, 100s.

Edstone, ½ fee held by Agnes de Aillesbury, 50s.

Morton Bagot, ½ fee held by Alfred Trussell, 50s.; and ½ fee held by the prior of Kenilworth, 50s.

Wolverton, ⅐ fee held by the heirs of John Hastyng, 16s.8d.

Coton with Churchover, ½ fee held by the abbot of Combe, 50s.

Ditchford Ferry, ⅓ fee held by Henry de Sutton, 20s.

Oxhill, 1 fee held by the heirs of John Keynes and the abbot of Bordesley, 100s.

Oldberrow [recte Henley?] in Arden, ¼ fee held by William Beauchamp, 100s.

Oldberrow, 1 fee held by the abbot of Evesham, 100s.

Rowington, ¼ fee held by the abbot of Reading, 15s.

Botley, 1 fee held by John Malory, 100s.

844 Writ, for fees, 9 Aug. 1403.

CAMBRIDGE. Inquisition. Caxton. 18 Sept.

He held in his demesne as of fee the following, extending at the amounts shown:

Orwell and Arrington, 2 fees formerly held by the heirs of the earl of Winchester, £11.

Litlington, ¼ fee and ½ fee held by William Neuton, 30s. and 50s.

Bottisham, 1 fee held by the prior of Anglesey, William Wulff, Maurice Tone, Robert Passelewe, William Magote, Geoffrey Porter, John Jennys and William Mittleweye, 100s.

Horseheath, 1 fee held by the heirs of Richard Horset, 100s.

Harlton, 1 fee formerly held by the heirs of Richard Huntyngfeld, 100s.

He also held in right of Anne his wife:

Chippenham, ½ fee held by the abbot of Walden, 50s.

Fulbourn, 1 fee held by William Fulbourne, 100s.

Thriplow, ½ fee held by John Barrington, 50s.

Sawston, 3 fees held by John de Huntyngdon, £15.

Linton, 2 fees held by Robert Busteler, knight, and Thomas Sewale, £12 10s.

Haslingfield, ½ fee held by the prioress of Stratford, 50s.

He also held the right to present a servant to a corrody in the hospital of St. John of Jerusalem in Chippenham, with a sufficiency in victuals, clothing and lodging for his status there. The corrody is called 'Maundesvylestool' and is worth 100s. yearly. Eleanor, daughter of Humphrey earl of Hereford, the mother of Anne, and her predecessors from time immemorial presented when it was vacant whomsoever they wished, and the master of the house received them.

845 HUNTINGDON. Inquisition. Papworth St. Agnes. 19 Sept. 1403.

He held in his demesne as of fee, extending at the amounts shown:

Great Gransden, ½ fee formerly held by Warin Bassyngbourne and William Waleys, 60s.

Grafham, ½ fee held by the heirs of John Hemyngford, 60s.

Woolley, ½ fee held by John Styvecle, 40s.

Sawtry and Papworth [Cambs], 1¼ fees held by Thomas Hemyngton and Reynold Beaumys, £6.

Grafham. Offord, Hemingford and Thurning [Northants], ⅓ fee formerly held by Berengar le Moigne, 30s.

Stilton, ½ and ⅛ fee held by the prior of Bushmead, 60s.

Wood Walton, ⅔ fee held by Robert Bevill, 40s.

Folksworth, 1 fee held by Maud Pakenham, 60s.

Great Gidding, Luddington [Northants], Winwick, Litelhay, and Hail Weston, 1¹⁄₅₀ fees held by the prior of Huntingdon, 106s.

Papworth [Cambs], ⅓ fee held by the same prior and Geoffrey Cobbe, 30s.

Clapton [Northants], 1 fee held by the abbot of Thorney, £6.

Great Gransden, 1 fee held by John Wytherfeld, 50s.

Winwick, 1 fee held by Eleanor Knyvet, 100s.

Stilton, ⅑ fee held by Richard de Hemyngton, 10s.

Wood Walton, ⅓ fee held by John Bevyll, 40s.

He also held the advowsons of:

St. Neot's priory, temporalities worth £10 when it falls vacant; and a corrody there for one to receive as much as a monk there should or does receive, worth 100s. yearly.

Stonely priory, temporalities 10 marks.

Huntingdon, priory of St. Mary, of the honour of Gloucester in the dower of Anne his wife of the inheritance of Thomas her late husband, temporalities £10.

846 Writ, for fees, 9 Jan. 1403.

GLOUCESTER AND THE ADJACENT MARCH OF WALES. Inquisition. Thornbury. 21 Sept.

He held the following in the dower of Anne his wife, extending at the amounts shown:

Rendcomb and Hardwicke, 2½ fees held of him by Thomas de la Mare and Robert de la Mare, £73.

Doynton, 2 fees held by William Tracy, £60.

Charfield, 1 fee held by Robert le Veel, £20.

Eastleach Turville, 1 fee held by the heirs of William Lecche, £40.

Tytherington, 1 fee held by William de Clynton, £40.

Badgeworth and Shurdington, 1 fee lately held by Richard Talbot and 1 held by Lord Daudeley, £40.

Eldersfield [Worcs], 1 fee held by Thomas Berkeley of Coberley, £40.

Chaddesley Corbett [Worcs], 1 fee once held by William Corbet, £40.

Oxenton and Aston on Carrant, ½ fee once held by Lord Tiptoft, £40.

Kemerton, Aston on Carrant and Boddington, 1 fee once held by William de Bello Campo, £40.

Mangotsfield, 1 fee formerly held by Edmund Blount, £10.

'Bykynton', 1½ fees held by Matthew Gournay, £40.

Kemerton, 1 fee held by John de Bures, £20.

Dixton and Alderton, 2 fees held by John de Akelesdon, £10.

Shurdington, ⅕ fee held by William Cropet, 100s.

Dodington, ½ fee held by the heirs of Maud Cantelo, £34.

Shenington [Oxon], ⅕ fee held by John Pecche, 100s.; ⅕ fee held by Ralph de Stafford, 100s.; and ⅕ fee once held by Lambert de la More, 100s.

Bentham, 1 fee held by Henry de Harletre, 100s.

Lydney, ⅕ fee held by Robert de Lydon, 100s.

Sutton, ⅕ fee held by Richard de Sutton, 100s.

Walcot [Oxon], ½ fee held by the heirs of Senar de Walcote, 100s.

Walton Cardiff, 1 fee held by Edward de Kerdyf, £25; and 1 fee held by the abbot of Tewkesbury, £25.

Reddington, 1 fee held by Simon Basset, £10.

Crowell [Oxon], ⅓ fee held by Alan de Crawelle, 40s.

Hethe [Oxon], ½ fee held by the heirs of Baldwin de Lisle, 40s.; and ⅛ fee once held by the heirs of Thomas Tox, 20s.

Enborne [Berks], 1/15 of the marshall's fee, once held by Andrew de la Beche, 20s.

Iron Acton, 1 fee held by Robert de Poyntz, £30.

Little Marshfield, ⅓ fee held by James de Berkeley, £10.

Oldland, Upton Cheyney and Beach, ⅓ fee held by John de Bitton, £10.

Didmarton, Welford on Avon and Eastleach, 1 fee called 'Chamburleyns', £30.

Sharcott, Norcott and Preston, 2 fees held by Thomas de Raly, £48.

Siddington, ½ fee called 'Barebastes', 100s.

Kemerton and Baunton, 2 fees held by John de Dyclysdon, £70.

Also in the dower of Anne his wife the advowsons of North Cerney, extending at £10, and Rendcomb, 100s.

He held the following knight's fees in his demesne as of fee:

Tockington and Swell, 6 fees held by Nicholas Poyntz, £170.

Meysey Hampton with its members, 8½ fees held by lord le Seymor, £200.

Milton, ⅛ fee once held by Robert Feryby, 13s.4d.

And in the March of Wales belonging to the lordship of Newport:

Ebbw, 1 fee held by the duke of Lancaster, £10.

Basaleg, 1 fee held by Lawrence Berkeroulles, £10.

Coedcernyw, ½ fee once held by John ap Rees, 100s.

St. Brides, ½ fee once held by John de la More, 100s.

St. Mellons, ½ fee now held by Edmund Weldeyeve and his wife, 100s.

Began, ¼ fee held by John Kemeys, 40s.

Caerwent, 1 fee held by Geoffrey Lucy, £10.

And the advowsons of:

Michaelstone-y-Vedw, extending at 100s.

Machen, £6 13s.4d.

Bedwas, 100s.

Malpas priory, the patronage, a cell of Montacute, value unknown.

Barnsley, alternate presentations, in right of Anne his wife, £13 6s.8d.

Shirenewton, also in right of Anne, £13 6s.8d.

847 Writ, for fees, 11 Aug. 1403.

Essex. Inquisition. Chelmsford. 10 Sept.

He held the following:

Stambourne, ¼ fee and ½ fee once held by Alice Gestnyngthorp.

Great Burstead, ½ fee held by the abbot of Stratford.

Bardfield, ¼ fee held by the heirs of John Geney.

Morrell Roding, 1 fee held by Thomasia widow of William de Wauton, knight.

Chrishall, ¾ fee held by the heir of John de la Pole.

Gestingthorpe and Gosfield, 1 fee held by the heirs of John Butteturte.

Epping, Bentfield and Thorpe le Soken, 2 fees held by the heirs of Robert le Brus.

Cottered, ¼ fee held by the heirs of Martin le Chamberleyn.

Stanford Rivers, ½ fee held by the heir of John le Grace.

In right of the inheritance of Anne his wife he also held the following advowsons, extending when they occur at the amounts shown:

Chipping Ongar, 40s.; Barnston, 10 marks; South Fambridge, 100s.; Debden, £20; Quendon, 100s.; Shenfield, £8; Pleshey, free chapel in the castle, 100s.; Great Baddow, free chapel, 20s.; West Thurrock, 20 marks; Pleshey, college of Holy Trinity, temporalities £10; Wix, priory, temporalities 20 marks; Wethersfield, 20 marks.

848 Hertford. Inquisition. Bishop's Stortford. 11 Sept.

He held the following in right of the inheritance of Anne his wife:

Farnham, 1 fee formerly held by Walter Arderne.

North Mimms, 1½ fees once held by Thomas de Swanlond; and 1½ fees held by William de Kestevene, clerk.

Shenley, ¾ fee formerly held by Richard Salman.

Bushey, 1 fee once held by Geoffrey Jarpevylle and 1/10 fee once held by Aubrey de Byssheye, both formerly held by Edward prince of Wales.

Hoddesdon, 1 fee once held by Thomas de Bassynbourne.

Thorley, 1⅕ fees once held by Thomas Chirberge, knight, and ¼ fee held by the prior of Merton.

Stapleford, 1 fee formerly held by Walter atte Lee, knight.

Ayot St. Lawrence, 1 fee formerly held by Richard de Penbregge.

Enfield and Sawbridgeworth, 1 fee formerly held by Jordan de Elsyng.

Enfield, 1 fee which John Wroth formerly held.

Gilston, 1/20 fee held by John Davy and ½ fee held by John Dyeghere.

Sawbridgeworth, ½ fee formerly held by Hamelin de Matharm.

Bishop's Stortford, ½ fee once held by John Boys.

Bollington and Farnham, ½ and ¼ fee held by Fulk de Baa.

Sawbridgeworth, ½ fee held by Geoffrey de la Mare.

Hyde by Sawbridgeworth, ½ fee held by Geoffrey Josselyn.

Hunsdon, ¼ fee held by John de Goldyngton.

Barkway, ½ fee formerly held by Edmund Lancastre.

Hinxworth and Ashwell, 1 fee formerly held by John Gyldesburgh, knight.

Bushey and Digswell, 1 fee once held by Alice de Perrers.

Gilston, ½ fee formerly held by the heirs of John de Roos, ½ fee held by William Armurer and 1/10 fee formerly held by Peter de Goldyngton.

Digswell, ½ fee held by William Melksop.

Berden [Essex], ¼ fee held by the heirs of Lawrence Tany.

U

849 Writ, for fees, 5 Sept. 1403.

KENT. Inquisition. Tonbridge. 19 Sept.

He held the following:

Haleford, ¼ fee held by the heirs of Hugh le Despenser, John Haille and Simon Colebrant.

Pembury, ¼ fee held by Thomas Colpeper.

Crombury, ½ fee held by the heir of William Brampton.

Pimp, 1 fee held by the heirs of John de Pympe.

Henhurst, ½ fee held by the heirs of Gilbert de Henhurst and by John son of John Gervays.

Barming, ½ fee held by John son of Thomas Bermyng.

Brenchley, ½ fee held by Richard de Knolle; and ½ and 1/10 fee held by John de Pekham.

Hadlow, ½ fee held by John Colepepir, 1/6 fee held by Richard atte Berne and William Bakere of Peckham, 1/6 fee held by Richard de Bromfeld and 1/5 fee held by Thomas Fromond.

Ifield, 1 fee held by the heirs of Alice de Columbers.

Tonbridge, ½ fee held by the prior and convent of Tonbridge and John Berden.

Barming, ½ fee held by the heirs of Lora Payferot.

Shipbourne, ¼ fee held by the heirs of Roger Bavent.

Tonbridge, 1/6 fee held by Richard de Bromfeld.

Hadlow, 1/16 fee held by the heirs of Roger Swyft of the serjeanty of Tonbridge to the value of 6 fees.

Nettlestead, Pembury. Blackland and Helthe, 2 fees held by the heirs of Philip de Pympe and Thomas le Gegge.

Filston, ¾ fee held by the heirs of John de Vieleston.

Upper Hardres, Hartanger and Barfreston, 1 fee held by the heirs of Robert de Hardres.

Clowes and Ebolestone, ½ fee held by the heirs of John atte Welle.

Dodingdale, ¼ fee held by the heirs of John de Poldre.

Lackendon and Well, ½ fee held by Robert de Clyfford, esquire, for the life of his wife Joan, widow of Thomas de Garwynton, with reversion to the heirs of Thomas.

Chekeswell, Petts Wood and Ranscombe, 1 fee held by the heirs of William de Ore.

East Barming, ½ fee held by the heirs of Roger le Kent.

Tonbridge, ½ fee held by Roger Bardon.

Hadlow, 1/8 fee held by the heirs of Hugh de Causton and William Frankeleyn.

Leigh, Bidborough and Yalding, 1 fee held by the heirs of George Chaunz.

Mereworth, Old Hay and Cliffe, 2 fees held by William Beauchamp, knight, and 1/3 fee held by the heirs of Henry de Leybourne.

Trimworth and the suburbs of the city of Canterbury, 1½ fees held by the master of New College, Maidstone.

Filston, 'Witton', Penshurst and Chiddingstone, ¼ fee held by the heirs of John de Sheperham.

Eltham, ½ fee held by the heirs of Gilbert Vescy and ½ fee held by the heirs of John Hidle.

Milton and Filston, 1 fee held by William Septvantz, knight.

Ditton, Siffleton and Brompton, 1¼ fees held by the heirs of Ralph de Ditton.

Crundale, High Halden, Bethersden and Cranbrook, 1 fee held by the heirs of John de Hadelo.

Little Wigborough [Essex], 2 fees held by William Septvantz, knight.

Whitstable, 1/3 fee held by the heirs of Robert Grauntcourt, John son of John de

Bellinge, John Sprynge, John Badekyn, Walter de la Haye, Richard Leger, Thomas Bollynge and John son of Richard Bollynge.

Dodingdale, $\frac{1}{4}$ fee held by John son of William Berton of Ickham in right of his wife, daughter of Richard de Merton.

Sheldwich, 1 fee held by the earl of Oxford and the heirs of Lawrence de Huntyngfeld.

Bridge and Nackington, $\frac{1}{2}$ and $\frac{1}{4}$ fee held by the lord de Roos and the prior of St. Gregory's, Canterbury.

Blean, $\frac{1}{2}$ fee held by the master of the hospital of St. Thomas, Eastbridge, Canterbury.

He also held the advowsons of Tonbridge priory, annual value when it occurs £12 6s.8d.; Great Hardres, 66s.8d.; and Cowden, 100s.

In right of Anne his wife he held:

Harbilton in Harrietsham by Ospringe, $\frac{3}{4}$ fee of the honour of Mandeville, formerly held by William de Pympe and John Sistede.

Swingfield, 1 fee once held by Robert de Swynfeld.

Otterden, $\frac{1}{4}$ and $\frac{1}{10}$ fee once held by William de Otrenden.

Sevington, $\frac{1}{4}$ fee once held by John Satrendon.

Maytham and Rolvenden, 2 fees once held by William de Pympe.

Rolvenden, 2 fees once held by Richard atte Lese and the heirs of Henry Auger.

Dodingdale, $\frac{1}{2}$ fee in the manor.

Rolvenden, $\frac{1}{2}$ fee in the manor once held by Hawise de Mayhamme and once by William Pympe and 1 fee once held by Roger de Cassyngham.

Saynden, $\frac{1}{4}$ fee once held by the heirs of Joce de Otrenden.

Swingfield, $1\frac{1}{2}$ fees once held by William Aboke.

Two fees in the county held by the prior and convent of Bilsington.

Lossenham, $\frac{1}{4}$ fee once held by Henry Fitzauger.

Lowden in Rolvenden, 3 fees once held by Richard atte Lese, knight.

Knock and Ockley, $\frac{1}{2}$ fee held by the abbot and convent of Robertsbridge.

Staplehurst, $\frac{1}{4}$ fee once held by Robert de Marke and John Somery.

850 MIDDLESEX. Inquisition. Westminster, in St. Margaret's church. 22 Sept. 1403.

He held the following in right of the inheritance of Anne his wife:

Greenford and Stickleton, 2 fees formerly held by John de Bealmont and the prioress of Ankerwyke.

Enfield, $\frac{1}{5}$ fee once held by Jordan de Elsyng and once by John de Raria and $\frac{1}{5}$ fee once held by Jordan de Elsyng and formerly by Thomas Frescamp.

Northolt and Ickenham, 1 fee except a twentieth part, once held by Roger de la Doune and once by Adam Fraunceys.

South Mimms, 1 fee once held by Arnold Maundevile and held by the heirs of Roger Leukenore.

Stickleton, Islington and Hatton by Hounslow, $\frac{1}{2}$ fee held by the heirs of Robert de Norhthampton and once by Richard de Norhampton.

Stickleton, 1 fee held by the nuns of Ankerwyke and once by Hugh de Messenden.

Islington, 1 fee in the manor held by the heirs of John de Berners.

Date of death and heir as above.

851 Writ, for fees, 9 Aug. 1403.

STAFFORD. Inquisition. Wolverhampton. 17 Sept.

He held the following:

Blore and Grindon, 2 fees held by John Basset, knight; and 1 fee which the earl of Lincoln sometime held, 50s.

Ellastone, 1 fee held by Nicholas de Langford.

Tean, 1 fee held by the heirs of Ralph Basset of Sapcote.

Hopton and Tean, 2 fees held by John Savage and Maud his wife.

Madeley, 1 fee held by the heirs of Ralph Basset of Madeley.

Bramshall, 1 fee held by Thomas Erdeswyke.

Dilhorne, 1 fee held by Humphrey de Stafford.

Mitton, Ingestre and Gratwich, 2½ fees held by the heir of William Sheteswynde, knight.

Colton, 1 fee held by Thomas de Grosill, knight.

Bromley Bagots, 1 fee held by John Bagot, knight.

Tixall, 1 fee held by Roger Wostneys.

Salt, 1 fee held by Ivo de Salt.

Milwich, 1 fee held by the heirs of Ralph Olyvere.

Aston by Stone and Burston, 4 fees held by Robert Marschall and others.

Walton, 1 fee held by Henry de Walton.

Standon and Weston, ½ fee held by William de Weston.

Haughton and High Offley, 3 fees held by Humphrey de Halghton.

Tillington, ½ fee held by Thomas de Hopton and others.

Swynnerton, 1 fee held by the heirs of Henry de Verdoun.

Standon and Weston, 2 fees held by the heirs of Humphrey de Staundon.

Church Eaton, ⅓ fee held by the heir of Henry de Boring.

Hilderstone, 1 fee held by the heirs of Robert Bagot.

Burslem, ½ fee formerly held by Nicholas lord de Audeley.

Saredon, Shareshill and Pateshull, 3 fees held by William Shareshull, knight.

Stretton and Dunston, 1¼ fees once held by Richard de Stratton.

Dunston and Lower Drayton, ½ fee held by the heirs of William de Stafford.

Barton, ½ fee held by the heirs of Hugh de Leghe.

Blymhill and Brincton, ⅔ fee held by the heirs of John Bagot.

Acton Trussell, ⅔ fee held by Fulk de Pennebruk.

Wilbrighton, 1 fee held by Henry de Wilbrighton.

Church Eaton and Orslow, 1 fee held by the heirs of John Bryngton.

Barton, ½ fee held by the heir of Roger Taylour.

Syerscote and Wichnor, 1¼ fees held by the heirs of Res ap Greff', £6 10s.

Hamstall Ridware, part fee held by the heir of Roger Rydeware.

Oakley, ⅓ fee held by Thomas Erkyngton, 44s.

Mavesyn Ridware, ⅓ fee held by John Cameroy, 25s.

Rickerscote, ½ fee held by Humphrey de Stafford.

And the following advowsons:

Stafford, the free chapel, extending at 20s.

Stone, priory, £10.

Bradley, £8.

Spittal Pool, the chapel, in the dower of Anne his wife, [no value given].

852 BERKSHIRE. Inquisition. Faringdon. 26 Sept. 1403.

He held in right of the inheritance of Anne his wife:

Woodspean, two parts of the manor, of the king in chief, service unknown, annual value £6.

Date of death and heir as above.

He held the following in his demesne as of fee:

Denchworth and Padworth, 1 fee held of him by Amery Feteplace, 20s.

Hanney, ¼ fee, held by Hugh de Sancto Mauro, 5s.

Long Wittenham, 1 fee held by the heir of Robert de Stanford, 10s.

Enborne, $\frac{1}{20}$ fee held by John de Haveryng, 40s.

Hanney, 2 fees once held by the earl of Oxford; £40; and 1 fee held by William de Ripariis, 20s.

Stanford in the Vale, ⅛ fee held by [blank] atte Wyke, 2s.6d.

853　Writ 9 Aug. 1403.

OXFORD. Inquisition. Deddington. 27 Sept.

He held in right of the inheritance of Anne his wife:

Deddington, the manor, of the king in chief by the service of a third part of 2 knight's fees, annual value £13 6s.8d.

Great Haseley, the manor, of the honour of Wallingford by knight service, annual value £26 13s.4d.

Pyrton, the manor, of the honour of Wallingford by knight service, annual value £16 13s.4d.

He also once held in right of Anne the manor of Kirtlington, but granted it on 1 Jan. last to Nicholas Bradeshawe for life, and he still lives.

Date of death and heir as above.

He held the following (extending at the amounts shown):

Lower Heyford and Hampton Gay, 1 fee held by the heirs of William de Campo Arnulphi, 30s.

Shiplake, ½ fee held by Roger de Ingelfeld, 10s.

Swinbrook, ½ fee held by the heirs of Geoffrey de Cruce, 66s.8d.

Hethe, ½ fee held by the heirs of Theobald de Verdon, £10.

Finmere, 1 fee held by Robert de Fynmere, 20s.

Burford, ½ fee held by the heirs of William Fernacourt, 10s.

And in right of the inheritance of Anne his wife:

Kingham, ½ fee held by the lady of Langley and ½ fee held by the heirs of John Beaufo, each 50s.

Wendlebury, 1 fee formerly held by Amery de Sancto Amando, 100s.

Stonor, 1 fee once held by Edmund de Stonhore, 100s.

Latchford, ½ fee held by William Pyppard, 50s.

Haseley, the advowson, annual value when it occurs £40.

> C 137/38, 39, no.41
> E 149/80, no.3
> E 152/386, 389–91

EDWARD HASTYNGES, KNIGHT

854　Writ for proof of age of Edward Hastynges, knight, brother of Hugh, esquire, son of Hugh, knight, son of Hugh, knight, younger brother of John Hastynges, son of Hugh, knight, and heir of the same Hugh, father of John. 27 May 1403.

YORK. Proof of age. Carleton. 9 June.

The jurors say that he was born in the manor of Fenwick and baptised in the chapel of St. Mary in the Fields in the parish of Campsall on 21 May 1382, and was aged 21 on 21 May last.

Thomas Seintpoule, aged 46 years and more, has often been told by John abbot of Selby, the child's godfather and therefore knows.

Thomas Dilcock, 60 and more, has seen the abbot show a book in which this date of the birth was entered.

Nicholas de Brayton, 60 and more, had a son Nicholas born on 6 Dec. next before the birth of Edward. Had he lived he would now have been 21.

William Dawson, 50 and more, was in Pontefract on the day that Edward was born, and there saw a man unknown to him, who had been arrested for casting the evil eye on the horse of his neighbour, John de Hirn, and he then heard that Anne de Hastynges had been delivered of a male child, whom he afterwards heard called Edward.

John Britesvill, 50 and more, remembers because a wood called 'Wellowpark' was sold to divers persons by Hugh, Edward's father, on that 21 May.

Thomas Crull, 56 and more, heard Thomas late prior of Drax tell some bystanders at Drax that he was going to ride to the manor of Fenwick to be a godfather of Edward.

William de Thornton, 70 and more, remembers that John son of Joan Askern, now parish clerk of Campsall and aged 22 years and more, was born in the year preceding the birth of Edward, whose wet nurse Joan was, and John owing to his age expects this year to be ordained priest.

William de Knottyngley, 50 and more, having been summoned by the escheator to attend this proof of age, met a woman called Joan Parker, aged 80 and more and worthy of credence, and she swore that she was present at the birth and stayed with Hugh, the child's father for 3 years, and has since lived in Norton for 18 years, so that she knows that Edward was born 21 years ago.

Roger Chapman, 50 and more, says that there was an earthquake through all England when Edward was born in May 21 years ago.

John de Belton, 51 and more, says that Edward was born in the year after the rebellion of the commons of England at London, which was in the summer 22 years ago.

Thomas Tubholm, 56 and more, had a daughter Maud born on 3 May next before the birth of Edward, and she is now 21.

William de Belwode, 60 and more, was riding to Doncaster on 21 May 1382 when he fell from his horse and broke two ribs, and he heard that Edward was born on that day at the manor of Fenwick.

C 137/40 no.43

RICHARD SON AND HEIR OF THOMAS LATE EARL OF WARWICK

855 Writ for proof of age, 26 Jan. 1403.

WORCESTER. Proof of age. Worcester. 5 Feb.

He was born at Salwarpe and baptised there on 25 Jan. 1382, and was therefore 21 on the same day last past. The witnesses having been separately examined say that they know this for the reasons given:

Henry Bruyn, aged 50 years, was at Salwarpe on that day and saw Elizabeth le Despenser, the godmother, present in the church.

Henry Haggeley, 50, was an esquire of Henry Wakfeld, then bishop of Worcester, who baptised Richard.

John Power, 50, was an esquire of Walter prior of Worcester, who having heard of the birth sent a silver goblet with 100s. for the baptism.

Ralph Ardern, 43, says that his father and mother were at the house of Thomas earl of Warwick at Salwarpe and told him of the birth, and that Peter Holt received £10 for taking the news to the earl.

Thomas Throgmarton, 43, had a son John of the same age.

John Wassheburn, 50, saw Roger abbot of Evesham with the bishop at the baptism.

Thomas Lyttelton, 50, saw Alice formerly wife of Richard Stury, knight, at the baptism.

John Braas, 44, saw the bishop holding Richard at the font.

William Folyot, 50, saw Henry Bruyn carrying before Richard after the baptism a sword, which Hugh earl of Stafford gave to Richard on that day.

John Froxmere, 40, saw Thomas abbot of Pershore with the bishop at the baptism.

John Clynton, 50, carried a torch before Richard at the baptism.

William Botiller, 40, saw John Beauchamp of Holt, knight, at the baptism carrying two cloths of gold with the arms (*de exeunte*) of King Richard.

C 137/40, no.44

JOHN SON AND HEIR OF JOHN DE LEVYNGTON

856 Writ for proof of age, stating that he is in the ward of Mary widow of William de Stapulton, who should be warned. 7 Feb. 1403.

[Endorsed] Mary de Stapulton was summoned by John Brodsell and William Ryott and was present.

CUMBERLAND. Proof of age. Carlisle. 10 March (or 1 Sept.: Saturday before St. Gregory the pope).

The jurors say that he is aged 21 years and 4 months and more, having been born at Carlisle on 26 March 1380 [Monday after Lady Day 3 Richard II] and baptised in the church of St. Mary there. Duly examined, they say that they remember this for the following reasons:

John de Dalston, aged 50 years and more, heard mass at St. Mary's that day and saw the baptism.

William de Hoton, 46 and more, because that day the house(?) of Thomas Boteler, chaplain, was burnt down, and he came by the church to extinguish the fire and several men told him of the baptism.

Richard de Louthyre, 44 and more, bought a horse from Roger Cosour for 40s. at the church on that day and saw the baptism.

Thomas de Raghton, 52 and more, had a son Richard baptised after John de Levyngton.

Adam de Melle, 47 and more, came to the church to bury Margery his sister on that day and saw the baptism.

Adam de Denton, 48 and more, was coming to mass on that day when his arm was severely injured by a horse, and several men told him of the baptism.

John Cotyngham, 60 and more, going to mass on that day broke his right shin in a fall, and common talk was then of the birth.

Robert de Heymour, 43 years and more, was in the church for the marriage of John Roys and Maud daughter of Richard Orfare, and saw the baptism.

John Dalemour, 49 and more, because on that day at Carlisle John Williamson was killed by Thomas Dissed(?), who fled to the church after the felony, and he went in pursuit and was told of the baptism.

William de Britby, 50 and more, because on that day the cathedral bell-tower was blown down by a great wind, and he came there and saw the baptism.

William Bewcham, 50(?) and more, because his brother heard mass in the church on that day and the baptism was common talk there.

John Egglisfeld,, 60 and more, because John his brother was drowned that day in the river Eden, and he came to the church and saw the baptism.

C 137/40, no.45

JOHN DEYNCOURT, KNIGHT

857 Writ for proof of age of John Deyncourt, knight, brother and heir of Ralph Deyncourt, son and heir of William Deyncourt, deceased. 16 July 1403.

[Endorsed] Ralph earl of Westmorland, who held two parts of the lands, was summoned to attend the proof by John Laxston and William Pillay.

YORK. Proof of age. Stillingfleet. 13 Dec.

William Coupland, aged 56 years and more, John Waghen, 55 and more, and William Carter, 50 and more, remember that John Deyncourt, knight, was born at Middleham on 28 Feb, 1382 and baptised on 1 March in the church there, because on that 28 Feb. 21 years ago John son of William Coupland was promoted to priest's orders at York as appears by his letters shown to them.

William Hertesheved, 53 and more, William Baxster, 58 and more, Robert Magson, 58 and more, William Kampsall, 50 and more, and William Broun, 53 and more, were witnesses to livery of seisin of a messuage and 2 a. in Middleham to John Bryce on that day, and they then heard of the birth of John.

William de Morton, 56 and more, William Gayle, 54 and more, William Wryght, 50 and more, and William Smyth, 58 and more, remember because they were present on 1 March that year at the burial of Isabel late wife of John Perot at Middleham, saw John baptised and asked the bystanders about the birth.

C 137/40, no.46

NICHOLAS SON AND HEIR OF JOHN MOLYNS

858 Writ for proof of age; by the grant of John Frank he was in the ward of John Bernard, who should be warned of the inquisition. 27 Nov. 1402.

SOMERSET. Proof of age. Ilchester. 15 March 1403.

The jurors say that Nicholas is aged 21 years and more, having been born at South Petherton on 24 June 1380, and baptised in the church of St. Peter there.

Robert Lambrouk, 64, knows because he was present in the church when John Hayward, chaplain, baptised Nicholas and wrote the day and year in a missal in the church.

John Mucheldever, 54, came with Nicholas, then prior of Muchelney abbey, to the church, where the prior was godfather, and he saw the date written in the missal.

John Mede, 60, was present and had a son William born in the same year.

John Peny, 48, came to the church on that day, and on the Sunday before he had married Alice daughter of Robert Lambrouk.

John Warmwell, 44, was with Robert Lambrouk in the church and contracted marriage with Margery his daughter.

Henry Humerford, 60, John Holme, 64, Robert Boton, 68, and Philip Batte, 55, were at a fair at South Petherton on that feast [Midsummer day], they were called from it to bear witness and were present when John Hayward wrote the date.

John Bryce, 50, John Wodehous, 56, John Bokerell, 60, were present in the church at the baptism and were called to bear witness; and on that day John Molyns granted to John Spore and Edith his wife 3 a. in South Petherton for their lives by a charter so dated.

C 137/40, no.49

ELIZABETH WIDOW OF ROBERT SCALES, KNIGHT

859 Writ to assign dower, 5 March 1403.

CAMBRIDGE. Assignment of dower, in the presence of Lawrence Trussebut and William Lampet, next friends of Robert son and heir of Robert Scales. Haslingfield. 7 May.

One chamber with 1 chimney called 'le Squyerschambre' next to a chamber called 'le Knyghteschambre' inside the moat with all the rooms from the 'Knyghteschambre' to the end of the bridge, with free ingress and egress within the moat; a garden also within, to the west end of the hall, called the 'Kychengarden' with fruit and pasture; a third part of a dovecot in the same garden; 1 house called 'le Stots. . .' situated between the 'couhous . . .stable' under one roof; half a barn called 'le Oteberne' in the west, with a house called 'le Chauffhouse' by the barn on the south; a third part of the large barn; a third part of a barton by the 'Aldefelde'; and a third part of a barn there; all with free ingress and egress.

Farm of free tenants: Walter Phelip for a tenement bought from Thomas Bradfeld, formerly of John Hied(?), 6¼d. and half a farthing; John Stacy, 22d.; Margery Asshby, 11½d.; John Jake, 47½d.; John Knyght, chaplain, 9d.; Agnes Bysshop, 15s.; Thomas Robat, 3s.4d.; . . . and 1 capon; Thomas Pappeworth, 17½d.; . . .; William Amys, 3s.10d.; John Ey, senior, 17d. and half a farthing; Thomas Rown, 3s.8¼d.; Henry Masoun, 23d. and half a farthing; John Shymmyng, 9½d.; Agnes Scot of Barrington, 1d.; Thomas Serle 1 capon.

Total . . .

Farm of servile tenants . . .

[Part of two more paragraphs, torn and illegible].

C 137/40, no.51

OSBERT SON AND HEIR OF OSBERT DE MUNDEFORD

860 Writ for proof of age, 22 Oct. 1402.

NORFOLK. Proof of age. Hockwold. 21 Nov.

The jurors say that he was aged 21 on 25 Sept. last, having been born at Hockwold and baptised there on 25 Sept. 1381.

[The statements by the following jurors are illegible] Thomas Moncheney and William Eyre, each aged 50 years and more, Stephen Bate and Robert Kavell, each 40 and more, John Phelipp, senior, and John Stede, each 45 and more, William Mountford and John Waterman, each 60 and more, John Freman and William Ferers, each 48 and more.

John Cheseman and John Norman, each 43 and more, remember the date because Thomas Norman, brother of John, died on that day after 9 and before 3 o'clock.

C 137/40, no. 52

JOAN WIDOW OF EDMUND DUKE OF YORK

861 LONDON. Assignment of dower. 12 Dec. 1403.

£96 8s. 10½d., being a third part of £289 6s. 8d. payable from the custom of wools and woolfells since 28 Nov. 1402 by the collectors.

Edward now duke of York was warned to be present by Hugh Battesford and Walter Staunton.

862 Writ to assign dower, 22 May 1403.

LINCOLN. Assignment of dower.

From Grantham, where his rents and services, with soc, lands and tenements, tolls and perquisites of court extended at £100 12s. 3d.:

Great Ponton, with its appurtenances in Denton, Belton, Harlaxton and Harrowby, with lands, tenements, rents, services, wards, marriages, reliefs, escheats and all other appurtenances, annual value £21 1s. 10d.

Harlaxton, £4 8s. ½d. from various lands and tenements called the fee of 'Brewes' so let to farm to John Grene of Grantham.

Grantham, a third part of the tolls of markets and fairs, and of forfeitures, escheats, and other profits and commodities arising from perquisites of courts with soc of the same.

From Stamford, where all lands and tenements extend at £80: 2 watermills £4 6s. 8d.; houses and shops of various tenants, £4 17s. 6d., viz Roger Fraunceys 16s., William Dobyn 14s., John Draper 9s., Robert Massthorp 3s., William Tyerd 13s. 4d., John Spillesby 12d., William Fletcher 10s., John Algode 5s., John Cadeney 14d., John Chaloner, senior, 8s., John Barker 2s., John Forster 2s., John Pitt 6s., Nicholas Tabard 6s. and Robert Asshborne 12d.; from various demesne lands let to farm 55s. 11d., viz John Longe 17s., Henry Cok 5s. 4d., Gilbert Apethorp 6s. 3d., William Stacy 6s. 8d., John Apethorp 4s., Richard Bonde 4s., John Gervays 3s., John Cobto of Ryhall 2s. 8d., John Carter 2s., Richard Benefeld 3s. and Robert Grafton 2s.; and a third part of all wastes, tolls of markets and fairs, forfeitures, escheats and perquisites of courts there.

863 Writ to assign dower, 22 May 1403.

NORTHAMPTON. Assignment of dower.

Fotheringhay: from all the lands etc. of the duke in Fotheringhay where the castle and manor extend at £80:

From various free tenants, 20s. 1½d.: viz abbot of Sawtry 10s.; John Knyvet 8d.; Henry Bracy 6s. 8d.; William Webster 2s. 3d.; and rent of 'Swanneholme' 6d.

Rents of cottagers, 9s. 6½d.: James Sumpter 7s.; John So. . . 12d.; Robert Derby 6d.; and William Hauseman 12d.

Rents of servile tenants, £13 8s.: viz Thomas Austyn 36s. 8d.; William Taillour

36s.8d.; John Horne 36s.8d.; Walter Holand 18s.4d.; John Hoghton 18s.; John Olneye and William Lessy 13s.4d.; William Taunt 26s.8d.; Hugh Grovelane 15s.; John Hoghton 26s.8d.; Robert de Vye 26s.8d.; and John del Chambre 13s.4d.

Farm of bakery and mills, 31s.1¼d.; farm of fisheries from William Hunne and Nicholas Petit, 8s.9¼d.; and from Robert Wyrtrynham, clerk, farmer of the castle land there, 4s.2d.

A third part of all the demesne lands: 'Parkewong', 'Darnwellwong' and 'Langethor-newellwong'; ½ a. under 'Chalkehill'; 12 a. in 'Toftewong' by 'Tofteshall'; 'Littilbury-morewong'; 4 a. called 'Leys' in 'Westondewong'; 12 a. in 'Risshcroft' by the mill; 'Curtellwong', le Conynghere', 'Cunnlynshade', 7 selions on the 'Curtellwong'; 38 a. meadow in the meadow called 'Wyldeholme' to the north; 7 a. meadow in 'Horsec-roft' to the west; 10 a. in 'Westmedowe' to the west; and 60 a. in the meadow called 'Arneweys' to the south with the meadows called 'Fremannesmedowe' and 'Warmyng-tonmedowe'.

A third part of the moor and pasture, namely 'Estmore' and 'Oxmore'; a third of the park on the east, with a third of the . . . and of the woods belonging to the lordship, with a third of the profits from the perquisites of court, and a third of all casual profits whatsoever.

Nassington and Yarwell, a third part of the lordship extending at £68 yearly, com-prising £12 18s.8d. from assize rents at Yarwell; 13s.9d. from rents of tofts there; 39s.9d. small rents; 12d. from Wansford; £7 6s.2d. from various tenants of the fee called 'Doddisfee' in Nassington, viz Thomas Chaddelerove 14s., Robert Levyng 8s., Robert Bilby 9s., Henry Chaddelrode 9s.6d., Henry Bracy 16s., William Wryght 26s., John Welden 6s., William Kay 3s.6d., John Cole 8s., John Brown 20s.2d., Agnes Norman 8s., William Brown 8s., John Mounteyn 8s. and John Taillour 12d.; with one third of the profits of courts and of all casual revenues.

864 Writ to assign dower, 22 May 1403.

YORK. Assignment of dower. 13 Aug.

Firstly, Conisbrough, Braithwell, and Clifton, the manors and vills, with all their members, lands and tenements, rents, services, wards, marriages, reliefs, escheats, knight's fees, advowsons, mills, suits of court of free tenants and villeins with their offspring, with hall of pleas at Conisbrough, the pond called 'Casteldame', the park of Conisbrough with game, agistment and pannage, 'housebot', 'haibot', 'feirebot' in the park, with all other profits of the offices of the bailiwick of Conisbrough, as of the offices of reeves of Conisbrough, Braithwell and Clifton.

Then, Hatfield, the vill and lordship with a third part of the manor, two long chambers, a bakery with other small chambers adjoining, a granary in the site of the manor, with half the long stable, a third of the garden towards the north, next to the bounds there, and of a granary next to the church, that is in the east end; with the park of Hatfield with game, agistment and pannage, with 'housebot', 'haibot' and 'fairebot' in the park.

Dowsthorpe, the vill, with all its members, lands and tenements . . . villeins with their offspring [as above under Conisbrough], with all the fishery of 'Countesmer' with a park in 'Counteyseng' lying next to Tudworth with free ingress and egress to the fisheries and with sufficient ground to draw and dry their nets and bow(?) (*ad tractand' et siccand' recia arcumquaque*), a third part of the warren and the chase of Hatfield, namely the bailiwick of Clownes with all other profits whatever of the offices of reeves of Hatfield and Dowsthorpe.

Similarly Holmfirth, the town and lordship, with all its members, appurtenances and mills, and the wood called 'Owtwode' of Wakefield in the west of that wood, with lands, tenements etc. [as above under Conisbrough], and all other profits of the office of reeve of Holmfirth, saving always free ingress and egress to Edward duke of York to the same for cutting, carting and selling the great timber for repairing houses and for large fuel.

Also £133 6s. 8d. from the grant of £400 yearly from the customs of wool in Kingston upon Hull, and £33 6s. 8d. from the grant of £100 from the same customs.

C 137/40, nos. 53, 54

PETRONILLA WIDOW OF HUGH MORTYMER

865 SHROPSHIRE. Assignment of dower in the manor of Quatt by the escheator, who afterwards took her oath not to marry without the king's licence.

1 chamber where the manor formerly was, length 36 feet, width 15 feet; 1 little toft annexed to it, length 14 feet, width 10 feet; 1 close called 'Home close', 4 a., annual value 5s.; 1 pasture called 'Byrches', 4 a., 4s.; 1 pasture called 'Westfeldes', 16 a., 10s.; 1 messuage with garden and ½ virgate held by John Hancokes, 3s.; 1 messuage, 1 garden and ½ virgate held by Roger Fuller, 3s.; 1 messuage, 1 garden and 1 virgate held by Thomas Piers, 10s.; 1 messuage, 1 garden and 1 virgate held by John Wygan, 5s.; 1 messuage, 1 garden and ½ virgate held by John Tandy, 4s.; 1 messuage, 1 garden and ½ virgate held by Richard Hulle, 5s.; 1 messuage, 1 garden and ½ virgate held by Constance Bacon, 6s.; 1 cottage held by John Webbe, 2s.; 1 cottage and ½ virgate held by John Harlewyn . . . 1 lb. cumin; 1 ruinous cottage and 1 a., nil; 1 cottage and ½ virgate held by Walter Turnour, 10d.(?); and 1 fishery opposite the tenement of Hugh Dodmaston and 1 a., nil.

Total 59s. 10d.

C 137/40, no. 55

ELEANOR WIDOW OF AMERY DE ST. AMAND

866 BEDFORD. Assignment of dower from the manor of Harlington. 23 March 1403.

Site of the manor. Firstly assigned within the site of the manor: 1 barn, 1 . . . called . . . with garden, with ingress and egress protected by the common way to the spring within the site.

Rents of freemen, villeins and rent-paying cottars: 10s. from William Huntewene senior for his rent and all other services and customs; 16s. 11d. from John Oseberne; 13s. 8d. from Richard Archer; 13s. from John Martyn; 11s. 6½d. from Robert atte Hale; 4s. 9½d. from Thomas Boltere beyond 2s. 3¼d. paid to the king; 14s. from. . . Cholestre; . . .9½d. from Edmund Croy; 12s. 6d. from William Longe; 5s. 5½d. . . .; 4s. 6d. from John Lyncolne; 16¼d. from John Buckeby, senior; 19s. 10d. from William . . .; 7¼d. from Eleanor Matheu beyond 2s. 6¾d. paid to the king; and 4s. from various . . .

Total £7 . . . ¼d.
[22 lines mostly illegible].

C 137/40, no.57

HUGH DE ANNESLEY KNIGHT

867 Commission to Hugh de Shirley, Thomas Frisby, John Curson, Peter de la Pole and the escheator to enquire what he held in Nottinghamshire. 3 June 1403 [*CPR 1401–5*, p.278].

NOTTINGHAM. Inquisition before Thomas Frysby, John Curson and the escheator. Kingston upon Soar. 16 June.

He held 1 messuage and 3½ bovates in Ruddington, which were once of Roger Perpointe, and 'Magotdoghterland' in his demesne as of fee of the king in chief of the castle of Castle Donington, parcel of the duchy of Lancaster, by knight service, annual value 13s.4d.

He died on 23 Sept. 1401. Hugh de Annesley his son and heir is aged 8 years. John de Clyfton, clerk, has held since he died, title unknown. What lands he held of others is likewise unknown.

C 137/40, no.58

WILLIAM DE LAWYS

868 YORK. Inquisition *ex officio*. Richmond castle. 3 March 1403.

William de Lawys of North Cowton died about 5 years ago holding 2 messuages and 30 a. arable and meadow in his demesne as of fee in North Cowton, annual value 5s.

Thomas his son and heir is an idiot. John de Lawys has held and taken the profits to the date of this inquisition, and is answerable to the king for them.

C 137/40, no.59

ELIZABETH WIDOW OF NICHOLAS PYCHARD

869 ESSEX. Inquisition *ex officio*. Castle Hedingham. 4 Nov. 1402.

She held the manor of Eyston Hall in Belchamp Walter for life by the grant of John de Veer, late earl of Oxford, grandfather of Robert de Veer, duke of Ireland, with reversion to himself and his heirs, annual value 66s.8d. Owing to the death of Elizabeth and the forfeiture of the duke it should belong to the king.

She died on 7 May 1395. John Baryngton, John Aylemer and Richard Ferrour have occupied the manor and taken the profits since her death, by the grant of Aubrey de Veer, uncle and heir of Robert.

E 149/81, no.8

ROBERT DE WHATTON

870 NOTTINGHAM. Inquisition *ex officio*. Bingham. 28 Aug. 1403.

He held 1 messuage in Wiverton Hall in his demesne as of fee of the honour of Peverel by a rent of 2s. payable by equal parts at the court of Peverel at Nottingham at Easter and Michaelmas, and by two attendances at that court, annual value 40s.

He died about Michaelmas 1398. John de Kneveton and Agnes, formerly wife of Robert, have taken the issues since then. John his son and heir is aged 7 years and more.

E 149/81, no.12

JOHN CHARNELS

871 LEICESTER. Inquisition taken at Leicester in the court of the honour of Leicester and the duchy of Lancaster by William Byspham, feodary in Warwickshire and elsewhere in the honour and duchy, by virtue of the king's letters under the duchy seal. 23 Jan. 1403.

John Charnels of Bedworth, esquire, held in his demesne as of fee certain lands and tenements in Pailton, [Warwickshire], and by his charter enfeoffed William Pareys, parson of Widdrington, John de Grenehull of Attleborough and William Clerkes of Green End to them and their heirs. They granted them by charter on 26 April 1386 to John Charnels, Elizabeth his wife, and the heirs and assigns of John, and they were so held until he died.

The feodary having heard that John was sole tenant in his demesne as of fee and that he had died without heirs took the premises into the king's hands. They are held of the king of the duchy of Lancaster.

E 149/82, no.6

ELIZABETH CHEDDAR

872 WILTSHIRE. Inquisition. Calne. 8 Feb. 1403.

Elizabeth wife of Richard Chedder is the granddaughter and heir of Robert Cauntelo, formerly husband of Maud Cauntelo, being the daughter of his son Robert.

E 152/391, no.2

JULIANA CHAUMBERLEYN

873 Writ 8 Nov. 1403.
CAMBRIDGE. Inquisition. Babraham. 24 Nov.

She held in her demesne as of fee of the king in chief 1 messuage and 20 a. 1½ roods in Sawston as a thirtieth part of a knight's fee, annual value 3s.4d.

She died on 16 April last. John Prat her son and next heir is aged 30 years and more.

C 137/41, no.1

E 149/82, no.11

THOMAS SOUTHAM

874 Writ, *devenerunt*, asking what lands he had acquired in Stapenhill and elsewhere. 8 June 1404.

DERBY. Inquisition. Measham. 6 Aug.

He lately acquired in Stapenhill 34 a. and a parcel of meadow in the fields of Heathcote called 'Cadlowesyche', annual value 32s.; 1 messuage, 2 virgates and 1 a. meadow called 'Kirkemedewe', annual value 50s.; and 1 messuage and 15 a., annual value 12s. Of whom they are held and by what service is unknown. They came into the hands of the abbot and convent of Burton on Trent and so remain, without royal licence.

C 137/41, no.2

CHRISTINA WIDOW OF GEOFFREY ALEYNS OF CROMER

875 Writ 3 Feb. 1404.

NORFOLK. Inquisition. Thorpe Market. 1 July.

She held the manor of East Beckham of the king in chief in fee tail as an eighth part of a knight's fee by the grant of Roger Virly, Simon de Blyklyngge, Peter de Lyngwode and William de Tonne, chaplain of Aylsham, by licence of Edward III [*CPR 1350–4*, p.486] to Geoffrey and Christina and the heirs of their bodies, with successive remainders to Roger brother of Geoffrey and his heirs, William their brother and his heirs, and the right heirs of Christina, annual value 45s.

She held in fee tail 1 messuage, 35 a. and 24s.2d. rent in Shipden, payable by equal parts at Easter and Michaelmas, of Walter de Walyngton, Simon Felbrygge, knight, John Reynold, John Herdyng and the heirs of Robert Herward, with remainders as above, service unknown, annual value 13s.

She died on 8 July 1392, and all should descend to Cecily daughter and heir of Robert Aleyns, son of Roger, because Geoffrey and Christina died without heirs. Cecily was aged 15 on 2 Feb. last and is married to Edward son of Edward Durdaunt of Buckinghamshire.

Edward Durdaunt, deceased, Benjamin Everard of Shipden and William Ulp of East Beckham held the premises and took the profits from the death of Christina until 2 Feb. last.

C 137/41, no.5

ROBERT ROBELL

876 Writ 12 April 1404.

NORFOLK. Inquisition. Norwich. 15 July.

Robert Robell of Great Yarmouth held a quarter of the manor of Hempstead, except

6½ a. which James Jeneye now holds, in his demesne as of fee of the king in chief by the service of half a quarter of a knight's fee, annual value 23s. 3½d.

He held 3 a. and half a messuage in Hempstead of the prior of Hickling of his manor of Netherhall by a rent of 2d., annual value 16d.

He died on 24 Feb. 1404. Thomas his son and next heir is aged 23 years and more.

C 137/41, no. 7

CONSTANCE WIFE OF JOHN WATIRSHIPE

877 Writ 10 March 1404.

KENT. Inquisition. Canterbury. 19 March.

As fourth sister and heir of William Cundy of Sandwich Constance took a quarter of £30 rent from the farm of the city of Canterbury to herself and her heirs, granted to Cundy by letters patent of Edward III [*CPR 1354–8*, p. 326], £10 at Easter and £20 at Michaelmas.

She died on 26 Feb. last. Joan wife of Thomas Mayhew of Sandwich and Margaret wife of Robert Fygge of the Isle of Thanet are her daughters and next heirs, both aged 24 years and more.

C 137/41, no. 8

ROGER DE BURLETON

878 Writ 20 Oct. 1403.

SHROPSHIRE. Inquisition. Shrewsbury. 19 Nov.

He held in his demesne as of fee 1 tenement in Leighton of the king in chief in socage, by a rent of 40d. payable by the sheriff by equal parts at Lady Day and Michaelmas, annual value 13s. 4d.

He died on 16 Oct. last. William his son and heir is aged 14 years and more.

C 137/41, no. 9
E 149/83, no. 7

STEPHEN BAROWE

879 Writ 19 April 1404.

HEREFORD. Inquisition. Hereford. 10 May.

He held in fee tail of the king in chief 1 messuage, 96 a. arable, 3 a. meadow and 100s. rent in Lower Bullinghope, Clehonger and Hereford as a fifth part of a knight's fee, annual value 113s. 4d.

He died on 19 March last. Henry his son and heir is aged 40 years and more.

C 137/41, no. 10
E 149/83, no. 3

WILLIAM SOLERS

880   Writ 28 Sept. 1403.

GLOUCESTER. Inquisition. Chipping Campden. 8 Oct.

He held one quarter of 3 messuages, 2½ virgates and 7 a. meadow in Weston Subedge in his demesne as of fee of the king in chief by knight service, annual value 7s.

He died on 21 May last. John his son and heir was aged 13 at Christmas last.

C 137/41, no.11

KATHERINE ONE OF THE DAUGHTERS AND HEIRS OF THOMAS DE MALTON

881   Writ 8 Feb. 1404.

YORK. Inquisition. York castle. 3 April.

She held half of a ruinous messuage, 4 waste tofts and 24 bovates of waste land in Great Givendale and of 4 bovates of waste land in Little Givendale of the king in chief by one quarter of the serjeanty of finding a crossbowman in York castle for 40 days when there is war in Yorkshire, annual value 13s.4d.

She died on 15 June 1379. Elizabeth wife of Hugh Standyssh, esquire, of Lancashire, aged 60 years and more is her sister and heir because she has no surviving issue. The lands have been in the king's hands since Katherine's death.

C 137/41, no.12, mm.1,2

THOMAS DE PLUMLAND

882   Writ 11 May 1404.

YORK. Inquisition. York castle. 12 March 1405.

The lands named in the last inquisition [the bovates not being described as 'waste'] with the addition of one quarter of a wood in Great Givendale, and again valued at 13s.4d., came into the king's hands owing to the death of Katherine de Malton and the minority of Thomas de Plumland her son and heir, and so they remain.

He died on 7 Feb. 1379. Elizabeth his aunt, wife of Hugh Standyssh, his heir is aged 60 years and more.

C 137/41, no.12, mm.3,4

JOHN SON OF HUGH HASTYNGES, KNIGHT

883   Writ 18 Oct. 1403.

HAMPSHIRE. Inquisition. Winchester. 6 Nov.

He held 2 a. in Sutton Scotney in the field called 'Hentechele' between the lands formerly of William le White on both sides in his demesne as of fee of the king in chief by knight service, annual value 12d.

He died on 31 Aug. 1393. Edward Hastynges is next heir, being the brother of Hugh, esquire, son of Hugh, knight, son of Hugh, knight, younger brother of John. He was aged 21 on 24 May last.

C 137/41, no.13, mm.3,4

HUGH HASTYNGES, KNIGHT

884 Writ 18 Oct. 1403.

HAMPSHIRE. Inquisition. Winchester. With same jurors as last. 6 Nov.
He held 2 a. in Sutton Scotney [as in last].
He died on 2 Nov. 1396. Edward Hastynges, knight, his brother and heir, was aged 21 on 24 May 1403.
The escheators have held the land and taken the profits for the king since the death of Hugh.

C 137/41, no.13, mm.1,2

THOMAS DE LANGTON

885 Writ 28 Jan. 1404.

LINCOLN. Inquisition. Alford. 4 March.
He held a fifth part of the lordship and soke of Mumby in his demesne as of fee of Anne late queen of England, of the honour of Richmond by knight service, annual value £14.
It was in the queen's hands owing to his death and the minority of his son John. The queen took the profits from Thomas's death until her own death. Since then John Bell of Boston has held it by virtue of letters patent of Richard II.
He also held in his demesne as of fee the manor and advowson of Langton, of John duke of Lancaster and Thomas earl of Kent by knight service, annual value £10. The duke, the earl and their executors held them until 25 April 1393 owing to the minority of the heir.
John his son and next heir was aged 21 on 6 Jan. last.

C 137/41, no.14

JOHN SON AND HEIR OF THOMAS DE LANGTON

886 Writ for proof of age; his lands being in the custody partly of John Bell of Boston and partly of the executors of John duke of Lancaster and Thomas earl of Kent, they should be warned. 17 March 1404.
[Endorsed] John Bell was warned at Mumby and the executors at Langton, all on 29 March by Thomas Swynshed and Robert Walton
LINCOLN. Proof of age. Partney. 8 April.
The jurors say that John son of Thomas de Langton, who held in chief of the honour of Richmond, was 21 on 29 Dec. last, having been born at Langton by Sausthorpe and baptised in the church there on 29 Dec. 1381 [sic].
Being separately examined, they say that they know for the reasons given below:
John Northorp of Sausthorpe, aged 60 years and more, was in the church at the

baptism and says that the name and date of birth were written in a great missal in the church.

Walter son of Robert Langton, 44 and more, had a son William born on the next day.

Walter Tateshale of Langton, 49 and more, was sent to find John de Marham, chaplain, who was a godfather.

Hugh Justice of Sausthorpe, 50, was bailiff of Thomas the father in Langton and accounted for the issues of the manor from Michaelmas before the birth and had an acquittance, by the date of which he knows when John was born.

Henry Godeale of Sausthorpe, 48, purchased for himself and his heirs 1 a. in Langton at Easter after the birth and knows by the date of the charter.

Henry Cutman, 50, had a daughter married on 1 Nov. following the birth.

John Pylett, 44, and Thomas South, 50, were in the church at the baptism with a jug of wine and also with dinner, and John Northorp and John Marham were godfathers, and they and all the other people there ate and drank.

Alexander Stacy, 54, and Richard Abott, 50 and more, were witnesses to a charter by which the father bought a messuage for himself and his heirs at Midsummer before the birth,

Thomas son of Nicholas de . . ., 48, and William Gylyott, 42, set out for Lincoln at Michaelmas before the birth, and it rained so heavily and the waters rose so much that they scarcely avoided being drowned.

C 137/45, no.53

KATHERINE WIDOW OF JOHN SON OF JOHN WARBLETON

887 Writ 12 Feb. 1404.

HAMPSHIRE. Inquisition. Basingstoke. 15 April.

She held 80 a. waste assart in the heath in Hazeley in her demesne as of fee of the king by a rent of 4s. 10¾d. payable by the sheriff, annual value nil.

Jointly enfeoffed with her late husband she held the manor of Sherfield upon Loddon by the gift of John Foxle, knight, made with the king's licence [*CPR 1401–5*, p.466] to them for their lives with remainder to Thomas de Warbleton, her husband's son, and his heirs male. It is held of the king in grand serjeanty by the service of being marshal of the whores, of dismembering evildoers when condemned, and of measuring gallons and bushels in the king's household, annual value £13 2s. 2½d.

She also held for life by the gift and grant of Arnold Brocas, clerk, with remainder to the right heirs of her husband: 1 messuage and 1 carucate in Chineham of Thomas de Ponynges, Lord St. John, service unknown, annual value 40s.; 1 messuage and 1 carucate in Preston Candover of John de Camoys, service unknown, annual value 20s.; 1 messuage and 60 a. in Basingstoke of the king of the manor of Basingstoke by a rent of 20s. payable to that manor, annual value 10s.; and 1 messuage, 40 a. arable and 4 a. meadow in Stratfield Turgis of Edward Boclond of his manor of Heckfield by a rent of 1d., annual value 10s.

Thomas son of John Warbleton had issue William and died. Katherine died on 7 Feb. last. William, son of John, son of Thomas and Katherine, her next heir, is aged 22 years and more.

888 Writ, *plenius certiorari*, citing an inquisition before Robert Loxle concerning the manor of Warbleton [*CIPM* XVI, no.179] and inquiring who were the heirs of John and Alice Warbleton. 3 Dec. 1403.

SUSSEX. Inquisition. East Grinstead. 8 Jan. 1404.

John Warbelton, father of John, and Alice his wife had an heir of their bodies, namely John Warbelton. John the father died. John the son married Katherine daughter of John Foxle, knight. They had issue Thomas. John the son died. Thomas married Joan daughter of John Hay, knight. They had issue William Warbleton, who still lives. Thomas is dead.

William son of Thomas is next heir of John, father of John, and Alice, being son of Thomas, son of John, son of John, son of John, father of John and Alice.

889 SURREY. Inquisition. Tandridge. 7 Jan. 1404.

Findings as in last.

C 137/41, no.15
E 149/83, no.14

WILLIAM WARBLETON

890 Writ for proof of age; William More who has the wardship of the lands should be warned. 3 Dec. 1403.

HAMPSHIRE. Proof of age of William Warbleton, son of Thomas, son of John, son of John and Alice, and heir of John, father of John, and Alice. Basingstoke. 11 Jan. 1404.

Thomas Coufold, aged 60 years and more, and Thomas Baldok, 52 and more, say that he is 21, having been born at Sherfield upon Loddon on 6 April 1381 and baptised that day in St. Leonard's church there. They remember because that day they were retained for life by Katherine Warbleton, then lady of Sherfield.

William Tighale, 51 and more, and William Burgeys, 49 and more, remember by the date, 5 April, of a bond by which they bound themselves in a sum of money to Katherine Warbleton.

John Leche, 45 and more, and Stephen Waspell, 62 and more, were in the church to hear mass and saw the baptism.

John Shipver, 48 and more, and Stephen Sherveld, 64 and more, were wrestling together within the site of the manor of Sherfield on that day, and John broke Stephen's shin.

Thomas Gregory, 48 and more, and Thomas Leche, 46 and more, had a dispute and reached agreement by indenture on that day, and know the age of William by the date of the indenture.

William Overton, 53 and more, and Robert Many, 61 and more, were at Sherfield that day with several others practising archery beside the churchyard, and the same day dined with Katherine and heard the common talk about the birth and the baptism.

C 137/41, no.15, mm.7, 8

ROGER DE PYCHEFORD

891 Writ 8 Feb. 1404.

STAFFORD. Inquisition. Stafford. 26 June.

He held a quarter of the manor of Blymhill in his demesne as of fee by knight service jointly with Hawise his wife, who survives, of Edmund brother and heir of William earl of Stafford, who is under age in the king's ward, annual value of the quarter £4.

He died on 29 Jan. 1397. William his son and heir is aged 30 years and more. Hawise has held and taken the profits since his death.

C 137/41, no.16

THOMAS GORGES

892   Writ 20 April 1404.

HAMPSHIRE. Inquisition. Titchfield. 10 June.

He held the manor of Knighton in the Isle of Wight in his demesne as of fee of Edward duke of York of his castle of Carisbrooke by knight service, annual value £20. The island was granted to the duke by Richard II. [*CPR 1396–9*, p.150].

He died on 15 April last. John his son and heir was aged 6 years on 22 Nov. 1403.

893   Writ 20 April 1404.

DEVON. Inquisition. Exeter. 12 May.

He held the manor of Braunton Gorges in his demesne as of fee. From it he granted a rent of 20 marks to Elizabeth, widow of his brother Bartholomew, whose heir he was, in dower for life. In return for this she released to him all the rights and claims she had in his lands throughout England. He also granted 40s. rent for life from the manor to John Copleston. Later he enfeoffed Thomas Beauchamp, knight, John Manyngforde, Richard Sutton, Robert Veel and their heirs and assigns. It is held of the king in socage by the service of rendering a barbed arrow whenever and as often as the king hunts in the forest of Exmoor; annual value beyond the rents £10 7s.4d.

Date of death and heir as above.

894   Writ 20 April 1404.

DORSET. Inquisition. Dorchester. 24 May.

He held in his demesne in fee tail to himself and his heirs male by the gift of Walter Waleys:

Sturminster Marshall, a quarter of the manor and the advowson. Long before he died, by his deed dated 7 Jan. 1403 he granted the quarter manor, but not the advowson, to Robert Grey, John Fauntleroy, junior, Edmund Elyot, clerk, and Robert Veel, describing it as his manor of Sturminster Marshall, to hold for their lives, by a rent of a rose at Midsummer for 3 years, and after 3 years, if they wished to retain it, by a rent of £40 payable by equal parts at the four principal terms. If the rent were wholly or partly in arrears for 15 days he might re-enter and hold it. He bound himself and his heirs in warranty to the feoffees. The manor and advowson are held of the king in socage by the service of rendering a pair of gilt spurs or 6d. whenever the king comes to the forest of Purbeck; annual value 20 marks.

Upper Kingcombe, 1 messuage, 4 carucates, 7 a. meadow and 2 a. wood. By his charter dated 2 June 1401 and shown to the jurors he granted and confirmed these premises described as all his lands, tenements, meadows, feedings, pastures, moors, woods, rents and services in Upper Kingcombe to Robert Veel for life, on condition that he paid Thomas, his heirs and assigns a rent of 26s.8d. during the life of John Sparwe and 13s.4d. yearly to the same John Sparwe, who still lives, to be held of the

king as he himself had held it. So Robert Veel was seised of it. By another charter dated
20 Dec. 1402 likewise shown to the jurors, reciting this grant and confirmation, Robert
Veel regranted all the premises to Thomas and paid a certain sum of money, and Thomas
again granted and confirmed them to Robert Veel for his life and one year more, paying
to Thomas and his heirs a rent of a rose at Midsummer . . . during his life 13s.4d.
for all services. Thomas bound himself and his heirs to warranty to Robert Veel, who
was then seised of the premises. They are held of the heirs of Guy de Briene, knight,
as of his manor of 'Ray. . .', service unknown, annual value 40s.

   Bridport, 1 messuage called 'la Glebe' and the advowson. Long before he died he
granted this messuage to John Hayward *alias* Saymour for life, by his charter shown
to the jurors, for a rent of 1 belt (*cingulum*) or 2d. to him and his heirs at Midsummer.
[They are held of the king in socage *deleted*], annual value 4s.

   Date of death and heir as above.

895   Writ 20 April 1404.
SOMERSET. Inquisition. Wells. 13 May.
   He held the manor of Wraxhall with its members of Flax Bourton and Nailsea in
his demesne as of fee. Long before his death he enfeoffed Thomas Beauchampe, knight,
John Copelston, Richard Sutton, Robert Veel, their heirs and assigns, on condition
that they should re-enfeoff him, Agnes his wife, who is still alive, and his heirs male,
but they held it and made no re-enfeoffment. The manor is held of the earl of Devon
by knight service, annual value £60.

   He died on 16 April. John his son and heir was aged 7 years on 11 May last.
                                                                    C 137/41, no.17
                                                                    E 149/83, no.13

WILLIAM SON AND HEIR OF HENRY DE HETON, KNIGHT

896   12 Feb. 1404.
NORTHUMBERLAND. Inquisition. Morpeth. 26 March.
   Henry de Heton, knight, held half the vill of Hartley, a place called Brierdene, the
castle and manor of Chillingham, and 1 husbandland in Doxford. Owing to his death
and the minority of William his son and heir, the half vill and place being held of the
king in chief, all were taken into the king's hands and so remain. William the son died
under age.

   The half and place are worth 20 marks yearly. Chillingham is held of Henry de Percy,
earl of Northumberland, by knight service, annual value these days 20 marks. The
husbandland is held of Richard de Arundell, knight, in socage, annual value 12s.

   William the son died on 27 Sept. 1401. Joan, aged 15 years and more, and married
to Robert de Rotherford, Elizabeth, aged 12 years and more, and Margaret, 9 years
and more, are the daughters of Henry de Heton, and sisters and next heirs of William.
                                                                    C 137/41, no.18

JOHN DODYNGSELLES, KNIGHT

897   Writ 6 Jan. 1404.
RUTLAND. Inquisition. Oakham. 19 Jan.
   He held in his demesne as of fee 8 messuages and 8 virgates in Morcott, annual value

4 marks; and 1 messuage and 1 carucate in Barrowden, annual value 26s. 8d.; of whom and by what service is unknown.

He died on 4 Dec. 1403. Edward his son and heir was aged 14 on 4 March 1403.

898   Writ 6 Jan. 1404.
WARWICK. Inquisition. Southam. 24 Jan.
He held the manor of Long Itchington in his demesne as of fee of the king in chief by the service of half a knight's fee, annual value 35 marks 10s.
Date of death and heir as above.

899   Writ 6 Jan. 1404.
NOTTINGHAM. Inquisition. Epperstone. 24 Jan.
He held the manor of Epperstone in his demesne as of fee of Thomas Chaworth, knight, by suit of court at the castle of Tickhill and payment of 3s. yearly of common farm and 'Shyreftothe', annual value £6 10s.4d.
Date of death and heir as above.

900   Writ 6 Jan. 1404.
HERTFORD. Inquisition. Hitchin. 31 Jan.
He held half the manor of Pirton called Oddingselles in his demesne as of fee of the king in chief by knight service, amount unknown, annual value £20.
Date of death and heir as above.

901   Writ 6 Jan. 1404.
OXFORD. Inquisition. Burford. 24 Jan.
He held in his demesne as of fee the manor of Broadwell of the king in chief as half a knight's fee, annual value 20 marks; and 5 virgates in Great Rollright of Hugh Lord Burnell, service unknown, annual value 20s.
Date of death and heir as above.

902   Writ, for fees, 24 Feb. 1404.
WARWICK. Inquisition. Long Itchington. 24 Sept.
He held the following of his manor of Long Itchington:
Maxstoke, the castle and manor, held of him by John Russell, knight, and Elizabeth his wife in right of Elizabeth for her life, with reversion to William de Clynton, knight, as one fee, annual value 40 marks.
Solihull, half the manor and lordship with a third part of the liberty of the lordship and the whole advowson, held by Sibyl widow of Hugh le Despenser, knight, for life, with reversion to Edward Boteller, knight, and Anne his wife in right of Anne, as half a fee, annual value 40 marks; the other half of the manor and lordship with a third part of the liberty, held by John Dencourt, Lord Deincourt, in right of his wife as half a fee, annual value £22.
Stoneythorpe, the manor, held by William Hore by knight service, 10 marks.
Slowley and Arley, the manors, held by Ralph Racheford, knight, as one fee, 40 marks.
Bascote, the manor, held by Thomas Seyvyll by knight service, 18 marks 6s.8d.
Stockton, the manor, held by Thomas ap Gryffyth as one fee, £20.

Solihull, 100s. rent and a third part of the liberty, held by William de Clynton, knight, by knight service, amount unknown.

Collyweston in Northamptonshire, the manor, held by Edward Boteller, knight, and Anne his wife in her right as one fee, 40 marks.

Long Itchington, lands and tenements, held by Guy Breton as half a fee, 100s.; and various lands, held by the prior of Maxstoke as a quarter fee, 5 marks.

Edward his son and next heir was aged 11 and no more on 17 Feb. 1404.

Writ to Thomas Frysby to receive the attorneys of Mary widow of John Dodyngselles to seek reasonable dower, and send in their names, 16 Feb. 1404.

[Endorsed] He had received Nicholas Dene and Thomas Throp as attorneys of Mary and executed the writ.

C 137/42, no.19
E 149/83, no.2
E 152/395, no.1

CLARICE YORKE, FORMERLY WIFE OF RICHARD WYNDESORE

903 Writ 12 April 1404.

BERKSHIRE. Inquisition. Abingdon. 22 May.

She held for life of the king in chief by knight service 1 ruinous messuage, 2 carucates, 10 a. meadow and 5s. rent in West Hagbourne of the inheritance of Richard son of Brian de Wyndesore, with reversion to him, annual value 5 marks.

She died on 22 April last [*sic*]. Richard son of Brian, her next heir, is aged 5 years and more.

She also held jointly with John Yorke, her son, to him and his heirs, 5 messuages, 80 a. arable and 4 a. meadow in the same place of Richard son of Brian by knight service, annual value 20s. John her son is aged 24 years and more.

C 137/42, no.20
E 152/395, no.2

JOAN WIDOW OF WILLIAM BARON GREYSTOKE

904 Writ 20 Sept. 1403.

WESTMORLAND. Inquisition. Appleby. 15 Oct.

She held in dower from all the lands of William Baron Greystoke, of the inheritance of Ralph Baron Greystoke, knight, son and heir of William, the advowson of Dufton taxed according to the new tax at 6s. yearly. It is held of the Lord Clifford in chief as parcel of the manor of Dufton by homage and fealty.

She died on 1 Sept. last. Ralph her son and heir is aged 40 years and more.

905 Writ 20 Sept. 1403.

YORK. Inquisition. Malton. 7 Oct.

She held in dower of the inheritance of Ralph Baron Greystoke, knight:

Nidd, 8 messuages and 8 bovates, annual value 53s.4d.; 2 a., 12d.; and a third part
of a mill, 6s.8d.; all of the archbishop of York of his manor of Ripon by fealty.

Welbury by East Harlsey, the manor, of Walter Lord Fauconberg of his manor of
Skelton in Cleveland, annual value £10, and he holds of the king in chief.

Butterwick in Grindalythe, the manor, with its members in Sherburn, Hertfordlythe,
Boythorpe, Flixton, Folkton and Flotmanby, with the advowson of Folkton, of Peter
de Malo Lacu of his manor of Bainton by knight service, and he holds of the king in
chief, annual value £9.

Crossthwaite in Teesdale, the manor, of Henry Fitzhugh, knight, of his manor of
Kirby Ravensworth, by a rent of 4s., annual value £6. Fitzhugh holds it of the earl
of Richmond of the honour of Richmond, and the earl of the king in chief.

Scagglethorpe, £4 2s.6d. in rents, of Ralph Hastyngs, knight, of his manor of
Slingsby, and he holds of Lord de Moubray of his manor of Hovingham by knight
service, and Moubray of the king in chief.

Date of death and heir, as aged 46 years and more, as above.

906 Writ 20 Sept. 1403.

NORTHUMBERLAND. Inquisition. Morpeth. 9 Oct.

She held in dower of the inheritance of Ralph Baron Greystoke Morpeth castle and
manor, with the advowsons of Morpeth and of the hospital of St. Mary Magdalen there
called Catchburne 'spitell'; 5 husbandlands and 5 cottages in Horsley; half of the
demesne lands and of 4 husbandlands and 4 cottages in Tranwell; a third part of half
the demesne arable and meadow, husbandlands and cottages in Long Benton; and a
rent of 17s.4d. in Killingworth, payable by equal parts at Whitsun and Martinmas;
all of which William Baron Greystoke died seised of to himself and his heirs. There
is a weekly market on Wednesdays at Morpeth and a fair at St. Mary Magdalen without
tolls. All are held of the king in chief by knight service, annual value £20 and no more
because of destruction and burning by the Scots.

She also held of the king in chief by knight service of the same inheritance by the
grant of Robert Herle, knight, to William and herself and the heirs of William:

Benridge, the manor, annual value 60s.

Outchester, Benwell, Eachwick, East Heddon, Heddon on the Wall and Middleton
Morel, 2½ knight's fees, and half the manor of Angerton, annual value £10 and no more
for the same reason.

Date of death and heir, aged 46 years and more, as above.

907 Writ 20 Sept. 1403.

CUMBERLAND. Inquisition. Penrith. 16 Oct.

She held nothing in Cumberland.

Date of death and heir, aged 40 years and more, as above.

C 137/42, no.21
E 149/82, no.13
E 152/380, no.1

ROBERT GOUSHILL, KNIGHT

908 Writ 6 Aug. 1403.

SUSSEX. Inquisition. Bramber. 4 Oct.

He held in the dower of Elizabeth his wife, from the lands of Thomas duke of
Norfolk, her former husband, all of the king in chief, services unknown:

Knepp, the manor, annual value £7 17s.

Shoreham, the borough, £17.

Findon, the manor, £30.

West Grinstead, the manor, £10.

Southease, meadow, 33s.4d.

Washington, assize rent of 20s. from Robert Peter.

Lower Beeding, assize rents of 6d. from Robert Maynard from the manor, and 7s. from John Wylman.

Bramber, assize rent of 12d. from Thomas Palmer.

West Grinstead and Burbeach, the hundreds, and Wyndham and Fishergate, the half hundreds, annual values unknown.

He died on 20 [recte 21] July. Joan and Elizabeth his daughters and heirs are aged 2 years and more and 1 year and more.

909 Writ 6 Aug. 1403.

NOTTINGHAM. Inquisition. Nottingham. 24 Oct.

He held 10 marks rent from Nottingham castle in dower of Elizabeth his wife, from the annuity of £20 of her former husband, Thomas duke of Norfolk, according to the law and custom of England.

Date of death, 20 July, and heirs as above.

910 DERBY. Inquisition. Bretby. 23 Oct. 1403.

He held in the dower of Elizabeth his wife from the lands of Thomas duke of Norfolk, her late husband, with reversion to Thomas his son, of whom is unknown:

Bretby, the castle and manor, annual value £25.

Rosliston and Coton in the Elms, the manors, annual value £28 10s.7d.

Repton, Linton, Milton, Willington, Ashbourne and 'Howes', 12 messuages, 14 bovates and £10 rent, annual value £14 10d.

Date of death, 20 July, and heirs as above.

911 Writ 6 Aug. 1403.

BEDFORD. Inquisition. Bedford. 4 Oct.

He held in the dower of Elizabeth his wife, of the king in chief as parcel of the barony of Bedford:

Haynes, the manor and a third part of the park of the manor, service unknown, annual value £10.

Stotfold, the manor, service unknown, annual value £16.

Date of death, 21 July, and heirs as above.

912 BUCKINGHAM. Inquisition. Wing. 13 Oct. 1403.

He held the manors of Penn, Linslade and Southcott in the dower of Elizabeth his wife, Linslade and Southcott of the king in chief by knight service, annual value 100s., Penn, annual value £10.

He also held the manor of Wing in right of Elizabeth because Richard earl of Arundel gave it to Thomas duke of Norfolk, Elizabeth then his wife and the heirs of their bodies. Of whom it is held and by what service is unknown.

Date of death, 21 July, and heirs as above.

913   Writ 6 Aug. 1403.

HUNTINGDON. Inquisition. Huntingdon. 19 Jan. 1404.

He held in the dower of Elizabeth his wife a third part of the manor of Alconbury, of whom is unknown, annual value of the third part £17 15s.7d.

Date of death, 20 July, and heirs as above.

914   CAMBRIDGE. Inquisition. Cambridge. 8 Oct. 1403.

He held in the dower of Elizabeth his wife, of whom is unknown:

Kennett and Kentford, the manor, annual value 20 marks.

Cherry Hinton, a third part of the manor, £10 4s.5d.

Ickleton, 6s.8d. rent.

Date of death, 20 July, and heirs as above.

915   Writ 6 Aug. 1403.

LINCOLN. Inquisition. Gainsborough. 17 Oct.

He held in the dower of Elizabeth his wife, of whom is unknown, a third part of the manor of Epworth, annual value of the third, £50.

Date of death, 20 July, and heirs as above.

916   Writ 6 Aug. 1403.

LEICESTER. Inquisition. Hallaton. 22 Oct.

He held in the dower of Elizabeth his wife:

Witherley, the manor, of whom is unknown, annual value £10.

Goscote, the hundred, of the king in chief, 40s.

Melton Mowbray, a third part of the manor, of whom is unknown, annual value 10 marks, 10s.6d.

Date of death, 20 July, and heirs as above.

917   WARWICK. Inquisition. Coventry. 13 Oct.

He held in the dower of Elizabeth his wife a third part of the manors of Kineton and Caludon, of whom is unknown, annual value together, £10.

Date of death, 20 July, and heirs as above.

918   Writ 6 Aug. 1403.

ESSEX. Inquisition. Saffron Walden. 23 Oct.

He held in the dower of Elizabeth his wife, of whom is unknown:

Chesterford, the manor, annual value £30.

Dovercourt with Harwich, a third part of the manor, £9 11s.2d.

Romford, the manor, £10.

He also held in right of Elizabeth, who held jointly with Thomas duke of Norfolk, her former husband, the manor of Prittlewell, of whom is unknown, annual value 24 marks.

Date of death, 20 July, and heirs as above.

919   HERTFORD. Inquisition. Hertford. 20 Oct. 1403.

He held nothing in Hertfordshire.

Date of death, 20 July, and heirs as above.

920 Writ 6 Aug. 1403.

RUTLAND. Inquisition. Oakham. 13 Sept.

He held in the dower of Elizabeth his wife a third part of a toft and of two virgates in Alesthorp by Burley, of Robert de Plesyngton, lord of Burley, service unknown, annual value 3s. 4d.

Date of death, 21 July, and heirs as above.

921 NORTHAMPTON. Inquisition. Chipping Warden. 17 Sept. 1403.

He held in the dower of Elizabeth his wife:

Chalcombe, a third part of the manor, of the bishop of Lincoln of his castle of Banbury, service unknown, annual value of the third part beyond ancient annuities 6s.8d.

Northampton, 8s. rent from various tenements held of the king in burgage.

Date of death, 21 July, and heirs as above.

922 Writ 6 Aug. 1403.

NORFOLK. Inquisition. Kenninghall. 6 Sept.

He held the manor of Kenninghall with the hundred of Guiltcross in right of Elizabeth duchess of Norfolk his wife, who held it jointly with John [*recte* William] Mountegu, her former [i.e. first] husband, by the gift of William Mountegu, earl of Salisbury, to John [*recte* William] and Elizabeth and their heirs male. Elizabeth widow of the earl of Salisbury holds a third part in dower. It is held of the king in chief by a rent of 40d. blanch farm of the castle of Norwich, annual value £40 4d.

Date of death, 20 July, and heirs as above.

923 SUFFOLK. Inquisition. Earl Soham. 7 Sept. 1403.

He held in the dower of Elizabeth his wife, assigned to her in chancery, of the king in chief, services unknown:

Walton, a third part of the manor, the annual value of the whole manor being £80 17s.4d.

Earl Soham, the manor, annual value £28.

Bungay, the manor and borough, £70 5s.1d.

Earl Stonham, the manor, £46 17s.4½d.

Dunningworth, the manor, £16.

Kelsale, the manor, £60.

Peasenhall, the manor, £18.

Staverton, the manor, £36 16s.3¼d.

Hollesley, the manor, £40 17s.7d.

Hoo, the manor, with the hundred of Loes, £33 1s.¼d.

Cratfield, Stow Park and Berwick, £6 in rents.

Kennett and Kentford, 72 a. arable and 8 a. meadow called 'Londmedwe', part of the manor, which is partly in Cambridgeshire, the arable at 2d. the a. and no more because stony and sandy, the meadow 2s. the a.

Date of death, 20 July, and heirs as above.

924   Writ 6 Aug. 1403.

YORK. Inquisition. Thirsk. 24 Oct.

He held a third part of the manors of Thirsk, Hovingham and Kirkby Malzeard in the dower of Elizabeth his wife, of whom is unknown, annual value £36.

Date of death, 20 July, and heirs as above.

925   Writ 6 Aug. 1403.

HEREFORD AND THE ADJACENT MARCH OF WALES. Inquisition. Hereford. 15 Oct.

He held a third part of the castle of Swansea, of the lordship and manor of Kilvey and of the lordship of Gower in the dower of Elizabeth his wife, of whom is unknown, annual value together 200 marks.

Date of death, 20 July, and heirs as above.

926   Writ 6 Aug. 1403.

SHROPSHIRE. Inquisition. Bridgnorth. 4 Oct.

He held the manors of Stottesdon, annual value £20, and Kingswood, annual value 100s., in the dower of Elizabeth his wife, how and of whom is unknown.

Date of death, 20 July, and heirs as above.

C 137/42, no.22
E 149/80, no.2
E 152/380, no.2, 382, 389, no.5

JOHN ROSSALE

927   Writ 21 Dec. 1403.

SHROPSHIRE. Inquisition. Shrewsbury. 31 Dec.

He held in his demesne in fee tail jointly with Eleanor his wife, who survives him, by the grant of William Walleford and William Russell, chaplains, to them and their heirs, half the manors of Rossall, Yagdon and Sleap by Bilmarsh with the advowson of the free chapel of Rossall, together with the reversion of the other halves of the manors which Beatrice his mother holds. They are held of Thomas earl of Arundel by knight service; annual values of the halves, Rossall 6 marks, Yagdon 20s., Sleap 13s.4d.

He died on 21 July last. Eleanor formerly the wife of Nicholas Dagworth, knight, and Alice wife of John Inggelfeld, his sisters and next heirs, are aged 26 and 22 years.

C 137/42, no.23

JOAN WIFE OF WILLIAM HORNEBYE AND WIDOW OF EDWARD DE STOCKE

928   Writ 22 Feb. 1404.

WILTSHIRE. Inquisition. Marlborough. 28 Feb.

John de Nubury, chaplain, Adam Blake, chaplain, and Thomas Hungerford, citizen and merchant of Salisbury, by their charter with royal licence [*CPR 1354–8*, pp.308–9] granted the manor of Rushall with the advowson to Edward de Stocke and Joan, then his wife, and the heirs of the body of Edward, with successive remainders to Thomas son of Walter de Hungerford and the heirs of Thomas, William de Lucy, knight, and his heirs, Edmund brother of William de Lucy and his heirs, Thomas de Stocke and his heirs, and the right heirs of Edward.

Edward de Stocke died without heirs. Joan then held it for life, of the king as one quarter of a knight's fee, annual value 20 marks.

She died on 18 Feb. last. Thomas son of Walter de Hungerford is dead. It should remain to Walter Hungerford, knight, son and heir of Thomas son of Walter, aged 25 years and more.

C 137/42, no.24
E 152/397

ROGER LESCROPE, KNIGHT

929 Writ 16 Dec. 1403.

LEICESTER. Inquisition. Melton Mowbray. 1 July 1404.

He held in his demesne as of fee jointly with Margaret his wife the manors of Edmondthorpe and Wymondham, with 1 messuage and 1 carucate in Barkestone, by the grant of John de Gunwardby and Benet de Goteham, clerk, by a fine of 1386 [CP 25(1) 289/54, no.150] to them and their heirs with remainder to the right heirs of Margaret. Edmondthorpe is held of the king of the honour of Leicester by knight service, annual value 100s.; Wymondham is similarly held, annual value £4; the messuage and carucate are held of William Lord de Roos, service unknown, annual value 20s.

He also held in his demesne as of fee 9s. 3d. rent in Medbourn with the advowson, of the king in chief by a rent of 2d. payable by the sheriff at the exchequer at Easter, annual value of the advowson 20 marks.

He died on 3 Dec. 1403. Richard his son and next heir was aged 10 years on 31 May last.

930 Writ 14 March 1404.

BUCKINGHAM. Inquisition. High Wycombe. 15 April.

Richard Lescrope, knight, held the manor of Hambleden with the advowson for the life of Juliana wife of Stephen Spore and 1 year more with reversion to John de Gunwardby and Benet de Gotham, clerk, and the heirs of John. They granted the reversion to Roger Lescrope and Margaret his wife, their heirs and the right heirs of Margaret by a fine [as above, no.929]. Richard released his rights to them and they entered and so held them until Roger died. They are held of William earl of Salisbury of the honour of Christchurch, service unknown; annual values, manor £40, advowson £20.

Date of death and heir, aged 9 years on 31 May, as above.

931 Writ 16 Dec. 1403.

YORK. Inquisition. York castle. 5 Aug. 1404.

He held in his demesne as of fee:

Caldwell, the manor, of the earl of Richmond by knight service, annual value £8.

Croft and Bolton upon Swale, the manors, of the same earl, annual values 100s. and 40s.

Uckerby, the manor of Lord Deincourt and Henry de Hedelame, annual value 60s.

Ellerton on Swale, the manor, of the lord of Richmond castle, service unknown, annual value £20.

Kirkby Fleetham, the manor, of the earl of Richmond, service unknown, annual value £7.

Great Fencote, the manor, of Henry Fitzhugh, service unknown, annual value £10.

Low Bolton in Wensleydale, the manor, of the lord of Richmond castle, service unknown, annual value £20.

West Bolton in Wensleydale, the manor, of Ralph earl of Westmorland, service unknown, annual value 100s.

Redmire and Preston under Scar, half the manors, of the earl of Richmond and Henry Fitzhugh respectively, services unknown, annual values 100s. and £6.

Brettanby, Jolby, Wensley and Sutton Howgrave, the manors, of the earl of Richmond, services unknown, annual values, 113s.4d., 10s., £10 and 100s.

Dishforth, the manor, of Henry Percy, earl of Northumberland, service unknown, annual value 40s.

West Burton and Walden, 1½ carucates, and Aysgarth, 1 carucate, of Thomas Mounford, services unknown, annual value 100s.

Richmond, a free rent of £7 13s.4d., 3 messuages, 4 tofts, 3 shops and 40 a., of the earl of Richmond, service unknown, annual value £9.

Hudswell, 2 small closes and 3 a., of the abbot of St. Agatha's, service unknown, annual value 8s.

Bellerby, 2 messuages, 2 cottages, 6 bovates and 20 a. meadow, of Stephen Lescrope, lord of Masham, service unknown, annual value 10s.

Date of death and heir, aged 10 years on 31 May, as above.

932 Writ 16 Dec. 1403.

HERTFORD. Inquisition. Sawbridgeworth. 26 June 1404.

He held nothing in Hertfordshire.

Date of death and heir, aged 10 years on 31 May, as above.

C 137/43, no.25
E 149/82, no.10

JOHN TREYGOS

933 Writ 8 Sept. 1404.

KENT. Inquisition. West Malling. 10 March 1405.

Long before he died he granted the manor of Boxley by his deed to Nicholas de Carreu, John Asshurst and John Blachemerden, clerk, their heirs and assigns. They still hold it in peaceful seisin, and he only had it by their licence and at their will.

He died on 24 Aug. last. Thomas Leukenore is next heir of blood, being the son of Roger Leukenore, son of Joan, daughter of Margaret Doyle, sister of Henry Treygos, father of John. He is aged 12 years and more, and by right of inheritance the manor would descend to him.

934 Writ 8 Sept. 1404.

SUSSEX. Inquisition. Angmering. 3 Jan. 1405.

Long before he died he recognised by a fine [CP 25(1) 240/80, no.13] that the manors of Goring, Preston, Dedisham, Barkham, Parham, Walderton, Wiggenholt, Greatham and Cootham were the right of Nicholas de Carreu, John Estephenes, Thomas Harlyng, clerk, William Pymour, clerk, Thomas Suthtoune, clerk, Thomas Lyttewynne and the heirs of Thomas Lyttewynne. Thomas Lyttewynne by his deed released his rights to the others. William Pymour died. The survivors assigned to Alice widow of Edward Tregos the manors of Preston, Barkham, Wiggenholt and Parham, and 20s. rent from Goring, for life in dower; and she was given seisin by Thomas Asshehurst in accordance with their letters to him [CCR 1399–1402, p.298]. So she has held these manors until the present time.

John Tregos after this assignment and livery of seisin to Alice, by the licence and will of Nicholas Carreu, John Estephenes, Thomas Harlyng and Thomas Suthtoune, entered the manors of Goring, Dedisham, Greatham, Walderton and Cootham, the possession of which they confirmed by their deed to John Tregos, his heirs and assigns.

Afterwards by his deed John Tregos granted to Nicholas de Carreu, John Asshurst and John Black the manors of Goring, Dedisham, Greatham, and Walderton and certain lands and tenements . . . by the name of 'Wyntric' with their appurtenances to them, their heirs and assigns. So they were seised of them and still hold in peaceful seisin, without . . . John Tregos . . . [several lines illegible].

Date of death and heir as above.

C 137/43, no.26

JOHN SON OF ROGER LESTRAUNGE OF KNOCKIN

935 LONDON. Inquisition. 31 May 1403.

He held nothing in his demesne as of fee beyond that which appears in the inquisition taken under Richard II. [CIPM XVII, no.1098]. John Keresley held for life by the grant of Roger Lestraunge 12 cottages in an alley next to Holborn bridge in the parish of St. Andrew, Holborn, to the east of a garden of Christina widow of Stephen Pulham. They are held of the king in free burgage as all London is, annual value 6s.8d. After the death of John Keresley they should revert to Roger Lestraunge as son and heir of John son of Roger.

John Keresley died on 30 Jan. 1403. Richard son of John son of Roger is heir.

E 152/383, no.3

MAUD WIDOW OF JOHN SON OF ROGER LESTRAUNGE OF KNOCKIN

936 Writ 10 Oct. 1403.

OXFORD. Inquisition. Bicester. 21 Dec.

She held the manor of Bicester with the advowson of the priory for life jointly with John her late husband, of the prince [of Wales] of his honour of Wallingford by knight service, by the grant of Richard Edevenet, Richard Wythyford and John Bannebury, clerks, to them and the heirs and assigns of John; annual value £10.

She died on 20 Sept. 1400. Richard son and next heir of both John and Maud is aged 21 years and more. Since the death of Maud, Nicholas Hauberk, knight, has occupied the manor with the advowson of the priory, and still holds and takes the profits, title unknown.

937   BERKSHIRE. Inquisition. Hungerford. 28 Jan. 1404.

Roger Lestraunge of Knockin held the manor of Avington in his demesne as of fee, and granted it to John Lestraunge and Maud and the heirs of their bodies [licence, *CPR 1370–4*, p.187]. She died seised of it, of the king in chief as a sixth part of a knight's fee, annual value 100s.

Date of death, heir and tenure by Nicholas Hauberk as above.

938   Writ 10 Oct. 1403.

MIDDLESEX. Inquisition. Charterhouse. 7 May 1404.

She held the manors of Colham and Uxbridge for life jointly with John her late husband, of the prince [of Wales] of his honour of Wallingford by knight service, by the grant of Richard Edevenet, Richard Wythyford and John Bannebury, clerks, to them and the heirs and assigns of John; annual value £40.

Date of death, heir, and tenure by Nicholas Hauberk as above.

939   Writ 10 Oct. 1403.

NORTHAMPTON. Inquisition. Oundle. 14 Jan. 1404.

Roger Lestraunge of Knockin, knight, held the manor of Wadenhoe and granted it to John and Maud and the heirs of their bodies. It is held of the king in chief by knight service, annual value £20.

Date of death, heir, and tenure by Nicholas Hauberk as above.

940   Writ 10 Oct. 1403.

BUCKINGHAM. Inquisition. Amersham. 10 June 1404.

She held 2 watermills under one roof in Denham for life jointly with John her late husband, by the grant of Richard Edvenet, Richard Withiford and John Bannebury, clerks, to them and the heirs and assigns of John. They are held of the abbot of Westminster by the rent of a red rose at Midsummer, annual value 60s.

Date of death, heir, and tenure by Nicholas Hauberk as above.

941   Writ 10 Oct. 1403.

CAMBRIDGE. Inquisition. Cambridge. 19 June 1404.

She held the manor and advowson of Milton for life jointly with John her late husband, of the bishop of Ely by the rent of a pair of gilt spurs, price 6d., or 6d., by the grant of Richard Edvenet, Richard Wythyford and John Bannebury, clerks, to them and the heirs and assigns of John; annual value £45.

Date of death, heir, and tenure by Nicholas Hauberk as above.

942   Writ 10 Oct. 1403.

STAFFORD. Inquisition. Stafford. 24 Jan. 1404.

She held the manor of Shenstone for life jointly with John her late husband, of Robert Plessy, knight, service unknown, by the grant of Robert de Kendale, William Wolascote and John de Longeforde to them and the heirs and assigns of John; annual value £40.

Date of death, heir, and tenure by Nicholas Hauberk as above.

943 Writ 10 Oct. 1403.

SHROPSHIRE. Inquisition. Shrewsbury. 20 Dec.

She held in her demesne as of fee jointly with John her late husband, of the earl of Arundel, services unknown:

Myddle, the manor, by the grant of Philip de la Lee, parson of Myddle, Roger Hampton, vicar of Ellesmere, and Richard Edevenet, parson of Llanymynech, to them and the heirs of their bodies; annual value £6 13s.4d. and no more because almost wasted by the Welsh rebels.

Knockin, the castle and lordship, by the grant of the same, annual value 100s. and no more for the same reason.

Hardwick and Marton, the manors, by the grant of Richard de Whithiford, chaplain, annual value £4 and no more for the same reason.

Date of death, heir, and tenure by Nicholas Hauberk as above.

C 137/43, no.27

RICHARD SON AND HEIR OF JOHN LESTRAUNGE

944 Writ for proof of age, ordering that Nicholas Haweberk who had custody of the lands should be warned. 8 Aug. 1404.

[Endorsed] He was warned by John Pichard and William Hamme.

LONDON. Proof of age. Guildhall. 16 Aug.

Richard, son and heir of John, son of Roger Lestraunge of Knockin, was born in London in the parish of St. Bartholomew the Less in Broad Street ward and baptised in that church on 1 Aug. 1381 [sic] and so was aged 22 on 1 Aug. last.

Geoffrey Creek, aged 60, was in the church and saw Richard earl of Arundel acting as godfather.

Thomas Whyte, 45, was also there and saw William de Monte Acuto, earl of Salisbury, as the other godfather.

John Goldesburgh, 46, saw Elizabeth le Despenser, the godmother, there.

Henry Anketill, 44, says that Katherine atte Hull, who was staying in a house of his, was a matron of Maud, Richard's mother, and told him of the birth.

Nicholas Luffenham, 50, saw Nicholas Bleseworth, then an esquire of John son of Roger, carrying a torch before Richard to the church.

John Cole, 44, saw Beatrice atte Lee carrying a bowl of water before Richard to the church for the baptism.

William Weston, 43, had a son called Geoffrey who was baptised then.

William Rybode, 48, met John Bereford, an esquire of Maud, going to Elizabeth to ask her to be a godmother.

Roger Hillom, 60, was present in the church and saw him having 4 godfathers and 2 godmothers whence there was a multiplicity of promises.

John Staunton, 56, saw Richard earl of Arundel on that day after the baptism making a gift to Richard.

John Wolverlee, 70, was an esquire of the earl of Salisbury, and brought Richard that day . . . as a gift from the earl.

Walter Banham, 42, saw Elizabeth le Despenser on that day . . .

C 137/45, no.49

ELIZABETH WIFE OF ROBERT DE WYLUGHBY, KNIGHT

945   Writ 20 Dec. 1403.

HERTFORD. Inquisition. St. Albans. 26 Dec.

She held in her demesne as of fee 40 a. arable and 6 a. wood in Flaunden, annual value 10s., and 4s. rent of free tenants there payable by equal parts at the four terms, all of the honour of Wallingford, service unknown.

She died on 5 Nov. 1395. Robert her husband held the lands by the courtesy of England, and after he died they were taken into the king's hands owing to the minority of John Nevell, her son and heir. He is next heir and aged 21 years and more.

946   Writ 20 Dec. 1403.

BEDFORD. Inquisition. Bedford. 28 Dec.

She held in her demesne as of fee:

Dilwick, the manor, annual value 20 marks, and the park there, annual value nil because she granted an annual fee of £4 to Gilbert Drye, the parker, for life.

Wootton, the manor, annual value 12 marks.

Renhold, the manor, with the wood of Cardington, annual value 33 marks.

Potton, certain lands and tenements called Potton Burdetts held by various tenants, annual value 5 marks.

Stratton, £10 rent from the manor payable by equal parts at Easter and Michaelmas.

Bedford, perquisites of the court held every 3 weeks, annual value 10s.

Bromham, rent of 26s.8d. from various tenants.

All were held in chief of Richard II of the barony of Bedford, except the lands in Potton which are held of the earl of Pembroke of the honour of Huntingdon, service unknown.

Date of death, tenure by Robert, and heir as above.

947   BUCKINGHAM. Inquisition. Chesham. 27 Dec. 1403.

She held in her demesne as of fee of Henry prince of Wales of the honour of Wallingford, services unknown:

Latimer, the manor, annual value £16 13s.4d.

North Crawley, view of frankpledge held once yearly after Michaelmas, annual value 20d.

Broughton, view of frankpledge, annual value 2s.

Date of death, tenure by Robert, and heir as above.

948   Writ 20 Dec. 1403.

NORTHAMPTON. Inquisition. Wellingborough. 29 Dec.

She held in her demesne as of fee:

Corby, the manor and advowson, 40s. rent in East Carlton with the advowson, and the hundred of Corby, of the king in chief by a rent of £10 8s. payable at the exchequer by the sheriff, annual value beyond the rent 10 marks 6s.8d.

Bozeat, the manor, of Reynold Grey of Ruthin, knight, service unknown, annual value £8.

Burton Latimer by Finedon, the manor and advowson, of William Latymer, knight, by a rent of 1 oz. of silk, annual value £6.

Northampton, a garden called 'Latymersplace', of the king in burgage by a rent of 7s. payable to the bailiffs of the town, annual value 4s.

Date of death, tenure by Robert, and heir as above.

949 Writ 20 Dec. 1403.

LINCOLN. Inquisition. Swaton. 28 Dec.

She held the manor of Helpringham called Thorpe Latimer with Bicker hamlet in her demesne as of fee of Henry Lord Beaumont, the heir of the lord of Kyme, Thomas Lord Bardolf and William Lord Willoughby, service unknown, annual value £27.

She granted the manor of Scredington to William Pylett to hold for life and one year more at a rent of £8, which rent she held. The manor is held of William Dysny, service unknown, annual value £8.

Afterwards she married Robert de Wilughby and had issue Margaret.

Date of death, tenure by Robert, and heir as above.

C 137/43, no.28

E 149/82, no.8

DENISE WIDOW OF ROBERT DE STODHOWE

950 Writ, *plura*, 5 May 1404.

YORK. Inquisition. Northallerton. 20 May.

She held nothing beyond what was stated in an inquisition taken after her death and returned to the chancery [*CIPM* XVI, no.927], except the advowson of a chantry in Pocklington held of the earl of Northumberland in socage, annual value nil.

Robert de Stodhowe, her next heir, son of Robert her son, is aged 21 years and more.

C 137/43, no.29, mm.3,4

ROBERT DE STODHOWE

951 Writ 5 May 1404.

YORK. Inquisition. Northallerton. 20 May.

Robert de Stodhowe, son of Denise widow of Robert de Stodhowe, held in his demesne in fee tail jointly with Elizabeth his wife:

Yapham, 4 bovates, granted to him by Denise on his marriage to Elizabeth, as being worth a rent of 20s., annual value 12s.4d.

Wombwell, 3 messuages, 2½ bovates and 11s. rent, of John Anneslay, knight, in socage, annual value 40s.

Studdah, the manor of Stephen Lescrop in socage, annual value 40s.

Hudswell in Richmondshire, 1 cottage and 60 a., of the abbot of St. Agatha's in socage, annual value 17s.

Birdsall, half a carucate, of whom is unknown, annual value 7s.

Harmby, a strip, of Richard Lescrop, knight, in socage, annual value 7s.

The 4 bovates in Yapham are part of 8 bovates there taken into the king's hands on the death of Denise owing to the minority of Robert son of Robert. They were granted to Henry Percy, son of the earl of Northumberland, to hold from the death of Denise to the full age of Robert, together with his marriage for a certain yearly farm. Elizabeth

held the 4 bovates from the death of Robert her husband until they were demised to
Henry Percy, and took the profits, and she is answerable for them to the king. On
the death of Henry Percy they were taken into the king's hands by Thomas Egmanton,
late escheator, and so they remain.

Robert de Stodhowe, son of Denise, died about 23 Nov. 1383. Robert his son and
heir is aged 21 years and more.

952   Writ, *melius sciri*, as it was not stated how he was heir to Denise. 5 May 1404.

YORK. Inquisition. Northallerton. 20 May.

Robert son of Robert, son of Robert de Stodhowe, late husband of Denise, is her
next heir, namely the son of Robert her son.

C 137/43, no.29, mm.1,2,5,6

ROBERT SON OF ROBERT DE STODHOWE

953   Writ for proof of age, 3 June 1404.

YORK. Proof of age. 18 June 1404.

John Clervaux, 52 years and more, says that Robert de Stodhowe, son of Robert,
son of Denise, wife of Robert de Stodhowe, was born at Croft and baptised in the
church there on 5 April 1381 [*sic* 4 Richard II; probably 1383, 6 Richard II]. He
remembers because on that day he was retained with the bishop of Norwich to accom-
pany him on his voyage to Flanders.

Robert son of Robert Thorpe, 43 and more, was chamberlain of John Clervaux,
Robert's grandfather, in whose house at Croft Robert was born.

Richard de Dele, 60 and more, was present in the church and saw the baptism by
John Bet, chaplain of that church.

Robert de Spellowe, 50, remembers because his house in Croft was accidentally
burnt down on that same day.

John Belamy, 61 and more, was building his new house in Croft and saw Beatrice,
wife of John Clervaux the grandfather, carrying Robert in his arms to the church to
be baptised.

Ivo de Croft, 44 and more, married his wife Elizabeth on that day.

Simon Robertson of Croft, 61 and more, had a daughter Beatrice baptised in the
church immediately after the baptism of Robert, and she is now aged 21 years and more
by 27 weeks [*sic*].

John de Bretanby, 60 and more, went to the church to hear mass, and saw Robert
de Hippeswell, vicar of East Cowton, raise Robert from the font, and the vicar gave
a red cow as a godfather's present.

Thomas Bell of Croft, 60 and more, heard mass at the church, and afterwards went
with Robert Rukeby, chaplain, the other godfather, to the houe of John Clervaux the
grandfather to see the child's mother, who was very ill, and he carried a lantern with
a candle.

William Cabery, 67 and more, was a servant of John Clervaux senior, uncle of
Robert, and carried a basin, ewer and towel for washing the hands of the godfathers
and godmother after the baptism.

William Stable of Croft, 60 and more, says that on that day Robert de Stodhowe the father bought an ambling palfrey from him for 100s. to give to the bishop of Durham.

William Greyson of Croft, 66 and more, was fishing in the Tees that runs by the vill of Croft, and caught a pike three foot long and more, and gave it as a present to the boy's father.

C 137/43, no.29, mm.7.8

ELIZABETH WIFE OF HENRY SUTHILL AND FORMERLY WIFE OF ROBERT DE STODEHOWE

954   Writ 5 May 1404.

YORK. Inquisition. Northallerton. 20 May.

Elizabeth held jointly with Robert de Stodowe, sometime her husband:

Wombwell, 3 messuages, 2½ bovates and 11s. rent, of John Anneslay, knight, in socage, annual value 40s.

Studdah, the manor, of Stephen Lescrop in socage, annual value 40s.

Hudswell in Richmondshire, 1 cottage and 60 a., of the abbot of St. Agatha's in socage, annual value 17s.

Birdsall, ½ carucate, of whom is unknown, annual value 7s.

Harmby, a strip of arable, of Richard Lescrop, knight, in socage, annual value 7s.

She died about 1 May 1401. Robert de Stodowe, her son and heir, to whom the reversion of the premises belongs, is aged 21 years and more. They were taken into the king's hands on her death because he was a minor and Robert the father held elsewhere of the king in chief.

C 137/43, no.29, mm.9,10

THOMAS SON AND HEIR OF RALPH DE LOMLEY, KNIGHT

955   Writ 25 Jan. 1404.

YORK. Inquisition. York castle. 6 Aug.

On the day of his forfeiture Ralph de Lomley, knight, was seised in fee tail by the grant of Marmaduke de Thweng, lord of Danby, made to his son Marmaduke, ancestor of Ralph, and the heirs of his body, whose heir Ralph was, namely the son of Isabel, sister of Thomas, brother of Robert, brother of William, son of Robert, son of Marmaduke, son of Marmaduke, of the following lands held of Henry de Percy, earl of Northumberland, by knight service, annual value £26:

Kilton, the castle and manor.

Kirkleatham and Coatham, the manor, with the advowson of Kirkleatham.

Hinderwell, the advowson on alternate vacancies, and 2s. rent called 'Windmill-henge'.

Kilham, the services of his tenants.

Denton, the homage and service of Walter de Buketon, knight, and his heirs for 6 bovates.

Kilton Thorpe, the homage and service of Robert Constable and all his free tenants.

By the grant of the same Marmaduke and Lucy his wife, to their son Marmaduke and the heirs of his body, he held:

Great Moorsholme, 1 messuage, 17 tofts and 13 bovates, of the king in chief by knight service, annual value £4.

Little Moorsholme, 1 bovate, 12 a. and 2 tofts, also of the king by knight service, annual value 30s.

Kilton Thorpe, Brotton, Skinningrove and Liverton, 8 messuages and 16 bovates, of the same, annual value 50s.

Thwing on the Wold near Bridlington and Octon near Swaythorpe, the manors, with half the advowson of Thwing, of the same, annual value £20.

Runswick and Yarm, half the wreck of the sea between, and a yearly rent of salt payable from East Coatham marsh, that is from every brine pit that is boiled half a skep of salt.

Thwing, Kilham, Harpham, North Grimston, Binnington, Bempton, Steeton, Scagglethorpe, Kirkleatham, Tocketts, Mossdale, Kirklevington, Glaphowe, Newton under Roseberry, Easington, Newton in Whitby Strand, Acklam, Marton, Tollesby, Faceby with Sexhow, High Worsall with Staindale and Little Busby with Tanton, 7½ knight's fees, of the king in chief.

John de Chestre and William de Chestre were jointly enfeoffed of the manor of Hempholme in Holderness, to them, their heirs and assigns, on the day of the forfeiture of Ralph, because in 1384 he gave the manor to John Fullour, chaplain, and John de Sadbergh, and their heirs and assigns, and they held it from then until 1 Nov. 1393 when they conveyed it to John de Chestre and William de Chestre, his brother, with other lands in Northumberland and in the bishopric of Durham which they had of the grant of Ralph, to them their heirs and assigns, and Ralph occupied it only at their will. Owing to his occupation it was taken into the king's hands on his forfeiture. It is held of the fee of St. John of Beverley, service unknown, annual value 40 marks.

Ralph and John Chestre were jointly enfeoffed, to themselves, their heirs and assigns, of the manor of Glaphow by the grant of Elizabeth de Botreux. It is held of the king in chief by knight service, annual value 13s.4d.

All are in the king's hands owing to the forfeiture of Ralph and the minority of Thomas his son and heir.

Thomas died under age on 31 May 1400. John de Lomley, knight, son and now heir of Ralph and brother and heir of Thomas, was aged 20 on 2 Feb. last.

956 Writ 25 June 1404.

NORTHUMBERLAND. Inquisition. Newcastle upon Tyne castle. 2 Oct.

Ralph de Lomley, knight, by his charters dated 29 June 1384 and shown to the jurors granted his lands, tenements and the services of both free tenants and villeins and their families in West Chevington, East Chevington, Morwick, Reaveley, Longhirst and Old Moor to John Fullour, chaplain, and John Sadbergh, their heirs and assigns. They held them until 1 Nov. 1393 and then enfeoffed John de Chestre, chaplain, and William de Chestre his brother, their heirs and assigns. They held them until the death of Ralph. He occupied the lands only at the will of these two, but on account of his occupation they were taken into the king's hands on his forfeiture and so remain. No lands are in the king's hands owing to the minority of Thomas de Lomley, his heir.

The West Chevington lands are held of the king in chief by knight service and a payment of 13s.4d. for castle ward at Bamburgh, annual value 4 marks; lands in East Chevington of the manor of Hadston by knight service; lands in Morwick by knight service of the barony of Warkworth and a rent of 13s.4d. to the earl of Northumberland, annual value 8 marks; lands in Old Moor and Longhirst of the barony of Bothal by knight service, annual value nil; and those in Reaveley of the lord of Ingram, service unknown, annual value nil.

Date of death and heir as above.

957 Commission to Robert Conyers, knight, Gilbert Elvet and the escheator in Northumberland to inquire into his holdings in the bishopric of Durham. 4 March 1404 [*CPR 1401–5*, p.425].

DURHAM. Inquisition before Robert Conyers, knight, and Gilbert Elvet. Durham. 3 April.

Ralph de Lomley, knight, John de Chestre, chaplain, and William de Chestre jointly held the manor of Stanley with Shield Row to themselves, their heirs and assigns of the bishop of Durham, service unknown, by the grant of Richard de Kilkenny. Robert de Laton, knight, and Katherine his wife have an annual rent of £10 from the manor for the life of Katherine. The annual value is nil beyond this rent.

He held no more in the bishopric because long before his death by his charter shown to the jurors and dated 20 May 1384 he granted the manors of Stranton, Murton and Monk Hesleden, and various lands and tenements in Hawthorn, Bishop Wearmouth, Tunstall and Sunderland, pasture and fisheries in Wearmouth, the manor of Little Lumley, lands, tenements and fisheries in Great Lumley and Chester le Street, Rickleton manor, lands tenements and pasture in Greencroft, Butterby manor, lands and tenements in Croxdale, and lands, meadows and pastures in Barmpton, with messuages and lands in South Street in Durham, to John Fullour, chaplain, and John de Sadbergh, their heirs and assigns. They held them from that date until 1 Nov. 1393 and then by their charter granted them to John de Chestre, chaplain, and William de Chestre his brother, with other lands in Northumberland and Yorkshire, to them, their heirs and assigns. So they were held until Ralph died. He did not hold or occupy any of them except at the will of these two, but owing to his occupation they were taken into the king's hands on his forfeiture and so remain. Nothing was taken into the king's hands owing to the minority of Thomas his son and heir.

He held nothing in the quarter manor of Seaton Carew except by the grant of John de Chestre and Thomas Creler, chaplains, to hold at their will, as they held by the grant of Thomas Potter and Isabel his wife.

The manor and castle of Little Lumley, Butterby, Morton and Hesleden are held of the bishop of Durham, annual value £20; the manor of Stranton of the heirs of Thomas de Clifford, annual value £40; all the other premises of the bishop of Durham, except certain lands in Hawthorn and 1 messuage in Durham which are held of the prior of Durham, annual value £10. The services are all unknown.

Date of death and heir as above.

C 137/43, no.30

ALICE DE BAGGESOVERE

958 Writ 24 April 1404.

SHROPSHIRE. Inquisition. Bridgnorth. 15 May.

William le Yonge, Richard le Yonge, clerk, his brother, Roger Attenassh, parson of the chapel of Badger, and William Stretey, clerk, granted the manor of Badger with the advowson of the free chapel there to John de Baggesovere and Alice his wife and the heirs male of their bodies, with remainder to the right heirs of William son of Philip de Baggesovere. John died without heirs male by Alice, and William son of Philip died without heirs of his body, so the remainder descended to Annabel and Eleanor, sisters and heirs of William son of Philip. Annabel had a daughter Katherine, now wife of Thomas Sevile, and died. Eleanor had two daughters, Elizabeth and Katherine, and died. Elizabeth is wife of Thomas Maundevile. Katherine had two daughters, Isabel and Elizabeth, and died. Elizabeth is the wife of Ralph Fraunceys. Isabel had two daughters, Katherine and Margaret, and died. Katherine is the wife of William Mercher, Margaret the wife of John de Overton.

Alice held the property until 25 March last, when she died. It then descended to Katherine wife of Thomas Sevile, aged 40 years and more; Elizabeth wife of Thomas Maundevile, 30 years and more; Elizabeth wife of Ralph Fraunceys, 26 years and more; Katherine wife of William Mercher, 20 years and more; and Margaret wife of John de Overton, 18 years and more.

The vill of Ackleton, part of the manor, is held of William de Beuchampe of his manor of Worfield, service unknown; 1 carucate, 30 a. meadow and 40 a. wood, parcel of the manor, are held of Elizabeth Ersedekon of the lordship of Richards Castle, service unknown; the remainder of the manor, with the advowson, of the prior of Wenlock, service unknown; annual value of the manor 10 marks.

Ralph de Arden her kinsman and next heir is aged 30 years and more.

C 137/44, no.31
E 149/83, no.9

WALTER ROMESYE, KNIGHT

959 Writ 28 Nov. 1403.

HAMPSHIRE. Inquisition. Ringwood. 6 Dec.

He held the manor of Rockbourne of the king in chief by knight service jointly with Alice his wife, who survives, for their lives, by the grant of Thomas Bonham and John Wykyng, with successive remainders to Thomas son of Thomas Romesye and his heirs male, Walter brother of Thomas son of Thomas and his heirs male, and the right heirs of Margaret Byset, mother of Walter, knight, as appears by the king's licence [*CPR 1399–1401*, p.451] and by charters and muniments shown to the jurors; annual value £20.

Similarly he held 2 messuages, 1 carucate, 20 a. meadow, 10 a. wood and rents of £12 and 12 quarters of salt in Romsey, East Dean, Hyde and Marshwood by the grant of John Wykyng, John Fauntleroy and John Toper, chaplain, with successive remainders to Thomas son of Thomas Romseye and his heirs male, Walter brother of Thomas and his heirs male, and the right heirs of Walter, knight, as appears by a fine [CP 25(1) 290/59, no.49] shown to the jurors; annual value £16.

One messuage and 20 a. are held of Henry Popham and his heirs by fealty, the remainder of the abbess of Romsey by fealty.

He died on 25 Nov. Thomas son of Thomas Romseye, his next heir, is aged 13 years and more.

960 Writ 28 Nov. 1403.

DORSET. Inquisition. Cerne Abbas. 1 Jan. 1404.

He held of the king in chief two knight's fees in South Perrott and Clifton Maybank, which Philip Mabank held of him of the manor of Rockbourne in Hampshire. He held them jointly with Alice his wife by the same grant and with the same remainders as that manor [as in last], annual value when they occur £10.

He also held jointly with Alice for their lives by the grant, by a deed shown to the jurors, of William Fillol, deceased, by the rent of a rose, with reversion to the heirs of William: 10 marks rent from the manor of Bradford Bryan, formerly of Hugh Mohaut; 2 messuages and 40 a. in Thornhill by Holt which Nicholas Crouk, deceased, held for life, annual value 26s. 8d.; 2 messuages and 40 a. in Petersham by Wimborne Minster, annual value 20s.; and 12 a. in Barnsley formerly of John le Hoppere, deceased, annual value 6s.

In the dower of Alice from Ralph atte Hyde, sometime her husband, he held a third part of the manor of Allington, and 19 messuages, 80 a. arable and 40 a. meadow in Knitson, Herston, Newton, Swanage, Woolgarston and Moreton, with reversion to William Bonevylle, knight, and his heirs, annual value 100s.

He died on 25 Nov. Thomas son of Thomas his son and his next heir is aged 13 years and more.

961   Writ 28 Nov. 1403.
WILTSHIRE. Inquisition. Wilton. 3 Jan. 1404.
He held 1 a. in Coombe Bissett, parcel of the half manor of Coombe Bissett, in his demesne as of fee of the king in chief by knight service, annual value 4d.

Jointly with Alice his wife for their lives he held half the manor of Coombe Bissett, except the 1 a., of the king in chief, by the grant by a fine made with royal licence [CP 25(1) 290/59, no.49; *CPR 1401-5*, p.15] of John Wykyng, John Fauntleroy and John Toper, chaplain, with successive remainders to Thomas Romesye, son of Thomas, son of Walter, and his heirs male, Walter brother of Thomas and his heirs male, and the right heirs of Walter, knight, on the side of Margaret Byset, his mother; annual value 100s.

Date of death and heir as above.

962   Writ 28 Nov. 1403.
SOMERSET. Inquisition. Bridgwater. 8 Jan. 1404.
He held in his demesne as of fee:

Langridge, 9 a., a weekly market on Thursdays and a yearly fair for three days, the eve, feast and morrow of St. Mary Magdalen, of the king in chief, annual value 8d.

East Cranmore and Catcott, 2 knight's fees, of the abbot of Glastonbury by knight service. William Hangford, knight, holds 1 fee in East Cranmore, Walter Cadecote the other in Catcott; annual value nil except for wards, marriages, reliefs or escheats when they occur.

High Littleton, 1d. rent from 1 messuage, 1 carucate, 6 a. meadow and 10 a. wood, which John Boteler holds for life by the grant of Walter Romesye with reversion to him. They are held of the earl of March of the honour of Gloucester.

Shepton Mallet, 5s. rent from 1 messuage and 16 a., which John Babyngton holds for life by the grant of Walter. This rent with the reversion of the holding Walter granted to Richard Dumer for life, and John Babyngton attorned to Richard Dumer. It is held of Matthew Gourney, knight, by fealty.

Under the fine of 1402 [above, no.959] he held jointly with Alice his wife the manor of Oakleigh, a third part of the manor of Mudford, and 2 messuages, 3 carucates, 25 a. meadow, 70 a. wood and rents of £6 10s., 1 lb. wax and ½ lb. pepper in Otterhampton, Combwich and Pipplepen. They recognised the right of John Fauntleroy, John

Wykyng and John Toper, who in turn granted to them for their lives with successive remainders of Oakleigh and the third part of Mudford to Thomas son of Thomas Romesye and his heirs male, Walter brother of Thomas the son and his heirs male, and the right heirs of Walter, knight, and of the other holdings to Walter brother of Thomas and his heirs male, Thomas the son and his heirs male, and the right heirs of Walter, knight.

Oakleigh is held of John Lorty, knight, and his heirs by fealty; the third part of Mudford of Michael earl of Suffolk by knight service and a rent of 6s. of his manor of Haselbury; 1 messuage and 1 carucate in Pipplepen of John Lorty by fealty and suit of court twice yearly at North Perrott; the remainder in Otterhampton and Combwich of John Twychet, knight, by knight service of his manor of Nether Stowey.

Date of death and heir as above.

C 137/44, no.32
E 149/83, no.10

IVO DE HARLESTON

963 Writ 12 Nov. 1403.
ESSEX. Inquisition. Thaxted. 19 Nov.

He once held in his demesne as of fee:

Steeple Bumpstead, the manor called Waltons: 1 toft and 15 a., parcel of the manor, of the king in chief as a twenty-fifth part of a knight's fee and by 3s. rent payable by the sheriff, annual value 3s.; and the rest of the manor of the abbot of Westminster, service unknown, annual value £10.

Wimbish, the manor called Waltons, *alias* Tiptoft, of Edward duke of York and Philippa his wife, service unknown, annual value 10 marks.

Roydon, the manor called Downhall, of the prior of St. John of Jerusalem in England by fealty and a rent of 5s. 1d. payable by equal parts at Easter and Michaelmas, annual value £4.

Long before his death he granted to Reynold Grey, lord of Ruthin, Master Ivo Souche, clerk, William Par, knight, Payn Typtot, knight, Ralph Braylesforde, William Alkebarowe and Robert Parys, clerk, their heirs and assigns, all his lands in Wimbish, Roydon, Steeple Bumpstead, Birdbrook, Sturmer and Wixoe, except those which were of the fee of the earl of March. The tenants attorned to them, and they regranted the lands to Ivo by the name of Eudo de Harleston, Eleanor his wife, and the heirs of their bodies, with remainder to his right heirs. So they held and the tenants attorned to them. Eleanor survives him.

He died on 10 Nov. John son of Ivo and Eleanor and next heir is aged 1 year and more.

964 HERTFORD. Inquisition. Ware. 17 Nov. 1403.

He held nothing in Hertfordshire.

Date of death and heir as above.

965 Writ 12 Nov. 1403.
BEDFORD. Inquisition. Tempsford. 22 Nov.

He held the manor of Dunton Chamberlain in his demesne as of fee of the king in chief as a twelfth part of a knight's fee, annual value £10.

Date of death and heir as above.

966   Writ 12 Nov. 1403.

CAMBRIDGE. Inquisition. Babraham. 26 Nov.

He held in his demesne as of fee of the king in burgage a manor in St. Clement's parish in Cambridge, extending into Yen Hall, Newnham, Coton, Chesterton, Water-beach and Fordham, which long before he died he granted to Reynold Lord Grey of Ruthin and others [as in no.963 above], and they regranted it to him and Eleanor his wife and the heirs of their bodies, with remainder to his right heirs. So Eleanor now holds it, annual value £10.

Date of death and heir as above.

C 137/44, no.33
E 149/82, no.7

JOHN MOUCHE

967   Writ, *melius sciri*, referring to a writ sent to William Walweyn, escheator, who was superseded before holding an inquisition, 24 April 1405.

HEREFORD AND THE ADJACENT MARCH OF WALES. Inquisition. Hereford. 12 Dec.

He held the manor of Trefecca in the March in west Wales (Westwallis), of whom and by what service is unknown, annual value 20 marks.

He died on 3 Nov. 1403. Fulk son of John and Elizabeth his wife and his next heir was aged 14 at his father's death.

968   Writ 1 Dec 1403.

SHROPSHIRE AND THE ADJACENT MARCH OF WALES. Inquisition. Shrewsbury. 18 Dec.

He held for life by the courtesy of England of the inheritance of Elizabeth daughter and heir of Fulk Corbet, knight, sometime his wife, with remainder to Fulk their son as heir of Elizabeth:

Yockleton, Shelve and Wentnor, the manors, with one quarter of the forest of Caus, of the king in chief by knight service, annual value £30 and no more because they lie in the borders of the county which are raided by Welsh rebels, devastated and partly burnt from day to day. Joan wife of John Barras, esquire, once the wife of Robert de Harley, held a rent of £60 for life with Robert her husband taken in equal parts from these three manors and the quarter of the forest by a fine of 1334 [8 Edward III, *recte* 38 Edward III, 1364: CP 25(1) 195/16, no.43] between Fulk son of Robert Corbet of Moreton Corbet and Robert and Joan Harley. After the death of Robert her husband, Joan Harley disclaimed £20 of this rent on condition of receiving £40 yearly for life from Fulk son of Robert Corbet, then the tenant of these manors. After the death of Fulk, owing to the insufficiency of the revenues she freely released £10 to John Mouche, then tenant of the manors, and so received £30 yearly for life. Joan and John Barras, now her husband, held this until the death of John Mouche.

Wattlesborough, the manor, of the earl of Stafford, a minor in the king's ward, of the castle of Caus by knight service, annual value £10 at present and no more because it lies on the bounds of the March and the tenants have withdrawn from fear of the malice and damage of the Welsh rebels.

Hem, the manor, of the king in chief by a rent of 3s. payable through the sheriff, annual value 40s. and no more.

Bretchel, the hamlet, of John de Eyton by a rent of 10s., annual value 20s. and no more.

He held the lordship of Mochdre in the March in his demesne as of fee of Edward lord of Powys by knight service of his castle of Welshpool, annual value nil because totally wasted by the rebels. Long before he died he gave by his charter to Thomas Lee, William Lee and Griffin Mouche, their heirs and assigns, a rent of £40 from this lordship, and they held it in peace until the lordship was devastated by the Welsh rebels.

He died on 3 Nov. Fulk son of John and Elizabeth and next heir of both is aged 14 years and more. He was born at Wattlesborough on 31 Aug. 1388 and baptised in the church of Alberbury.

C 137/44, no.34
E 149/83, no.8

JOAN WIDOW OF ANTHONY DE LUCY, KNIGHT

969 Writ 20 Oct. 1403.

LINCOLN. Inquisition. Whaplode. 27 Oct.

She held for life in dower of Anthony her former husband a third part of the manor of Fleet, except for various lands worth £4, with reversion to Robert de Haryngton of Aldingham, knight, and Walter Fitzwauter of Woodham Walter, knight, as kinsmen and heirs of Anthony.

John de Multon of Egremont, knight, once held in his demesne as of fee this third part with the other two parts and other manors and lands in Lincolnshire. He died without heirs of his body and the lands descended to Elizabeth, Joan and Margaret as his sisters and heirs. The third part with other parcels was assigned to Margaret. She died and it descended to Anthony as her son and heir. He married Joan and died without issue. It descended to Maud his sister and heir. She married Gilbert de Umfraville, earl of Angus, and after the death of Anthony, Maud and Gilbert entered and afterwards assigned the third part less the parts mentioned above to Joan in dower. Maud died without heirs of her body. Robert Haryngton and Walter Fitzwauter are her next heirs. Robert is son of John, son of Elizabeth, sister of Margaret, mother of Anthony and Maud, aged 40 years and more; Walter Fitzwauter is son of Walter, son of John, son of Joan, the other sister of Margaret, aged 24 years and more.

The third part is held of Robert and Walter, annual value 20 marks, and they hold it with the rest of the manor of the king of the duchy of Lancaster by knight service.

She died at Clerkenwell in the suburbs of London on 1 Sept. last.

C 137/44, no.35

THOMASIA WIDOW OF JOHN CHICHESTRE

970 Writ 8 June 1404.

SOMERSET. Inquisition. Crewkerne. 21 June.

John Eve, chaplain, Henry Stoute and Thomas Yeo, clerk, held the manors of Beggearn Huish and Dunwear in their demesne as of fee, and by their deed granted them after the death of John Chichestre to Thomasia for life with remainder to the heirs of the bodies of John and Thomasia. She held them and married William Talbot, knight. They are held of John, son and heir of John earl of Huntingdon, of his manor of Barnstaple in Devon by knight service; annual values, Beggearn Huish 100s.,

Dunwear £20. Barnstaple is in the king's hands owing to the minority, being held of the king in chief of the crown by knight service.

She died on 31 July 1402. John son of John Chichestre and Thomasia and son and heir of both is aged 17 years. William Talbot has held the lands since her death, title unknown.

971 Writ 8 June 1404.
DEVON. Inquisition. Exeter. 18 June.

John Eve, chaplain, Henry Stoute and Thomas Yeo, clerk, held the manors of Raleigh by Barnstaple and Ruxford Barton in their demesne as of fee with 1 messuage, 4 ferlings and 60 a. wood in Coxleigh, and granted them to Thomasia for life after the death of John, with remainder to the heirs of John and Thomasia. Raleigh is held of John, son of John earl of Huntingdon, of the manor of Barnstaple by knight service, annual value £20. Barnstaple, held of the king in chief of the crown by knight service, is in the king's hands owing to the minority. Ruxford is held of Philip Courtenay of his manor of Bradninch by knight service, and the holdings in Coxleigh of William Beaumont of his manor of Shirwell by knight service, annual values 10 marks and 13s.4d.

She married William Talbot, knight. Date of death, heir and tenure by William Talbot as above.

C 137/44, no.36

JOHN CAWODE

972 Writ 5 Oct. 1403.
YORK. Inquisition. Cawood. 3 Nov.

He held in his demesne as of fee of the king in chief by knight service, as parcel of a third part of the vill of Cawood, which his ancestors held in chief 1 capital messuage, annual value nil; herbage in the site, 12d.; 95 a. 2 roods at 6d., 47s.9d.; 13a. 1 rood of meadow at 12d., 13s.3d.; 4½ a. 2 parts of a rood of pasture at 6d., 2s.4d.; rents of free tenants payable by equal parts at Whitsun and Martinmas, 14d.; 16 messuages and 22 a. held by various tenants at will payable similarly, 27s.; 12 waste tofts, 12d.; 1 ruinous windmill, nil; 3 fishgarths in the river Ouse, nil; and 2 oak trees to be received each year from the foreign wood of the archbishop of York at Cawood, 20d.

He died on 9 Sept. last. Peter his son and heir is aged 10 years and more.

CECILY WIDOW OF JOHN CAWODE

973 YORK. Assignment of dower in the presence of Thomas Brokett and Thomas Gower, to whom the king committed the lands. 19 March 1404.

In Cawood: 18 a. in 'Davydleys' with the lane there; 6 a. held by Thomas Smyth; 3½ a. by Vincent Tailliour; 3 a. by John Henman; 1 rood by Thomas Gybbounman; 5 a. called 'Bonsall' by John Huton; 2½ a. by William Hokday; ⅓ rood by William Clerk; 2½ a. in 'Claywyk'; 2 a. meadow in 'Northenge'; 1 a. meadow held by Richard Enot in 'Esthenge'; 3 roods there held by Thomas Smyth; ½ a. by Cecily Cook; ½ rood by William Clerk; a third part of 2 pieces of pasture in 'Griscroft'; the holdings of Matthew

Shall, Thomas Smyth, John Croxton, William Brome, John Chubbok and John Car-
lele; wastes held by Thomas Barker, Henry Lowys, Marjory Boys and Maud de Rome;
1 fishgarth in the Ouse called 'Sandded'; a third part of assize rents of free tenants,
22d., namely from Richard Hemyngburgh 12d., Walter del Hall 6d. and William
Trusse 4d.; with the court, common rights and other profits and easements belonging
to the third part, which third part is worth 32s. yearly.

C 137/44, no.37
E 152/380, no.5

THOMAS EARL OF KENT

974   Writ 23 Jan. 1404.
LEICESTER. Inquisition. Hallaton. 24 March.
   He held the castle and vill of Castle Donington to himself and his heirs by the grant
of Edward III to Edmund earl of Kent, his ancestor [*CChR* IV, pp.2–5], he being the
son of Thomas, son of Joan princess of Wales, sister of John, brother of Edmund,
son of Edmund.
   There are the site of the castle, annual value nil; a watermill, £3; a park, nil beyond
the cost of the enclosure and the fee of the parker; a fishery in the Trent, 13s.4d.; 3
carucates, 40s.; 40 a. meadow at 12d.; rent of free tenants, 40s. payable by equal parts
at Michaelmas and Lady Day; rent of burgesses, customary tenants and cottars, £36
10s.4d. payable similarly; and perquisites of court with 2 views of frankpledge, 40s.
They are held of Henry prince of Wales of his county of Chester, service unknown.
   He died on 7 Jan. 1400. Edmund his brother and heir is aged 21 years and more.
The castle and vill were taken into the king's hands and so remain. Who has taken the
profits is unknown.

975   Writ 3 July 1404.
NOTTINGHAM. Inquisition. Nottingham. 20 Oct.
   By the grant of Edward III to Edmund earl of Kent, his ancestor [as above, no.974]
he held to himself and his heirs:
   Ollerton, the manor, annual value in lands, meadows, pastures, demesnes, rents,
services, farms, perquisites of courts, woods, mill and all other profits and liberties
50s. Immediately after his death it was taken into the king's hands owing to his
forfeiture, and from that time Thomas Basse occupied it to the king's use of the duchy
of Lancaster until 1 July 1403. Then the king by letters patent [*CPR 1401–5*, p.260]
granted to Edmund de Holand, now earl of Kent, brother and heir of the late earl,
livery of all his inheritance in the county, except for the wapentake of Ollerton. Of
whom it is held is unknown.
   Ollerton, the wapentake, annual value in rents, services and all other appurtenances
£4, but of whom it is held and by what service is unknown. Thomas Basse held it until
30 Sept. 1404, and William de Lake since that date, both to the king's use.
   Plumtree, the wapentake, annual value £4, but of whom and by what service is
unknown. It was held like the manor of Ollerton by Thomas Basse until 1 July 1403,
and since then by Edmund earl of Kent.
   He died on 7 Jan. 1400. Edmund his brother and next heir was aged 21 on 6 Jan.
last.

976 DERBY. Inquisition. Ashford. 18 Oct. 1404.

By the grant of Edward III to Edmund earl of Kent, his ancestor [as above, no.974] he held to himself and the heirs of his body:

Risley, the wapentake, of whom and by what service is unknown, annual value 30s. Owing to his forfeiture it was taken into the king's hands. Thomas Basse until 30 Sept. 1403 and since then William de Leeke have occupied it to the king's use of the duchy of Lancaster, and taken the profits.

Ashford, the manor, extending in Ashford, Longstone, Sheldon, Wardlow and Holme, of whom and by what service is unknown, annual value £60. It was taken into the king's hands, and Thomas Beaufort held it by the king's grant until 1 July 1403, when by letters patent [as in no.975] the king granted all his inheritance in this county, except the wapentake of Risley, to Edmund now earl of Kent.

Ticknall, certain lands, of whom held and by what service is unknown, annual value 40s. Thomas Basse occupied them until 30 Sept. 1403, and since then Richard, the bailiff of Castle Donington castle, both to the king's use of the duchy of Lancaster.

He held the manor of Chesterfield jointly with Joan his wife of the king in chief by knight service, by the grant of Thomas earl of Kent and Alice his wife by a fine [CP 25(1) 289/56, no.243] to them and their heirs. Joan has held it since his death, annual value £60.

Date of death and heir as above [no.975].

977 Writ 3 July 1404.
LINCOLN. Inquisition. Bourne. 7 Oct.

By the grant of Edward III to Edmund earl of Kent, his ancestor [as above, no.974] he held to himself and his heirs, of the king in chief by knight service:

Greetham, the manor and the lordship called the honour of Greetham, extending in Greetham, Minting, Gautby, Thurlby, Langton, Stenwith and many other places; annual value in rents, farms, perquisites of court, woods and other profits £40. They were taken into the king's hands on his death, and William de Wyllughby, lord of Eresby, has taken the issues and profits by the king's grant [CFR XII, p.43], for how long is unknown.

Hay, the fee, with the ward of Lincoln castle, and rents, farms, foreign services, courts and views of frankpledge in Billingborough and Bitchfield, with fees, advowsons and 2 shops with solars in the bailiwick of Lincoln belonging to the fee, annual value 106s.8d. They were taken into the king's hands on his death and have since been held by the escheators.

Caistor, Beesby and Market Deeping, the manors, annual values £52, £32, and £202, with the advowson of the church of St. Nicholas, South Kelsey.

Also by the grant of Edward III he held, but of whom and by what services is unknown:

Keelby and Brattleby, the manors, annual values £14 and £13 6s.8d., and the free court called rere-county held at Lincoln every six weeks, annual value 20s.

The manors of Caistor, Beesby, Market Deeping, Keelby and Brattleby, the advowson and the free court came into the possession of Edmund de Holand, now earl of Kent, in virtue of the entails by his predecessors and the letters patent of 1 July 1403 [CPR 1401–5, p.260] shown to the jurors, granting him all his lands in Lincolnshire except the manor and honour of Greetham, the fee of Hay, lands in Stenwith, the manors of Horbling, Sedgebrook and Thurlby, and the free court of Hay; and he has taken the profits of the manors of Caistor etc. since then.

Francis de Courte, knight, had the issues of the manors of Caistor, Beesby and Keelby by the king's grant from the death of the earl until 1 July 1403. Thomas Rempston held the manor of Market Deeping for one year after the earl's death to the king's use, and then the king granted it to Joan, the earl's widow, who held it until 1 July 1403. Henry now bishop of Lincoln took the issues and profits of the manor of Brattleby until the same 1 July, and the escheators held and took the issues of the rere-county to the king's use.

He also held of the king in chief by knight service jointly with Joan his wife the castle and manor of Bourne with its members, and £30 rent from the manor of Skellingthorpe, to them and the heirs of their bodies by the grant of Thomas Holand, late earl of Kent, and Alice his wife by a fine [CP 25(1) 289/56, no.243]. Edward I granted Bourne to John de Wake, knight, and Joan his wife, [CPR 1292–1301, p.303] and Thomas was his lineal descendant, being the son of Thomas, son of Joan princess of Wales, daughter of Margaret, sister of Thomas, son of John and Joan de Wake. The annual value of the castle and manor is £70. Joan his widow has held them since the death of Thomas by virtue of the fine.

Date of death and heir as above.

978 MIDDLESEX. Inquisition. Westminster. 7 July 1404.

He held in his demesne as of fee of the king in chief 2 messuages, 1 hide and 1 'bordel' of half a hide, and half a virgate in the parish of Stepney at Mile End, and common pasture for 60 swine in the forest of Havering by the service of finding a leash each year for the king's greyhounds when the king hunts in person in the forest between 15 Aug. and 8 Sept. After his death John Cassey entered without licence and enfeoffed John Potter and George Benet, citizens and cordwainers of London, and they have held them without licence until the present; annual value 60s.

[Cf. CPR 1405–8, p.20].

C 137/44, no.38
C 137/51, no.56

EDMUND HOLAND

979 Writ for proof of age, 18 April 1404.

HAMPSHIRE. Proof of age. Winchester. 22 May.

The jurors say that Edmund Holand, brother and heir of Thomas earl of Kent, was born at Brockenhurst on 6 Jan. 1382 and baptised on the 8th in the church of St. Thomas the Apostle there; and he is therefore aged 21.

They remember the date because:

William Frebody, aged 50 years and more, held a lighted torch at the font during the baptism.

Thomas Colyngton, 42 and more, on that day brought 12 partridges to Thomas de Holland, the father of Edmund.

Robert atte More, 46 and more, killed a deer on that day in the New Forest near Brockenhurst with two white greyhounds.

John Wallop, 50 and more, on that day took two swans to Brockenhurst and gave them to Alice countess of Kent, the mother of Edmund.

John Payn, 56 and more, on that day served in the hall of Thomas the father at Brockenhurst manor, and there cut the thumb of his left hand with a knife.

William Escote, 50 and more, held a lighted torch at the font.

John Polayn, 60 and more, brought a wild boar, killed in the said forest, to the town and presented it to Thomas the father.

John Harryes, 50 and more, presented 12 capons and 24 hens (*pulcrones*) to the mother.

Thomas Tauk, 42 and more, held a torch at the font.

John Shottere, 50 and more, carried a torch before Edmund when he was brought to the church for the baptism, and there lit it and gave it to William Frebody at the font.

Thomas Brangwyn, 46 and more, provided a silk purse.

Robert Barbour of Romsey, 50 and more, carried a torch before Edmund to the church, and gave it to William Escote at the font.

C 137/44, no.38, mm.9,10

RICHARD DE LA POLE

980 Writ 2 Jan. 1404.

NORTHAMPTON. Inquisition. Northampton. 12 Jan.

He held the manor of Grafton in fee tail by a fine of 1384 [CP 25(1) 289/54. no.113] by which Michael de la Pole, knight, granted it to William de la Pole and his heirs male, with successive remainders to Richard de la Pole and his heirs male, and Thomas de la Pole and his heirs male, all being the sons of Michael. William died without heirs long ago. Richard held it and died without heirs on 18 Dec. last, and so it remains to Thomas who is aged 26 years and more.

He also held the advowsons of Bugbrooke and Grafton. All are held of the king in chief as a fifth part of a fee; annual values, manor £18, advowson of Bugbrooke 20 marks when it occurs, Grafton 10 marks.

Michael earl of Suffolk, his brother and next heir, is aged 30 years and more.

981 Writ 2 Jan. 1404.

BUCKINGHAM. Inquisition. Buckingham. 14 Jan.

He held the manor of Marsh in his demesne in fee tail of the king in chief by the grant of Michael de la Pole his father by the fine of 1384 [above, no.980]. It is held by knight service, annual value 20 marks. He also held 11s.4d. rent from a tenement called 'Gracielord' and land called 'Powereslond' in Mursley to himself and his heirs and assigns, of the king in chief by knight service. Altogether the manor and rent constitute a fifth part of a knight's fee.

He died on 27 Dec. last without heirs male of his body. Thomas is his heir under the fine and aged 26 years and more. Michael earl of Suffolk is heir to the rent of 11s.4d., being next heir in blood, and aged 30 years and more.

C 137/44, no.39
E 149/82, no.9
E 152/394

THOMAS BEAUPYNE

982 Writ 5 Feb. 1404.

DORSET. Inquisition. Wareham. 15 March.

He held the manor of Sturminster Marshall called 'Beauchampsmanere' in his demesne as of fee and granted it to Philip Wodeman and William Basket for their lives by a rent of 12 marks, and he granted the rent with the reversion of the manor to Thomas Harewell, Robert Orchard and William Pynche, and the heirs and assigns of Thomas Harewell. Afterwards by a fine of 1403 [CP 25(1) 51/53, no.16] between Harewell, Orchard and Pynche, and Henry Darleston, clerk, Thomas Colston, and Thomas Beaupyne and Margaret his wife, the reversion after the deaths of Philip Wodeman and William Basket was granted to Thomas Beaupyne and Margaret for their lives, with successive remainders to William Venour and Elizabeth his wife and the heirs of their bodies, the heirs of Thomas Beaupyne and Margaret, the heirs of Margaret, and the right heirs of William Venour.

Thomas died holding the rent and reversion jointly with Margaret. The manor is held of the King in chief by knight service, annual value nil beyond the rent.

Margery wife of John Harewell, Elizabeth wife of William Venour, Margaret wife of William Worfton, and Agnes wife of John Bluet, his daughters and heirs, are aged 30, 26, 24, and 19 years and more.

983 Writ 5 Feb. 1404.

BRISTOL. Inquisition. Guildhall. 26 March.

In right of Margaret his wife he held 1 messuage in St. Thomas Street of Thomas Berkelegh, Lord Berkeley, by a land-gavel rent of 6d. yearly, annual value 40s.; 2 messuages in West Tucker Street of the same by 4s. land-gavel, annual value 20s.; and 1 messuage in Redcliffe Street by 12d. land-gavel, annual value 4 marks.

He died on 11 Nov. last, heirs as above. Margaret has held the messuages in her own right in free burgage since his death.

984 Writ 5 Feb. 1404.

SOMERSET. Inquisition. Ilchester. 17 March.

By a fine of 1403 [CP 25(1) 201/33, no.26] between Thomas Harewell, Robert Orchard and William Pynche, and Henry Darleston, clerk, Henry Colston and Thomas Beaupyne and Margaret his wife, Thomas and Margaret were granted the manor and hundred of North Petherton except for 12s. rent, which was also granted with the homages and services of John Paulet, knight, John Popham, John Payn and Matthew de Clyvedon and their heirs, for their lives, with successive remainders to John Bluet and Agnes his wife and the heirs of their bodies, the heirs of the body of Agnes, the heirs of the bodies of Thomas Beaupyne and Margaret, the heirs of the body of Margaret, and the right heirs of John Bluet.

By another fine of the same date [no.23] between the same parties Thomas Beaupyne and Margaret were granted for their lives the manors of Beer Crocombe and East Capland, with 4 messuages, 50 a. arable, 20 a. meadow, 50 a. pasture and 20 a. wood in Hisbare and Buckland St. Mary and the advowsons of Beer Crocombe and East Capland, with successive remainders to John Harewell and Margery his wife, and the heirs of their bodies, the heirs of the body of Margery, the heirs of the bodies of Thomas Beaupyne and Margaret, the heirs of her body, and the right heirs of John Harewell.

By a third fine of the same date [no.24] between the same parties the manors of

Morton, which was held for life by Richard Walronde and Alice his wife with reversion to Thomas Harewell, and Knowle, with 2 messuages in Bedminster, and the advowson of Knowle, were granted to Thomas Beaupyne and Margaret for their lives, with successive remainders to William Venour, Elizabeth his wife and the heirs of their bodies, the heirs of the body of Elizabeth, the heirs of the bodies of Thomas Beaupyne and Margaret, the heirs of the body of Margaret, and the right heirs of William Venour.

By a fourth fine of the same date [no. 28] between the same parties the manor and advowson of Bawdrip, and 1 messuage, 1 carucate and 4 a. meadow in Chilton Trinity, which Isabel Pare held for life of the inheritance of Thomas Harewell and which should revert to him after her death, were granted to Thomas Beaupyne and Margaret for their lives, with successive remainders to William Worfton and Margaret his wife and the heirs of their bodies, the heirs of Margaret Worfton, the heirs of the bodies of Thomas Beaupyne and Margaret, the heirs of the body of Margaret, and the right heirs of William Worfton.

The manor and hundred of North Petherton are held of the king in chief by knight service, annual value 22 marks; the manors of Beer Crocombe and East Capland, and the other holdings with them, of John Lorty, knight, by knight service, annual value 24 marks; and the manor of Knowle with the holdings in Bedminster etc. of Thomas de Berkeley, knight, Lord Berkeley, by knight service, annual value 100s.

Richard Wallronde and Alice his wife held the manor of Morton for life of Henry Darleston, clerk, Thomas Colston and Thomas and Margaret Beaupyne, by a rent of 10 marks, and they hold it of the abbot of St. Mary Graces by the Tower of London of his manor of Blagdon by knight service, annual value 10 marks beyond the rent. The manor and advowson of Bawdrip are held of Richard de Sancto Mauro by knight service, annual value 20 marks.

Isabel Pare still lives and renders a rose at Midsummer and 2s. at Michaelmas for the premises in Chilton Trinity to Henry Darleston, clerk, Thomas Colston and Thomas and Margaret Beaupyne. It is held of Simon Michell and John Hugyn by a rent of 1 lb. cumin at Michaelmas, annual value beyond this 40s.

Date of death and heirs as above.

985 Writ, *plura*, 16 June 1404.

SOMERSET. Inquisition. Ilchester. 7 July.

John Harewell and Thomas Colston held 4 marks rent payable by equal parts at Easter and Michaelmas from 1 messuage, 1 carucate and 4 a. meadow in Washford, which John Gyst holds for life with reversion to them; and 40s. rent payable at the same terms from 2 messuages, 1 carucate and 16 a. meadow in Idson, which Thomas Haule and Margery his wife hold for life with reversion to them. They granted the rents and reversions to Thomas Beaupyne, Margaret his wife and the heirs of Thomas, and John Gyst, Thomas Haule and Margery attorned to them, and so Thomas Beaupyne held them.

The premises in Washford are held of the abbot of Cleeve by knight service and a rent of 10s., and are worth no more beyond the above 4 marks and 10s. The premises in Idson are held of the heirs of Walter Romesey, knight, by a rent of 1d. at Michaelmas, annual value, beyond that and the rent of 40s., 10s.

Apart from these he held no more than was stated in the inquisitions already returned.

Date of death and heirs as above.

C 137/44, no.40
C 137/45, no.60
E 149/83, no.11

ISABEL WIDOW OF RICHARD PONYNGES, KNIGHT

986 Writ 4 Dec. 1403.

SUFFOLK. Inquisition. Brandon. 21 Dec.

She held the manor of Wrentham called Northall for life by the grant of Thomas Kynardesle, Thomas Blast, John Walyngton, Thomas Flintham, William Wysebech and Thomas Ikham to Richard, her late husband and herself, and the heirs of Richard. It is held of the earl of Arundel by knight service, annual value 20 marks.

She died on 11 April 1394. Robert de Ponynges, their son, is next heir and aged 21 years and more. William Lescrop, earl of Wiltshire, held it from her death until 21 May 1399 by the king's grant [*CPR 1391–6*, p.513]. Then Lescrop granted the custody of all the lands of Richard and Isabel to Humphrey Stafford and William Percy, knights, William Makenade and Thomas Blast, who still hold it and take the issues.

987 NORFOLK. Inquisition. Brandon. 21 Dec.

She held in dower of Richard a third part of a quarter of the manor of Wilton and Hockwold of the earl of Arundel by knight service, annual value 4 marks; and a third part of a quarter of the manor of Flitcham, of whom and by what service is unknown, annual value 40s.

Date of death, heir and tenure since her death, as above.

C 137/45, no.41, mm.1–3

RICHARD PONYNGES, KNIGHT

988 Writ, *plura*, 6 Dec. 1403.

SUSSEX Inquisition. Crawley. 10 Dec.

Thomas de Ponynges, knight, brother of Richard, held in his demesne as of fee 1 messuage and 40 a. in Southwick and Kingston by Sea, and granted them to John atte Hyde and the heirs of his body. He held them and had issue Richard atte Hyde. After the death of John, Richard held and had issue Alice, and she died seised of them on 7 Oct. 1393 without heirs of her body. They should revert to Robert de Ponynges as heir of Thomas, that is son of Richard, brother of Thomas. They were taken into the king's hands because he was in the king's ward on account of other lands held in chief. They are held of Joan widow of John Sandes, knight, service unknown, annual value 30s.

Thomas also held in his demesne as of fee 1 messuage, 24 a. arable, 5 a. meadow and 26 a. pasture in Twineham and gave them to Sarah wife of Simon Smethe for life to hold by a rent of a rose at Midsummer. She held them until she died on 16 Nov. 1395. Then they descended to Robert, who was in the king's ward. They are held of the earl of Arundel, service unknown, annual value 13s.4d.

Alice widow of Nicholas Wylcombe, senior, held in dower of William Bonet, formerly her husband, a third part of the manor of Chyngton, which Nicholas Wylcombe, junior, as heir of William Bonet, son of Alice, sister of William, granted to Richard Ponynges and his heirs. Alice attorned to him. She died on 5 Oct. 1390. It came to Robert as son and heir of Richard, under age in the king's ward, and is held of the prior of Michelham, service unknown, annual value 13s.4d.

Richard survived Thomas his brother, and held all the reversions. Robert de Ponynges is aged 21 years and more.

C 137/45, no.41, mm.4, 5

ALICE DAUGHTER AND HEIR OF RICHARD ATTE HYDE

989 Writ, *plenius certiorari*, enquiring what she held for life of the inheritance of Robert de Ponynges. 6 Dec. 1403.

SUSSEX. Inquisition. Crawley, with the same jurors as above [no.988]. 10 Dec.

She held 1 messuage and 60 a. [*sic*] in Southwick and Kingston by Sea [otherwise as above, no.988] of Joan widow of John Sandes, knight, by knight service and a rent of 2s. to her manor of Kingston by Sea, annual value 30s.

The escheators have held them since her death and are answerable for the profits. Robert de Ponynges, son of Richard, his next heir, is aged 21 years and more.

C 137/45, no.41, mm.6, 7

ROBERT SON AND HEIR OF RICHARD PONYNGES, KNIGHT

990 Writ for proof of age. He is in ward of Humphrey de Stafford and William Percy, knights, William Makenade and Thomas Blast by the grant of William Lescrop, knight, to whom Richard II granted the wardship, and they should be warned. 6 Dec. 1403.

DORSET. Proof of age of Robert son and heir of Richard Ponynges, knight, and Isabel his wife. Dorchester. 31 Dec.

John Pusele, aged 50 years and more, says that Robert was 21 on 2 Dec. 1403, and he knows because he saw him born at Okeford Fitzpaine on 3 Dec. (Wednesday after St. Andrew) 1382 in the house of Robert Fitzpayn there, and baptised in the church of St. Andrew at Okeford on the same day. He had a son Nicholas baptised there on that day.

Nicholas Kene, 48, and William Mayne, 52, saw Robert born in the house of Robert Fitzpayn, and baptised in the church there, and they immediately rode to Woodsford in the same county, and told Guy de Briene, senior, knight, kinsman of Isabel, mother of Robert, and he gave them each 40s.

Nicholas Mautravers, 55, John Bolde, 47, and William Spenser, 61, immediately rode to Ifield in Sussex and told Richard de Ponynges, the father of Robert, and he gave them 20s. each.

John Nypred, 55, had a son buried in that church on the day of the baptism.

William Davy, 48, and Thomas Kene, 56, were retained in the council of Richard the father of Robert in the year before the birth, with a robe and a pension for life, and remember by the date of the pension.

John Busy, 48, and John Stylle, 52, say that on that day Guy de Briene, junior, knight, rode in all haste to Okeford and was godfather, and Walter Mourdon, then parson of Okeford, entered the date in a missal in the church.

Richard Lust, 54, had a son John baptised in the church on that day and knows by counting the years from that baptism.

The escheator warned Humphrey Stafford and William Percy, knights, William Makenade and Thomas Blast, as required by the writ. Humphrey was present, the others not. He said nothing against the proof, and Robert should have his lands.

C 137/45, no.41, mm.8, 9

SARAH WIDOW OF SIMON SMETHE

991 Writ, *melius sciri*, asking what she held for life of the inheritance of Robert Ponynges, and who has held and taken the profits since her death. 6 Dec. 1403.

Sussex. Inquisition. Crawley, with the same jurors as above [no.988]. 10 Dec.

She held for life 1 messuage, 24 a. arable, 5 a. meadow and 26 a. pasture in Twineham by the grant of Thomas de Ponynges, deceased. She died on 17 Nov. 1395. They are held of the earl of Arundel, service unknown, annual value 13s.4d. They belong to Robert as heir of Thomas, being the son of Richard, brother of Thomas de Ponynges. He was a minor in the king's ward on account of other lands held in chief.

The escheators have held since the death of Sarah. Robert son and heir of Richard is aged 21 years and more.

C 137/45, no.43

ELIZABETH WIDOW OF WILLIAM DE BURLE

992 Similar writ, 6 Dec. 1403.

Sussex. Inquisition. Crawley, with the same jurors as above [no.988]. 10 Dec.

She held for life 11s. rent in Little Perching of the inheritance of Robert Ponynges by the grant of William de Perchyng, who granted the reversion to Michael de Ponynges and his heirs. She attorned to him and died on 26 May 1399. It belongs to Robert as son of Richard, son of Michael. He is a minor in the king's ward. Of whom it is held and by what service is unknown. Thomas Camell has held and taken the profits since she died.

Robert Ponynges son and heir of Richard is aged 21 years and more.

C 137/45, no.44

ALICE WIDOW OF NICHOLAS WYLCOMBE

993 Writ, *melius sciri*, enquiring what she held in dower of the inheritance of Richard Ponynges. 6 Dec. 1403.

Sussex. Inquisition. Crawley, with the same jurors as above [no.988]. 10 Dec.

After the death of William Bonet, her husband, she held in dower from him a third part of the manor of Chyngton of the inheritance of Robert de Ponynges, which third part and the reversion Nicholas Wilcombe, son of Alice sister of William Bonet, granted after the death of William to Richard de Ponynges and his heirs. Alice attorned to Richard and died on 27 May 1399. They belong to Robert, who is in the king's ward, as son and heir of Richard.

They are held of the prior of Michelham, service unknown, annual value 13s.4d. Thomas Camell has held them and taken the profits since the death of Alice. Robert is the son and next heir of Richard and aged 21 years and more.

C 137/45, no.45

WALTER SON AND HEIR OF ELEANOR HOLT

994 Writ for proof of age; William Phelip, junior, who was granted the wardship by letters patent [*CPR 1401–5*, p.89] should be warned. 14 Oct. 1403.

[Endorsed] He was warned by John Dounyng and Robert Talbot.

WORCESTER. Proof of age. Redditch. 29 Dec.

The jurors say that Walter Holt, son and heir of Eleanor, daughter of Nicholas Dirnassall, was born at Yardley and baptised in the church there on 22 July 1381 and was therefore 21 [*sic*: the 1 written over erasure] on 23 July last. They remember this for the reasons given:

Richard Rudyng, aged 50 years, was in the church and saw John Preston, chaplain, baptise Walter.

Richard Beawmond, 48, was told about the baptism by his father who was in the church.

Edward Eggeok, 43, says that John his father built a dovecote at Edgiock on that day.

Roger Wodelowe, 44, married Agnes his wife in that church on that day.

William Braderugge, 44, had a son John baptised there on that day.

William Jones, 45, was in the market at Dudley on that day to buy four oxen for his plough.

John Wodeward, 44, mowed a meadow in Yardley on that day.

Henry Chamberleyn, 50, had a son Richard who died on that day.

John Bulnacre, 44, fell from his horse and broke his shin on that day.

Hugh Cotter, 53, says that the abbot of Bordesley dined with the prior of Studley on that day.

William Rouke, 56, was robbed of 20 marks on the Ridge Way on that day.

John Rouke, 43, was serving with his father on that day.

C 137/45, no.46

JOHN SON AND HEIR OF ROBERT CARBONELL, KNIGHT

995   Writ for proof of age; Richard Burgh who has custody of the lands by the grant of the executors of Margaret duchess of Norfolk should be warned. 26 April 1404.

[Endorsed] He was warned by Warin atte Lane and John Fullere.

NORFOLK. Proof of age. Bradeston. 28 May.

The jurors say that he was aged 21 on 23 April last, having been born at Bradeston on 23 April 1382, and baptised in the font of St. Michael's church there.

John Palmer, aged 50 years and more, remembers because his wife Margaret was with Margery Carbonell, the mother, at the birth, and was wet nurse.

Robert Dallyng, 50 and more, was present in the rectory with William Morgate, then rector of Bradeston, when he was told of the birth, and went to the church with him and saw the baptism.

Henry Pye and Thomas Cole, each 57 and more, heard the rector say mass that day, and afterwards saw the baptism and John Fastolf, knight, and others raise John from the font, and the bystanders said he was born that day.

Thomas But and John Heylesdon, each 59 and more, went that day to the manor of John Fastolf in Tunstall by Bradeston to petition him, and were told that he was at Bradeston, hastened there and met him, and he being godfather told them of the birth.

John Stratton and John Grygges, each 52 and more, met several people coming from the church, including Cecily Goodfellow, the common midwife in those parts, who was carrying a child in her arms wrapped in a fine cloth and told them that he was the son of Robert and baptised John.

John Rysyng and John Lyghtfote, each 56 and more, were walking in the fields near the manor of Bradeston looking for certain animals of theirs, and met John Hawe, the bailiff of that manor, who said that he had their beasts impounded at the manor, and told them of the birth and baptism.

Geoffrey atte Lee and Thomas Camplyen, each 54 and more, met the wife of John Palmer of Bradeston coming from the manor and hurrying home, and she told them of the baptism and that she was with Margery the mother at the birth.

C 137/45, no.47

THOMAS SON AND HEIR OF THOMAS FRAMBALD

996 Writ for proof of age, 8 Dec. 1403.

BEDFORD. Proof of age. . . . 1403–4 (5 Henry IV).

The jurors say that Thomas the son was born at Battlesden on 17 June 1381 and baptised there on the same day, and is now aged 22 years and more.

Paul Hereford, aged 60 years and more, 1st juror . . .

William Haukyns, 52 and more, Richard Ballard, 51 and more, and . . . , 56 and more, remember because they were attending the court of Thomas the father as jurors when the birth was announced.

Nicholas Bylmyn, 60 and more, Adam Hert, 50 and more, John Bowebrek, 54 and more, and Simon Pekham, 55 and more, say that Thomas the father asked the then rector to write the day and year of the birth in a martyrology, and so it is now recorded and they know the date.

Thomas Steer, 50 and more, John Ballard, 52 and more, Robert Porton, 53 and more, and Richard Graunt, 56 and more, say that Thomas the father let to farm a several pasture called 'le Overle' to them, and told them of the birth when making the indenture, and they went to the church for the baptism.

C 137/45, no.48

JOHN SON AND HEIR OF ELIZABETH DE NEVYLL

997 Writ for proof of age; Ralph Lord Nevyll, Gerard Braybroke, junior, and John Walshe, knights, and John Warrewyk, who were granted custody of the lands, should be warned. 2 Jan. 1404.

YORK. Inquisition for proof of age. Middleham. 18 Jan.

The jurors say that John son and heir of Elizabeth, widow of John de Nevyll of Raby, knight, was born at Middleham castle in the tower called 'Barontoure' and baptised in the church of St. Mary, Middleham, on 12 June 1381, and is now aged 21 years and more, and this they remember for the following reasons:

Richard de Esyngwalde, aged 52 years and more, met William Chamberlane riding in haste to Raby, and, when asked the reason for his haste, he said that Elizabeth had borne a son and he was taking the news to the father, John de Nevyll.

John de Maunby, 44 and more, was doorkeeper of the castle on the day that John was baptised.

Thomas Broune, 47 and more, sold a Flanders chest to William Kylkenny on that day for the use of Elizabeth.

William de Skeltone, 51 and more, says that Henry Fitzhugh, knight, father of the present Henry Fitzhugh, knight, was godfather of John and gave him a basin and six goblets of silver after the baptism.

William Taillour, 47 and more, had a daughter Isabel born and baptised in the same church on the same day.

William Symson, 52 and more, saw Thomas Ullesby, chaplain, writing the day and year of the birth in the calendar of Elizabeth's great primer.

John Thomson, 48 and more, says that Euphemia de Ketulwell, his neighbour, who is still alive, was nurse to John.

Thomas Frere, 45 and more, was shown 100s. in gold by William Chamberlayne who had been given it by John the father for being the first to bring him the news.

Richard Kykerarde, 45 and more, was in the church and saw the baptism.

John Dent, 49 and more, saw William Wylde, William Chamberlayne, John Butteler, John Hoton, William Grene and William Burton carrying six wax torches at the baptism.

Richard Ingelande, 62 and more, saw John Alwent, chaplain in Coverham abbey, write the day and year of the birth in a psalter, and Alwent who was present confirmed this.

John Hudeson, 56 and more, on that day took the holding in which he lives from Richard Baysi, then steward of the court of John the father.

The escheator sent to inform Ralph Lord de Nevyll, knight, . . . [torn off] because in London at the parliament. The others named in the writ have no properties in this bailiwick where they could be warned.

C 137/45, no.50

HENRY SON AND HEIR OF JOHN DE BELLO MONTE, KNIGHT

998   Writ for proof of age; Katherine de Bello Monte, who has the wardship by the grant of Edward duke of York, should be warned. 15 May 1404.

[Endorsed] Katherine was warned by Thomas Holme and Thomas Warner at Linwood on 22 May.

LINCOLN. Proof of age in the presence of Thomas de Enderby, attorney of Katherine de Bello Monte, keeper of the lands by the grant of Edward duke of York to whom the king gave them. Folkingham. 31 May.

The jurors say that he is 21 years of age and more, and was born in Folkingham castle on 16 Aug. 1381, and baptised in the church there, and this they know because:

Nicholas Davy of Threekingham, aged 64 years and more, with others held torches at the baptism.

Thomas Seywyll of Pointon, 63 and more, was in the church and saw Adam, sometime prior of Sempringham, baptising Henry.

Robert Bozom of Pointon, 60 and more, was present and saw the Lady Hawise Luterell who was the godmother.

John Saperton of Pickworth, 50 and more, was in the church and was surprised that Henry did not bear the same name as his godfather, Thomas la Warre.

John Palmer of Spanby, 50 and more, says that William Sunbery, parker of Folkingham, took rabbits from the warren of Quarrington in his bailiwick for the dinner of those who were at the baptism.

John Ouseby of Oseby, 50 and more, had a discussion with the midwife and other women, through which they found a good wet nurse.

John Fordham of Billingborough, 65 and more, was in the church and says that Adam de Leverington, formerly prior of Sempringham, was the other godfather.

William Amyson of Billingborough, 45 and more, saw Margaret wife of Geoffrey Cook of Irnham carrying Henry to the church for the baptism.

William Bawdewyn of Billingborough, 50 and more, says that immediately after the baptism Thomas la Warre, the godfather, gave Henry a silver cup.

John Kyrketon of Swaton, 60 and more, saw Henry carried to the church with four unlighted torches around him.

William Birthorp of Walcot, 60 and more, saw Adam, the other godfather, immediately after the baptism give a little purse of gold.

John Stowe of Folkingham, 60 and more, saw four men carrying torches without lights to the church around Henry, and afterwards the torches were carried lighted from the church to the castle.

John Robinson of Folkingham, 60 and more, immediately after the baptism saw Thomas de Bostone, then rector, write the day and place of birth in a great breviary of the church.

C 137/45, no.51

MARGARET WIFE OF THOMAS SEGRAVE AND ISABEL WIFE OF WILLIAM ULKERTHORP, DAUGHTERS AND HEIRS OF JOHN FRECHEVYLE SON AND HEIR OF JOHN FRECHEVYLE OF PALTERTON

999 Writ for proof of age; Robert de Stokley, who was granted custody of the lands by Richard II [*CPR 1381–5*; p.175], should be warned. 5 July 1403.

[Endorsed] He was warned by John Balton and William Preston.

DERBY. Proof of age. Chesterfield. 20 Oct.

The jurors say that Margaret was born at Nettleworth and baptised in the church of Warsop on 12 May 1383 and is therefore aged 20 years and more. Isabel was born at Nettleworth and baptised at Warsop on 26 Jan. 1385, and is therefore aged 18 years and more.

Roger Somur of Scarcliffe, aged 60 and more, knows this because on the first occasion he was in company with John their father at Pleasley Park, saw a sitting hare, shot it in the head with an arrow and sent it to Beatrice the mother of Margaret on the day of the birth; and on the day of Isabel's birth William Netylworth, grandfather of Isabel, bought a black horse from him for 40s.

Ralph de Glapwell, 44 and more, came to the house where Margaret was born on that day, and on the day that Isabel was born met a forester of Sherwood carrying on his shoulder a quantity of game, and he said that he was going to Beatrice who had borne Isabel on that day.

John de Ufton, 62 and more, when Margaret was born took two pheasants to Nettleworth and presented them to Beatrice the mother; and on the day of the birth of Isabel he met William Netylworth, the grandfather, in the fields of Palterton.

Richard Pereson of Scarcliffe, 46 and more, went to Lady Deincourt who was staying at Elmeton, and a woman from Nettleworth was there who said that Beatrice had given birth to Margaret, and immediately he was free from the chains of his punishment, praised be the Lord; and on the second occasion he presented two hens to Beatrice mother of Isabel.

William de Chaumbur, 41 and more, was staying with the lady of Longford at Park Hall and bought a palfrey for her from a chaplain celebrating in the church of Warsop, and he was in the church and heard the parish chaplain baptising, and afterwards the chaplain told him that it was a daughter of John Frechevyle; and on the second occasion he heard Nicholas Goushyll, knight, saying at Chesterfield that Beatrice had given birth to Isabel and, John the father being dead, Margaret and Isabel were co-heirs.

William son of Thomas de Plesley had a dispute with Richard son of John de Scarkelyff, and it was settled at Scarcliffe on the day of Margaret's birth, of which the midwife came and told them; and on the Sunday after Isabel's birth he was in the company of William de Netylworth, the grandfather, who noted the date in a psalter.

Ralph Smyth of Stony Houghton, 52 and more, was staying with John the father of Margaret, who carried her to the church at Warsop; and on the second occasion he was at Nottingham to buy wine and other victuals, and when he returned home he asked what the child was called and was told Isabel.

John Symson of Pleasley, 46 and more, bought oats for his horses from John the father who told him of the birth of Margaret on that day; and on the second occasion, learning that Beatrice had borne Isabel, he sent her a lamb.

Peter de Kestewon, 46 and more, was at Nettleworth on his way to Lincoln and saw Margaret baptised; and on the second occasion he bought 50 quarters of pease at Langwith by Nettleworth and heard of the birth of Isabel.

Ralph Cachehors, 60(?) and more, on the first occasion was building a house at Woodthorpe when William de Netylworth, the grandfather, gave him a beam and told him of the birth; and he was at Nettleworth on the day of the baptism of Isabel and gave a hare to William the grandfather, who told him that his family had been increased because Beatrice his daughter had given birth to Isabel.

John del Marsh, 57 and more, bought certain lands and tenements on the day that Margaret was born, and he was godfather to Isabel but was so ill that he was unable to be present on that day.

Peter Gylesson of Barlborough, 51 and more, was present at a grant by the abbot and convent of Welbeck of an annuity of 40s. from the lands of the abbey at Cuckney to William de Netylworth, the grandfather, for life, and William told the abbot that his daughter had given birth to Margaret the week before; and on the second occasion he was buying a virgate at Pleasley Park by Nettleworth when a servant of William told him of the birth of Isabel.

C 137/45, no.52

ALICE WIFE OF WILLIAM BERNDHURST

1000 Writ 16 June 1404.

GLOUCESTER. Inquisition. Gloucester. 23 July.

Peter Bythoutethyate formerly held the manor of Whittington with the advowson of the king in chief by knight service, and granted it to Richard Croupes, senior, for life with successive remainders to Richard his bastard son, Alice wife of William Barndhurst by the name of Alice Croupes, and the right heirs of Richard senior, who married Isabel and had issue Margaret. She married Robert Lynham, and they had issue

Margery, Alice and Elizabeth. After the death of Richard senior the right in fee simple descended to Margaret, and after her death to her three daughters. On the death of Richard senior, Richard junior entered and held the manor until he died, when Alice entered in accordance with the grant. She married Edmund Hakelyt. Of the three daughters of Margaret, Alice married William Carter of Great Rissington, and Margery married John Gros of Oxford.

Edmund Hakelyt died, and afterwards by a fine of 1373 [CP 25(1) 78/76, no.520] between Edward le Despenser, knight, and William and Alice Carter, the reversion of a third part of the manor, after the death of Alice, was granted to Edward le Despenser. He married Elizabeth and had issue Thomas le Despenser, knight, to whom the right descended. He married Constance and had issue Richard and died. Richard, who has the reversion of this third part, is now in the king's ward.

John Groos and Margery, and Elizabeth her sister, by their charter dated at Oxford on 25 March 1373, granted their reversion of two parts to William Smyth, perpetual vicar of Brixworth in Northamptonshire, and Nicholas Wakere of Leafield in Oxfordshire. Alice attorned to them. William Smyth by deed dated at Brixworth on 1 June 1374 quitclaimed to Wakere.

Alice afterwards married William Barndhurst. By a fine made in 1375 and confirmed in 1376 [CP 25(1) 78/77, no.540] the reversion of two parts of the manor was conveyed by Nicholas Wakere to John Dauntesey, knight, after the death of Alice and William Barndhurst who held for life. By fine of 1380 [CP 25(1) 78/79, no.26] John Dauntesey conveyed this reversion to Elizabeth wife of Edward le Despenser, knight, for life, with remainder to Thomas his son. Elizabeth is still alive, and Richard son and heir of Thomas is aged 8 years and more.

Alice died on 1 June. Who is her next heir is unknown. The annual value of the whole manor and advowson is 20 marks.

C 137/45, no.61, m.1
E 152/392, no.1

ANNE WIDOW OF EDMUND EARL OF STAFFORD

1001　Writ to assign dower, 30 Dec. 1403.

CALAIS. [Assignment of dower].

Assignment of 22s. 2¾d. rent in sterling, being a third part of a rent of 5 marks which Thomas, sometime earl of Stafford, held from a house in the parish of St. Nicholas, which he had let to farm for a hundred years to Henry Tamworth, his heirs and assigns, for that yearly sum.

C 137/45, no.61, mm.2,3

MARGARET WIDOW OF GILES DAUBENEY, KNIGHT

1002　SOMERSET. Assignment of dower, Joan queen of England, to whom the king granted the custody of all the lands of Giles Daubeney [CPR 1401–5, p.263], being warned but not attending. South Petherton. 11 Nov. 1403.

Assigned: a third part of all the lands, tenements, rents and services which he held in the manor of South Petherton in the vill of South Petherton, and a third part of the same in the hamlets of Barrington, Dommett, Chillington and Southarp, members of the manor; and a third part of the issues and profits of the hundred of South Petherton; as dower of all the holdings of her late husband, Giles, in Somerset, in accordance with the law and custom of England and with the writ.

C 137/45, no.64

ELIZABETH DE LANCASTRE, COUNTESS OF HUNTINGDON

1003   Writ to assign dower from the lands of John de Holand, earl of Huntingdon, as advised and agreed by parliament [*Rot. Parl.* III, p.533]. 10 June 1404.

HUNTINGDON, Assignment of reasonable dower to John de Cornewayll, knight, and Elizabeth Lancastre, countess of Huntingdon, his wife. Huntingdon. 21 June.

Assigned: 10 marks from the farm of the county out of the £20 payable by equal parts at Easter and Michaelmas by the sheriff, which Richard II granted to the earl of Huntingdon by letters patent, to maintain his title, style, name and honour [*CChR* V, p.309]. The earl held no lands or advowsons in the county from which dower should or could be assigned.

1004   Similar writ, 10 June 1404.

SOMERSET. Assignment of dower to Elizabeth Lancastre, countess of Huntingdon, and John de Cornewaill, knight, her husband. Crewkerne. 21 June.

Assigned: a third part of the issues, fines, liberties and profits of the hundreds of Stone and Catsash with the office of the beadleries, which Richard II granted to the earl of Huntingdon [*CPR 1391–6*, p.102]. He held no more in Somerset.

1005   DEVON. Assignment of dower to John de Cornewaille and Elizabeth Lancastre, countess of Huntingdon, his wife, from the lands of John de Holand, earl of Huntingdon, citing the writ of 10 June 1404 in full. Fremington. 22 Sept. 1404.

Dower from the manor and borough of South Molton, the castle, manor and borough of Barnstaple, the manor of Dartington, the manors of Fremington and Combe Martin, the borough of Winkleigh and the manors of Newton Tracey and Blackborough, which were granted to the earl and his heirs by Elizabeth by letters patent of Richard II [*CPR 1385–9*, pp.494–5]:

South Molton, the manor, hundred and borough, and Barnstaple, the manor and borough, except knight's fees and advowsons.

Winkleigh and Blackborough, 38s. 1½d. rent.

Fremington, a third part of the manor, except knight's fees and advowsons, comprising: 'le Oldecourte' with chapel and chamber annexed, a third part of the demesne arable, meadow and wood, 'Knollewode', 'Heyly', 'Ileslond', 'Underchelspark', 'Chelspark', 'Comereslond', 'Brodmede', 'Dertrich', Newton Down by West Collacott, a close west of the church, and 3 a. at 'Carswelle manis' next to the close, a third part of the profits of mill, fishery, rabbit warren, court, view of frankpledge, tolls, customs of port, and clay of the hundred (*argilli hundr*'), with all the profits, and the rents, services and tenures of Hugh Basselyng of Newton Tracey, Walter Beste, John Pocok, Henry Smyth, John Wynard, Richard Hille of High Bickington, John Brigge, Walter atte Leye, Richard Whetene, Geoffrey None, senior, Adam Burell, Richard Puddyng, William Swyfte of 'West Halys', Thomas Swyfte, Roger Dyker, Richard Dyker, John Dyker, Alexander atte More, William atte Merssh of 'Esthalys', Thomas Callicote, Walter Josse, Robert Dranesfeld, John Wybbury, William Swyft, Thomas

atte Lake, Robert Jarde, William Michaell, John Matyn, John Holmoncote, William
Spyrlyngton, Ralph Spencer, John Bampell, William Whicher, Alexander Huchecok,
Alexander Smert, John Morecok, John atte Wille, John Loveybounde, Richard
Loveybounde, Richard Johan, the lands of 'Pyeson', John Wynter, Stephen Vygge,
Geoffrey Welywroght, John Hurt, Thomas Coke, Roger Spyrlyngton, Hugh
Shupherde, Henry Lange of Fremington, Thomas Sefare, John in the Haye, Stephen
Taillour, Walter Welywrought, Alexander Welywrought, John Harry, Richard Morys
and William Hoper, tenants and villeins with their families and services, and a rent
of 21 bushels of wheat.

The manor, hundred and borough of South Molton with the manor and borough
of Barnstaple, the rent 38s. 1½d., and the third parts are worth annually together £96
9s. 9¾d., in allowance for Barnstaple castle, Dartington, Combe Martin, Winkleigh,
Newton Tracey and Blackborough manors, and two parts of Fremington, excluding
knight's fees and advowsons, £192 19s. 7½d.

From the advowsons in the same places, those of South Molton, value . . ., of
Dartington £50, and the chantry of the free chapel of Mortehoe, and the free chapels
on the bridge at Barnstaple and of the castle there £100.

From the knight's fees of all the above-named manors, the following all held with
others of the manor of Barnstaple:

Coryton, ½ fee held by William Coryton.
Nether Exe, 1 fee held by Thomas Flemmyng.
Up Exe, ½ fee held by Fulk Fitzwaryn.
Sourton and North Russell, 2 fees held by William Speke.
Sourton, Thorne and Kimworthy, 1 fee held by . . . Tremayn.
Sutcombe and Merton, 1 fee held by Ivo Fitzwaryn.
Peadhill, ½ fee held by the heirs of Thomas Peadehill.
Loxbeare, ½ fee held by John Keynes.
Milford, ½ fee held by John Devyle.
Ashwater, 1 fee held by William Carmynowe and ½ fee held by the heirs of William
Avenell.
Henscott, 3 parts of a fee held by Richard Heyngescote.
Buckland, 1½ fees held by John Fill.
Hartley and East Buckland, 1 fee held by John Fill.
Roborough, 1 fee held by the heirs of Alexander Cloynge.
Hagginton, 1 fee held by the heir of Robert Penrys.
'Southquarm', 1 fee held by Hugh Courtenay.
Luscott, ½ fee held by the prior of Taunton.
Wilsham, ¼ fee held by John Copleston.
Cowley, ½ fee held by William Bonevyle.
Horton and Newland, ¼ fee held by the heirs of Walter Horton.
Tavistock, ¼ fee held by the heirs of John Kayle.
Crackaway, ¼ fee held by Roger Pym.
[No values given].

C 137/45, no. 65

ROBERT HEMNALE, KNIGHT

1006   NORFOLK. Inquisition. Heacham. 21 Dec. 1403.

He held the manor of Hempnall in Hempnall, and 40s. rent in Fritton, Morning-
thorpe and Long Stratton, annual value 10 marks, and 3s. 4d. rent from the manor of

John Lestraunge, knight, in Burnham Westgate called Reynham's, all in his demesne as of fee of the king in chief by knight service.

He proposed to make an enfeoffment to exclude the king by fraud and collusion from the wardship and marriage of his heir, as appears by his first will dated 24 Oct. 1389, and also by his last will dated at Belaugh on 24 Sept. 1391 [*sic*], which is of record in the court of the archbishop of Canterbury in London.

He died on 15 Sept. 1391. William his son and heir was then aged 4 years and more. He was an idiot all his life and died on 18 Dec. 1402. Ralph Hemenale is next heir and aged 30 years and more.

John Muryell and Hugh Lancastre, clerks, Simon Blyaunt, and John de Berton, rector of Downham Market, have held the lands since his death and taken the profits, title unknown.

John West and Nicholas Baron purchased a manor in Hillington called Bury's without the king's licence. It is held of the king in chief, annual value, with the advowson of Stibbard belonging to it, £10. [*Cf. CCR 1402–5*, p.114].

1007 SUFFOLK. Inquisition *ex officio*. Ixworth. 30 May 1404.

He held the manor of Cotton called Champains in his demesne as of fee of John Karenet by knight service, annual value £20.

He also held in his demesne as of fee, services unknown:

Cotton, the manor called 'Cumpaynes', annual value 10 marks, and the manor called Gipswich, 20 marks.

Thornham Magna, the manor called Hemenhall, 40 marks.

Wickham Skeith, the manor of Skeith's, £20.

Stonham Aspall, the manor, £40.

Yaxley, the manor called Boles, 20 marks.

Date of death and heirs as above. Hugh Lancastre and John Berton, clerks, and Simon Blyaunt have taken the issues of these manors since he died, title unknown.

C 137/45, nos.66,67

E 152/393

THOMAS TOUNLONDE

1008 KENT. Inquisition *ex officio*. Woodchurch. 7 Oct. 1403.

He held in his demesne as of fee 1 messuage, 48 a. arable, 12 a. wood and 20s. rent in Woodchurch, Warehorne, Kenardington, Ruckinge and Newchurch in Romney marsh; except for a third part which Alice, widow of John his father, holds in dower. They are held of the king in chief of the castle of Dover by a rent of 5s. for the guard of the castle. A rent of 7d. is payable to the abbot and convent of Boxley, annual value of the rest 15s.4d., the third part 7s.8d.

He died on 26 July last. William his brother and heir is aged 18 years and more since 6 Dec. last.

C 137/45, no.69

NICHOLAS GOUSHILL, KNIGHT

1009 DERBY. Inquisition *ex officio*. Clowne. 7 Nov. 1403.

Long before his death he gave all his lands in Killamarsh by charter to Henry Shirley, parson of Barlborough. They are held of Nicholas de Longeford, knight, as parcel of the manor of Killamarsh, service unknown. Nicholas holds of the king of the honour of Peverel by the service of finding a horse, value 5s., and a sack with a goad (*unum saccum cum uno stimulo*) for 40 days with the king's army for war in Wales.

He died on 21 July last.

[Subscribed] No reason for seisin (*Non habet causa seisine*).

E 149/83, no.6

JOHN DE CLYFTON, KNIGHT

1010 NOTTINGHAM. Inquisition. Nottingham. 12 Oct. 1403.

He held nothing in the county.

He died on 21 July last. Gerard his son and heir is aged 14 years and more.

E 152/389, no.6

ROBERT BRAYBROOK

1011 LONDON. Inquisition *ex officio*. 20 Sept. 1404.

Robert Braybrook, bishop of London, died on 27 Aug. 1404.

He held 12 shops with solars above in the parish of St. Faith in Paternoster Row, in Faringdon ward, annual value 8 marks; and 2 shops with cellars and solars above in St. Peter Cornhill parish, annual value 15s.

E 149/83, no.4

CHRISTINA DAUGHTER OF THOMAS GOLOFFRE

1012 SOMERSET. Inquisition *ex officio*. Ilchester. 7 July 1404.

Christina daughter of Thomas Goloffre, son and heir of John Goloffre and Christina his wife, sister and heir of Walter Englyssh, held in her demesne as of fee 1 messuage and 24 a. arable and meadow in Ashington of the lady de Sturye of her manor of Ashington by knight service, annual value 10s. She is an idiot from birth, unable to distinguish good from evil and evil from good.

E 149/83, no.12

JOHN DE THORNTON

1013 Writ 21 Oct. 1404.

YORK. Inquisition. Sutton on the Forest. 4 Nov.

He held of the king in chief by knight service 1 close called Launde by Sutton on the Forest, containing 30 a., annual value 40s.

He died on 21 July last. John his son and heir is aged 24 years and more.

C 137/46, no.1

THOMAS ENFELD

1014 Writ 28 Feb. 1405.

ESSEX. Inquisition. Chipping Ongar. 27 March.

He held in his demesne as of fee of the king in chief by knight service 44 a. arable

2A

and 36 a. wood in Fyfield, the arable as a thirtieth part of a knight's fee, the wood as a twentieth part, annual value 20s.

He died on 1 March last [*sic*]. Thomas his son and next heir was aged 3 years on 18 Oct. last.

C 137/46, no.2

MAUD WIDOW OF ROBERT DE LA MARE, KNIGHT

1015   Writ 24 April 1405.

HERTFORD. Inquisition. Hitchin. 19 May.

She held in her demesne as of fee a manor in Offley called Delamers of the manor of Hitchin as half a knight's fee, annual value £10.

She died on 20 April last. Willelma widow of John Roches, her daughter and next heir, is aged 40 years and more.

1016   Writ 24 April 1405.

GLOUCESTER. Inquisition. Gloucester. 13 May.

She held in her demesne as of fee:

Cherington, the manor and 2 carucates, of the prince [of Wales] as half a knight's fee, annual value £4.

Minchinhampton, 1 messuage and 1 carucate of the abbess of Caen by a rent of 10s., annual value nil beyond the rent.

She died on 19 April (Easter), heir as above.

1017   Writ 24 April 1405.

OXFORD. Inquisition. Oxford. 30 April.

She held in her demesne as of fee of the prince [of Wales]:

Marsh Baldon, the manor and advowson, in chief by knight service, annual value 20 marks.

Lower Heyford, the manor and half the advowson, of the honour of Wallingford by knight service, annual value £20.

She died on 19 April, heir as above.

1018   Writ 24 April 1405.

WILTSHIRE. Inquisition. Foxley. 7 May.

She held the manor of Market Lavington in her demesne in fee simple of the king in chief as half a knight's fee, annual value 20 marks, including 12 marks in assize rents payable by free and servile tenants at the four terms.

She also held in her demesne as of fee 2 virgates and pasture called Nabal's in the lordship of Stanton St. Quintin, of the duchy of Lancaster, of the honour of Trowbridge, service unknown, annual value nil.

She died on 19 April, heir as above.

C 137/46, no.3
E 152/400

JOHN COK OF LATCHINGDON

1019 Writ 20 Jan. 1405.

ESSEX. Inquisition. Maldon. 13 July 1406.

He held in his demesne as of fee 1 messuage and 20 a. in Latchingdon of the prior of Christchurch, Canterbury, annual value 2s.; and 150 a. of arable and marsh there of the king of the honour of Dover, service unknown, annual value 12s.6d.

He died on 13 May 1404. Peter his son and heir is aged 30 years and more.

C 137/46, no.4

THOMAS BERKELEY OF COBERLEY

1020 Writ 20 April 1405.

GLOUCESTER. Inquisition. Gloucester. 9 May.

He held the manor of Stoke Orchard in his demesne as of fee of the king in chief in grand serjeanty, annual vaue £20; and the manor of Coberley with the advowson, of Richard Chedder as half a knight's fee, annual value £20.

He died on 12 April. Margaret wife of Nicholas Mattesdon, aged 30 years and more, and Alice wife of Thomas de Brugge, 26 years and more, are his daughters and heirs.

1021 Writ 20 April 1405.

DERBY. Inquisition. Repton. 7 May.

He held the manor of Chilcote in his demesne as of fee of Thomas de Erdyngton as half a knight's fee, annual vaue £18 3s.4d.

Date of death and heirs as above.

1022 Writ 20 April 1405.

WORCESTER. Inquisition. Upton on Severn. 5 May.

He held the manor of Eldersfield in his demesne as of fee of Elizabeth widow of Edward le Despenser, knight, as one knight's fee, annual vaue £30.

Date of death and heirs as above.

C 137/46, no.5
E 149/85, no.8

ROBERT CORBET SENIOR, KNIGHT

1023 Writ 8 Dec. 1404.

STAFFORD. Inquisition. Kings Bromley. 19 Dec.

He held the manor of Kings Bromley in his demesne as of fee of the king in chief at fee farm of 100s. at the exchequer and by fealty, annual value £10.

He died on 5 Dec. Robert Corbet, knight, his son and next heir, is aged 50 years and more.

1024 Writ 8 Dec. 1404.

OXFORD. Inquisition. Oxford. 18 Dec.

He held nothing in Oxfordshire.

Date of death and heir, aged 40 years and more, as above.

1025 BERKSHIRE. Inquisition. Grandpont. 17 Dec. 1404.

Jointly with Maud his wife he held the manor of Tubney, extending in Tubney, Frilford, Abingdon and Uffington, with the advowson of Tubney, of the abbot of Abingdon in socage by knight service [*sic*], annual value 10 marks; and also jointly with Maud various lands and tenements in Denchworth of the duchy of Lancaster by knight service, annual value 10 marks.

Date of death and heir, aged 40 years and more, as above.

1026 Writ 8 Dec. 1404.

NORFOLK. Inquisition. Harling. 31 Dec.

With Beatrice his former wife he held the manor of Little Dunham to them and the heirs of their bodies by the grant of Robert de Swelyngton and Margaret his wife and John Garlek and Sarah his wife by a fine [CP 25(1) 167/175, no. 1596]. It is held of William Bowet, service unknown, annual value £8.

He died on 5 Dec. Guy son of Robert and Beatrice and heir to this manor is aged 30 years and more.

1027 SUFFOLK. Inquisition. Lavenham. 30 Dec. 1404.

He held the manor of Assington in his demesne as of fee of the king in chief of the honour of Hatfield Peverel as half a knight's fee, annual value £11; and 60 a. in Cornard and Assington of the abbot of Bury St. Edmunds, service unknown, annual value £3.

He died on 5 Dec. Robert Corbet, knight, his son and next heir, is aged 40 years and more.

1028 Writ 8 Dec. 1404.

SHROPSHIRE. Inquisition. Shrewsbury. 22 Dec.

He held the manor of Hadley with the hamlet of Hatton in his demesne as of fee of Thomas earl of Arundel and Surrey of his manor of Wroxeter by a rent of one sparrowhawk. There are the site with all buildings, close and adjacent gardens, annual value nil; a dovecot, nil; a park, of which the underwood nil; pasture, nil except in summer; 80 a. arable lying fallow; 10 a. meadow, of which herbage in summer 10s.; and assize rents of 16 marks payable by equal parts at Lady Day and Michaelmas.

Date of death and heir as in last.

Richard Saundres, his bailiff, has held the manor and taken the profits since his death, title unknown.

1029 Writ 8 Dec. 1404.

GLOUCESTER. Inquisition. Chipping Campden. 9, 13 or 16 Dec. [Tuesday St. Lucy the virgin, but St. Lucy, the 13th, was a Saturday in 1404].

He held the manor of Ebrington with the hamlets of Hidcote Bartrim, Farmcote, Peasley and Little Farmcote, parcels of the manor, in his demesne as of fee of the duchy of Lancaster, service unknown. There are the site with buildings, close and garden, annual value nil; 3 carucates lying fallow, 60s.; 100 a. meadow, herbage in summer £8; and assize rents of £20 payable by equal parts at Lady Day and Michaelmas.

Date of death as above. Robert his son and heir is aged 30 years and more.

William Bayly, his bailiff, has held and taken the profits since his death, title
unknown.

C 137/46, no.6

E 149/85, no.6

E 152/402, no.6

AGNES WIDOW OF JOHN WYLY

1030   Writ 9 March 1405.

WILTSHIRE. Inquisition. Upavon. 17 March.

She held in her demesne as of fee:

Calstone Wellington and Quemerford, 1 messuage and 2 carucates of arable and
meadow of the king in chief by a rent of 58s.4d., annual value beyond the rent 66s.8d.

Cherhill, 1 messuage, 1 watermill and half a virgate, and Calstone Wellington, 20
a. meadow, of the treasurer of Salisbury Cathedral by a rent of 20s. at Michaelmas
and suit at the prebendal court of Calne at two law days on reasonable summons, annual
value 13s.4d.

Avebury, 40 a., of the priory of Avebury by a rent of 13s.4d. at Michaelmas, annual
value beyond the rent 6s.8d.

She died on 16 Feb. last. Katherine wife of William Pershut, her daughter and next
heir is aged 30 years and more.

C 137/46, no.7

WALTER CATECOTE

1031   Writ 24 March 1405.

SOMERSET. Inquisition. Wells. 7 April.

He held the manor of Catcott in his demesne as of fee of Thomas Romesye, kinsman
and heir of Walter Romesye, that is son of Thomas son of Walter, in the king's ward,
and of John Vernay, Robert Orcherd, John Pokeswellys, John Wyveliscombe, senior,
and Christina wife of Richard Clopton, heir of Thomas Tryvet deceased, by knight
service, annual value 10 marks.

He also held the manor of East Harptree, with its members of Eastwood, Coley,
Shrowle and Sherborne, for life by the courtesy of England in right of Joan formerly
his wife, of Elizabeth widow of Edward le Spencer of the honour of Gloucester by
knight service, annual value £20.

He died on 9 March. Alice wife of William Hampton, the daughter and next heir
of Walter and Joan his late wife, is aged 25 years and more.

C 137/46, no.8

E 152/404

DAVID HOLGRAVE

1032   Writ 7 Aug. 1405.

NORTHUMBERLAND. Inquisition. Morpeth. 29 Aug.

He held the castle and manor of Bothal jointly with Helen his wife by the grant of

John Worth and Blanche his wife by a fine of 1387–8 [CP 25(1) 181/14, no.25], to
them and the heirs of their bodies, with remainder to the right heirs of Helen. Helen
died without heirs of her body by him, and David died holding them of the king of
the crown by the service of 3 knight's fees in a barony [*in baronia*], rendering for
cornage for the keeping of the castle of Newcastle upon Tyne 115s.4d. The annual
values are: the castle nil, the manor 20 marks and no more these days because of the
Scottish war and the king's army lying there recently.

He died on 13 June. Robert de Ogle, knight, the son and heir of Helen, is aged 30
years and more. The escheator has held them and taken the profits since his death.

C 137/46, no.9
E 152/408, no.1

THOMAS WESTON, CHAPLAIN

1033 Writ 2 Nov. 1404.
GLOUCESTER. Inquisition. Chipping Campden. 30 Jan. 1405.

He held in his demesne as of fee of the king in chief by knight service 1 messuage
and 1 virgate in Weston Subedge, annual value 10s.

He died on 29 July last. John Grene the next heir, is aged 30 years and more. He
has held and taken the profits, title unknown.

1034 Writ, *melius sciri*, asking how John Grene is the heir. 22 Oct. 1405.
GLOUCESTER. Inquisition. Winchcomb. 16 Nov.

John Grene is next heir of Thomas Weston, chaplain, namely son of John Grene,
brother of Thomas Weston.

C 137/46, no.10
E 148/85, no.10

THOMAS STUYCHE

1035 Writ 28 Jan. 1405.
SHROPSHIRE. Inquisition. Wellington. 5 Feb.

He held in his demesne as of fee:

Longslow, half the hamlet, of the king in chief by the service of a quarter of a knight's
fee, comprising 1 messuage, with buildings and gardens, annual value nil; 10 a. arable,
6s.8d.; 3 a. meadow, of which the herbage in summer 3s.4d.; and assize rents of 13s.4d.
payable at Lady Day and Michaelmas.

Stirchley, the hamlet, of William Lord Ferrers of Groby of his manor of Stoke upon
Tern by a rent of 18d., annual value in assize rents 20s. payable at Lady Day and
Michaelmas.

Broughton, 1 messuage and 5 a., of the dean of St. Chad's, Shrewsbury, service
unknown, annual value 3s.4d. in time of peace, now nil owing to the war and damage
by the rebels.

He died on 24 Jan. William his son and heir is aged 23 years and more.

C 137/46, no.11
E 149/86, no.5

JOHN BRISTOWE

1036 Writ 28 March 1405.

LONDON. Inquisition. 13 June.

He held nothing of Richard II because he died on 19 June 1369. He then held of the king in free burgage, as all London is, two tenements in Seacoal Lane, annual value 4 marks. He was a freeman of the city of London and by custom of the city by his testament, proclaimed and enrolled in the hustings on 15 July 1370, gave and left them to Agnes his wife for her life; to be sold by his executors after her death for the health of his soul and for other works of charity, as appears in his will. He named as executors Agnes his wife, Master Richard Asshewell, and William Kyryell, tanner. If after the death of Agnes they did not sell the tenements, or were no longer living, he wished the tenements to be sold by the executors of the executors under the supervision of four parishoners of St. Sepulchre in the suburbs and two persons next in blood to himself, and the money to be spent as stated. They on 15 March 1391 sold them to Marion Blakwyn and her heirs.

Agnes held them from his death until 15 March 1391. Since then Marion Blakwyn has done so.

Nicholas his brother and next heir is aged 60 years and more.

C 137/46, no.12

RICHARD TORELL

1037 Writ 12 May 1405.

SUSSEX. Inquisition. Midhurst. 8 July.

He granted the manors of Eastcourt and Westcourt in Bepton to John Tyrell, Walter Tyrell, John Mymmes and Geoffrey Mareschal, clerks, and Adam Reyner. They held them in their demesne as of fee and received the rents and services of the free tenants and villeins. All the tenants, including the priors of Tortington, Portsmouth and Southwick, William Turgess and William atte Chambre attorned to them. The manors are held of the earl of Arundel of his manor of 'Toteshale' by a rent of 3s.4d. at Michaelmas.

He died on 11 May last. Thomas his son was aged 9 years on 21 Sept.

1038 Writ 12 May 1405.

LONDON. Inquisition. 15 July.

He held nothing in the city.

Date of death as above. Thomas his son and heir was aged 8 years on 21 Sept.

1039 Writ 12 May 1405.

ESSEX. Inquisition. Brentwood. 1 June.

He held in his demesne as of fee of the king in chief in petty serjeanty the manor called Torells in Little Thurrock by the service of the napery at the coronation, annual value £8.

On 18 Feb. 1405 he granted by charter to John Tyrell, Walter Tyrell, John Mymmes, clerk, Geoffrey Marischall, clerk, and Adam Reyner the manor of West Thurrock, two parts of the manor of Shellow Bowells, and all other lands, tenements, rents and services in West Thurrock and Stifford with the advowson of Stifford at the third vacancy, and the reversion of the third part of the manor of Shellow Bowells which Margaret widow of Roger Marischal holds for life and which should revert to him and his heirs, to them, their heirs and assigns. They held them before the death of Richard without fraud or collusion. The manor of West Thurrock with the holdings etc. are held of John Lyghtfot and other tenants of the manor and lordship of West Thurrock, service unknown. The two parts of Shellow Bowells with the reversion of the third are held of Joan de Bohun, countess of Hereford, service unknown.

Date of death and heir, aged 8 on 21 Sept., as above.

1040   HERTFORD. Inquisition *ex officio*. Bishop's Stortford. 30 June 1410.

Richard Torell of Essex, esquire, who held of the king in chief, died on 11 May 1405 holding the reversion of various lands called Bertrams in Standon after the death of Robert Marchall, knight, in virtue of a grant in fee tail to him and the heirs of his body. They should have descended to Thomas Torell, his son and heir, who is under age in the king's ward. They are held of the earl of March, also in the king's ward, of his manor of Standon, service unknown, annual value £4.

Richard Perers, esquire, entered on the death of Richard Torell and took the profits, title unknown, until Midsummer last, and he is answerable to the king because he refuses to pay them to the escheator. From Midsummer the escheator will answer for them.

C 137/46, no.13
E 149/85, no.2 and 95, no.3

JOHN FROME

1041   Writ 24 Nov. 1404.

BUCKINGHAM. Inquisition. Buckingham. 11 Feb. 1405.

He held in his demesne as of fee:

Buckingham, the manor, of the earl of Stafford of the honour of Gloucester by the service of two knight's fees, annual value £40.

Padbury, 1 tenement and 1 carucate, of Walter FitzRychard by a rent of 3s.4d., annual value 40s.

Lenborough, 2½ carucates, of the abbot of Reading by a rent of 6s., annual value 53s.4d.

He died on 22 Nov. 1404. Isabel wife of Bernard Mussenden and Joan wife of William Fillole, his daughters and heirs, are aged 22 years and more and 18 years and more.

1042   Writ 24 Nov. 1404.

DORSET. Inquisition. Dorchester. 26 Jan. 1405.

He held in his demesne as of fee:

Woodlands, the manor, with the hundred of Knowlton, parcel of the manor, of Edmund earl of March, in the king's ward, of the manor of Pimperne by knight service, annual value £20.

Winterborne Belet, 1 messuage and 1 carucate, of the abbot of Milton by knight service, annual value 10 marks.

Stafford, 1 messuage and 60 a., of Robert Byngham of his manor of West Stafford, service unknown, annual value 5s.

Kingston, 2 messuages, 3 a. and 13s. rent, of Robert Grey of his manor of Kingston, service unknown, annual value 8s.

Winterborne Herringston, 3 messuages and 40 a., of Alice Bryene of her manor of Sutton Poyntz by a rent of one pair of gilt spurs or 6d. at Easter, annual value 40s.

Winterborne Whitchurch, a rent of a rose from 1 messuage and 6 bovates, which Richard Frome and Joan his wife hold for life by his grant with reversion to him and his heirs, held of Alice widow of Guy Brien, junior, of her manor of Sutton Poyntz, service unknown.

Date of death and heirs as above.

C 137/46, no.14

JOAN WIFE OF EDWARD LOVETOFT

1043 Writ 2 Feb. 1405.

LINCOLN. Inquisition. Corby. 16 Feb.

She held in her demesne as of fee:

Skillington, the manor, of the archbishop of York by knight service, annual value 40s.

Owmby, the manor, of Alice Basset of the castle of Castle Bytham by knight service, annual value 20s.

She died on 28 Dec. last. Margaret wife of John Cheyne, knight, her daughter and heir, was 32 on 22 Jan. last.

1044 Writ 27 Jan. 1405.

HUNTINGDON. Inquisition. St. Neots. 13 Feb.

She held for life 1 messuage, 150 a. arable, 2 a. meadow, 4 a. wood and 10s. rent in Southoe, and £10 assize rents from the manor of Orton Waterville payable at the four terms by equal parts, by the grant of Ellis parson of Southoe and Richard Moigne, chaplain, in the time of Edward III to Joan and Edward Lovetoft and the heirs of Edward. They are held of the king in chief as a third part of a knight's fee, annual value 20s., and after her death belong to Margaret wife of John Cheyne, knight, daughter and heir of Edward.

Robert Toweslond and John de Southo, chaplains, William Philyppot of Ashwell and Richard Fraunceys of Little Paxton held the manor of Boughton, and granted it to Joan and Simon Burgh, then her husband, for their lives with reversion to themselves. Robert Toweslond and the others granted the reversion to John Cheyne, knight, Margaret his wife, and their heirs, and failing them the right heirs of Margaret. Simon and Joan attorned to John and Margaret Cheyne, and so Joan held it for life with reversion to them. It is held of the king of the honour of Huntingdon as half a knight's fee, annual value 30s.

Date of death and heir as above.

C 137/47, no.15
E 149/84, no.3

ELIZABETH DABRIGGECOURT

1045 Writ 2 Oct. 1404.

BERKSHIRE. Inquisition. Grandpont by Oxford. 8 Oct.

She held of the king in chief 12 tenements in 'le Wyke' and Beech Hill in the parish of Stratfield Saye, service unknown, annual value 6 marks.

She died on 26 Sept. last. John her son and heir is aged 26 years and more.

1046 Writ, *plenius certiorari*, her status in the tenements not being stated in the above inquisition. 28 Oct. 1404.

BERKSHIRE. Inquisition. Reading. 11 Nov.

She held the 12 tenements in 'le Wyke' and Beech Hill jointly with Nicholas Dabriggecourt, her late husband, by the grant of Nicholas Careu, John de Salesbury, Robert Corby and William de Brentyngham, to them and their heirs, the heirs of the body of Elizabeth, and failing such the right heirs of Nicholas, annual value 6 marks.

Date of death and heir as above.

1047 Writ 2 Oct. 1404.

HAMPSHIRE. Inquisition. Basingstoke. 15 Oct.

She held the manor and advowson of Stratfield Saye jointly with Nicholas Dabriggecourt, knight, formerly her husband, by the grant of Nicholas Carreu, John de Salesburi, Robert Corby and William de Brantyngham, for which the king's licence had been obtained, to them and their heirs, the heirs of the body of Elizabeth, and failing such the right heirs of Nicholas. The manor is held of the king in chief as one knight's fee. There are 200 a., annual value 40s.; 100s. assize rent payable equally at the four principal terms; 1 park, the pasture grazed by the deer, annual value nil beyond the enclosure and the fee of the parker; 30 a. meadow, 30s.; 100 a. pasture, 20s.; 2 watermills, 40s.; 1 fulling mill, 6s. 8d.; and 1 dovecot, 40d.

She held 1 watermill in Bramley of Thomas Ponynges, Lord St. John, as a twentieth part of a knight's fee, annual value 6s. 8d.

She died on 28 Sept., heir as above.

1048 Writ, *plenius certiorari*, who was next heir of Nicholas not being stated in the above inquisition. 28 Oct. 1404.

HAMPSHIRE. Inquisition. Odiham. 3 Nov.

She held the manor and advowson of Stratfield Saye [as above, no. 1047] as one knight's fee, owing to the forfeiture by John de Stoutevill, a Frenchman. There are 300 a. [*sic*], annual value 40s.; 100s. in assize rents payable by equal parts at the four principal terms; 1 park, the pasture grazed by the deer, annual value nil beyond the enclosure and the fee of the parker; 30 a. meadow, 40s.; 100 a. pasture, 20s.; 2 watermills, 40s.; and 1 fulling mill, 6s. 8d.

She held 1 watermill in Bramley [as above, no. 1047].

John is the son of Nicholas and Elizabeth and their next heir in accordance with the grant to them. He is aged 26 years and more. Elizabeth died on 28 Sept. last.

C 137/47, no. 16
E 149/86, no. 8
E 152/402, no. 4

THOMAS LA ZOUCHE

1049   Writ 23 Nov. 1404.

BUCKINGHAM. Inquisition. Doddershall. 31 Dec.

By the grant of William la Zouche, his father, he held the manor of Middle Claydon for life of the king in chief of the honour of Peverel by knight service, and the manor of Ellesborough for life of Reynold de Grey by a rent of 1d. William la Zouche, now lord of Harringworth, his kinsman, that is the son of William, son of William, by a fine of 9 Feb. 1402 [not found] granted the reversion of these manors, which Thomas held for life of the inheritance of William, to Henry bishop of Lincoln, William de Wilughby and Thomas de Rempston, knights, Thomas Frysby, Ralph Flemyng, William Palmer, William Danby, and John Toly and William Glen, clerks, and the heirs of the bishop. The manors should remain to them. The annual values are Middle Claydon £10, Ellesborough 10 marks.

He died on 30 Oct. William la Zouche, his kinsman and heir, namely son of William his brother, is aged 30 years and more.

1050   Writ 12 Nov. 1404.

BEDFORD. Inquisition. Dunstable. 10 Dec.

He held the manor of Westoning of the king by the service of a quarter of a knight's fee by the grant of John bishop of Lincoln, Simon Warde, John de Holt and John Thame, by a fine of 1373 [CP 25(1) 5/65, no.19] to William and Elizabeth la Zouche, his father and mother, with remainder to him (Thomas) and the right heirs of his father. William and Elizabeth died seised, and then Thomas held it until he died on 30 Oct. 1404. The annual value is £8.

William la Zouche, lord of Harringworth, aged 30 years and more, is next heir, as above.

1051   Writ, *melius sciri*, the original writ being lost and not delivered to the escheator. 24 Jan. 1405.

HERTFORD. Inquisition. St. Albans. 28 Jan.

He held for life with remainder to John la Zouche, knight, son of William la Zouche, knight, deceased, and Margaret wife of John, who are both still living, and the heirs of the body of John, by the grant of John bishop of Lincoln, by a fine of 1392 [CP 25(1) 289/56, no.246] shown to the jurors, granting the remainder after his death to William la Zouche and his heirs:

Wheathampstead, 1 carucate, of the abbot of Westminster by a rent of 20s., annual value 53s.4d.

Redbourn, 80 a., of the abbot of St. Albans by a rent of 13s., annual value at 4d., 26s.8d.

Date of death and heir, aged 28 years and more, as above.

1052   Writ 12 Nov. 1404.

KENT. Inquisition. Eynsford. 5 Dec.

He held for life with remainder to John la Zouche, knight, Margaret his wife, and the heirs of John [as above, no.1051] in accordance with the same fine:

Ightham, the manor and advowson, of Thomas archbishop of Canterbury by homage and fealty, annual value £10.

Eynsford, the manor, of the same archbishop by a rent of 12d. annual value £8.
Date of death and heir as above [no. 1050].

1053 Writ 12 Nov. 1404.
SUFFOLK. Inquisition. Sudbury. 10 Jan. 1405.
He held the manor of Aveley for life with remainder to John la Zouche, knight,
Margaret his wife and the heirs of John [as above, no. 1051] by the same fine, of Robert
Corbet, knight, service unknown, annual value 100s. It should remain to John and
Margaret.
Date of death and heir as above [no. 1050].

1054 Writ 12 Nov. 1404.
HAMPSHIRE. Inquisition. King's Somborne. 14 Jan. 1405.
He held the manor of King's Worthy for life with remainder to John la Zouche,
knight, Margaret his wife and the heirs of John [as above, no. 1051] by the same fine,
of the king by a rent of a pair of gilt spurs or 6d. payable by the sheriff at Michaelmas,
annual value £12 10s. It should remain to John and Margaret.
Date of death and heir as above [no. 1050].

C 137/47, no. 17
E 149/84, no. 1

THOMAS DE LA MARE

1055 Writ 29 March 1405.
BERKSHIRE. Inquisition. Aldermaston. 6 April.
He held the manors of Aldermaston and Sparsholt for life by the grant of Master
Walter de Stratton, parson of Shillingford, and Thomas de Arnewyk by a fine of 1342
[CP 25(1) 11/60, no. 8], by which the manor of Sparsholt was granted, without the
advowson, to Robert Achard for life with successive remainders to Peter Achard,
Elizabeth his wife and the heirs of their bodies, John his brother for life, Peter de la
Mare and Joan his wife for their lives, Thomas son of Peter and his heirs, and finally
Richard, son of Peter and brother of Thomas, and his heirs; and the manor of Alder-
maston was granted to Robert Achard and Agnes his wife for their lives with successive
remainders to Peter Achard and his heirs by Elizabeth his wife, Peter de la Mare and
Joan his wife, Thomas de la Mare and his heirs, and Richard and his heirs.
Both are held of the king by knight service, amount unknown, annual values,
Sparsholt 120 marks, Aldermaston £20.
He died on 29 March. Robert his son and heir is aged 26 years and more.

C 137/47, no. 18
E 152/402, no. 8

JOHN DAUNTESEY, KNIGHT

1056 Writ 6 Feb. 1405.
HERTFORD. Inquisition. Hitchin. 7 July 1405 [Tuesday, St. Thomas the Martyr, but
the Translation of St. Thomas must be intended].

He held by the courtesy of England in right of his former wife a third part of the manor of Minsden of the king in chief by knight service, amount unknown, annual value 4 marks.

He died on 6 Jan. last. Walter his son and heir was aged 12 years and more on 29 Sept. last.

1057 Writ 6 Feb. 1405.

WILTSHIRE. Inquisition. Marlborough. 10 March.

He held the manor of Marden in his demesne as of fee of the king in chief by the rent of a rose, annual value 13 marks.

He had also held in his demesne as of fee the manors of Dauntsey and Bremilham with the advowsons, the manors of Smithcot and Wilsford, the advowson of the chapel of Smithcot, two parts of the manor of Winterbourne Dauntsey with the reversion of the third part which Thomas Blount and Joan held in the dower of Joan, and two parts of certain lands and tenements in Marden, formerly of Nicholas Botiller, with the reversion of the third part also held by Thomas and Joan Blount in the dower of Joan. These on 6 March 1395 he granted to Philip Dauntesey, John Wekkelescote, vicar of Seagry, John Frye of Little Somerford and William Byllyn of Christian Malford. The first three died and on 1 July 1402 William Byllyn granted them to Amice wife of Robert Bardolf, knight, Richard Mawardyn, Roger Lynde, William Lynde, Walter Whyte, vicar of Hilmarton, John Thornbury, parson of Crudwell, and their heirs; and so they held them.

The manors of Dauntsey and Bremilham are held of the abbot of Malmesbury, service unknown, annual values £16 and £4; Smithcot of the lord of Castle Combe, service unknown, annual value 10 marks; Wilsford of the countess of Salisbury, service unknown, annual value 100s.; Winterbourne Dauntsey of Lady Despenser, senior, of the honour of Gloucester, service unknown, annual value £4.

He died on 2 Feb. last. Walter his son and heir is aged 14 years and more.

1058 Writ, *plura*, 26 July 1405.

WILTSHIRE. Inquisition. Marlborough. 10 September.

Besides the manor of Marden mentioned in the other inquisition, he held in his demesne as of fee of the king in chief by knight service the manor of Smithcot with the advowson of the chapel there, annual value 10 marks.

He held in his demesne as of fee the manors of Dauntsey and Bremilham, with the advowsons, of the abbot of Malmesbury, service unknown, annual values £16 and £4; the manor of Wilsford of the countess of Salisbury, service unknown, annual value 100s.; and two parts of the manor of Winterbourne Dauntsey, with the reversion of the third part which Thomas and Joan Lynford [*sic*] hold in the dower of Joan, of the honour of Gloucester as half a knight's fee.

Walter his son and heir is aged 14 years and more.

Walter White, vicar of Hilmarton, and others unknown were enfeoffed, as is rumoured by some, long before the death of John Dauntesey in certain parts of these manors and lands, but what parts and how is unknown; but he took all the rents and profits during his life, and since his death Edmund his brother has taken them.

1059 Writ 6 Feb. 1405.

LONDON. Inquisition. 10 March.

Long before his death he held in free burgage, as is all London, various messuages and shops by the courtesy of England after the death of Elizabeth his wife, one of the daughters and heirs of John Beverle, esquire, with reversion to Walter their son: 1 messuage in the parishes of St. Michael le Querne and St. Faith in Paternoster Row, annual value 20s.; 2 shops with solar above in St. Alban, Wood Street, 20s.; 1 messuage in St. Michael le Querne, 20s.; and half a messuage with 6 shops in St. Alban, Wood Street, 40s. By his charter dated 1 June 1402 he granted them all to Amice wife of Robert Bardolf, knight, Edmund Dauntesey and William Lynde for the term of his own life.

He died on 2 Feb. last. Walter son of John and Elizabeth was 14 years of age on 12 Aug. last.

C 137/47, no.19
E 149/85, no.4
E 152/401, no.3

JOHN KENNE

1060 Writ 12 Jan. 1405.

NORTHAMPTON. Inquisition. Northampton. 11 Feb.

He held half the manor of Grimsbury in his demesne as of fee of the king in chief by knight service, annual value 6 marks.

He died on 18 Nov. last. John his son and heir is aged 26 years and more.

1061 Writ 6 March 1405.

GLOUCESTER. Inquisition. Gloucester. 16 March.

He held in his demesne as of fee:

Sandhurst, 2 messuages, 40 a. arable, 10 a. meadow and 4s. rent at Brawn, of the king in chief by a rent of 12d. payable by the sheriff at Michaelmas and suit at the king's court at King's Barton by Gloucester every three weeks, annual value 7 marks.

Minsterworth, 1 messuage and 1 virgate, of John Hathewy in socage by a rent of 22d., annual value 20s.

Hardwicke, 40 a. arable and pasture, of Thomas de Brugge by knight service, annual value 20s.

Date of death and heir as above.

1062 Writ 6 March 1405.

SOMERSET. Inquisition. Stogursey. 23 March.

He held the following manors with the knight's fees and advowsons belonging to them jointly with Alice his wife, described as Alice daughter of Reynold Perl of Bristol, who survives, to them and his heirs and assigns, by the grant of Thomas Garenter and John Walsch, chaplains:

Kenn, of Lady la Despenser senior, that is Anne Lady la Despenser, who was under age in the king's ward, of the honour of Gloucester by knight service, annual value £10, of which 100s. is in assize rents payable by equal parts at Michaelmas and Hockday.

East Huish, by Kingston Seymour, of the same lady of the same honour by knight service, annual value 6 marks, of which 40s. is in assize rents payable as above.

Kingston Seymour, of the king of the duchy of Lancaster of the honour of Trowbridge by knight service, annual value 100s., of which 53s.4d. is in assize rents payable as above.

He also held in his demesne as of fee 1 messuage and 1 carucate in Berrow and 1 messuage and 18 a. in Wrington, both of the abbot of Glastonbury, service unknown, annual values 40s. and 10s.

Date of death and heir as above.

Writs to assign dower to Alice formerly his wife, now the wife of John Everdon, in all three counties. 21 June 1407 [*CCR 1405–9*, p.197].

C 137/47, no.20
E 149/85, no.11

WILLIAM HERON, KNIGHT

1063 Writ 18 Nov. 1404.

BUCKINGHAM. Inquisition. Buckingham. 28 Feb. 1405.

He held nothing in Buckinghamshire.

He died on 30 Oct. last. John Heron, knight, son of John, knight, his brother, is his next heir and aged 24 years and more.

1064 Writ 18 Nov. 1404

HERTFORD. Inquisition. Bishop's Stortford. 9 May 1405.

He held the manor of Sawbridgeworth in his demesne as of fee to himself, his heirs by Elizabeth his late wife, and her right heirs, by a fine of 1396 [CP 25(1) 290/57, no.286]. It is held of the king in chief by the service of one knight's fee. There are a ruinous capital messuage with adjacent garden, annual value nil beyond the maintenance of the buildings; 500 a. arable at 3d., £6 5s.; 15 a. meadow at 18d., 22s.6d.; 20 a. pasture at 2d., 3s.4d., and no more because they lie in common; 100 a. wood, of which the underwood nil because it cannot be cut; assize rents, £6 13s.8d. payable at the four terms, 2 capons, 1 lb. wax, 3 large arrows, and 1 sparrowhawk or 2s., from the manors of Rickling and Elsenham in Essex; summer, autumn and winter works, 35s.6d.; and pleas and perquisites of courts, nil beyond the expenses of the steward.

Date of death and heir as above.

1065 Writ 18 Nov. 1404.

NORTHAMPTON. Inquisition. Northampton. 19 Feb. 1405.

He held nothing in Northamptonshire.

Date of death and heir as above.

1066 Writ 18 Nov. 1404.

SUSSEX. Inquisition. Ditchling. 10 March 1405.

He held the manor of Hamsey of Thomas earl of Arundel as one knight's fee, by what title or how is unknown. There are the site, annual value nil; assize rents payable by equal parts at Hockday and Michaelmas, 40s.; 150 a. arable at 2d., 25s.; 40 a. several pasture at 1d., 3s.4d.; 40 a. meadow at 4d., 13s.4d., and no more because marsh and often under water so that it cannot be mown; hill pasture for 300 sheep, 6s.8d.; 60 a. wood and pasture in a place near Hewenstreet, nil because occupied by the earl of Arundel's game; and a tenement with park called Pyecombe in Offham, which belonged to Michael Pikombe and is held of the manor of Hamsey as an eighth part of a knight's fee, annual value 6s. 8d.

Date of death and heir as above.

1067 SUSSEX. Inquisition. Steyning. 28 Feb. 1405.

He held the manors of Buxted and Streat by the grant of Thomas archbishop of York, John bishop of Salisbury and Thomas Percy, knight, to him, Elizabeth his wife and their heirs, with remainder to the right heirs of Elizabeth, by a fine of 1396 [CP 25(1) 290/57, no. 286]. Buxted is held of William Walays, knight, by the service of half a knight's fee, and the payment to the archbishop of Canterbury at his manor of South Malling of 33s. 8¾d. yearly, annual value £4. Streat is held of Thomas earl of Arundel by the service of half a knight's fee, annual value 10 marks.

Date of death and heir as above.

1068 Writ, *plenius certiorari*, as the title to the manor of Hamsey was not stated in the above [no. 1066]. 8 May 1405.

SUSSEX. Inquisition. Uckfield. 12 June.

By a fine of 1341 [CP 25(1) 237/59, no. 7] Thomas Hethe, parson of Rotherfield, conveyed the manor of Hamsey to Geoffrey de Say, knight, and Maud his wife and their heirs male, with remainder to the right heirs of Geoffrey. They had two sons, William and John. William had a daughter, Elizabeth, and died without male heirs. After the deaths of Geoffrey and Maud John entered the manor and granted it to Thomas Crewe, his heirs and assigns, on condition that he re-enfeoff John de Say, Elizabeth his wife and their heirs, with remainder to his right heirs. This re-enfeoffment was often requested but not carried out during the lifetime of John. John died without heirs of his body. William Heron, knight, married Elizabeth heir of John, being the daughter of William his brother. They entered and peacefully held the manor. She died without heirs, and William Heron enfeoffed Simon Davy, vicar of Framfield, and Walter atte Broke, their heirs and assigns. They granted it to him to hold at their pleasure, and so he held it at his death, 30 Oct. last.

1069 Writ 18 Nov. 1404.

KENT. Inquisition. Deptford. 27 Feb. 1405.

He held the manors of Birling, Burham, Cudham and West Greenwich, and lands in Ryarsh and West Malling, with lands in other counties, in his demesne as of fee in virtue of a grant to him, Elizabeth his wife and their heirs, with remainder to her right heirs, by Thomas archbishop of York, John bishop of Salisbury and Thomas Percy, knight, by a fine of 1396 [CP 25(1) 290/57, no. 286]. The manors are held of the king in chief by knight service, and comprise:

Birling: 1 capital messuage with garden, annual value 3s. 4d.; 80 a. arable on the hills at 1½d., 10s.; 78 a. pasture at 1d., 6s. 6d.; 50 a. arable beside the manor at 3d., 12s. 6d.; 32 a. meadow at 2s., 64s.; 16 a. several pasture at 12d., 16s.; assize rents £14, comprising at Michaelmas £8 5s. and at Easter 115s.; a park, number of acres unknown, value beyond the keeping of the game 10s.; 2 leets yearly after Easter and Michaelmas, 13s. 4d.; and perquisites of court, 5s.; tenants have to plough both winter and Lent 78 a. at 6d., 39s.; and the parker takes wages of 2d. a day, or 14d. a week.

Cudham: 66 a. arable at Berry 2d., 11s.; 34 a. arable at 1d. because they are hilly and stony, 2s. 10d.; 100 a. arable in 'Northberdenne', 'Southberdenne', 'Thornfold' and 'Mede' at 3d., 25s.; 100 a. pasture for sheep at 1d., 8s.4d.; 1 a. 1 rood meadow, 2s.; a park, extent unknown, pasture beyond the keeping of the game 10s., the parker taking 14d. weekly, or 2d. daily; wood, nil because cut; 2 leets after Easter and Michaelmas, 13s.4d.; assize rents of free tenants, £12; perquisites of court, nil; and rents at Ewell by West Malling beyond 100s. payable to the bishop of Rochester, 50s.½d.

Burham: 1 messuage with adjacent garden, 2s.; 111 a. arable at 2d., 18s.6d.; 79 a. pasture at 1½d. because hilly, 9s.10½d.; 21 a. several pasture at 4d., 7s.; 15 a. salt pasture at 12d., 15s.; assize rents, £14 payable at Easter and Michaelmas except for 18s. at Midsummer and 18s. on 21 Dec.; 80 hens at Christmas at 1½d., 10s.; 400 eggs at Easter at 4d. a 100, 16d.; the tenants have to plough 60 a. in winter and Lent, 13s.4d.; and 1 watermill, 6s.8d. and no more because old and weak.

West Greenwich: 1 capital messuage, nil; 140 a. arable at 6d., 70s.; 40 a. at 4d., 13s.4d.; 20 a. several pasture for cows at 2s., 40s.; 25 a. meadow at 4s., 100s.; 50 a. wood of which 10 a. may be cut each year at 2s. an a., rest nil; assize rents, £7 8d. of which 75s.4d. at Martinmas and 65s.4d. at Lammas; perquisites of court, nil beyond the expenses of the steward; and 2 leets after Hockday and Martinmas, 2s.

John Herleston, knight, holds the manor of Fredville for life by the grant of Geoffrey de Say, with reversion in virtue of the above fine to the heirs of Elizabeth, annual value when it occurs 100s.

Date of death and heir as above [no.1063].

1070 Writ 18 Nov. 1404.

NORTHUMBERLAND. Inquisition. Newcastle upon Tyne castle. 8 April 1405.

He held in his demesne in fee tail the manor of Eshott, 160 a. in Clifton and Coldwell, and 114 a. in Duddoe, by the grant of William Meryngton and Roger del Bothe, clerks, with successive remainders failing heirs male, to Gerard Heron and his heirs male, William Heron, esquire, and his heirs male, Nicholas Heron and his heirs male, and the right heirs of William Heron, knight. William, knight, Gerard, and William, esquire, are dead. Nicholas survives. They are held of John Scrope, knight, and Elizabeth his wife, in right of Elizabeth, of the barony of Mitford by knight service, annual value 20 marks.

He also held in fee simple the manor of Hartside, 50 a. in Glanton and 100 a. in Whittingham of Joan, Margaret and Elizabeth, daughters and heirs of Alan de Heton, knight, by knight service, annual value 5 marks; and 56 a. in Thornton of the prior of St. John of Jerusalem of the hospital of Chibburn, annual value 13s.4d.

He died on 20 [sic] Oct. last, heir as above, aged 33 years and more.

C 137/48, no.21, mm.1–15
E 152/399, and 405, nos.1,3

ELIZABETH WIFE OF WILLIAM HERON, KNIGHT

1071 Writ 18 Nov. 1404.

BUCKINGHAM. Inquisition. Buckingham. 28 Feb. 1405.

She held nothing in Buckinghamshire.

She died on 8 July 1399. Her next heirs are William de Clynton, knight, son of William de Clynton, knight, son of John de Clynton, knight, and Idonea his wife, one aunt of Elizabeth; Mary wife of Otto de Worthyngton, and Maud her sister,

2B

daughters of Thomas de Alden, knight, and Elizabeth his wife, another aunt; and Roger Fyenles, son of William de Fyenles, knight, son of William de Fyenles and Joan his wife, her third aunt. Idonea, Elizabeth and Joan were sisters of William de Say, knight, father of Elizabeth. William de Clynton is aged 26 years and more, Mary 34 years and more, and Maud 28 years and more. Roger will be 20 on 14 Sept. next.

1072 Writ 18 Nov. 1404.

HERTFORD. Inquisition. Bishop's Stortford. 9 May 1405.

Jointly with William Heron, her husband, who survived her, she held the manor of Sawbridgeworth by a fine of 1396 [details and extent as in no. 1064 above].

Date of death and heirs as above [no. 1071].

William Heron, knight, held it and took the profits from her death until 30 Oct. last by virtue of the fine.

1073 Writ 18 Nov. 1404.

NORTHAMPTON. Inquisition. Northampton. 19 Feb. 1405.

She held nothing in Northamptonshire.

Date of death and heirs as above [no. 1071].

1074 Writ 18 Nov. 1404.

SUSSEX. Inquisition. Steyning. 28 Feb. 1405.

She held the manors of Buxted and Streat jointly with William Heron, knight, her husband, by a fine of 1396 [details as in no. 1067 above].

Date of death and heirs as above [no. 1071].

William Heron, knight, held them and took the profits from her death until 30 Oct. last.

1075 SUSSEX. Inquisition. Ditchling. 10 March 1405.

She held the manor of Hamsey in her demesne as of fee of Thomas earl of Arundel as 1 knight's fee, and a tenement called Pyecombe in Offham [extent and details as in no. 1066 above].

Date of death and heirs as above [no. 1071].

William Heron, knight, held then and took the profits from her death until 30 Oct. last.

1076 Writ 18 Nov. 1404.

KENT. Inquisition. Deptford. 28 Feb. 1405.

She held in her demesne as of fee the manors of Birling, Durham, Cudham and West Greenwich, with lands and tenements in Ryarsh and West Malling, and the reversion of the manor of Fredville, by a fine of 1396 [details as in no. 1069, above].

Date of death and heirs, except age of William de Clynton given as 28 years and more, as above [no. 1071].

C 137/48, no. 21, mm. 16–26
E 152/399, and 405, nos. 2, 4

WILLIAM HERON, KNIGHT

1077   Writ, for fees, 18 Nov. 1404.

BUCKINGHAM. Inquisition. Buckingham. 18 Nov. 1404.

He held in his demesne as of fee one knight's fee in each of Crafton, Chetwode, and Leckhampstead, and half a fee in Gayhurst.

1078   Similar writ 18 Nov. 1404.

HERTFORD AND ESSEX. Inquisition. Bishop's Stortford. 9 May 1405.

He held in his demesne as of fee 4¾ knight's fees in Sawbridgeworth and Kimpton, and the advowson of Sawbridgeworth, value of the last nil apart from the spiritual benefit.

Similarly he held 2 knight's fees in Essex in Rickling, Elsenham and Great Saling.

1079   Similar writ 18 Nov. 1404.

NORTHAMPTON. Inquisition. Northampton. 19 Feb. 1405.

He held in his demesne as of fee 2 knight's fees in Hartwell.

1080   Similar writ 18 Nov. 1404.

SURREY. Inquisition. Southwark. 28 April 1405.

He held 2 knight's fees in Hatcham and Bredinghurst in accordance with the fine of 1396, to himself, Elizabeth his wife and the heirs of Elizabeth [as above in no. 1067].

1081   SUSSEX. Inquisition. Ditchling. 10 March 1405.

Owing to his death 7 knight's fees are in the king's hands in Hamsey, Offham, Allington, Coombes, Saddlescombe, Fulking, Perching, Newtimber, Brighton and Kingston near Lewes, held in accordance with the fine of 1396 [as above in no. 1067].

1082   Similar writ 18 Nov. 1404.

KENT. Inquisition. Elham. 30 March 1405.

Owing to his death 36 knight's fees were taken into the king's hands, in Waldershare, Southwood, Appleton, Swanton, Appledore, Otterpley, Henden, Eynton, Binbury, Thornham, Bearsted, Kearsney, Pevington, Tremhatch, Fairbourne, Little Delce, Paddlesworth, Coldred, Birling, Heppington, Wickham, Patrixbourne, Hammill, Baracre, Nackington, Bishopsbourne, Hougham, Coldred, Bethersden, Harbourne, Whitfield, Aldglose, Staple, Speldhurst, Easole, Lydden, Old Romney, Ripple, Horsmonden, Gutteridge Field, Stourmouth, and Horton Kirby by Farningham, and he also held the advowson of the priory of Combwell, all in virtue of the fine of 1396 [as above in no. 1067].

1083   Similar writ 18 Nov. 1404.

NORFOLK AND SUFFOLK. Inquisition. Hempton. 18 May 1405.

He held in his demesne as of fee 12 knight's fees in Reedham, Stratton, Taverham, Attlebridge, Kerdiston, Sall, Reepham, Stinton, Heydon, Corpusty, Creake, Stanhoe, Choseley, East and West Rudham, New Houghton, Bagthorpe, Barmer, Syderstone, Marham, Gayton, Letton, Middleton, Clenchwarton, Shouldham and Thorpe Market, and the advowson of the priory of Coxford in Norfolk, extending at £60, the priory nil apart from spiritual benefits.

He also held 1 fee in Brandeston in Suffolk.

All the tenants are living.

Writs to partition the lands of Elizabeth Heron, 26 June 1405 [*CFR* XII, p.315].
C 137/48, no.21, mm.27–39
E 149/85, no.12

WALTER PEDWARDYN, KNIGHT

1084 Writ 20 June 1405.

WESTMORLAND. Inquisition. Appleby. 10 Aug.

He held by the courtesy of England after the death of Isabel his wife, because they had children, a sixth part of a quarter of the manor of Kendal of the king in chief as a sixth part of half a knight's fee, with reversion to Robert Pedwardyn, knight, son and heir of Isabel and himself, annual value 40s.

He died on 11 June last. Robert his son is aged 50 years and more.

1085 Writ 20 June 1405.

NORTHAMPTON. Inquisition. Northampton. 18 July.

He held the manor of Clipston in his demesne as of fee of the earl of Lincoln as a sixth part of a knight's fee, annual value 10 marks.

He died on 11 June last. Robert Pedwardyn, knight, his son and heir, is aged 60 years and more.

1086 Writ 20 June 1405.

HAMPSHIRE. Inquisition. Alton. 21 July.

He held the manor of South Warnborough in his demesne as of fee of the king in chief as part of the barony of Burton Pedwardine in Lincolnshire, annual value £11.

Date of death and heir, aged 50 years and more, as above.

1087 Writ 8 July 1405.

YORK. Inquisition. Hotham. 28 Aug.

He held by the courtesy of England a half of a third part of 2 bovates in Lund, of Henry Percy, late earl of Northumberland, by knight service, annual value 5s.; the homage and service of John de Grene, chaplain, who held various lands in Whixley and Garrowby by knight service of him as he of the king in chief; and a fee farm of 42s.7½d. from the manor of Lund.

Date of death and heir, age not given, as above.

1088 Writ 20 June 1405.

LINCOLN. Inquisition. Boston. 3 Aug.

He held in his demesne as of fee:

Burton Pedwardine, the manor with its members, South Warnborough manor in Hampshire and other lands, of the king in chief by the service of one barony, annual value apart from the manor of South Warnborough £8 4s.2d.

Nocton, half the manor, with the advowson of Flixborough, of the king in chief by the service of half, an eighth, a thirty-second, a hundred and sixtieth and a hundredth of a hundred and sixtieth of the barony of Darcy, annual value 100s.

The manor of Burton and the half manor of Nocton are worth no more because Walter, son of Walter, takes £20 for life by the grant of Walter his father.

'Thorntoft', the manor, of Ralph earl of Westmorland of the earldom of Richmond as a third part of a knight's fee, annual value 66s. 8d.

Friskney, the manor, held partly of Gilbert Umfravyll, under age in the king's ward, of his manor of Croft by knight service, partly of Maud de Cromewell by knight service, and partly of Richard Corbet of Caus, also in the king's ward, of his manor of Dalby by knight service, annual value of the three parts 100s.

Date of death and heir, aged 50 years and more, as above.

C 137/48, no. 22
E 149/84, no. 5
E 152/406, no. 3

ISABEL WIFE OF WALTER PEDWARDYN, KNIGHT

1089   Writ 8 July 1405.

WESTMORLAND. Inquisition. Appleby. 10 Aug.

She held a sixth part of a quarter of the manor of Kendal of the king in chief as a sixth part of half a knight's fee, annual value 40s. She married Walter Pedwardyn and had issue Robert Pedwardyn, knight. Walter held it until 11 June by the courtesy of England.

She died on 19 July 1404. Robert her son and heir is aged 50 years and more.

1090   Writ 8 July 1405.

YORK. Inquisition. Hotham. 28 Aug.

She held the lands in Lund, Whixley and Garrowby, as detailed above [no. 1087]. Walter held by the courtesy of England until 11 June.

Date of death and heir as above.

1091   Writs to the chancellor of the duchy of Lancaster for Walter Pedwardyn, knight, and for Isabel his wife, 8 July; and to the escheator, enclosing these. 9 July 1405.

LANCASHIRE. Inquisition. Lancaster. 13 Oct.

She held in fee and inheritance the homage and services of Robert de Haveryngton, knight, for the manor of Thornham, and a rent of 6s. 8d. from the manor payable by equal parts at Whitsun and Martinmas; the homage and services of Thomas de Metham for the manor of Ashton, and a similar rent of 6s. 8d. from the manor at the same terms; and the advowson of the priory of Conishead and of the church of Warton, alternate presentation of the latter with John de Hothum, knight, he having the first and Isabel the second presentation. These fees and advowsons make up a sixth part of a quarter of the manor of Kendal in Westmorland, and were assigned to her as her share of the manor. They are held of the king in chief as a sixth part of half a knight's fee.

She died as above, and then Walter held by the courtesy of England until he died on 11 June last. Robert their son and heir is aged 50 years and more.

C 137/48, no.22
E 149/84, no.6
E 152/406, no.4

THOMAS SON OF RALPH DE LUMLEY, KNIGHT

1092   Writ 26 Jan. 1404.

WESTMORLAND. Inquisition. Kendal. 6 Sept.

The manor of Helsington in Kendal, and a quarter of the manor of Kirkby in Kendal, except the castle of Kendal, were taken into the king's hands owing to the death of Ralph de Lumley, knight, and because of the minority of Thomas his son and heir, and so they remain. They are held of the king in chief as an eighth part of a knight's fee, annual value £30.

Margaret de Roos gave them to Marmaduke de Thweyng, ancestor of Ralph, whose heir the elder Thomas was, and the heirs of his body. Marmaduke held them in his demesne as of fee, and they descended to Marmaduke his son, Robert his son, William his son, Robert his brother, Thomas his brother, Isabel their sister, the mother of Ralph, and so to Thomas, and John de Lumley, knight, brother and heir of Thomas. Thomas was the son and heir of Ralph and died on 31 May 1400 under age.

John, knight, is son and heir of Ralph and brother of Thomas. He was aged 20 on 2 Feb. 1404, and is now 20 years and more.

C 137/49, no.23

MARGARET WIFE OF ROGER SON OF THOMAS GREY

1093   Writ 6 March 1405.

SUFFOLK. Inquisition. Henhow. 1 May.

Thomas de Grey, knight, held the manor of Stansfield and gave it to Roger his son, Margaret wife of Roger, and the heirs of their bodies, with remainder to the heirs of Thomas. Roger survived his father and died without heirs. Then John Lakyngethe, knight, and the said Margaret, then his wife, granted their rights in Stansfield to William Forde and Walter Brugge, clerks, and John Hethe for the life of Margaret. She died on 29 June 1399.

Between 6 and 13 Jan. 1400 Richard Basyngham, in the name of Fulk de Grey, kinsman and heir of Thomas de Grey, that is son of Fulk, brother of Roger, son of Thomas, entered the manor of Stansfield, claiming the right of inheritance of Fulk, and also claiming of the last earl of Warwick whatever rights he had in that manor, as guardian of Fulk son of Fulk, he being under age. Fulk was 17 on 28 Oct. 1399, and Fulk the father died long before Margaret.

The manor except for a quarter called 'Narfordestenement' is held of the earl of March, who is in the king's ward, as a third part of a knight's fee. The quarter is held of the countess of Warwick of her manor of Panworth as a quarter of a knight's fee. This manor was in the king's hands long before the death of Margaret owing to the forfeiture of Thomas earl of Warwick.

Thomas de Grey, clerk, held a tenement in Denston of the earl of March by the service of a fiftieth part of a knight's fee. He died long before the death of Margaret, and then the earl of March, father of the present earl, took this tenement with the ward of Fulk son of Fulk, as kinsman and heir of Thomas de Grey, clerk, that is son of Fulk, brother of Thomas. The wardship and marriage he granted to various persons.

The annual value of Stansfield manor is altogether 16 marks, the three quarters held of the earl of March £8, and the quarter called 'Narfordes' 4 marks; and owing to the death of Margaret the king should hold this manor for the reasons and in the form abovesaid.

Adam de Clyfton, the brother and next heir of Margaret, is aged 60 years and more. Agnes widow of Thomas Mortymer, knight, received the profits from the death of Margaret until her death in Whitweek 1403, her executors from then until 25 March 1404, and John son of Thomas White since 27 Jan. 1405. They are answerable to the king for the profits.

[Cf. *Cf. CIM* VII, no.264].

C 137/49, no.24

ROGER MORTEMERE, ESQUIRE

1094 Writ 21 Dec. 1404.

HEREFORD. Inquisition. Weobley. 31 July 1405.

He held:

Tedstone Wafer, the manor, of the king in chief of the honour of Brecon, service unknown, annual value 106s.8d.

'Coldehampton', certain lands, of the abbot of Reading in right of his church of St. Mary, Reading, service unknown, annual value 40s.

Stoke Prior in the liberty of Leominster, a watermill called 'Marschemulle', of the same abbot in right of his church, service unknown, annual value 20s.

Bodenham, a parcel of land, of Thomas Lucy, knight, of his manor of Bodenham, service unknown, annual value 4s.

Bromyard, lands, meadow and pasture in the lordship called 'Badurnes', of John Trevenant, late bishop of Hereford, in right of his church of St. Ethelbert king and martyr in Hereford, service unknown, annual value 24s.

Edvin Loach, 1 carucate, of John Blakeney, service unknown, annual value 10s.

Saltmarsh, lands, meadow and pasture so-called, of John Trevenant, late bishop of Hereford, service unknown, annual value 36s.

He died on 13 Dec. 1402. John Mortymer, his son, was aged 14 years on 13 Dec. last. John ap Harry has held the manor of Tedstone Wafer, the lands in 'Coldehampton', the mill in Stoke Prior and the lands in Bodenham since his death and still holds them, title unknown; John Mortymer, bastard son of Roger, has held the lands called 'Badurnes' and those in Edvin Loach; and Philip Dombulton those called Saltmarsh; and they have taken the profits, titles likewise unknown.

C 137/49, no.25

JOAN WIFE OF THOMAS WEST

1095 Writ 29 April 1404.

GLOUCESTER. Inquisition. Acton Turville. 10 June.

Ralph Welyngton held in his demesne as of fee the manor of Frampton Cotterell in chief of Richard II, and the manors of Sandhurst and Ablington of the abbot of Gloucester, services unknown. He married Joan and died without heirs. They descended to John Welyngton as brother and heir of Ralph and, he being under age, were taken into the king's hands. The king in chancery assigned in dower to Joan a third part of each manor with 3 a. wood in Sandhurst and 5 a. wood in Frampton Cotterell.

John Welyngton died without heirs, whereupon the two parts of the manors with the reversion of the third parts descended to Isabel wife of William Beaumount, then of full age, as one sister and heir, and John Wroth, son of Margaret the other sister, under age. Annual values of the third parts: Frampton Cotterell £9, Sandhurst £4, Ablington 53s.4d.

She died on 24 April. Isabel is aged 30 years and more, John Wroth 12 years and more. Thomas West, son of Thomas West, is son and next heir of Joan, age unknown.

1096   Writ, *plura*, 18 July 1404.

GLOUCESTER. Inquisition. Chipping Sodbury. 10 Oct.

Ralph de Welyngton held certain lands and tenements in Sandhurst called Moorslade. He married Joan and died without heirs of his body. They were taken into the hands of Richard II owing to the minority of John brother and heir of Ralph, because he held other lands in chief by knight service. Afterwards a third part of Moorslade was assigned to Joan in dower. John died without heirs of his body and the reversion of the third descended to Isabel wife of William Beaumont and John Wroth as above, ages as above.

The third part is held of the abbot of Gloucester, service unknown, annual value 3s.4d.

1097   Writ 29 April 1404.

DEVON. Inquisition. Torrington. 28 June.

Ralph Welyngton held the manor of Huntshaw in his demesne as of fee of the duchy of Cornwall by knight service. He married Joan and died without heirs. The manor was taken into the hands of Richard II owing to the minority of John Welyngton, his brother and heir. She was assigned a third part with 100 a. wood in dower, annual value £4 18s.

Date of death, heirs of Ralph, and her heirs, as above [no. 1095].

1098   DEVON. Partition. Huntshaw. 27 July 1405.

Partition of the lands and tenements which Joan widow of Thomas West held in dower of Ralph Welyngton, sometime her husband, of the inheritance of Isabel wife of William Beaumont, one sister and heir of John Welyngton, brother and heir of Ralph, and John Wroth, son of Margaret, the other sister, in the presence and with the assent of William Beaumont and Isabel, and Walter Pollard, attorney of John Wroth, knight, to whom the king granted the custody of the lands of John Wroth [*Cf. CPR 1399–1401*, p.391].

Assigned and delivered to William Beaumont and Isabel:

Wiggadon, 6d. rent from free tenants, and 1 ferling which Thomas Jon holds.

Guscott, half a ferling held by Robert Burgh and 1 ferling held by William Peirs.

Haddacott, 3 plots (*clavas*) held by William Hadyncote, 1 plot held by John Twechene, 1 plot held by Simon Hugh, and a third part of a messuage, 10 a. and 1 cornmill held by Henry atte Mille.

'Keyrlond', 'Radweye' and 'Wodewallys', certain parcels of the demesne there so-called, comprising by estimation 1 ferling and held by Ivo Frend, and a third part of a messuage there held by Simon Vynhagh.

'Babbecary', 1 cottage and 2 a. held by Alice Grenecomb, and 1 cottage and 2 a. held by Robert Burgh.

Wayhead, 7d. rent from all the lands there; and 34 a. wood there of which 26 a. lie between the wood of John [Wroth], son of Margaret, on the east and the wood of the same John on the west, and 8 a. between the wood of the same John on the east and the king's highway on the west, which amount to 48s. 4¾d.; all to be held by William Beaumont as Isabel's share of the lands by the law and custom of England.

Assigned and delivered to John Wroth, son of Margaret, as his share to hold by the law and custom of England:

Wayhead, 1 messuage, 1 dovecot and 2 ferlings held by Adam Knokeworthy.

Hill, 2½ ferlings held by John Welyngton.

Haddacott, 1 ferling held by John Twechene, villein, with all his family there; and 24 a. wood extending at 40s.

Writ to give seisin to William Beaumont, who has paid 13s. 4d. and given fealty. 21 Feb. 1405.

[Text of oath of fealty]: *Vour jurrez que vous serez foiall et loial, et foi et loialtee porterez a nostre segnur le Roi Henry et a ses heirs Rois Dengleterre et loialment ferez et loialment comistrez les services dues des terres lesqueux vous clamez tenir de luy come de droit de vostre femme et les queux il vous rende si Dieux vous aide, et ses seintz.*

Writ, ordering return of the partition to the chancery. 18 Oct. 1406.

C 137/49, no. 26
E 149/83, no. 1

MARGARET WIDOW OF THOMAS DE ERDYNGTON, KNIGHT

1099　Writ 3 Feb. 1405.

DORSET. Inquisition. Sturminster Marshall. 9 Feb.

She held a third part of the manor of Corfe Mullen in dower after the death of Thomas, with reversion to Thomas their son. It is held of the countess of Kent of her manor of Queen Camel by knight service, annual value of the third part 8 marks.

She died on 14 Jan. last. Thomas the son and heir is aged 30 years and more.

1100　Writ 3 Feb. 1405.

WARWICK. Inquisition. Solihull. 10 Feb.

She held in dower a third part of the manors of Erdington and Hunscote, and a third part of a messuage and of a virgate in Withybrook, by assignment of Thomas de Erdyngton, son and heir of her husband and herself, with reversion to himself. Erdington is held of Hugh Lord Burnell by knight service, annual value of the third part £4; Hunscote of John Stafford of Brownshill, knight, service unknown, annual value of the third part 8s. 8d.; the messuage and land also of John Stafford, service unknown, annual value of the third part 7s.

Date of death and heir as above.

1101   Writ 19 Jan. 1405.

LEICESTER. Inquisition. Leicester. 24 Jan.

She held to herself and the heirs of Thomas, her late husband, and herself:

Barrow upon Soar, the manor, of the king in chief by knight service, annual value 40 marks.

Houghton on the Hill, the manor, of Lord la Zouche of Harringworth by knight service, annual value £10.

Branston by Leicester, the manor, of Thomas Harcourt, knight, or of the heirs of John Burdet, knight, of which or by what service is unknown, annual value £10.

Date of death and heir as above.

1102   Writ, *melius sciri*, as to how the above manors were held, 1 Feb; and writ, *plura*, 3 Feb. 1405.

LEICESTER. Inquisition. Mountsorrell, 9 Feb.

She did hold more than previously returned, namely in dower by assignment of Thomas son and heir of Thomas, her late husband, and herself, with reversion to him:

Knossington, a third part of the manor, of John de Ordeby, knight, service unknown, annual value of the third part 40s.

Sysonby, 1 messuage and 3 virgates, not of the king in chief but of whom and by what service is unknown, annual value 13s.4d.

Barrow upon Soar, 1 messuage, half a virgate and a third part of 12 a. meadow, of the king in chief as a sixtieth part of a knight's fee, annual value 13s.4d.

Quorndon, a third part of a service rent of 3s., of the king in chief as a two-hundredth part of a knight's fee.

She held the manor of Barrow, with the above premises in Barrow and the rent in Quorndon, of the king in chief as half a knight's fee by the grant of William Walssh and Thomas Wild, chaplains, to Thomas and herself, and the heirs of their bodies, by licence of Edward III [*CPR 1374–7*, pp.116–7], with remainder to the right heirs of Giles de Erdyngton, knight, whose heir Thomas was.

C 137/49, no.27
E 149/86, no.13

THOMAS RALEIGH

1103   Writ 20 Oct. 1404.

WILTSHIRE. Inquisition. Cricklade. 21 Nov.

He held in his demesne as of fee one parcel of dry and hilly meadow in 'Asshetonmede' in Ashton Keynes by Cricklade, containing 20 a., of the earl of Gloucester of his manor of Shorncote in socage, service unknown, annual value 8s.

He died on 18 Oct. last. William his son and heir was aged 1 year on 16 Nov. last.

1104   Writ 20 Oct. 1404.

HAMPSHIRE. Inquisition. Newport. 15 Nov.

He held in his demesne as of fee:

Walpen, the lordship, and a windmill belonging to it in the Isle of Wight, of Edward duke of York of the castle of Carisbrooke as one knight's fee. The island was granted to the duke by letters patent of Richard II [*CPR 1396–9*, p.150]. In the lordship are various tenants, villein and free, and the annual value with the windmill is £19 6s. payable by equal parts at Lady Day and Michaelmas.

Wode and Chillingwood, various lands, tenements and woods so-called in the Isle, of the same duke of the same castle, as an eighth and a thirteenth of a knight's fee, annual value £6 13s.4d. payable at the same terms.

Haven Street, 2 small crofts of land and heath in the Isle, of John Hore by a rent of 12d., annual value 12d.

Date of death and heir as above, age 1 year on 16 Nov. next.

1105   Writ 20 Oct. 1404.
OXFORD. Inquisition. Banbury. 10 Nov.
He held in his demesne as of fee:
Mollington, the manor of 'Spaldyngfe', of the king in chief by knight service, annual value 65s.
Williamscot, 1 virgate, of the bishop of Lincoln by knight service, annual value 10s.; and Cropredy, 2 a. meadow, of the same by knight service, annual value 6s.8d.
Great Bourton, the manor called 'Sagesfe' of the lord of Nottingham of his manor of Vipont, service unknown, annual value 20s.
By his charter dated at Claydon he granted to John de Wetherley, dean of Astley, and Thomas Kyngeslond all his manor of Claydon and 'Laundesfe', to them, their heirs and assigns. They granted it to Joan his wife for life, with remainder to his right heirs.
Date of death and heir as above, age 1 year on 16 Nov. last.

1106   Writ 20 Oct. 1404.
WARWICK. Inquisition. Burton Dassett. 3 Nov.
He held in his demesne as of fee half a toft and 28 a. in Shuckburgh, of whom and by what service is unknown, annual value 40d.
By his charter dated at Farnborough, 4 July 1403, he granted to John de Wytherley, dean of Astley, and Thomas Kyngeslond all his manor of Farnborough, with all his lands, tenements, rents and services there in Avon Dassett, Warmington, Upton, Hardwick in Tysoe, North End, Kington in Claverdon and Napton on the Hill, with all the villeins with all their services, suits, families, cattle, liberties, free customs, common pastures, woods, hays, mills, waters and ponds, to them, their heirs and assigns.
Date of death and heir as above, age 1 year on 16 Nov. next.

1107   Writ 20 Oct. 1404.
GLOUCESTER. Inquisition. Cirencester. 10 Nov.
He held in his demesne as of fee:
Turkdean, 1 messuage and 2 carucates, in chief of the honour of Wallingford, service unknown, annual value 50s.
Norcott, the manor, of the manor of Shorncote, which Elizabeth widow of Edward le Despenser holds in dower as one quarter of a knight's fee, annual value 30s.
Lassington, two parts of the manor and of the advowson, of the archbishop of York, service unknown; annual values, two parts of manor 50s., advowson nil, but the church is worth £10.
Ley, a third part of the manor, of Lord Talbot in socage, annual value 5 marks.

Edgeworth, the manor and advowson, of Lord Talbot of his manor of Painswick, service unknown; annual values, manor £4, advowson nil, but the church 10 marks.

Date of death and heir as above, age 1 year on 16 Nov. next.

1108 Writ 20 Oct. 1404.

HEREFORD. Inquisition. Hereford. 22 Nov.

He held a quarter of the manor of Westhide of the heirs of Adam Everyngham, knight, lord of Everingham, annual value £4.

Date of death and heir as above, age 1 year on 16 Nov. last.

1109 DEVON. Inquisition. Barnstaple. 14 Nov. 1404.

He held the manor of West Hagginton, not in demesne but in fee and right, of Edward Courtenay, earl of Devon, by knight service. Long before he died he granted it by his deed shown to the jurors to Thomas Kyngeslond for life for a rent of £8 6s. 8d. payable by equal parts at Easter and Michaelmas, with remainder to Agnes wife of Thomas and John their son for their lives at a rent of £11; annual value £8 6s. 8d.

Also long before his death he granted to Thomas Kyngeslond for life for a rent of £18, payable by equal parts at Easter and Michaelmas:

Charles, the manor, held, not in demesne but in fee and right, of the earl of Devon by knight service, annual value £8.

West Buckland, the manor, similarly held of the heir of [the lord of] Rose Ash by knight service, annual value £4 6s.

Walson, 1 messuage, 1 carucate and 40 a. wood, similarly held of the heir [of the lord] of Cobham Week by knight service, annual value 40s.

Curtisknowle, half the manor, similarly held of Clarice widow of John Bera by knight service, annual value 50s.

He also held by knight service half a knight's fee in Clannaborough, half a fee in Whitsleigh and a quarter fee in Thorne of the said heir of Cobham Week, annual value nil.

Date of death and heir as above, age 1 year on 16 Nov. next.

> C 137/49, no. 28
> E 149/84, no. 9
> E 152/397, no. 1 and 402, no. 2

ALICE WIDOW OF WALTER ROMESYE, KNIGHT

1110 Writ 16 Dec. 1404.

WILTSHIRE. Inquisition. Salisbury. 30 Dec.

She held for life half the manor of Coombe Bissett, except 1 a., of the king in chief by knight service by the grant of John Wykyng, John Fantleroy and John Toper, chaplain, to Walter and herself, with successive remainders to Thomas Romesye, son of Thomas, son of Walter, and his heirs male, Walter brother of Thomas and his heirs male, and the right heirs of Walter on the side of Margaret Byset, his mother, by a fine [CP 25(1) 290/59, no. 49] made with the king's licence; annual value 100s.

Walter Romesye, knight, died on 25 Nov. 1403. Alice died on 13 Dec. last. Thomas son of Thomas, their [grandson and] heir, was 15 on 28 Oct. last.

1111   Writ 16 Dec. 1404.

HAMPSHIRE. Inquisition. Romsey. 29 Dec.

She held the manor of Rockbourne for life of the king in chief by knight service by the grant of Thomas Bonham and John Wikyng. By their deed they granted that this manor, which should have reverted to them on the death of Walter and Alice Romesye, should remain to Thomas son of Thomas and the heirs male of his body, then to Walter brother of Thomas and his heirs male, and failing them to the right heirs of Margaret Byset, mother of Walter Romesye, knight, by royal licence [*CPR 1399–1401*, p.451] shown to the jurors with other muniments; annual value £20. Walter and Alice attorned to Thomas son of Thomas.

Similarly and with the same remainders she held 2 messuages, 1 carucate, 20 a. meadow, 10 a. wood and rents of £12 and 12 quarters of salt in Romsey, East Dean, Hyde and Marshwood by the grant of John Wykyng, John Fantleroy and John Toper, chaplain, by a fine [as in no.1110 above]; annual value £16. One messuage and 20 a. are held of Henry Popham and his heirs by fealty, the rest of the abbess of Romsey by fealty.

Dates of death and heir as above.

1112   Writ 16 Dec. 1404.

SOMERSET. Inquisition. Taunton. 13 Jan. 1405.

She held jointly with Walter Romesye, knight, her late husband, by the grant of John Wykyng, John Fauntleroy and John Toper, chaplain, in accordance with the fine of 1402 [as in no.1110]:

Oakleigh, the manor, of John Lorty, knight, by fealty, with successive remainders to Thomas son of Thomas Romesye and his heirs male, Walter brother of Thomas the son and his heirs male, and the right heirs of Walter, knight; annual value £12.

Otterhampton, Combwich and Pipplepen, 2 messuages, 3 carucates, 25 a. meadow, 70 a. wood and rents of £6 10s., 1 lb. wax and ½ lb. pepper: 1 messuage and 1 carucate in Pipplepen of John Lorty, knight, by fealty and suit of court at North Perrott twice yearly; the remainder in Otterhampton and Combwich of John Twychet, knight, by knight service of his manor of Nether Stowey; annual values, Pipplepen 60s., Otterhampton and Combwich £8. The successive remainders to these premises were to Walter brother of Thomas and his heirs male, Thomas son of Thomas and his heirs male, and the right heirs of Walter, knight.

Mudford, a third part of the manor, of Michael earl of Suffolk of his manor of Haselbury by knight service and a rent of 6s.8d., with successive remainders as for Oakleigh; annual value £4.

Dates of death and heir as above.

C 137/49, no.29
E 149/86, no.7

AGNES WIDOW OF CHRISTOPHER SHUCKBURGH, FORMERLY WIFE OF ROGER DE NORTHWODE, KNIGHT

1113   Writ 28 May 1405.

KENT. Inquisition. Sittingbourne. 10 June.

She held for life the manor of Stonepit in the isle of Sheppey, 5 marks rent from various lands in Thornham and a marsh in Iwade called Chetney Marshes, by the grant of John de Cobeham, Lord Cobham, who granted the reversion of the manor of Stonepit to Richard Noke and his heirs. Christopher Shuckburgh and Agnes attorned to him. Noke granted the reversion to Richard Cheyne, Robert Sharp, Nicholas atte Cherche, William Elys of Sheppey, deceased, Bartholomew Seyntleger, Thomas son of John Chiche of Canterbury and Stephen Peytefyn, their heirs and assigns, and Christopher and Agnes attorned to them. So she died seised of this manor with reversion to them; annual value 100s. A rent of 39s. 2d. from 40 a. and a marsh called 'la Wilghe', parts of the manor, were held of Roger earl of March of his castle of Tonge as a twentieth part of a knight's fee. The rest of the manor was held of the archbishop of Canterbury of his church of Canterbury by knight service.

Lord Cobham granted the rent of 5 marks from the lands in Thornham, after her death, to the master and chaplains of his chantry of Cobham by royal licence. Thomas Lodelowe, knight, William Haldenne, Reynold de Cobeham, clerk, and John Ydele granted to the master and chaplains of Cobham and their successors the reversion of two parts of 200 a. marsh in Iwade which Christopher Shokkebourgh and Agnes held for her life by the grant of John de Cobeham, knight, to whom the reversion formerly belonged [CPR 1367–70, p. 277], royal licence having been obtained; annual value 10s. Of whom the rent of 5 marks is held and by what service is unknown. Christopher and Agnes attorned to Thomas Lodelowe, knight, and the others.

Richard Sheme, vicar of Eastchurch, and Peter Haddelay granted the manor of Horton by Canterbury to Roger de Northwode and Agnes then his wife and the heirs of Roger, by a fine of 1360 [CP 25(1) 105/170, no. 1308]. Afterwards Roger Northwode son and heir of John de Northwode, knight, son and heir of Roger de Northwode, knight, granted the reversion of this manor to Thomas Chicche of Beverley, Gilbert Manfeld, citizen of London, Nicholas Potyn, John Dreylonde, William Emery and William Makenade, and the heirs and assigns of William Makenade, and Christopher and Agnes attorned to them.

She held the manors of Yokes and Wichling with the advowson of Wichling and other lands and tenements in dower of Roger de Northwode, knight, her second [sic] husband by assignment in chancery in March 1362 made with the assent of John de Northwode, his son and heir, and the reversion of the manors was granted by Roger son of John to John son of Roger Digge and Juliana his wife, and Christopher and Agnes attorned to them.

The reversion of the advowson of Wichling was granted to Bartholomew Seynt Leger and Stephen Peyteveyn, and Christopher and Agnes attorned to them. It is held of John Seyntcler and Margaret his wife of their manor of Ospringe by knight service, annual value nil beyond the presentation.

Agnes died on 27 May last. Agnes formerly wife of Stephen Peytevyn, aged 24 years, Margaret wife of Walter Roo, aged 24 years and more, her daughters, and Peter Rede, son of Juliana, a third daughter, aged 34 years [sic], are her next heirs.

[Partly worn and illegible; some details from CCR 1402–5, pp. 462, 467, 468; 1405–8, pp. 264, 360, 362].

1114   Writ, melius sciri, as the above inquisition did not say how or of whom the rent in Thornham and the marsh in Iwade were held. 10 July 1405.

KENT. Inquisition. Sittingbourne. 21 July.

The 5 marks rent is not held of anyone by any service, but is rent from various lands and tenements in Thornham. The marsh is held of Humphrey of Lancaster, knight, of his manor of Milton by a rent of 1 pair of gloves, price 1d., at Easter. He holds the manor by the grant of the king, his father.

C 137/49, no.30

ELEANOR WIDOW OF REYNOLD COBHAM, KNIGHT, FORMERLY WIFE OF JOHN DE ARUNDELL, KNIGHT

1115 Writ 21 Jan. 1405.

WILTSHIRE. Inquisition. Salisbury. 20 Feb.

She held in dower of the inheritance of Reynold Cobham, son of Reynold Cobham, her late husband, the manor of Langley Burrell of the duchy of Lancaster of the honour of Trowbridge by knight service, annual value £10.

She died on 10 Jan. last.

1116 Writ 16 Feb. 1405.

WILTSHIRE. Inquisition. Wilton. 19 March.

She held jointly with John de Arundell, knight, to them and his heirs:

Sherrington and Codford, the manor of the king in chief by knight service, annual value £13 5s. of which assize rents of free and unfree tenants payable at the four terms amount to £9 13s.4d.

Elston, half the manor, also in chief by knight service, annual value 10 marks, of which similar assize rents 100s.

Boyton, the manor and advowson, of the heir of the earl of Salisbury, under age in the king's ward, annual value £10, assize rents £7.

Corton, the manor, of the same, annual value 60s., assize rents 36s.8d.

Winterbourne Stoke, the manor, of the same, annual value 40s., assize rents 26s.8d.

Coate, the manor, of the same, annual value £4, assize rents 52s.

Hill Deverill, the manor, of the heir of the earl of March, under age in the king's ward, annual value 40s., assize rents 26s.8d.

She also held jointly to them and their heirs Great Somerford, the manor. Long before her death she granted this manor with the advowson by her charter in pure widowhood to John Chelreye for life, he paying her £8 by equal parts at the four terms. So she held the rent of £8. The manor is held of Lord Tiptoft of his manor of Castle Combe by the service of half a knight's fee.

She died on 10 Jan. last. John Arundell, esquire, aged 20 years and more on 1 Aug. last, is kinsman of both John Arundell, knight, and Eleanor, being the son and heir of their son, John Arundell, knight, junior.

1117 Writ, *plenius certiorari*, as the holdings are said to be of greater value than stated in the above inquisition. 10 July 1405.

WILTSHIRE. Inquisition. Wilton. 13 Oct.

John Arundell, knight, held jointly with Eleanor, to them and the heirs of their bodies the manor of Sherrington and Codford and half the manor of Elston of the king in chief by knight service, annual values Sherrington and Codford £18, half of Elston £8; the manor of Boyton with the advowson, annual value £17, and the manors of Corton, 100s., Winterbourne Stoke, 60s., and Coate, £6, of the heir of John earl of Salisbury, under age in the king's ward; the manor of Hill Deverill, 100s., of the heir of the earl of March, under age in the king's ward, by knight service; and the manor and advowson of Great Somerford of the Lord Tiptoft of his manor of Castle Combe as half a knight's fee, annual value £8.

1118   Writ 16 Feb. 1405.
SOMERSET. Inquisition. Ilchester.
   She held for life jointly with John Arundell, formerly her husband, of the king in chief by knight service, with remainder after her death to his right heirs:
   Cucklington, the manor, annual value £10, and the advowson.
   Stoke Trister, the manor, annual value £10, and the advowson.
   Bayford, the manor, annual value £4 3s.4d.
   Selwood, the bailiwick of the forester, annual value 10s.
   She also held jointly to them and their heirs Hendford, the manor, annual value £30, and 57s. rent from lands in Yeovil, of the heir of the earl of March, under age in the king's ward.
   Date of death and heir as above [no. 1116].

1119   Writ 16 Feb. 1405.
GLOUCESTER. Inquisition. Gloucester. 26 March.
   She held in her demesne as of fee:
   Stonehouse, the manor, of the bishop of Worcester, service unknown, annual value £20, of which £12 is in assize rents payable by equal parts at the four principal terms.
   Minchinhampton, 1 toft, 1 dovecot, 1 carucate, 2 a. meadow and 100s. rent, of Hugh Waterton and Katherine his wife of the manor of Minchinhampton in socage by a rent of 43s.3½d. and suit of court there every three weeks, annual value nil beyond the rent.
   Shurdington, 1 messuage and 1 virgate, annual value 60s., and 100s. rent, of Thomas de Fornevale and Ankaret his wife by a rent of 6d.
   Date of death and heir as above [no. 1116].

1120   Writ 26 Jan. 1405.
DORSET. Inquisition. Dorchester. 27 Feb.
   She held:
   Witchampton, the manor. William Warre and Henry Stroude, clerk, held it by the feoffment of Eleanor Arundel to them and their heirs and assigns. They granted it to her for life with remainder to Richard Arundel, knight, and the heirs of his body, and failing such heirs to the heirs of the body of Eleanor. It is held of the heir of Roger de Mortuo Mari, earl of March, under age in the king's ward, annual value £24, of which £21 10s.5d. is in assize rents. Richard is still living, aged 26 years and more.
   Loders, rent of a rose from the manor and from certain lands, meadows, pasture, woods, rents and services which she held in Eggardon, Litton Cheney, Woolcombe and West Moors, and which John Quinton holds for life by her grant with reversion to her heirs. They are held of the abbot of Forde by knight service, annual value £10.
   Frome Whitfield, £32 rent from the manor payable at the four terms. The manor is held for life by Robert Veel by her grant, with reversion to her heirs. He is still living. It is held of the earl of Hereford by knight service, annual value £32 beyond the rent.
   Lytchett Matravers, rent of a rose at Midsummer from 1 messuage, 22 a. and 3 plots of land and pasture, held by John Kent, Alice his wife and William their son, who is still living, for their lives, by the grant of Eleanor, with reversion to her heirs, annual

value . . . 6s.8d.; and the rest of the manor held of the heir of the earl of March, annual value £13 6s.8d.

Philipston, the manor, of the abbess of Wilton by a rent of 25 quarters of salt, annual value £4.

Worth Matravers, the manor, of the earl of Hereford by knight service, annual value £8.

Langton Matravers in Purbeck, the manor, of the heir of the earl of Salisbury, annual value £10.

East Morden, the manor, of the king in chief by a rent of 8s. payable by the sheriff, annual value £10.

Wootton Fitzpaine, the manor, of the heir of Henry Lorty by knight service, annual value £10.

Wimborne St. Giles, the manor called French's, of the heir of the earl of March by knight service, annual value 4 marks.

Winterborne St. Martin, half a toft, 60 a. arable and 20 a. pasture, of Roger Seymour of . . .hamp(?). . ., annual value 10s.(?).

Date of death and heir as above [no.1116].

[Partly worn and illegible; cf. no.766 above].

1121   Writ 21 Jan. 1405.

KENT. Inquisition. West Malling. 11 March.

She held in dower of Reynold Cobeham, knight, of the inheritance of Reynold his son and heir:

Aldington by Maidstone, the manor, of the king of the castle of Rochester by a rent of 14s. payable on St. Andrew's day for the ward of the castle, annual value 60s.

Hiltesbury, the manor, with the advowson of Lullingstone, of the prior of Leeds of his manor of Leeds by suit of court there at Michaelmas, annual value 40s.

East Shelve and Boardfield, the manor, partly of the king of the castle of Dover by a rent of 3s.9d. for ward of the castle every 24 weeks, annual value 40s., and the remainder of the abbot of Faversham and John Champeyne in gavelkind, service unknown, annual value £8.

Westwell, a tenement in called Westwell, of Thomas Swynbourne, knight, of his manor of Boughton Aluph in gavelkind, and of others, names and services unknown, annual value 40s.

Orkesden, the manor, in gavelkind of the archbishop of Canterbury, Lady la Zouche, William son of Nicholas Keryel, knight, and others, names and services unknown, annual value 66s.8d.

Bowzell, the manor, in gavelkind of the archbishop, John Frenyngham, George Modell, Reynold de Pekham and others, names and services unknown, annual value 40s.

Date of death and heir, aged 20½ years, as above [no.1116].

1122   Writ 14 Feb. 1405.

KENT. Inquisition. West Malling. 1 June.

Eleanor widow of Reynold Cobham *alias* Eleanor Mautravers held the manor of Postling to herself and the heirs of herself and John de Arundell, senior, sometime

2C

her husband. It is held of the king of the castle of Dover by a rent of 20s. for ward of the castle, annual value £38.

Date of death and heir, no age given, as above [no.1116].

C 137/49, no.31, mm.1–16
E 149/85, no.5
E 152/403

JOHN ARUNDEL

1123   Writ for proof of age of John, son of John Arundel, junior, knight. By the grant of the prince of Wales he is in the ward of Thomas Nevill, Lord Furnival, who should be warned. 8 Aug. 1406.

[Endorsed] He was warned at Ditton by William Spelyng, Thomas Neel, Henry Aleyn and John Fynton.

BUCKINGHAM. Proof of age. Colnbrook. 12 Aug.

John Arundel, kinsman [grandson] and heir of Eleanor Arundel, was born at the manor of Ditton on 1 Aug. 1385 and baptised in St. Mary's church, Datchet, and he is therefore aged 21 years and more. Asked how they knew this the jurors said:

William Spelyng, aged 58 years and more, on that day went to the house of John Benet, vicar of Datchet, to ask him to be godfather.

Thomas Neel, 55 and more, carried a torch at the baptism.

Henry Aleyn, 58 and more, was a butler of Margery then Lady Moleyns, lady of that manor, and delivered bread and wine and sent it for the baptism.

John Sperman, 56 and more, on that day was sent to London by Margery Lady Moleyns to discover where John the father could be found.

John Bakere of Colnbrook, 42 and more, in that month took at farm the house in Colnbrook, where he now lives, of William West of that place for 10 years from the ensuing Michaelmas.

William Skynnere of Iver, 59 and more, had a daughter born that day who is now dead.

John Hale of Langley Marish, 41 and more, had a new shop in Colnbrook on that day.

Robert Dastrell, 43 and more, at that time purchased to himself and his heirs a tenement in the parish of St. Mary there by a charter of feoffment.

William Randolf, 45 and more, had a daughter Joan married to John Wellys in St. Mary's church, Datchet, in the following week.

Walter Clerk of Horton, 51 and more, knows because in that week his wife Isabel was delivered of his eldest son John.

Richard Auger, 54 and more, was in the church and held a cloth for drying of hands after the baptism.

John Fynton of Datchet, 52 and more, was a servant of Lady Moleyns and carried two bottles of wine to the church for the people there to drink.

C 137/49, no.31, mm.17–8

WALTER COKESEY, KNIGHT

1124   Writ 24 June 1405.

WARWICK. Inquisition. Monks Kirby. 13 July.

He held the manor of Hunningham by the law of England after the death of Isabel his wife, whose inheritance it was, with remainder to Walter Cokesey, knight, their son and heir. It is held of earl of Warwick, service unknown, annual value 8 marks payable by equal parts at Lady Day and Michaelmas, and was let at this farm to William Aleyn for a term of years.

He died on 13 June last. Walter Cokesey, knight, the son, was aged 21 years on 18 Oct. last.

ISABEL WIFE OF WALTER COKESEY, KNIGHT

1125 Writ 17 July 1405.
WARWICK. Inquisition. Coventry. 20 July.

Walter and Isabel held the manor of Hunningham in the right of Isabel, to her and her heirs, of the earl of Warwick, service unknown, annual value 8 marks. It was let to William Aleyn for a term of years at this farm.

She died on 25 June 1403. Walter Cokesey, knight, the son, was 21 years of age on 18 Oct. last. Walter senior held it and took the profits, until he died on 13 June last, as tenant by the law of England. On that day the escheator took it into the king's hands, and so it remains.

WALTER COKESEY, KNIGHT

1126 Writ 24 June 1405.
WORCESTER. Inquisition. Worcester. 29 June.

Jointly with Isabel his wife, who is still living [sic], he held for their lives by the grant of Henry Haggeley, Thomas Belue, William Boteler and John Mall:

Goldicote, the manor, of the abbot of Pershore, service unknown, annual value £10.

Lower Sapey, the manor, of the barony of Burford, service likewise unknown, annual value 20s.

Upthorpe and Alderminster, 100s. rent, of the abbot of Pershore, service unknown. Henry Haggeley and the others held this rent by the grant of Walter, and gave it to them in full recompense for the dower which Isabel might have had after the death of Walter, with remainder after their deaths to Walter son and heir of Walter, knight, Maud then his wife, and the heirs of Walter, and failing such heirs to the right heirs of Walter, knight.

He also held for life, without impeachment of waste, by the grant of the same Henry Haggeley and the others, with remainder to his son Walter and his heirs, and failing them to his own right heirs:

Cooksey, the manor, of the earl of Warwick, service unknown, annual value £10.

Caldwall, the manor, of the prior of Maiden Bradley, service unknown, annual value 100s.

Orleton, Overton, Netherton, Bastwood, and Stockton on Teme, the manors, of Katherine Musard, service unknown, annual values 5 marks, 20s., 20s., 40s. and 2s.

Sutton, the manor, of the barony of Burford, service unknown, annual value 100s.

Kidderminster, 1 messuage and 6 a. called Park Hall, of the king in chief as a fortieth part of a knight's fee, annual value 3s.

Harpley, 100s. rent, of the barony of Burford, service unknown.

Purshull, 30s. rent, of Matthew Gurney, knight, service unknown.

Droitwich, 21 lead vats for salt water (*bullar' plumborum aque salse*) and 1 salt pan (*salinam*) with appurtenances, of the king in chief in socage, annual value 10 marks. Date of death and heir as above [no.1124].

> C 137/50, no.32
> E 149/86, no.14
> E 152/407, no.3

JOAN WIDOW OF JOHN MOHUN, KNIGHT

1127 Writ 6 Oct. 1404.

OXFORD. Inquisition. Oxford. 12 Nov.

She held the manor of Goring in her demesne in fee tail to herself and the heirs of John Mohun and herself of the prince of Wales of the honour of Wallingford by knight service by the grant of William Fordham, chaplain, and Maud de Borton by a fine of 1346 [CP 25(1) 190/19, no.64], service unknown, annual value £10.

She died on 4 Oct. last. Elizabeth countess of Salisbury, one daughter of John de Mohun and Joan, aged 30 years and more, Philippa wife of Edward duke of York, a second daughter, aged 26 years and more, and Richard Straunge, son of Maud widow of John Straunge, knight, the third daughter, are next heirs. Maud died in the lifetime of Joan. Richard is aged 22 years and more.

1128 Writ 6 Oct. 1404.

DEVON. Inquisition. Exeter. 30 Dec.

William de Houthorp and Richard Cok, chaplain, granted the reversion of the manor of Ugborough, which Reynold de Mohun held for life of the inheritance of William de Houthorp, and that of the manor of Bradworthy, which Patrick de Mohun similarly held, both of which should have reverted to them on the death of the Mohuns, to John de Mohun of Dunster, knight, and Joan his wife, the heirs of their bodies and the right heirs of John, by a fine of 1348 [CP 25(1) 287/43, no.422]. Reynold died, and they held Ugborough until John granted it by his deed to Nigel Loryng, knight, his heirs and assigns.

John de Mohun and Patrick died. Joan entered Bradworthy and held it peacefully in fee tail until, by her indenture shown to the jurors, she granted it to William Cary, his heirs and assigns, for the term of her life. She held it of John de la Pomeray, knight, of his manor of Berry Pomeroy by knight service, annual value 106s.8d.

Date of death and heirs as above.

1129 DORSET. Inquisition *ex officio*. Wimborne Minster. 4 Nov. 1404.

She held one quarter of the manor of Sturminster Marshall, of whom and by what service is unknown; annual value £20.

She died on 4 Oct. Who is heir and of what age is also unknown.

1130 Writ and writ for fees, both 22 Oct. 1404.

DORSET. Inquisition. Sherborne. 22 Nov.

She held in her demesne in fee tail to herself and the heirs of the bodies of herself and John de Mohun of Dunster, knight, the manor of Sturminster Marshall and a third part of the hundred of Loosebarrow by the grant of William de Houtorp and Richard Coke, chaplain, by a fine of 1348 [as above, no.1128].

They are held of the manor of Kingston Lacy, which is parcel of the duchy of Lancaster, as a third part of a knight's fee, annual value together 20 marks.

John died long before. Joan died on 4 Oct. last. Philippa wife of Edward duke of York, one daughter, aged 28 years and more, Elizabeth widow of William de Monte Acuto, late earl of Salisbury, another daughter, aged 40 years and more, and Richard Lord Strange, son of Maud wife of John le Strange, a third daughter, aged 21 years and more, are their next heirs.

1131   Writ 22 Oct. 1404.

HAMPSHIRE. Inquisition. Odiham. 26 Nov.

She held the manor of Greywell in her demesne in fee tail to herself, the heirs of the bodies of John Mohun and herself, and the right heirs of John, by the grant of William de Houthorp and Richard Cok, chaplain, by a fine of 1348 [CP 25(1) 287/43, no.428]. It is held of the king of the manor of Odiham by the services of rendering £4 yearly in gold or silver, finding 10 men for autumn works for one day in autumn, and suit of court at Odiham every three weeks; annual value 20 marks.

John died long ago. Joan died on 4 Oct. Heirs as above; ages, Philippa 24 years and more, Elizabeth 40 and more, Richard 21 and more.

1132   Writ and writ for fees, 6 and 22 Oct. 1404.

WARWICK. Inquisition. Stratford on Avon. 30 Oct.

She held the manors of Long Compton and Whichford with the advowson of Whichford in her demesne in fee tail to herself, the heirs of the bodies of John Mohun and herself, and the right heirs of John, by the grant of Ivo de Clynton by a fine of 1348 [CP 25(1) 247/58, no.27]. They are held of the earl of Hereford by the service of half a knight's fee; annual values, Whichford manor £16, the church £20, Long Compton £20.

John died long ago, Joan on 4 Oct. Heirs as above; ages, Philippa 28 years and more, Elizabeth 40 and more, and Richard 21 and more.

1133   Writ 6 Oct. 1404.

SOMERSET. Inquisition. Taunton. 15 Oct.

She held the castle of Dunster, the manors of Kilton, Minehead and Carhampton, and the hundred of Carhampton for life, with remainder to Elizabeth Lutrell, John Wermyngton and the heirs of Elizabeth, of the king in chief by knight service, by the grant of Simon archbishop of Canterbury, formerly bishop of London, and Aubrey de Veer and John Burgherssh, knights, by a fine of 1376 shown to the jurors [CP 25(1) 200/27, no.90]; annual value 300 marks.

Hugh Lutrell, knight, son of Elizabeth Lutrell, her next heir, is aged 38 years.

Joan died on 4 Oct. Heirs as above, [ages as in no.1131].

The escheator has taken all the premises into the king's hands.

1134   Commission to John Hull and William Hankeford, reciting the last inquisition and enquiring whether she held on the day of her death, whether John Wermyngton and Elizabeth Lutrell are dead or not, and what is the name and surname of Lord Strange. 24 Oct. 1404 [CPR 1401–5, pp.506–7].

SOMERSET. Inquisition taken by John Hull. Taunton. 13 Jan. 1405.

Simon late bishop of London and Aubrey de Veer and John de Burgerssh, knights, held the castle of Dunster, the manors of Kilton, Minehead and Carhampton, and the hundred of Carhampton in their demesne as of fee to them and the heirs of Simon by the grant of John de Mohun and Joan by a fine of 1374–5 [CP 25(1) 200/27, no.85]. After the death of John de Mohun they granted them by another fine [CP 25(1) 200/27, no.90] to Joan for life with remainder to Elizabeth Lutrell and John Wermyngton and the heirs of Elizabeth. So Joan held them, but long before her death she granted them for her life to Edward then earl of Rutland and Philippa his wife, and Elizabeth countess of Salisbury for a rent of 400 marks. So she held the rent at her death.

Elizabeth Lutrell and John Wermyngton died long before Joan. The name of Richard Straunge, son and heir of John Lord Strange, is Richard Straunge. He, Philippa and Elizabeth are her heirs.

Hugh Lutrell, knight, aged 38 years and more, is son and heir of Elizabeth Lutrell.

1135   Further commission to John Hull and William Hankeford, saying that she held more than was reported in the original inquisition. 24 Oct. 1404 [CPR 1401–5, p.507].

SOMERSET. Inquisition taken by John Hull with the same jurors as last. Taunton. 13 Jan. 1405.

Repeats the last verdict and adds that the castle, manors and hundred are one and not divided.

William Houthorp and Richard Cok, chaplain, formerly held the manor of Cutcombe in their demesne as of fee and granted it to John and Joan de Mohun and their heirs. She held it in fee tail of the king in chief by knight service; annual value £10.

Date of death and heirs as above, [ages as in no.1131].

C 137/50, no.33
E 149/84, no.8
E 152/402, no.1

ELIZABETH SEYNTOMER

1136   Writ 13 Feb. 1405.

WILTSHIRE. Inquisition. Salisbury. 22 Feb.

Long before she died she held in her demesne as of fee 4 messuages, 1 carucate and 8 a. meadow in Stanton St. Quintin, and granted them to Thomas Hobbes and Joan his wife, who are still living, for their lives, with reversion to her own right heirs. They are held of the king in chief by the service of a twelfth part of a knight's fee, annual value 40s. The king pardoned the grant by letters patent on 4 Feb. last [CPR 1401–5, p.491]. She died seised of the reversion.

She held in fee tail to herself and the heirs male of her body, by the grant of Gilbert Gaveler, clerk, and Thomas Hobbes, with remainder failing heirs male to Robert More, Joan his wife and the heirs of their bodies, and failing them the right heirs of Elizabeth, by a fine of 1405 [CP 25(1) 290/61, no.81]:

Bramshaw and Britford, the manors, except 3 messuages, 40 a. arable, 10 a. meadow and 20s.4d. rent in Britford, of Thomas West, knight, in chief by knight service. There are assize rents of £20 payable by equal parts at the four terms; 2 messuages; 2 carucates in demesne, 2 parts being sown each year, worth £4, and the 3rd part nil because in a fallow field; 30 a. several meadow from Lady Day to Lammas, each a. as mowed

20d., then nil because common; 100 a. pasture on the hills, 16s.8d.; 40 a. of great wood nil, but pasture there 10s.; and pleas and perquisites of court 10s.

Burton, the manor, of the duke of York by knight service. There are assize rents, 100s.; 1 carucate, of which 2 parts are worth 30s. each year, the third part nil; 20 a. meadow with herbage at 20d. the a., but after mowing nil because common; and pleas and perquisites of court, 12d.

Eastrop, Cricklade, Calcutt, Ampney, Moredon, Marston, Highworth, Blunsdon St. Andrew, Stratton St. Margaret, Haydon, Haydon Wick, Widhill, Sevenhampton, Pynchet and Great and Little Chelworth, 20 messuages, 1 mill, 3 carucates, 80 a. meadow, 100s. rent, and the advowson of St. Sampson, Cricklade, comprising:

Eastrop, 1 messuage and 20 a., of the rector of Edington, service unknown, annual value 5s.

Moredon, 4 messuages and half a carucate, of the heir of Nicholas Mordon, service unknown, annual value 10s.

Blunsdon St. Andrew, Stratton St. Margaret and Haydon Wick, 4 messuages and 20 a., of Ivo Fitzwareyn, service unknown, annual value 10s.

Haydon and Widhill, 2 messuages and 30 a., of William Walrond, service unknown, annual value 13s.4d.

Pynchet, 1 mill, of John Berkle, service unknown, annual value 12d. for the fishery and no more because the mill lies deserted and broken.

Great Chelworth, 1 messuage and 10 a., of Oliver Servyngton, service unknown, annual value 8s.

Cricklade, Calcutt, Ampney, Marston, Highworth, Sevenhampton and Little Chelworth, all the rest, with the advowson of Cricklade, of Edward duke of York, service unknown, annual value, beyond the 100s. rent, 40s.

She died without heirs male on 5 Feb. last. Joan wife of Robert More, her daughter and next heir, is aged 22 years and more. In virtue of the fine the lands should remain to this Robert and Joan.

1137 Writ 13 Feb. 1405.
BERKSHIRE. Inquisition. Newbury. 5 March.

She held in her demesne in fee tail to herself and her heirs male, with successive remainders to Robert More and Joan his wife, the heirs of their bodies and her right heirs, by the grant of Gilbert Gaveler, clerk, and Thomas Hobbes by a fine of 3 Feb. last [as above, no.1136]:

Thatcham, 1 messuage, 2 mills, 1 carucate, 20 a. meadow, 19 a pasture and 30s. rent, and 1 a. pasture in Newbury all in the liberty of the abbot of Reading and held of the abbot, service unknown, annual value 40s. beyond the 30s. rent.

Date of death, heir and succession to the estates as above.

C 137/50, no.34

STEPHEN WYNSLADE

1138 Writ 1 April 1405.
SOMERSET. Inquisition. Wells. 27 April.

Robert FitzPagan was seised in his demesne as of fee of the manor and hundred of Frome, and by a fine of 1314 [CP 25(1) 198/17, no.1] granted it to Nicholas Braunche and Robergia his wife and the heirs of their bodies, with reversion in default to the heirs of Robert. So Nicholas and Robergia were seised of them. They had a son Andrew and a daughter Eleanor, who married Richard Wynselade of Gloucestershire and had issue Stephen. After the death of Nicholas and Robergia Andrew entered and held in fee tail in virtue of the fine.

By a fine of 1335 [CP 25(1) 199/22, no.9] Andrew Braunche and Joan his wife granted to Richard de Wynselade and Eleanor his wife, with remainder to the heirs of Eleanor, 7 messuages, 162 a. arable, 18 a. meadow, 80 a. pasture, 51 a. wood, 58s.6½d. in rents and a third part of a mill in Frome, Rodden and Marston Bigott, parcel of the manor of Frome. Richard and Eleanor were then seised of the premises.

Andrew had issue Thomas and died. After his death the manor and hundred of Frome, except the messuages, etc. mentioned above, were taken into the king's hands owing to the minority of Thomas in accordance with an inquisition of 1349 [CIPM IX, no.353].

Richard and Eleanor died, whereupon Stephen de Wynselade entered the messuages, etc. in Frome, Rodden and Marston Bigott as son and heir in virtue of the fine and of an inquisition of 1355 [CIPM X, no.232].

Then Thomas son of Andrew died under age without heirs of his body, and Stephen de Wynselade entered the manor and hundred as next heir, that is son of Eleanor, sister of Andrew, father of Thomas, in virtue of the fine of 1314, as found in an inquisition of 1360 [CIPM X, no.611], and by authority of a writ of livery of seisin of Edward III [CCR 1360–4, p.75].

Afterwards Stephen, by the name of Stephen de Wynselade, lord of Frome Braunche, merchant of Somerset, at Bristol on 1 July 1375 acknowledged before Walter Derby, then mayor of Bristol, and Thomas Denbawe, clerk of recognisances there, that he owed Guy de Bryan, knight, £20,000 [sic] for 220 marks borrowed from Guy which he had to pay on 2 Feb. 1366. Whether the 220 marks was paid to Guy on that day or not is unknown, but Guy had execution in virtue of the said bond (statutum) of the manor and hundred and of the 7 messuages, etc., until the sum mentioned in the bond should be paid.

Guy granted and assigned to Philip, his younger son, all his status in the manor and hundred until such time as he, Guy, should be satisfied of this sum. Philip died in possession but he and Guy Bryan had no other status in the manor and hundred except the execution of this bond.

So Stephen died on 18 Dec. 1404 holding them all in his demesne in fee tail in virtue of the fines; annual value of the manor and hundred of Frome £30, of the 7 messuages, etc. £10. All are held of the king in chief by knight service.

Elizabeth wife of Edmund de Liversegge, daughter and next heir of Stephen, is aged 28 years and more.

[Very faded, some words illegible].

C 137/50, no.35

ALEXANDER MOUNTFORT

1139   Writ 25 Nov. 1404.

LINCOLN. Inquisition. Great Limber. 26 Jan. 1405.

He held in his demesne in fee simple to himself, his heirs and assigns, by the grant of Thomas Mountfort, knight, his father, 12 messuages, 3 tofts, 25 bovates, 3 a. arable and meadow and 42s. rent in Riby of Edmund earl of Kent of his manor of Brattleby by knight service, that is by homage and fealty alone, annual value 9 marks.

He died on 1 Oct. 1395. Thomas his brother and next heir was of full age, 21 years, on 7 Jan. last. Thomas earl of Kent held his property from the death of Alexander until his own forfeiture, owing to the minority of the heir. Since the earl's forfeiture Richard Clyderowe has held it from 26 Feb. 1400, with all the chattels in the hands of the earl there, in virtue of letters patent of that date [*CPR 1399–1401*, p.222, letters quoted in full].

THOMAS MOUNTFORT

1140 Writ for proof of age, ordering that Richard Clyderowe be warned. 16 Feb. 1405.

YORK. Proof of age of Thomas brother and heir of Alexander Mountfort in the presence of Richard Clyderowe. Richmond. 4 April.

Thomas is aged 21 years and more, having been born in the manor of Hackforth and baptised in the church of Hornby on 7 Jan. 1382 [Wednesday morrow of Epiphany 5 Richard II, but the morrow of Epiphany was a Tuesday in 1382, and Wednesday in 1383; 23 and 22, not 21, years before 1405].

The jurors say that they remember this because:

John Ellerton of Aldborough, aged 64 years and more, with several others carried torches at the baptism.

Henry Bellerby of Manfield, 47 and more, was present in the church when John, sometime prior of St. Martin's [Richmond], baptised Thomas.

Robert Hilton of Melsonby, 49 and more, was present and Lady Joan Burgh was godmother.

Robert Skipton of Langton, 50 and more, was present in the church, John de Rukewyk, abbot of Jervaulx, was godfather, and he was surprised that Thomas was not given his godfather's name.

Ralph Foxholys of Richmond, 53 and more, remembers because William Jaklyn, parker of Tanfield, took rabbits in the warren of Richmond for the dinner of those who were present at the baptism.

Robert Walker of Bedale, 58 and more, consulted the midwife and other women to find a good wet nurse.

Thomas Forester of Richmond, 65 and more, was in the church, and John Whitgray, sometime vicar of Catterick, was the other godfather.

William Smythson, senior, of Newsham, 53 and more, saw Margaret wife of John Neston of Patrick Brompton carry the infant to the church.

John de Colburn, 52 and more, remembers because immediately after the baptism the abbot of Jervaulx, godfather, gave the baby a silver-gilt goblet with cover.

Thomas Kyrkeby of Whitwell, 50 and more, saw Thomas carried to the church with four unlighted torches around him.

John Buk of Wold Newton, 55 years and more, saw John Whitgray, the other godfather, give a little purse full of gold immediately after the baptism.

Hugh Clergenet of Richmond, 60 and more, saw four men carrying four torches with him to the church and returning from the church to the manor with the four torches alight.

C 137/50, no.36

WILLIAM DE PAR, KNIGHT

1141 Writ 10 Oct. 1404.

WESTMORLAND. Inquisition. Kendal. 16 Oct.

He held a quarter of the manor of Kendal of the king in chief as a quarter of a knight's fee by the courtesy of England in right of his late wife Elizabeth, kinswoman and heir of Thomas de Roos, knight, and daughter of John de Roos, son of Thomas, annual value £40.

The following were his tenants, with their holdings:

Thomas de Pykeryng, the manor of Killington by knight service and a rent of 6s. 7d. payable at Easter and Michaelmas by equal parts, annual value beyond that 100s.; and 2 tenements in Helsington and Levens, rent 1d., annual value beyond that 20s.

Joan widow of Christopher de Lancastre, the hamlet of Strickland Roger, rent 13s. 5d., annual value beyond that 20s.

Richard de Restwald, the manor of Little Strickland, rent 24s. 8d., annual value beyond that 40s.

Ellis de Kirkeby, chaplain, 1 tenement and 12 a. in Strickland Ketel, rent 3s., annual value beyond that 5s.; and 2 tenements and 12 a. in the hamlet of Bradleyfield, rent 5d., annual value beyond that 40d.

Hugh Ward and Lawrence de Berwik, 2 tenements in Strickland Ketel, rent 4s. and 1 lb. wax, annual value beyond that 8s.

Hugh Ward, 2 tenements and 20 a. in Bradleyfield, rent ¼ lb. pepper, annual value beyond that 40d.

Richard Gilpyne, the hamlet of Ulthwaite, rent 3s. 6d., annual value beyond that 20s.

Elizabeth widow of Robert Thomlynson, 1 tenement and 6 a. in Strickland Ketel, rent ½ lb. cumin, annual value beyond that 4s.; and 2 tenements and 20 a. in Tranthwaite, rent 7s. 3d. and 1 lb. cumin, annual value beyond that 10s.

John de Bethom, knight, and John de Berwyk, the manor of Burton, rent 31s., annual value beyond that 100s.

Margaret widow of Roger de Levens, 3 tenements and 40 a. in the hamlet of Likebergh, rent 23d., annual value beyond that 3s.

Helen widow of Roger de Stirkeland, 1 tenement and 6 a. in Strickland Ketel, rent 9s. 6d., annual value beyond that 6s.

John de Berwyke, 6 tenements and 60 a. in the hamlet of Stainton, rent 4d., annual value beyond that 40s.

Robert Layburn, knight, son and heir of Thomas de Layburn, knight, and Joan his wife, the manor of Cunswick, rent ½ lb. cumin, annual value beyond that 100s.

Robert Layburn, knight, 2 tenements in the hamlet of Bradleyfield, rent 1 lb. pepper, annual value beyond that 20s.; and 3 tenements and 20 a. in the hamlet of Sleddale by a rent of 1 sparrowhawk or 12d. at Lammas, annual value beyond that 40s.

John de Wyndesore, 4 tenements and 40 a. in the hamlet of Haverbrack, rent 2s., annual value beyond that 20s.

Henry de Guype, 6 tenements and 40 a. of arable and meadow in the hamlet of Crook, rent 9s. 5d., annual value beyond that 20s.

John de Croft, knight, the manor of Leighton, rent 1 sparrowhawk or 12d. at Lammas, annual value beyond that 20s.

William Baynebrig, 1 tenement and 6 a. in the hamlet of Crook, rent 18d., annual value beyond that 2s.

John de Wyndesore, half the hamlet of Dillicar, rent 3s., annual value beyond that 20s.

William de Walton, 1 tenement and 6 a. in the hamlet of Crook, rent 12d., annual value beyond that 3s.

John de Burgh, 2 tenements and 20 a. in Strickland Ketel, rent 3s. 8d., annual value beyond that 20s.

Henry de Ullaythorne, senior, the manor of Middleton, rent 27s., annual value beyond that 20s.; and Henry de Ullaythorne, junior, 1 tenement and 6 a. in Middleton, rent 1d., annual value beyond that 6s.

Adam Cade, 1 tenement and 6 a. in Middleton, rent 10d., annual value beyond that 6s.

Joan widow of Christopher de Lancastre, the manor of Strickland Roger, rent 26s.11½d., annual value beyond that 40s.

Adam de Bourebank, 1 tenement and 20 a. in Barton, rent 27s.10d., annual value beyond that 4s.

Richard de Bellyngham, 4 tenements and 40 a. arable and meadow in Strickland Ketel, rent 8s.9d., annual value beyond that 20s.

John de Preston of Kendal, the manor of Preston Richard by knight service, annual value 100s.

Stephen de Cottesford, 3 tenements and 40 a. arable and meadow in Melkinthorpe by knight service, annual value 20s.

William de Haybergh, kinsman and heir of William de Haybergh, 1 tenement and 6 a. in the hamlet of Crook by knight service, annual value 6s.

Richard Cayrons, 3 burgages in Kendal, rent 15d. and suit of court at Kendal every 3 weeks, annual value beyond that 2s.

Also the following in Kendal, showing the number of burgages, the rent, and the annual value beyond the rent: John de Burgh, 5, 19d., 40d.; William de Osmonderlaw, 1, 4d., 8d.; Thomas son of Thomas de Roos, 1, 3d., 6d.; Emma de Halbank, 1, 3d., 9d.; Hugh Ward, 1, 3d., 12d.; Adam Towere, 1, 3d., 12d.; John de Wyndesore, 1, 6d., 12d.; Thomas de Levens, 1, 3d., 12d.; John de Roos, 1, 11d., 12d.; Thomas Clerk, 2, 8d., 2s.; Thomas Hubard, 1, 3d., 12d.; Richard Mercer, chaplain, 1, 3d., 12d.; Richard Robynson, 1, 3d., 12d.; John Bell and Christina his wife in her right, 2, 12d., 12d.; John Bakstre, 1, 4d., 12d.; William Alexanderman and Joan his wife in her right, 1, 2½d., 12d.; John de Warton, 1, 2½d., 12d.; Robert de Siggiswyk, 2, 6d., 2s.; Hugh Gylewhene, 1, 4d., 12d.; Ellis de Kirkeby, chaplain, 1, 3d., 12d.; Alice de Burgh, 1, 4d., 12d.; Richard Clerkson, 1, 3d., 12d.; Robert de Levens, 1, 4d., 12d.; Hugh Ward, 1, 1d, 6d.; Robert Marsshall, 1, 2d., 8d.; Sybil de Levens, 1, 1d., 8d.; Robert Thomlynson, 1, 1d., 8d.; Agnes de Otteway, 1, 2d., 8d.; William Taillour, 1, 2d., 8d.; John de Dokwra, 1, 2d., 12d.; John Hogeson, chaplain, 1, 3d., 10d.; Adam Waryner, 1, 9d., 2s.; Thomas Rokane, 1, 4½d., 12d.; John Dogeson, 'fisher', 1, 1½d., 12d.; Robert de Dokwra, 1, 23½d., 4s.; and Hugh Ward and Nicholas Robynson, 1 by a rose at Midsummer.

He also held the advowson of the hospital of St. Leonard by Kendal, extending at 40s.

He died on 3 Oct. last. John son and heir of Elizabeth and himself is aged 22 years and more.

[Exchequer copy only] From 3 to 29 Oct., 27 days at 2s.2½d., 59s.7½d.

C 137/50, no.37
E 149/84, no.4

PETER COURTENAY, KNIGHT

1142 Writ 7 Feb. 1405; and further writ ordering the return of the inquisition. 24 March.

DORSET. Inquisition. Sherborne. 4 April.

He held in the right of Margaret his wife, who survives him:

Maiden Newton, the manor, of Henry Popham by knight service of his manor of Sutton Waldron, annual value £10.

Thorpe, 3 messuages, Notton, 5 messuages, and Crockway, 9 messuages, of John Lyle of his manor of Newton Lisle by a rent of 1d., annual value 100s.

He died on 2 Feb. last. Edward Courtenay, earl of Devon, is his kinsman and next heir, being the son of Edward his brother, and aged 50 years and more.

1143   Writ 7 Feb. 1405.

HAMPSHIRE. Inquisition. Broughton. 18 March.

He held the wardenship of the bailiwick of Buckholt, part of the forest of Clarendon, for life by the king's grant [CPR 1399–1401, p.75], annual value 100s.

In right of Margaret his wife, who survives him, he held:

Pennington, the manor, of the heir of John atte Hale by knight service, annual value 100s.

Bedenham, half the manor, of the bishop of Winchester by knight service, annual value £4.

Flexland, the manor, formerly of Philip de Throkelesford, of the prior of Southwick by knight service, annual value 100s.

Binsted, the manor, formerly of the same Philip, of Elizabeth Julers, countess of Kent, by knight service, annual value £10.

Date of death and heir, aged 35 years and more, as above.

1144   Writ 7 Feb. 1405.

WILTSHIRE. Inquisition. Upavon. 17 March 1405.

He held the keepership of the park of Melchet with the forest of Grovely for life of the king by his grant [as above, no.1143] without rent, annual value £10.

In the right of Margaret his wife, who survives him, he held:

Little Cheverell, the manor with the advowson of church and chantry, with £11 in rents from lands in Maddington and Shrewton, parts of that manor, of the countess of Salisbury by knight service, annual value £20.

Hardenhuish, the manor and advowson, annual value £10; and various lands in Ogbourne Maizey, annual value £4, of the king of the duchy of Lancaster by knight service.

Date of death and heir, age 35 years and more, as above.

1145   Writ 7 Feb. 1405.

DEVON. Inquisition. Exeter, 6 March.

He held 1 a. in Alphington with the advowson in his demesne as of fee to himself and his heirs of the king in chief by knight service, annual value 4d.

He held to himself and his heirs male with successive remainders, failing such heirs, to Philip his brother and his heirs male, and the right heirs of Hugh de Courtenay, formerly earl of Devon, grandfather of Edward earl of Devon:

Honiton, the manor, except the advowson, by the grant of Robert Vaggescomb, formerly canon of Exeter, parson of Parkham, William Bampton, formerly parson of Churchill, William Ponton, formerly portioner of Waddesdon, Henry de Burton and John Hudresfild, of the king in chief by knight service, annual value £20.

Moretonhampstead and Milton Damerel, the manors and advowsons, by the grant of Robert Vaggescomb, canon of Exeter and rector of Parkham; Moretonhampstead of the king in chief by knight service, annual value 20 marks; and Milton Damerel of the earl of Devon of the honour of Plympton, service unknown, annual value £6.

Alphington and Bolberry, the manors, except for the 1 a. and advowson mentioned above, by the grant of Hugh de Segrave by way of exchange for the manor of Nuneham Courtenay in Oxfordshire; Alphington of the earl of Devon of the honour of Oke-hampton, service unknown, annual value £20; and Bolberry of the same of the honour of Plympton, service unknown, annual value £10.

North Pool, the manor, by the grant of William Chabesie and Richard Brankes-combe, of Elizabeth le Despenser of the honour of Gloucester, service unknown, annual value £6.

He died on 2 Feb. 1405 without heirs of his body. All should go to Philip. Edward is alive and is next heir of Hugh, being son of Edward, son of Hugh. Edward is aged 40 years and more, Philip 50 years and more.

He also held the priory of Otterton jointly with Richard Amys, prior of Stogursey, John Kyrchehille, parson of Aller, and Richard Bacwill, parson of Lydford, for his life and to his executors for 1 year after, at farm of the king for 200 marks by a grant of 10 March 1401 [*CPR 1399–1401*, p.444]. Alexander Clyvedon and John Kyrchehele, clerk, are his executors. The priory is worth 200 marks annually.

1146 Writ 7 Feb. 1405.

SOMERSET. Inquisition. Taunton. 10 March.

He held to himself and his heirs male, with remainder in default of such heirs to Philip his brother and his heirs male:

East Coker, the manor and advowson, by the grant of Robert Vaggescomb, William Bampton and William Ponton, clerks, Henry Burton and John Hodresfeld, of the king in chief by knight service, annual value 20 marks.

Hardington Mandeville, 1 a. and the advowson, by the grant of the same, of John Wadham, knight, of his manor of Hardington, service unknown, annual value 6d.

Stewley, the manor, half by the grant of John Southdon, clerk, the other half by the grant of John Syward, clerk; all of Robert Hulle of his manor of Trull by knight service, annual value 10 marks.

West Capland, the manor, by the grant of William Domfravill and John Baret, of John earl of Somerset of his manor of Curry Rivel, service unknown, annual value 100s.

He held jointly with Richard Amys, prior of Stogursey, John Kirchill, parson of Aller, and Richard Bakwell, parson of East Lydford, 10 messuages, 1 carucate and half the great tithe of the parish of Martock, as parcel of the alien priory of Otterton in Devon, by the grant of the abbot of Mont St. Michel in Normandy, lord and chief patron of the priory, to hold with all the property, tithes, offerings, obventions and possessions, both spiritual and temporal, with fees, advowsons, franchises, liberties etc. for his life and 1 year more, confirmed by Richard II on 10 June 1397 and by Henry IV on 2 Oct. 1399, to hold for a rent of 200 marks; and the king further granted on 10 March 1401 that he might hold them from 1 Oct. 1400 during the war with France without payment of the farm of 200 marks, or any other payment [*CPR 1396–9*, p.148; *1399–1401*, pp.41, 444]. The messuages, land and half the tithe of Martock with the priory therefore belong to his executors for 1 year after his death. They are Alexander Clyvedon and John Kerchill, clerk.

Jointly with Margaret his wife he held by the grant of Robert son of Robert Hill, Richard Virgo, William Buttes, clerk, James Taunton and William Worcestre, for their lives with successive remainders to William Botreaux, son of Elizabeth daughter of John St. Lo and the said Margaret then wife of John, the heirs of the bodies of Peter and Margaret, and the right heirs of Margaret by a fine of 1391 [CP 25(1) 201/31, no.20; cf. no.17]:

Aller, the manor, with the advowson of the church and chapel or chantry, of Thomas Broke by knight service, annual value £20.

Cricket St. Thomas, the manor and advowson, of Richard Seymour, service unknown, annual value 100s.

Yeovilton, the manor, of Peter Cuysaunce, service unknown, annual value 40s.

Shipham, the manor and advowson, of Matthew Gournay by knight service, annual value 100s.

Cheddar and Leigh, the manor, of the bishop of Bath by knight service, annual value 100s.

Wells, a messuage, of the bishop of Bath in burgage.

He also held jointly with Margaret by the grant of Master Edmund Seyntcler, Robert Cheddre and John Leppeyet, parson of Backwell, to them and the heirs of Margaret:

Standerwick, the manor, of Matthew Gournay by knight service, annual value 10 marks.

Rodden, the manor, of the king of the duchy of Lancaster by knight service, annual value £6.

He held in right of Margaret:

Publow, the manor, of Lady Despenser of the honour of Gloucester, service unknown, annual value 20 marks.

Newton St. Loe, the manor, of the king of the duchy of Lancaster by knight service, annual value £10.

Chelwood, the manor, of the earl of Salisbury, service unknown, annual value £4.

Philip Courtenay is still living, aged 48 years and more.

Date of death and heir, aged 40 years and more, as above.

C 137/50, no.38
E 149/85, no.1

MARGARET WIDOW OF ROGER CORBET OF MORETON CORBET, KNIGHT

1147 Writ, *melius sciri*, referring to the inquisition of 12 Jan. 1396 [*CIPM* XVII, no.607]. 14 Feb. 1405.

SHROPSHIRE. Inquisition. Shrewsbury. 21 Feb.

She held in her demesne as of fee:

Shawbury, the manor, of Richard II in chief by knight service, annual value £7 12d.

Moreton Corbet, the manor, of Joan wife of Richard de Peshale, knight, by knight service of her manor of Chetwynd, annual value £12 10s.6d.

Upton Waters, the manor, of the baron of Wem of his manor of Tyrley, service unknown, annual value 60s.3d.

Evelith by Shifnal, 1 messuage and half a virgate, of Joan de Peshale of her manor of Chetwynd, service unknown, annual value 20s.

Lawley, the manor, of the baron of Wem of his manor of Hinstock, service unknown, annual value £4.

Bletchley, the vill, of Lord Ferrers of Groby of his manor of Stoke, service unknown, annual value 63s.

'Culses', the manor, of the baron of Wem of his manor of Tyrley, service unknown, annual value 40s.

Booley upon Hine Heath, the vill, of the abbot of Shrewsbury, service unknown, annual value 10s.

Rowton and Amaston, the vills, of Hugh Lord Burnell at fee farm, annual value beyond the farm 20d.

Shrewsbury and the suburbs, 6 messuages, of Richard II in free burgage, annual value 50s.

Sowbach, 1 messuage and 1 carucate, of Robert Lee of his manor of Stanton upon Hine Heath, service unknown, annual value 20s.

Wytheford, 2 messuages formerly of Richard Crowe, annual value 20s.; 1 messuage formerly of Richard Tudour, 4s.; 1 messuage of Edith de la Haye, 5s.; and 1 cottage, 12d.; all of Richard II, service unknown.

She died on 14 Nov. 1395. Robert her son and heir is aged 21 years and more.

Thomas Stones, then escheator, took the wardship of Robert and all her lands, and took the profits until Richard II granted them by letters patent [*CPR 1396–9*, p.219] to Thomas Percy, earl of Worcester, to hold until the full age of the heir without rendering anything to the king. So he held until 10 Feb. 1401 when he gave the wardship to John Boerley, having given him the marriage of Robert by his letters of 14 Oct. 1399.

ROBERT SON AND HEIR OF MARGARET CORBET

1148   Writ for proof of age, John Boerley to be warned to be present. 7 March 1405. SHROPSHIRE. Proof of age. Wellington. 12 March.

Robert son and heir of Margaret, widow of Roger Corbet of Moreton Corbet, knight, was born at Moreton Corbet on 8 Dec. 1383, and baptised in the church there, and was aged 21 on that date last past. The jurors say that they know this for the following reasons:

Philip de Willeley, aged 52, was then at Moreton as an esquire of Nicholas abbot of Shrewsbury, who baptised Robert.

William Thornhull, 50, came that day to talk to the abbot about his own business and saw the baptism.

John Hodenet, 56, on the day of the birth took a doe with his greyhounds in the chase of Brockhurst. John Don told him of the birth, whereupon he sent the doe to Robert.

Thomas de Eyton, 44, was an esquire of Ralph abbot of Haughmond, one of the godfathers of Robert, and saw him standing with the abbot of Shrewsbury throughout the ceremony.

William de Coton, 50, was present at the baptism and held a candle throughout the ceremony.

Griffin Wareyn, 46, had a son of the same age.

William Frensshe, 53, on that day granted Roger the father 1 messuage and 1 carucate for life, and immediately gave seisin.

Richard Horton, 42, on that day struck John Foxley, bailiff of Roger Corbet of the manor of Moreton, on the head with a sword, for which transgression he paid the bailiff 100s.

William Smethecote, 49, was then steward of the household of Roger and stayed with him for the whole of the following year. The abbot of Shrewsbury gave him 13s.4d. for his work on that day.

Richard Walleford, 50, saw Margery wife of John Herebert carrying Robert to the baptism wrapped in a white cloth.

William Hethe, 42, came that day from the hundred court of Bradford and dined with Henry vicar of Moreton who told him of the baptism.

John Williamson, 55, says that on that day Isabel his wife went from Shawbury to Moreton to be the nurse and fell into a ditch called 'Fylledych' opposite the church.

John Boerley was informed of the proof and warned to be present by Roger Monselowe, John Dermyn, William Forster and William Bent. He came himself and raised no objection to the delivery of the lands to Robert, and no objection on behalf of the king to the proof.

C 137/50, no.39

JOHN DE CRADDELEY

1149 Writ, *plenius certiorari*, as the service for the premises held in chief was not specified in the earlier inquisition [no.713 above]. 10 July 1405.

NOTTINGHAM. Inquisition. Nottingham. 20 Sept.

He held 1 messuage, 2 cottages and 9 bovates in Ratcliff on Soar and Kingston on Soar in his demesne as of fee of the king in chief in socage in petty serjeanty by 13s. rent payable by the sheriff.

C 137/50, no.40

JOHN PULLELEY

1150 Writ, *devenerunt*, on outlawry. 1 April 1405.

SHROPSHIRE. Inquisition. Bridgnorth. 11 April.

He died on 7 May 1398. On the day of his outlawry for felony he had held 1 messuage and 1 virgate in 'Le More' by Bridgnorth of the inheritance of Alice then his wife, daughter of William Picheford, and now the wife of John Donvowe of Bridgnorth. They are held of the prebendary of Erdington by a rent of 10s., came into the hands of Edward III on his outlawry, and remained in the King's hands; annual value beyond the rent 3s.4d.

The king has held and taken the profits by the sheriff since the outlawry.

C 137/50, no.41

THOMAS COLVYLE, KNIGHT

1151 Writ 9 Aug. 1405.

YORK. Inquisition. Coxwold. 1 Sept.

William Darell and Peter de Lythom, chaplains, granted two parts of the manor of Coxwold with the reversion of the third part which Margaret Darell held for life in dower, to Thomas Ughtrede, senior, knight, for life, with successive remainders to

Thomas Colvyle father of Thomas, knight, and his heirs male, George his brother and his heirs male, William brother of George and his heirs male, the heirs male of Thomas Ughtrede, senior, and the right heirs of Thomas Colvyle the father, as appears in an indenture shown to the jurors.

So Thomas Ughtrede, senior, held two parts of the manor and Margaret one part. After their deaths Thomas Colvyle the father was seised of the whole manor in fee tail. Thomas Colvyle, knight, succeeded him and died on 28 May last without male heirs, holding the whole manor. George and William died without male heirs. Thomas Ughtrede is kinsman and next heir of Thomas Ughtrede, knight, being the son of William, son of Thomas, son of the first Thomas. He is aged 21 years and more.

The manor was held of the late Lord Mowbray of his manor of Thirsk by the service of rendering one targe or shield of arms of the lord at Whitsun, annual value £12.

John Percehay of Kildale, the next heir, is aged 40 years and more.

1152   YORK. Inquisition *ex officio*. Coxwold. 13 Sept. 1405.

He held the manor of Nunwick in his demesne as of fee, annual value £10. It should descend to John Percy of Kildale as next heir, but he rebelled on 1 May last, and therefore the escheator took it into the king's hands as forfeit.

He died on 21 May. Master William de Cawode and John Cooke of Nunwick have taken the profits since 21 May.

1153   YORK. Inquisition *ex officio*. Same place, date and jurors as last.

He died on 21 May holding in his demesne as of fee:
Upsland, the manor, annual value 100s.
Kilburn, 30 a. arable and 2 a. meadow, annual value 26s.8d.
Thirsk, 2 messuages and 3 roods, annual value 13s.4d.
Coxwold, 4 a. meadow called 'Lassart', annual value 6s.8d.
They should descend to John Percy of Kildale as next heir, but he rebelled with Ralph Hastynges, John Fauconberge, John Colvill and John FitzRandolph, knights, who were condemned at Durham on 20 July.

The escheator took the premises, and William Yheverslay has taken the profits since 20 July.

1154   Writ, ordering return of an inquisition already taken *ex officio*. 28 Oct. 1405.
YORK. Inquisition *ex officio*. Nunwick. 14 Sept. 1405.

He died seised in his demesne as of fee of the manor of Nunwick, annual value £10. It should have descended to John Percy of Kildale as next heir, but he rebelled against the king before the death of Thomas, with Ralph Hastynges, John Fauconberge, John Colvill and John FitzRandolph, knights, and many others who were executed as rebels. The escheator therefore held the manor as forfeit to the king.

1155   Writ, *plura*, 10 Feb. 1406.
YORK. Inquisition. Richmond. 5 March.

He held in his demesne as of fee:
Coxwold near Newburgh, the manor, comprising 1 messuage, 4 bovates and a close called 'Lasarte', of Lord Mowbray of his manor of Thirsk by knight service, annual value 40s.

2D

Upsland, the manor, of Henry Fitzhugh, knight, by knight service, annual value 100s.

Yearsley, the manor, of Lord Mowbray of his manor of Thirsk, service unknown, annual value 10 marks.

Nunwick near Ripon, the manor, of the archbishop of York of his manor of Ripon, service unknown, annual value £10.

Thirsk, 4 messuages and 4 bovates, of Lord Mowbray, service unknown, annual value 40s.

Kilburn, 4 messuages and 4 bovates, of the manor of Kilburn, service unknown, annual value 40s.

The heir was John Percy, aged 40 years and more. He on 21 May rebelled with Ralph Hastynges and others [as above], and the premises are therefore forfeit.

1156 Writ 7 Feb. 1406.

YORK CITY. Inquisition before William Frost, warden. 21 April.

He held in his demesne as of fee 6 messuages, 1 garden, 1 dovecot and half the advowson of Old St. Mary's of the king in burgage as is all the city, annual value £6.

He died on 28 May 1405. John Percy of Kildale is his kinsman and heir, being the son of Mary, daughter of John, brother of Thomas, father of Thomas, father of Thomas, father of this Thomas, aged 50 years and more.

1157 DERBY. Inquisition *ex officio*. Bolsover. 20 Oct. 1405.

He held half the manor of Bolsover for life by the king's grant [*CPR 1399–1401*, p.23], annual value £18.

He died on 21 May last.

C 137/51, no.43
E 149/86, no.15

THOMAS EARL MARSHAL

1158 Writ, *melius sciri*, as to what he held jointly with Constance his wife, the king's niece. 7 Aug. 1405.

WESTMORLAND. Inquisition. Appleby. 17 Aug.

They held the manor of Long Marton jointly to them and the heirs of their bodies, except for knight's fees and advowsons, by the grant of Robert late bishop of London, William late bishop of Winchester, Richard bishop of Salisbury, formerly bishop of Chichester, Edward duke of York, then earl of Rutland, and John Lord Lovell, with other manors and lands, and with remainder to the right heirs of John earl of Huntingdon. It is not held of the king in chief, but of whom is unknown; annual value £10.

He died aged 19 years and more without heirs by Constance.

1159 Similar writ 7 Aug. 1405.

HERTFORD. Inquisition. Great Gaddesden. 1 Sept.

They held the manor of Great Gaddesden, except knight's fees and advowsons, jointly by the same grant [above, no. 1158]. It is not held of the king in chief, but of whom is unknown; annual value 40 marks.

Death as above.

1160   Similar writ 7 Aug. 1405.
BUCKINGHAM. Inquisition. Great Gaddesden. 1 Sept.
They held jointly by the same grant [above, no. 1158]:
Linslade and Southcott, two parts of 10 virgates, 3 a. wood and of 25s. 7d. rent, with the reversion of the third part held by Elizabeth duchess of Norfolk in dower, with remainder, failing heirs of their bodies, to the right heirs of Thomas his father. They are not held of the king in chief, but of whom and by what service is unknown; annual value 100s.
Great Gaddesden, 1 messuage and 42 a., part of the manor, which extends in both Buckinghamshire and Hertfordshire, with remainder to the right heirs of the earl of Huntingdon. It is not held of the king in chief, but of whom and by what service is unknown; annual value 40s.

Death as above.

1161   Similar writ 7 Aug. 1405.
RUTLAND. Inquisition. Oakham. 17 Aug.
Thomas and Constance held jointly by the same grant [above, no. 1158] 2 messuages, 400 a. arable, 40 a. meadow, 40 a. pasture and 20 a. wood in Stretton, with remainder to the right heirs of Thomas his father. They are not held of the king in chief, but of whom and by what service is unknown; annual value 40s.

Death as above.

1162   Similar writ 7 Aug. 1405.
WARWICK. Inquisition. Kineton. 13 Aug.
They held jointly two parts of the manor of Kineton, with the reversion of the third part which Elizabeth duchess of Norfolk holds in dower, except knight's fees and advowsons, by the same grant [above, no. 1158], with remainder to the right heirs of Thomas his father. The manor is held of the king in chief by a rent of £12, and is worth £12 yearly beyond that.

Death as above.

1163   Similar writ 7 Aug. 1405.
SUFFOLK. Inquisition. Mildenhall. 28 Aug.
They held jointly by the same grant [above, no. 1158] the manor of Icklingham, except knight's fees and advowsons, with remainder to the right heirs of John earl of Huntingdon. It is held of the earl of Kent, service unknown, annual value 20 marks.

Death as above.

1164   Similar writ 7 Aug. 1405.
CAMBRIDGE. Inquisition. Cambridge. 18 Aug.
They held jointly by the same grant [above, no. 1158] two parts of the manor of Cherry Hinton, except knight's fees and advowsons, and of 20s. rent in Ickleton with reversion of the third parts which Elizabeth duchess of Norfolk holds in dower, with

remainder to the right heirs of Thomas his father. They are not held of the king in chief, but of whom and by what service is unknown; annual value of the manor £20.
  Death as above.

1165 HUNTINGDON. Inquisition *ex officio*. Huntingdon. 14 June 1405.

He held the manor of Fen Stanton to himself and his heirs, of whom and by what service is unknown; annual value £132 11d.

1166 HUNTINGDON. Inquisition. Huntingdon. 17 Aug. 1405.

Thomas and Constance held jointly by the same grant [above, no. 1158] two parts of the manor of Old Weston and Alconbury, except knight's fees and advowsons, with reversion of the third part which Elizabeth duchess of Norfolk holds in dower, with remainder to the right heirs of Thomas his father. It is not held of the king in chief but of whom and by what service is unkown; annual value of the manor £20.
  Death as above.

1167 HUNTINGDON. Inquisition. Fen Stanton. 26 May 1411.

He held the manor of Fen Stanton in fee tail to himself and his heirs of the king in chief by knight service, amount unknown, annual value 200 marks.
  He died on 8 June 1405. John de Moubray, his brother and heir, is under age, being 20 on 10 Aug. last.
  Queen Joan has held the manor since his death.

1168 Writ, *melius sciri*, as to what he held jointly with Constance his wife, the king's niece. 7 Aug. 1405.
SOMERSET. Inquisition. Bridgwater. 12 Sept.

They held jointly by the same grant [above, no.1158] the manor of Haselbury Plucknett, except knight's fees and advowsons, with remainder to the right heirs of John earl of Huntingdon. It is not held of the king in chief, but of whom and by what service is unknown; annual value 40 marks.
  Death as above [no.1158].

1169 Similar writ 7 Aug. 1405.
YORK. Inquisition. Norton. 17 Sept.

They held jointly by the same grant [above, no.1158]:
  Burton in Lonsdale, two parts of the manor, except knight's fees and advowsons, with the reversion of the third part which Elizabeth duchess of Norfolk holds in dower, with remainder to the right heirs of Thomas his father. The manor is held of the king in chief by knight service, annual value 40 marks.
  Langton, the manor, except knight's fees and advowsons, with remainder to the right heirs of John earl of Huntingdon, also held of the king in chief by knight service, annual value £20.
  Death as above [no.1158].

1170 YORK. Inquisition. South Cave. 20 Aug. 1405.

Thomas Earl Marshal, was of age long before the death of Thomas son of Thomas Dayvell of South Cave, who held the manor of South Cave and lands in Swanland of the earl by knight service, and lands, tenements and services in Spaldington, Howden and 'Endewode', of whom is unknown, annual value of all £7 5s.4¼d.

Thomas Dayvell junior died on 21 April last, and was of age a quarter of a year before that. The earl, owing to the minority of John brother and heir of Thomas, took his lands and was in full possession on the day of his forfeiture. John is brother and heir of Thomas son of Thomas and aged 16 years and more.

1171   Writ, similar to above, no.1158. 7 Aug. 1405.
NORTHAMPTON. Inquisition. Northampton. 15 Aug.

Thomas and Constance held jointly by the same grant [above, no.1158] two parts of 24s. rent in Northampton, with the reversion of the third part which Elizabeth duchess of Norfolk holds in dower, with remainder to the right heirs of Thomas his father. It is held of the king in free burgage.

Death as above [no.1158].

1172   BEDFORD. Inquisition. Willington. 6 Oct. 1405.

He held in his demesne as of fee, of whom and by what services is unknown:

Willington, the manor, annual value 40 marks beyond the following grants for life made by his father, Thomas Earl Marshal and of Nottingham, and confirmed by the king [*CPR 1399–1401*, p.109]: to John Tunstall on 1 Sept. 1394 2d. daily or 60s.10d. yearly, and on 13 Feb. 1397 40s. payable by equal parts at Easter and Michaelmas, and to John Cauley 10 marks payable by equal parts at Easter and Martinmas.

Bromham, lands and tenements, annual value 6 marks.

Stotfold, lands and tenements, annual value 60s.

He died on 8 June 1405.

1173   HEREFORD AND THE ADJACENT MARCH OF WALES. Inquisition. Hereford. 11 April 1407.

He held nothing in the county or the adjacent March.

He died on 8 June 1405, heir unknown.

C 137/51, no.44
E 149/84, no.2 and 86, no.16
E 152/398, and 407, no.2

AGNES WIDOW OF GEOFFREY PRIOUR

1174   Writ 10 Feb. 1405.
SURREY. Inquisition. Southwark. 20 June.

She held in her demesne as of fee 1 messuage and 16 a. in Mitcham by the service of receiving the king's distraints taken for debt in the hundred of Wallington, rendering 5s. for aid by the sheriff by equal parts at Easter and Michaelmas, and suit of court at the hundred every three weeks, annual value nil beyond the rent and services.

She died on 3 Feb. last. Agnes wife of Richard Heryngman, aged 30, and William son of Walter Heryngham, aged 24 years and more, are her next of kin and heirs.

C 137/31, no.45
E 149/86, no.9

JOHN BUSSEBRIGGE

1175   Writ 26 April 1405.

SURREY. Inquisition. Guildford. 2 May.

He held 1 tenement in Ewhurst in his demesne as of fee of the king in chief in socage by a payment of 14s. called 'shereyvegheld' to the sheriff. There are 1 site, annual value nil; 20s. rent payable by equal parts at the four principal terms; 40 a. arable at 4d., 13s.4d.; and 50 a. wood at 1d., 4s.2d.

He died on 23 April last. Robert his son and heir is aged 30 years and more.

C 137/51, no.46
E 149/86, no.10

ROBERT PERVYNG, KNIGHT

1176   Writ 8 May 1405.

CUMBERLAND. Inquisition. Penrith. 28 Sept.

He held in his demesne in fee tail by the grant of Robert Pervyng, senior, formerly parson of Hutton:

Blackhall, the manor, to himself and his heirs male, with successive remainders failing such heirs to Adam son of John Pacok and his heirs male, John the brother of Adam and his heirs male, Thomas the brother of John and his heirs male, and the right heirs of Robert Pervyng, junior, by a fine of 1337 [CP 25(1) 35/9, no.23]. It is held of the king in chief by a cornage rent of 4s.6½d. payable at the exchequer of Carlisle on 15 Aug., suit at the county court each month, 16s.1d. at the exchequer of Carlisle for the purpresture of Inglewood, 31s. for the allowance of the foresters of Inglewood and 4s.4d. for the allowance of the king's bailiffs of Cumberland ward; annual value beyond that £10.

Stainton, the manor, to himself and his heirs male by the same grant and with the same remainders. It is also held of the king in chief, by a cornage rent of 8s. payable at the exchequer of Carlisle on 15 Aug. and 2s.8d. for the allowance of the king's bailiffs of the county of Cumberland; annual value beyond that 20s. and no more because devastated by the recurring invasions of the Scots.

Botcherby, the manor, to himself, Isabel his wife and the heirs of his body, with successive remainders to Adam Pacok and the others as above by another fine of 1337 [CP 25(1) 35/9, no.22]. It is held of the king by a cornage rent of 6s.2d. payable at the exchequer of Carlisle on 15 Aug.; annual value beyond that 100s.

He also held to himself and his heirs and assigns 1 messuage in Carlisle of the king in house-gavel of 1d., annual value beyond that 2d.

John and Thomas, brothers of Adam Pacok, died without heirs male of their bodies. Adam Pacok held the manors in virtue of the fines, and had issue Robert Pervyng, knight, and Margaret wife of Thomas Bowet, senior. Robert Pervyng, knight, died without heirs of his body. Margaret wife of Thomas Bowet, Maud formerly wife of John Walker of Cockermouth, and Thomas Qwytlokman are heirs of Robert Pervyng, junior.

Margaret Bowet is one heir of Robert Pervyng, junior, namely daughter of Adam Pervyng *alias* Adam Pacok, father of Robert Pervyng, knight. Adam was son of Joan, sometime wife of John Pacok, sister and heir of Robert Pervyng, junior.

Maud formerly wife of John Walker of Cockermouth is another heir, being the daughter of Alice de Wode, daughter of Emma de Skateby, another sister and heir of Robert Pervyng, junior. She is aged 30 years and more.

Thomas Qwytlokman is son and heir of Margaret Pape, another daughter of Alice, daughter of Emma de Skateby; also aged 30 years and more.

He died on 10 April last. To the messuage in Carlisle Margaret wife of Thomas Bowet is next heir and of full age, being 30 years and more.

C 137/51, no.47

JOHN CHALERS, KNIGHT

1177 Writ, *plenius certiorari*, as to his status in the manor of Whaddon, not given in the earlier inquisition [*CIPM* XVI, no.529]. 1 Dec. 1404.

CAMBRIDGE. Inquisition. Whaddon. 27 Dec.

He held the manor of Whaddon in his demesne as of fee.

C 137/51, no.48

THOMAS SON OF JOHN CHALERS

1178 Writ for proof of age. William Castelacre, knight, and Margery widow of John Chalers, to whom Richard II granted the wardship [*CPR 1383–91*, p.227], should be warned. 17 Dec. 1404.

[Endorsed] Margery was warned by William Owyn and Henry Rokyng. William Castelacre, knight, is dead.

CAMBRIDGE. Proof of age. Whaddon. 27 Dec.

The jurors say that Thomas was born on 17 Sept. 1381 at Whaddon and baptised in St. Mary's church there. Asked how they remembered the date they said:

Thomas Eyr, aged 46, was in the church to hear mass and saw Thomas baptised.

John Pynk, 48, was coming from the church to his home and met Thomas being carried to the church in a woman's arms.

Henry Frost, 48, said that John Chalers the father caused him to settle a dispute with his neighbour, Peter Molde, in the manor house of John Chalers when Thomas was carried to the church for the baptism.

John Lelye, 52, said that his wife was at the birth and caught a serious fever.

Ellis Ropere, 48, was farmer of the lands of John Chalers in Meldreth, took his rent to Whaddon and there saw Thomas being carried to church in the arms of Marion Dymmok.

William Coupere, 46, heard mass in the church and held the book for the priest at the baptism.

Robert Sherman, 53, was receiver of rents of the manor of Whaddon and by his receipt for the payment of the rent has evidence of the age.

William Dycon, 55, was with John Chalers when he was first told that his wife was delivered of a son.

Robert Chapman, 43, had a house burnt down on that day.

Thomas Rous, 60, had a son John born on the Thursday after that day.

John Dette, 56, on the Tuesday after that day set out for the court of Rome.

William Hitchyn, 55, on that day purchased one acre lying in the field of Whaddon, and knows by the date of the charter.

C 137/51, no.48

CECILY WIFE OF GUY WHITYNTON

1179 Writ for proof of age of Cecily, sister and heir of Richard son of John Brounyng, kinsman and heir of Thomas Rodberugh, who held of William earl of Stafford. John Bray, esquire, to whom Richard II granted the wardship [*CPR 1391–6*, pp.281–2], should be warned. 13 Feb. 1405.

GLOUCESTER. Proof of age. Gloucester. 3 March 1405.

[Headed] Of full age, sixteen years and more.

John Bray, esquire, warned by John Brasyer and William Bailly, did not come.

The jurors said that Cecily was born at Leigh on 10 April 1389 and baptised there and they remember because:

Thomas Walton, aged 60, on that day assisted John Preston, the chaplain, in the church after the baptism.

John Walton, 55, went to find John Preston, the chaplain, and made him come to the church, and was himself present.

William Russell of Corse, John Hall and John Colseye, all 60 and more, on that day settled various disputes between themselves and saw the baptism.

John Clervowe, John White and John Hull, all 40 and more, on that day rode towards Gloucester past the church and met Cecily being carried from the church after the baptism in the arms of Margaret Merssh, her godmother.

John Marchall, Walter Hathewey, William Sketeby and Nicholas Ruyhale, all 40 and more, were neighbours of John Brounyng the father, and it was common talk that she was born, and they saw her carried to and from the church to the home of John Brounyng.

C 137/51, no.49

FULK DE GREY

1180 Writ for proof of age of Fulk, son of Fulk, brother of Roger son of Thomas Grey, knight, kinsman and heir of Thomas. John Pelham and John Typtoft, knights, who had the wardship [*CFR* XII, p.240], should be warned. 29 May 1405.

[Endorsed] They were so warned.

CAMBRIDGE. Proof of age. Caxton. 22 July.

The jurors say that he was born on 28 Oct. 1382 at Haddenham and baptised in Trinity church there, and so is of full age. This they know for the following reasons:

John Ware, aged 46, had a son born and baptised in that church on the same day.

Walter Crysp, 54, had a son ordained in that year who said his first mass in that church about the following 30 Nov.

William Pernel, 48, because his eldest son died within a week of the day of the birth.

John Brache, 47, was married after the following Midsummer.

Edward Brond, 62, was on a pilgrimage to Canterbury with Fulk's father when his mother was pregnant and gave birth.

William Redberd, 58, bought certain lands and tenements in Haddenham from the father on 9 Nov. following the birth and knows by the date of the charters.

Geoffrey Waryn, 63, because his wife's father died on 31 Oct. of the previous year and was buried in that church. He made the tomb.

John Gelyn, 54, set off for Santiago [de Compostela] on 2 Feb. following.

Thomas Smyth, 66, because a stranger was killed by accident at Haddenham on 26 Nov. following the birth and he was there with the king's coroner.

John Mannyng, 48, was in the church at the baptism and held the book for the priest.

Richard Mestylon, 60, paid Fulk the father £10 at Christmas after the birth, and he has a receipt which gives the date.

William Outelawe, 62, says that Fulk affirmed, maintained and declared it (*eum affirmavit, tenuit et nominavit*) before the bishop in the church of Sutton in the same county, whence he well knows that Fulk son of Fulk de Grey is of full age.

C 137/51, no.50

CECILY DURDAUNT

1181   Writ for proof of age of Cecily wife of Edward Durdaunt, daughter of Robert Aleyns, son of Roger Aleyns, brother of Geoffrey Aleyns of Cromer. Margery Moleyns, to whom Richard II granted the wardship [but see *CFR* XI, p.53], should be warned. 26 Jan. 1405.

[Endorsed] Margery Moleyns is dead.

NORFOLK. Proof of age. Beckham. 23 Feb.

The jurors say that Cecily was born at Beckham and baptised in the church there on 2 Feb. 1388, and is now aged 16 years. They say that they remember for the following reasons:

Roger Symondesson, aged 58 years and more, because on 11 April in that year he married Margaret his wife.

Richard Watteson, 51 and more, because on 9 May 1388 Robert [*sic*] father of Robert Aleyns died.

Robert Glyve, 60 and more, because on 4 Jan. in that year going from Aylmerton to Cromer he fell, breaking his right arm.

Richard Mawclerk, 66 and more, because his son, Robert, now deceased, was born on the preceding 20 Oct.

Thomas Shirforde, 40 and more, because on 8 May in that year his son John was drowned in the sea near Cromer.

John Capron, 67 and more, because on 6 April 1388 Agnes his sister broke her left shin on her way to the mill at Cromer.

Thomas Howes, 70 and more, because his son Richard died on 6 Jan. 1388.

John Bonde, draper, 60 and more, because on 4 May 1388 Margaret his daughter was born.

John Shepherd, 66 and more, because he married Margaret his wife on 6 Jan. 1389.

Robert Ulpe, 68 and more, because on 4 May in that year his son Henry was drowned near Cromer.

John Anneseye, 57 and more, because Peter his son, now deceased, was born on 10 May 1388.

William Ulpe, 68 and more, because his son John died on 12 April 1388.

C 137/51, no.51

THOMAS UGHTREDE

1182 Writ for proof of age of Thomas son of William, son of Thomas Ughtrede, knight, who held of Thomas Moubray. John and William Sandford, who were granted the wardship, should be warned. 29 May 1405.

[Endorsed] They were warned by John West and William Fox.

LINCOLN. Proof of age in the presence of William FitzRoger, attorney of John and William Sandford, to whom the king committed the wardship by letters patent [*CFR* XII, p.171]. Great Limber. 16 June.

Robert Pye of Riby, aged 46 years and more, says that Thomas was born at Riby and baptised in the parish church there on 6 Jan. 1382. He knows because he held a book from which the priest read at the baptism.

William Launde of Laceby, 40 and more, knows the date because his wife was churched on that day in Laceby church.

John Bryd of Bradley, 40 and more, knows because his son was buried [the remainder is illegible].

C 137/51, no.52

MAUD CORBET

1183 STAFFORD. Assignment of dower to Maud widow of Robert Corbet, knight, in the presence of Henry Swan, attorney of Robert Corbet, knight, son and heir of Robert. King's Bromley. 1 Feb. 1405.

King's Bromley, 1 watermill, annual value 5 marks, and 1 parcel of 3 a. meadow called 'Halle Medowe', annual value 26s. 8d., as the value of the third part of the manor.

C 137/51, no.33

ELEANOR WIDOW OF IVO DE HARLESTON

1184 Writ to assign dower in the presence of John Foljaumbe and John Pygot, clerk, who were granted the wardship [*CFR* XII, p.235; *CPR 1401–5*, p.367], the former escheator having been removed before he could execute the writ. 26 May 1405.

BEDFORD. Assignment of dower in the presence of Thomas Lounde, attorney of John Foljaumbe and John Pygot, clerk, and John Croyser, attorney of Eleanor. 8 Sept.

Dunton, a third part of the manor called Dunton Chamberlains inside the great ditch called the 'Mote' on the south side, as appears by the bounds there placed, with free ingress and egress by the gate of the site; a grange called the 'Greteberne', a third part of the lower part of a house called 'le Bakhous' by the great gate of the manor, and 1 stable at the upper end of the grange called the 'Wheteberne' next to the same gate, all as a third part of the hall; 2 chambers, 1 kitchen, 1 house called the long 'Shephous', the grange called the 'Wheteberne', and 2 parts of the house called the 'Bakhous', all belonging to the manor. All the close called the 'Foreyerd' within the gates and houses aforesaid is in common between John Foljaumbe, John Pygot and Eleanor.

Also a third part of the profits of the dovecot, a third part of a close called 'Wode-roveclos' by the bounds there placed, and the profits of the boughs of the trees growing on the south side of the door of the great grange which opens in 'Woderoveclos' to a bound by the kitchen of the manor on both sides of the ditch, and all the willows growing by the way leading from the manor to Dunton; a third part of the perquisites of the court; the rents and services of Robert Laurence, Richard Saltwelle, Richard Gylle, Richard Coupere and John Paternostre, junior, free tenants of the manor, as a third part of all the free tenancies; the rents and services of John Paternostre, senior and junior, for their lands in Dunton, and of Robert Abraham and William Paton, and a third part of those of John Roger, servile tenants, as a third part of all the servile tenancies of the manor; and the following parcels of demesne arable with the meadow, pasture and headlands of each, all lying to the south of their respective parcels: 5 a. at the end as a third part of 15 a. by the manor; 13 a. 1⅓ roods as a third of 40 a. called 'Borende' and 'Eldeponde'; 4 a. as a third of 12 a. called 'Rokisdole'; 6 a. as a third of 18 a. called 'Ladymauncell'; 4½ a. and ⅓ of ½ a. as a third of 14 a. called the 'Fourteenac-res'; 2 a. as a third of 6 a. called 'Shortlond Dole'; 5 a. as a third of 15 a. called 'Bradsik Dole'; 6 a. as a third of 18 a. called 'Delle Dole'; 2½ a. and ⅓ a. as a third of 8 a. next 'Delle Dole'; 1½ a. and ⅓ of ½ a. as a third of 5 a. called 'Shor. . .ode'; 12 a. as a third of 36 a. called 'Riggewey Dole'; and 1 a. of meadow called 'Berystardy' for a third part of 2 a. on 'Welyforlang'.

C 137/51, no.54

JOAN WIDOW OF EDMUND, DUKE OF YORK

1185 Writ to assign dower, the escheator having been removed before he could execute the writ of 28 Sept. 1402. 15 Jan. 1405.

MIDDLESEX. Assignment of dower, Richard Baynard, attorney of Edward now duke of York, son and heir of Edmund, having been warned. Westminster. 20 Feb.

Assignment of £94 8s.9½d. at the exchequer as a third part of the £283 6s.8d. granted by Edward III, with the arrears from 28 Sept. 1402 to date.

[Cf. no.626 above].

C 137/51, no.55

JOHN BERTELOT

1186 Writ, *melius sciri*, he being said to have alienated his lands and dissipated his goods owing to his idiocy, what they are and who now holds them. 6 March 1405.

HERTFORD. Inquisition. Hitchin. 19 May.

He was an idiot from birth, incapable of adminstering his property. He held in St. Albans by right of inheritance:

One messuage called 'Bertelottestenement' between the tenement of William Jolyf on one side and a messuage of the abbot of St. Albans on the other, annual value 20s.

Two shops in 'Heyrowe' between the tenements of Adam Stonham and the prioress of Sopwell, annual value 9d.

One messuage and 3 a. in Holywell Hill by 'Fullyngwelle Lane' between the lands of the abbot on both sides, annual value 12d. The 3 a. are in the field called 'Malebranche-feld' in St. Peter's parish, extending from the king's highway to the field formerly of John Randulf, between the land of Richard Wellyng and John Faunton, and are held of the abbot of St. Albans and the prioress of Sopwell, service unknown.

All descended to him after the death of Margaret wife of Robert Whight, as next heir of William Bertelot, his grandfather. Robert died on 10 Aug. 1402.

Joan wife of Alexander Smith, sister of John Bertelot, his next heir, is aged 50 years and more. Richard Wallyngford and Roger Bryde, fuller of St. Albans, have held them since 10 Aug. 1402, title unknown.

Geoffrey Felyngdon, chaplain of St. Albans, on 20 April last, after the messuage was taken into the king's hands by the escheator, knocked down, took and carried off from the messuage, without the king's licence and to the king's annual loss of 10s., a building made for John Bertelot worth 30s.

C 137/51, no.57

WILLIAM DE FERRARIIS

1187　Writ, *plenius certiorari*, stating that Edward III in parliament on 3 March 1337 granted [*CPR 1334–8*, p.418] the reversion of the manor of Walton upon Trent after the death of Queen Isabel his mother to Henry de Ferrariis and the heirs male of his body; that afterwards by an inquisition held on 6 Sept. 1358 [*CIPM* X, pp.358–9] it was found that Isabel had held the manor of Walton upon Trent for life with the advowson, with remainder to William son and heir of Henry de Ferrariis, and she had attorned for it; that by a second inquisition [*CIPM* X, p.358] it was found that she held the manor of Fakenham in Norfolk for life with reversion to the king; and that both were then in the king's hands and both William and Henry died before they were released. Inquire when they died, who is next heir, and what is his age. 30 Nov. 1404.

DERBY. Inquisition. Measham, [Leics]. 22 Dec.

William de Ferrariis died on 7 Jan. 1371. Henry was his son, and heir to the manor of Walton upon Trent with the advowson. He was then aged 14, and he died on 3 Feb. 1388. William his son and heir is aged 30 years and more.

[Cf. no.683 above].

C 137/51, no.59

JOHN DE HOLAND, EARL OF HUNTINGDON

1188　GLOUCESTER. Inquisition *ex officio*. Tetbury. 26 March 1405.

On the day of his death and forfeiture he held the manor of Tytherington of Edmund earl of Stafford of his manor of Thornbury, annual value 40 marks.

He died on 15 Jan. 1400. William de Clynton, knight, has taken the profits since his death, title unknown. John son of John Holand, his next heir, is aged 9 years and more.

Writ to assign dower to Elizabeth Lancastre, wife of John Cornewaill, knight, his widow.

C 137/51, no.60
E 149/85, no.7

PETER GRUBBE AND JULIANA HIS WIFE

1189 Writ, *plenius certiorari*, Peter Grubbe, citizen and fishmonger of London, and Juliana being said to have held property in free burgage which should have escheated for lack of heirs. 18 Oct. 1404.

LONDON. Inquisition. Guildhall. 10 Dec.

They held to themselves and the heirs of Juliana 1 messuage in the parish of All Hallows, Bread Street, by the gift of John Lynton, formerly parson of St. Vedast's, and John Adam and Thomas Polle, citizens and goldsmiths of London, annual value 4 marks.

Juliana died without heirs, and Peter died later.

1190 LONDON. Inquisition *ex officio*. 16 Jan. 1405.

Peter Grubbe, citizen and fishmonger, died on 14 Oct. 1400 holding 1 messuage in the parish of All Hallows, Bread Street, which escheated to the king as appears by the inquisition already returned.

William Grubbe, fishmonger, entered after his death and took the profits from 14 Oct. to 10 Dec. 1404; annual value 4 marks.

C 137/51, no.61
E 149/86, no.2

JOHN CHAPMAN OF GUSSAGE ST. ANDREW

1191 Writ, *plenius certiorari*, as the inquisition held under Richard II did not give his status in 1 messuage and 16 a. in Gussage St. Andrew [*CIPM* XVII, no.620]. 18 March 1405.

DORSET. Inquisition. Sturminster Marshall. 11 June.

He held this messuage and 16 a. in Gussage St. Andrew in his demesne as of fee of the king in chief by a rent of 1 lb. cumin, annual value 3s.6d.

He died on 27 July 1391. Robert Chapman, clerk, his son and heir, is aged 30 years and more.

C 137/51, no.62

WILLIAM WYKEHAM, BISHOP OF WINCHESTER

1192 LONDON. Inquisition *ex officio*. 12 Oct. 1404.

William Wykeham, bishop of Winchester, died on 27 Sept. last holding quitrents of £10 11s.8d. payable at Easter and Michaelmas from the following tenements in the parish of All Hallows the Less in Dowgate ward:

The house of John Beaufort, earl of Somerset, which the king granted him after the forfeiture of John earl of Huntingdon [*CPR 1399–1401*, p.546], 20s.

A tenement formerly of John Weston and now of Richard Northlode, knight, and Joan his wife, daughter and heir of Alice Perers, 20s.

A tenement formerly of Robert Turk, knight, 20s.

A tenement formerly of Henry Darcy and Margery his wife in the right of Margery, and now of Richard Torell, 53s.4d.

A tenement formerly of William Enot, citizen and draper, 10s.

A tenement of John Snypston, vintner, and Joan his wife, daughter of Simon Benfeld, 26s.8d.

Also the following in the parish of All Hallows the Great in the same ward:

The tenements in Greenwich Lane of the prior of the new hospital outside Bishopsgate, 20s.

A tenement of Philip Seynclere, knight, and Margaret his wife, formerly called Coldharbour, on both sides of the lane, 26s.8d.

A tenement of Nicholas Waterton, formerly of William Leyre, 20d.

A tenement of the prior of the hospital of St. Mary Elsing Spital within Cripplegate, formerly of John Norhampton, 7s.10d.

A capital messuage of two lanes in the Ropery now held by Robert Comberton, 5s.6d., and

A tenement of Robert Parys called the 'Castell in the Hope' in the parish of St. Margaret Moses in Friday Street, Bread Street ward, 1 lb. pepper at Easter.

E 149/85, no.13

1193   DORSET. Inquisition *ex officio*. Dorchester. 20 Oct. 1404.

William Wykeham, bishop of Winchester, held the manor of Piddlehinton, part of the possessions of the alien priory of Mortain, for life by the grant of Edward III [*CPR 1370–4*, p.219]. It has now come into the king's hands and belongs to the king.

There are assize rents of £11 3s. payable by equal parts at the four terms; 100 a. arable, of which 30 lie fallow and 70 at 4d. are worth 23s.4d. annually; common pasture for 300 sheep, 10s.; 2 a. meadow, herbage before harvesting 8s. but afterwards nil because common; a close anciently of the manor house, pasture 4s.; and perquisites of court 13s.4d.

He died on 27 Sept. last.

E 149/85, no.13

JOHN TREVENANT, BISHOP OF HEREFORD

1194   LONDON. Inquisition *ex officio*. 25 Oct. 1404.

He died on 29 March 1404 holding 1 house in St. Mary Mounthaw parish, Queenhithe ward, which would let for 5 marks 6s.8d., but was, and still is, vacant and unlet; and also 1 shop, parcel of the same, annual value 6s.8d.

E 149/86, no.1

JOAN WIFE OF JOHN DEYNCOURT

1195   Writ for proof of age. . . . 16 Feb. 1401.

OXFORD. Proof of age of Joan daughter and heir of Robert Grey of Rotherfield Greys, knight. . . . 23 Feb.

The jurors say that she was born and baptised at Rotherfield Greys on [20 July 1386] and was aged 14 years on 20 July last and know this for the following reasons:

Thomas Clobbere, aged 56 years and more, was granted 1 messuage in Rotherfield Greys on the Thursday after her birth by Richard Noke, and knows by the date of the charter.

William Padenhale, 35 and more, was granted various lands in the same place by Walter Braye on the Sunday after her birth, and also knows by the date of the charter.

Reynold Jory, 40 and more, had a son John baptised in the church of Henley upon Thames on the day that Joan was born.

William More, 40 and more, . . . was buried in Rotherfield Greys church on the day of the baptism.

John Aleyn, 45 and more, had a grange at Rotherfield Greys burnt down on the day of the baptism.

William Rede, 40 and more, married his wife Joan on that day.

John Durches, 69 and more, had a son who celebrated his first mass on that day.

Robert Newemore, 30 and more, was riding to Oxford . . .

Stephen Lytelmore, . . . John Croyle, . . . Nicholas Har. . . and John . . . [statements illegible].

C 137/64, no.84

INDEX OF PERSONS AND PLACES

The references are to entries not to pages.

Abbas Hall (Abessishalle), in Great Cornard, Suff, manor, 24
Abberley (Abbodele, Abbotele), Worcs, advowson, 515
manor, 502
Abbotsbury (Abbotesbury), Dors, inquisition at, 445
Abbott (Abott), John, 308
Richard, 886
Aberedw (Aberedewe), [Rad], manor, 506
Abergavenny (Bergavenny, Bergeveny), [Monm], castle and town, 463
Abergavenny (Bergavenny, Bergeveny), lordship, 463
Abingdon (Abyndon), Berks, 1025
abbot of, 350, 592, 799, 1025
inquisitions at, 131, 202, 318, 592, 903
manor, 799
Abinger, Surrey, Paddington in, q.v.
Ablington (Ablynton) [in Bibury], Glos, manor, 1095
Aboke, William, 146, 162, 166, 849
Abott see Abbott
Abovebrook, Richard, 527
Abovetheton, William, 828
Abraham, John, 662
Robert, 1184
Acaster Malbis (Acastremalbyssh), Yorks, manor, 568
Achard (Axhard), John, rector of Clyst Hydon, 104
Peter, Elizabeth his wife and John his brother, 1055
Robert, and Agnes his wife, 1055
Acklam (Acclum), Yorks, 955
Ackleton (Acleton) [in Badger], Salop, 958
Acle, Norf, Weybridge in, q.v.
Acre, Castle, (Castelacre), Norf, prior of, 406
Newton by, q.v.
Acton Burnell, Salop, 840–1
Ruckley in, q.v.
Acton, Iron, (Irenacton), Glos, 846
Acton Trussell, Staffs, 851
Acton Turville (Acton), Glos, inquisition at, 1095
Acton, John de, 831
Adam, John, John ap, 303, 522
John, citizen and goldsmith of London, 1189
William, 259, 299
Adderbury, East, (Adderbury), Oxon, manor, 801
Adderle, Ralph, 792
Addingham, Cumb, Salkeld, Little, in q.v.
Addington (Adyngton), Kent, manor, 12
Addington, Little (Little Adyngton), Northants, 334, 828
Adforton (Atforton) [in Leintwardine], Salop, [afterwards Heref], 61
Admond, John, 676

Adstone (Adeston) [in Canons Ashby], Salop, 825
Advent, Corn, Poldue in q.v.
Afflington (Alfrynton) [in Corfe Castle], Dors, 648
Aglaby, William de, 115
Aillemer see Aylemer
Aillesbury see Aylesbury
Aishford (Ayschford), Richard, and Alice his wife, 699
William, 105–6
Aiskew (Aiscogh) [in Bedale], Yorks, 221
Ake (Ak), William, parson of Lockington, 319
William de, of Lockington, and Alice (Hall) his wife, 655
Akelesdon (Akelyston), John de, 152, 846
Akenbergh (Bergh) [in Lockington], Yorks, manor, 419
Akenham, Suff, 303
Alayn see Aleyn
Alberbury (Alburbury), Salop, church, 968
Amaston, Breiddin, Bretchel, Eyton, Hayes and Rowton in, q.v.
Albon, John, 838
Alburgh (Aldeburgh), Norf, advowson, 302
Alby, Norf, advowson, 302
Alcester (Alycestre), Warw, 309, 527
Alconbury (Alcumbury, Alkemondebury, Alkenbury), Hunts, inquisition at, 333
manor, 271, 913, 1166
Aldborough, Yorks, 1140
Aldbourne, Sussex, manor, 370
Aldebury, Thomas, clerk, 342, 494, 500, 508–9, 511
Alden, Thomas de, knight, Elizabeth (Say) his wife and Maud his daughter, 1071
Mary daughter of see Worthyngton
Aldenham, Herts, 25
Alderbury (Alwardbury), Wilts, 410
Ivychurch in, q.v.
Aldermaston, Berks, inquisition at, and manor, 1055
Alderminster (Aldermerston), Worcs, 1126
Goldicote and Upthorpe in, q.v.
Aldersfield (Alderfeld) [in Wickhambrook], Suff, 834
Alderton (Aldryngton), Glos, 152, 846
Dixton in, q.v.
Alderton (Aldryngton), Northants, manor and advowson, 395
Aldglose (Aldelose) [in Hastingleigh], Kent, 1082
Aldham, Essex, Bourchiers in see Fordham, Little, formerly Bourchiers
Aldingham (Aldyngham), Lancs, 969
Aldington (Aldyngton by Maydeston) [in Thurnham], Kent, manor, 768, 1121
Aldridge (Allerwich), Staffs, manor, 774
Aldwincle (Aldewyncle), Northants, 828

2F

Busby, Little, (Little Buskby) [in Stokesley], Yorks, 955
Bush, John, 320
Bushbury, Staffs, Essington in, q.v.
Bushey (Bissheye, Byssheye, Risby), Herts, 140, 848
Bushmead (Bysshemede) [in Eaton Socon], Beds, prior of, 845
Busland (Buffeslond) [in Cadeleigh], Devon, 30
Buslingthorpe (Buslyngthorp), Lincs, manor, 83
BUSSEBRIGGE, JOHN, and Robert his son, 1175
Busshell, William, 678
Busshey (Bissheye, Busy, Byssheye), Aubrey de, 140, 848
　　John, 990
　　Walter de, 248, 298
Busteler, Robert, knight, 844
Busy see Busshey
But, Thomas, 995
Butlers (Botelers) [in Clifton Reynes], Bucks, 822
Butley (Buttele, Butteley), Suff, prior of, 302–3
Butley, Roger, 63
Butteler see Boteler
Butterby (Beautrove) [in Croxdale], Durh, manor, 957
Butterwick (Boterwik, Boterwyk) [in Owston], Lincs, 305
Butterwick (Botrewyk) [in Barton le Street], Yorks, 301
Butterwick (Botirwyke in Grindalythe) [in Foxholes], Yorks, manor, 905
Buttes, William, clerk, 1146
Butteturte see Buttourt
Buttington (Botyngton), [Mont], manor, 650
　　Teirtref and Trewern in, q.v.
Button (Boton), John de, 846
　　Robert, 858
Buttourt (Botourd, Butteturte, Buttort, Byttort), John, 53, 773–4, 847
　　Joyce daughter of see Burnell
　　John, knight, 425
Butveleyn see Boteveyllen
BUXHULL, Alan de, 21–2, 28, 668–71
　　ALAN DE, knight, son of, 21, 28, **668–71**
　　Amice daughter of see Beverley
　　Elizabeth daughter of see Lynde
　　Maud wife of see Montague
Buxted (Bokstede), Sussex, manor, 1067, 1074
Buysshop see Bysshop
Byde, Master William, 410
Byfield (Byfeld), Northants, 755
Bygot (Begot), John, and Isabel his wife, 302
　　John, knight, and John, knight, his son 427–9
Byker, Northumb, lordship, 73
Bykerstath, John de, 598
'Bykyngton' ('Bykynton') (unidentified), Glos, 152, 846
Byland [in Coxwold], Yorks, abbey, abbot of, 428
　　advowson, 301
Byllyngford, James de, 565
Byllyn, Bylmyn see Billyng
Byne [in West Grinstead], Sussex, 304
Byne, James, and Joan his wife, 304
Byngham, Robert, 1042
Bynkfelde, Henry de, 4
Byntre, William de, 305
Byrches, Richard atte, 529
Byset, Margaret see Romesy

Byspham, William, feodary of the duchy of Lancaster, 871
Byssheye see Busshey
Bysshop (Buysshop), Agnes, 859
　　Agnes wife of John, 342
　　Thomas, 28
Bytham, Castle, Lincs, Castle, 1043
Bythoutethyate, Peter, 1000
Byttort see Buttourt
Bywell, Northumb, Newton in, q.v.
Bywell, barony, 745, 756

Cabery, William, 953
Cachehors, Ralph, 999
Cadbury, North, Som, Woolston, North and South, in, q.v.
Cadbury (Cadebury), John, 28
　　Nicholas, and John his son, 476
Caddington, Beds, Markyate in, q.v.
Cade, Adam, 1141
Cadebury see Cadbury
Cadecote see Catecote
CADEHAY, GEOFFREY, 30
　　Beatrice daughter of see Gambon
　　Margaret and Emma daughters of, and Richard son of Emma, 30
Cadeleigh, Devon, Busland, Langley and Meadhayes in, q.v.
Cadeneye, John, 862
Cadon, John, 676
Caen (Cadamum) [France, dép. Calvados], abbess of, 391, 1016
Caereinion (Kareignon), [Mont], commote, 650
Caerwent (Kaerwent) [Monm], 846
　　Crick in, q.v.
Caister (Castre), Norf, manor, 793
Caistor (Castre), Lincs, manor, 977
Calais (Cales) [France, dép. Pas-de-Calais], castle, 762, 830
　　escheators in see Newport, John; Wotton, Lawrence
　　inquisitions at, 264, 492, 584–5, 729–30, 762, 830, 1001
　　'Mesondeustrete', 730
　　St. Mary's parish, 584–5
　　St. Nicholas's parish, 264, 762, 830, 1001
Calclogh, Hugh, esquire, 829
Calcote (Caldecote) [in Bishop's Cannings], Wilts, 388
Calcutt (Calcote) [in Cricklade], Wilts, 1136
Caldecote (Caldecot), Warw, 527
Caldecote, Thomas, 310
　　William de, 303
Caldecott (Caudelcote) [in Fritton], Suff, 303
Caldecott (Caldecote) [in Bow Brickhill], Bucks, 824
Caldeford, Richard, chaplain, 604
Caldewell, John, clerk, 405
Caldicot (Caldecote), [Monm], castle, 134, 154, 166, 170, 815
　　free chapel in, advowson of, 145
Caldwall (Caldewalle) [in Kidderminster], Worcs, manor, 1126
Caldwell (Caldewell) [in Stanwick], Yorks, manor, 931
CALEMAN, JOHN, of Horseheath, **693**
　　Agnes daughter of, 693
　　Elizabeth daughter of see Hatholf
Caliot, William, 119

Epsle (Epsley), William, and Joan his wife, and William, junior, 304

Epworth (Eppeworth in Haxholm), Lincs, 284
manor, 305, 580, 915
Lubbancroft, Pipercroft and Sulbyplace in, 305

Ercall, High, Salop, Isombridge and Roden in, q.v.

Erdeswyke, Thomas, 851

Erdington (Erdyngton) [in Aston], Warw, 773
manor, 1100
prebendary of, 1150

ERDYNGTON, Giles, knight, 1102
Thomas de, 527, 772, 1021, 1099, 1102
MARGARET wife of, 1099–1102
Thomas son of, 1099–1100, 1102

Erghum, Ralph, bishop of Bath and Wells, 304

Eridge (Erregge) [in Frant], Sussex, 2

Erkyngton, Thomas, 851

Erleigh (Erleygh), John, 142, 189, 836

Erlyngham, William, 390

Ermyte see Hermyte

Erpingham (Erpyngham), Norf, 302

Erringham (Iryngham) [in Old Shoreham], Sussex, 304

Ersedekon see Lercedekene

Erysshe see Iryssh

Escote, William, 979

Eshott (Esshete) [in Felton], Northants, manor, 1070

Eshton (Eschehoton) [in Gargrave], Yorks, 301

Eslington (Esselyngton) [in Whittingham], Northumb, manor, 412

Essa (Usse) [in Lanteglos by Fowey], Corn, manor, 731

Esselyngton, Robert de, and Elizabeth his wife, George his son and Elizabeth and Isabel his daughters, 412

Essex, county, escheator in see Leget, Helmyng
king's forests in, 196
sheriff of, 15, 49, 127, 816

Essex, earldom, or barony of the county, 128, 169, 498, 817

Essington (Esyngton) [in Bushbury], Staffs, 774

Est, William, 670

Estephenes, John, 934

'Esthalys' (unidentified), Devon, 1005

Estlee, Thomas, knight, 793

Estoft, Thomas de, 793

Eston see Aston

Esyngwalde, Richard de, 997

Etchingham (Echyngham), Sussex, court at, 21
Bellhurst and Burgham in, q.v.

Etheleston, Roger de, 597

Eton, Bucks, manor, 562

Ettington (Etyngdon), Warw, manor, 711
Fulready in, q.v.

Etton, Yorks, 301

Euyr, Ralph de, 301

Eve, John, chaplain, 970–1

Evelith (Ivelith next Shoffonhale) in Shifnal, Salop, 1147

Everard, Benjamin, of Shipden, 875

Evercreech (Evercriche), Som, manor, 393

Everdon, John, 1062
Alice, formerly Kene, wife of, 1062

Everingham (Everyngham), Yorks, lord of see Everyngham, Adam

Evershot (Evershott) [in Frome St. Quintin], Dors, inquisition at, 45

Everthorpe (Yverthorp) [in North Cave], Yorks, 606

Everton, Beds, 256

Everyngham, Adam, knight, lord of Everingham, 1108

Evesham, Worcs, abbot of, 843
Roger abbot of, 853
inquisition at, 502

Evesham, John de, 799, 803
Margaret wife of, 799

Evyle see Dayville

Ewart (Eworth) [in Doddington], Northumb, manor, 433

Ewell (Ewelle by Mallyng) [in West Farleigh], Kent, 1069

Ewell, Temple, Kent, Kearsney in, q.v.

Ewhurst (Ewerst), Surrey, 1175

Ewhurst (Ywherst) [in Shermanbury], Sussex, 304

Exe, Nether, (Netherexe), Devon, 1005

Exe, Up, (Upexe) [in Rewe], Devon, 1005

Exeter, bishop of see Stafford, Edmund

Exeter (Exon), Devon, inquisitions at, 363, 367, 479, 566, 788, 893, 971, 1128, 1145
canon of see Vaggescomb, Robert
East, North and South Gates, Paul Street (Poulestrete) and Smith Street (Smythestrete) in, 566

Exhall (Eccleshale), Warw, 527

Exmoor (Exemora, Exemore), Devon, forest, 363, 893

Exton, Som, 576

Ey, John, 859

Eyehurst (Iherste) [in Chipstead], Surrey, 741

Eyke (Eyk), Suff, advowson, 303
Staverton in, q.v.

Eyleston, Adam de, 664

Eynesford, Isabel, 650

Eynsford (Eynesforde), Kent, castle, 768
inquisition at, 1052
manor, 1052
Austin in, q.v.

Eynsham, Oxon, abbot of, 320
Thomas abbot of, 621

Eynton [in Thurnham], Kent, 1082

EYR, Thomas, 1178
WILLIAM, outlaw, 322–3, 665, 860
Isabel daughter of see Mone
Richard brother of, 322

Eyston Hall (Estonhalle) [in Belchamp Walter], Essex, manor, 196, 204, 485, 869

Eyton (Eton on Lugg), Heref, 523

Eyton (unidentified) Salop, 544

Eyton (Iton) [in Alberbury], Salop, 840–1

Eyton upon the Weald Moors, Salop, Wappenshall in, q.v.

Eyton (Iton), John de, 840, 968
Thomas de, 206, 1148

Eyvill see Dayville

Faceby [in Whorlton], Yorks, 955

Fadmoor (Fadmore) [in Kirkby Moorside], Yorks, 301

Fagwyr Goch alias Redwalls (Redeswalles) [in Morvil, Pemb], 484

Fairbourne (Farborne) [in Harrietsham], Kent, 1082

Fairefax (Ferefax), John, 573
John, clerk, 568
Richard, 568

Fairewode see Fairwode

Fairfield (Forfeld) [in Belbroughton], Worcs, 515

Hogyn, John, 829
Hoke, William atte, 415
Hokday, William, 973
HOLAND (Holland), EDMUND, earl of Kent [1401–8], 691, 974–7, **979**, 1139
John, 308
John, of Paston, 541, 543
JOHN, earl of Huntingdon [1387–1400], 446, 684, 970–1, 974, 1003–5, 1158, 1160, 1163, 1168–9, **1189**, 1192
 Elizabeth wife of see Lancaster
 John son of, 1189
John, knight, 516
Stephen, 828
Thomas, 527
Thomas, earl of Kent [1360–97], 976–7, 979
 Alice wife of, 467, 976–7, 979
 Joan daughter of, wife of Edmund duke of York see Edmund
THOMAS, earl of Kent [1397–1400], 11, 83, 108, 301, 411, 578, 885–6, **974–8**, 979, 1163
 Joan wife of, 976–7
Walter, 863
Holbeach (Holbech), Lincs, manor, 141, 184, 842
Holbech, John, 314
Holborn (Holborne), Midd, bridge and St. Andrew's parish in, 935
Holbrook (Holebrok) in Cottered, Herts, 443
Holbrook (Holbrok), Suff, 303
HOLBROOK (Holbrok), John, and Alice his wife, 303
 THOMAS, **321A**
Holcombe (Holecombe), Som, 389
Holcot (Holcote), Beds, 821, 835
Holderness (Holdernesse), Yorks, 416
 lordship, 419
Holderness (Holdernesse), Yorks, wapentake, 427
Holdych, Richard, 71
Holes, Hugh de, 477, 483–4
Holeweye, Robert, 843
Holgot Philip, 343
HOLGRAVE (Holgreve), DAVID, **1032**
 Helen wife of, 1032
  Robert son of see Ogle
 William, 530
Holkham (Hokham), Norf, 302, 793
 manor, 469
Holland, Lincs, 141, 184, 842
Holland see Holand
Hollesley (Holisle, Holislee), Suff, manor, 258, 923
Hollington (Holynton) [in Longford], Derb, 708
Hollington, Sussex, Cortesley and Filsham in, q.v.
Holme (Holm) [in Bakewell], Derb, 976
Holme (Holm) [in Caverswall], Staffs, manor, 376
Holme (Holm in Newton), afterwards Biggin, Warw, q.v.
Holme [in Almondbury], Yorks, 301
Holme, Paull, (Holme) [in Paull], Yorks, 416
Holme, South, (Holme, Southolme) [in Hovingham], Yorks, 301
Holme upon Spaldingmoor (Holme in Spaldyngmore), Yorks, 301
 Bursea in, q.v.
HOLME (Holm), John, 858
 Thomas, 998
 William, 345–6
  John brother of, 346
  Isabel daughter of see Rende
  WILLIAM son of, idiot, **345–6**

Holmesfield (Holmesfeld) [in Dronfield], Derb, manor, 572–3
Holmfirth (Holmefrith) [in Kirkburton], Yorks, 641, 864
Holmoncote, John, 1005
Holsworthy, Devon, Thorne in, q.v.
Holt (Wymborneholt), Dors, Petersham in, q.v.
Holt (Holt Market), Norf, 342, 527, 843, 855
 inquisitions at, 813, 833
HOLT (Holte), Henry, 44, 48
 John, 828, 1050
 Peter, 855
 Robert del, 597
 Thomas, 670–1
 WALTER, and Eleanor (Dirnasall) his mother, 552, **994**
Holton St. Mary (Oleton), Suff, 303
Holverston (Holveston), Norf, advowson, 302
Holwell (Haliwell) [in Earsdon], Northumb, 745
Home [in Wentnor], Salop, 840–1
Honeman, John, 191
Honibere (Honybear, Honybere) [in Stogursey], Som, manor, 481
Honiton (Honyton), Devon, manor and advowson, 1145
Hoo, Kent, 768
Hoo, Suff, manor, 258, 923
Hoo, William de, knight, 21–2, 303
HOOD, JOHN, idiot, and William, sons of William, **538**
Hook (Houke) [in Nately Scures], Hants, 466
Hook (Howke) [in Snaith], Yorks, manor, 623
Hoon (Hone) [in Marston on Dove], Derb, manor, 707–8
 see also 'Howes' (Hoon?)
Hooton Pagnell (Hoton Paynell), Yorks, manor, 68
Hope, [Mont], 825
Hope All Saints, Kent, Cockreed in, q.v.
Hopecrone, John, 272
Hoper see Houpere
Hopewas, Hugh de, chaplain, 57
Hoppegras, William, 837
Hoppere see Houpere
Hopsford (Happesford) [in Withybrook], Warw, 295
Hopton, Staffs, 851
Hopton Cangeford, Salop, Poston, Lower and Upper, in, q.v.
Hopton, Thomas de, 851
Horbling (Horblyng), Lincs, manor, 977
Horbury, William, clerk, 566
Hore, John, 1104
 William, 834
 William, knight, 902
Horewode, John, 80
Horiford (Horyford) [in Preston], Dors, 646
Hornby (Horneby), Yorks, manor, 1140
 Hackforth in, q.v.
Horncastle (Horncastell), Lincs, inquisition at, 112
Horndon, East, (Est Thorndon), Essex, 196
Horndon, West, (Westhorndon), Essex, 196
Horne, Henry de, 119
 John, 863
 John de, parson of Weston, 393
 Thomas and William, 119
HORNEBY, JOAN, formerly Stokke, wife of William, **928**
Horner, Robert, 531
 Maud daughter of see Despenser

Lane—*cont.*
  Warin atte, 995
Langbargh (Langebergh), Yorks, wapentake, 714
Langdon Hills (Langedon), Essex, 198
  manor, 196
Lange *see* Longe
'Langeforde' (*unidentified*), Sussex, 304
Langelegh, Thomas and William, 30
  Cf. Longley
Langenho, Maud de, 303
Langeston [in Walton], Suff, 303
Langeston, John de, 303
Langeton *see* Langton
Langford (Langeford), Beds, manor, 726
Langford (Langeford), Essex, manor, 15
Langford (Landford), Notts, manor, 691
Langford, Steeple, Wilts, Bathampton in, *q.v.*
Langford *see* Longford
Langham (*unidentified*), Norf, 793
Langham, Rut, 551
Langham, Suff, 564
Langham (Langenham) [in North Bradley], Wilts,
  manor, 473
Langham, John de, 519
Langley (Langele) [in Hampstead Norris], Berks,
  203-4
Langley (Langalegh) [in Cadeleigh], Devon, manor,
  30
Langley (Langele), Norf, abbot of, 201, 302, 368-
  9
Langley (Langelegh, Langeley, Langlegh) [in
  Shipton under Wychwood], Oxon, lady of,
  148, 183, 853
Langley (Langeley), Salop, advowson, 377
  manor, 375, 377, 399
Langley, Abbots, (Abboteslangley), Herts, 'le
  Hyde' in, 25
Langley Burrell (Langele Burell), Wilts, manor, 763,
  1115
Langley Marish (Langley), Bucks, 1123
  Colnbrook in, *q.v.*
Langridge (Langerugg), Som, 962
  market and fair, 962
Langrove [in Ilston, Glam], 300
Langton (Langeton), Lincs, 886, 977
  advowson, 885
  manor, 885-6
Langton, Yorks, 301, 1140
  manor, 1169
Langton, Church, (Langeton), Leics, manor and
  advowson, 436, 609
Langton, Great, Yorks, 221
Langton, Little, [in Great Langton], Yorks, manor,
  108-9
Langton Matravers (Langeton Walsche in Purbyk),
  Dors, 1120
  manor, 759, 766
  Knitson in, *q.v.*
LANGTON (Langeton), Ralph de, 597
  Robert de, and Walter his son and William his
    grandson, 886
  THOMAS DE, 885
    JOHN son of, 885, 886
Langwith (Langewath by Nettleworthe) [in
  Cuckney], Notts, 999
Lanivet, Corn, Reperry in, *q.v.*
Lanreath (Lanraython, Lanrethon), Corn, manor,
  31, 35, 38
Lansant, Robert, 802

Lantegloss by Fowey, Corn, Essa and Polruan in,
  q.v.
Larling (Lyrlinge), Norf, 793
Lascels, John, 624
  Roger, knight, 429
Lassington (Lassyndon), Glos, manor and
  advowson, 1107
Lasyngby, John, of Rounton, 429
Latchford (Lacheford) [in Great Haseley], Oxon,
  148, 152, 183, 853
Latchingdon (Lachyndon), Essex, 15, 1019
Latimer (Isenhampstede Latymer) [in Chesham],
  Bucks, manor, 947
Latimer (Latymer), lords *see* Latimer, William;
  Nevill, John
LATIMER (Latymer, Latymer Bochard),
  THOMAS, knight, 435-9, 609-13, 838
  ANNE, *formerly* Beysyn, wife of, 436-9, 609-
    13
  Edward brother of, 435, 609-10, 613
  William, 429, 452
  William, knight, 948
  William, Lord Latimer, 622-3, 803
Laton, Robert de, and Katherine his wife, 957
Latymer *see* Latimer
Launceston (Launceton), Corn, castle, 31-2, 38,
  211, 322, 731
Launde (le Launde) [in Moor Monkton], Yorks,
  manor, 622-4
Launde (le Londe) in Sutton on the Forest, Yorks,
  1013
Launde, Eleanor de la, 425
  William, of Laceby, 1182
  Cf. Lounde
'Laundesfe' (Lawn Hill in Clattercote?), Oxon, 1105
Laurence, John, of Poulton, 597
  Robert, 1184
  Thomas, 828
Laurenson, John, and John his son, 428
Lavendon, William, 828
Lavenham (Lavnham), Suff, inquisition at, 1027
Lavenham, John, 666
Laver, Little, (Lavare), Essex, 220
Laverstock (Larkestoke), Wilts, 218
Lavington, Market, (Lavyngton, Stepullavynton),
  Wilts, manor, 1018
  Fiddington in, *q.v.*
Lawford, Little, (Little Laweford, Lytellawford) [in
  Newbold on Avon], Warw, 295, 527
Lawford, Long, (Longelaweford) [in Newbold on
  Avon], Warw, 295
Lawkland (Loukelandes) [in Clapham], Yorks, 301
Lawley (Lauley) [in Wellington], Salop, manor,
  1147
Lawn Hill [in Clattercote], Oxon *see* 'Laundesfe'
Lawney, Robert, 666
Lawrenceholme (Laurenceholme) [in Wigton],
  Cumb, 232
Lawton, Alice, 678
LAWYS, John, 868
  WILLIAM DE, and Thomas, his son, idiot, 868
Laxston, John, 857
Laxton, Northants, manor, 17
Layburn *see* Leybourne
Layham (Lexham), Suff, 303
Laylondshire, John de, 598
Layston, Herts, Beauchamps (Affledwyck) in, *q.v.*
Lea Marston (Lee Marston), Warw, manor, 420,
  424-5

Newton Abbot (Nyweton Abbatis) [in Woolborough], Devon, inquisition at, 446

Newton Bank (Neuton in Craven) [in Gargrave], Yorks, 301

Newton Blossomville (Newenton Blosmevyll), Bucks, manor, 822
park, 821

Newton by Castle Acre (Nuton by Castelacre), Norf, manor, 70–1

Newton near Sudbury (Neutone by Sudbury), Suff, manor, 24

Newton, Cold, (Neuton Burdet), [in Lowesby], Leics, 296

Newton Down (Neuton Doun by Westcallicote) [in Fremington], Devon, 1005

Newton Flotman (Floteman Neuton), Norf, 302

Newton in Cleveland (Neuton under Onesburgh], Yorks, 955

Newton Lisle (Neweton Lyles, Nyton Lyles) [in Maiden Newton], Dors, 1142

Newton Longville (Newenton Langville), Bucks, 824
priory, 152
advowson of, 824
prior of, 824

Newton, Maiden, (Mayden Neweton), Dors, inquisition at, 471
manor, 1142
Newton Lisle, Notton and Thorpe in, q.v.

Newton Mulgrave (Newton in Whitbystrand), Yorks, 955

Newton, North, (Newton Plecy), [in North Petherton], Som, 576
inquisition at, 576

Newton Regis (Kyngesneuton), Warw, manor, 594

Newton St. Loe (Neuton Sentloo), Som, manor, 1146

Newton Tracey (Neweton by Barnestaple), Devon, advowson, 479
manor, 479, 1009

Newton, Wold, (Neuton), Yorks, 583, 1140

NEWTON (Neuton, Neutone, Neweton), THOMAS, citizen and mercer of London, 6
William, 844
William de, parson of Seagrave, 235, 269, 279, 282–3, 289

Newtonbury alias Dunton Chamberlains, q.v.

Neyland (Nelond), Norf, 793

Nicholaston (Nacleston, Nicolaston), [Glam], 300, 307

Nicolson, William, and Elizabeth (Normanton) his wife, 537
Avelina daughter of, 537
Joan daughter of see Camyn
Nicola daughter of see Baylyff

Nidd, Yorks, 905

Nidderdale (Niderdale), Yorks, chase, 289

Nocton, Lincs, manor, 1088

Noke, Richard, 1113, 1195

None see Noon

Nonington, Kent, Easole and Fredville in, q.v.

Noon (None), Edmund, knight, 793
Geoffrey, 1005

Norbury, John de, chaplain, 928

Norby [in Thirsk], Yorks, 301

Norchard (Orchard) [in Hartlebury], Worcs, 515

Norcott (Northcote) [in Preston], Glos, 846
manor, 1107

Nordley (Nordeleye) [in Astley Abbotts], Salop, 77

Noreys see Norreys

Norffolk (Nortfolk, Northfolk), John, 529, 673–4

Norfolk (Norff), county, 255, 275

Norfolk (Norff), countess and duchess of see Margaret
duke of see Mowbray
earl of see Thomas de Brotherton

Norham, Northumb, Thornton in, q.v.

Norham, William de, 434

Norhampton (Norhthampton), John, 313, 1192–3
Richard, 147, 850
Robert de, 147, 151, 163, 166, 187, 838, 850

Norman, Agnes, 863
John, 769, 793, 860
Thomas, 860

Normanton, Lincs, manor, 537

Normanton, Rut, 551

NORMANTON, THOMAS DE, 537
Elizabeth daughter of see Nicolson
Isabel and Margaret daughters of, 537

Norreys (Noreys), Geoffrey, 843
Henry le, of Speke, 596–7
John, 529

Norfolk see Norffolk

North End (Buryton Northende) [in Burton Dassett], Warw, 1106

Northall (Northalle) in Wrentham, Suff, manor, 986

Northallerton (Allerton), Yorks, inquisitions at, 714, 950–4
manor, 428
Worsall, High, in, q.v.

Northampton (Norhampton), Northants, 151, 163, 166, 187, 271–2, 505, 838, 921, 1171
inquisitions at, 66, 98, 102, 151, 187, 272, 290, 439, 458, 504, 610, 728, 980, 1060, 1065, 1073, 1079, 1085, 1171
reeve of, 610
'Kyngeshale' in, 439, 610
'Latymersplace' in, 948

Northcott Barton (Northcote) [in Ashreigney], Devon, 538

Northfolk see Norffolk

Northiam, Sussex, Morley in, q.v.

Northill (Northyevyll), Beds, manor and advowson, 101, 644
rector of see Warde, John
Ickwell in, q.v.

Northlond (Northlode), Richard, knight, 527, 1192
Joan (Perers) wife of, 1192

Northolt (Norhthalle), Midd, 147, 850

Northorp, John, of Sausthorpe, 886

Northumberland, county, sheriff of, 212, 412

Northumberland, earl of see Percy

Northwode, Roger, knight, 1113
Agnes daughter of see Peytefyn
Agnes wife of, afterwards Shukburgh, q.v.
John de, knight, son of, 1113
Juliana daughter of see Rede
Margaret daughter of see Roo
Roger de, knight, son of, 1113
William, parson of Anderby, 439, 611–2

Northwood Sheppey (Northwodeshepeye) [in Minster in Sheppey], Kent, manor, 768

Norton (Norton by Daventre), Northants, 63, 520
Muscott and Thrupp in, q.v.

Norton (Norton in Colneis), Suff, 303
Haugh, Little, in, q.v.

Norton [in Campsall], Yorks, 854
inquisition at, 1169

'Plomesyard' (*unidentified*), Suff, 303
Plowrigh, Hugh, 310
PLUMLAND, THOMAS DE, **882**
Plumpton [in Kingsbury], Warw, manor, 81, 317
Plumpton [in Ripon], Yorks, 301
Plumstead (Plumstede), Kent, manor, 764
Plumstede, Clement de, 302
Plumtree (Plumtre), Notts, 691
Plumtree (Plumtre), Notts, wapentake, 975
Plympton, honour, 1145
Plympton, Devon, castle, 105
Plympton St. Mary (Plympton), Devon, prior of, 744
Plymtree, Devon, Woodbeer in, *q.v.*
Pobelowe, Robert, clerk, 463
Pocklington (Pokelyngton, Poklyngton), Yorks, 622, 624, 687
  chantry, advowson of, 950
  inquisitions at, 392, 623
  Yapham in, *q.v.*
Pockthorpe (Pocthorp) [in Nafferton], Yorks, manor, 428
Pocock, John, 1005
Pointon (Poynton) [in Sempringham], Lincs, 998
Pokelyngton, Ralph, 100, 643
POKESWELL (Pokeswellys), JOHN, **684**, 1031
  Eleanor wife and John son of, 684
Poket, John, 307
Polayn, John, 979
Poldre, John de, 849
Poldue (Poldu) [in Advent], Corn, manor, 31, 35, 38
POLE (Polle, Poole), John, (de la), 310, 847
  Michael, knight, 980–1
    Michael, earl of Suffolk [1398–1415], son of, 70, 85, 962, 980–1, 1112
    RICHARD son of, **980–1**
    Thomas son of, 980–1
    William son of, 980
  Peter de la, 867
  Thomas, citizen and goldsmith of London, 1189
  Walter de la, and Elizabeth his wife, 473, 475
Polebrook (Pokebrok), Northants, 838
Polesworth, Warw, Pooley, Stipershill and Warton in, *q.v.*
Pollard, John, 34
  Walter, 1098
Polle *see* Pole
Polruan [in Lanteglos by Fowey], Corn, manor, 731
Polton (Pulton), John, 439
  Walter de, chaplain, 471, 476
Pomeray, John de, knight, 322, 1128
Pontefract (Pontefratt), Yorks, 854
  Carleton in, *q.v.*
Ponteland, Northumb, manor, 581
  Benridge and Callerton in, *q.v.*
Pontesbury, Salop, manor, 650
  Horton in, *q.v.*
Ponton, Great, (Great Pauncton, Great Paumpton, Great Paunmton), Lincs, 141, 184, 842, 862
  Ganthorpe in, *q.v.*
Ponton, Little, (Little Pauncton, Little Paunton), Lincs, 141, 184, 842
PONTON (Pauncton, Paunton), JOHN, outlaw, and Richard his brother, **566**
  Philip de, 141, 184, 842
  William, portioner of Waddesdon, 1145–6
Ponynges *see* Poynynges

Pool, North, (Northpole), [in South Pool], Devon, manor, 1145
Poole *see* Pole
Pooley (Poley) [in Polesworth], Warw, manor, 594
Pope (Pape), Margaret (Wode), 1176
  Thomas son of *see* Qwytlokman
  Roger, 534
  William, 662
POPHAM, Henry, 413, 959, 1111, 1142
  John, 984
  PHILIP, and Philip his father, Elizabeth his mother and Philip his son, **349–50**
Poret, Henry, 307
Poringland, Great *or* Little, (Porringlond, Poryngland), Norf, 302
  advowson, 302
Porter, Ellis, 434
  Geoffrey, 844
  John, of Whaplode, 719
Porteynon (Portenan), [Glam], 300, 307
Portisham, Dors, Shilvinghampton in, *q.v.*
Porton, Robert, 996
Portskewett (Porscuet), [Monm], 259, 299
  Harpson in, *q.v.*
Portsmouth (Portesmouth), Hants, prior of, 1037
Postling (Postlynge), Kent, manor, 769, 1122
Poston, Lower, (Littel Posthorn) [in Hopton Cangeford], Salop, 612
Poston, Upper, (Muchel Posthorn), [in Hopton Cangeford], Salop, 612
Potsgrove (Potesgrave), Beds, 835
Potter, John, citizen and cordwainer of London, 978
  Thomas, and Isabel his wife, 957
Potterne, Wilts, Marston in, *q.v.*
Potterspury (Potterespyrye), Northants, manor, 504–5
  Yardley Gobion in, *q.v.*
Potton, Beds, 452
Potton Burdetts (Bordelettesfee) [in Potton], Beds, 946
Potyn, Nicholas, 1113
POULET (Paulet), John, 651
  IDONEA wife of, **651–4**
  John son of, 651, 653–4
  John, knight, 984
  Nicholas, 476
Poulton (Pulton), Glos, 522
Poulton (Pulton) [in Warrington], Lancs, 597
Pounfreyt, Henry, 625
Poutrell, John, 672
  Juliana daughter of *see* Cotiler
Power (Powair), Alice, 843
  Henry, 50–1
  John, 855
  Robert, 670–1
  Walter, esquire, 509
Powse, William, 315
Powys, lord of *see* Charlton
POYLE, Mabel, 591
  THOMAS, knight, **590–3**
  John brother of, 52, 590, 592
Poyns (Poyntz), Nicholas, 846
  Robert, 846; escheator in Gloucestershire, 432A
POYNYNGES (Ponynges), Michael, [Lord Poynings 1339–69], 992
  RICHARD, knight, Lord Poynings [1375–87], 599, 702, 986–7, **988**, 989–93
  ISABEL wife of, **986–7**, 990, 992–3

Yerd (Jarde), John in the, 308
  Robert, 1005
YEVELE, HENRY and Richard, **97**
Yheverslay, William, 1153
Ynge, William, 303
Ynglysthorp, John, 198
Yockleton (Yokelton) [in Westbury], Salop, 840–1
  manor, 968
Yokes (Yoke) [in Frinsted], Kent, manor, 1113
Yokflete, Thomas, clerk, 272
Yongare, John, 530
Yonge, John, of Theddlethorpe, 316
  Richard le, clerk, 958
  Thomas, 774
  Thomas, dean of St. Mary's, Warwick, 527
  William le, 958
York, archbishops of *see* Arundel, Thomas; Scrope,
  Richard le
York (Ebor'), Yorks, 857
  castle, 881
    inquisitions at, 381–2, 535, 624, 881–2, 931,
      955, 1156
    inquisitions at, 108, 113–4, 411, 468, 568
    St. Mary's abbey, abbot of, 305, 623
      advowson of, 1156
    streets and places in
      Bishophill (Bysshophill), 113–4, 468
      Finkle Street (Fenkelstrete), 113
      Micklegate (Mykellyll), 113–4
    warden of *see* Frost, William
    Copmanthorpe in, *q.v.*
York, county, 641
  escheators in *see* Egmanton, Thomas; Godard,
    John; Graa, Thomas
  sheriff of, 641

York, dukes of *see* Edmund and Edward
YORKE, CLARICE, *formerly* Windesore, and
  John her son, **903**
Youlgrave, Derb, Stanton in, *q.v.*
Yoxford (Yexforth, Yokesford), Suff, 303, 564
  Stickingland in, *q.v.*
Yoxhale, John de, 420
Ysonde, Henry, 828
Ystrad Marchall (Southstramarghell), [Mont], com-
  mote, 650
Yvyngho, Nicholas de, chaplain, 57

ZOUCHE (Souche, Zouch), HUGH LA, knight,
  53–5
  Alan father of, 53
  Joan wife of, 55
  Joyce sister of, 53
  Master Ivo la, 963; chancellor of Cambridge Univ-
    ersity, 310
  William la, [Lord Zouche of Harringworth, 1352–
    82], 1049–50
    Elizabeth wife of, 1050, 1121
    John son of, and Margaret his wife, 1051–4
    THOMAS son of, 16–9, 356–9, **1049–54**
      MARY (Dengayne), *formerly* Bernak, wife
        of, 16–9, **356–9**
  William la, [Lord Zouch of Harringworth, 1382–
    96], son of William, 1049–50
  William la, knight, [Lord Zouch of Harring-
    worth, 1396–1414], son of William, 19, 333–4,
    356, 406, 768, 824, 838, 1049–50, 1101

INDEX OF SUBJECTS

Most subjects are grouped under inclusive headings. The main groups are: Areas of local administration; Arms and armour; Buildings and architectural features; Clergy and religious; Disasters; Household goods and clothing; Land; Law courts; Liberties of tenants; Livestock; Officials and servants; Religious houses and institutions; Rents, services and serjeanties; Rights of Lordship; Tenures; Trades and occupations; Writs. All *see under* references are to the Index of Persons and Places.

Printed in the United Kingdom by Her Majesty's Stationery Office at Edinburgh Press
Dd   0238613   C5   8/87   (241869)